3D Games

Real-time Rendering and Software Technology

VOLUME ONE

ACM SIGGRAPH Series

This book is published as part of the SIGGRAPH Book Series with ACM Press Books, a collaborative effort among ACM SIGGRAPH, ACM Press, and Pearson Education Ltd. The SIGGRAPH Books Series publishes books on theory, practice, applications, and imaging in computer graphics and interactive techniques, some developed from courses, papers, or panels presented at the annual ACM SIGGRAPH conference.

Editor: Stephen Spencer, The Ohio State University

MEMBERSHIP INFORMATION

Founded in 1947, ACM is the oldest and largest educational scientific society in the information technology field. Through its high-quality publications and its services, ACM is a major force in advancing the skills and knowledge of IT professionals throughout the world. From a dedicated group of 78, ACM is now 85,000 strong, with 34 special interest groups, including SIGGRAPH, and more than 60 chapters and student chapters.

For more than 25 years, SIGGRAPH and its conferences have provided the world's forum for the interchange of information on computer graphics and interactive techniques. SIGGRAPH members come from many disciplines and include researchers, hardware and software systems designers, algorithm and applications developers, visualization scientists, educators, technology developers for interactive visual communications, animators and special-effects artists, graphic designers, and fine artists.

For further information about ACM and ACM SIGGRAPH, contact:

ACM Member Services
1515 Broadway, 17th floor
New York, NY 10036-5701
Phone: 1-212-626-0500
Fax: 1-212-944-1318
E-mail: acmhelp @ acm.org

ACM European Service Center
108 Cowley Road
Oxford, OX4 1JF, United Kingdom
Phone: +44-1865-382388
Fax: +44-1865-381388
E-mail: acm_europe @ acm.org

URL: http://www.acm.org

3D Games

Real-time Rendering and Software Technology

ALAN WATT AND
FABIO POLICARPO

ACM Press • SIGGRAPH Series
New York,   New York

ADDISON-WESLEY

An imprint of PEARSON EDUCATION

Harlow, England · London · New York · Reading, Massachusetts · San Francisco · Toronto · Don Mills, Ontario · Sydney
Tokyo · Singapore · Hong Kong · Seoul · Taipei · Cape Town · Madrid · Mexico City · Amsterdam · Munich · Paris · Milan

Pearson Education Ltd
Edinburgh Gate
Harlow
Essex CM20 2JE
England

and Associated Companies throughout the world

Visit us on the World Wide Web at:
www.pearsoneduc.com

First edition 2001

ISBN 0201-61921-0

British Library Cataloguing-in-Publication Data
A catalogue record for this book can be obtained from the British Library

Library of Congress Cataloging-in-Publication Data
Watt, Alan H., 1942-
     3D games: real-time rendering and software technology/Alan Watt and Fabio Policarpo.-- 1st ed.
        p. cm. -- (SIGGRAPH series)
     Includes bibliographical references and index.
     ISBN 0-201-61921-0
     1. Computer games--Programming. 2. Computer graphics. 3. C++ (Computer program language) I. Title: Three D games. II. Policarpo, Fabio. III. Title. IV. Series.

     QA76.76.C672 W39 2001
     794.8'1693--dc21

                                                                                    00-062080

10 9 8 7 6 5 4 3 2
05 04 03 02 01

Cover designed by Dionea Watt

Typeset in 9/12pt Stone serif by 42
Printed and bound in Great Britain by Biddles Ltd., Guildford and King's Lynn

Fabio – Para meus avós, Carlos Maia (em memória)
e Dirce Policarpo, pelo apoio durante toda minha vida.

Contents

Preface   xiii

Foundations

1   Mathematical fundamentals of 3D computer graphics   1

  1.1   Manipulating three-dimensional structures   2

  1.2   Vectors and computer graphics   9

  1.3   Rays and computer graphics   14

  1.4   Bi-linear interpolation of polygon properties   21

  1.5   A basic maths engine using SIMD instructions   22

**2   Modelling and representation 1 – comparative review and polygon
mesh models**   31

  2.1   Introduction   31

  2.2   Polygonal representation of three-dimensional objects   36

  2.3   High-level methods – constructive solid geometry   47

  2.4   High-level creation using modellers/editors   51

3   Modelling and representation 2 – the economics of polygon meshes   53

  3.1   Compressing polygonal models   53

  3.2   Compressing the geometry   54

  3.3   Encoding connectivity   56

  3.4   Triangle strips   57

  3.5   Local vs. global algorithms   59

3.6   Using vertex buffers   60

3.7   Level of detail (LOD) processing   62

4   **Representation and modelling 3 – landscape specialisations**   68

4.1   Introduction   68

4.2   Simple height field landscapes   69

4.3   Procedural modelling of landscapes – fractals   70

4.4   Terrain LODs: triangle bintrees   72

4.5   Rendering of landscapes by ray casting   76

5   **Modelling and representation 4 – Bézier, B-spline and subdivision surfaces**   79

5.1   Introduction   79

5.2   Bézier curves   82

5.3   B-spline curves   91

5.4   Rational curves   104

5.5   From curves to surfaces   107

5.6   Modelling or creating patch surfaces   116

5.7   Rendering parametric surfaces   131

5.8   Practical Bézier technology for games   139

5.9   Subdivision surfaces   153

5.10 Scalability – polygon meshes, patch meshes and subdivision surfaces   170

Classical 3D graphics

6   **Classic polygon mesh rendering technology**   172

6.1   Coordinate spaces and geometric operations in the graphics pipeline   173

6.2   Operations carried out in view space   179

6.3   Algorithmic operations in the graphics pipeline   189

6.4   Rendering examples   212

7   **Classic mapping techniques**   215

7.1   Introduction   215

7.2   Two-dimensional texture maps to polygon mesh objects   218

7.3   Two-dimensional texture domain to bi-cubic parametric patch objects   227

7.4   Bump mapping   227

7.5   Environment or reflection mapping   231

7.6 Three-dimensional texture domain techniques 238

7.7 Comparative examples 243

8 Anti-aliasing theory and practice 245

8.1 Introduction 245

8.2 Aliases and sampling 246

8.3 Jagged edges 249

8.4 Sampling in computer graphics compared with sampling reality 250

8.5 Sampling and reconstruction 252

8.6 A simple comparison 252

8.7 Pre-filtering methods 254

8.8 Supersampling or post-filtering 256

8.9 Anti-aliasing in texture mapping 258

8.10 The Fourier transform of images 264

Real-time rendering

9 Visibility processing of complex scenes 270

9.1 Introduction 270

9.2 Why trees? 274

9.3 BSP trees 277

9.4 Bounding volume hierarchies 279

9.5 BSP trees and polygon objects 280

9.6 Specialisations for building interior-type environments 295

9.7 Portals and mirrors 296

9.8 Advanced view frustum culling 301

9.9 Exact visibility 305

9.10 Dynamic objects and visibility 312

10 Lighting in games 314

10.1 Light maps 315

10.2 Dynamic lighting effects with light maps 320

10.3 Dynamic lights 322

10.4 Switchable/destroyable light sources 322

10.5 Fog maps/volumetric fog 322

10.6 Lighting case studies 323

11 Shadows in games 329

11.1 The nature of shadows 329

11.2 Classical shadow algorithms 333

11.3 Shadows in games 340

12 Multi-pass rendering 346

12.1 Introduction 346

12.2 Multi-pass functionality 347

12.3 Multi-pass algorithms 351

12.4 Multi-pass sampling approaches 361

12.5 Multi-texture 363

12.6 Multi-texture example 365

Control of objects

13 Motion control – kinematic 368

13.1 Introduction 368

13.2 Pre-scripting animation – linear interpolation and elapsed time 370

13.3 Pre-scripted animation – interpolation problems 372

13.4 Pre-scripted animation – explicit scripting 373

13.5 Interpolation of rotation 376

13.6 Using quaternions to represent rotation 378

13.7 The camera as an animated object 386

13.8 Particle animation 387

13.9 Particle animation and computer games 389

13.10 Articulated structures 392

14 Control by dynamic simulation 402

14.1 Dynamics in off-line animation – the famous example 402

14.2 Initial value problems vs. boundary value problems 403

14.3 Topic areas 404

14.4 Motivations for dynamic simulations 405

14.5 Basic classical theory for particles 406

14.6 Basic classical theory for rigid bodies 408

14.7 The practicalities of dynamic simulations 418

14.8 Numerical integration 431

15   Collision detection   437

   15.1 Broad phase/narrow phase algorithms   440

   15.2 Bounding volume hierarchies   444

   15.3 Broad phase collision detection with AABBs   445

   15.4 Broad phase collision detection with OBBs   449

   15.5 Broad phase collision detection with local or object
         spatial partitioning   451

   15.6 Narrow phase collision detection   453

   15.7 Single phase approaches   459

16   Interactive control   467

   16.1 Interaction and animation   467

   16.2 Controller module   467

   16.3 User–object interaction – 6 DOF control with simple sampling 470

   16.4 User–object animation – a four-key car simulation   473

   16.5 Object–object interaction   476

   16.6 Camera–object interaction   477

   16.7 Objects with simple autonomous behaviour   478

   16.8 User–scene interaction   482

17   Behaviour and AI   484

   17.1 Established approaches and architectures   487

   17.2 Agents and hierarchies   490

   17.3 Examples of agent architectures   493

   17.4 Cognitive modelling and situation calculus   498

   17.5 The role of sensing – vision as an example   503

   17.6 Learning architectures   505

2D technology

18   Two-dimensional techniques   516

   18.1 Image pyramids   516

   18.2 Wavelet transform   518

   18.3 Image transforms and basis matrices   525

   18.4 Wavelets and computer games   526

   18.5 Image metamorphosis – morphing   531

19 Image-based rendering   540

19.1 Introduction   540

19.2 Reuse of previously rendered imagery   541

19.3 Varying rendering resources   547

19.4 Using depth information   551

19.5 View interpolation   559

19.6 Four-dimensional techniques – the Lumigraph or light field
      rendering approach   564

19.7 Photo-modelling and IBR   566

Software technology

20 Multi-player game technology   572

20.1 Introduction   572

20.2 Definitions   573

20.3 Implementation of multi-player games   574

20.4 The origin and nature of problems in multi-player games   576

20.5 Reducing the information in messages   580

20.6 Multi-player implementation using client–server   586

21 Engine architecture   595

21.1 Game programming in C++   595

21.2 Managing and evolving complexity in games   602

21.3 Engine design and architecture   603

21.4 Fly3D software architecture   604

22 Fly3D SDK reference   617

22.1 Introduction   617

22.2 Globals reference   618

22.3 Objects reference   622

Appendix A Fly3D SDK tutorials   749

References   779

Index   788

Preface

This book aims to be a comprehensive treatment of current 3D games technology. It concentrates on:

real-time rendering, or the necessary enhancements of 3D graphics to enable rendering at interactive rates;

those topics from other areas that are beginning to be used in games; namely AI, physics and collision detection;

the software technology of games – engine architecture and multi-player technology.

The text is written around an actual engine that implements most of the described techniques. The intention is that you can try out your own ideas by writing source code and experiment with existing demonstrations by writing plug-ins and altering existing ones.

A quick feature list of the engine is:

- BSP/PVS render management
- Light maps for static geometry (pre-computed lighting with soft shadows)
- Normal maps (dot product texture blending) for dynamic objects
- Diffuse and specular vertex lighting for dynamic objects
- Volumetric fog with fog maps
- Detail textures
- Multi-texture support
- Collision detection
- Dynamic coloured lights with distance attenuation
- Dynamic shadows – light map or stencil shadow volumes
- Physically based simulations
- Animated meshes (vertex morph)
- Tri-strips and fans
- Subdivision surfaces

- Dynamic LODs using bi-quadric Bezier meshes
- Cartoon-like rendering with dynamic cartoon lighting
- Multi-player support (TCP/IP) with client/server architecture (using DirectPlay)
- 3D sound support (using DirectSound)
- Mouse and keyboard input (using DirectInput)
- Intel® Pentium3 vector and matrix maths optimisation
- Complete plug-in directed

The book can be read forwards or backwards. For example, if you wish to build up detailed implementation experience, you could start with Chapter 21 (Engine Architecture), familiarise yourself with the engine and development environment and start writing new plug-ins using the theoretical chapters for reference when required. Alternatively you could take a more conventional approach studying the theoretical aspects first before moving on to implementation.

Chapters are grouped into sections that are more or less self contained. These are:

- **Modelling and foundation maths** This section deals with the basic mathematics required to handle objects in three-dimensional space and the theory of object representation.
- **Classical 3D graphics** Although much of the material in this section has migrated onto hardware, it is still necessary to have an appreciation of what the hardware does to be able to use it effectively.
- **Real-time rendering** This section deals with the technology developed by the games industry and the virtual reality industry which enables complex scenes to be rendered, to a reasonably high quality, in real time on a low-cost graphics processor.
- **Control of objects** Mainstream techniques used to control the movement of objects are described in this section. This ranges from simple low-level control through to behavioural animation using AI technology. The material on AI is in the form of a debate concerning the potential use of the technology in the future.
- **2D technology** A potentially important solution to the complexity problem in 3D graphics, in terms of both the creation cost and the rendering cost, is the use of image-based rendering techniques.
- **Software technology** This section deals with the techniques needed to write a multi-player game using the currently popular first-person shooter genre as an example. We examine the software architecture of a games engine and look at the design of the engine. Finally a comprehensive reference manual for the engine is given.

The book is not intended to be a 'how to program' in C++ and OpenGL text and we assume a reasonable knowledge of C or C++. Detailed examples of various algorithms implemented in C++ are sprinkled throughout the text. These are extracted from the engine and are reproduced in the text for convenience. A quick read will give some feel for the structure of the algorithms. In most cases to fully comprehend the code requires them to be studied in conjunction with Chapter 21 and the Reference Manual.

The graphics API/library used is OpenGL. Pentium 3 code is given alongside the C++ equivalent for efficient matrix operation in Chapter 1 and DirectPlay utilities are used in Chapter 20. Clearly these facilities need separate study and the purpose of the examples is to give a 'flavour' of their use in the applications.

The following material has been reproduced with permission of the copyright holders:

Figure 2.1: 3D models by Viewpoint Digital, Inc. from *Anatomy*, Viewpoint's 3D Dataset™ Catalogue, 2nd edn.
Figure 2.2: Courtesy of Agata Opalach.
Figure 2.5: Beatty and Booth Tutorial, *Computer Graphics*, 2nd edn, The Institute of Electrical and Electronics Engineers, Inc.: New York © 1982 IEEE.
Figure 10.9: James, G., 1996, *Modern Engineering Mathematics*, 2nd edn, Addison-Wesley: Harlow, courtesy of Pearson Education Ltd.
Figure 18.11: Thompson, D., 1942, *On Growth and Form*, Cambridge University Press.
Figure 19.9: Courtesy of Steven M. Seitz.

Acknowledgements

The authors would like to thank (in alphabetical order)

In Brazil:

- Althayr Rodrigues for the sound files.
- Edison Bezerra (Ed) for helping a lot with the reference documents and several program tests.
- Eduardo Grandele (Duda) for the ship powerups models and textures.
- Francisco Meirelles (Chico) for several level textures and always keeping me going ahead.
- Gilliard Lopes for help on the tutorials and chapter reviews.
- Henrique Vidinha for the cover image, several test levels and nice 3D models (missiles, car, ship and robots).
- Marcio Tatagiba (ZNP) for working on the Bronto model with Conseqüencia Animação.
- Marcos Bezerra for the laser texture and several multi-player tests.
- Marina Morato for several texture maps including the great ship and car textures.
- Michael Stanton for helping with the computer networks-related material.
- Pedro Burglin for the font texture map generation utility.
- Conseqüencia Animação for the Bronto player model used on the cover, spine and colour plate 13.2.
- Intel (especially Ruy Castro and Luis Picinini) for programming support/tools and the very fast computers used in this project.
- Soter for a lot of the time its employees spent on this book.

In the UK:

- Dionea Watt for the cover layouts.
- Julie Knight and Keith Mansfield (Pearson Education) for their help and forbearance.

Alan Watt and Fabio Policarpo
July 2000

Mathematical fundamentals of 3D computer graphics

1.1 Manipulating three-dimensional structures

1.2 Vectors and computer graphics

1.3 Rays and computer graphics

1.4 Bi-linear Interpolation of polygon properties

1.5 A basic maths engine using SIMD instructions

The role of three-dimensional computer graphics in the context of computer games is to supply tools that enable the building of worlds, populating them with characters and objects, having these games objects interact with each other and 'reducing' the action to a two-dimensional screen projection in real time. None of this can be accomplished without a knowledge of the basic mathematics of three-dimensional space and the purpose of this chapter is to introduce the fundamental tools required to make calculations about three-dimensional objects and to move them around.

At their lowest level, three-dimensional objects are represented as a set of points. In most cases these points are the vertices of polygonal facets – the approximation to the real or imagined surface – and we embed the points in a data structure that specifies their connectivity required to represent a polygon. Usually we do this simply by listing the points in the order that they are encountered as we move around the boundary of the polygon. As far as the mathematics is concerned we only have information concerning the position of each point in three-dimensional space – our object is just a 'cloud' of points and we can, for example, move our object around by applying the same displacement or translation to each point. Our first topic of study will therefore be transformations.

Manipulating three-dimensional structures

Transformations are important tools in generating three-dimensional scenes. They are used to move objects around in an environment, and also to construct a two-dimensional view of the environment for a display surface. This chapter deals with basic three-dimensional transformations and the three-dimensional geometry that we will be using later in the text.

In computer graphics the most popular method for representing an object is the polygon mesh model. This representation is fully described in Chapter 2. We do this by representing the surface of an object as a set of connected planar polygons and each polygon as a list of (connected) points. This form of representation is either exact or an approximation depending on the nature of the object. A cube, for example, can be represented exactly by six squares. A cylinder, on the other hand, can only be approximated by polygons; say six rectangles for the curved surface and two hexagons for the end faces. The number of polygons used in the approximation determines how accurately the object is represented and this has repercussions in modelling cost, storage and rendering cost and quality. The popularity of the polygon mesh modelling technique in computer graphics is undoubtedly due to its inherent simplicity and the development of inexpensive shading algorithms that work with such models.

Despite its not insignificant disadvantages this representation has become the *de facto* standard in three-dimensional computer graphics and this is reflected in the routine availability of 3D cards in modern PCs which perform hardware rendering of polygons.

A polygon mesh model consists of a structure of vertices, each vertex being a three-dimensional point in so-called world coordinate space. Later we will be concerned with how vertices are connected to form polygons and how polygons are structured into complete objects. But to start with we shall consider objects just as a set of three-dimensional vertices and look at how these are transformed in three-dimensional space using linear transformations.

Three-dimensional geometry in computer graphics—affine transformations

In this section we look at three-dimensional affine transformations. These are the transformations that effect rotation, scaling, shear and translation. Affine transformations can be represented by a matrix and a set of affine transformations can be combined into a single overall affine transformation. Technically we say that an affine transformation is made up of any combination of linear transformations (rotation, scaling and shear) followed by translation.

Objects are defined in a world coordinate system which is conventionally a right-handed system. A right-handed and left-handed three-dimensional coordinate system is shown in Figure 1.1. Right-handed systems are the standard mathematical convention although left-handed systems have been, and still are, used

Figure 1.1
(a) Right-handed and
(b) left-handed coordinate
systems.

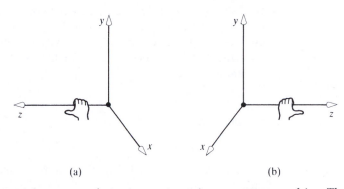

(a)   (b)

in the special context of viewing systems in computer graphics. The difference between the two systems is the sense of the z axis as shown in the figure. Rotating your fingers around the z axis, from the positive x axis to the positive y axis, gives a different z direction for your thumb depending on which system is used.

It is often convenient to define objects in their own local coordinate system. There are three reasons for this. When a three-dimensional object is modelled it is useful to build up the vertices with respect to some reference point in the object. In fact a complex object may be broken down into parts and have a number of local coordinate systems, one for each sub-part. It may be that the same object is to appear many times in a scene and a definition with a local origin is the only sensible way to set this up. Instancing an object by applying a mix of translations, rotation and scaling transformations can then be seen as transforming the local coordinate system of each object to the world coordinate system. Finally, when an object is to be rotated, it is easier if the rotation is defined with respect to a local reference point such as an axis of symmetry.

A set of vertices or three-dimensional points belonging to an object can be transformed into another set of points by a linear transformation. Both sets of points remain in the same coordinate system. Matrix notation is used in computer graphics to describe the transformations and the convention in computer graphics is to have the point or vector as a column matrix, preceded by the transformation matrix $\textbf{\textit{T}}$.

Using matrix notation, a point $\textbf{\textit{V}}$ is transformed under translation, scaling and rotation as:

$$\textbf{\textit{V}}' = \textbf{\textit{V}} + \textbf{\textit{D}}$$
$$\textbf{\textit{V}}' = \textbf{\textit{S}} \, \textbf{\textit{V}}$$
$$\textbf{\textit{V}}' = \textbf{\textit{R}} \, \textbf{\textit{V}}$$

where $\textbf{\textit{D}}$ is a translation vector and $\textbf{\textit{S}}$ and $\textbf{\textit{R}}$ are scaling and rotation matrices.

These three operations are the most commonly used transformations in computer graphics. A body moving around in three-dimensional space can only undergo rotation and translation and scaling is used in object modelling. To enable the above transformations to be treated in the same way and combined, we use a system called homogeneous coordinates which increases the dimensionality of the space. The practical reason for this in computer graphics is to enable us to include translation as matrix multiplication (rather than addition) and thus have a unified scheme for linear transformations. In a homogeneous system a vertex:

$V(x,y,z)$

is represented as

$V(w.X,w.Y,w.Z,w)$

for any scale factor $w \neq 0$. The three-dimensional Cartesian coordinate representation is then:

$x = X/w$

$y = Y/w$

$z = Z/w$

If we consider w to have the value 1 then the matrix representation of a point is

$$\begin{bmatrix} x \\ y \\ z \\ 1 \end{bmatrix}$$

Translation can now be treated as matrix multiplication, like the other two transformations and becomes:

$$V' = T\,V$$

$$\begin{bmatrix} x' \\ y' \\ z' \\ 1 \end{bmatrix} = \begin{bmatrix} 1 & 0 & 0 & T_x \\ 0 & 1 & 0 & T_y \\ 0 & 0 & 1 & T_z \\ 0 & 0 & 0 & 1 \end{bmatrix} \begin{bmatrix} x \\ y \\ z \\ 1 \end{bmatrix}$$

This specification implies that the object is translated in three dimensions by applying a displacement T_x, T_y and T_z to each vertex that defines the object. The matrix notation is a convenient and elegant way of writing the transformation as a set of three equations:

$x' = x + T_x$

$y' = y + T_y$

$z' = z + T_z$

The set of transformations is completed by scaling and rotation. First scaling:

$$V' = S \, V$$

$$S = \begin{bmatrix} S_x & 0 & 0 & 0 \\ 0 & S_y & 0 & 0 \\ 0 & 0 & S_z & 0 \\ 0 & 0 & 0 & 1 \end{bmatrix}$$

Here S_x, S_y and S_z are scaling factors. For uniform scaling $S_x = S_y = S_z$, otherwise scaling occurs along these axes for which the scaling factor is non-unity. Again the process can be expressed less succinctly by a set of three equations:

$$x' = x.S_x$$
$$y' = y.S_y$$
$$z' = z.S_z$$

applied to every vertex in the object.

To rotate an object in three-dimensional space we need to specify an axis of rotation. This can have any spatial orientation in three-dimensional space, but it is easiest to consider rotations that are parallel to one of the coordinate axes. The transformation matrices for anti-clockwise (looking along each axis towards the origin) rotation about the X, Y and Z axes respectively are:

$$R_x = \begin{bmatrix} 1 & 0 & 0 & 0 \\ 0 & \cos\theta & -\sin\theta & 0 \\ 0 & \sin\theta & \cos\theta & 0 \\ 0 & 0 & 0 & 1 \end{bmatrix}$$

$$R_y = \begin{bmatrix} \cos\theta & 0 & \sin\theta & 0 \\ 0 & 1 & 0 & 0 \\ -\sin\theta & 0 & \cos\theta & 0 \\ 0 & 0 & 0 & 1 \end{bmatrix}$$

$$R_z = \begin{bmatrix} \cos\theta & -\sin\theta & 0 & 0 \\ \sin\theta & \cos\theta & 0 & 0 \\ 0 & 0 & 1 & 0 \\ 0 & 0 & 0 & 1 \end{bmatrix}$$

The z axis matrix specification is equivalent to the following set of three equations:

$$x' = x \cos\theta - y \sin\theta$$
$$y' = x \sin\theta + y \cos\theta$$
$$z' = z$$

Figure 1.2 shows examples of these transformations.

The inverse of these transformations is often required. T^{-1} is obtained by negating T_x, T_y and T_z. Replacing S_x, S_y and S_z by their reciprocals gives S^{-1} and negating the angle of rotation gives R^{-1}.

Figure 1.2
Examples of linear transformations.

(a) Identity
$$\begin{bmatrix} 1 & 0 & 0 & 0 \\ 0 & 1 & 0 & 0 \\ 0 & 0 & 1 & 0 \\ 0 & 0 & 0 & 1 \end{bmatrix}$$

(b) *Z*-axis rotation
$$\begin{bmatrix} 0.866 & 0.5 & 0 & 0 \\ -0.5 & 0.866 & 0 & 0 \\ 0 & 0 & 1 & 0 \\ 0 & 0 & 0 & 1 \end{bmatrix}$$

(c) *X*-scale
$$\begin{bmatrix} 2 & 0 & 0 & 0 \\ 0 & 1 & 0 & 0 \\ 0 & 0 & 1 & 0 \\ 0 & 0 & 0 & 1 \end{bmatrix}$$

(d) Translation
$$\begin{bmatrix} 1 & 0 & 0 & 2 \\ 0 & 1 & 0 & 2 \\ 0 & 0 & 1 & 0 \\ 0 & 0 & 0 & 1 \end{bmatrix}$$

(e) Rotation followed by translation
$$\begin{bmatrix} 1 & 0 & 0 & 2 \\ 0 & 1 & 0 & 2 \\ 0 & 0 & 1 & 0 \\ 0 & 0 & 0 & 1 \end{bmatrix} \begin{bmatrix} 0.866 & 0.5 & 0 & 0 \\ -0.5 & 0.866 & 0 & 0 \\ 0 & 0 & 1 & 0 \\ 0 & 0 & 0 & 1 \end{bmatrix} = \begin{bmatrix} 0.866 & 0.5 & 0 & 2 \\ -0.5 & 0.866 & 0 & 2 \\ 0 & 0 & 1 & 0 \\ 0 & 0 & 0 & 1 \end{bmatrix}$$

(f) Translation followed by rotation
$$\begin{bmatrix} 0.866 & 0.5 & 0 & 0 \\ -0.5 & 0.866 & 0 & 0 \\ 0 & 0 & 1 & 0 \\ 0 & 0 & 0 & 1 \end{bmatrix} \begin{bmatrix} 1 & 0 & 0 & 2 \\ 0 & 1 & 0 & 2 \\ 0 & 0 & 1 & 0 \\ 0 & 0 & 0 & 1 \end{bmatrix} = \begin{bmatrix} 0.866 & 0.5 & 0 & 2.732 \\ -0.5 & 0.866 & 0 & 0.732 \\ 0 & 0 & 1 & 0 \\ 0 & 0 & 0 & 1 \end{bmatrix}$$

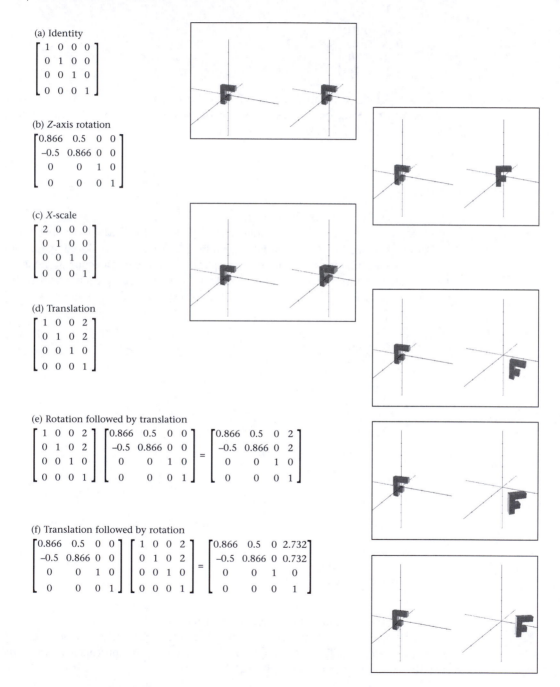

Any set of rotations, scaling and translations can be multiplied or concatenated together to give a net transformation matrix. For example if:

$$\begin{bmatrix} x' \\ y' \\ z' \\ 1 \end{bmatrix} = M_1 \begin{bmatrix} x \\ y \\ z \\ 1 \end{bmatrix}$$

and

$$\begin{bmatrix} x'' \\ y'' \\ z'' \\ 1 \end{bmatrix} = M_2 \begin{bmatrix} x' \\ y' \\ z' \\ 1 \end{bmatrix}$$

then the transformation matrices can be concatenated:

$$M_3 = M_2 M_1$$

and

$$\begin{bmatrix} x'' \\ y'' \\ z'' \\ 1 \end{bmatrix} = M_3 \begin{bmatrix} x \\ y \\ z \\ 1 \end{bmatrix}$$

Note the order: in the product $M_2 M_1$ the first transformation to be applied is M_1. Although translations are commutative, rotations are not and

$$R_1 R_2 \neq R_2 R_1$$

This is demonstrated in Figures 1.2(e) and 1.2(f).

A general transformation matrix will be of the form:

$$\begin{bmatrix} a_{11} & a_{12} & a_{13} & t_x \\ a_{21} & a_{22} & a_{23} & t_y \\ a_{31} & a_{32} & a_{33} & t_z \\ 0 & 0 & 0 & 1 \end{bmatrix}$$

The 3×3 upper left sub-matrix A is the net rotation and scaling while T gives the net translation.

The ability to concatenate transformations to form a net transformation matrix is useful because it gives a single matrix specification for any linear transformation. For example, consider rotating a body about a line parallel to the z axis which passes through the point $(T_x, T_y, 0)$ and also passes through one of the vertices of the object. Here we are implying that the object is not at the origin and we wish to apply rotation about a reference point in the object itself. In other words, we want to rotate the object with respect to its own coordinate system known as a local coordinate system (see also next section). We cannot simply apply a rotation matrix because this is defined with respect to the origin and

Figure 1.3
Two stages in building up the rotation of an object about one of its own vertices. The rotation is about an axis parallel to the z axis at point P $(T_x, T_y, 0)$. (a) Original object at $(T_x, T_y, 0)$. (b) Translate to the origin. (c) Rotate about the origin. (d) Translate to $p(T_x, T_y, 0)$.

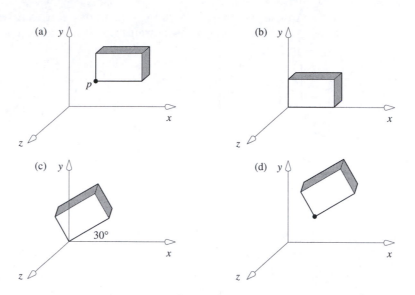

an object not positioned at the origin would rotate and translate – not usually the desired effect. Instead we have to derive a net transformation matrix as follows:

(1) translate the object to the origin,

(2) apply the desired rotation, and

(3) translate the object back to its original position.

The net transformation matrix is:

$$
\mathbf{T_2 R T_1} =
\begin{bmatrix}
1 & 0 & 0 & -T_x \\
0 & 1 & 0 & -T_y \\
0 & 0 & 1 & 0 \\
0 & 0 & 0 & 1
\end{bmatrix}
\begin{bmatrix}
\cos\theta & -\sin\theta & 0 & 0 \\
\sin\theta & \cos\theta & 0 & 0 \\
0 & 0 & 1 & 0 \\
0 & 0 & 0 & 1
\end{bmatrix}
\begin{bmatrix}
1 & 0 & 0 & T_x \\
0 & 1 & 0 & T_y \\
0 & 0 & 1 & 0 \\
0 & 0 & 0 & 1
\end{bmatrix}
$$

$$
=
\begin{bmatrix}
\cos\theta & -\sin\theta & 0 & (-T_x\cos\theta + T_y\sin\theta + T_z) \\
\sin\theta & \cos\theta & 0 & (-T_x\sin\theta - T_y\cos\theta + T_y) \\
0 & 0 & 1 & 0 \\
0 & 0 & 0 & 1
\end{bmatrix}
$$

This process is shown in Figure 1.3 where θ is 30°.

1.1.2

Transformations for changing coordinate systems

Up to now we have discussed transformations that operate on points all of which are expressed relative to one particular coordinate system. This is known as the world coordinate system. In many contexts in computer graphics we need to derive transformations that take points from one coordinate system into another. The commonest context is when we have a number of objects each specified by a set of vertices in a coordinate system embedded in the object itself. This is known as a local coordinate system. Every object will have a convenient local coordinate system; for example, a complex object that is basically cylindrical in shape may have a coordinate axis that coincides with the long axis of the cylinder. If we wish to bring a number of such objects together and position them in a scene then the scene would take the world coordinate system and we would apply translations, rotations and scale transformations to the objects to position them in the scene. Thus we can consider that the transformations operate on the object or equivalently on the local coordinate system of the object. Transformations that emplace an object with a local coordinate system into a position in a world coordinate system are called modelling transformations.

Another important context that involves a change of coordinate system is the transformation from the world coordinate system to the view coordinate system – a viewing transformation. Here we have a new coordinate system – an object if you like – defined with respect to the world coordinate system and we have to transform the vertices in the world coordinate system to this new system.

Consider two coordinate systems with axes parallel, that is, the systems only differ by a translation. If we wish to transform points currently expressed in system 1 into system 2 then we use the inverse of the transformation that takes the origin of system 1 to that of system 2. That is, a point $(x,y,z,1)$ in system 1 transforms to a point $(x',y',z',1)$ by:

$$\begin{bmatrix} x' \\ y' \\ z' \\ 1 \end{bmatrix} = \begin{bmatrix} 1 & 0 & 0 & -T_x \\ 0 & 1 & 0 & -T_y \\ 0 & 0 & 1 & -T_z \\ 0 & 0 & 0 & 1 \end{bmatrix} \begin{bmatrix} x \\ y \\ z \\ 0 \end{bmatrix}$$

$$= \boldsymbol{T}_{12} = (\boldsymbol{T}_{21})^{-1}$$

which is the transformation that translates the origin of system 1 to that of system 2 (where the point is still expressed relative to system 1). Another way of putting it is to say that the transformation generally required is the inverse of the transformation that takes the old axes to the new axes within the current coordinate system.

This is an important result because we generally find transformations between coordinate systems by considering transformations that operate on origins and axes. In the case of viewing systems a change in coordinate systems involves both translation and rotation and we find the required transformation in this way by considering a combination of rotations and translations.

1.2

Vectors and computer graphics

Vectors are used in a variety of contexts in computer graphics. They are used, for example, in shading where a vector associated with a surface is compared with the position of a light source. We would represent the velocity of a moving object, such as a car in a computer game, with a vector. A vector is an entity that possesses magnitude and direction. Velocity possesses both a magnitude (sometimes called the speed) and a direction and this distinguishes it from a scalar quantity, which only has magnitude. An example of a scalar is the temperature of a point in space. A three-dimensional vector is written as a triple:

$$\boldsymbol{V} = (v_1, v_2, v_3)$$

where each component v_i is a scalar. In programming with vectors we consider them as single entities or data structures; but at the lowest level of code vector manipulations will generally involve the same calculations on each of the components of the vector.

1.2.1 Addition of vectors

Addition of two vectors $\boldsymbol{V}$ and $\boldsymbol{W}$, for example, is defined as:

$$\begin{aligned} \boldsymbol{X} &= \boldsymbol{V} + \boldsymbol{W} \\ &= (x_1, x_2, x_3) \\ &= (v_1 + w_1,\ v_2 + w_2,\ v_3 + w_3) \end{aligned}$$

Geometrically this is interpreted as follows. The 'tail' of $\boldsymbol{W}$ is placed at the 'head' of $\boldsymbol{V}$ and $\boldsymbol{X}$ is the vector formed by joining the tail of $\boldsymbol{V}$ to the head of $\boldsymbol{W}$. This is shown in Figure 1.4 for a pair of two-dimensional vectors together with an alternative, but equivalent, interpretation. A common example of the application of vector addition is given in Chapter 14. This is the (vector) addition of forces, a calculation that has to be made if more than one force is simultaneously applied to a body in a dynamic simulation. Because the forces generally act in different directions, vector addition must be used to calculate the net force.

Figure 1.4
Two geometric
interpretations of the sum
of two vectors.

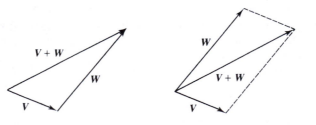

1.2.2 Length of vectors

The magnitude or length of a vector is defined to be

$$|\boldsymbol{V}| = (v_1^2 + v_2^2 + v_3^2)^{1/2}$$

and we interpret this geometrically as the distance from its tail to its head.

We normalise a vector to produce a unit vector which is a vector of length equal to one. The normalised version of $\boldsymbol{V}$ is:

$$\boldsymbol{U} = \boldsymbol{V}/|\boldsymbol{V}|$$

which is a vector of unit length having the same direction as $\boldsymbol{U}$. We can now refer to $\boldsymbol{U}$ as a direction. Note that we can write:

$$\boldsymbol{V} = |\boldsymbol{V}|\boldsymbol{U}$$

which is saying that any vector is given by its magnitude times its direction. Normalisation is used frequently in computer graphics because we are interested in calculating and representing the orientation of entities, such as adjacent surfaces, and comparative orientation requires normalised vectors.

1.2.3

Normal vectors and cross-products

In computer graphics considerable processing is carried out using vectors that are normal to a surface. For example, in a polygon mesh model (Chapter 2) a normal vector is used to represent the orientation of a surface when comparing this with the direction of the light. Such a comparison is used in reflection models to compute the intensity of the light reflected from the surface. The smaller the angle between the light vector and the vector that is normal to the surface, the higher is the intensity of the light reflected from the surface (Chapter 6).

A normal vector to a polygon is calculated from three (non-collinear) vertices of the polygon. Three vertices define two vectors $\boldsymbol{V}_1$ and $\boldsymbol{V}_2$ (Figure 1.5) and the normal to the polygon is found by taking the cross product of these:

$$\boldsymbol{N}_\mathrm{p} = \boldsymbol{V}_1 \times \boldsymbol{V}_2$$

The cross product of two vectors $\boldsymbol{V}$ and $\boldsymbol{W}$ is a vector $\boldsymbol{X}$ and is defined as:

$$\boldsymbol{X} = \boldsymbol{V} \times \boldsymbol{W}$$
$$= (v_2w_3 - v_3w_2)\boldsymbol{i} + (v_3w_1 - v_1w_3)\boldsymbol{j} + (v_1w_2 - v_2w_1)\boldsymbol{k}$$

where $\boldsymbol{i}$, $\boldsymbol{j}$ and $\boldsymbol{k}$ are the standard unit vectors:

$$\boldsymbol{i} = (1,0,0)$$
$$\boldsymbol{j} = (0,1,0)$$
$$\boldsymbol{k} = (0,0,1)$$

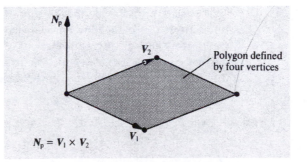

Figure 1.5
Calculating the normal vector to a polygon.

that is, vectors oriented along the coordinate axes that define the space in which the vectors are embedded.

Geometrically, a cross-product, as we have implied, is a vector whose orientation is normal to the plane containing the two vectors forming the cross-product. When determining the surface normal of a polygon, the cross product must point outwards with respect to the object. In a right-handed coordinate system the sense of the cross-product vector is given by the right hand rule. If the first two fingers of your right hand point in the direction of V and W then the direction of X is given by your thumb.

If the surface is a bi-cubic parametric surface (Chapter 5), then the orientation of the normal vector varies continuously over the surface. We compute the normal at any point (u,v) on the surface again by using a cross-product. This is done by first calculating tangent vectors in the two parametric directions (we outline the procedure here for the sake of completeness and give full details in Chapter 5). For a surface defined as $Q(u,v)$ we find:

$$\frac{\partial}{\partial u} Q(u,v) \text{ and } \frac{\partial}{\partial v} Q(u,v)$$

We then define:

$$N_s = \frac{\partial Q}{\partial u} \times \frac{\partial Q}{\partial v}$$

This is shown schematically in Figure 1.6.

Figure 1.6
Normal N to a point on a parametric surface $Q(u,v)$.

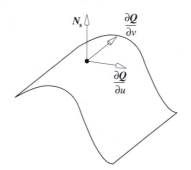

1.2.4 Normal vectors and dot products

The most common use of a dot product in computer graphics is to provide a measure of the angle between two vectors, where one of the vectors is a normal vector to a surface or group of surfaces. Common applications are shading (the angle between a light direction vector and a surface normal) and visibility testing (the angle between viewing vector and a surface normal).

The dot product of vectors V and W is a scalar X which is defined as:

$$X = V.W$$
$$= v_1w_1 + v_2w_2 + v_3w_3$$

Figure 1.7
The dot product of the two vectors is related to the cosine of the angle between them:

$$\cos = \frac{V.W}{|V||W|}$$

(b) $|X| = V.W$ is the length of the projection of **W** onto **V**.

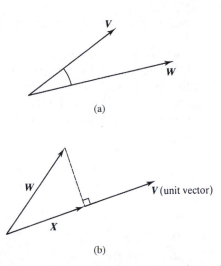

(a)

(b)

Figure 1.7(a) shows two vectors. Using the cosine rule we have:

$$|V - W|^2 = |V|^2 + |W|^2 - 2|V||W|\cos\theta$$

where θ is the angle between the vectors. Also it can be shown that:

$$|V - W|^2 = |V|^2 - 2V\cdot W + |W|^2$$

thus

$$V\cdot W = |V||W|\cos\theta$$

giving

$$\cos\theta = \frac{V\cdot W}{|V||W|}$$

or the angle between two vectors is the dot product of their normalised versions.

We can use the dot product to project a vector onto another vector. Consider a unit vector **V**. If we project any vector **W** onto **V** (Figure 1.7(b)) and call the result **X**, then we have:

$$|X| = |W|\cos\theta$$

$$= |W|\frac{V\cdot W}{|V||W|}$$

$$= V\cdot W \tag{1.1}$$

because **V** is a unit vector. Thus the dot product of **V** and **W** is the length of the projection of **W** onto **V**.

A property of the dot product used in computer graphics is its sign. Because of the relationship of the dot product of **V** and **W** (where **V** and **W** are of any length) to $\cos\theta$ the sign of $V\cdot W$ is:

$$V\cdot W > 0 \quad \text{if } \theta < 90 \text{ degrees}$$
$$V\cdot W = 0 \quad \text{if } \theta = 90 \text{ degrees}$$
$$V\cdot W < 0 \quad \text{if } \theta > 90 \text{ degrees}$$

Vectors associated with the normal vector

There are three important vectors that are associated with the surface normal. They are the light direction vector L, the reflection vector or mirror vector R and the viewing vector V. The light direction vector L is a vector whose direction is given by the line from the tail of the surface normal to the light source; which in simple shading contexts is defined as the point on the surface that we are currently considering. This vector is shown in Figure 1.8(a). The reflection vector R is given by the direction of the light reflected from the surface due to light incoming along direction L. Sometimes called the mirror direction, geometric optics tells us that the outgoing angle equals the incoming angle as shown in Figure 1.8(b).

Consider the construction shown in Figure 1.9. This shows:

$$R = R_1 + R_2$$
$$R_1 = -L + R_2 \qquad\qquad [1.1]$$

Thus

$$R = 2R_2 - L$$

from Equation 1.1

$$R_2 = (N \cdot L)N$$

and

$$R = 2(N \cdot L)N - L$$

The reflection vector is used in certain types of texture mapping (Chapter 7) and in the global rendering algorithm called ray tracing.

Figure 1.8(c) shows a view vector V. Note that this vector has any arbitrary orientation and we are normally interested in that component of light incoming in direction L that is reflected along V. This will depend in general on both the angles ϕ_v and θ_v. We also note that the intensity of outgoing light depends on the incoming angles ϕ_i and θ_i, and this is usually described as a bi-directional dependence because two angles, (ϕ_v, θ_v) and (ϕ_i, θ_i) in three-dimensional space are involved.

Rays and computer graphics

In computer graphics we are interested in an entity called a ray (mathematically known as a directed line segment) that possesses position, magnitude and direction. Rays are used in rendering in ray tracing and ray casting (Chapter 4) and also in general computational geometry calculations such as those required in collision detection (Chapter 15). If a user fires a missile then we can easily find the surface that the missile first intersects by representing its path as a ray.

If we imagine a ray to be a physical line in three-space, then its position is the position of the tail of the line, its magnitude the length of the line between its

Figure 1.8
Vectors associated with the
normal vector. (a) *L*, the
light direction vector,
(b) *R*, the reflection vector,
(c) *V*, the view vector, is a
vector of any orientation.

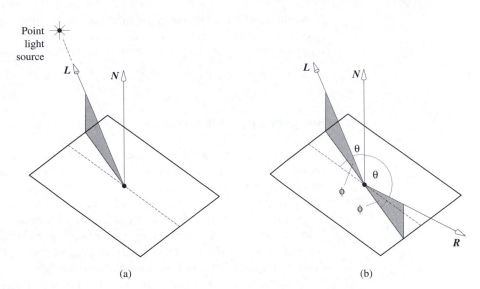

(a)   (b)

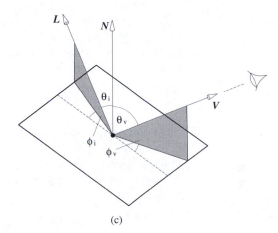

(c)

Figure 1.9
Construction of the
reflection vector *R*.

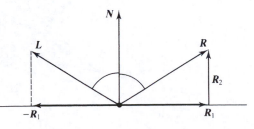

head and tail and its direction the direction of the line. A ray can be specified by two points or by a single point, and a vector. If the end points of the ray are (x_1, y_1, z_1) and (x_2, y_2, z_2) respectively then the vector is given by:

$$\mathbf{V} = (x_2 - x_1, y_2 - y_1, z_2 - z_1)$$

1.3.1 Ray geometry – intersections

The most common calculation associated with rays is intersection testing – we see whether a ray has hit an object and, if so, where. Here we test a ray against all objects in the scene for an intersection. This is potentially a very expensive calculation and the most common technique used to make this more efficient is to enclose objects in the scene in bounding volumes – the most convenient being a sphere – and test first for a ray/sphere intersection. The sphere encloses the object and if the ray does not intersect the sphere it cannot intersect the object. Another common bounding volume is a box.

Spheres and boxes are also used to bound objects for collision detection tests in computer animation (Chapter 15). Pairs of objects can collide only if their bounding volumes intersect. The motivation here is the same as that for ray tracing – we first cull away pairs that cannot possibly collide before we undertake detailed intersection checking at the individual polygon level. Checking for sphere/sphere intersection is trivial and for boxes – if they are axis aligned – then we only need limit checks in the x, y and z directions.

1.3.2 Intersections – ray–sphere

The intersection between a ray and a sphere is easily calculated. If the end points of the ray are (x_1, y_1, z_1) and (x_2, y_2, z_2) then the first step is to parametrise the ray (Figure 1.10):

$$
\begin{aligned}
x &= x_1 + (x_2 - x_1)t = x_1 + it \\
y &= y_1 + (y_2 - y_1)t = y_1 + jt \\
z &= z_1 + (z_2 - z_1)t = z_1 + kt
\end{aligned}
$$

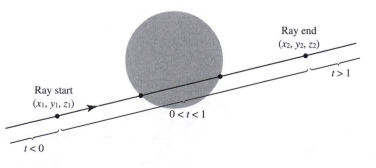

Figure 1.10
Values of parameter t along a ray.

where

$$0 \leq t \leq 1$$

A sphere at centre (l,m,n) of radius r is given by:

$$(x - l)^2 + (y - m)^2 + (z - n)^2 = r^2$$

Substituting for x, y and z gives a quadratic equation in t of the form:

$$at^2 + bt + c = 0$$

where:

$$a = i^2 + j^2 + k^2$$
$$b = 2i(x_1 - l) + 2j(y_1 - m) + 2k(z_1 - n)$$
$$c = l^2 + m^2 + n^2 + x_1^2 + y_1^2 + z_1^2 + 2(-lx_1 - my_1 - nz_1) - r^2$$

If the determinant of this quadratic is < 0 then the line does not intersect the sphere. If the determinant equals 0 then the line grazes or is tangential to the sphere. The real roots of the quadratic give the front and back intersections. Substituting the values for t into the original parametric equations yields these points. Figure 1.10 shows that the value of t also gives the position of the points of intersection relative to (x_1,y_1,z_1) and (x_2,y_2,z_2). Only positive values of t are relevant and the smallest value of t corresponds to the intersection nearest to the start of the ray.

Other information that is usually required from an intersection is the surface normal although, if the sphere is being used as a bounding volume, only the fact that an intersection has occurred, or not, is required.

If the intersection point is (x_i,y_i,z_i) and the centre of the sphere is (l,m,n) then the normal at the intersection point is:

$$\mathbf{N} = \left(\frac{x_i - l}{r}, \frac{y_i - m}{r}, \frac{z_i - n}{r} \right)$$

1.3.3

Intersections – ray–convex polygon

If an object is represented by a set of polygons and is convex then the straightforward approach is to test the ray individually against each polygon. We do this as follows:

(1) Obtain an equation for the plane containing the polygon.
(2) Check for an intersection between this plane and the ray.
(3) Check that this intersection is contained by the polygon.

A more common application of this operation is clipping a polygon against a view frustum (Chapter 6). Here the 'ray' is a polygon edge and we need to find the intersection of a polygon edge and a view frustum plane so that the polygon can be split and that part outside the view frustum discarded.

For example, if the plane containing the polygon is:

$$Ax + By + Cz + D = 0$$

and the line is defined parametrically as before, then the intersection is given by:

$$t = -(Ax_1 + By_1 + Cz_1 + D)/(Ai + Bj + Ck) \qquad [1.2]$$

(See Section 9.5.2 on how to derive A, B, C and D.)

We can exit the test if $t < 0$. This means that the ray is in the half-space defined by the plane that does not contain the polygon (Figure 1.11(a)). We may also be able to exit if the denominator is equal to zero which means that the line and plane are parallel. In this case the ray origin is either inside or outside the polyhedron. We can check this by examining the sign of the numerator. If the numerator is positive then the ray is in that half-space defined by the plane that is outside the object and no further testing is necessary (Figure 1.11(b)).

The straightforward method that tests a point for containment by a polygon is simple but expensive. The sum of the angles between lines drawn from the point to each vertex is $360°$, if the point is inside the polygon, but not if the point lies outside.

There are three disadvantages or inadequacies in this direct approach. We cannot stop when the first intersection emerges from the test unless we also evaluate whether the polygon is front- or back-facing with respect to the ray direction. The containment test is particularly expensive. It is also possible for errors to occur when a ray and a polygon edge coincide.

All of those disadvantages can be overcome by a single algorithm developed by Haines (1991). Again we use the concept of a plane that contains a polygon defining a half-space. All points on one side of the plane are outside the polyhedron. Points on the other side may be contained by the polyhedron. The logical intersection of all inside half spaces is the space enclosed by the polyhedron. A ray that intersects a plane creates a directed line segment (unbounded in the

Figure 1.11
(a) A ray in the half-space that does not contain the object ($t < 0$). (b) A possible exit condition. The ray is parallel to the plane containing the polygon currently being tested. It is either inside or outside the object.

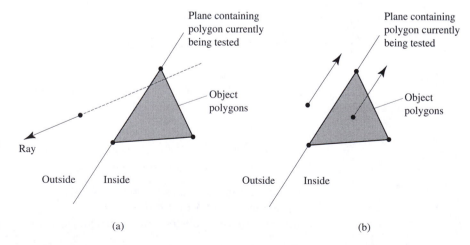

direction of the ray) defined by the intersection point and the ray direction. It is easily seen that the logical intersection of all directed line segments gives the line segment that passes through the polyhedron. Proceeding as before, we exit from the test when a parallel ray occurs with an 'outside' origin. Otherwise the algorithm considers every polygon and evaluates the logical intersection of the directed line segments. Consider the example shown in Figure 1.12. For each plane we categorise it as front-facing or back-facing with respect to the ray direction. This is given by the sign of the denominator in Equation 1.2 (positive for back-facing, negative for front-facing). The conditions that form the logical intersection of directed line segments are embedded in the algorithm which is:

{initialize t_{near} to large negative value
      t_{far} to large positive value}

if *{plane is back-facing}* **and** *($t < t_{far}$)*
then *$t_{far} = t$*

if *{plane is front-facing}* **and** *($t > t_{near}$)*
then *$t_{near} = t$*

if *($t_{near} > t_{far}$)* **then** *{exit – ray misses}*

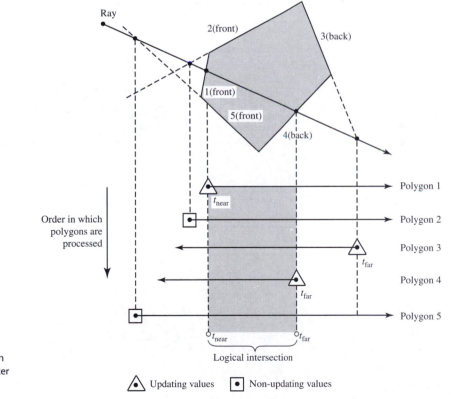

Figure 1.12
Ray–convex polyhedron intersection testing (after Haines (1991)).

Intersections – ray–box

Ray–box intersections are important because boxes may be more useful bounding volumes than spheres, particularly in hierarchical schemes. Also, generalised boxes can be used as an efficient bounding volume.

Generalised boxes are formed from pairs of parallel planes, but the pairs of planes can be at any angle with respect to each other. In this section we consider the special case of boxes forming rectangular solids, with the normals to each pair of planes aligned in the same direction as the ray tracing axes or the object space axes.

To check if a ray intersects such a box is straightforward. We treat each pair of parallel planes in turn, calculating the distance along the ray to the first plane (t_{near}) and the distance to the second plane (t_{far}). The larger value of t_{near} and the smaller value of t_{far} is retained between comparisons. If the larger value of tnear is greater than the smaller value of t_{far}, the ray cannot intersect the box. This is shown, for an example, in the xy plane in Figure 1.13. If a hit occurs then the intersection is given by t_{near}.

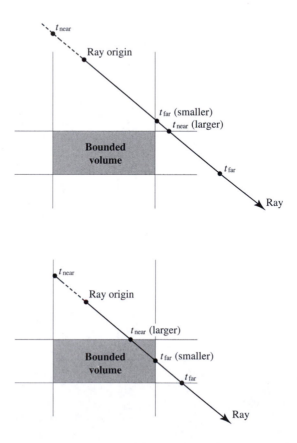

Figure 1.13
Ray–box intersection.

A more succinct statement of the algorithm comes from considering the distance between the intersection points of a pair of parallel planes as intervals. Then if the intervals intersect, the ray hits the volume. If they do not intersect the ray misses.

Again, because our convex polygon is reduced to a rectangular solid, we can define the required distances in terms of the box extent. Distances along the ray are given for the x plane pairs as follows: if the box extent is (x_{b1}, y_{b1}, z_{b1}) and (x_{b2}, y_{b2}, z_{b2}) then:

$$t_{1x} = \frac{x_{b1} - x_1}{x_2 - x_1}$$

is the distance along the ray from its origin to the intersection with the first plane, and:

$$t_{2x} = \frac{x_{b2} - x_1}{x_2 - x_1}$$

The calculations for t_{1y}, t_{2y} and t_{1z}, t_{2z} are similar. The largest value out of the t_1 set gives the required t_{near} and the smallest value of the t_2 set gives the required t_{far}. The algorithm can exit at the y plane calculations.

1.4 Bi-linear interpolation of polygon properties

In mainstream rendering techniques – that is rendering polygons – various properties required for interior pixels are interpolated from the values of these properties at the vertices of the polygon (that is, the pixels onto which the vertices project). Such interpolation is known as bi-linear interpolation and it is the foundation of the efficiency of this kind of shading.

Referring to Figure 1.14, the interpolation proceeds by moving a scan line down through the pixel set representing the polygon and obtaining start and end values for a scan line by interpolating between the appropriate pair of vertex properties. Interpolation along a scan line then yields a value for the property at each pixel. The interpolation equations are (for the particular edge pair shown in the illustration):

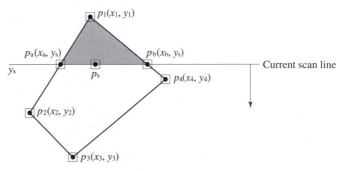

Figure 1.14
Interpolating a property at a pixel from values at the vertex pixel.

$$p_a = \frac{1}{y_1 - y_2} \left[p_1 (y_s - y_2) + p_2 (y_1 - y_s) \right]$$

$$p_b = \frac{1}{y_1 - y_4} \left[p_1 (y_s - y_4) + p_4 (y_1 - y_s) \right]$$

$$p_s = \frac{1}{x_b - x_a} \left[p_a (x_b - x_s) + p_b (x_s - x_a) \right]$$

These would normally be implemented using an incremental form, the final equation, for example, becoming:

$$p_s = p_s + \Delta p$$

with the constant value Δp calculated once per scan line.

1.5 A basic maths engine using SIMD instructions

The above manipulations are easily implemented in standard code. In this section we look at an optimised implementation. We note that 4×4 matrix multiplication involves a total of 64 products and 48 sums and a 4×1 vector matrix product involves 16 multiplications and 12 sums. SIMD (single instruction multiple data) instructions enable four multiplications or four additions to take place simultaneously, and we use this facility in the following implementation.

The following code segment defines a vector and a matrix class with several methods and operators used in the above text. It contains the minimum set of operations required in three-dimensional graphics. We use Intel assembler instructions for faster performance when a SIMD symbol is defined for the compiler (Pentium3 or greater). If no SIMD is defined, it uses standard single data floating-point operations which are much slower.

```
#pragma pack(16)       // 16 byte data align

#define SIMD

class vector4;               // 4 floats
class mat4x4;                // 16 floats

class vector4
{
    public:
            float x,y,z,w;

        vector4() { ; }; // un-initialised constructor

        // initialises a vector from 3 or 4 floats
        vector4(float x0,float y0,float z0,float w0=1.0f)
        { x=x0; y=y0; z=z0; w=w0; };
```

```
// set value from 3 or 4 floats
void vec(float x0,float y0,float z0,float w0=1.0f)
{ x=x0; y=y0; z=z0; w=w0; };

// clears vector to (0,0,0,1)
void null(void)
{ x=y=z=0.0f; w=1.0f; };

// indexes the ith component
float& operator[](int i)
{ return (&x)[i]; };

// evaluates the magnitude of the vector
float length(void)
{ return (float)sqrt(x*x+y*y+z*z); };

// inverts the vector
void negate(void)
{ x=-x; y=-y; z=-z; };

// normalises the vector
void normalize(void)
{
float len=(float)sqrt(x*x+y*y+z*z);
if (len==0.0f)
        return;
x/=len; y/=len; z/=len;
}
// evaluates the cross-product
void cross(vector4& v1,vector4& v2)
{
#ifdef SIMD
        __asm
        {
        mov esi,v1
        mov edi,v2

        movaps xmm0,[esi]
        movaps xmm1,[edi]
        movaps xmm2,xmm0
        movaps xmm3,xmm1

        shufps xmm0,xmm0,0xc9
        shufps xmm1,xmm1,0xd2
        mulps xmm0,xmm1

        shufps xmm2,xmm2,0xd2
        shufps xmm3,xmm3,0xc9
        mulps xmm2,xmm3

        subps xmm0,xmm2
```

```
                           mov esi,this
                           movaps [esi],xmm0
                           }
#else
        x=v1.y*v2.z-v1.z*v2.y;
        y=v1.z*v2.x-v1.x*v2.z;
        z=v1.x*v2.y-v1.y*v2.x;
        w=1.0f;
#endif
        }
        // defines an operator: vector4+=vector4 for vector addition
        void operator+=(vector4& v)
        {
#ifdef SIMD
                __asm
                {
                mov esi,this
                mov edi,v
                movaps xmm0,[esi]
                addps xmm0,[edi]
                movaps [esi],xmm0
                }
#else
                x+=v.x; y+=v.y; z+=v.z; w+=v.w;
#endif
        }
        // defines an operator: vector4-=vector4 for vector
        // subtraction
        void operator-=(vector4& v)
        {
#ifdef SIMD
                __asm
                {
                mov esi,this
                mov edi,v
                movaps xmm0,[esi]
                subps xmm0,[edi]
                movaps [esi],xmm0
                }
#else
                x-=v.x; y-=v.y; z-=v.z; w-=v.w;
#endif
        }
        // defines an operator vector4*=vector4 for the dot product
        void operator*=(vector4& v)
```

```
        {
#ifdef SIMD
                __asm
                {
                mov esi,this
                mov edi,v
                movaps xmm0,[esi]
                mulps xmm0,[edi]
                movaps [esi],xmm0
                }
#else
                x*=v.x;  y*=v.y;  z*=v.z;  w*=v.w;
#endif
        }




        // defines an operator: vector4+vector4   for vector addition
        vector4 operator+(vector4& v)
        {
                __declspec(align(16)) vector4 ret;
#ifdef SIMD
                __asm
                    {
                    mov esi,this
                    mov edi,v
                    movaps xmm0,[esi]
                    addps xmm0,[edi]
                    movaps ret,xmm0
                    }
#else
                ret.x=x+v.x;  ret.y=y+v.y;  ret.z=z+v.z;  ret.w=w+v.w;
#endif
            return ret;
        }
        // defines an operator: vector4-vector4 for vector
        // subtraction
        vector4 operator-(vector4& v)
        {
                __declspec(align(16)) vector4 ret;
#ifdef SIMD
                __asm
                    {
                    mov esi,this
                    mov edi,v
```

```
                                movaps xmm0,[esi]
                                subps xmm0,[edi]
                                movaps ret,xmm0
                                }
#else
                ret.x=x-v.x; ret.y=y-v.y; ret.z=z-v.z; ret.w=w-v.w;
#endif
            return ret;
        }
        // defines an operator: vector4*vector4 for dot product
        vector4 operator*(vector4& v)
        {
                __declspec(align(16)) vector4 ret;
#ifdef SIMD
                __asm
                    {
                    mov esi,this
                    mov edi,v
                    movaps xmm0,[esi]
                    mulps xmm0,[edi]
                    movaps ret,xmm0
                    }
#else
                ret.x=x*v.x; ret.y=y*v.y; ret.z=z*v.z; ret.w=w*v.w;
#endif
            return ret;
        }


        // defines an operator: vector4*mat4x4 to multiply a vector
        // and a matrix
        vector4 operator*(mat4x4& m)
        {
            __declspec(align(16)) vector4 a;
#ifdef SIMD
                __asm
                {
                        mov esi, this
                        mov edi, m

                        movaps xmm0,[esi]
                        movaps xmm1,xmm0
                        movaps xmm2,xmm0
                        movaps xmm3,xmm0

                        shufps xmm0,xmm2,0x00
```

```
                        shufps  xmm1,xmm2,0x55
                        shufps  xmm2,xmm2,0xAA
                        shufps  xmm3,xmm3,0xFF

                        mulps   xmm0,[edi]
                        mulps   xmm1,[edi+16]
                        mulps   xmm2,[edi+32]
                        mulps   xmm3,[edi+48]

                        addps   xmm0,xmm1
                        addps   xmm0,xmm2
                        addps   xmm0,xmm3

                        movaps  a,xmm0

                }
#else
                float *f=(float *)this;
                a.x = x*f[0]  + y*f[4]  + z*f[8]   + w*f[12];
                a.y = x*f[1]  + y*f[5]  + z*f[9]   + w*f[13];
                a.z = x*f[2]  + y*f[6]  + z*f[10]  + w*f[14];
                a.w = x*f[3]  + y*f[7]  + z*f[11]  + w*f[15];
#endif
        return a;
        }
};
class mat4x4
{
public:
        float m[4][4];
        // clears all matrix elements to zero
        void null(void)
        {
        memset(&m,0,sizeof(m));
        }
        // sets the matrix to an identity matrix
        void load_identity(void)
        {
        memset(m,0,sizeof(m));
        m[0][0]=m[1][1]=m[2][2]=m[3][3]=1.0;
        }
        // sets up a  matrix as a rotation of rad around vector vec
        void set_rotation( vector4& dir, float rad );
        // operator mat4x4*max4x4
        inline mat4x4 operator*(mat4x4& m1)
        {
            __declspec(align(16)) mat4x4 m2;
#ifdef SIMD
```

```
            __asm
            {
                mov edi,m1
                movaps xmm4,[edi]
                movaps xmm5,[edi+16]
                movaps xmm6,[edi+32]
                movaps xmm7,[edi+48]

                mov esi,this
                mov     eax,0

                LOOP:
                movaps xmm0,[esi+eax]
                movaps xmm1,xmm0
                movaps xmm2,xmm0
                movaps xmm3,xmm0

                shufps xmm0,xmm2,0x00
                shufps xmm1,xmm2,0x55
                shufps xmm2,xmm2,0xAA
                shufps xmm3,xmm3,0xFF

                mulps xmm0,[edi]
                mulps xmm1,[edi+16]
                mulps xmm2,[edi+32]
                mulps xmm3,[edi+48]

                addps xmm0,xmm1
                addps xmm0,xmm2
                addps xmm0,xmm3

                movaps m2+eax,xmm0

                add eax, 16
                cmp     eax, 48
                jle LOOP
            }
    #else
            int i,j,k;
            float ab;
            for(i=0; i<4; i++)
                    for(j=0; j<4; j++)
                    {
                    ab=0.0f;
                    for(k=0; k<4; k++)
                            ab+=m[i][k]*m1.m[k][j];
                    m2.m[i][j]=ab;
                    }
    #endif
        return m2;
```

```
        }
        // defines an operator: mat4x4*vector4 to multiply a matrix
        // and a vector
        vector4 operator*(vector4& v)
        {
            __declspec(align(16)) vector4 a;
#ifdef SIMD
            __asm
            {
                    mov esi, v
                    mov edi, this

                    movaps xmm0,[esi]
                    movaps xmm1,xmm0
                    movaps xmm2,xmm0
                    movaps xmm3,xmm0

                    shufps xmm0,xmm2,0x00
                    shufps xmm1,xmm2,0x55
                    shufps xmm2,xmm2,0xAA
                    shufps xmm3,xmm3,0xFF

                    mulps xmm0,[edi]
                    mulps xmm1,[edi+16]
                    mulps xmm2,[edi+32]
                    mulps xmm3,[edi+48]

                    addps xmm0,xmm1
                    addps xmm0,xmm2
                    addps xmm0,xmm3

                    movaps a,xmm0
            }
#else
            float *f=(float *)this;
            a.x = v.x*f[0] + v.y*f[4] + v.z*f[8] + v.w*f[12];
            a.y = v.x*f[1] + v.y*f[5] + v.z*f[9] + v.w*f[13];
            a.z = v.x*f[2] + v.y*f[6] + v.z*f[10] + v.w*f[14];
            a.w = v.x*f[3] + v.y*f[7] + v.z*f[11] + v.w*f[15];
#endif
            return a;
        }
    };
```

A simple example:

```
    main()
    {
        vector4 v1(1,2,3,4);
        vector4 v2(5,6,7,8);
```

```
        vector4 v3;
        mat4x4 m1,m2,m3;

        m1.load_identity();
        m2.load_identity();
        printf("v1=(%f,%f,%f,%f)\n",v1.x,v1.y,v1.z,v1.w);
        printf("v2=(%f,%f,%f,%f)\n",v2.x,v2.y,v2.z,v2.w);

        v3=v1+v2;
        printf("add=(%f,%f,%f,%f)\n",v3.x,v3.y,v3.z,v3.w);

        v3=v1-v2;
        printf("sub=(%f,%f,%f,%f)\n",v3.x,v3.y,v3.z,v3.w);

        v3=v1*v2;
        printf("dot=(%f,%f,%f,%f)\n",v3.x,v3.y,v3.z,v3.w);

        v3.cross(v1,v2);
        printf("cross=(%f,%f,%f,%f)\n",v3.x,v3.y,v3.z,v3.w);

        v3=v1*m1;
        printf("vecmat=(%f,%f,%f,%f)\n",v3.x,v3.y,v3.z,v3.w);

        m3=m1*m2;
        printf("matmul=(%f,%f,%f,%f)\n                    (%f,%f,%f,%f)\n
(%f,%f,%f,%f)\n         (%f,%f,%f,%f)\n",
                m3.m[0][0],m3.m[0][1],m3.m[0][2],m3.m[0][3],
                m3.m[1][0],m3.m[1][1],m3.m[1][2],m3.m[1][3],
                m3.m[2][0],m3.m[2][1],m3.m[2][2],m3.m[2][3],
                m3.m[3][0],m3.m[3][1],m3.m[3][2],m3.m[3][3]);
    }
```

prints:

```
    v1=(1.000000,2.000000,3.000000,4.000000)
    v2=(5.000000,6.000000,7.000000,8.000000)

    add=(6.000000,8.000000,10.000000,12.000000)

    sub=(-4.000000,-4.000000,-4.000000,-4.000000)

    dot=(5.000000,12.000000,21.000000,32.000000)

    cross=(-4.000000,8.000000,-4.000000,0.000000)

    vecmat=(1.000000,2.000000,3.000000,4.000000)

    matmul=(1.000000,0.000000,0.000000,0.000000)
            (0.000000,1.000000,0.000000,0.000000)
            (0.000000,0.000000,1.000000,0.000000)
            (0.000000,0.000000,0.000000,1.000000)
```

Modelling and representation 1 – comparative review and polygon mesh models

2.1 Introduction

2.2 Polygonal representation of three-dimensional objects

2.3 High-level methods – constructive solid geometry

2.4 High-level creation using modellers/editors

2.1 Introduction

We begin this chapter with a general discussion on modelling and representation in computer graphics and take a comparative look at the main representational methods used. Although most of these methods are not currently used by the games industry, it is important to understand their usage and advantages in mainstream computer graphics. And it is certainly the case that at the time of writing (2000) the games industry is beginning to look seriously at bi-cubic parametric representations as a way of levering visual complexity without a vast increase in polygon count.

Modelling and representation is a general phrase which can be applied to any or all of the following aspects of objects:

- creation of a three-dimensional computer graphics representation;

- the technique or method or data structure used to represent the object;

- manipulation of the representation – in particular changing the shape of an existing model.

The ways in which we can create computer graphics objects are almost as many and varied as the objects themselves. For example, we might construct an object using an interactive modelling program. This might use some interface based on a sweeping technique where so-called ducted solids are created by sweeping a cross-section along a spine curve. If we are interested in representing a real existing object we may take data directly from a device such as a laser ranger or a three-dimensional digitiser.

The representation of an object is very much an unsolved problem in computer graphics. We can distinguish between a representation that is required for a machine or renderer and the representation that is required by a user or user interface. Representing an object using polygonal facets – a polygon mesh representation – is the most popular machine representation. It is, however, an inconvenient representation for a user or creator of an object. Despite this, it is used as both a user and a machine representation. Other methods have separate user and machine representations. For example, bi-cubic parametric patches and constructive solid geometry (CSG) methods, which constitute user or interface representations, may be converted into polygon meshes for rendering.

The polygon mesh form suffers from many disadvantages when the object is complex and detailed. The predominant disadvantage is that the number of polygons in an object representation can be anything from a few tens to hundreds of thousands. This has serious ramifications in rendering time and object creation cost and in the feasibility of rendering the object in real time. Even with the advent of fast hardware renderers, a high polygon count causes a bottleneck on the CPU–3D card bus.

Other serious problems accrue in animation where a model has both to represent the shape of the object and be controlled by an animation system which may require collisions to be calculated or the object to change shape as a function of time. Despite this the polygon mesh is the *de facto* representation in both mainstream computer graphics and the computer games industry. Its inertia is due in part to the development of efficient algorithms and hardware to render this description. This has resulted in a somewhat strange situation where it is more efficient – as far as rendering is concerned – to represent a shape with many simple elements (polygons) than to represent it with much fewer (and more accurate) but more complicated elements such as bi-cubic parametric patches (see Chapter 5).

The ability to manipulate the shape of an existing object depends strongly on the representation. Polygon meshes do not admit simple shape manipulation. Moving mesh vertices immediately disrupts the 'polygonal resolution' where a shape has been converted into polygons with some degree of accuracy that is related to the local curvature of the surface being represented. For example, imagine twisting a cube represented by six squares. The twisted object cannot be represented by retaining only six polygons. Another problem with shape manipulation is scale. Sometimes we want to alter a large part of an object which may involve moving many elements at the same time; other times we may require a detailed change.

Different representational methods have their advantages and disadvantages but there is no universal solution to the many problems that still exist. Rather, particular modelling methods have evolved for particular contexts. A good example of this tendency is the development of constructive solid geometry methods (CSG) popular in interactive computer-aided design (CAD) because they facilitate an intuitive interface for the interactive design of complex industrial objects as well as a representation. CSG is a constrained representation in that we can only use it to model shapes that are made up of allowed combinations of the primitive shapes or elements that are included in the system.

The advances in rendering hardware have led to a consumer expectation of higher and higher quality graphics. Using a bare polygon mesh model, the only way in which we can increase the detail quality is to increase the number of polygons. This is illustrated by the models in Figure 2.1. The ultimate impracticality of this extrapolation has led to hybrid methods for very complex and unique objects such as a human head. For example, in representing a particular human head we can use a combination of a polygon mesh model and photographic texture maps. The solid form of the head is represented by a generic polygon mesh which is pulled around to match the actual dimensions of the head to be modelled. The detailed likeness is obtained by mapping a photographic texture onto this mesh. The idea here is that the detailed variations in the geometry are suggested by the texture map rather than by detailed excursions in

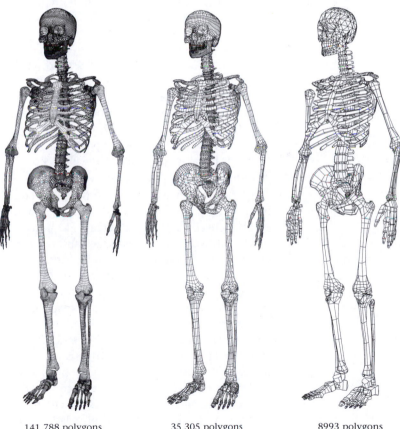

Figure 2.1
The art of wireframe – an illustration from Viewpoint Digital's catalogue.
Source: '3D models by Viewpoint Digital, Inc.' *Anatomy*, Viewpoint's 3D Dataset™ Catalog, 2nd edn.

141 788 polygons   35 305 polygons   8993 polygons

the geometry. Of course, it is not perfect because the detail in the photograph depends on the lighting conditions under which it was taken as well as the real geometric detail, but it is a trick that is increasingly being used. Another common application of photographic texture maps is terrain modelling, as we describe in Chapter 4. Whether we regard the texture mapping as part of the representation or as part of the rendering process is perhaps a matter of opinion; but certainly the use of photographic texture maps in this context enables us to represent a complex object like a human head with a small number of polygons plus a photograph.

This compromise between polygonal resolution and a photographic texture map can be taken to extremes. A recent football game consists of players whose heads are modelled with just a cube onto which a photographic texture is mapped.

We now list in order of approximate frequency of use the mainstream models used in computer graphics. Although in the majority of games applications only the first tends to be used at the moment, the second category is starting to be introduced.

(1) Polygonal.   Objects are approximated by a net or mesh of planar polygonal facets. With this form we can represent, to an accuracy that we choose, an object of any shape. However, the accuracy is somewhat arbitrary in this sense; consider Figure 2.1 again: are 142 000 polygons really necessary, or can we reduce the polygonal resolution without degrading the rendered image, and if so by how much? The shading algorithms are designed to visually transform the faceted representation in such a way that the piecewise linear representation is not visible in the shaded version (except on the silhouette edge). Connected with the polygonal resolution is the final projected size of the object on the screen. Waste is incurred when a complex object, represented by many thousands of polygons, projects onto a screen area that is made up of only a few pixels.

(2) Bi-cubic parametric patches (Chapter 5).   These are 'curved quadrilaterals'. Generally we can say that the representation is similar to the polygon mesh except that the individual polygons are now curved surfaces. Each patch is specified by a mathematical formula that gives the position of the patch in three-dimensional space and its shape. This formula enables us to generate any or every point on the surface of the patch. We can change the shape or curvature of the patch by editing the mathematical specification. This results in powerful interactive possibilities. The problems are, however, significant. When we change the shape of individual patches in a net of patches there are problems in maintaining 'smoothness' between the patch and its neighbours. Bi-cubic parametric patches can either be an exact or an approximate representation. They can only be an exact representation of themselves, which means that any object, say a car body panel, can only be represented exactly if its shape corresponds exactly to the shape of the patch. This somewhat torturous statement is necessary because when the representation is used for real or existing objects, the shape modelled will not necessarily correspond to the surface of the object.

A significant advantage of the representation is its economy. An example of the same object represented by both bi-cubic parametric patches and by polygonal facets is shown in Figure 5.28 (a) and (c). This clearly shows the complexity/number of elements trade-off, with the polygon mesh representation requiring 2048 elements against the 32-patch representation.

(3) CSG (constructive solid geometry). This is an exact representation to within certain rigid shape limits. It has arisen out of the realisation that very many manufactured objects can be represented by 'combinations' of elementary shapes or geometric primitives. For example, a chunk of metal with a hole in it could be specified as the result of a three-dimensional subtraction between a rectangular solid and a cylinder. Connected with this is the fact that such a representation makes for easy and intuitive shape control – we can specify that a metal plate has to have a hole in it by defining a cylinder of appropriate radius and subtracting it from the rectangular solid, representing the plate. The CSG method is a volumetric representation – shape is represented by elementary volumes or primitives. This contrasts with the previous two methods which represent shape using surfaces. An example of a CSG represented object is shown in Figure 2.14.

(4) Spatial subdivision techniques. This simply means dividing the object space into elementary cubes, known as voxels, and labelling each voxel as empty or as containing part of an object. It is the three-dimensional analogue of representing a two-dimensional object as the collection of pixels onto which the object projects. Labelling all of three-dimensional object space in this way is clearly expensive, but it has found applications in computer graphics. We are now representing the three-dimensional space occupied by the object; the other methods we have introduced are representations of the surface of the object.

(5) Implicit representation. Occasionally in texts implicit functions are mentioned as an object representation form. An implicit function is, for example:

$$x^2 + y^2 + z^2 = r^2$$

which is the definition for a sphere. On their own these are of limited usefulness in computer graphics because there are a limited number of objects that can be represented in this way. Also, it is an inconvenient form as far as rendering is concerned. However, we should mention that such representations do appear quite frequently in three-dimensional computer graphics – in particular in ray tracing where spheres are used frequently – both as objects in their own right and as bounding objects for other polygon mesh representations.

Implicit representations are extended into implicit functions which can loosely be described as objects formed by mathematically defining a surface that is influenced by a collection of underlying primitives such as spheres. Implicit functions find their main use in shape-changing animation – they are of limited usefulness for representing real objects. An example of an object modelled initially as a collection of spheres is shown in Figure 2.2

(Colour Plate). The Salvador Dali imitation on the left is an isosurface formed by considering the interaction of the spheres shown on the right. Given the spheres the isosurface is easily defined. The radius of each sphere is proportional to its radius of influence. The dark spheres represent negative generators which are used to 'carve' concavities in the model. (Although we can form concavities by using only positive generators, it is more convenient to use negative ones as we require far fewer spheres.) The example illustrates the potential of the method for modelling organic shapes. Deformable object animation can be implemented by displaying or choreographing the spheres that generate the object. The problem with using implicit functions in animation is that there is not a good intuitive link between moving groups of generators and the deformation that ensues because of this. Of course, this general problem is suffered by all modelling techniques where the geometry definition and the deformation method are one and the same thing.

Above, we have arranged the categories in order of popularity. Another useful comparison is: with voxels and polygon meshes the number of representational elements per object is likely to be high (if accuracy is to be achieved) but the complexity of the representation is low. This contrasts with bi-cubic patches where the number of elements is likely to be much lower in most contexts but the complexity of the representation is higher.

2.2 Polygonal representation of three-dimensional objects

This is the classic representational form in three-dimensional graphics. An object is represented by a mesh of polygonal facets. In the general case an object possesses curved surfaces and the facets are an approximation to such a surface (Figure 2.3). Polygons may contain a vertex count that emerges from the technology used to create the model, or we may constrain all polygons to be triangles. It may be necessary to do this, for example, to gain optimal performance from special-purpose hardware or graphics accelerator cards (Chapter 3).

Polygonal representations are ubiquitous in computer graphics. There are two reasons for this. Creating polygonal objects is straightforward (although for complex objects the process can be time consuming and costly) and visually

Figure 2.3
Approximating a curved surface using polygonal facets.

effective algorithms (now embedded in hardware) exist to produce shaded versions of objects represented in this way. As we have already stated, polygon meshes are strictly a machine representation – rather than a convenient user representation – and they often function in this capacity for other representations which are not directly renderable. Thus bi-cubic parametric patches, CSG and voxel representations are often converted into polygon meshes prior to rendering.

There are certain practical difficulties with polygon meshes. Foremost amongst these is accuracy. The accuracy of the model, or the difference between the faceted representation and the curved surface of the object, is usually arbitrary. As far as final image quality is concerned, the size of individual polygons should ideally depend on local spatial curvature. Where the curvature changes rapidly, more polygons are required per unit area of the surface. These factors tend to be related to the method used for creating the polygons. If, for example, a mesh is being built from an existing object, by using a three-dimensional digitiser to determine the spatial coordinates of polygon vertices, the digitiser operator will decide on the basis of experience how large each polygon should be. Sometimes polygons are extracted algorithmically (as, for example, in the creation of an object as a solid of revolution or in a bi-cubic patch subdivision algorithm) and a more rigorous approach to the rate of polygons per unit area of the surface is possible.

One of the most significant developments in three-dimensional graphics was the emergence in the 1970s of shading algorithms that deal efficiently with polygonal objects, and at the same time, through an interpolation scheme, diminish the visual effect of the piece-wise linearities in the representation. This factor, together with recent developments in fixed program rendering hardware, has secured the entrenchment of the polygon mesh structure.

In the simplest case, a polygon mesh is a structure that consists of polygons represented by a list of linked (x,y,z) coordinates that are the polygon vertices (edges are represented either explicitly or implicitly as we shall see in a moment). Thus the information we store to describe an object is finally a list of points or vertices. We may also store, as part of the object representation, other geometric information that is used in subsequent processing. These are usually polygon normals and vertex normals. Calculated once only, it is convenient to store these in the object data structure and have them undergo any linear transformations that are applied to the object.

It is convenient to order polygons into a simple hierarchical structure. Figure 2.4(a) shows a decomposition that we have called a conceptual hierarchy for reasons that should be apparent from the illustration. Polygons are grouped into surfaces and surfaces are grouped into objects. For example, a cylinder possesses three surfaces: a planar top and bottom surface together with a curved surface. The reason for this grouping is that we must distinguish between those edges that are part of the approximation – edges between adjacent rectangles in the curved surface approximation to the cylinder, for example – and edges that exist in reality. The way in which these are subsequently treated by the rendering process is different – real edges must remain visible whereas edges that form part of the approximation to a curved surface must be made invisible. Figure 2.4(b) shows a more formal representation of the topology in Figure 2.4(a).

An example of a practical data structure which implements these relationships is shown in Figure 2.4(c). This contains horizontal as well as vertical hierarchical links, necessary for programmer access to the next entity in a horizontal sequence. It also includes a vertex reference list which means that actual vertices (referred to by each polygon that shares them) are stored only once. Another difference between the practical structure and the topological diagram is that access

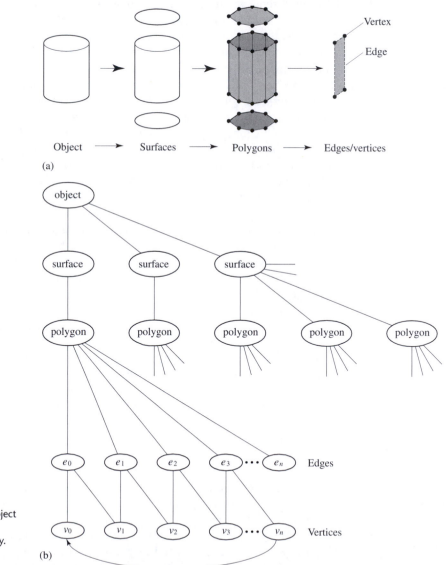

Figure 2.4
Representation of an object as a mesh of polygons.
(a) Conceptual hierarchy.
(b) Topological representation.

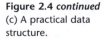

Figure 2.4 *continued*
(c) A practical data
structure.

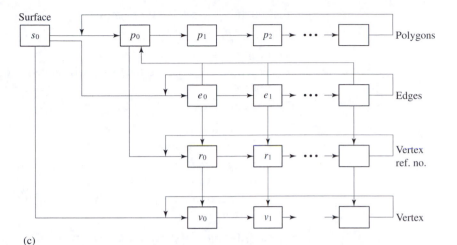

(c)

is allowed directly to lower-level entities. Wireframe visualisations of an object
are used extensively and to produce a wireframe image requires direct access to
the edge level in the hierarchy. Vertical links between the edges and the polygons, levels can be either backward pointers or forward pointers depending on
the type of renderer that is accessing the structure. In a scan line renderer, edges
are the topmost entity whereas in a Z-buffer renderer polygons are. A Z-buffer
renderer treats polygons as independent entities, rendering one polygon at a
time. A scan line renders all those polygons that straddle the scan line being rendered.

The approach just described is more particularly referred to as a vertex-based
boundary model. Sometimes it is necessary to use an edge-based boundary
model, the most common manifestation of which is a winged-edge data structure (Mantyla, 1988). An edge-based model represents a face in terms of a closing sequence of edges.

The data structure just described encapsulates the basic geometry associated
with polygonal facets of an object. Information required by applications and
renderers is also usually contained in the scene/object database. The following
list details the most common attributes found in polygon mesh structures. They
are either data structure pointers, real numbers or binary flags. It is unlikely that
all of these would appear in a practical application, but a subset is found in most
object representations.

- Polygon attributes
  (1) Triangular or not
  (2) Area
  (3) Normal to the plane containing the polygon
  (4) Coefficients (A,B,C,D) of the plane containing the polygon
      where $Ax + By + Cz + D = 0$
  (5) Whether convex or not

    (6) Whether it contains holes or not

- Edge attributes

  (1) Length

  (2) Whether it is an edge between two polygons or an edge between two surfaces

  (3) Polygons on each side of the edge

- Vertex attributes

  (1) Polygons that contribute to the vertex

  (2) Shading or vertex normal – the average of the normals of the polygons that contribute to the vertex

  (3) Texture coordinates (u,v) specifying a mapping into a two-dimensional texture image

All these are absolute properties that exist when the object is created. Polygons can aquire attributes as they are passed through the graphics pipeline. For example, an edge can be tagged as a silhouette edge if it is between two polygons with normals facing towards and away from the viewer.

A significant problem that crops up in many guises in computer graphics is the scale problem. With polygonal representation this means that, in many applications, we cannot afford to render all the polygons in a model if the viewing distance and polygonal resolution are such that many polygons project onto a single pixel. This problem bedevils flight simulators, computer games and virtual reality applications. An obvious solution is to have a hierarchy of models and use the one appropriate to the projected screen area. There are two problems with this. The first is that in animation (and it is in animation applications that this problem is most critical) switching between models can cause visual disturbances in the animation sequence – the user can see the switch from one resolution level to another. The other problem is how to generate the hierarchy and how many levels it should contain. Clearly we can start with the highest-resolution model and subdivide; but this is not necessarily straightforward. We look at this problem in more detail in Chapters 3 and 4.

2.2.1   Creating polygonal objects

Much of the labour in games development involves building scenes or levels, objects and characters. Many applications enabling levels to be built are available. In this section we will look at the very basic options available to build polygon mesh objects considering single polygons as the unit of creation. (A particular way of building simple levels by joining boxes together is given in Section 2.4).

Although a polygon mesh is the most common representational form in computer graphics, modelling, although straightforward, is somewhat tedious. The popularity of this representation derives from the ease of modelling, the emergence of rendering strategies (both hardware and software) to process polygonal objects and the important fact that there is no restriction whatever on the shape or complexity of the object being modelled.

Interactive development of a model is possible by 'pulling' vertices around with a three-dimensional locator device but in practice this is not a very useful method. It is difficult to make other than simple shape changes. Once an object has been created, any one polygon cannot be changed without changing its neighbours also. Thus most creation methods use either a device or a program; the only method that admits user interaction is number 4 on the following list of four common examples of polygon modelling methods:

(1) using a three-dimensional digitiser or adopting an equivalent manual strategy;

(2) using an automatic device such as a laser ranger;

(3) generating an object from a mathematical description;

(4) generating an object by sweeping.

The first two modelling methods convert real objects into polygon meshes, the next two generate models from definitions. We distinguish between models generated by mathematical formulae and ones generated by interacting with curves which are defined mathematically.

Manual modelling of polygonal objects

The easiest way to model a real object is manually using a three-dimensional digitiser. The operator uses experience and judgement to emplace points on an object which are to be polygon vertices. The three-dimensional coordinates of these vertices are then input into the system via a three-dimensional digitiser. The association of vertices with polygons is straightforward. A common strategy for ensuring an adequate representation is to draw a net over the surface of the object – like laying a real net over the object. Where curved net lines intersect defines the position of the polygon vertices. A historic photograph of this process is shown in Figure 2.5. This shows students creating a polygon mesh model of a car in 1974. It is taken from a classic paper by early outstanding pioneers in computer graphics – Sutherland, Sproull and Schumacker (1974).

Figure 2.5
The Utah Beetle – an early example of manual modelling. *Source*: Beatty and Booth Tutorial: *Computer Graphics*, 2nd edn, The Institute of Electrical and Electronics Engineers, Inc.: New York © 1982 IEEE

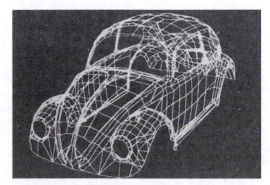

2.2.3   Automatic generation of polygonal objects

A device that is capable of creating very accurate or high-resolution polygon mesh objects from real objects is a laser ranger. In one type of device the object is placed on a rotating table in the path of the beam. The table also moves up and down vertically. The laser ranger returns a set of contours – the intersection of the object and a set of closely spaced parallel planes – by measuring the distance to the object surface. A 'skinning' algorithm, operating on pairs of contours, converts the boundary data into a very large number of triangles (Figure 2.6(a). Figure 2.6(b) is a rendered version of an object polygonised in this way. The skinning algorithm produced, for this object, over 400 000 triangles. Given that only around half of these may be visible on screen and that the object projects onto about half the screen surface implies that each triangle projects onto one pixel on average. This clearly illustrates the point mentioned earlier that it is extremely wasteful of rendering resources to use a polygonal resolution where the average screen area onto which a polygon projects approaches a single pixel. For model creation, laser rangers suffer from the significant disadvantage that in the framework described – fully automatic rotating table device – they can only accurately model convex objects. Objects with concavities will have surfaces that will not necessarily be hit by the incident beam.

Figure 2.6
A rendered polygonal object scanned by a laser ranger and polygonised by a simple skinning algorithm. (a) A skinning algorithm joins points on consecutive contours to make a three-dimentional polygonal object from the contours. (b) A 400 000 polygonal object produced by a skinning algorithm.

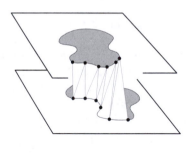

2.2.4   Interactive/mathematical generation of polygon objects

Many polygonal objects are generated through an interface into which a user puts a model description in the form of a set of curves that are a function of two-dimensional or two-parameter space. The most popular paradigm is that of sweeping a cross-section in a variety of different ways. There are two benefits of this approach. The first is fairly obvious. The user works with some notion of shape which is removed from the low-level activity of constructing an object from individual polygonal facets. Instead shape is specified in terms of notions that are connected with the form of the object – something that Snyder (1992) calls 'the logic of shapes'. A program then takes the user description and transforms it into polygons. The transformation from the user description to a polygon mesh is straightforward. A second advantage of this approach is that it can

Figure 2.7
Straight spine objects –
solid of revolution vs
cross-sectional sweeping.
(a) A solid of revolution
generated by sweeping a
(vertical) cross-section.
(b) The same solid can be
generated by sweeping a
circle, whose radius is
controlled by a profile curve
up a straight vertical spine.
(c) Non-circular cross-
section.

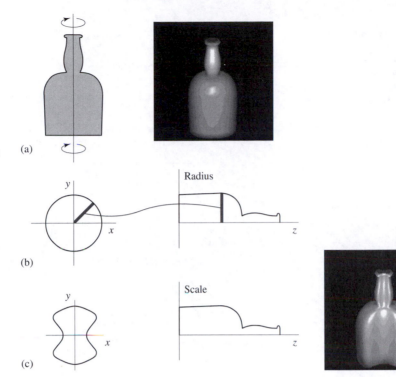

be used in conjunction either with polygons as primitive elements or with bi-cubic parametric patches (see Chapter 5).

The most familiar manifestation of this approach is a solid of revolution where a, say, vertical cross-section is swept through 180°, generating a solid with a circular horizontal cross-section (Figure 2.7(a)). The obvious constraint of solids of revolution is that they can only represent objects possessing rotational symmetry.

A more powerful generative model is arrived at by considering the same solid generated by sweeping a circle, with radius controlled by a profile curve, verti-cally up a straight spine (Figure 2.7(b)). In the event that the profile curve is a constant, we have the familiar notion of extrusion or lofting. This immediately removes the constraint of a circular cross-section and we can have cross-sections of arbitrary shape (Figure 2.7(c)).

Now consider controlling the shape of the spine. We can incorporate the notion of a curved spine and generate objects that are controlled by a cross-sectional shape, a profile curve, and a spine curve as Figure 2.10 demonstrates.

Other possibilities emerge. Figure 2.8 shows an example of what Snyder calls a rail product surface. Here a briefcase carrying-handle is generated by sweeping a cross-section along a path determined by the midpoints of two rail curves. The long axis extent of the elliptical-like cross-section is controlled by the same two

Figure 2.8
Snyder's rail curve product surfaces. *Source*: J.M. Snyder, *Generative Modelling for Computer Graphics and CAD*, Academic Press, 1992.

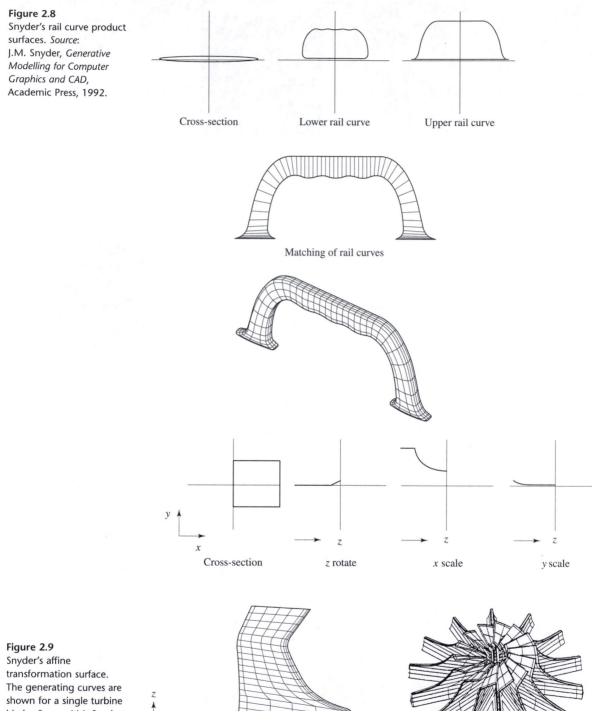

Cross-section   Lower rail curve   Upper rail curve

Matching of rail curves

Cross-section   *z* rotate   *x* scale   *y* scale

Figure 2.9
Snyder's affine transformation surface. The generating curves are shown for a single turbine blade. *Source*: J.M. Snyder, *Generative Modelling for Computer Graphics and CAD*, Academic Press, 1992.

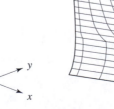

curves – hence the name. A more complex example is the turbine blade shown in Figure 2.9. Snyder calls this an affine transformation surface, because the spine is now replaced by affine transformations, controlled by user-specified curves. Each blade is generated by extruding a rectangular cross-section along the z axis. The cross-section is specified as a rectangle and three shape-controlling curves, functions of z, supply the values used in the transformations of the cross-section as it is extruded. The cross-section is, for each step in z, scaled separately in x and y, translated in x, rotated around, translated back in x, and extruded along the z axis.

A complicated shape is thus generated by a general cross-section and three curves. Clearly implicit in this example is a reliance on a user/designer to be able to visualise the final required shape in three dimension so that he or she is able to specify the appropriate shape curves. Although for the turbine blade example this may seem somewhat of a tall order, we should bear in mind that shapes of such complexity are the domain of professional engineers where the use of such generative models for shape specification will not be unfamiliar.

Certain practical problems emerge when we generalise to curved spines. There are three difficulties in allowing curved spines that immediately emerge. These are illustrated in Figure 2.10. Figure 2.10(a) shows a problem in the curve to polygon procedure. Here it is seen that the size of the polygonal primitives depends on the excursion of the spine curve. The second is how do we orient the cross-section with respect to a varying spine (Figure 2.10(b))? And finally, how do we prevent cross-sections self-intersecting (Figure 2.10(c))? It is clear that this

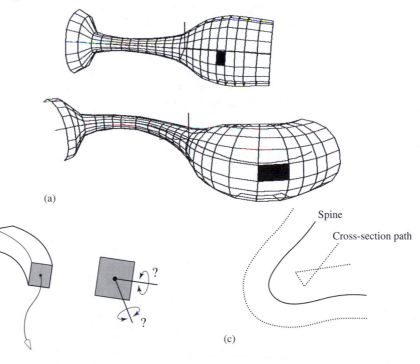

(a)

Figure 2.10
Three problems in cross-sectional sweeping. (a) Controlling the size of the polygons can be problematic. (b) How should the cross-section be orientated with respect to the spine curve? (c) Self-intersection of the cross-section path.

Spine

Cross-section path

(b)

(c)

will occur as soon as the radius of curvature of the path of any points traced out by the cross-sectional curve exceeds the radius of curvature of the spine. We will now look at approaches to these problems.

Consider a parametrically defined cubic along which the cross-section is swept. This can be defined (see Section 5.2) as:

$$Q(u) = au^3 + bu^2 + cu + d$$

Now if we consider the simple case of moving a constant cross-section without twisting it along the curve we need to define intervals along the curve at which the cross-section is to be placed and intervals around the cross-section curve. When we have these we can step along the spine intervals and around the cross-section intervals and output the polygons.

Consider the first problem. Dividing u into equal intervals will not necessarily give the best results. In particular, the points will not appear at equal intervals along the curve. A procedure, known as arc length parametrisation (see Section 13.4), divides the curve into equal intervals, but this procedure is not straightforward. Arc length parametrisation may also be inappropriate. What is really required is a scheme that divides the curve into intervals that depend on the curvature of the curve. When the curvature is high the rate of polygon generation needs to be increased so that more polygons occur when the curvature twists rapidly. The most direct way to do this is to use the curve subdivision algorithm (see Sections 5.7.1 and 5.8.1) and subdivide the curve until a linearity test is positive.

Now consider the second problem. Having defined a set of sample points we need to define a reference frame or coordinate system at each. The cross-section is then embedded in this coordinate system. This is done by deriving three mutually orthogonal vectors that form the coordinate axes. There are many possibilities.

A common one is the Frenet frame. The Frenet frame is defined by the origin or sample point, P, and three vectors T, N and B (Figure 2.11). T is the unit length tangent vector:

$$T = V/|V|$$

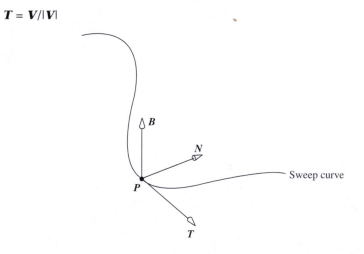

Figure 2.11
The Frenet frame at sample
point P on a sweep curve.

where V is the derivative of the curve:

$$V = 3au^2 + 2bu + c$$

The principal normal N is given by

$$N = K/|K|$$

where:

$$K = V \times A \times V/|V|^4$$

and A is the second derivative of the curve

$$A = 6au + 2b$$

Finally B is given by

$$B = T \times N$$

2.3

High-level methods – constructive solid geometry

The CSG approach is a powerful high-level tool that is found in many modelling packages. It does not manipulate polygons directly but produces polygon models after the modelling or design phase is complete. This is something of an over-simplification since the model has to be rendered during the design process itself. It is a high-level representation that functions both as a shape representation and as a record of how it was built up. The 'logic of the shape' in this representation is in how the final shape can be made or represented as a combination of primitive shapes. The designer builds up a shape by using the metaphor of three-dimensional building blocks and a selection of ways in which they can be combined. The high-level nature of the representation imposes a certain burden on the designer. Although with hindsight the logic of the parts in Figure 2.14 is apparent, the design of complex machine parts using this methodology is a demanding occupation.

The motivation for this type of representation is to facilitate an interactive mode for solid modelling. The idea is that objects are usually parts that will eventually be manufactured by casting, machining or extruding and they can be built up in a CAD program by using the equivalent (abstract) operations combining simple elementary objects called geometric primitives. These primitives are, for example, spheres, cones, cylinders or rectangular solids and they are combined using (three-dimensional) Boolean set operators and linear transformations. An object representation is stored as an attributed tree. The leaves contain simple primitives and the nodes store operators or linear transformations. The representation defines not only the shape of the object but its modelling history – the creation of the object and its representation become one and the same thing. The object is built up by adding primitives and causing them to combine with existing primitives. Shapes can be added to and subtracted from – to make holes – the current shape. For example, increasing the diameter of a hole through a rectangular solid means a trivial alteration – the radius of the cylinder primitive defining the hole is simply increased. This contrasts with the polygon mesh representation where the same operation is distinctly non-trivial. Even although the constituent polygons of the cylindrical surface are easily accessible in a hierarchical scheme, to generate a new set of polygons means reactivating whatever modelling procedure was used to create the original polygons. Also, account has to be taken of the fact that to maintain the same accuracy more polygons will have to be used.

Boolean set operators are used both as a representational form and as a user interface technique. A user specifies primitive solids and combines these using the Boolean set operators. The representation of the object is a reflection or recording of the user interaction operations. Thus we can say that the modelling

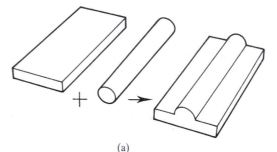

(a)

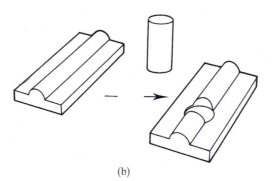

(b)

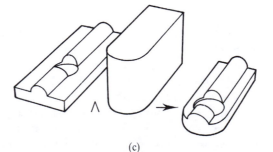

(c)

Figure 2.12
Boolean operations between solids in CSG modelling: (a) union, (b) subtraction and (c) intersection.

All the colour images in this section are reproduced on the CD. Differences between images in certain studies (anti-aliasing, for example) which are not too apparent on the page are visible when viewed on a monitor.

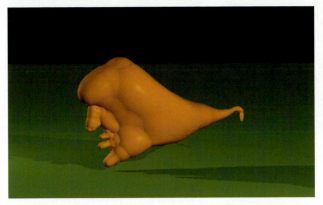

An object (based on a famous Salvador Dali painting)

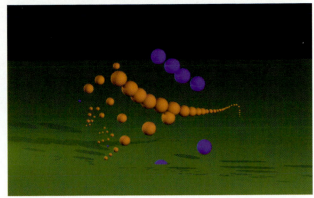

Point generators – the radius of each sphere is the influence of each generator

Figure 2.2
An example of an implicit function modelling system. (Courtesy of Agata Opalach.)

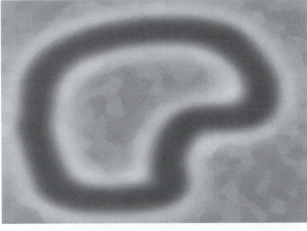

(a)

(b)

(c)

Figure 4.2
Building a simple landscape and car track. (a) A height field constructed in a paint package. (b) Ground texture. (c) A view of the rendered landscape

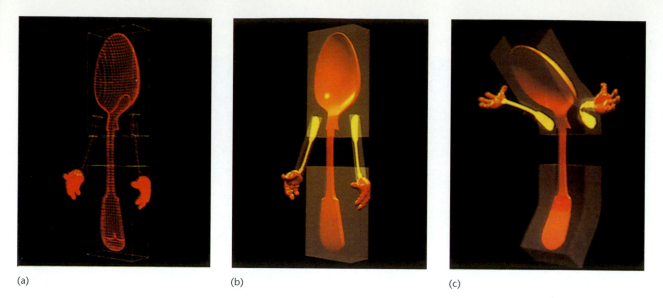

(a)   (b)   (c)

Figure 5.39
FFD applied to a polygon mesh object. (a) Wireframe of the object (b) The object rendered with the trivariate patch grid shown as semi-transparent grey boxes (c) moving the control points in the patch causes the object model to deform in an appropriate manner.

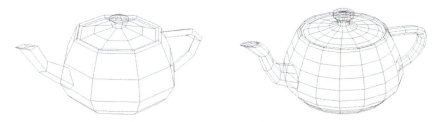

Polygons for the 128 and 512 rendered images.

Figure 5.50
Parametric patch rendering at different levels of uniform subdivision (128, 512, 2048 and 8192 polygons).
(Courtesy of Steve Maddock)

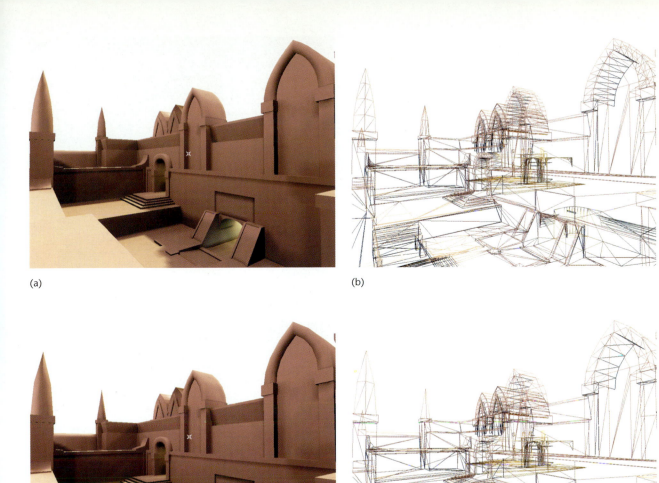

(a)

(b)

(c)

(d)

Figure 5.52
Two consecutive LODs (generated from a Quake 3 level) shown in wireframe and rendered. These are generated by down-sampling the pre-calculated Bezier mesh. Only light map rendering is used to emphasize the silhouette edges.

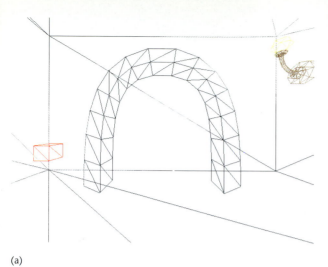

(a)

(b)

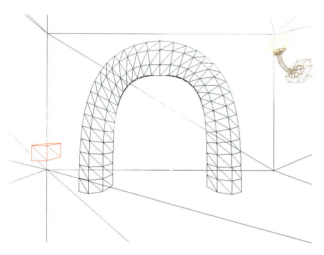

(c)

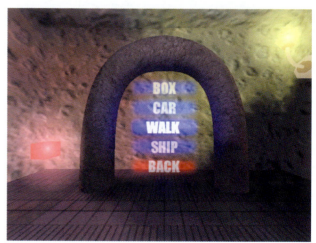

(d)

Figure 5.53
Rendered imagery for uniform and non-uniform subdivision.
2 levels of uniform subdivision

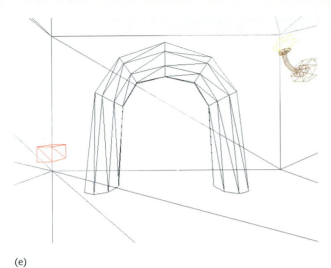

(e)

(f)

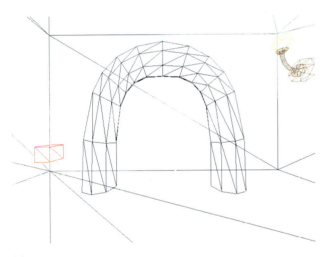

(g)

(h)

Figure 5.53
Rendered imagery for uniform and non-uniform subdivision.
2 levels of non-uniform subdivision

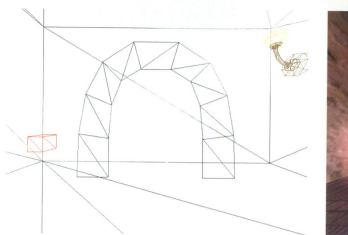

Figure 5.55
No subdivision in the cross-section. The arch is completely flat. Despite this when viewed from the front it still looks curved.

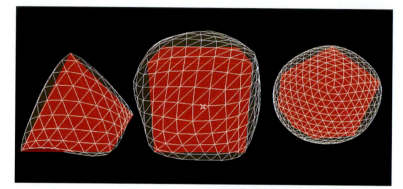

Figure 5.61
Three objects (shown as solid rendered) after three levels of butterfly subdivision.

Figure 6.28
The 'traditional' way of illustrating Phong shading. k_a and k_d are constant throughout k_s is increasing from left to right and the exponent is increasing from top to bottom. The model attempts to increase 'shininess' by increasing the exponent. This makes the extent of the specular highlight smaller, which could also be interpreted as the reflection of a light source of varying size. (The light is a point source.)

Figure 6.36
An office scene, together with a wireframe visualization, that has been shaded using the constant ambient term only.

Figure 6.37
The same scene using flat shading. Flat shading shows the polygonal nature of the surfaces due to discontinuities in intensity.

(a)

Figure 6.38
Main defects in Gouraud interpolation. (a) Colour image. The two defects in this image (described in detail in the text) are: Mach banding (may not be visible in the reproduction) and the interpolation artefact on the back wall.

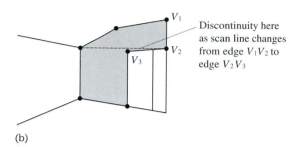

V_1

Discontinuity here
as scan line changes
from edge V_1V_2 to
edge V_2V_3

V_2

V_3

(b)

(c)

Figure 6.38
(b) Dotted line shows the position of the discontinuity. (c) New wireframe triangulation necessary to eliminate the interpolation artefact.

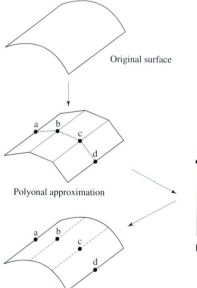

Original surface

Polyonal approximation

a b

c

d

Reflected light intensity
is piecewise linear

This produces Mach bands in the image

Figure 6.39
Mach bands in Gouraud shading.

Figure 6.40
The same scene using Phong shading. A glaring defect in Phong interpolation is demonstrated in this figure. Here the reflected light from the wall light and the image of the light have become separated due to the nature of the interpolation.

Figure 6.41
Stylised rendering using a colour LUT/one-dimensional texture map.
(Car model created by Henrique Vidinha for FLY3D.)

(a)

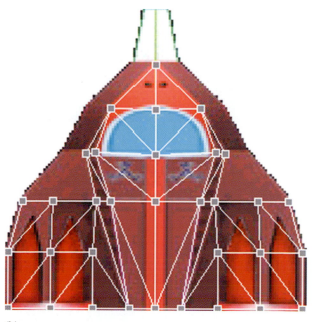

(b)

Figure 7.6
Interactively tuning a texture mapping. (a) Polygon mesh superimposed on mapped object. (b) Interaction can be achieved by picking and dragging vertices on an orthographic projection. (Created by Francisco Meireles for FLY3D.)

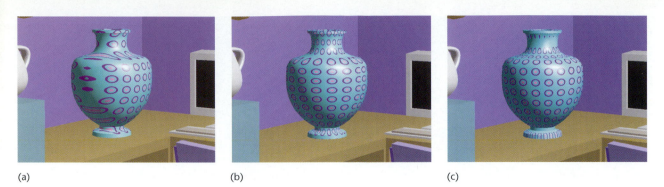

(a) (b) (c)

Figure 7.5
Examples of two-part texture mapping with a solid of revolution. The intermediate surface are: (a) a plane (or no surface); (b) a cylinder, and (c) a sphere.

(a)

Figure 7.9
Agglomerating part maps into a single texture map. a) The single map, b) and c) Two views of the object. (Texture map created by Marina Morato and model Henrique Vidinha for FLY3D.)

(b)

(c)

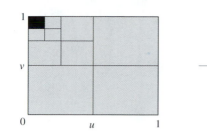

Texture map   1 Bézier patch

Figure 7.10   (Left) Texture map. (Right) One Bezier patch on the object. (Below) Recursive teapot. (Courtesey of Steve Maddock)

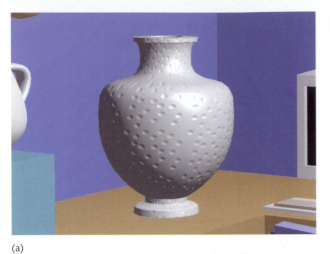

(a)

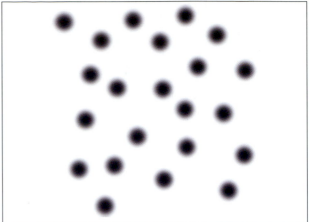

(b)

(c)

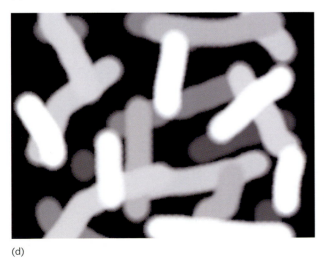

(d)

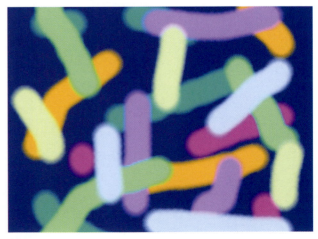

(e)

Figure 7.11
Bump mapping. (a) A bump mapped object together with the bump map. (b) A bump mapped object from a procedurally generated height field. (c) Combining bump and colour mapping. (d) The bump and colour map for (c).

Figure 7.20 Imitating marble – the classic example of a three-dimensional procedural texture.

Figure 7.23
The office scene with 'traditional' two-dimensional texture.

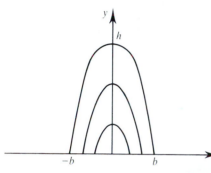

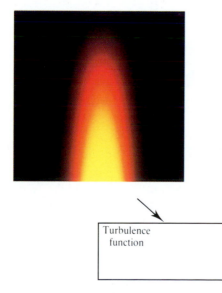

Turbulence
function

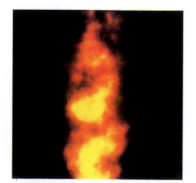

Figure 7.21 Modelling and simulating flame using a turbulence function. (Above) Unturbulated flame. (Right) Turbulated flame.

Figure 7.24
The same scene with shadow and environment mapping
(the teapot) added.

Shadow map

Environment map

Figure 7.25
This is a comparison between generating reflections using environment mapping (left) and ray tracing (right).

Figure 8.13 Mip-map used in Figure 7.10.
(Courtesy of Steve Maddock)

(a)

(b)

(c)

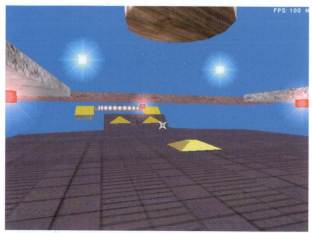

(d)

Figure 8.16

A set of comparison images showing the increase in quality available from mip-mapping. (a) uses no filtering. (b) uses simple neighbourhood filtering where the 4 closest pixels are linearly interpolated to give the final value. (c) mip-mapping with a single map. (d) mip-mapping by linearly interpolating between two maps (tri-linear interpolation).

Figure 10.1 A frame rendered using a light map derived from radiosity solution. The original solution took approximately 1 hour to calculate.
(Courtesy Mark Eastlick)

(a)

(b)

(c)

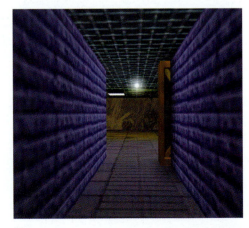

(d)

Figure 10.3
Partially updating light maps. A door opening sequence shows static objects – behind the door – being appropriately re-lit as the door opens.

Figure 10.4
A moving light illuminates a nearby static object.

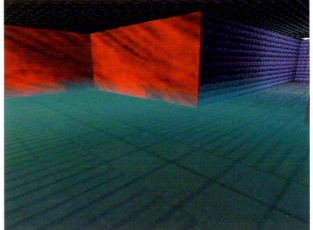

Figure 10.6
Same technique as Figure 10.5 but this time the fog object is a box.

(a)   (b)

Figure 10.5
Volume fog
(a) A spherical fog object implemented by finding those polygons enclosed by the sphere then finding if the polygon/camera rays intersect the fog sphere.
(b) Viewing from inside the fog sphere.

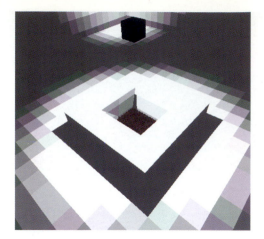

(a)

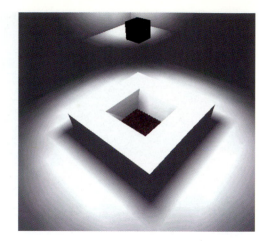

(b)

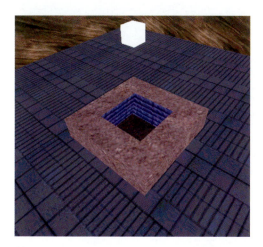

(c)

(d)

(e)

Figure 11.7
Shadows and static objects. Shadows for static objects are pre-calculated as part of the light map. (a) The light map with the shadow calculation applied. (b) As the previous image but this time texture filtering is applied. (c) Shows the texture map applied. (d) The texture map blended with the image in a). (e) The texture map blended with the image in b)

(a)

(b)

(c)

(d)

Figure 11.8
Comparing texture filtered shadows with explicitly generated soft shadows. (a) No soft shadows, no texture filtering. (b) Soft shadows, no texture filtering. (c) No soft shadows, texture filtering. (d) Soft shadows, texture filtering.

Figure 11.9
Simple arbitrary shape, constant surge shadow option
(see also Figure 11.10).

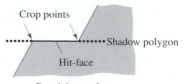

Crop points

Shadow polygon

Hit-face

Receiving surface

(a) Option 1 – using Z_{equal} – shadow
polygon coincident with hit face but
artifacts and cropping occurs

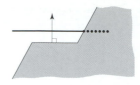

(b) Option 2 – displace shadow
polygon above the hit face and
used $Z_{less\ than\ equal}$ – shadow
polygon still (partially) cropped

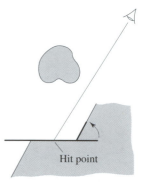

Hit point

(c) Option 3 – no Z buffer comparison – requires
a ray intersection from camera to hit point.
Shadow is only drawn if there are no intervening
objects in the path of the ray

(a)

(b)

(c)

Figure 11.10
Showing the visual discrepancies of different options for fast shadow generation for moving objects. (a) Using Z_{equal} produces cropping and
z-buffer artefacts. (b) Discrepancies in a) are partially alleviated by 'floating' the shadow polygon above the hit surface – cropping still
occurs. (c) Z-buffer comparisons are avoided by using a ray intersect between the camera and the hit surface

Figure 11.12
A shadow calculated by firing a ray from the light source through each vertex of 5 bounding boxes. Note that because the 5 bounding boxes are processed separately they will generate shadow polygons that may separate and overlap depending on the nature of the receiving surface.

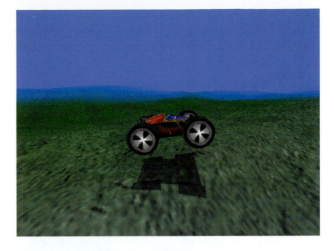

(a)

(b)

(c)

Figure 12.1
Showing a simple multi-pass technique for planar reflections.
(a) The stencil mask for the mirror. (b) The scene rendered 'into' the mirror the scene rendered and the component from b) added.

(a)

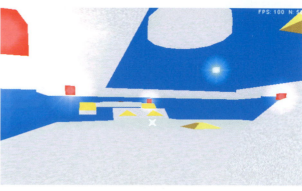

(b)

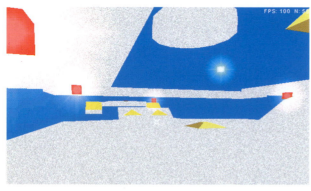

(c)

(d)

(e)

(f)

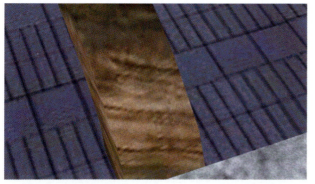

(g)

Figure 12.6

A simple multi-texture effect – adding 'grain' to texture.
(a) Shows a simple detail map made up of a random dark pattern on a white background. (b) Shows a scene using conventional texture – no detail phase added. (c) shows the detail only added to the previous image. (d) shows the previous image using tri-linear filtering. Compared to the previous image we can see that for deep mip-map levels the detail turns to almost solid white (as we would expect). (e) shows the scene with detail added and should be compared with b). (f) zoom without detail texture. (g) zoom with detail texture.

Figure 13.2
An example of manual animation of a character. (Courtesy of Consequência Animação)

Figure 13.8
Showing the effect of using equal parametric intervals in conjunction with a pursuit strategy. (a) A multi-segment Bezier curve shown superimposed on a track. (b) The car pursuing a grey object. (c) The grey object is travelling at uniform velocity in parametric space equal intervals make it speed up and slow down (as can be seen from the unequal spacing between the grey spheres). The pursuit strategy then causes the car to overshoot.

(a)

(b)

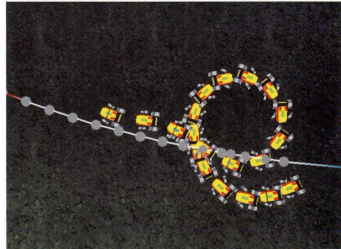

(c)

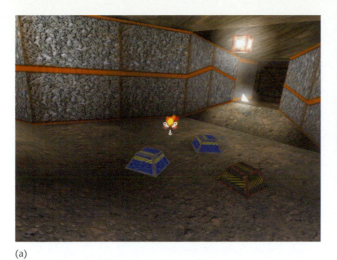
(a)

(b)

(c)

(d)

Figure 13.17
Four frames in a particle explosion. This is a fairly standard implementation of a particle system based on a single emitter.

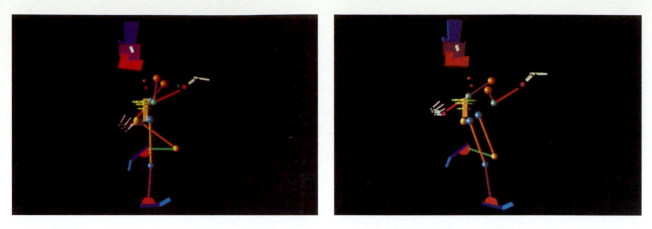

Figure 13.21
Simple characterization using an articulated structure – the flamboyant gait was animated using forward kinematics.

Figure 16.6
Typical motion of the simple car model shown as superimposed frames.

 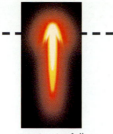

build a $^1/_2$
cross-section

construct a full
cross-section

select a row from the
previous image and rotate
to construct the other
crosss-section

two orthogonal cross-sections shown in perspective

three emplacements of the
billboard – the axis of the long
cross-section is aligned with the
view vector

the same image viewed from
the camera

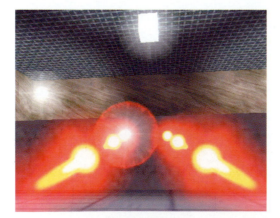

the billboards in action

Figure 19.5
A dynamic billboard built from two
orthogonal planes. (Created by
Marcos Bezerra for FLY3D.)

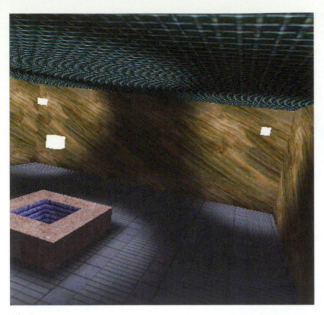
(a)

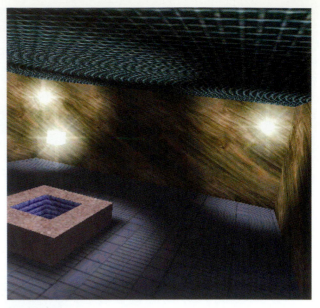
(b)

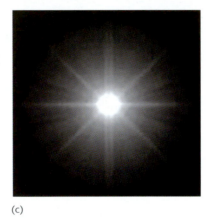
(c)

Figure 19.7
The ubiquitous lens flare effect. (a) Scene without the effect. (b) Scene with the effect. (c) The billboard used to produce lens flare

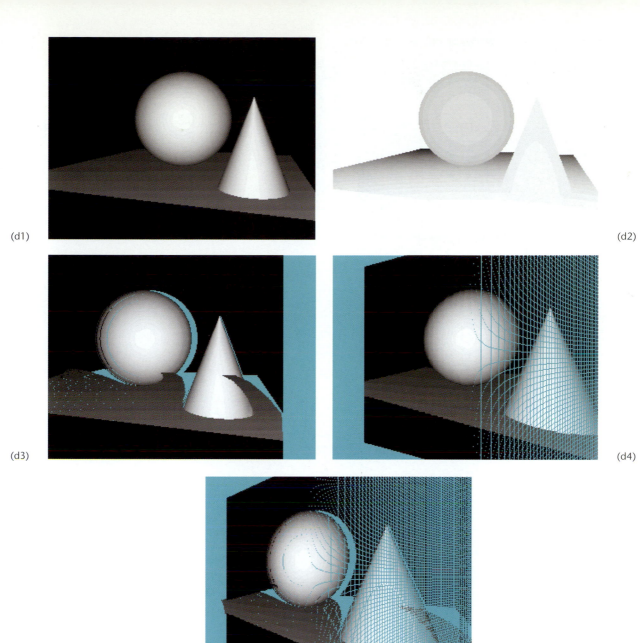

Figure 19.12 (d1 and d2)
A simple scene and the corresponding Z-buffer image.

Figure 19.12 (d3)
Artefacts due to translation (only) in this case are holes (cyan) caused by missing information and image folding.

Figure 19.12 (d4)
Artefacts due to rotation (only) are holes caused by increasing the projected area of surfaces. Note how these form coherent patterns.

Figure 19.12 (d5)
Artefacts caused by both rotation and translation.

1   Overlapping frames from a rotating camera

2   'Stitched' into a cylindrical panoramic image

3   A section of which is warped into a planar polygon

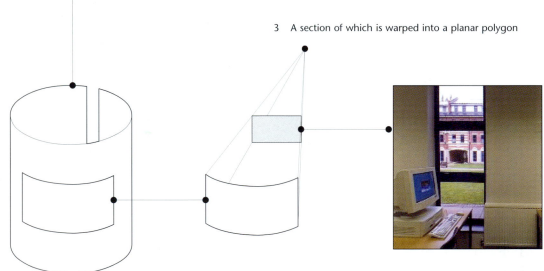

Figure 19.24   QuickTime® VR system, (Courtesy of Guy Brown.)

information and representation are not separate – as they are in the case of deriving a representation from low-level information from an input device. The low-level information in the case of CSG is already in the form of volumetric primitives. The modelling activity becomes the representation. An example will demonstrate the idea.

Figure 2.12 shows the Boolean operations possible between solids. Figure 2.12(a) shows the union of two solids. If we consider the objects as 'clouds' of points the union operation encloses all points lying within the original two bodies. The second example (Figure 2.12(b)) shows the effect of a difference or subtraction operator. A subtract operator removes all those points in the second body that are contained within the first. In this case a cylinder is defined and subtracted from the object produced in Figure 2.12(a). Finally, an example is shown of an intersect operation (Figure 2.12(c)). Here a solid is defined that is made from the union of a cylinder and a rectangular solid (the same operation with the same primitives as in Figure 2.12(a)). This solid then intersects with the object produced in Figure 2.12(b)). An intersect operation produces a set of points that are contained by both the bodies. An obvious distinguishing feature of this method that follows from this example is that primitives are used not just to build up a model but also to take material away.

Figure 2.13 shows a CSG representation that reflects the construction of a simple object. Three original solids appear at the leaves of the tree: two boxes

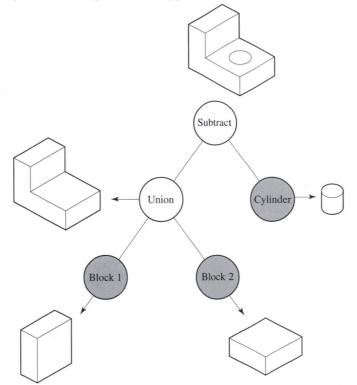

Figure 2.13
A CSG tree reflecting the construction of a simple object made from three primitives.

and a cylinder. The boxes are combined using a union operation and a hole is 'drilled' in one of the boxes by defining a cylinder and subtracting it from the two-box assembly. Thus the only information that has to be stored in the leaves of the tree is the name of the primitive and its dimensions. A node has to contain the name of the operator and the spatial relationship between the child nodes combined by the operator.

The power of Boolean operations is further demonstrated in the following examples. In the first example (Figure 2.14(a)) two parts developed separately are combined to make the desired configuration by using the union operator followed by a difference operator. The second example (Figure 2.14(b)) shows a complex object constructed only from the union of cylinders, which is then used to produce, by subtraction, a complex housing.

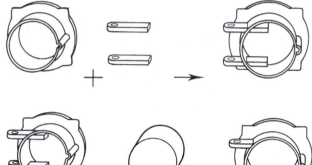

(a)

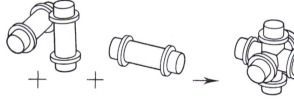

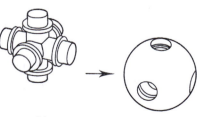

(b)

Figure 2.14
Examples of geometrically complex objects produced from simple objects and Boolean operations.

2.4

High-level creation using modellers/editors

The previous sections described modelling methods that are commonly embedded in modellers/editors. Such software will generally contain many high-level facilities, and may, for example, include a CSG-type facility where an object can be constructed by combining a group of primitive objects.

A simple example built up in three stages is shown in Figure 2.15. The basic building block is a box. The level is constructed by joining boxes together, dragging vertices to convert the boxes into truncated rectangular pyramids and then deleting shared faces to create the final environment. This example is explained in greater detail in Section A.2; here we intend only to demonstrate the general principles used in the construction.

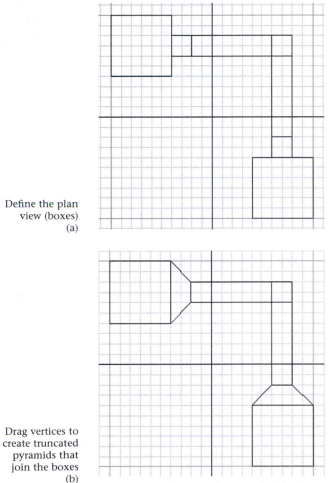

Define the plan
view (boxes)
(a)

Drag vertices to
create truncated
pyramids that
join the boxes
(b)

Figure 2.15
Three stages in building a
simple (box-like) level.

Figure 2.15 *continued*

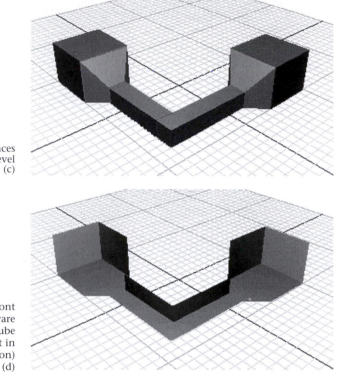

Delete the adjacent faces
to create the final level
(c)

The level with the front
faces removed (beware
of the Necker Cube
illusion prominent in
this illustration)
(d)

The rationale of using such facilities is that the artist wants to work with as powerful and high-level tools as are appropriate in an application. However, the further the artist gets away from low-level polygon manipulation the less control he or she has over polygon count. Steed (1998) points out that using, for example, CSG methods can result in 'extraneous faces that are hard to find'.

In games development an artist will undertake the building of the polygon models to be used in the game, employing such tools as fit the application. The same person will also be responsible for maintaining the polygon count within design limits and may also employ tools such as vertex merging to reduce the number of polygons that may have been produced by a high-level facility such as an extrusion tool. Clearly the manual optimisation of polygon counts for a particular model is something of a black art and defies a theoretical approach; an excellent treatment of this topic is given in Steed (1998).

Modelling and representation 2 – the economics of polygon meshes

3.1 Compressing polygonal models

3.2 Compressing the geometry (information per vertex)

3.3 Encoding connectivity

3.4 Triangle strips

3.5 Local vs. global alogorithms

3.6 Using vertex buffers

3.7 Level of detail (LOD) processing

3.1 Compressing polygonal models

Currently graphics processors are not limited by the so-called pixel fill rate but by the bandwidth of the channel that transfers information into the graphics sub-system. This means that in general 3D cards are capable of rendering more triangles/second than can be transformed across the bus. For example, to transfer a complex scene database of 1 million triangles at 30 Hz and 36 bytes/triangle would require 1080 MB/sec throughput between the processor and the graphics hardware.

There are three ways of reducing the information per polygon:

(1) We can reduce the information sent per polygon vertex.

(2) We can reduce the number of vertices, and the common way of doing this is to generate so called 'tri-strips' for the polygon object.

(3) We can reduce the number of polygons per object according to the number of pixels onto which it projects. This is called level of detail or LOD.

The first two approaches could be categorised as compression methods whereas the third may well expand the total data required to represent the object, an appropriately detailed model being selected in real time.

Ideally we would like to be able to achieve information reduction off-line and limit the computation that is to be done in real time to display the compressed model. This is exactly the same as the notion of asymmetric methods in video compression, where a lengthy off-line compression method enables both a high compression ratio and a decompression or decode time which is realisable in real time. Most approaches are therefore asymmetric.

As in two-dimensional image compression, techniques can be either lossy or lossless. The distinction between these options, however, is more difficult to specify in the three-dimensional domain. An approximate specification is that techniques in the first category, which may, for example, involve coarsening the numerical accuracy of geometric coordinates or colour values, are lossy. Tristrips, on the other hand, are lossless. The geometry is simply encoded in a more efficient manner. In the third category we select a three-dimensional polygonal resolution for the object that is appropriate to its area of projection on the screen. Whether this technique is lossless or not depends crucially on the application. An implementation that resulted in a visual discontinuity (popping), as the representation changed from one level to the other, could certainly be termed lossy because such an artefact would not occur if we only ever rendered the high-detail model.

3.2 Compressing the geometry (information per vertex)

We begin by considering the minimum information required per vertex in a basic application if no compression techniques are adopted. An absolute minimum information set is:

(x,y,z) three-dimensional screen space coordinate of the vertex (12 bytes)

(u,v) texture (colour) coordinates (8 bytes)

(u,v) light map coordinates (8 bytes)

and we note that the use of light maps means that we do not have to use vertex normals which are otherwise required for Gouraud or Phong shading.

This can only be reduced further by sharing texture coordinates – many applications use the same coordinates for both colour and light maps (in our implementation texture and light maps use different (u,v) coordinates, but fog maps share the light map coordinates) and by standard lossless or entropy-reducing data compression techniques.

Common lossless classical data compression techniques are, for example, run length encoding where a stream of data is encoded as duples representing the value of a recurring data item together with the number of times it occurs (the run). Alternatively the data volume can be reduced in most cases by encoding the difference between successive data items and some predicted value rather than their absolute value. Entropy reduction means encoding data items using a symbol whose bit length is inversely proportional to the frequency of occurrence of the data item in the application. In this case the data stream would consist of a sequence of numbers representing the components of each vertex.

Geometry and colour information can be further subject to both lossy and lossless compression techniques. The consequence of loss of accuracy in position specification results in vertices moving (shape change or distortion) and loss of accuracy in colour information means a shift away from the original desired colour. For example, for an object about the size of an automobile engine 10 bits per positional component implies an accuracy of 0.5 mm.

Deering (1995) suggests on the basis of empirical visual tests that the model's local space specification should be restricted to 16 bits per component and then be subjected to delta compression or encoding. Delta compression means encoding the difference between consecutive component values and the deltas themselves can be subject to a variable length code, a common technique being Huffman coding. A requirement of variable length coding to represent the deltas is that each element is preceded by a specific-length data field indicating the bit length of the following code. Deering points out that the deltas of position components are not statistically uncorrelated. If the number of bits required to represent the largest delta is n, then on average $n - 1.4$ bits is required to represent the other two components and because of this he used a single length field to indicate the bit length of Δx, Δy and Δz.

Chow's (1997) method also starts from a basis of 16 bits per component but automatically finds the best quantisation (in the range 3 to 16 bits) for an object. This proceeds by normalising all the position components to the range [−0.5,0.5],

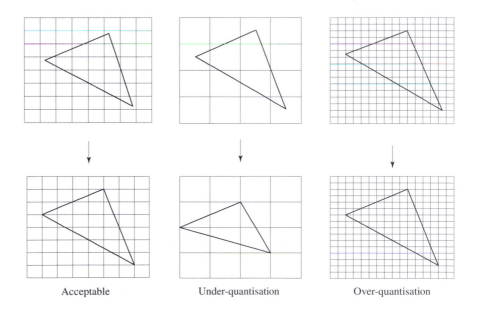

Figure 3.1
A 2D analogy of the 3D quantisation process (after Chow (1997)).

Acceptable   Under-quantisation   Over-quantisation

a process equivalent to enclosing the object in a unit cube subdivided into voxels of dimension $1/2^{16}$. For a particular object an appropriate quantisation q of the unit cube exists. Figure 3.1 shows for a simple two-dimensional example an 'acceptable' value for q, a value of q that is too low resulting in under-precision and a value of q that is too high resulting in over-precision. The quantisation is reduced from 16 bits according to a user-specified error threshold e. This is approximately the range that the user wants to tolerate the vertices moving through when the quantisation is reduced. This is done by finding the average triangle side length and then choosing the quantisation level q such that $1/e$ is within $1/2^q$ by testing all values of q between 3 and 16. These values can then be further compressed by delta and Huffman encoding.

3.3 Encoding connectivity

We can consider (conventional) ways of defining vertex connectivity in a mesh. In some applications the connectivity is implicit or understood. For example, a height field; conventionally used to represent terrain, the mesh connectivity is understood to be formed from a rectangular array (this special case is considered in detail in Chapter 4). We only need store the height of each vertex – no connectivity information is encoded. At the other extreme, for a general object, we specify a pointer for each vertex into an array of vertex positions. Consider the storage costs (and therefore the bandwidth requirements) of this simple scheme. If we assume that we have quantised the vertex components to (an average of) 10 bits then for an object of n vertices we have:

vertex cost = $30n$ bits

A theorem due to Euler shows that, in general, for a triangle mesh there are (at most) twice as many triangles as there are vertices. Thus we have, for a scheme where each triangle vertex points into a list of n vertices:

connectivity cost = $6n \log_2 n$ bits

and

total cost = $(30n + 6n \log_2 n$ bits$)$

The advantage of this common approach can be seen by considering the (more expensive) alternative to this common data structure. This is to store each triangle as a list of three vertices *without* explicit connectivity information and simply recover this from geometric tests on the vertices. Such a scheme requires $180n$ bits per object ($2n$ triangles $\times$ 90 bits/triangle). Each vertex will now appear on average six times.

Rossingnac (1999) suggests the following scheme which does not use explicit connectivity information and does not duplicate vertex data. Each triangle has a vertex descriptor which is either the 30-bit vertex data or a pointer to an already encountered vertex. A one-bit flag indicates which type of descriptor the vertex consists of. Again we have $6n$ elements in the structure but $5n$ of these are pointers to previous elements. The total cost is now:

vertex cost $(1 + 30)n$ bits

pointer cost $(1 + \log_2 n)\ 5n$ bits

where in each case 1 extra bit is required for the flag. If we subtract $30n$ – the vertex storage cost – from this, we have the equivalent connectivity cost of this scheme:

$6n + 5n\log_2 n$ bits

which compares with the connectivity cost of the conventional scheme of:

$6n\log_2 n$ bits

and is lower for objects of more than 64 vertices.

3.4 Triangle strips

Triangle strips or tri-strips are a way of compressing the vertex connectivity information in a triangle mesh. Tri-strips 'order' triangles so that consecutive triangles share an edge, reducing the vertices per strip from $3n$ (if n triangles were sent separately) to $n + 2$ because it is only necessary to specify one new vertex per triangle (Figure 3.2). This, however, is a theoretical lower bound which for a complex model will only be approached by an algorithm that finds 'good'

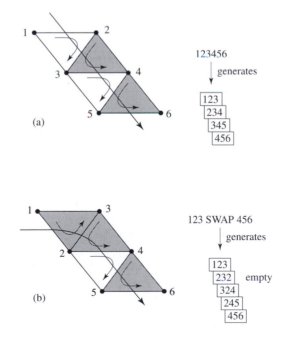

Figure 3.2
Tri-strip representation.
(a) A tri-strip with alternate windings. The strip is represented by the sequence 123456. (b) A tri-strip with two consecutive anti-clockwise windings is represented by 123 SWAP 456.

tri-strips. Figure 3.2(a) shows a simple case where we note that the triangles must exhibit alternate 'winding'. The second example (Figure 3.2(b)) shows a case where this condition is not met. More precisely we say that the triangulation must be sequential, which means that a path (known as the Hamiltonian path) must exist in which no three triangle edges crossed by the path are incident on the same vertex.

Note that although a triangle mesh is a three-dimensional entity, in what follows we consider it as a planar graph where we are only interested in the connectivity of the vertices and not the value of their associated three-dimensional coordinates.

An implementation of this method enables two consecutive vertices to be stored in a buffer which forms in effect a FIFO queue, and a triangle is drawn for every three vertices in the sequence. The class of meshes that can be represented by a sequential triangulation is very limited and the constraint can be relaxed by allowing two of the registers to be swapped. Thus in the case of Figure 3.2(b) we represent the sequence by 123 SWAP 456. The SWAP command (implemented in GL but not in OpenGL) swaps the order of the latest two vertices in the buffer which in effect inserts an empty triangle, as the sequence in Figure 3.2(b) shows. The use of such a facility enables longer tri-strips to be generated at the cost of the insertion of one vertex (compared to the two-vertex cost of starting a new strip) together with the 1-bit cost of the command insertion.

The practical benefit of this facility manifests itself when we generate as long a tri-strip as possible from a triangle mesh. For example, Figure 3.3(a) shows a triangulation that can be represented by a single tri-strip if the SWAP facility is used. Whether a tri-strip can be generated from such a mesh depends on its topology; Figure 3.3(b) shows a mesh which requires two strips. It is not difficult to see from these simple examples that the main problem with tri-strip implementation is achieving the minimum number of strips for any triangle mesh. Algorithms that do this have the clumsy title of 'stripification' algorithms.

Figure 3.3
Tri-strips and triangular meshes. (a) A mesh that can be represented by a single tri-strip that re-references some vertices. (b) A mesh requiring two tri-strips (after an illustration in Bar-Yehuda and Gotsman (1996)).

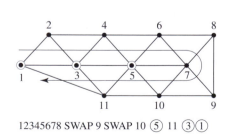

12345678 SWAP 9 SWAP 10 ⑤ 11 ③①

(a)

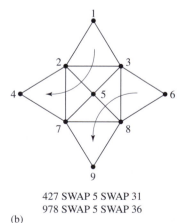

427 SWAP 5 SWAP 31
978 SWAP 5 SWAP 36

(b)

If the sequence representing the mesh in Figure 3.3(a) is examined it can be seen that the vertices 1, 3 and 5 are repeated and this immediately raises the question: can we invoke a scheme that stores repeated vertices so that they do not have to be retransmitted to the graphics hardware? The generalisation of this problem comes from Euler's theorem on graphs which shows that the number of triangles in a mesh is at most twice the number of vertices. Thus in the basic scheme described we would, on average, have to send each vertex twice. This observation has led to the suggestion that a mesh buffer storing repeated vertices should be used, as we describe in Section 3.6.

3.5   Local vs. global algorithms

The first appearance of an algorithm for constructing tri-strips from meshes appears to be due to SGI (Akeley *et al.* 1990). The algorithm constructs a path through the triangles by choosing a neighbour to the current triangle which is itself adjacent to the least number of (unvisited) neighbours. If the algorithm encounters more than one triangle with the same least number of neighbours then it looks ahead one level and applies the same test.

Evans *et al.* (1996) categorise the SGI approach as a local algorithm and introduce the concept of a global algorithm where they conduct a global analysis of a mesh using a technique they term 'patchification'; this approach depends on the observation that many polygon mesh models exhibit large areas which consist of connected quadrilaterals (Figure 3.4). The algorithm is based on finding these patches and then triangulating these row-wise or column-wise at a cost of 3 SWAPs per turn. Patches are found by 'walking' through the structure and counting, for each face, the number of adjacent polygons in the north, south, east and west directions. Each face is visited exactly twice, once for the north–south direction, and once for the east–west direction. This information enables rectangular collections of adjacent polygons to be formed in order of decreasing size. To prevent the formation of patches that are too small, a cut-off threshold is set and the patchification process is terminated when this is reached. A local algorithm can then be used on the remaining algorithms. An obvious disadvantage of the approach is its reliance on quadrilaterals whose appearance in a mesh depends on the nature of the mesh and the modelling method used to create it.

Figure 3.4
Many meshes exhibit large rectangular areas consisting of quadrilaterals. These areas are found and triangulated along rows and columns.

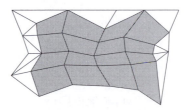

3.6 **Using vertex buffers**

As we have already implied, tri-strips need to be made as long as possible to exploit their compression potential. There have been many approaches to this problem and no one 'standard' solution. When a mesh produces a number of tri-strips, vertices from adjacent strips are reused and this leads to the obvious approach that vertices should be stored on graphics hardware memory to enable reuse locally. This is exactly the approach taken in Deering (1995), Bar-Yehuda and Gotsman (1996) and Evans *et al.* (1996).

Deering uses a stack buffer of size 16 and allows random access to any vertex stored in the stack. Connectivity information is now embedded in stack commands as follows:

- 1 bit/vertex to indicate whether the vertex is to be read from the stack;
- 4 address bits/vertex for stacked vertices;
- 1 bit/(new) vertex to indicate whether the vertex is to be pushed onto the stack;
- 2 bits/vertex to indicate how to continue.

If each vertex is reused once then the cost is 11/2 bits/vertex (again assuming twice as many triangles as vertices). Of course, the approach depends on the stack 'never becoming full' – vertices for reuse must be in the stack. The trade-off here is the size of the stack address field, the largest component in the list above, against the number of vertices that can be reused.

Bar-Yehuda and Gotsman (1996) investigate the relationship between 'rendering time' and buffer size and show that a buffer size of $12.72\sqrt{n}$ suffices to generate a minimum sequence for any triangle mesh of n vertices in time n. This compares to the non-buffered scheme which will generate a sequence which may require up to $2n$ time. In other words, buffer size can be traded against rendering cost expressed as the number of vertices transmitted per mesh.

Bar-Yeduda and Gotsman's algorithm uses a stack for the mesh buffer. A triangle mesh is converted into a representation that is sequence of stack commands of the form:

push(v)	the vertex sent down the pipeline is pushed onto the stack
draw(v1,v2,v3)	draw a triangle with vertices v1, v2 and v3. These will be stack indices – the vertices must already be in the stack
pop(k)	pop the stack k times

The only command that transfers vertices into the graphics sub-system is the push command. The triangles are rendered by the draw command and the order in which they appear in the sequence no longer relates to a tri-strip configuration. Nevertheless, only one vertex is transmitted per triangle.

To convert meshes into a sequence of stack commands they use a recursive procedure which relies on a well-known graph theory algorithm – the planar separator theorem. This considers the triangle mesh as a graph where the nodes of the graph are the triangle vertices and the edges of the graph the edges of the triangles. The theorem states that a class of graphs with n vertices have a separator $(g(n),ß)$ $(1/2 \leq ß < 1)$, if for any graph $G(V,E)$ vertices in the class V can be partitioned into three sets U, S and W such that no edge in E joins a vertex in U with a vertex in W, $|U| \leq ßn$, $|W| < ßn$ and $|S| < g(n)$. The class of planar graphs

has a $\left(\dfrac{7}{3} \sqrt{n}, \dfrac{2}{3} \right)$ separator computable in $O(n)$ time.

This means that such a graph can be split into three sub-graphs such that one separates the other in the way described. In addition, the two separated sub-graphs contain fewer than two-thirds the number of vertices than the original and the

separating graph contains fewer than $\dfrac{7}{3} \sqrt{n}$. An example of the theorem is shown in Figure 3.5.

Figure 3.5
An example of the planar separator theorem.

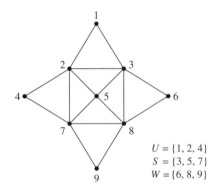

$U = \{1, 2, 4\}$
$S = \{3, 5, 7\}$
$W = \{6, 8, 9\}$

At the heart of the algorithm that produces the stack sequence is a process that finds the set S in $O(n)$ time. The algorithm that converts the data into a sequence of stack commands is run off-line to convert the mesh. It is a simple recursive procedure:

```
draw_sequence(M(V))

        if |V| ≠ 0 then

        find U, S and W
        output("push("S")")
        push(stack,S)

        for all triangles t of M having one vertex in S, and the other two in
        stack

            output("draw("index(v1(t)) index (v2(t)) index(v3(t))")")
```

draw_sequence (M(U))
draw_sequence (M(V))

output("*pop*("|S|")")
pop(stack,|S|)

Thus for the mesh in Figure 3.5 the following sequence is generated:

push(3) push(5) push(7) push(2) draw(2,3,5) draw(2,5,7) push(1) draw(1,2,3)
pop(1) push(4) draw(2,4,7) pop(2) push(8) draw(3,5,8) draw(5,8,7) push(6)
draw(3,6,8) pop(1) push(9) draw(7,8,9) pop(5)

where for ease of interpretation the *draw* indices are given as triangle vertices instead of stack indices and the number in the *pop* command equals the number of *pops*. Only *push()* implies the transmission of a vertex and the number of *push()*s is equal to 9, the number of vertices. This compares with using two tri-strips, which requires, for the same example, 12 vertices (plus the delimiters for the separate strips) to be passed to the graphics hardware.

3.7 Level of detail (LOD) processing

As we have discussed, polygon mesh models are well established as the *de facto* standard representational form in computer graphics but they suffer from significant disadvantages, notably that the level of detail, or number of polygons, required to synthesise the object for a high-quality rendition of a complex object is very large. And if the object is to be rendered on screen at different viewing distances, the pipeline has to process thousands of polygons that project onto a few pixels on the screen. As the projected polygon size decreases, the polygon overheads become significant and in real-time applications this situation is intolerable. High polygon counts per object occur either because of object complexity or because of the nature of the modelling system.

As early as 1976, one of the pioneers of 3D computer graphics, James H Clark, wrote:

> It makes no sense to use 500 polygons in describing an object if it covers only 20 raster units of the display . . .. For example, when we view the human body from a very large distance, we might need to present only specks for the eyes, or perhaps just a block for the head, totally eliminating the eyes from consideration . . . these issues have not been addressed in a unified way.

Did Clark at that time realise that, not many years after he had written the paper, that 500 000 polygon objects would become fairly commonplace and that complex scenes might contain millions of polygons?

Existing systems tend to address this problem in a somewhat ad hoc manner. For example, many systems adopt a two or three level representation switching in surface detail, such as the numbers on the buttons of a telephone as the viewer moves closer to it. This produces an annoying visual disturbance as the detail blinks on and off. More considered approaches are now being put forward, and lately there has been a substantial increase in the number of papers published in this area.

An obvious solution to the problem is to generate a polygon mesh at the final level of detail and then use this representation to spawn a set of coarser descriptions. As the scene is rendered an appropriate level of detail is selected. Certain algorithms that use this principle have emerged from time to time in computer graphics. An example of a method that facilitates a polygon mesh at any level of detail is bi-cubic parametric patches (Section 5.7.1). Here we take a patch description and turn it into a polygon description. At the same time we can easily control the number of polygons that are generated for each patch and relate this to local surface curvature. This is exactly what is done in patch rendering where a geometric criterion is used to control the extent of the subdivision and produce an image free of geometric aliasing (visible polygon edges in silhouette). The price we pay for this approach is the expense and difficulty of getting the patch description in the first place. But in any case we could build the original patch representation and construct a pyramid of polygon mesh representations off-line.

The idea of storing a 'detail pyramid' and accessing an appropriate level is established in many application areas. Consider the case of mip-mapping, for example (Chapter 8). Here texture maps are stored in a detail hierarchy and a fine-detail map selected when the projection of the map on the screen is large. In the event that the map projects onto just one pixel, then a single pixel texture map – the average of the most detailed map – is selected. Also, in this method the problem of avoiding a jump when going from one level to another is carefully addressed and an approximation to a continuous level of detail is obtained by interpolation between two maps.

An important consideration in the discussion of LODs is smoothness of the on-screen transition from one level to another. If the difference between successive LODs is large then there will be a popping effect on the screen. Methods to try to overcome this vary from the simple approach of blending one image in at the same time as fading the other out to trying to implement a continuous LOD method, which by definition does not exhibit discrete changes.

Another consideration is the selection of an appropriate level. Here we need to use some (screen-based) error criterion that measures in some way the error between the geometry projected at some LOD and that of the finest LOD. Unfortunately screen-based criteria are view dependent by definition and have therefore to be calculated for each frame.

The diversity of current approaches underlines the relative newness of the field. A direct and simple approach for triangular meshes derived from voxel sets was reported by Schroeder *et al.* in 1992. Here the algorithm considers each vertex on a surface. By looking at the triangles that contribute to or share the vertex, a number of criteria can be enumerated and used to determine whether these triangles can be merged into a single one exclusive of the vertex under consideration. For example, we can invoke the 'reduce the number of triangles

Figure 3.6
A simple vertex deletion criterion. Delete *V*? Measure *d*, the distance from *V* to the (average) plane through the triangles that share *V*.

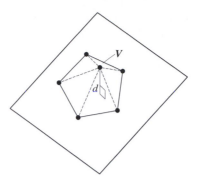

where the surface curvature is low' argument by measuring the variance in the surface normals of the triangles that share the vertex. Alternatively we could consider the distance from the vertex to an (average) plane through all the other vertices of the sharing triangles (Figure 3.6). This is a local approach that considers vertices in the geometry of their immediate surroundings.

A more recent approach is the work of Hoppe (1996) which we will now describe. Hoppe gives an excellent categorisation of the problems and advantages of mesh optimisation, listing these as follows:

- **Mesh simplification.** This involves reducing the polygons to a level that is adequate for the quality required. (This, of course, depends on the maximum projection size of the object on the screen.)

- **Level of detail approximation.** A level is used that is appropriate to the viewing distance. In this respect, Hoppe adds: 'Since instantaneous switching between LOD meshes may lead to perceptible "popping", one would like to construct smooth visual transitions, *geomorphs*, between meshes at different resolutions.'

- **Progressive transmission.** This is a three-dimensional equivalent of the common progressive transmission modes used to transmit two-dimensional imagery over the Internet. Successive LOD approximations can be transmitted and rendered at the receiver.

- **Mesh compression.** Analogous to two-dimensional image pyramids, we can consider not only reducing the number of polygons but also minimising the space that any LOD approximation occupies. As in two-dimensional imagery, this is important because a LOD hierarchy occupies much more memory than a single model stored at its highest level of detail.

- **Selective refinement.** A LOD representation may be used in a context-dependent manner. Hoppe gives the example of a user flying over a terrain – the terrain mesh need only be fully detailed near the viewer.

Addressing mesh compression, Hoppe takes a 'pyramidal' approach and stores the coarsest level of detail approximation, together, for each higher level, with the information required to ascend from a lower to a higher level of detail. To make the transition from a lower to a higher level, the reverse of the transformation that constructed the hierarchy from the highest to the lowest level is stored and used. This is in the form of a vertex split – an operation that adds an additional vertex to the lower mesh to obtain the next mesh up the detail hierarchy. Although Hoppe originally considered three mesh transformations – an edge collapse, an edge split and an edge swap – he found that an edge collapse is sufficient for simplifying meshes.

The overall scheme is represented in Figure 3.7(a) which shows a detail pyramid which would be constructed offline by a series of edge collapse transformations that take the original mesh M_n and generate through repeated edge collapse transformations the final or coarsest mesh M_0. The entire pyramid can then be stored as M_0 together with the information required to generate from M_0 to any finer level M_i in the hierarchy. This inter-level transformation is the reverse of the edge collapse and is the information required for a vertex split. Hoppe quotes an example of an object with 13 546 faces which was simplified to an M_0 of 150 faces using 6698 edge collapse transformations. The original data is then stored as M_0 together with the 6698 vertex split records. The vertex split records themselves exhibit redundancy and can be compressed using classical data compression techniques.

Figure 3.7
Hoppe's (1996) progressive mesh scheme based on edge collapse transformations.

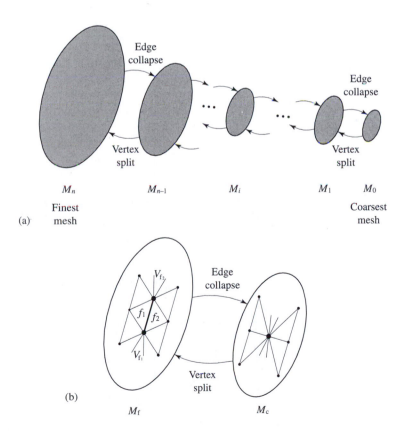

Figure 3.7(b) shows a single edge collapse between two consecutive levels. The notation is as follows:

V_{f1} and V_{f2} are the two vertices in the finer mesh that are collapsed into one vertex V_c in the coarser mesh

where $V_c \in \left\{ V_{f1},\ V_{f2},\ \dfrac{V_{f1} + V_{f2}}{2} \right\}$

From the diagram it can be seen that this operation implies the collapse of the two faces f_1 and f_2 into new edges.

Hoppe defines a continuum between any two levels of detail by using a blending parameter α. If we define:

$$d = \frac{V_{f1} + V_{f2}}{2}$$

then we can generate a continuum of geomorphs between the two levels by having the edge shrink under control of the blending parameter as:

$$V_{f1} := V_{f1} + \alpha d \quad \text{and} \quad V_{f2} := V_{f2} - \alpha d$$

Texture coordinates can interpolated in the same way, as can scalar attributes associated with a vertex such as colour.

The remaining question is: how are the edges selected for collapse in the reduction from M_i to M_{i-1}? This can be done either by using a simple heuristic approach or by a more rigorous method that measures the difference between a particular approximation and a sample of the original mesh. A simple metric that can be used to order the edges for collapse is:

$$\frac{|V_{f1} - V_{f2}|}{|N_{f1}.N_{f2}|}$$

Figure 3.8
The result of applying the simple edge elimination criterion described in the text – the model eventually breaks up.

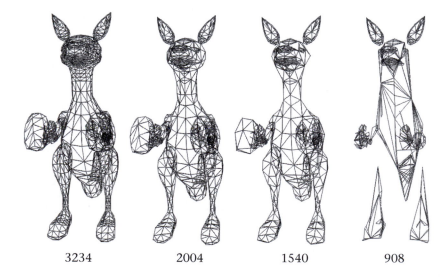

| 3234 | 2004 | 1540 | 908 |

that is, the length of the edge divided by the dot product of the vertex normals. On its own this metric will work quite well, but if it is continually applied the mesh will suddenly begin to 'collapse' and a more considered approach to edge selection is mandatory. Figure 3.8 is an example that uses this technique.

Hoppe casts this as an energy function minimisation problem. A mesh M is optimised with respect to a set of points X which are the vertices of the mesh M_n together (optionally) with points randomly sampled from its faces. (Although this is a lengthy process it is, of course, executed once only as an off-line pre-process.) The energy function to be minimised is:

$$E(M) = E_{dist}(M) + E_{spring}(M)$$

where

$$E_{dist} = \sum_i d^2(x_i, M)$$

is the sum of the squared distances from the points X to the mesh – when a vertex is removed this term will tend to increase.

$$E_{spring}(M) = \sum k||v_j - v_k||^2$$

is a spring energy term that assists the optimisation. It is equivalent to placing on each edge a spring of rest length zero and spring constant κ.

Hoppe orders the optimisation by placing all (legal) edge collapse transformations into a priority queue, where the priority of each transformation is its estimated energy cost ΔE. In each iteration, the transformation at the front of the queue (lowest ΔE) is performed and the priorities of the edges in the neighbourhood of this transformation are recomputed. An edge collapse transformation is only legal if it does not change the topology of the mesh. For example, if V_{f1} and V_{f2} are boundary vertices, the edge $\{V_{f1}, V_{f2}\}$ must be a boundary edge – it cannot be an internal edge connecting two boundary points.

4 Representation and modelling 3 – landscape specialisations

4.1 Introduction

4.2 Simple height field landscapes

4.3 Procedural modelling of landscapes – fractals

4.4 Terrain LODs: triangle bintrees

4.5 Rendering of landscapes by ray casting

4.1 Introduction

Landscapes or terrains are a common entity in computer games. They are, of course, found in flight simulators and it is this area that has led to most of the research and development in the field. The main reasons why landscapes have received special consideration, beyond that given to standard polygon mesh models, is that they tend to be very large and they usually have the special property that they are built by superimposing a height field on a regular grid pattern in the xy plane. In this case very large means that they consist of polygons that may be in the order of a pixel extent when rendered – causing a bottleneck on the CPU–3D card bus. Another problem is that they are not susceptible to conventional LOD methods for polygons. Their total extent in screen space is large and this means that ideally the size of a landscape polygon needs to decrease as a function of viewing distance (Figure 4.1). In other words, the LOD should ideally vary not only as a function of the local surface curvature but globally across the model.

The most popular form of landscape model is a height field based on a uniform grid. However, we will look in the next section at a classic procedural method for terrain generation – fractals – which generates a (non-uniform) triangle mesh. LOD approaches to terrain exploit the normal height field representation of landscape data and the approaches are generally more straightforward than those for 'arbitrary' polygon meshes.

Figure 4.1
A landscape may occupy all of screenspace and require a LOD scheme that varies across the terrain.

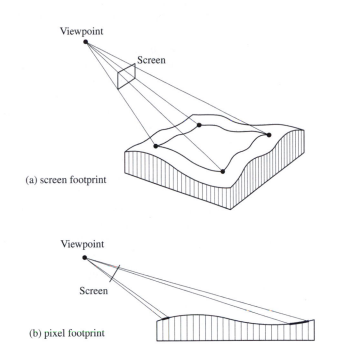

Viewpoint

Screen

(a) screen footprint

Viewpoint

Screen

(b) pixel footprint

An important consideration of landscape models is their 'ease of following'. Landscapes in computer games have to be continually accessed if objects are to be animated and checked for collision with the terrain.

In many terrain modelling applications – real flight simulation, for example, landscapes are textured using aerial photographs.

4.2 Simple height field landscapes

The easiest way to generate a height field is to use a painting package with the understanding that the grey scale is to represent height. Figure 4.2(a) (Colour Plate) shows such an image created for a car track. The height field values can be mapped into a suitable colour, depending on the nature of the landscape, and a texture map applied (Figures 4.2(b) and (c)). The coherences due to the tiling are apparent in the static landscape. However, they become much more noticeable in motion. For example, consider a car driven around in circles. If the camera is fixed relative to the car, it also rotates in a circular motion with respect to the landscape. The coherences in the texture pattern then become apparent and concentric circles 'jump out' of the landscape.

4.3 Procedural modelling of landscapes – fractals

In this section we will look at a common example of generating polygon mesh objects procedurally. Fractal geometry is a term coined by Benoit Mandlebrot (1977, 1982). The term was used to describe the attributes of certain natural phenomena, for example coastlines. A coastline viewed at any level of detail – at microscopic level, at a level where individual rocks can be seen or at 'geographical' level – tends to exhibit the same level of jaggedness; a kind of statistical self-similarity. Fractal geometry provides a description for certain aspects of this ubiquitous phenomenon in nature and its tendency towards self-similarity.

In three-dimensional computer graphics, fractal techniques have commonly been used to generate terrain models and the easiest techniques involve subdividing the facets of the objects that consist of triangles or quadrilaterals. A recursive subdivision procedure is applied to each facet, to a required depth or level of detail, and a convincing terrain model results. Subdivision in this context means taking the midpoint along the edge between two vertices and perturbing it along a line normal to the edge. The result of this is to subdivide the original facets into a large number of smaller facets, each having a random orientation in three-dimensional space about the original facet orientation. The initial global shape of the object is retained to an extent that depends on the perturbation at the subdivision and a planar four-sided pyramid might turn into a 'Mont Blanc'-shaped object.

Most subdivision algorithms are based on a formulation by Fournier *et al.* (1982) that recursively subdivides a single line segment. This algorithm was developed as an alternative to more mathematically correct, but expensive procedures, suggested by Mandlebrot. It uses self-similarity and conditional expectation properties of fractional Brownian motion to give an estimate of the increment of the stochastic process. The process is also Gaussian and the only parameters needed to describe a Gaussian distribution are the mean (conditional expectation) and the variance.

A procedure recursively subdivides a line $(t1,f1)$, $(t2,f2)$ generating a scalar displacement of the midpoint of the line in a direction normal to the line (Figure 4.3(a)). To extend this procedure to, say, triangles or quadrilaterals in three-dimensional space, we treat each edge in turn, generating a displacement along a midpoint vector that is normal to the plane of the original facet (Figure 4.3(b)). Using this technique we can take a smooth pyramid, say, made of large triangular faces and turn it into a rugged mountain.

Fournier categorises two problems in this method – internal and external consistency. Internal consistency requires that the shape generated should be the same whatever the orientation in which it is generated, and that coarser details should remain the same if the shape is replotted at greater resolution. To satisfy the first requirement, the Gaussian randoms generated must not be a function of the position of the points, but should be unique to the point itself. An invariant point identifier needs to be associated with each point. This problem can be

Figure 4.3
An example of procedural generation of polygon mesh objects – fractal terrain. (a) Line segment subdivision. (b) Triangle subdivision.

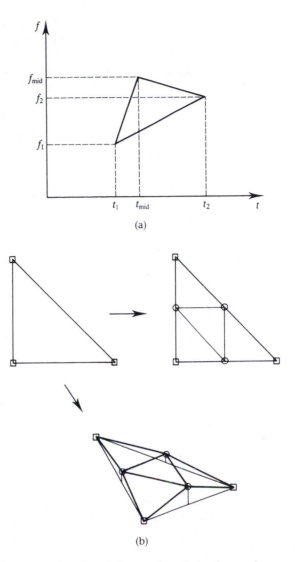

(a)

(b)

solved in terrain generation by giving each point a key value used to index a Gaussian random number. A hash function can be used to map the two keys of the end points of a line to a key value for the midpoint. Scale requirements of internal consistency mean that the same random numbers must always be generated in the same order at a given level of subdivision.

External consistency is harder to maintain. Within the mesh of triangles, every triangle shares each of its sides with another; thus the same random displacements must be generated for corresponding points of different connecting triangles. This is already solved by using the key value of each point and the hash function, but another problem still exists, that of the direction of the displacement.

If the displacements are along the surface normal of the polygon under consideration, then adjacent polygons which have different normals (as is, by definition, always the case) will have their midpoints displaced into different positions. This causes gaps to open up. A solution is to displace the midpoint along the average of the normals to all the polygons that contain it but this problem occurs at every level of recursion and is consequently very expensive to implement. Also, this technique would create an unsatisfactory skyline because the displacements are not constrained to one direction. A better skyline is obtained by making all the displacements of points internal to the original polygon in a direction normal to the plane of the original polygon. This cheaper technique solves all problems relating to different surface normals, and the gaps created by them. Now surface normals need not be created at each level of recursion and the algorithm is considerably cheaper because of this.

Another two points are worth mentioning. Firstly, note that polygons should be constant shaded without calculating vertex normals – discontinuities between polygons should not be smoothed out. Secondly, consider colour. The usual global colour scheme uses a height-dependent mapping. In detail: the colour assigned to a midpoint is one of its end point's colours. Which one is chosen is determined by a Boolean random which is indexed by the key value of the midpoint. Once again this must be accessed in this way to maintain consistency, which is just as important for colour as it is for position.

4.4 Terrain LODs: triangle bintrees

We now return to height field terrain models and consider how to exploit this structure to facilitate an LOD approach.

A uniform height field is conveniently triangulated by a representation known as a triangle bintree (Figure 4.4). Each triangle is a right-angled isosceles triangle. The children of any node are formed by splitting the triangle along an edge formed by joining the right-angled apex (indicated in the figure by a dot) to the base to form two more right-angled child triangles.

This structure is employed in the work of Duchaineau *et al.* (1997) and Lindstrom *et al.* (1996). The key idea is that a particular LOD representation for a terrain database is a single level in the triangle bintree and the vertices in the bintree level are associated with the corresponding height field data $z(x,y)$ (Figure 4.5). This association is conveniently defined as:

$$w(v) = (x,y,z(x,y))$$

where:

$z(x,y)$ is the value of the height field at the point (x,y), the bintree domain coordinates of v

Thus a LOD mesh is *always* a recursive bintree decomposition. This differs from the object unique meshes which are obtained from the LOD methods described

Figure 4.4
A triangle bintree.

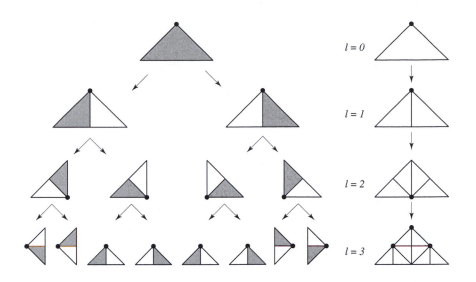

$l = 0$

$l = 1$

$l = 2$

$l = 3$

Figure 4.5
Vertices of the bintree are
assigned values from the
height field $z(x,y)$.

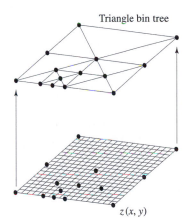

Triangle bin tree

$z(x, y)$

in Chapter 3; and this attribute enables, for example, more rigorous level selection, as we shall see in this section.

The triangle bintree can thus be considered as a complete set of LOD representations – one for each level in the tree.

In Duchaineau *et al.*'s approach the root of the tree contains two triangles – forming what they call a diamond – and the leaves (may) contain triangles whose vertices are formed from adjacent vertices in the height field grid – the lowest level of detail. Any triangle in the structure has a base, and right and left neighbours (Figure 4.6). These have following properties. Either the neighbours

Figure 4.6
Split operation possible when a triangle and its base neighbour are from the same level (after Duchaineau *et al.* (1997)).

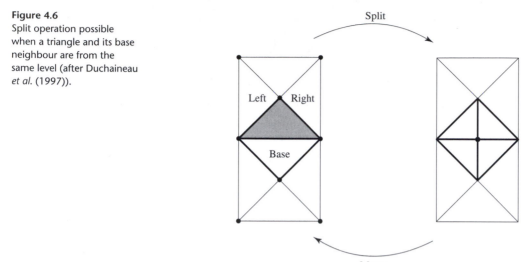

are from the same level, or from the next coarsest level (base neighbours), or from the next finer level (left and right neighbours). A split and merge operation defines a transition down or up a level. Splitting adds a vertex and merging removes one. For example, when a triangle and its base neighbour are from the same level a simple split operation (Figure 4.6) is possible by adding a new vertex.

A difficulty that immediately arises is that a triangle cannot be split as shown in the previous figure if its base neighbour is from a coarser level. Such a situation, shown in Figure 4.7, requires that the base triangle must be split first in a recursive sequence. Duchaineau *et al.* refer to such splits as *forced splits* and they use them subsequently in an optimisation procedure.

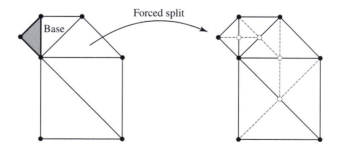

Figure 4.7
A triangle with a base neighbour from a coarser level. In this case four splits are required (after Duchaineau *et al.* (1997)).

Figure 4.8
Vertex morphing a split. The new vertex $w(v_c)$ is 'moved' into position from the midpoint of the base line $(w(v_0), w(v_1))$.

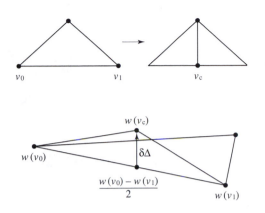

For temporal continuity such splits and merges are easily animated by vertex morphing. Consider Figure 4.8 which shows a new vertex v_c being formed. This can be moved into its new position over some time interval as:

$$w_a = (1 - t) \ \frac{w(v_0) - w(v_1)}{2} \ + tw(v_c)$$

The overall scheme consists of a pre-processing phase and an on-line phase. The on-line phase consists of an algorithm that updates the previous frame's bintree by split and merge operations, stopping when a geometric screen space (view-dependent) error criterion is satisfied. The pre-processing phase constructs a set of view-dependent error bounds which are used by the on-line phase.

This structure takes the form of a set of nested bounding volumes for triangles in the representation. These are all of the form of extruded triangles (or wedgies) that contain two faces parallel to the contained triangle and displaced from each vertex by a thickness E_T. These are built from the bottom up with E_T initially set to zero. A one-dimensional case is shown for two consecutive levels in Figure 4.9. E_T is defined as:

$$E_T = \text{max\_of } (E_{T0} - E_{T1}) + \left| z(v_c) - \frac{z(v_0) - z(v_1)}{2} \right|$$

At run-time the refinement process is controlled by projecting these into screen space and using a criterion that depends on the maximum projected thickness.

The run-time process is a series of split and merge operations controlled by two queues. The merge queue is used to implement frame to frame coherence where the starting point for building the current frame's triangulation is taken as the previous. The split algorithm proceeds by keeping priorities for every triangle in the triangulation and repeatedly forcing a split of the highest-priority

Figure 4.9
At any level a bounding
volume (wedgie) contains all
its child bounding volumes.

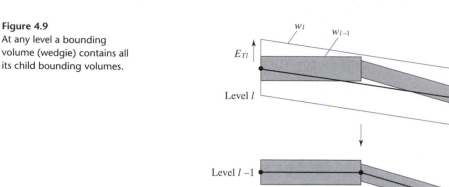

triangle. As the triangulation is built a priority queue is maintained and the following operations are carried out as long as the screen space projection is inaccurate:

(1) Find the highest-priority triangle T in the queue.
(2) Force split T.
(3) Update the queue by removing T and other split triangles.
(4) Add any new triangles to the queue.

Another approach that uses triangle bintrees is due to Lindstrom *et al.* (1996). In this work the authors use a bottom-up approach starting at the finest resolution and merging triangles according to the magnitude of the projection of the $\delta\Delta$ vector shown in Figure 4.8. An efficient scheme for considering the worst case or maximum delta projection of all vertices at a particular recursive level is described.

4.5 Rendering of landscapes by ray casting

From time to time in the games development community voxels have been suggested as an alternative graphics primitive to polygons. Certain advantages immediately accrue with this representation. Textured mapped uniform height fields are similar to voxel-based data. We can simply consider each cell as a voxel with a variable z dimension, and use a voxel rendering algorithm to produce the projected image. The work that we now describe is typical of voxel rendering and is due to Cohen-Or *et al.* (1996).

The basic algorithm is called ray casting and, as the name implies, a ray is generated from the viewpoint through each pixel and cast into world space. The hit point on the terrain then gives the colour for the pixel from which the ray has emanated (Figure 4.10). Now the well-known inefficiency of ray casting (or in general ray tracing) is the cost of the intersection testing. In a naïve algorithm the geometry of each ray would be separately calculated, then tested against all objects in the scene for intersection. In this, considerable use can be made of ray coherence and Cohen-Or *et al.* calculate an intersection by stepping incrementally along a ray and comparing its height within the height of the terrain immediately below the current ray length value until an intersection occurs. This operation is performed in a plane containing the ray and the current pixel column, which immediately leads to the efficiency advantage shown in Figure 4.10. Here we see that if we cast rays in a column from the bottom pixel upwards, each ray can be started from a vertical displacement from the hit point of the previous ray. Because the ray intersection is calculated by incrementally traversing each ray, the total ray cast time is considerably reduced by shortening the traversal.

Another advantage that accrues from this simple scheme is that it 'automatically' implements a form of LOD. Figure 4.1(b) shows that for normal viewing angles the pixel 'footprint' increases as the distance from the viewpoint, or equivalently the height of the pixel in the screen space column. The terrain voxels are non-uniformly sampled by the pixel rays; those close to the viewpoint may be oversampled, those distant undersampled. Cohen-Or *et al.* exploit this

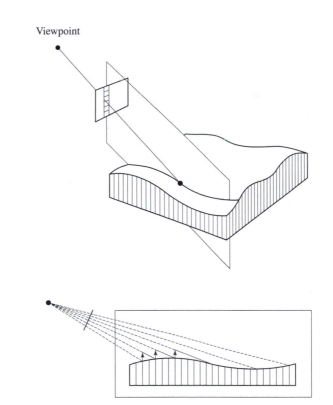

Figure 4.10
Rays are incrementally traversed in a plane containing the ray and the current pixel column. Each ray starts from the previous hit point.

characteristic by having a multi-resolution representation of the data equivalent to the common mip-map approach in texture mapping. Rays then sample a level whose voxels (x,y) extent varies according to the height of the ray in the pixel column. The important point here is that the incrementation values can also be increased as lower-resolution maps are accessed, making the traversal time per ray tend to a constant. This is important for maintaining a stable frame-generation time.

Modelling and representation 4 – Bézier, B-spline and subdivision surfaces

5.1   Introduction

5.2   Bézier curves

5.3   B-spline curves

5.4   Rational curves

5.5   From curves to surfaces

5.6   Modelling or creating patch surfaces

5.7   Rendering parametric surfaces

5.8   Practical bézier technology for games

5.9   Subdivision surfaces

5.10 Scalability – polygon meshes, patch meshes and subdivision surfaces

5.1   Introduction

In Chapter 2 we concentrated on the polygon mesh representation where a polygon was, for example, a (flat) quadrilateral made up of four vertices joined by four straight lines. This chapter is devoted entirely to a representational form where the primitive element – a bi-cubic parametric patch – is a curvilinear quadrilateral. It has four corner points joined by four edges which are themselves cubic curves. The interior of the patch is a curved (cubic) surface where every point on the surface is defined. This contrasts with the polygon mesh approximation where surface points on an object are only defined at the polygon vertices.

The original motivation for such a representation in computer graphics was as a basis for interactive design in CAD. Here we may obtain the model by an interactive process – a designer building up a model by interacting with a program. In many CAD applications the representational form is transformed *directly* into a real object (or a scaled-down model of the real object). The computer graphics representation is used to control a device such as a numerical milling machine which sculpts the object in some material. This is exactly the opposite of the 'normal' computer graphics modelling methodology – instead of transforming a real object into a representation we are using the computer graphics model to make the real object.

Now patch representations are being used more and more as alternatives to the polygon mesh model. Despite problems which will become apparent during the chapter, they offer the potential of complexity reduction – a net of patches can represent a complex shape with far fewer elements than a net of planar polygons.

The immediate advantages of this representation are:

- It has the potential of three-dimensional shape editing or modelling. Real-time shape changing – sometimes known as soft body animation – has long been one of the goals of computer graphics and will undoubtedly find applications in computer games.

- By using a fast patch to polygon conversion algorithm, it can be used with existing polygon rendering hardware.

- It facilitates an 'automatic' LOD representation. This can be bound by screen-based criteria or by processing time available. That is, a quality of model is rendered depending on the time available.

- If patch processing algorithms migrate onto hardware then the inherent economy of representation implies a solution to the CPU–graphics processor bus bottleneck. The complexity explosion of polygons/object is then local to the graphics processor.

- The lighting resolution for static objects can be made independent of the LOD. (This factor is dealt with in detail in Section 5.8.2)

- It is an exact analytical representation (this is possibly more important in CAD applications than in computer games).

- It is a more economical representation.

Given these advantages it is somewhat surprising that this form is not the mainstream representation in computer graphics. It is certainly no more difficult to render an object represented by a net of patches and so we must conclude that its lack of popularity in mainstream computer graphics (it is, of course, used in industrial CAD) is due to the mathematical formalities associated with it.

The exactness of the representation factor needs careful qualification. A real object (or a physical model of a real object) can be represented by a net or mesh of patches (Figures 5.28 and 5.40 show two such objects) but the representation may not be completely 'exact'. In the first example, the teapot cannot have a perfectly circular cross-section because the representational method, in this case the Bézier form or Bernstein basis, cannot represent a circle exactly. The patches representing the face in the second example may not everywhere be coincident with the real object. We can obtain a suitable set of points that lie in the surface of the object from a three-dimensional digitiser and we could, say, use the same set of points that we would use to build a polygon mesh model. We then use an interpolation technique, known as surface fitting, to determine a set of patches that represent the surface. However, the patch surface and the object surface will not necessarily be identical. The exactness of the fit depends both on the nature of the interpolation process and how closely the physical surface conforms to the shape constraints of the bi-cubic patch representation. But we do end up with an object representation that is a smooth surface which has certain advantages over the polygon mesh representation – the silhouette edge problem, which accounts for the most prominent visual defect in rendered polygon mesh objects, is cured.

The most common current applications of the bi-cubic parametric patch representation are not to build very complex models but as a representation for fairly simple objects in industrial CAD or CAGD applications. The real value of the representation here is that it can be used to transform an abstract design, built up within an interactive program, directly into a physical reality. The description can be made to drive a sculpting device such as a numerically controlled milling machine to produce a prototype object without any human intervention. It is this single factor more than any other that makes bi-cubic parametric patches important in CAD.

Possibly the greatest potential advantage of a patch representation is in interactive modelling where a shape can be changed 'naturally' using an editing tool. It is possible to model and edit subtly shaped objects such as a human face with a net of patches. An adequate representation of such an object using a polygon mesh would need an extremely high polygonal resolution. A natural extension of this is shape-changing animation where an object deforms or changes shape in real time.

We distinguish between objects that are represented by a single patch and objects whose form demands that they are represented by a net of patches. A single patch is straightforward but the objects that we can design with a single patch are restricted. Shape-editing an object that is represented by a net of patches is much more difficult. One problem is that if we have to alter the shape of one patch in a net, we have to maintain its smoothness relationship with the neighbouring patches in which it is embedded. Another difficulty is yet another manifestation of the scale problem. Say we want to effect a shape change that involves many patches. We have to move these patches together and maintain their continuity with all their neighbouring patches.

Despite these difficulties we should recognise that this representation has a strong potential for shape editing compared with the polygon mesh representation. This is already an approximation and pulling vertices around to change the shape of the represented object results in many difficulties. The accuracy of the polygon mesh representation changes as soon as vertices are moved, resulting perhaps in visual defects. It is almost certain that we would always have to move groups of points rather than moving a single polygon vertex around in three-space. Pulling a single vertex would just result in a local peak.

The analytical representation of patches differs according to the formulation and some have been named after their instigators. One of the most popular formulations is the Bézier patch developed in the 1960s by Pierre Bézier for use in the design of Renault cars. His CAD system, called UNISURF, was one of the first to be used. In what follows, we will concentrate mainly on the Bézier patch.

The usual approach in considering parametric representation is to begin with a description of three-dimensional space curves and then to generalise to surfaces or patches. A three-dimensional space curve is a smooth curve that is a function of the three spatial variables. An example would be the path that a particle traced as it moved through space. Incidentally curves by themselves also find applications in animation, as we demonstrate in Chapter 13. For example, we can script the path of an object in three-dimensional computer animation by using a space curve. We can model a 'ducted' solid by sweeping a cross-section along a space curve, as we saw in the previous chapter.

5.2 Bézier curves

In this section we will look at the pioneering developments of Bézier, who was amongst the first to develop computer tools in industrial design. We will draw on Bézier's own descriptions of the evolution of his method, not just because of their historical interest but because they give a real insight into the relationship between the representation, the physical reality and the requirements of the designers who were to use his methods.

Bézier's development work was carried out in the Renault car factory in the 1960s and he called his system UNISURF. Car designers are concerned with styling free-form surfaces which are then used to produce master dies which produce the tools that stamp out the manufactured parts. Many other industries use free-form surfaces. Some parts such as ships' hulls, airframes and turbine blades are constrained by aerodynamic and hydrodynamic considerations and shapes evolve through experience and testing in wind tunnels and test tanks – but a designer still needs freedom to produce new shapes albeit within these constraints. Before the advent of this representational form, such free-form surfaces could not be represented analytically and once developed could only be stored for future reproduction and evolution by sampling and storing as coordinates.

Prior to Bézier's innovation the process of going from the abstract design to the prototype was lengthy and involved many people and processes. The following description, abstracted from Bézier's account in Piegl's book (1993), is of the process of car design at the time:

(1) Stylists defined a general shape using small-scale sketches and clay mock-ups.

(2) Using offsets (world coordinates in computer graphics terminology) mea-sured on the mock-up, designers traced a full-scale shape of the skin of the car body.

(3) Plasterers built a full-scale model, weighing about 8 tons, starting from ply-wood cross-sections duplicating the curves of the drawing . . . the clay model was then examined by stylists and sales managers, and modified according to taste.

(4) When at last the model was accepted, offsets were again measured and the final drawings were made. . . During this period, which could be a year or more, tooling and production specialists often suggested minor changes to avoid difficult and costly operations during production.

(5) The drawings were finalised, and one three-dimensional master was built as the standard for checking the press tools and stamped parts.

(6) The plaster copies of the master were used for milling punches and dies on copy-machine tools. . ..

Bézier's pioneer development completely changed most aspects of these processes by enabling a representation of free-form surfaces. Before, a designer would produce curves using, say, a device such as a French curve. The designer used his or her skill and experience to produce a complete curve that was built up a step at a time using segments along some portion of the French curve. A curve so generated could not be stored in any convenient way except as a set of samples. Bézier's development was a definition that enabled such curves to be represented as four points, known as control points, and an implicit set of basis or blending functions. When the four points are injected into the definition, the curve is generated or reproduced. This has two immediate consequences. The definition could be used to directly drive a numerically controlled milling machine and the part is produced exactly without the intervention of compli-cations and delays. (Numerically controlled milling machines had been in exis-tence since 1955 and were another motivation for the development of CAGD.) The definition could be used as a basis of a CAD program in which modifications to the curve could be seen in a computer visualisation.

Bézier describes an intriguing difficulty that he experienced at the time:

When it was suggested that these curves replace sweeps and French curves, most stylists objected that they had invented their own templates and would not change their methods. It was therefore solemnly promised that their secret curves would be translated into secret listings and buried in the most secret part of the computer's memory, and that nobody but them would keep the key of the vaulted cellar. In fact, the standard curves were flexible enough and secret curves were soon forgotten; designers and draughtsmen easily understood the polygons and their relationship with the shape of the corresponding curves.

Many simultaneous developments were occurring in other industries – notably aircraft and ship manufacture, and much of the research was carried out

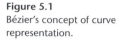

Figure 5.1
Bézier's concept of curve
representation.

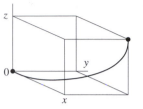

Curve 'contained' by a cube

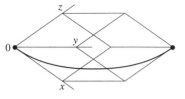

Drawing the cube into a
parallelepiped changes the curve

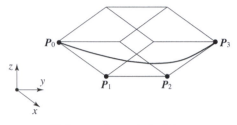

Vertices used as control points

under the auspices of particular manufacturers, who, like Bézier at Renault, developed their own CAD systems and surface representations suited to their own requirements. This has led to a number of parametric definitions of surfaces and the interested reader is best referred to Piegl's book in which each chapter is written by a pioneer in this field.

Bézier states that one of the most important requirements of his representation was that it should be founded on geometry and that the underlying mathematics be easily understood. He introduced the concept of a space curve being contained in a cube which when distorted into a parallelepiped distorts the curve (Figure 5.1). The curve is 'fixed' within the parallelepiped as follows:

● The start and end points of the curve are located at opposite vertices of the parallelepiped.

● At its start point the curve is tangential to 0X.

● At its end point the curve is tangential to 0Z.

This geometric concept uniquely defines any space curve (if it is understood that the curve is a polynomial of a certain degree) and also gives an intuitive feel for how the curve changes shape as the parallelepiped changes. Now the parallelepiped, and thus the curve, can be completely defined by four points – known as **control points** – P_0, P_1, P_2 and P_3 – which are just vertices of the parallelepiped as shown in the figure. Given that the position of the end points of the curve is fixed and its behaviour at the end points is determined, the shape that the curve traces out in space between its extremities needs to be defined. A parametric definition was chosen which means that the space curve $Q(u)$ is defined in terms of a parameter u ($0 \leq u \leq 1$). As u varies from 0 to 1 we arrive at values for the position of a point on $Q(u)$ by scaling or blending the control points. That is, each point on the curve is determined by scaling each control point by a cubic polynomial known as a basis or blending function. The curve is then given by:

$$Q(u) = \sum_{i=0}^{3} P_i B_i(u) \qquad [5.1]$$

and in the case of a Bézier curve the basis or blending functions are the Bernstein cubic polynomials:

$B_0(u) = (1 - u)^3$
$B_1(u) = 3u \, (1 - u)^2$
$B_2(u) = 3u^2 \, (1 - u)$
$B_3(u) = (u)^3$

Figure 5.2 shows these polynomials and a Bézier curve (projected into the two-dimensional space of the diagram).

A useful intuitive notion is the following. As we move physically along the curve from $u = 0$ to $u = 1$ we simultaneously move a vertical line in the basis function space that defines four values for the basis functions. Weighting each basis function by the control points and summing, we obtain the corresponding point in the space of the curve. We note that for any value of u (except $u = 0$ and $u = 1$) all the functions are non-zero. This means that the position of all the control points contribute to every point on the curve (except at the end points). At $u = 0$ only B_0 is non-zero. Therefore:

$$Q(0) = P_0$$

similarly

$$Q(1) = P_3$$

Figure 5.2
Moving along the curve by increasing u is equivalent to moving a vertical line through the basis functions. The intercepts of this line with the basis functions give the values of B for the equivalent point.

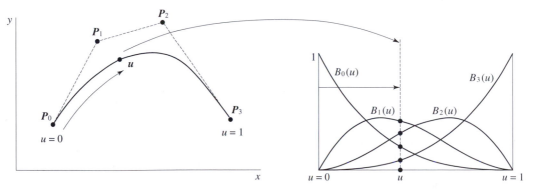

Space of curve

Space of basis functions

We also note that:

$$B_0(u) + B_1(u) + B_2(u) + B_3(u) = 1$$

Joining the four control points together gives the so-called control polygon and moving the control points around produces new curves. Moving a single control point of the curve distorts its shape in an intuitive manner. This is demonstrated in Figure 5.3. The effect of moving the end points is obvious. When we move the inner control points P_1 and P_2 we change the orientation of the tangent vectors to the curves at the end points – again obvious. Less obvious is that the positions of P_1 and P_2 also control the magnitude of the tangent vectors and it can be shown that:

$$Q_u(0) = 3(P_1 - P_0)$$
$$Q_u(1) = 3(P_2 - P_3)$$

where Q_u is the tangent vector to the curve (first derivative) at the end point. It can be seen that the curve is pulled towards the tangent vector with greater magnitude which is controlled by the position of the control points.

Bézier curves find uses not just in highly technical applications but also in popular software. Drawing packages that are found nowadays in word processors and DTP applications almost always include a sketching facility based on Bezier curves. Another well-known application of Bézier curves is shown in Figure 5.4. Here a typeface is in the process of being designed. The outline of the filled character is a set of Bézier curves to which the designer can make subtle alterations by moving the control points that specify curves that describe the outline.

Bézier's original cube concept, encapsulating a curve of three spatial variables, seems to have been lost and most texts simply deal with the curves of two spatial variables enclosed in a control polygon. Applications where three-dimensional space curves have to be designed, three-dimensional computer animation for example, can have interfaces where two-dimensional projections of

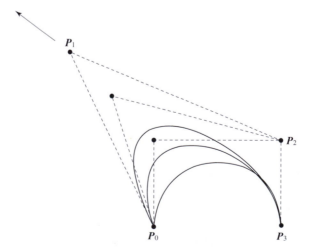

Figure 5.3
Effects of moving control point P_1.

Figure 5.4
Using Bézier curves in font design. Each curve segment control points are symbolised by O + + O.

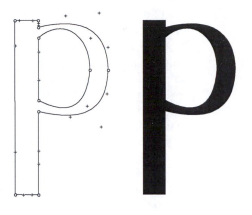

the curve are used. An example of this application is given in Section 13.4. (Note that for a three-dimensional curve the parallelepiped determines the plane in which the tangents to the curve – the edges of the control polygon – are oriented.)

At this point it is useful to consider all the ramifications of representing a curve with control points. The most important property, as far as interaction is concerned, is that moving the control points gives an intuitive change in curve shape. Note from Figure 5.3 that although the shape of the curve is changed most in the region near to the control point being moved, all of the curve is affected to some extent. In general, moving either of the two middle control points affects all parts of the curve. In some applications this 'non-locality' of control is a disadvantage and it is one of the motivations for using an alternative representation – the B-spline form.

Another way of putting it is to say that the curve mimics the shape of the control polygon. An important property from the point of view of the algorithms that deal with curves (and surfaces) is that a curve is always enclosed in the convex hull formed by the control polygon. The convex hull of a two-dimensional space curve is illustrated in Figure 5.5 and can be considered to be the polygon

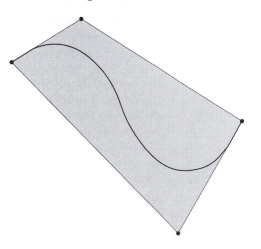

Figure 5.5
Convex hull property for cubic spline. The curve is contained in the shaded area formed from the control points.

formed by placing an elastic band around the control points. This follows from the fact that the basis functions sum to unity for all u.

Now consider transforming curves. Since the curves are defined as linear combinations of the control points, the curve itself is transformed by any affine transformation (rotation, scaling, translation etc.) in three-dimensional space by applying the appropriate transformations to the set of control points. Thus to transform a curve we transform the control points then compute the points on the curve. In this context note that it is not easy to transform a curve by computing the points then transforming (as we might do with an implicit description). For example, it is not clear in scaling, how many points are needed to ensure smoothness when the curve has been magnified. Note here that perspective transformations are non-affine, so we cannot map control points to screen space and compute the curve there. However, we can overcome this significant disadvantage by using rational curves, as we describe later in the chapter.

Finally, a useful alternative notation to the summation form is the following. First, we expand equation 5.1 to give:

$$Q(u) = P_0(1 - u)^3 + P_1 3u(1 - u)^2 + P_2 3u^2(1 - u) + P_3 u^3$$

This can then be written in matrix notation as:

$$Q(u) = UB_zP$$

$$= [u^3 \ u^2 \ u \ 1] \begin{bmatrix} -1 & 3 & -3 & 1 \\ 3 & -6 & 3 & 0 \\ -3 & 3 & 0 & 0 \\ 1 & 0 & 0 & 0 \end{bmatrix} \begin{bmatrix} P_0 \\ P_1 \\ P_2 \\ P_3 \end{bmatrix} \qquad [5.2]$$

5.2.1   Joining Bézier curve segments

Curve segments, defined by a set of four control points, can be joined to make up 'more complex' curves than that obtainable from a single segment. This results in a so-called piecewise polynomial curve. An alternative method of representing more complex curves is to increase the degree of the polynomial, but this has computational and mathematical disadvantages and it is generally considered easier to split the curve into cubic segments. Connecting curve segments implies that constraints must apply at the joins. The default constraint is positional continuity, the next best is first order (or tangential continuity). The difference between positional and first-order continuity for a Bézier curve is shown in Figure 5.6. Positional continuity means that the end point of the first segment is coincident with the start point of the second. First-order continuity means that the edges of the characteristic polygon are collinear as shown in the figure. This means that the tangent vectors, at the end of one curve and the start of the other, match to within a constant. In shaded surfaces, maintaining only positional continuity would possibly result in the joins being visible in the final rendered object.

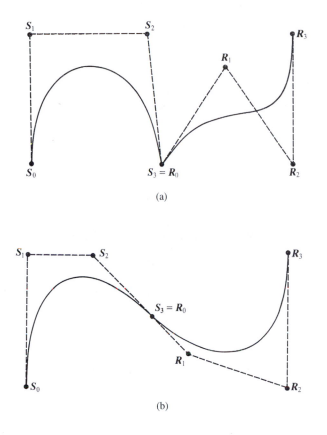

Figure 5.6
Continuity between
Bézier curve segments.
(a) Positional continuity
between Bézier points.
(b) Tangential continuity
between Bézier points.

(a)

(b)

If the control points of the two segments are $\boldsymbol{S}_i$ and $\boldsymbol{R}_i$ then first-order continuity is maintained if:

$$(\boldsymbol{S}_3 - \boldsymbol{S}_2) = k(\boldsymbol{R}_1 - \boldsymbol{R}_0)$$

Using this condition a composite Bézier curve is easily built up by adding a single segment at a time. However, the advantage of being able to build up a composite form from segments is somewhat negated by the constraints on local control that now apply because of the joining conditions.

Figure 5.4 is an example of a multi-segment Bézier curve. In this case a number of curves are joined to represent the outline of the character and first-order continuity is maintained between them. It is useful to consider the ramifications for an interface through which a user can edit multi-segment curves and maintain continuity. Figure 5.7 shows some possibilities. The illustration assumes that the user has already constructed a two segment curve whose shape is to be altered around the area of the join point $\boldsymbol{S}_3/\boldsymbol{R}_0$. To maintain continuity we must operate simultaneously on $\boldsymbol{R}_1$, $\boldsymbol{R}_0/\boldsymbol{S}_3$ and $\boldsymbol{S}_2$. We can do this by:

● maintaining the orientation of the line $\boldsymbol{R}_1,\boldsymbol{S}_2$ and moving the join point up and down this line (Figure 5.7(a);

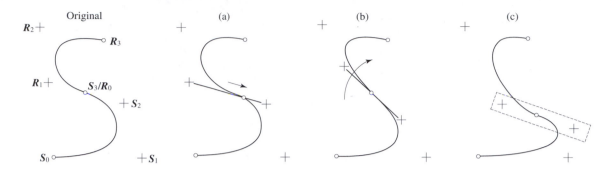

Figure 5.7
Examples of possible shape editing protocols for a two-segment Bézier curve. (a) Maintain the orientation of R_1S_2 and move any of the three control points R_1, S_3/R_0, S_2 along this line. (b) Rotate the line R_1S_2 about S_3/R_0. (c) Move the three control points R_1, S_3/R_0, S_2 as a 'locked' unit.

● maintaining the position of the join point and rotating the line R_1,S_2 about this point (Figure 5.7b);

● moving all three control points as a locked unit (Figure 5.7(c)).

These three editing possibilities or constraints will enable the user to change the shape of curves made up of any number of segments while at the same time maintaining first-order continuity between the curve segments. We will see later that this complication of Bézier curves can be overcome in another way – by using B-spline curves.

5.2.2 Summary of Bézier curve properties

● A Bézier curve is a polynomial. The degree of the polynomial is always one less than the number of control points. In computer graphics we generally use degree 3. Quadratic curves are not flexible enough and going above degree 3 gives rise to complications and so the choice of cubics is the best compromise for most computer graphics applications.

● The curve 'follows' the shape of the control point polygon and is constrained within the convex hull formed by the control points.

● The control points do not exert 'local' control. Moving any control point affects all of the curve to a greater or lesser extent. This can be seen by examining Figure 5.2 which shows that all the basis functions are everywhere non-zero except at the point $u = 0$ and $u = 1$.

● The first and last control points are the end points of the curve segment.

● The tangent vectors to the curve at the end points are coincident with the first and last edges of the control point polygon.

● Moving the control points alters the magnitude and direction of the tangent vectors – the basis of the intuitive 'feel' of a Bézier curve interface.

● The curve does not oscillate about any straight line more often than the control point polygon – this is known as the variation diminishing property. This has implications concerning the nature of the surface that can be represented.

- The curve is transformed by applying any affine transformation (that is, any combination of linear transformations) to its control point representation. The curve is invariant (does not change shape) under such a transformation.

5.3 B-spline curves

Two drawbacks associated with Bézier curves that are overcome by using B-spline curves are their non-localness and the relationship between the degree of the curve and the number of control points. The first property – non-localness – implies that although a control point heavily influences that part of the curve closest to it, it also has some effect on all the curve and this can be seen by examining Figure 5.2. All the basis functions are non-zero over the entire range of u. The second disadvantage means that we cannot use a Bézier cubic curve to approximate or represent n points without the inconvenience of using multiple curve segments (or by increasing the degree of the curve).

Like a Bézier curve, a B-spline curve does not pass through its control points. A B-spline is a complete piecewise cubic polynomial consisting of any number of curve segments. (For notational simplicity we will consider only cubic B-splines. We can, however, have B-splines to any degree.) It is a cubic segment over a certain interval, and going from one interval to the next, the coefficients change. For a single segment only, we can compare the B-spline formulation with the Bezier formulation by using the same matrix notation.

The B-spline formulation is:

$$Q_i(u) = UB_sP$$

$$= [u^3\ u^2\ u\ 1]\frac{1}{6}\begin{bmatrix} -1 & 3 & -3 & 1 \\ 3 & -6 & 3 & 0 \\ -3 & 0 & 3 & 0 \\ 1 & 4 & 1 & 0 \end{bmatrix}\begin{bmatrix} P_{i-3} \\ P_{i-2} \\ P_{i-1} \\ P_i \end{bmatrix} \quad [5.3]$$

where Q_i is the ith B-spline segment and P_i is a set of four points in a sequence of control points. Alternatively we can write:

$$Q_i(u) = \sum_{k=0}^{3} P_{i-3+k}B_{i-3+k}(u) \quad [5.4]$$

where i is the segment number and k is the local control point index – that is, the index for the segment i. The value of u over a single curve segment is $0 \leq u \leq 1$. Using this notation we can describe u as a local parameter – locally varying over the parametric range of 0 to 1 to define a single B-spline curve segment.

Thus in this notation we see that a B-spline curve is a series of m-2 curve segments that we conventionally label $Q_3, Q_4, \ldots, Q_m$ defined or determined by $m+1$ control points $P_0, P_1, \ldots, P_m$, $m \geq 3$. Each curve segment is defined by four control points and each control point influences four and only four curve segments. This is the local control property of the B-spline curve, the main advantage over Bézier curves.

Here we must be careful. Barsky (Bartels *et al.*, 1998) points out that comparing Bézier curves and B-spline curves can be misleading because it is not a comparison of like with like but a comparison of a single-segment Bézier curve (which may have the control vertex set extended and the degree of the curve raised) with a piecewise or composite B-spline curve. A single-segment Bézier curve is subject to global control because moving a control point affects the complete curve. In a composite B-spline curve, moving a control point only affects a few segments of the curve. The comparison should be between multi-segment Bézier curves and B-splines. The difference here is that to maintain continuity between Bézier segments the movement of the control points must satisfy constraints, while the control points of a B-spline composite can be moved in any way.

A B-spline exhibits positional, first derivative and second derivative (C^2) continuity and this is achieved because the basis functions are themselves C^2 piecewise polynominials. A linear combination of such basis functions will also be C^2 continuous. We define the entire set of curve segments as one B-spline curve in u:

$$Q(u) = \sum_{i=0}^{m} P_i B_i(u)$$

In this notation i is now a non-local control point number and u is a global parameter discussed in more detail in the next section.

Uniform B-splines

Equation 5.4 shows that each segment in a B-spline curve is defined by four basis functions and four control vertices. Hence there are three more basis functions and three more control vertices than there are curve segments. The join point on the value of u between segments is called the knot value and a uniform B-spline means that knots are spaced at equal intervals of the parameter u. Figure 5.8 shows a B-spline curve that is defined by (the position of) six control vertices or control points $P_0, P_1, \ldots, P_5$. It also shows the effect of varying the degree of the polynomials, and curves are shown for degree 2, 3 and 4. We are generally interested in cubics and this is a curve of three segments with the left-hand end point of Q_3 near P_0 and the right-hand end point of Q_5 near P_5. (Thus we see that a uniform B-spline does not in general interpolate the end control points, unlike a Bézier curve. Also, it is the case that a Bézier curve more closely approximates its control point polygon. However, the continuity maintaining property of the B-spline curve outweighs these disadvantages.)

Figure 5.8
A three-segment B-spline cubic curve defined by six control points.

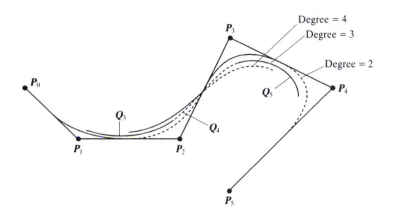

The notation gives us the following organisation (where each curve segment is shown as an alternating full/dotted line):

Q_3 is defined by P_0 P_1 P_2 P_3 which are scaled by B_0 B_1 B_2 B_3

Q_3 is defined by P_1 P_2 P_3 P_4 which are scaled by B_1 B_2 B_3 B_4

Q_3 is defined by P_2 P_3 P_4 P_5 which are scaled by B_2 B_3 B_4 B_5

The fact that each curve segment shares control points is the underlying mechanism whereby C^2 continuity is maintained between curve segments. Figure 5.9 shows the effect of changing the position of control point P_4. This pulls the segment Q_5 in the appropriate direction and also affects, to a lesser extent, segment Q_4 (which is also defined by P_4). However, it does not affect Q_3 and this figure demonstrates the important locality property of B-splines. In general, of course, a single control point influences four curve segments.

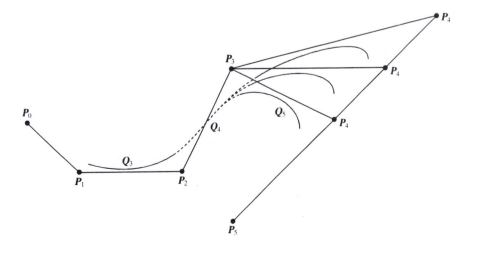

Figure 5.9
Demonstrating the locality property of B-spline curves. Moving P_1 changes Q_5 and Q_4 to a lesser extent. Q_3 is unchanged.

Figure 5.10
The uniform cubic B-spline $B_i(u)$.

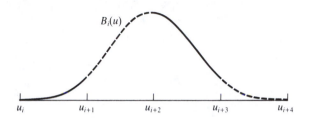

We now consider the underlying basis functions that define the curve. Each basis function is non-zero over four successive intervals in u (Figure 5.10). It is in fact a cubic, itself composed of four segments. The B-spline is non-zero over the intervals $u_i, u_{i+1}, \ldots, u_{i+4}$ and centred on u_{i+2}. Now each control point is scaled by a single basis function and if we assume that our knot values are equally spaced, then each basis function is a copy or translate and the set of basis functions used by the curve in Figure 5.8 is shown in Figure 5.11.

Figure 5.11
The six B-splines used in constructing the curve of Figure 5.8. They are all translates of each other.

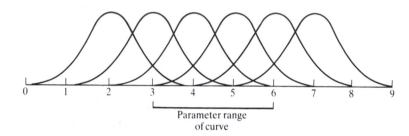

The basis functions sum to unity in the range $u = 3$ to $u = 6$ in this case, the values of the parameter u over which the curve is defined. A consequence of this is that the entire B-spline curve is contained within the convex hull of its control points. If we consider a single segment in the curve, then this defines a parameter range u_i to u_{i+1}. The basis functions that are active in the ith parametric interval, u_i to u_{i+1}, that is, the functions that define a single curve segment, are shown highlighted in Figure 5.12. This gives a useful interpretation of the behaviour of the functions as u is varied. In general, for values of u that are not knot values, four basis functions are active and sum to unity. When a knot value $u = u_i$ is reached, one basis function 'switches off' and another 'switches on'. At the knot value there are three basis functions that sum to unity.

Figure 5.12
The four B-splines that are non-zero or active for the first curve segment in Figure 5.8.

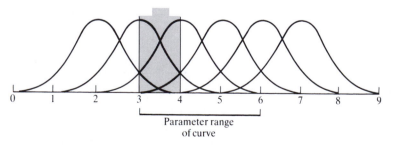

At this stage we can summarise and state that a B-spline curve is made up of $m - 2$ segments defined by the position of $m + 1$ basis functions over $m + 5$ knot values. Thus in Figure 5.7 we have three segments, six control points and six basis functions over 10 knot values.

Now consider again Figure 5.12. In the parameter range $u_i \leq u \leq u_{i+1}$ we evaluate the four B-splines B_i, B_{i-1}, B_{i-2} and B_{i-3} by substituting $0 \leq u \leq 1$ and computing:

$$B_i \quad = \frac{1}{6} \ u^3$$

$$B_{i-1} = \frac{1}{6} \ (-3u^3 + 3u^2 + 3u + 1)$$

$$B_{i-2} = \frac{1}{6} \ (3u^3 - 6u^2 + 4)$$

$$B_{i-3} = \frac{1}{6} \ (1-u)^3$$

It is important to note that this definition gives a single segment from each of the 4 B-spline basis functions over the range $0 \leq u \leq 1$. It does *not* define a single B-spline basis function which consists of four segments over the range $0 \leq u \leq 4$.

We now come to consider the end control vertices and note again that the curve does not interpolate these points. In general, of course, a B-spline curve does not interpolate any control points. We can make a B-spline curve interpolate control points by introducing multiple vertices. However, this involves a loss of continuity, as we shall see. Intuitively we can think of increasing the influence of a control point by repeating it. The curve is attracted to the repeated point. A segment is made by basis functions scaling control points. If a control point is repeated it will be used more than once in the evaluation of a single segment. For example, consider Figure 5.13 and compare it with Figure 5.8. The last control point in the example in Figure 5.8 is now repeated three times. There are now five segments and P_5 is used once in the determination of Q_5, twice in Q_6 and three times in Q_7. The curve now ranges over $3 \leq u \leq 8$. At $u = 8$ the curve is coincident with P_5.

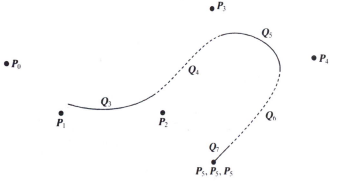

Figure 5.13
Demonstrating the effect of multiple end control points. P_5 is repeated three times, forcing the curve to interpolate it.

Figure 5.14
Demonstrating the effect of multiple intermediate control points. (a) P_3 is duplicated. (b) P_3 is triplicated.

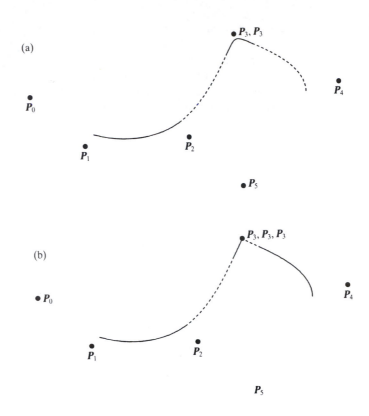

Such a technique can be used to make the curve interpolate both the intermediate control points and the end points. Figure 5.14(a) shows the effect of introducing multiple intermediate control points. In this figure P_3 has been doubled. P_3 is almost interpolated and an extra segment is introduced. The continuity changes from C^2G^2 to C^2G^1. This means that the continuity across the two segments is reduced by one although the continuity within each segment is still C^2. Figure 5.14(b) shows P_3 made into a triple control point. This time the curve interpolates the control point and the curve becomes a straight line on either side of the control point. The continuity reduces now to C^2G^0.

5.3.2   Non-uniform B-splines

In the previous section we considered a family of curves that we referred to as uniform B-splines because the basis functions were translates of each other. We now look at non-uniform B-splines.

A non-uniform B-spline is a curve where the parametric intervals between successive knot values are not necessarily equal. This implies that the blending functions are no longer translates of each other but vary from interval to interval. The most common form of a non-uniform B-spline is where some of the

Figure 5.15
A non-uniform B-spline that interpolates the end points by using a knot vector [0,0,0,0,1,2,3,3,3].

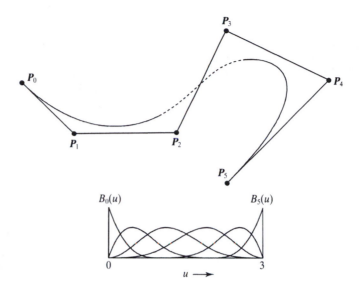

intervals between successive knot values are reduced to zero by inserting multiple knots. This facility is used to interpolate control points (both end points and intermediate points) and it possesses certain advantages over the method used in the previous section – inserting multiple control points. In particular a control point can be interpolated without the effect that occurred with multiple control vertices – namely straight line curve segments on either side of the control point.

Consider the curve generated in Figure 5.8. The knot values for this curve are $u = 3, 4, 5, 6$. We define a knot vector for this curve as [0,1,2,3,4,5,6,7,8,9] and a useful parametric range (within which the basis functions sum to unity) as $3 \leq u \leq 6$. The interval between each knot value is 1. If non-uniform knot values are used, then the basis functions are no longer the same for each parametric interval, but vary over the range of u. Consider Figure 5.15. This uses the same control points as Figure 5.8 and the B-spline curve is still made up of three segments. However, the curve now interpolates the end points because multiple knots have been inserted at each end of the knot vector. The knot vector used is [0,0,0,0,1,2,3,3,3,3]. The basis functions are also shown in the figure. The curve now posses nine segments Q_0 to Q_8. However, Q_0, Q_1, Q_2 are reduced to a single point. Q_3, Q_4 and Q_5 are defined over the range $0 \leq u \leq 3$. Q_6, Q_7 and Q_8 are reduced to a single point $u = 3$. In practice the knot sequence [0,0,0,0,1,2, . . . $n - 1,n,n,n,n$] is often used. That is, interpolation is forced at the end points but uniform knots are used elsewhere. A second example showing the flexibility of a B-spline curve is given in Figure 5.16. Here we have nine control points and 13 knots. The knot vector is [0,0,0,0,1,2,3,4,5,6,6,6,6].

In general, a knot vector is any non-decreasing sequence of knot values u_0 to u_{m+4}. As we have seen, successive knot values can be equal and the number of identical values is called the multiplicity of the knot. Causing a curve to inter-

Figure 5.16
Showing the flexibility
of B-spline curves.
The knot vector is
[0,0,0,0,1,2,3,4,5,6,6,6,6].

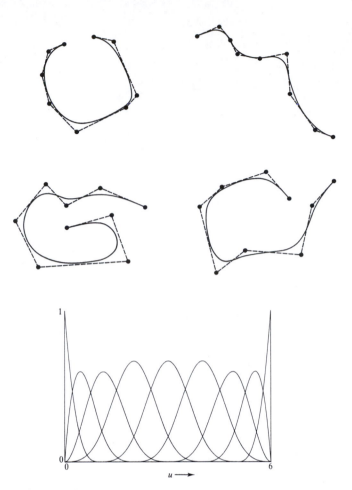

polate the end points by using multiple control vertices does not have precisely the same effect as using multiple control vertices and Figure 5.17 shows the final control point P_5 in our standard example interpolated using both a multiple control point and a knot vector with multiplicity 4 on the final knot value.

Figure 5.17
Comparing multiple knots
with multiple control points.
(a) The curve is generated
by a knot vector with
multiplicity 4 on the start
and end values. (b) P_5 is
repeated three times.

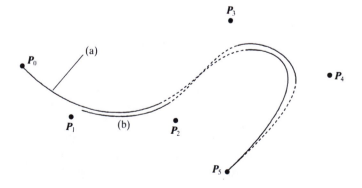

Note that if we use the knot vector [0,0,0,0,1,1,1,1] then we have single-segment curve interpolating $\boldsymbol{P}_0$ and $\boldsymbol{P}_3$. In this instance the basis functions are the Bézier basis functions (Figure 5.2) and the resulting curve is a Bézier curve. Thus we see that a Bézier curve is just a special case of a non-uniform B-spline.

The effect of a multiple knot on the shape of a basis function is easily seen. Consider Figure 5.18(a), which shows the uniform B-spline basis function defined over the knots 0, 1, 2, 3, 4. As we have explained in the previous section, this is itself made up of four cubic polynomial segments defined over the given ranges. These are generated by using Equation 5.4 and translating each cubic segment by 0, 1, 2, 3 and 4 units in u. Alternatively we can use:

$$
B_0(u) = \begin{cases}
b_{-0}(u) = \dfrac{1}{6}\, u^3 & 0 \leq u \leq 1 \\[2ex]
b_{-1}(u) = -\dfrac{1}{6}\, (3u^3 - 12u^2 + 12u - 4) & 1 \leq u \leq 2 \\[2ex]
b_{-2}(u) = \dfrac{1}{6}\, (3u^3 - 24u^2 + 60u - 44) & 2 \leq u \leq 3 \\[2ex]
b_{-3}(u) = -\dfrac{1}{6}\, (u^3 - 12u^2 + 48u - 64) & 3 \leq u \leq 4
\end{cases}
$$

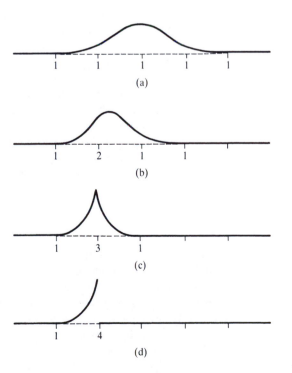

Figure 5.18
The effect of knot multiplicity on a single cubic B-spline basis function.
(a) All knot multiplicities are unity: [0,1,2,3,4].
(b) Second knot has multiplicity 2: [0,1,1,2,3].
(c) Second knot has multiplicity 3: [0,1,1,1,2].
(d) Second knot has multiplicity 4: [0,1,1,1,1].

Compared with Equation 5.4 note that this defines a single B-spline basis function over the range $0 \le u \le 4$. If we double the second knot and use [0,1,1,2,3], $b_{-1}(u)$ shrinks to zero length and the function becomes asymmetric as shown in Figure 5.18(b). The double knot eliminates second derivative continuity but first derivative continuity remains. Tripling the second knot by using knot vector [0,1,1,1,2] gives the symmetrical function shown in Figure 5.18(c) which now only has positional continuity. Quadrupling this knot [0,1,1,1,1] produces the function shown in Figure 5.18(d) where even positional continuity is eliminated.

If we now return to the context shown in Figure 5.15, the first basis function is defined over 0, 0, 0, 0, 1 and is asymmetric with no positional continuity. The second is defined over a set of knot values that contains a triple knot – [0,0,0,1, 2], the third over the sequence [0,0,1,2,3] and is also asymmetric. In this case all functions are asymmetric and summarising we have:

Knot vector	Basis function
0 0 0 0 1	B_0
0 0 0 1 2	B_1
0 0 1 2 3	B_2
0 1 2 3 3	B_3
1 2 3 3 3	B_4
2 3 3 3 3	B_5

We can further see from this set of basis functions that they sum to unity over the entire range of u and that at $u = 0$ and $u = 3$ the only non-zero basis functions are B_0 and B_5 (both unity) which cause the end points to be interpolated by Q_3 and Q_5 respectively.

We now consider altering the knot multiplicity for interior knots where the issue of continuity changes becomes apparent. Consider the examples given in Figure 5.19. This is the same example as we used in Figure 5.7 except that an extra control point has been added to give us a four segment curve. The knot vector is [0,1,2,3,4,5,6,7,8,9,10] and Figure 5.19(a) shows the curve. Figure 5.19(b) shows the effect of introducing a double knot using vector [0,1,2,3,4,4,5,6,7,8,9]. The number of segments is reduced to three. Q_4 shrinks to zero. The convex hulls containing Q_3 and Q_5 meet on edge $P_2 P_3$ and the join point between Q_3, Q_4 and Q_5 is forced to lie on this line. In Figure 5.19(c) a triple knot is introduced – [0,1,2,3,4,4,4,5,6,7,8]. The curve is reduced to two segments. Q_4 and Q_5 shrink to zero at P_3. There is only positional continuity between Q_3 and Q_6 but the segments on either side of the control point P_3 are curved. This should be compared with Figure 5.13 produced using a triple control vertex. In Figure 5.19(d) a quadruple knot is introduced – [0,1,2,3,4,4,4,4,5,6,7]. Positional continuity is destroyed. The curve reduces to a single segment. To see what this means we have introduced another control point so that another segment Q_7 now appears. There is now a gap between the end of Q_3 and the start of Q_7. They have no control points in common.

We now consider a recursive method for generating the basis or blending functions for non-uniform B-splines. The method, known as the Cox de Boor algorithm (De Boor, 1972; Cox, 1972), remarkably is able to generate uniform or non-uniform B-splines of any degree using a single recursive formula. Because the functions are no longer translates of one another the computation is more expensive. For a cubic (fourth order) curve we can define the recursion in its unwound form. Extending the notation of a B-spline to include order as the second subscript, we define the basis function for weighting control point P_i as $B_{i,j}(u)$ and the recurrence relationships for a cubic B-spline is:

$$B_{i,1}(u) = \begin{cases} 1, & u_i \le u \le u_{i+1} \\ 0, & \text{otherwise} \end{cases}$$

$$B_{i,2}(u) = \frac{u - u_i}{u_{i+1} - u_i} B_{i,1}(u) + \frac{u_{i+2} - u}{u_{i+2} - u_{i+1}} B_{i+1,1}(u)$$

$$B_{i,3}(u) = \frac{u - u_i}{u_{i+2} - u_i} B_{i,2}(u) + \frac{u_{i+3} - u}{u_{i+3} - u_{i+1}} B_{i+1,2}(u)$$

$$B_{i,4}(u) = \frac{u - u_i}{u_{i+3} - u_i} B_{i,3}(u) + \frac{u_{i+4} - u}{u_{i+4} - u_{i+1}} B_{i+1,2}(u)$$

When knots are repeated a quotient of 0/0 can occur in the Cox de Boor definition and this is deemed to be zero. Computationally the numerator is always checked for zero and the result set to zero irrespective of the denominator value. The choice of a particular knot set in commercial CAD systems that use B-splines is usually a predefined part of the system.

5.3.3 Summary of B-spline curve properties

- Some of the properties that we listed for Bézier curves apply to B-spline curves. In particular, the curve follows the shape of the control point polygon and is constrained to lie in the convex hull of the control points.
- The curve exhibits the variation diminishing property.
- The curve is transformed by applying any affine transformation to its control point representation.

In addition, B-splines possess the following properties:

- A B-spline curve exhibits local control – a control point is connected to four segments (in the case of a cubic) and moving a control point can only influence these segments.

Figure 5.19
The effect of interior knot multiplicity on a B-spline curve. (a) A four-segment B-spline curve. The knot vector is [0,1,2,3,4,5,6,7,8,9,10]. All B-splines are translates of each other.

(a)

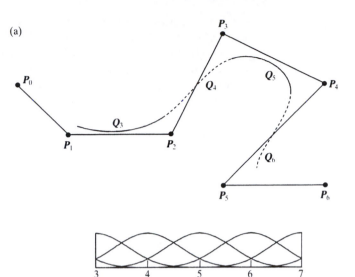

(b)

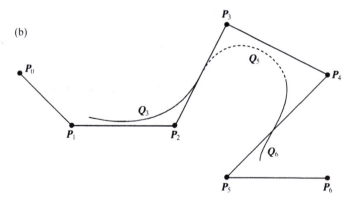

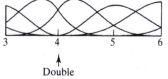

(b) Knot vector is [0,1,2,3,4,4,5,6,7,8,9]. Q_4 shrinks to zero.

Double
knot

Figure 5.19 *continued*
(c) Knot vector is
[0,1,2,3,4,4,5,6,7,8].
Q_4 and Q_5 shrink to zero.
Continuity between Q_3 and
Q_6 is positional.

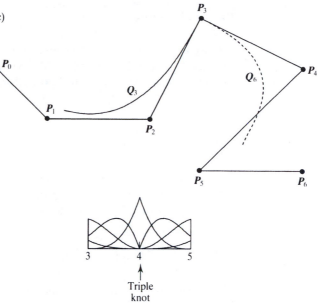

(d) Knot vector is
[0,1,2,3,4,4,4,4,5,6,7,8].
The curve reduces to a
single segment Q_3. Another
control point has been
added to show that the
curve now 'breaks' between
P_3 and P_4.

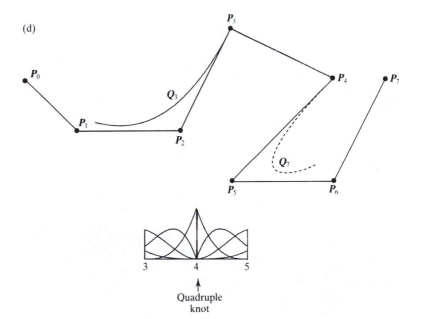

Rational curves

A rational curve is a curve defined in four-dimensional space – known as projective space – which is then projected into three-dimensional space. The advantage of the rational over the non-rational form will become clear in course of the treatment.

Rational Bézier curves

Let us start by considering the projection of a three-dimensional Bézier curve into two-dimensional space, specifically onto the plane $z = 1$ (Figure 5.20). We do this by dividing by $z(u)$ to define a two-dimensional (rational) curve $\boldsymbol{R}(u)$:

$$\boldsymbol{R}(u) = \left(\frac{x(u)}{z(u)} , \frac{y(u)}{x(u)} \right)$$

The curve is defined in three-dimensional (projective) space as:

$$\boldsymbol{Q}(u) = \sum_{i=0}^{3} \boldsymbol{P}_i B_i(u)$$

where

$$\boldsymbol{P}_i = (x_i, y_i, z_i)$$

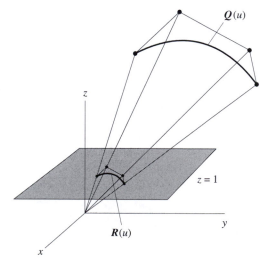

Figure 5.20
Projection of a three-dimensional Bézier curve, $Q(u)$, onto the plane $z = 1$ giving the two-dimensional curve $R(u)$.

Now a special notation is used for writing the three-dimensional control points of a rational curve in two-dimensional space, which is:

$$\boldsymbol{P}_i^w = (w_i x_i,\ w_i y_i,\ w_i)$$

and we write our three-dimensional curve as

$$\boldsymbol{Q}(u) = \sum_{i=0}^{3} \begin{bmatrix} w_i x_i \\ w_i y_i \\ w_i \end{bmatrix} B_i(u)$$

which is projected into two-dimensional space as:

$$\boldsymbol{R}(u) = \left(\frac{\sum w_i x_i B_i(u)}{\sum w_i B_i(u)},\ \frac{\sum w_i y_i B_i(u)}{\sum w_i B_i(u)} \right)$$

The same formula holds when we project a four-dimensional curve into three-dimensional space where each control point is now:

$$\boldsymbol{P}_i^w = (w_i x_i,\ w_i y_i,\ w_i z_i,\ w_i)$$

and we have

$$\boldsymbol{R}(u) = \frac{\sum w_i \boldsymbol{P}_i B_i(u)}{\sum w_i B_i(u)}$$

Rational curves enjoy all the properties of non-rational curves and indeed if the weights are set identically to 1 the form becomes the standard Bézier curve. Now consider the practical import of this form which allows control points to be weighted in this way. The effect of altering the value of a weight associated with a control point is shown in Figure 5.21. As the name suggests, increasing the weight of a control point gives it more influence. The way in which a weight value affects the curve is subtly different from the movement of a control point, as Figure 5.22 demonstrates. Changing the position of a control point moves points on the curve in a direction parallel to that defined by the control point displacement. However, changing the weight of a control point causes points on the curve to move towards that point in the manner shown in the figure. These factors can be used to significant advantage in design programs.

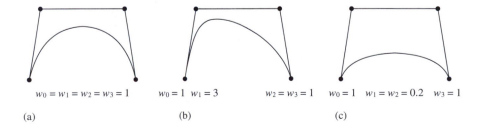

Figure 5.21
Varying the weights of a rational Bézier curve.

(a) $w_0 = w_1 = w_2 = w_3 = 1$

(b) $w_0 = 1$ $w_1 = 3$ $w_2 = w_3 = 1$

(c) $w_0 = 1$ $w_1 = w_2 = 0.2$ $w_3 = 1$

Figure 5.22
Rational Bézier curves: the different effect of control point movement and weight adjustment. (a) Movement of a control point causes any point on the curve to move in a parallel direction. (b) Adjustment of a weight causes any point on the curve to move along a line drawn from the curve point to the control point.

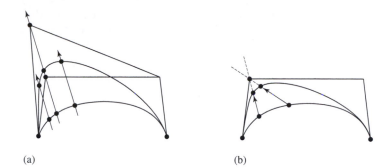

(a)　　　　　　　　　　　　　　(b)

Another important advantage of rational curves is that they can be used to represent conic sections precisely. A circle, or segments of it, is probably one of the most frequently used curves in CAD. A non-rational Bézier curve cannot represent a circle exactly. Finally, as we have already mentioned, we can only transform the control points of a non-rational curve under an affine transformation. The perspective transformation used in computer graphics is not affine, and non-rational curves whose control points are transformed into image space cannot be correctly generated in this space. Rational curves, however, because of the perspective division implicit in the construction of the curves, ensure that they are correctly handled in perspective views.

5.4.2 NURBS

NURBS stands for Non-Uniform Rational B-Splines and this representation is probably the most popular in CAD. In design applications it admits the following possibilities:

- interactive placement and movement of control points;
- interactive placement and movement of knots;
- interactive control of control-point weights.

Combining the rational curve advantages of the previous section with the properties of non-uniform B-splines, a NURBS curve is defined as a non-uniform B-spline curve on a knot vector where the interior knot spans are not equal. For example, we may have interior knots with multiplicity greater than 1 (that is, knot spans of length zero). Some common curves and surfaces, such as circles and cylinders, require non-uniform knot spacing and the use of this option generally allows better shape control and the ability to model a larger class of shapes.

A rational B-spline curve is defined by a set of four-dimensional control points:

$$\boldsymbol{P}_i^w = (w_i x_i,\ w_i y_i,\ w_i z_i,\ w_i)$$

The perspective map of such a curve in three-dimensional space is called a rational B-spline curve.

$$\boldsymbol{R}(u) = H\left[\sum_{i=0}^{n}\boldsymbol{P}_i^w B_{i,k}(u)\right]$$

$$= \frac{\displaystyle\sum_{i=0}^{n}\boldsymbol{P}_i w_i B_{i,k}(u)}{\displaystyle\sum_{i=0}^{n}w_i B_{i,k}(u)}$$

Rational B-splines have the same analytical and geometric properties as non-rational B-splines and if:

$w_i = 1$ for all i, then

$\boldsymbol{R}_{i,k}(u) = B_{i,k}(u)$

The w_i associated with each control point are called weights and can be viewed as extra shape parameters. It can be shown that w_i affects the curve only locally. If, for example, w_j is fixed for all $j \ne i$, a change in w_i only affects the curve over k knot spans (just as moving a control point only affects the curve over k spans). w_i can be interpreted geometrically as a coupling factor. The curve is pulled towards a control point $\boldsymbol{P}_i$ if w_i increases. If w_i is decreased the curve moves away from the control point.

A specialisation of rational B-splines is the generalised conic segment important in CAD. Faux (Faux and Pratt, 1979) shows that a rational quadratic form can produce a one-parameter (w) family of conic segments.

5.5 From curves to surfaces

The treatment of parametric cubic curve segments given in the foregoing sections is easily generalised to bi-parametric cubic surface patches. A point on the surface patch is given by a bi-parametric function and a set of blending or basis functions are used for each parameter. A cubic Bézier patch is defined as:

$$\boldsymbol{Q}(u,v) = \sum_{i=0}^{3}\sum_{j=0}^{3}\boldsymbol{P}_{ij}B_i(u)B_j(v)$$

(5.5)

Mathematically the three-dimensional surfaces are said to be generated from the Cartesian product of two curves. A Bézier patch and its control points are shown in Figure 5.23 where the patches are displayed using iso-parametric lines. The 16 control points form a characteristic polyhedron and this bears a relationship to the shape of the surface, in the same way that the characteristic polygon relates to a curve segment. From Figure 5.23(a) it can be seen intuitively that 12 of the control points are associated with the boundary edges of the patch (four of them specifying the end points). Only the corner vertices lie in the surface. In fact, if we consider the control points to form a matrix of 4×4 points then the four

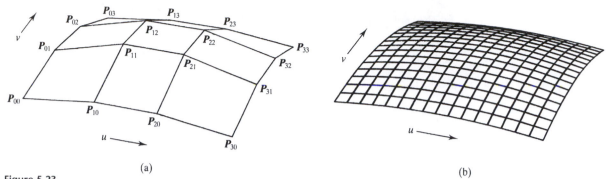

(a)

(b)

Figure 5.23
(a) A control polyhedron and (b) the resulting bi-cubic Bézier patch.

Figure 5.24
The effect of 'lifting' one of the control points of a Bézier patch.

groups of four points forming the edges of the matrix are the control points for the boundary curves of the patch. Thus the edges of the patch are made up of four Bézier curves. We can now see that the remaining four control points must specify the shape of the surface contained between the boundary edges.

The properties of the Bézier curve formulation are extended into the surface domain. Figure 5.24 shows a patch being deformed by 'pulling out' a single control point. The intuitive feel for the surface through its control points, and the ability to ensure first-order continuity are maintained. The surface patch is transformed by applying transformations to each of the control points.

The way in which the control points 'work' can be seen by analogy with the cubic curve. The geometric interpretation is naturally more difficult than that for

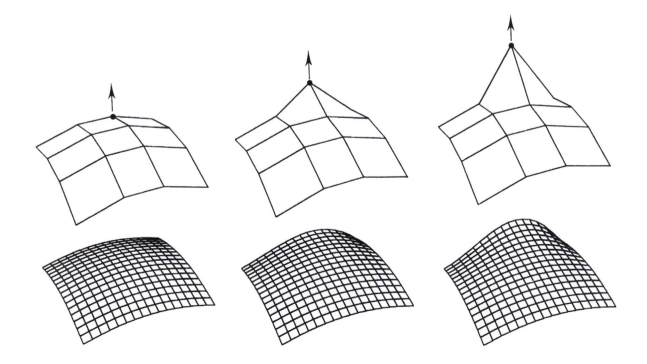

the curve and, of course, the purpose of the Bézier formulation is to protect the designer against having to manipulate tangent vectors and so on, but it is included for completeness.

The matrix specification of Equation 5.5 is:

$$\boldsymbol{P}(u,v) = [u^3 \; u^2 \; u \; 1] \; \boldsymbol{B}_z \; \boldsymbol{P} \; \boldsymbol{B}_z{}^T \begin{bmatrix} v^3 \\ v^2 \\ v \\ 1 \end{bmatrix}$$

where

$$\boldsymbol{B}_z = \begin{bmatrix} -1 & 3 & -3 & 1 \\ 3 & -6 & 3 & 0 \\ -3 & 3 & 0 & 0 \\ 1 & 0 & 0 & 0 \end{bmatrix}$$

$$\boldsymbol{P} = \begin{bmatrix} \boldsymbol{P}_{00} & \boldsymbol{P}_{01} & \boldsymbol{P}_{02} & \boldsymbol{P}_{03} \\ \boldsymbol{P}_{10} & \boldsymbol{P}_{11} & \boldsymbol{P}_{12} & \boldsymbol{P}_{13} \\ \boldsymbol{P}_{20} & \boldsymbol{P}_{21} & \boldsymbol{P}_{22} & \boldsymbol{P}_{23} \\ \boldsymbol{P}_{30} & \boldsymbol{P}_{31} & \boldsymbol{P}_{32} & \boldsymbol{P}_{33} \end{bmatrix}$$

It is instructive to examine the relationship between control points and derivative vectors at the corner of a patch. For example, consider the corner $u = v = 0$. The relationship between the control points and the vectors associated with the vertex $\boldsymbol{P}_{00}$ is as follows:

$$\boldsymbol{Q}_u(0,0) = 3\,(\boldsymbol{P}_{10} - \boldsymbol{P}_{00})$$
$$\boldsymbol{Q}_v(0,0) = 3\,(\boldsymbol{P}_{01} - \boldsymbol{P}_{00}) \qquad\qquad [5.6]$$
$$\boldsymbol{Q}_{uv}(0,0) = 9\,(\boldsymbol{P}_{00} - \boldsymbol{P}_{01} - \boldsymbol{P}_{10} + \boldsymbol{P}_{11})$$

Figure 5.25 shows these vectors at a patch corner. $\boldsymbol{Q}_u(0,0)$ is a constant times the tangent vector at $\boldsymbol{Q}(0,0)$ in the u parameter direction. Similarly $\boldsymbol{Q}_v(0,0)$ relates to the tangent vector in the v parameter direction. The cross-derivatives at each end point, sometimes called twist vectors, specify the rate of change of the tangent vectors with respect to u and v. It is a vector normal to the plane containing the tangent vectors.

Analogous to the control points in Bézier curves, patches are specified in terms of four end points, eight tangent vectors (two at each corner) and four twist vectors. Consider Figure 5.25(b) which shows the elements of the control point polyhedron that are involved in the derivatives. Four pairs of points specify the tangent vectors in u at each corner (two rows in the matrix), four pairs specify tangent vectors in v (two columns in the matrix) and all 16 elements specify the twist vectors.

If we set $\boldsymbol{Q}_{uv}(i,j) = 0$ then we have a so-called zero twist surface or a surface with four zero twist vectors. For such a surface the inner control points can be derived from the three adjacent edge points. For example, at the (0,0) corner we have:

$$0 = 9\,(\boldsymbol{P}_{00} - \boldsymbol{P}_{01} - \boldsymbol{P}_{10} + \boldsymbol{P}_{11})$$

Figure 5.25
Vectors at P_{00}. (a) Tangent
vectors at P_{00}. (b) Elements
of control point matrix
involved in vectors at P_{00}.

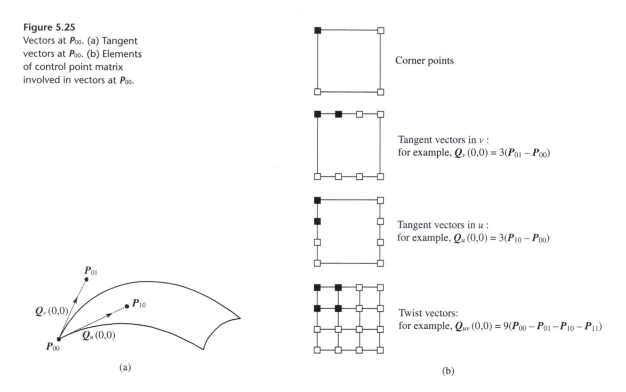

Corner points

Tangent vectors in v :
for example, $Q_v(0,0) = 3(P_{01} - P_{00})$

Tangent vectors in u :
for example, $Q_u(0,0) = 3(P_{10} - P_{00})$

Twist vectors:
for example, $Q_{uv}(0,0) = 9(P_{00} - P_{01} - P_{10} - P_{11})$

(a) (b)

This is important when we wish to derive the 16 control points of a patch when we only have knowledge of the boundary curves. This situation occurs in surface fitting or interpolation (Section 5.6.3) when we wish to fit a patch through a set of points in three space. We do this by first using curve interpolation to define the boundary curves of the patches – giving 12 of the control points for a patch – and estimating in some way the four internal control points. The zero twist solution is a particularly easy way to estimate what the four internal control points should be.

For shading calculations we need to calculate certain surface normals. One of the easiest ways to shade a patch is to subdivide it until the products of the subdivision are approximately planar (this technique is discussed fully later). The patches can then be treated as planar polygons and Gouraud or Phong shading applied. Vertex normals are calculated from the cross-product of the two tangent vectors at the vertex. For example:

$$a = (P_{01} - P_{00})$$

$$b = (P_{10} - P_{00})$$

$$N = a \times \mathbf{b}$$

A normal can be computed at any point on the surface from the cross-product of the two partial derivatives $\partial Q/\partial u$ and $\partial Q/\partial v$ but shading a patch by exhaustive calculation of internal points from the parametric description is computationally expensive and is subject to other problems. The advantages of using a parametric patch description of a surface are not contained in the fact that a precise world coordinate is available for every point in the surface – the cost of retrieving this information is generally too high – but in advantages that patch representation has to offer in object modelling.

However, we introduce an application in Section 10.6.1 (caching patch illumination using light maps) where we do require a value for the surface normal at any point on the patch surface. In this case we can calculate it from:

$$a = Q_u(u,v) = [3u^2 \ 2u \ 1 \ 0] \, \boldsymbol{B}_z \, \boldsymbol{P} \, \boldsymbol{B}_z{}^T \begin{bmatrix} v^3 \\ v^2 \\ v \\ 1 \end{bmatrix}$$

$$b = Q_u(u,v) = [u^3 \ u^2 \ u \ 1] \, \boldsymbol{B}_z \, \boldsymbol{P} \, \boldsymbol{B}_z{}^T \begin{bmatrix} 3v^2 \\ 2v \\ 1 \\ 0 \end{bmatrix}$$

$$\boldsymbol{N} = \boldsymbol{a} \times \boldsymbol{b}$$

Continuity and Bézier patches

The Bézier representation is excellent for single-segment curves and single-patch surfaces. When we want to make a curve (or surface) that is more complex, we have to join Bézier curves together using a continuity constraint. In Section 5.6 we will look at modelling issues in detail. In this section we will look at an issue that is crucial to modelling. This is the way in which we have to join patches together to maintain continuity over a surface and we will do this by developing a similar argument as we used for the joining of Bézier curve segments.

Maintaining first-order continuity across two patches is a simple extension of the curve joining constraints and is best considered geometrically. Figure 5.26 shows two patches, **S** and **R**, sharing a common edge. For positional or zero-order continuity:

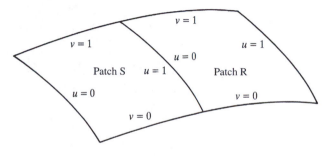

Figure 5.26
Joining two patches.

Figure 5.27
(a) Positional continuity between bi-cubic Bézier patches, and (b) tangential continuity between bi-cubic Bézier patches.

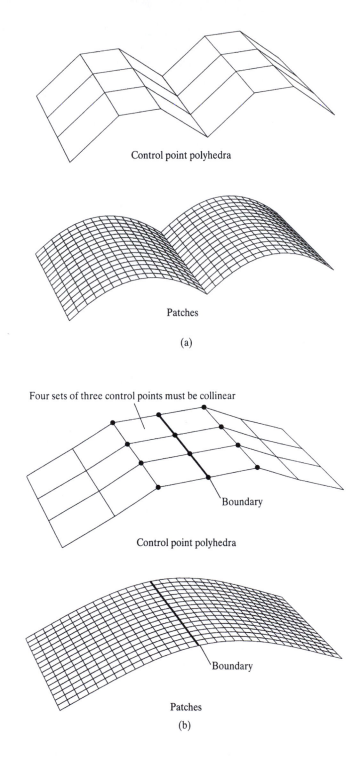

Control point polyhedra

Patches

(a)

Four sets of three control points must be collinear

Boundary

Control point polyhedra

Boundary

Patches

(b)

$$S(1,v) = R(0,v) \text{ for } 0 < v < 1$$

This condition implies that the two characteristic polygons share a common boundary edge (Figure 5.27) and:

$$S_{33} = R_{03}$$
$$S_{32} = R_{02}$$
$$S_{31} = R_{01}$$
$$S_{30} = R_{00}$$

or

$$S_{3i} = R_{0i} \; i = 0, \ldots, 3$$

To satisfy first-order (C1) continuity the tangent vectors at $u = 1$ for the first patch must match those at $u = 0$ for the second patch for all v. This implies that each of the four pairs of polyhedron edges that straddle the boundary must be collinear. That is:

$$(S_{3i} - S_{2i}) = k(R_{1i} - R_{0i}) \, i = 0, \ldots, 3$$

Faux in 1979 pointed out that in many contexts, this constraint is severe, if a composite surface is constructed from a set of Bézier patches. For example, a composite surface might be designed by constructing a single patch and working outwards from it. Joining two patches along a common boundary implies that eight of the control points for the second patch are already fixed and joining a patch to two existing patches implies that 12 of the control points are fixed.

A slightly less restrictive joining condition was developed by Bézier in 1972. In this patch corners have positional but not gradient continuity. However, tangent vectors of edges meeting at a corner must be co-planar. Even with this marginally greater flexibility, there are still problems with the design of composite surfaces.

It should be mentioned that although the foregoing treatment has dealt with rectangular patches, such patches cannot represent all shapes. Consider, for example, a spherically shaped object. Rectangular patches must degenerate to triangles at the poles. Farin points out that perhaps the main reason for the predominance of rectangular patches in most CAD systems is that the first applications of patches in car design were to the design of the outer body panels. Those parts have a rectangular geometry and it is natural to break them down into smaller rectangles and use rectangularly shaped patches.

5.5.2

A Bézier patch object – the Utah teapot

Possibly the most famous object in computer graphics is the so-called Utah teapot – an early example of a Bézier patch mesh. In this section we will describe this much-used object and use it to represent an important point concerning this representational form – its economy (compared to the polygon mesh model).

The University of Utah was the centre of research into rendering algorithms in the early 1970s. Various polygon mesh models were set up manually, including a VW Beetle, digitised by Ivan Sutherland's computer graphics class in 1971 (Figure 2.5).

In 1975 M. Newell developed the Utah teapot, a familiar object that has become a kind of benchmark in computer graphics, and one that has been used frequently in this text. He did this by sketching the profile of the teapot to estimate suitable control points for bi-cubic Bézier patches. The lid, rim and body of the teapot were then treated as solids of revolution and the spout and handle were modelled as ducted solids. This resulted, eventually, in the 32 patches.

The original teapot is now in the Boston Computer Museum, displayed alongside its computer alter ego. A full description of the model and details on the Computer Museum is given in Crow (1987).

A wireframe of lines of constant u and v is shown in Figure 5.28. The object is made up of 32 Bézier patches. A single patch is shown as a heavy line. (Also shown in this figure is a wireframe image made up of the Bézier curves that form the edges of the constituent patches and a composite control point polyhedron.) This representation consists of:

32 patches $\times$ 16 control points/patch
    = 288 vertices (approximately, most patches
        share 12 control points)
    = 288 $\times$ 3 real numbers (say)

Figure 5.28
The Utah teapot. (a) Lines of constant u and v. The teapot is made up of 32 Bézier patches. A single patch is shown shaded. (b) A wireframe of the control points. The shaded region shows the control polyhedron for the shaded patch. (c) A wireframe of the patch edges.

(a)

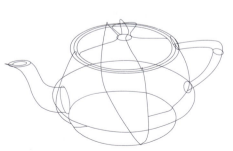

(c)

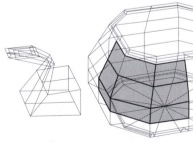

(b)

On the other hand a 'reasonable' polygon mesh representation would be:

approximately 2048 × four-sided polygons

= 2048 × 3 real numbers

Thus in the polygon mesh model, an inaccurate representation uses 2048/32 times as many primitive elements. This is a good demonstration of a point made in Chapter 2 – that throughout the two to three decades that three-dimensional computer graphics has been in existence, we prefer to deal with many simple primitives rather than far fewer more complex ones.

5.5.3

B-spline surface patches

To form a bicubic B-spline surface patch we need to evaluate:

$$Q(u,v) = \sum_{i=0}^{n} \sum_{j=0}^{m} P_{ij} B_{i,j}(u,v)$$

where P_{ij} is an array of control points and $B_{i,j}(u,v)$ is a bivariate basis function. We can generate $B_{i,j}(u,v)$ from:

$$B_{i,j}(u,v) = B_i(u)\,B_j(v)$$

where $B_i(u)$ and $B_j(v)$ are the previously defined univariate cubic B-splines. Thus we have:

$$Q(u,v) = \sum_{i=0}^{n} \sum_{j=0}^{m} P_{ij} B_i(u) B_j(v)$$

Analogous to B-spline curves we consider a B-spline patch to be made up of several rectangular surface patch segments. We now have two knot sequences in u and v, which taken together form a grid in parameter space.

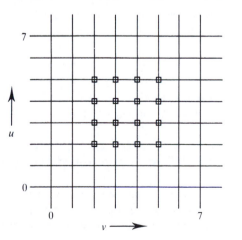

Figure 5.29
The 16 bivariate B-splines peak at the points shown in parametric space.

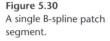

Figure 5.30
A single B-spline patch
segment.

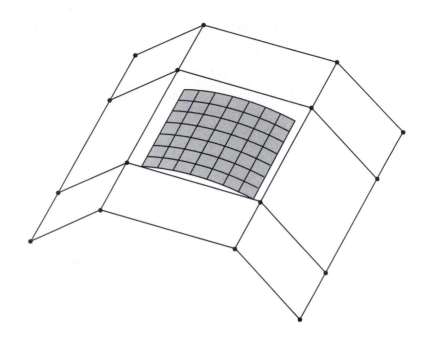

We consider uniform B-spline patches where the grid of knot values exhibit, equal intervals in the u and v parametric directions. First, consider a single patch segment. We shall use this phrase to mean the entity in two-parameter space that is analogous to a curve segment in single-parameter space. Thus we say that a general B-spline surface patch can made up of several patch segments, just as a B-spline curve is made up of a number of curve segments. In the case of a single B-spline curve segment we required four control points to define the segment. Extending into two-parameter space we now require a grid, P_{ij}, of 4×4 control points to form a single patch segment. These control points are blended with 4×4 bi-variate basis functions. Recall from Section 5.3.1 that a single B-spline segment requires a vector of eight knot values $u_0, . . ., u_7$. Thus a single patch segment requires a grid or knot array of 8×8 knot values (Figure 5.29) and the bi-variate basis functions peak at the knot values shown with a square.

Consider a simple example. Figure 5.30 shows a single B-spline patch segment determined by 16 control points. Note that the patch is confined to the region nearer the central four control points. Just as with B-spline curves, which do not interpolate their control points, a B-spline patch segment does not interpolate the inner four control points or any of the outer 12.

5.6 Modelling or creating patch surfaces

Modelling issues embrace both building up a parametric net description from scratch and editing or changing the shape of an existing description. One of the motivations for using a patch description is the ability to 'sculpt' an existing surface by altering its shape. Whereas modelling with a single patch, for example a Bézier patch, is straightforward, significant difficulties arise when dealing with a mesh of patches. The subject area is still very much a research topic and for that reason much of the material is outside the scope of this text. It is, however, an extremely important area and we will cover it as comprehensively as possible. In this section we will look at the following design or creation methods:

(1) Cross-section design: here we will look at a simplification of the sweeping techniques described in the previous chapter, restricting the objects to linear axis design.

(2) Interactive design by manipulating the control point polyhedron.

(3) Creating a patch net or mesh from a set of three-dimensional points representing a (usually) real object. We could call this surface interpolation, or surface fitting.

5.6.1   **Cross-sectional modelling with patches**

We will now look at an example where the design constraints enable us to work and interface with curves to derive an object made up of a net of patches.

Consider using an eight-patch surface to design containers or bowls that in cross-section have fourfold symmetry. That is, the final object can be considered to be made by sweeping some kind of cross section along a linear axis or spine. Many industrial objects fall into this category. We will develop a hierarchy of three manifestations of this design, each increasing in complexity in the nature of the variation of the cross-section. This is simply a repeat of the sweeping technique described in the previous chapter. However, this time the result of the modelling operation is a mesh of patches rather than a mesh of polygons. Here we will restrict our consideration to linear spines. Although the general sweeping techniques described for polygon meshes are extendible to patches, there are certain difficulties which are outside the scope of this text.

It may be that a patch model (rather than a polygon mesh representation) is important in this context because we want the ability to make global stylistic changes and also because we want a high quality visualisation of the object. Objects such as bottles have most of their shape defined in projection by their silhouette edge and we may not want to encounter the silhouette edge degradation that would come from using a polygon mesh model for the visualisation. We decide that to give us a reasonable degree of shape control the minimum number of patches that we can tolerate is eight.

The possibilities and the interactive protocol required are now dealt with. The illustrations show models constructed with eight patches. The formulae given relate in each case to a single patch.

Linear axis design – scaled circular cross-sections

Here we can have only circular cross-sections and the objects that we can design are of the form shown in Figure 5.31. (Actually, Bézier curves can only approximate a perfect circle, but we shall ignore this complication.) To derive the eight patches in this case we need only interact with a two-segment Bézier curve. This is known as a profile curve. This gives the control points for two patches and the other control points for the other six patches are obtained by symmetry. Such objects are also well known as solids of revolution.

If we take the z axis as the spine of the object the control points of a bottom patch are given by:

$$\begin{bmatrix} P_{00} & P_{01} & P_{02} & P_{03} \\ P_{10} & P_{11} & P_{12} & P_{13} \\ P_{20} & P_{21} & P_{22} & P_{23} \\ P_{30} & P_{31} & P_{32} & P_{33} \end{bmatrix} = \begin{bmatrix} T_{00} \\ T_{01} \\ T_{02} \\ T_{03} \end{bmatrix} [r_0 \ r_1 \ r_2 \ r_3] \begin{bmatrix} k \\ k \\ k \\ k \end{bmatrix} [z_0 \ z_1 \ z_2 \ z_3] \qquad [5.7]$$

where T_{00} T_{10} T_{20} and T_{30} are the control points for the quarter circle forming a cross-section segment circle and k is the unit vector in the z axis:

$T_{00} = (0, 1, 0)$
$T_{10} = (c, 1, 0)$
$T_{20} = (1, c, 0)$
$T_{30} = (1, 0, 0)$
$c = 0.552$ (approx.)

and the control points for the surface patch lie on circles of radius r_0 r_1 r_2 and r_3 at distances z_0 z_1 z_2 and z_3 along the z axis. The segments S_0S_1, S_2R_1 and R_2R_3 sweep out to form truncated cones. The designed surface is tangential to these conical sections at the top, bottom and join cross-section. We can derive the top patch similarly.

Figure 5.31
Linear axis design – circular cross-section, object is designed by a single profile curve.

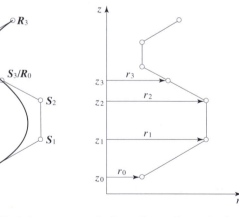

Profile design

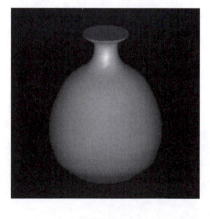

(r, v) coordinates of control points

Object

Figure 5.32
Linear axis design – scaled (non-circular) cross-section. Object is designed by one profile curve and one (1/4) cross-section curve.

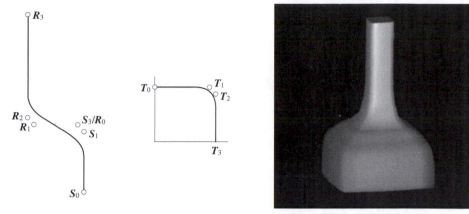

Profile design	Cross-section design		Object

Linear axis design – non-circular scaled cross-sections

This time we allow the quarter cross-section to be any shape and we design now with a profile curve as before and also a curve for the quarter cross-section (Figure 5.32). The cross-section maintains its shape and only varies in scale.

The control points for a bottom patch are again given by Equation 5.7 except that T_{00} T_{10} T_{20} and T_{30} are obtained from the cross-section design rather than being predefined.

Linear axis design – non-circular varying cross-sections

There are many options for blending different cross-section curves. An easy approach is to confine the blend to a single segment of the profile curve – the upper, say. Thus in this example the upper four patches will exhibit a varying cross-section while the lower four will have a constant cross-section as before.

Here we allow the cross-section to vary in shape and we design three cross-sections which form the top edge of the top patch, the common bottom/top

Figure 5.33
Linear axis design – non-circular varying cross-section. Object is designed by one profile curve and three cross-sections.

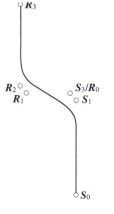

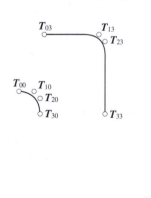

Profile design	Cross-section design	Object

Figure 5.34
Blending two different
cross-sections using the
profile curve.

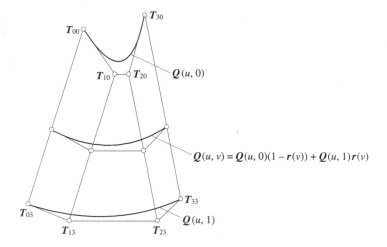

edge shared by both patches and the bottom edge of the bottom patch (Figure 5.33). Now we need to define intermediate curves from the top and bottom curves of a patch. This can be done simply by defining:

$$Q(u,v) = Q(u,0)(1 - r(v)) + Q(u,1)r(v)$$

where

$$r(0) = 0 \text{ and } r(1) = 1$$

Figure 5.34 is a representation of this procedure from which it can be seen that the curve $Q(u,v)$ has a characteristic polygon whose control points lie on lines joining the control points of the two cross-sections.

The control points of a patch are now given by

$$\begin{bmatrix} P_{00} & P_{01} & P_{02} & P_{03} \\ P_{10} & P_{11} & P_{12} & P_{13} \\ P_{20} & P_{21} & P_{22} & P_{23} \\ P_{30} & P_{31} & P_{32} & P_{33} \end{bmatrix} = \begin{bmatrix} T_{00} & T_{03} \\ T_{01} & T_{13} \\ T_{02} & T_{23} \\ T_{03} & T_{33} \end{bmatrix} \begin{bmatrix} 1 & 1-r_1 & 1-r_2 & 0 \\ 0 & r_1 & r_2 & 1 \end{bmatrix} \begin{bmatrix} k \\ k \\ k \\ k \end{bmatrix} \begin{bmatrix} z_0 & z_1 & z_2 & z_3 \end{bmatrix}$$

where T_{00} T_{10} T_{20} and T_{30} are the control points for the first cross-section (bottom edge) and T_{03} T_{13} T_{23} and T_{33} are the control points for the second cross-section (the common edge between the two patches).

5.6.2

Editing a patch net – altering an existing net

This approach to modelling with a parametric patch object is the one described in most textbooks. The idea is that given an existing patch model a designer interacts with a loop which enables the control points to be moved and the result of the movement displayed as a new surface. Sometimes it is described as 'free-form sculpting'. The designer can move one or a number of control points at will, modelling a surface as if it were some malleable material such as modelling clay. Leaving aside the practical problem of providing a three-dimensional editing system to facilitate control point movement, two fundamental problems arise.

First, what do we do when we are interacting with a mesh of patches rather than a single patch? Although single-patch design can cope with a number of practical problems – car body panels, for example, we may need to work with a net of patches. The problem is that we cannot move the control points of a single patch without regard to maintaining continuity with surrounding patches.

We considered this problem for curves in Section 5.2.1 and directly extending this method to patches we would move groups of nine control points as a single unit, as shown in Figure 5.35(a). This automatically ensures patch continuity but it has the effect of introducing plateaux into the surface. This is clearly seen with curves. Figure 5.35(b) shows a two-segment Bézier curve. If we move control points in collinear groups of three then we get a curved step effect (Figure 5.35(c)). What we may require is a deformation as shown in Figure 5.35(d).

The other problem that arises is locality of control. We have already discussed this with respect to a Bézier versus B-spline patch and we now consider the B-spline case in more detail. The difficulty centres around the need to be able to vary the **scale** of the deformation. Although moving a control point only changes those patches that share the point, the scale of the deformation in object space is related to the size of the patches. This suggests that we can control the scale by locally subdividing the patches in the region of the deformation if a fine change is required. Figure 5.36 shows a simple example of this technique where the scale of the deformation on the side of a cube is related to the number of patches that make up the face.

Consider the definition of a B-spline patch:

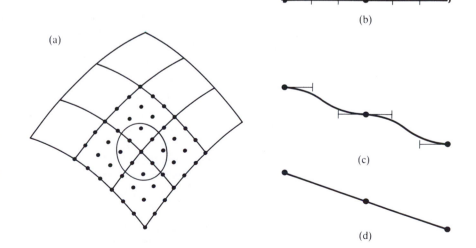

Figure 5.35
(a) Four adjoining Bézier patches and their control points. Continuity constraints imply that the central points cannot be moved without considering its eight neighbours. All nine points can be moved together and continuity maintained. (b) Undeformed two-segment curve. (c) Deformed curve by moving control points in collinear groups. (d) Desired deformation.

(a)

(b)

(c)

(d)

Figure 5.36
The scale of a deformation as a function of the number of (initially flat) patches used to represent the side of a cube.

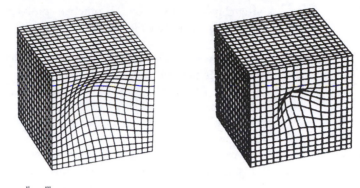

$$Q(u,v) = \sum_{i=0}^{n} \sum_{j=0}^{m} P_{ij} B_i(u) B_j(v)$$

This can be redefined by knot insertion (Farin, 1990) to a patch

$$Q(u,v) = \sum_{i=0}^{N} \sum_{j=0}^{M} R_{ij} B_i(u) B_j(v)$$

where

$N > n$ and $M > m$

The new control points are derived as described in Forsey and Bartels (1988). The problem is how to apply this strategy to the region of a surface that interests us. Forsey and Bartels do this by defining a minimal surface – the smallest section of the surface to which this refinement of control points can be applied. This minimal surface satisfies two constraints:

(1) Movement of the new control points produces deformations that are localised to this minimal surface.

(2) The derivatives at the boundary of the minimal surface remain unchanged.

This means that deformations within the refined surface will not affect the surface from which it is derived and continuity is everywhere maintained. The motivation for such an elaborate approach is to effect control point refinement only where required. The alternative would be control point refinement over the entire surface. This process can be repeated within the refined surface and so on until a satisfactory level of fine control is achieved – hence the term hierarchical.

A minimal surface is 16 patches defined by a 7 × 7 control points matrix (Figure 5.37(a)). The control points that are required if the centre four patches are refined to 16 are shown in Figure 5.37(b)). Here we note that 3 × 3 of the original control points are shared with the refined patches. A dynamic data structure of control points is created with the original surface at the root of a tree of overlays of control points. Editing the surface invokes a tree traversal and one of the important points of the scheme is that traversal can occur in either direction. Coarse refinement will carry previous fine refinements, in the same surface region, owing to the representation of control points in terms of offsets relative to a local reference frame.

Figure 5.37
(a) Sixteen patch minimal
surface with 49 control
points. (b) Central four
patches refined to 16
patches (after Forsey and
Bartels (1988)).

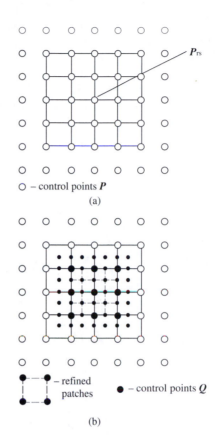

Global shape changing

Say that we are interested in global shape deformation; for example, taking a cylinder or tubular object and bending it into a toroidal-like body. Here we may need to operate, to some degree, on all the control points simultaneously.

Consider the strategy applied to a curve $Q(t)$ defined by four control points P_i. First, we enclose the curve in a unit square and divide up this region into a regular grid of points R_{ij}; $i = 0,. . .,3$; $j = 0,. . .,3$ as shown in Figure 5.38. If we consider the square to be uv space then we can write:

$$(u,v) = \sum_{i=0}^{3} \sum_{j=0}^{3} R_{ij} B_i(u) B_j(v)$$

Compare this identity with the equation for a bi-cubic parametric Bézier patch. This identity follows from the linear precision property of the polynomials $B_i(u)$ and $B_j(v)$ and it is expressing the fact that a set of co-planar control points will define a planar patch. If the grid of points R_{ij} is now distorted into the grid R_{ij}' (Figure 5.38) then the point (u,v) will be mapped into the point (u',v')

Figure 5.38

Global distortion of a planar curve (after Farin (1990)).

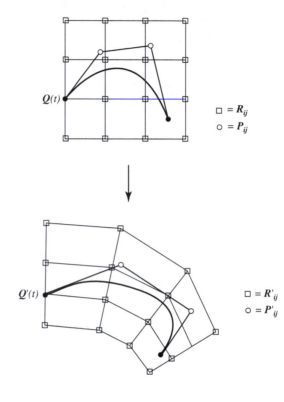

$$(u',v') = \sum_{i=0}^{3}\sum_{j=0}^{3} R'_{ij} B_i(u) B_j(v)$$

and we can use this equation to derive a new set of control points, P_i', for the new curve $Q'(t)$.

This is a method of changing the shape of the curve globally and indirectly. We are embedding the curve in a planar patch, distorting the patch by moving the control points of the patch, and at the same time changing the shape of the curve.

Now to extend this principle to operate globally on patches we embed the control points P_{ij} of the patch that we wish to deform in a **trivariate** Bézier hyperpatch, itself specified by a three-dimensional grid of control points, R_{ijk}, forming a unit cube. Thus we have:

$$(u',v',w') = \sum_{i=0}^{3}\sum_{j=0}^{3}\sum_{k=0}^{3} R_{ijk}' B_i(u) B_j(v) B_k(w) \qquad [5.8]$$

The unit cube grid is distorted globally in any way that we require and the new patch control points, P_{ijk}', are calculated.

An important aspect of this technique is that it can be applied to an object with any parametric representation. Thus we can embed B-spline patches in the trivariate Bézier space. We can also embed polygon mesh vertices in the same way. This gives us the concept of any point x embedded in a trivariate hyper-patch volume and then mapped to point x' by globally distorting the control grid of the trivariate patch. To use Equation 5.8 to do this we need to map x into (u,v,w) space and (u',v',w') back into Cartesian space. The conversions are:

$$x = x_0 + u\mathbf{u} + v\mathbf{v} + w\mathbf{w}$$

where

$$u = \mathbf{u}.(x - x_0)$$
$$v = \mathbf{v}.(x - x_0)$$
$$w = \mathbf{w}.(x - x_0)$$

x_0 defines the origin of (u,v,w) space and $\mathbf{u}$, $\mathbf{v}$ and $\mathbf{w}$ define the space. These values are set by the designer who positions the unit cube with respect to the object to be distorted.

The technique was originally developed by Bézier but most graphics-oriented treatments refer to a paper by Sederberg and Parry (1986) wherein the strategy is termed Free Form Deformation (FFD). Figure 5.39 (Colour Plate) shows an example of the technique in operation. The semi-transparent rectangular solids surrounding parts of the spoon object are the trivariate patches in which are embedded the vertices of the polygon mesh. The upper patch is specified by a grid of $3 \times 3 \times 7$ control points and note that there are many more polygonal vertices in the equivalent object space. Deforming the grid gives a 'natural' bending of the spoon character for use in animation.

5.6.3 Creating patch objects by surface fitting

In this section we look at taking a set of points in three-dimensional space representing an object and fitting and interpolating a patch surface through them. We will approach the topic by first considering the interpolation of curves then developing an algorithm for surface fitting.

Interpolating curves using B-splines

Fitting a B-spline curve (or surface) through existing data points finds two major applications in computer graphics. First in modelling: a set of sample data points can be produced by a three-dimensional digitising device, such as a laser ranger. The problem is then to fit a surface through these points so that a complete computer graphics representation is available for manipulation (for, say, animation or shape change) by a program. Second, in computer animation, we may use a parametric curve to represent the path of an object that is moving through three space. Particular positions of the object (key frame positions) may be defined and we require to fit a curve through these points. A B-spline curve is commonly used for this purpose because of its C^2 continuity property. In animation we are normally interested in smooth motion and a B-spline curve representing the position of an object as a function of time will guarantee this.

We state the problem of B-spline interpolation informally as follows: given a set of data points we require to derive a set of control points for a B-spline curve that will define a 'fair' curve that represents the data points. We may require the curve to interpolate all the points or to interpolate a subset of the points and pass close to the others. For example, in the case where data points are known to be noisy or slightly unreliable we may not require an exact interpolation through all the points. Different methodologies for fitting a B-spline curve to a set of data points are given in Bartels *et al.* (1987).

We can state the problem formally for the case where we require the curve to interpolate all the data points. If we consider the data points to be knot values in u then we have for a cubic:

$$\mathbf{Q}(u_p) = \sum_{i=0}^{m} \mathbf{P}_i B_i(u_p)$$

$$= D_p \quad \text{for all } p = 3,\ldots,m+1$$

where:

D_p is a data point

u_p is the knot value corresponding to the data point

The problem we now have is to determine u_p. The easiest solution, and the one we will adopt here, is to set u_p to p. This is called uniform parametrisation; it completely ignores the geometric relationship between data points and is usually regarded as giving the poorest interpolant in a hierarchy of possibilities described in detail in Farin (1990). The next best solution, chord length parametrisation, sets the knot intervals proportional to the distance between the data points. An advantage of uniform parametrisation, however, is that it is invariant under affine transformation of the data points.

Here we are specifying a B-spline curve through the data points. There are $m - 1$ data points to be interpolated and the curve is defined by $m + 1$ control points. If we consider a single component, say, x then we have:

$$x(u_p) = \sum_{i=0}^{m} \mathbf{P}_{xi} B_i(u_p)$$

$$= D_{xp} \quad \text{for all } p = 3,\ldots,m+1$$

where:

D_{xp} is the x component of the data point.

This defines a system of equations that we solve for $\mathbf{P}_{xi}$:

$$\begin{bmatrix} B_0(u_3) & \ldots & B_m(u_3) \\ \vdots & & \vdots \\ B_0(u_{m+1}) & \ldots & B_m(u_{m+1}) \end{bmatrix} \begin{bmatrix} \mathbf{P}_{x0} \\ \vdots \\ \mathbf{P}_{xm} \end{bmatrix} = \begin{bmatrix} D_{x3} \\ \vdots \\ D_{xm+1} \end{bmatrix}$$

This scheme results in $m - 1$ equations in $m + 1$ unknowns. For example, for $m = 5$ we have six control points to find from four data points. Various possibilities exist. The easiest approach is to select two additional points $\boldsymbol{P}_2$ and $\boldsymbol{P}_7$ to be interpolated. Clearly these can be two extra points inserted or be part of the data set, giving:

$$\begin{bmatrix} B_0(u_2) & B_m(u_2) \\ B_0(u_3) & B_m(u_3) \\ \vdots & \vdots \\ B_0(u_{m+1}) & B_m(u_{m+1}) \\ B_0(u_{m+2}) & B_m(u_{m+2}) \end{bmatrix} \begin{bmatrix} \boldsymbol{P}_{x0} \\ \vdots \\ \boldsymbol{P}_{xm} \end{bmatrix} = \begin{bmatrix} D_{x2} \\ D_{x3} \\ \vdots \\ D_{xm+1} \\ D_{xm+2} \end{bmatrix}$$

In this equation the matrix will have zero entries except in a band 3 $(k-1)$ entries wide along the main diagonal, and for uniform cubic B splines the matrix is:

$$\frac{1}{6} \begin{bmatrix} 4 & 1 & & & & \\ 1 & 4 & 1 & & & \\ & 1 & 4 & 1 & & \\ & & & \cdot & & \\ & & & & \cdot & \\ & & & & \cdot & \\ & & & 1 & 4 & 1 \\ & & & & 1 & 4 \end{bmatrix}$$

Interpolating surfaces

Interpolating surfaces means that we wish to interpolate a set of three-dimensional data points with a parametrically defined surface. We do this by first fitting a network of uv curves through the data points. Each data point is interpolated by a curve of constant u and v. These curves are B-splines interpolated through the data points using a standard B-spline curve interpolation technique. In the next stage the B-spline curves are converted to Bézier curves. This curve network is partitioned into individual mesh elements formed from four Bézier curve segments (Figure 5.40). These curve segments are the boundary edge of a Bézier patch and given these we can then derive the control points for the patch. Thus a set of points in 3 space are converted to a net of Bézier patches using a net of B-spline curves as an intermediary.

Now let us consider the first stage – deriving a net of curves that interpolate the data points. The main problem here is that we may have no knowledge of the topology of the points. (In curve interpolation we know that the points are sequential.) This is a problem that can only be solved in context and one approach is given in Watt and Watt (1992). Consider the case where the points have been obtained from a real object using a manual digitiser and the knowledge of which points to interpolate with curves is known. This is quite a common context and we will proceed with the second stage – that of deriving a net of Bézier patches from a B-spline curve network.

First, we need to convert the B-spline curves into multi-segment Bézier curves. If we first consider a single B-spline then the conversion to Bézier form is straightforward and is given by:

Figure 5.40
A schematic representation of surface fitting. (a) A set of points in three-space. (b) Fitting curves through the points in two parametric directions. (c) The grid of the curves from the boundaries of the patches. (d) A curve network obtained by interpolation through digitised points. (e) A rendered version of the patch model obtained from (d).

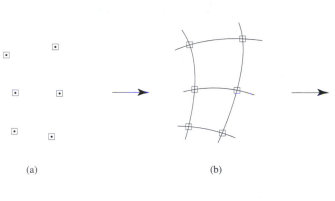

(a)

(b)

(c)

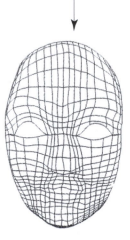

$$[P_0 \ P_1 \ P_2 \ P_3] = B^{-1}B_s \ [Q_0 \ Q_1 \ Q_2 \ Q_3]$$

$$= \frac{1}{6}\begin{bmatrix} 1 & 4 & 1 & 0 \\ 0 & 4 & 2 & 0 \\ 0 & 2 & 4 & 1 \\ 1 & 4 & 1 & 0 \end{bmatrix}\begin{bmatrix} Q_0 \\ Q_1 \\ Q_2 \\ Q_3 \end{bmatrix}$$

where

> P are the Bézier control points
>
> Q are the B-spline control points
>
> B is the Bézier matrix (Equation 5.2)
>
> B_s is the B-spline matrix (Equation 5.3)

(Note that a change of basis matrix can only be used for uniform B-splines. If the curve network consists of non-uniform B-splines then conversion has to proceed by knot insertion. This more general approach is described in Watt and Watt (1992).)

For a multi-segment B-spline curve we apply this formula repeatedly to the appropriate control points. For example, consider a two-segment B-spline curve defined by five control points $[Q_0\ Q_1\ Q_2\ Q_3\ Q_4]$. The conversion formula is applied twice for the control point sets $[Q_0\ Q_1\ Q_2\ Q_3]$ and $[Q_1\ Q_2\ Q_3\ Q_4]$.

Now consider a net of 5×5 two-segment B-spline curves with control points shown in figure 5.41(a). Application of the above scheme on a row by row basis yields five two-segment Bézier curves (Figure 5.41(b)). We now interpret these,

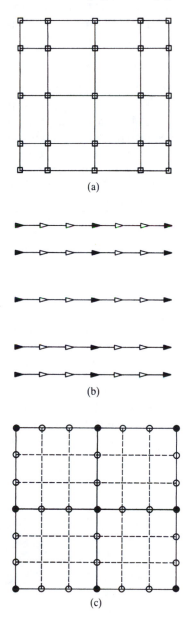

(a)

(b)

Figure 5.41
Converting a B-spline curve network to Bézier patches (after Farin (1990)).
(a) 5×5 two-segment B-spline curve network.
(b) Curve network converted row-wise to 5 two-segment Bézier curves.
(c) Curve network converted to 7×7 two-segment Bézier curves forming the boundaries of four Bézier patches.

(c)

column by column, and consider each column to be the control points of a B-spline curve. Each column is converted to a two-segment Bézier curve. This yields a net of 7×7 two-segment Bézier curves (Figure 5.41(c)). We know that the boundary edge of a Bézier patch is a Bézier curve and we interpret the unbroken lines in Figure 5.41c) as the boundaries of four Bézier patches. Thus we have converted a network of 5×5 two-segment B-spline curves into 2×2 Bézier patches. However, we have only defined the boundaries of each patch – that is, we have only determined 12 out of the 16 control points for each patch.

The question that now arises is: how are we to determine the inner four control points? We first consider their significance by reproducing Equation 5.6

$$Q_{uv}(0,0) = 9(P_{00} - P_{01} - P_{10} + P_{11})$$

This defines the twist of a surface as a mixed partial derivative and can be interpreted as a vector which is the deviation of the corner quadrilateral of the control polyhedron from a parallelogram (Figure 5.42). When the twist is zero this vector reduces to zero and the corner points of the quadrilateral are co-planar. An intuitive grasp of the effect of non-zero twist is difficult. It is easier to look at the geometric significance when a patch has zero twist at all four corners.

Then we have a translational surface where every quadrilateral of the control polygon is a parallelogram. The parallelograms are also translates of each other. Such a patch is called a translational surface because it is generated by two curves $C_1(u)$ and $C_2(v)$. Any isoparametric line in u is a translate of C_1 and any isoparametric line in v is a translate of C_2.

Thus the easiest solution to estimating the inner four control points is to assume that the patch is a translational surface, then the inner points are derivable from the boundary points. The implication of this, in terms of surface fitting, is that the boundary curves of the patch should more or less be translates of each other. In any practical situation this will depend on two factors: the shape of the object and the resolution of the uv curve network.

A visualisation of the overall process is shown in Figure 5.40. The original surface points were obtained from a real object. You can see in this figure how the validity of zero twist assumption varies across the surface of the object. The method gives us a correct surface with C^1 continuity overall, but it does not guarantee a 'good' shape. Alternative methods for determining the twist of a surface patch are given in Farin (1990).

Figure 5.42
The twist coefficients are proportional to the deviations of the control polygon subquadrilateral from a parallelogram.

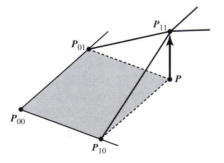

⟨5.7⟩

Rendering parametric surfaces

Algorithms that render surfaces represented by bi-cubic parametric patches divide naturally into two categories:

(1) those that render directly from the parametric description, or the equation describing the patch, and

(2) those that approximate the surface by a polygon mesh and use a planar polygon mesh renderer to render this approximation. Thus in this case rendering parametric surfaces reduces to a pre-processing operation or conversion operation.

Clearly with current games technology we would adopt the second option. For static objects we can perform the conversion offline. With dynamic objects we can use a fast conversion algorithms which will now be described.

⟨5.7.1⟩

Patch to polygon conversion

Deriving a polygon mesh from a patch mesh is conceptually simple. We simply subdivide the patches and use the corner points of the subdivision products as polygon. Each set of four vertices converts to two triangular facets (Figure 5.43). Thus in converting patches to polygons we go on subdividing until we decide that, to within some limit, the polygonal approximation is sufficiently close to the true (patch) surface. Herein there appears to be a contradiction. What is the point of going to the expense of a patch representation if we are then going to approximate it with polygonal facets? There are many justifications. The most common is that the application requires such a representation – this is mostly the case in CAD. The visualisation of the object can be an approximation but the designer needs to work with an accurate representation. We should also bear in mind that the representation allows us to control the accuracy of the polygonal approximation, as we shall see. This means that we have an 'automatic' LOD model as part of the conversion process.

This topic splits naturally into categories depending on the criterion used to determine the depth of the subdivision and exactly where it is applied on the patch surface. The main difference is whether the termination criteria operates in object space or screen space. Screen space termination criteria offer the potential of being able to adjust the polygonal resolution of the object to match the projected size of the object on the screen. In object space we compare the approximation against the true surface using object space metrics; in screen space we use pixel units as a metric. Screen space termination is dynamic in the sense that it depends on the view point or viewing distance.

Figure 5.43
The patch splitting process.
(a) Continue process until
flat and (b) convert the
vertices into two triangular
facets.

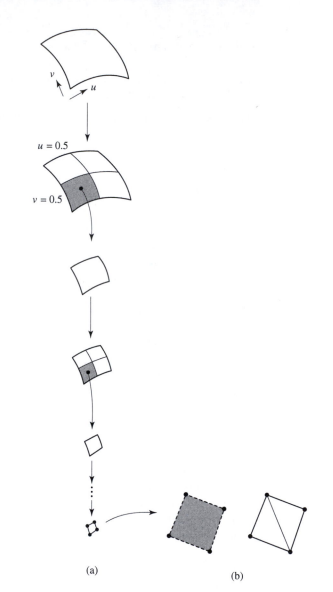

(a)

(b)

Object space subdivision

Dealing with object space first we can list the following simple categories:

(1) Object space – uniform subdivision. This is the simplest case and involves a user specifying a level at which uniform subdivision of all patches is to terminate.

(2) Object space – non-uniform subdivision. This means stopping the subdivision when the subdivision products meet a patch flatness criterion.

The second category is theoretically preferable – here you 'allocate' the degree of subdivision according to where it is required. More subdivision takes place in areas of high surface curvature. However, there is a high cost involved in testing for flatness which may outweigh the cost of unnecessary subdivisions.

Uniform subdivision proceeds as follows. The patch can be divided using iso-parametric curves. This yields a net or mesh of points at the intersection of these curves with each other and the boundary edges. This net of points can be used to define the vertices for a mesh of planar polygons which can then be rendered using a planar polygon renderer. There are two problems with this rudimentary approach. Visible boundary edges and silhouette edges may exhibit discontinu-ities. In general, a finer polygon resolution will be necessary to diminish the vis-ibility of piecewise linear discontinuities on edges than is necessary to maintain smooth shading within the patch. Another problem is that internal silhouette edges in the patch will generally be of higher degree than cubic. If special atten-tion is to be devoted to silhouette edges then this is best carried out in screen space as we shall see in the next section.

Now consider non-uniform subdivision. This simply means that areas of the patch that are 'flattish' are subject to few subdivisions. Areas where the local cur-vature is high are subject to more subdivisions. Effectively the patch is sub-divided to a degree that depends on local curvature. This is the approach adopted by Lane and Carpenter in Lane *et al.* (1980). It is demonstrated in Figure 5.44.

Patches are subdivided until the products of the subdivision submits to a flat-ness criterion. Such patches are now considered to be approximately planar polygons and are scan converted by a normal polygon renderer using the corner points of the patches as vertices for rectangles in the polygon mesh. The set of patches representing the surface can be pre-processed, yielding a set of polygons which are then scan converted as normal. This is the approach adopted in Clark (1979). Lane integrates this patch-splitting approach with a scan conversion algorithm.

There are two significant advantages to patch splitting:

(1) it is fast, and

(2) the speed can be varied by altering the depth of the subdivision. Alternatively we can bound the time taken for subdivision by that available within the frame for that task.

Figure 5.44
Uniform and non-uniform subdivision of a Bézier patch.

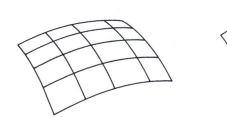
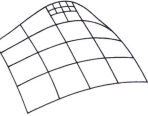

Figure 5.45
Tears produced by non-uniform subdivision of patches.

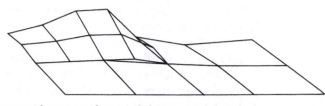

A disadvantage of non-uniform subdivision is that holes can appear between patches owing to the approximation of a patch boundary by a straight line. An example of this degenerative process is shown in Figure 5.45.

Subdivision algorithms are best considered for a curve. These are then easily extended or generalised to deal with a patch. The crux of the method is that rather than evaluate points along a curve, the curve is approximated by a piecewise linear version obtained by subdividing the control points recursively. This gives a finer and finer approximation to the curve. The level of subdivision/recursion terminates when a linearity criterion is satisfied. Lane *et al.* (1980) show that the piecewise linear approximation to the curve will eventually 'collapse' onto the curve providing enough subdivisions are undertaken.

A subdivision formula for the Bézier basis (or, in general, the Bernstein basis) is given in Lane and Riesenfeld (1980) and derived in Lane *et al.* (1980). (This process can be used for any basis by first converting the representation to the Bézier basis as described in Watt and Watt (1992).) A Bézier curve is subdivided into two curves by subdividing the control points, forming two new sets of control points R_i and S_i. The point R_3/S_0 is the end point of the first curve and the start of the second. The formula is:

$$R_0 = Q_0 \qquad\qquad S_0 = R_3$$
$$R_1 = (Q_0 + Q_1)/2 \qquad\qquad S_1 = (Q_1 + Q_2)/4 + S_2/2$$
$$R_2 = R_1/2 + (Q_1 + Q_2)/4 \qquad\qquad S_2 = (Q_2 + Q_3)/2$$
$$R_3 = (R_2 + S_1)/2 \qquad\qquad S_3 = Q_3$$

Figure 5.46 shows how, after a single subdivision, the piecewise linear curve joining the two new sets of control points is a better approximation to the curve

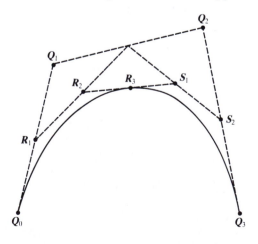

Figure 5.46
Splitting a bi-cubic Bézier curve.

Figure 5.47
Drawing the control points
at each level of subdivision.

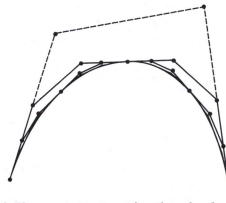

than the original. The approximation after three levels of subdivision is shown in Figure 5.47.

The curve-splitting process is easily extended to patches as illustrated in Figure 5.48. We consider the patch to be made up of four curves of constant u and four curves of constant v, whose control points are consecutive rows and consecutive columns of the control point matrix. We apply the curve-splitting formula separately to each of the four curves in u yielding two sub-patches of the original patch. Repeating the process for each of these two sub-patches, this time splitting the curves in v, and putting these divisions together divides the patch into four.

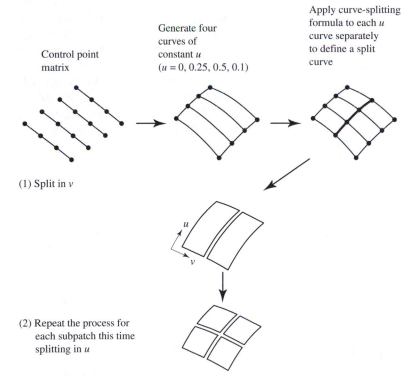

Control point
matrix

Generate four
curves of
constant u
($u = 0, 0.25, 0.5, 0.1$)

Apply curve-splitting
formula to each u
curve separately
to define a split
curve

(1) Split in v

(2) Repeat the process for
each subpatch this time
splitting in u

Figure 5.48
Using curve splitting to
subdivide a patch into four.

This efficient formula (which uses only additions and divide by twos) makes the subdivision rapid. The depth of the sub-division is easily controlled using a linearity criterion. The Bézier basis functions sum identically to 1.

$$\sum_{i=0}^{3} B_{i,n}(u) = 1$$

This means that the curve lies in the convex hull formed by the control points P_i. The piecewise linear subdivision product will coincide with the curve when it 'merges' with the line joining the two endpoints. The degree to which this is achieved, that is, the linearity of the line joining the four control points, can be tested by measuring the distance from the middle two control points to the end point joining line (Figure 5.49).

The philosophy of this test is easily extended to surface patches. A plane is fitted through three non-collinear control points. The distance of each of the other 13 control points from this plane is then calculated. If one of these distances lies outside a pre-specified tolerance, then the patch is further sub-divided. In effect, we are measuring the thickness of a bounding box – a rectangular solid enclosing the patch whose thickness is defined by the largest distance from the plane containing the corner points to the farthest control point. This is sometimes called the convex hull flatness test.

A practical problem that occurs, when considering non-uniform subdivision (subdivision until a flatness criterion is satisfied) compared with uniform subdivision to some pre-determined level, is the cost of the flatness test. It is debatable if it is a simpler and better, but less elegant approach simply to adopt uniform subdivision and ignore the fact that some areas are going to be unnecessarily sub-divided (because they are already flat). For a given image quality, the cost of testing for non-uniform subdivision will be greater than the extra rendering costs of uniform subdivision. The next illustration demonstrates this. Figure 5.50 (Colour Plate) shows a uniform subdivision approach for the Utah teapot at subdivisions of one, two and three. An important aspect of this image

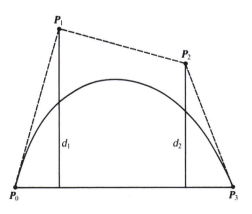

Figure 5.49
A cubic Bézier curve with control points P_0, P_1, P_2, P_3.

is that it shows predictably that the difference in quality between the rendered images is mainly visible along silhouette edges.

Let us now return to the problem of tears (Figure 5.45). Tears are a natural consequence of recursive or non-uniform subdivision. If one part of a surface patch is subdivided along a boundary shared by another patch that requires no further subdivision, then a gap between the two parts will naturally result. This 'tear' is then an unrepresented area and will appear as a gap or hole in the final rendering phase. The Lane/Carpenter algorithm does not deal with this problem. It can be minimised by making the flatness criterion more rigorous but herein lies the normal computational paradox. The philosophy of the sub-division approach is that areas of a surface are subdivided, to a degree that corresponds to local curvature. Large flat areas are minimally subdivided. Areas exhibiting fast curvature changes will be sub-divided down to sufficiently small polygons. Tightening the flatness criterion means that many more polygons are generated and the final rendering phase takes much longer.

Clark's method deals with this problem in a more elegant way by adopting a subdivision method that is initially constrained to the boundary curves. There are three steps involved:

(1) The convex curve hull criterion is applied to the boundary edges $u = 1$ and $u = 0$ and the patch is subdivided along the v direction until this is satisfied.

(2) The same method is then applied to the $v = 1$ and $v = 0$ boundaries.

(3) Finally the normal convex hull test is applied to the subdivision products and the process is continued, if necessary, along either the u or v directions.

Once a boundary satisfies the convex hull criterion it is assumed to be a straight line. Any further subdivision along this boundary will thus incur no separation.

A possible advantage of subdividing in the direction of the u or v boundaries, is that with some objects this will result in fewer patches. Consider, for example, subdividing a 'ducted' solid – a cylinder is a trivial example of such an object. Subdividing the cylinder along a direction parallel to its long axis will lead this algorithm to converge more quickly and with fewer patches than if the subdivision proceeds in both parametric directions. A disadvantage with this approach is that it is difficult to integrate with a scan line algorithm A scan line algorithm 'drives' or controls the order of subdivision depending on how the patches lie with respect to the scan lines.

Another aspect that requires consideration is the calculation of surface normals. These are, of course, required for shading. They are easily obtainable from the original parametric description, at any point (u,v) on the surface, by computing the cross-product of the u and v derivatives. However, if a subdivision method is being used to scan convert, then the final polygon rendering is going to utilise a Phong interpolation method and the vertex normals are easily calculated by taking the cross-products of the tangent vectors at the corner points. This will, in general, depending on the level of the subdivision, give non-parallel vertex normals for the 'flat' polygons, but all polygons contributing to a vertex will have the same normal. Two consequences can result from the fact that 'flat' polygons are being sent to a shader with non-parallel vertex normals. Firstly, erroneous shading effects can occur at low levels of subdivision. Secondly, the question of which vertex normal to use for culling arises. Problems occur because not all the polygons surrounding a vertex may be available since subdivision is taking place on the fly and an average vertex normal cannot be calculated as in polygon meshes. Cases can obviously result where one normal subtends an angle of greater than 90° with the view vector and one with an angle less than 90°. The only safe course of action is to cull a polygon by testing each of its vertex normals. If any vertex normal is 'visible' the polygon is not culled.

Image space subdivision

The methods of the previous section suffice for many applications, particularly in single object CAD work. In applications where the object can form projections of widely varying size in screen space it is better to consider controlling the depth of the subdivision using screen space criteria. We could call this approach view dependent or screen space controlled subdivision.

There are three simple ways in which we can do this. All of these involve projecting sample points from the patch, at its current level of subdivision, into screen space and comparing these against the projection of the polygon that is an approximation to the patch. The comparison is effected using pixel length units as the metric. The measurements are:

(1) Minimum pixel area occupied by a patch.

(2) The screen space flatness of the patch.

(3) The screen space flatness of the silhouette edge.

Minimum pixel area occupied by a patch

Once the patch projects onto a sufficiently small number of pixels, it is deemed to have been subdivided sufficiently. In the limit we can subdivide until the pieces are the size of a single pixel but this is clearly expensive.

Screen space flatness of the patch

For this test we can proceed exactly as in the object space test but use pixel-based metrics instead of object space units. In other words, we measure the thickness of the bounding box defined by the convex hull in pixel units. Alternatively we can use a less accurate but faster test. This criterion is illustrated in Figure 5.51 which shows a single patch at its current level of subdivision. Superimposed on this are three samples, v_0, $v_{0.5}$ and v_1, that lie in a curve of constant $u_{0.5}$. This curve – the boundary curve at the next level – lies in the true surface of the patch and the three points are the polygon vertices at the next level of subdivision. We can

Figure 5.51
Screen space subdivision termination increasing the flatness of the patch in screen space at its current level of subdivision.

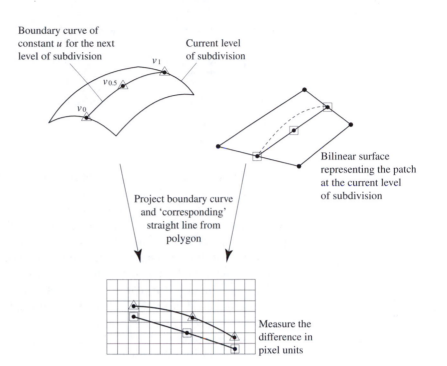

compare these points with points on the bi-linear patch formed from the four vertices. (A bi-linear patch is a non-planar quadrilateral where all lines of constant u and v are linear.) Comparing these samples of this curve with the straight line bisecting the bi-linear patch gives one estimate of the flatness of the patch in screen space. The procedure can be repeated for the curve $v_{0.5}$. As Figure 5.50 (Colour Plate) shows, the interior of an object is not much affected by the level of subdivision because the shading algorithm is specifically designed to diminish the visibility of polygon edges. This observation leads us to deduce that the subdivision needs to be concentrated near the silhouette edge.

5.8   Practical Bézier technology for games

5.8.1   Down-sampling bi-quadratic meshes

In this section we introduce two specialisations of Bézier surfaces suitable for games applications. These are bi-quadratic surfaces and objects generated from curves.

At the moment bi-cubic Bézier patch surfaces are too expensive for games platforms. Also, it may be the case that a simpler form is sufficient for games levels. The cubic form is traditionally used in CAD but in such applications the additional flexibility of the cubic form is definitely required.

A bi-quadratic Bézier patch is defined as:

$$Q(u,v) = \sum_{i=0}^{2} \sum_{j=0}^{2} P_{ij}B_i(u)B_j(v)$$

where the quadratic blending functions are

$B_0(u) = (1-u)^2$

$B_1(u) = 2(1-u)\,u$

$B_2(u) = u^2$

Thus we have a quadratic surface constructed by blending a 3×3 control point matrix with the above blending or basis functions. Four control points define the corner points of the patch and eight make up three sets of three control points which define the boundary curves of the patch. There is a single 'inner' control point (compared with four in the case of a bi-cubic patch.

The loss of shape flexibility compared to the bi-cubic is easily visualised in the case of a quadratic Bézier curve which has three control points – two end points and a single inner point. For example, it is obvious that unlike a cubic, a quadratic curve cannot cross the straight line joining the end points of the curve.

At the time of writing it appears that only Quake 3 uses Bézier technology and the developers have decided to implement bi-quadratics rather than bi-cubics.

In the following implementation we use quadratics for generic surfaces and cubics for loft surfaces. The reason for this is that most tools that enable curve modelling use cubics and so if you model a curve for a ducted solid this can be done in a conventional application. The class enables two options – adaptive subdivision or uniform subdivision which enables dynamic LOD at no cost. At run-time the desired subdivision level is selected based on distance from the viewer. This is done by down-sampling the high-resolution/subdivided mesh. The uniform subdivision finds independent levels of subdivision to be used in the u and v axis based on the surface curvature for each axis. Thus, for example, a cylinder will only subdivide in one axis.

The down-sampling approach differs from the patch recursive subdivision algorithm given in Section 5.7.1. In that 'traditional' method we start with a low-resolution definition and generate a higher-resolution representation. In this implementation we have the pre-calculated high-resolution structure and generate the desired lower-resolution model at run time by skipping rows and columns in the rectangular arrays that reference the control points.

The details are as follows:

The number of control points (np) in u and v are defined by the number of patches (ns):

cubic: $np = ns * 3 + 1$

quadratic: $np = ns * 2 + 1$

The surface is initially subdivided into the array *surf* based on a curve error factor (a subdivision *level* is selected for u and v directions).

The number of vertices (*nv*) in each direction is a function of the subdivision level (level):

$$nv = 2^{level} + 1$$

thus at level 0 we have two vertices (flat surface), and at level 0, we have three vertices. The possible number of vertices are:

2,3,5,9,17,33,etc. . .

Instead of looping on the *surf* array on increments of 1 which would draw the full resolution surface, we select an increment based on the number of levels to drop:

$$increment = 2^{droplevel}$$

If we are at level 2 (five vertices) and want to drop no levels (0 drop level) we increment by 1, and if we want to drop one level, the increment goes to 2.

If we want to drop two levels, the increment goes to 4 (getting the first and the last vertices of the five vertices).

Figure 5.52 (Colour Plate) shows a Quake 3 level rendered using this technique.

```
class FLY_API bezier_patch : public base_object
{
  public:
      int mode;           // 3 for quadratic and 4 for cubic
      vector *p;          // the surface control points
      vector *t;          // the surface texture control points
      int np,             // num points
        npu,              // num points in u dir
        npv,              // num points in v dir
        nsu,              // num segments in u dir
        nsv;              // num segments in u dir
      int levelu,levelv;  // subdivision level in u and v
      int nvertu,nvertv;  // surface num vertices in u and v
      int texpic,lm;      // texture and lightmap
      vector *surf;       // discretized surface
      vector pivot;       // the pivot position
  bezier_patch() { p=0; t=0; surf=0; reset(); };
  ~bezier_patch() { reset(); };

  // frees all memory
  void reset();
  // load from file
  int load_pch(char *file);
  // build control points from two curves (shape and path)
  void build_loft(bezier_curve *shape,bezier_curve *path,
  int texture,int lightmap,float tileu,float tilev);
  // evaluate point, normal or texture coordinates
```

```
        void evaluate(int evaltype,float u,float v,vector *dest);
        // generate the discrete surface
        void build_surface();
        // illuminate lightmap
        void illuminate(vector& p,float rad,vector& color,int shadows);
        // draw and simplifies based on col/row drop
        void draw(int nleveldrop=0);
        // return the mesh used for collision
        mesh *build_mesh();
    };

// frees all data allocated by the patch
void bezier_patch::reset()
{
    if (p)
        delete p;
    p=0;
    if (t)
        delete t;
    t=0;
    if (surf)
        delete surf;
    surf=0;
    np=npu=npv=nsu=nsv=0;
    mode=0;
    levelu=0;
    levelv=0;
    nvertu=0;
    nvertv=0;
}

// evaluates point, normal and texture coordinate
// patch can be cubic (mode=4) or quadratic (mode=3)
void bezier_patch::evaluate(int evaltype,float u,float v,vector *dest)
{
    if (p==0 || t==0)
        return;

    static float Bu[4],Bv[4],Bdu[4],Bdv[4];
    float u1,u2,v1,v2,f;
    int i,j,k,su,sv;

    vector point(0,0,0);
    vector textcoord(0,0,0,0);
    vector du(0,0,0),dv(0,0,0);

    switch(mode)
    {
    case 3: // quadratic
        if (FP_BITS(u)==FP_ONE_BITS)
```

```
      su=npu-3;
   else su=(int)(u*(npu-1))/2*2;
   u1=(u-(float)su/(npu-1))*nsu;

   if (FP_BITS(v)==FP_ONE_BITS)
      sv=npv-3;
   else sv=(int)(v*(npv-1))/2*2;
   v1=(v-(float)sv/(npv-1))*nsv;

   u2=1.0f-u1;
   Bu[0]=u2*u2;
   Bu[1]=2.0f*u1*u2;
   Bu[2]=u1*u1;

   v2=1.0f-v1;
   Bv[0]=v2*v2;
   Bv[1]=2.0f*v1*v2;
   Bv[2]=v1*v1;

   if (evaltype&PATCH_EVAL_NORMAL)
      {
      Bdu[0]= 2.0f*u1-2.0f;
      Bdu[1]= 2.0f-4.0f*u1;
      Bdu[2]= 2.0f*u1;

      Bdv[0]= 2.0f*v1-2.0f;
      Bdv[1]= 2.0f-4.0f*v1;
      Bdv[2]= 2.0f*v1;
      }
   break;
case 4: // cubic
   if (FP_BITS(u)==FP_ONE_BITS)
      su=npu-4;
   else su=(int)(u*(npu-1))/3*3;
   u1=(u-(float)su/(npu-1))*nsu;

   if (FP_BITS(v)==FP_ONE_BITS)
      sv=npv-4;
   else sv=(int)(v*(npv-1))/3*3;
   v1=(v-(float)sv/(npv-1))*nsv;

   u2=1.0f-u1;
   Bu[0]=u2*u2*u2;
   Bu[1]=3.0f*u1*u2*u2;
   Bu[2]=3.0f*u1*u1*u2;
   Bu[3]=u1*u1*u1;

   v2=1.0f-v1;
   Bv[0]=v2*v2*v2;
   Bv[1]=3.0f*v1*v2*v2;
   Bv[2]=3.0f*v1*v1*v2;
   Bv[3]=v1*v1*v1;
```

```
        if (evaltype&PATCH_EVAL_NORMAL)
          {
          u2=u1*u1;
          Bdu[0]=-3.0f + 6.0f*u1 - 3.0f*u2;
          Bdu[1]= 3.0f - 12.0f*u1 + 9.0f*u2;
          Bdu[2]= 6.0f*u1 - 9.0f*u2;
          Bdu[3]= 3.0f*u2;

          v2=v1*v1;
          Bdv[0]=-3.0f + 6.0f*v1 - 3.0f*v2;
          Bdv[1]= 3.0f - 12.0f*v1 + 9.0f*v2;
          Bdv[2]= 6.0f*v1 - 9.0f*v2;
          Bdv[3]= 3.0f*v2;
          }
      }
  for( i=0;i<mode;i++ )
    for( j=0;j<mode;j++ )
      {
      k=(sv+j)*npu+su+i;
      f=Bu[i]*Bv[j];
      if (evaltype&PATCH_EVAL_POINT)
        {
        point.x+=f*p[k].x;
        point.y+=f*p[k].y;
        point.z+=f*p[k].z;
        }
      if (evaltype&PATCH_EVAL_TEXTCOORD)
        {
        textcoord.x+=f*t[k].x;
        textcoord.y+=f*t[k].y;
        textcoord.z+=f*t[k].z;
        textcoord.w+=f*t[k].w;
        }
      if (evaltype&PATCH_EVAL_NORMAL)
        {
        du+=(Bdu[i]*Bv[j])*p[k];
        dv+=(Bu[i]*Bdv[j])*p[k];
        }
      }
  if (evaltype&PATCH_EVAL_POINT)
    *(dest++)=point;
  if (evaltype&PATCH_EVAL_TEXTCOORD)
    *(dest++)=textcoord;
  if (evaltype&PATCH_EVAL_NORMAL)
    {
    dest->cross(dv,du);
```

```cpp
            dest->normalize();
        }
    }
// finds the subdivision level for a quadratic curve
// segment based on curve error factor
int find_subdiv_level(vector v0,vector v1,vector v2)
{
        // finds subdivision level base on curve error factor
    int level;
    vector a, b, dist;
        float factor=flyengine->curveerr*flyengine->curveerr;
    for (level=0;level<8;level++)
    {
        a=(v0+v1)*0.5f;
        b=(v1+v2)*0.5f;
        v2=(a+b)*0.5f;
        dist=v2-v1;
        if (vec_dot(dist,dist)<factor)
         break;
        v1=a;
    }
    return level;
}
// builds the discrete surface points
void bezier_patch::build_surface()
{
    if (mode!=3 || p==0 || t==0)
        return;
    int i,j,k;
    vector normal;
    // finds level of subdivision in u direction
    levelu=0;
    levelv=0;
    k=0;
    for( j=0;j<nsv;j++,k+=2*npu )
    for( i=0;i<nsu;i++,k+=2 )
        if ((p[k]-p[k+2]).length()>0.1f)
        {
        levelu=find_subdiv_level(p[k],p[k+1],p[k+2]);
        break;
        }
    // finds level of subdivision in v direction
    k=0;
    for( j=0;j<nsv;j++,k+=2*npu )
    for( i=0;i<nsu;i++,k+=2 )
```

```
          if ((p[k]-p[k+2*npu]).length()>0.1f)
          {
          levelv=find_subdiv_level(p[k],p[k+npu],p[k+2*npu]);
          break;
          }

      // compute number of vertices in each direction
      nvertu=(1<<levelu)*nsu+1;
      nvertv=(1<<levelv)*nsv+1;
      if (nvertu<2) nvertu=2;
      if (nvertv<2) nvertv=2;

      // allocate surface points
      if (surf) delete surf;
      surf=new vector[nvertu*nvertv*2];

      // evaluate surface points
      k=0;
      for( j=0;j<nvertv;j++ )
         for( i=0;i<nvertu;i++,k+=2 )
            evaluate(PATCH_EVAL_POINT|PATCH_EVAL_TEXTCOORD,
               (float)i/(nvertu-1),(float)j/(nvertv-1),&surf[k]);
}
void bezier_patch::draw(int nleveldrop)
{
   if (surf==0)
      return;

   int i,j,k,l,mapcount=0;
   float *f1,*f2;
   int dropu,dropv,numstrips;

   // finds number of levels to drop in each direction
   if (levelu>=nleveldrop)
      dropu=nleveldrop;
   else dropu=levelu;
   if (levelv>=nleveldrop)
      dropv=nleveldrop;
   else dropv=levelv;

   // compute number of strips
   numstrips=(1<<(levelv-dropv))*nsv;

   // compute number of vertices to drop in each direction
   dropu=(1<<dropu);
   dropv=(1<<dropv);

   // number of floats to skip
   k=dropu*8;
   l=dropv*nvertu*2;
   glColor3ub(255,255,255);
```

```
// draw texture layer
if (flyengine->mapmode&MAPPING_TEXTURE)
   {
   tc->use(texpic);
   for( j=0;j<numstrips;j++ )
      {
      f1=(float * )&surf[j*l]; f2=f1+(l<<2);
      glBegin(GL_TRIANGLE_STRIP);
      for( i=0;i<nvertu;i+=dropu,f1+=k,f2+=k)
         {
         glTexCoord2fv(f2+4);
         glVertex3fv(f2);
         glTexCoord2fv(f1+4);
         glVertex3fv(f1);
         }
      glEnd();
      }
   mapcount++;
   }
// draw lightmap layer
if (flyengine->mapmode&MAPPING_LIGHTMAP &&
   flyengine->nlm!=0)
   {
   if (mapcount)
      {
      glBlendFunc(GL_ZERO,GL_SRC_COLOR);
      glDepthMask(GL_FALSE);
      glDepthFunc(GL_EQUAL);
      }
   tc->use(flyengine->lm[lm]->pic+flyengine->lmbase);
   for( j=0;j<numstrips;j++ )
      {
      f1=(float * )&surf[j*l]; f2=f1+(l<<2);
      glBegin(GL_TRIANGLE_STRIP);
      for( i=0;i<nvertu;i+=dropu,f1+=k,f2+=k)
         {
         glTexCoord2fv(f2+6);
         glVertex3fv(f2);
         glTexCoord2fv(f1+6);
         glVertex3fv(f1);
         }
      glEnd();
      }
   mapcount++;
   }
}
```

```
        // restore render state
        glDepthMask(GL_TRUE);
        glDepthFunc(GL_LESS);
        glBlendFunc(GL_SRC_ALPHA, GL_ONE_MINUS_SRC_ALPHA);
    }
```

5.8.2 Curves, objects and subdivision

In the foregoing sections we have assumed the general case in considering converting a patch representation into a polygon representation. We now consider making considerable complexity reduction for certain classes of objects, both in the representation and in the conversion to polygons or the subdivision.

In Section 5.6.1 we introduced the common method of modelling an object by sweeping a cross-section along a spine curve where both the spine curve and the cross-section can be Bézier curves, resulting in an entity which is known as a ducted solid. This can be used to generate a mesh of patches and the general algorithm applied to subdivide the patches. However, for regular ducted solids there is no need to represent the object in this way. We can simply retain the curves, or more precisely their control point array, as a generating formula and produce the primitives for rendering directly from the curve representation. The subdivision products are non-planar quadrilaterals which are then converted into triangles.

The idea is demonstrated in Figure 5.53 (see also the colour version of this figure) which shows two consecutive levels of uniform and non-uniform subdivision for an arch object. Both the spine and the cross-section curve are two-segment Bézier curves. Uniform subdivision can proceed as follows. We generate new control points and place a cross-section curve at each point. (A method for orientating the cross-section curves is given in Section 2.2.4.) Subdividing the cross-section curve and considering consecutive cross-sections gives us a net of (non-planar) quadrilaterals which can then be split into triangles.

For non-uniform subdivision of the curves we need a 'flatness' test and we subdivide recursively until this criterion is met. A simple (world space) test is to find the perpendicular distance from the midpoint of the curve to the line joining the endpoints and terminate the subdivision if this is within a threshold (Figure 5.54). If not, the subdivision function is called recursively with the two newly created segments.

Figure 5.55 (Colour Plate) shows a rendered image of the arch as a flat object. The entire arch is made from flat faces (no subdivision of the cross-section curve). It appears curved when rendered. This is because it still receives a high-resolution light map calculated from the original definition. Of course, with this example we can only view the object from the front but the apparent increase in the quality of the object representation due to the high-resolution light map is an advantage that can be exploited. We revisit this point in Chapter 10.

Figure 5.53
Converting a ducted solid
generator into triangles.

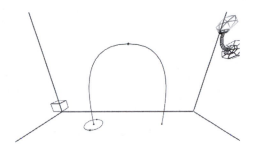

Generator: 3 Bézier curves

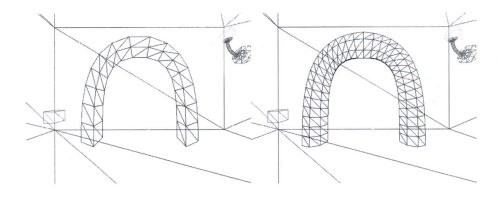

2 levels of uniform subdivision

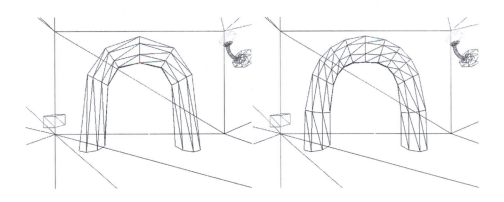

2 levels of non-uniform subdivision

Figure 5.54
Non-uniform curve
subdivision.

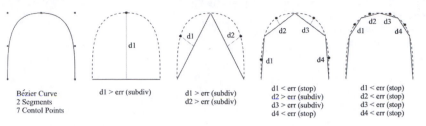

Bézier Curve 2 Segments 7 Contol Points	d1 > err (subdiv)	d1 > err (subdiv) d2 > err (subdiv)	d1 < err (stop) d2 > err (subdiv) d3 > err (subdiv) d4 < err (stop)	d1 < err (stop) d2 < err (stop) d3 < err (stop) d4 < err (stop)

Thus for this object we have a representation consisting of 11 floats (four control points for the spine and seven for the two-segment cross-section). This can be subdivided in real time to any level and the high-resolution light map applied to light it.

The following code performs uniform or non-uniform subdivision as described above.

```
class bezier_curve
{
   float distance(float *p,float *p1,float *p2);
   void subdiv(float u1,float u2,float *p1,float *p2,float *points,int&
npoints,float maxerror,int maxpoints);
   public:
      float *p;    // curve control points
      int np,      // number of control points
         ns,       // number of bezier segments ((np-1)/3)
         nd;       // curve dimensions (2->2D, 3->3D, etc...)
      vector pivot;      // curve pivot position

      void reset();
      void set_dim(int ndim);
      void add_point(float *f);
      void interpolate(float u,float *f);
      void interpolate_tangent(float u,float *f);
      float length();
      int load_bez(char *file);
      int adaptative_subdiv(float maxerror,float *points,int maxpoints);
      bezier_curve() { p=0; reset(); };
      virtual ~bezier_curve() { reset(); };
};

void bezier_curve::reset()
{
   if (p)
      delete p;
   p=0;
   ns=0;
   np=0;
}
```

```
void bezier_curve::set_dim(int ndim)
{
  reset();
  nd=ndim;
}
float bezier_curve::length()
{
  // returns the aproximate length of the curve
  if (ns==0 || nd==0) return 0;
  int i,j=ns*8,k,vv=1;
  float *v[2],len=0.0f,f;
  v[0]=new float[nd];
  v[1]=new float[nd];
  interpolate(0.0f,v[0]);
  for( i=1;i<j;i++ )
  {
    interpolate((float)i/(j-1),v[vv]);
    f=0.0f;
    for( k=0;k<nd;k++ )
       f+=(v[0][k]-v[1][k])*(v[0][k]-v[1][k]);
    len+=(float)sqrt(f);
    vv=!vv;
  }
  delete v[0];
  delete v[1];
  return len;
}
int bezier_curve::adaptative_subdiv(float maxerror,float *points,int
maxpoints)
{
  if (maxpoints<2) return 0;
  int npoints,i,j;
  float tmp;
  // start points list with two points (the curve edges)
  points[0]=0.0f;
  points[1]=1.0f;
  npoints=2;
  // subdiv curve recursively
  subdiv(0,1,&p[0],&p[nd*(np-1)],points,npoints,maxerror,maxpoints);
  // sort points
  for( i=1;i<npoints;i++ )
    for( j=i+1;j<npoints;j++ )
```

```
        if (points[j]<points[i])
        {
           tmp=points[i];
           points[i]=points[j];
           points[j]=tmp;
        }
   // sort number of points
   return npoints;
}
float bezier_curve::distance(float *p,float *p1,float *p2)
{
   // returns distance from point p to line defined by p1,p2
   float dot=0,len1=0,len2=0;
   int i;

   // alloc two vectors
   float *v1=new float [nd];
   float *v2=new float [nd];

   // compute length from (p1,p) and (p1,p2)
   for( i=0;i<nd;i++ )
   {
      v1[i]= p[i]-p1[i];
      v2[i]=p2[i]-p1[i];
      len1+=v1[i]*v1[i];
      len2+=v2[i]*v2[i];
   }
   len1=(float)sqrt(len1);
   len2=(float)sqrt(len2);

   // normalise
   if (len1>0)
      for( i=0;i<nd;i++ )
         v1[i]/=len1;
   if (len2>0)
      for( i=0;i<nd;i++ )
         v2[i]/=len2;

   // compute dot product
   for( i=0;i<nd;i++ )
      dot+=v1[i]*v2[i];

   // free vectors
   delete v1;
   delete v2;

   // return distance
   return (float)sqrt(len1*len1*(1.0f-dot*dot));
```

```
}
    void bezier_curve::subdiv(float u1,float u2,float *p1,float *p2,float
*points,int& npoints,float maxerror,int maxpoints)
    {
        // if points list is not full
        if (npoints<maxpoints)
        {
        // alloc a new point
        float *p=new float[nd];

        // compute segment midpoint coordinate
        float u=(u1+u2)*0.5f;

        // interpolare curve at the segment midpoint
        interpolate(u,p);

        // if error is bigger then maxerror
        if (distance(p,p1,p2)>maxerror)
            {
            // add point to points list
            points[npoints++]=u;
            // subdiv each segment recursively
            subdiv(u1,u,p1,p,points,npoints,maxerror,maxpoints);
            subdiv(u,u2,p,p2,points,npoints,maxerror,maxpoints);
            }

        // delete allocated point
        delete p;
        }
    }
```

5.9 Subdivision surfaces

Subdivision surfaces are B-spline surfaces that are defined by a polygon mesh, or equivalently a control point polyhedron, and a set of refinement rules which recursively generate new meshes by refining the previous. In this way a limit surface is generated. Their motivation is fairly obvious. Usually we employ a recursive subdivision algorithm to generate a polygonal representation of a B-spline (or other bi-cubic parametric) surface anyway. Why not employ the subdivision surface plus the refinement algorithm as the definition *per se* and eliminate the need for the closed form mathematical expression which defines the surface in terms of a set of basis or blending functions and a set of control points? The main advantage of this approach is that it eliminates the topological restrictions inherent in single patches. As we have seen, for many applications the alternative to a single patch – a net of patches – results in difficulties, particularly with continuity constraints.

We will now look at surfaces formed by subdivision. Following their histori-cal evolution we will start with Catmull-Clark surfaces then examine butterfly surfaces. The latter scheme, for reasons that will become clear, may be of greater utility in the games industry.

5.9.1 Catmull-Clark subdivision

It was Catmull and Clark (1978) who first noted that subdivision rules could be extended to include meshes of arbitrary topology. In particular, they showed that the limit surface is locally a bi-cubic uniform B-spline except at a number of points on the surface which they called 'extraordinary' points.

There are three ways in which in which subdivision rules are specified and we will now introduce these. In the original paper Catmull-Clark specified the rules 'algorithmically'. The start mesh is a polyhedron which has the same topology of the desired (limit) surface. The refinement rules are expressed as replacement operations on vertices and edges and are, following Catmull-Clarks' original con-vention:

(1) New vertices (face points) are placed at the centre of each original face. These are calculated as the average of the positions of original vertices of the face.

(2) New edge points are created. These are calculated as the average of the mid-points of the original edge with the average of the two new face points shar-ing the edge.

(3) New vertex points are formed as the average:

$Q/n + 2R/n + S(n − 3)/n$

where:

Q is the average of the new face points surrounding the old vertex

R is the average of the midpoints of the edges that share the old vertex

S is the old vertex point

n number of edges that share the vertex

(4) The new mesh is then formed by

(a) connecting each new face point to the new edge points of the edges that form the original face;

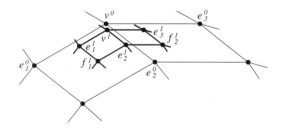

Figure 5.56
Notation of De Rose *et al.*
(1998).

(b) connecting each new vertex point to the new edge points of all original edges forming the original vertex.

De Rose *et al.* (1998) formulated these rules in a succinct convention which notates the subdivision level and the vertices. They denote the control mesh as M^0 and subsequent subdivision meshes as $M^1, M^2, \ldots$ and the generating formulae for edges and vertices (Figure 5.56) as:

$$e_j^{i+1} = \frac{v^i + e_j^i + f_{j-1}^{i+1} + f_j^{i+1}}{4}$$

(5.9)

$$v^{i+1} = \frac{n-2}{n} v^i + \frac{1}{n^2} \sum_j e_j^i + \frac{1}{n^2} \sum_j f_j^{j+1}$$

The final notation is perhaps the most popular because it enables an easy comparison between different schemes. This is the mask notation where a mask is shown simply as a black dot together with a set of coefficients. The vertices of the mask indicates where it is to be placed on the mesh and the coefficients define the subdivision rule. The dot gives the position of the new vertex whose position is given by the sum of the products of the mask weights and the corresponding vertex. Figure 5.57 gives the mask notation for the Catmull-Clark rules.

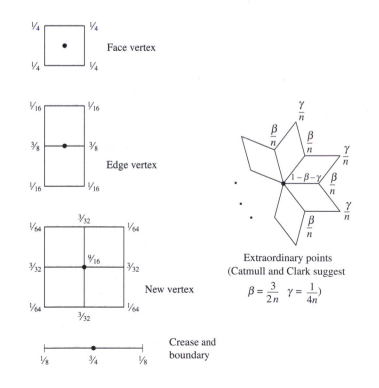

Figure 5.57
Masks for Catmull-Clark subdivision rules.

Figure 5.58
Extraordinary points in a subdivided mesh. The valence of these points in the control mesh is retained in the subdivided mesh.

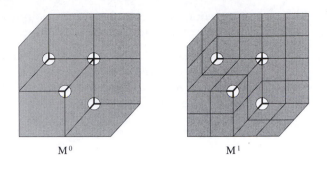

M^0 M^1

The valence of a vertex is defined as the number of edges incident on it and the vertices corresponding to the original control points retain the valence of these points. In general, after a few subdivision steps most vertices in a mesh will have vertices of valence 4 (for interior points) and 3 (on boundary points). Vertices in the surface which do not have valence 4 are called extraordinary points and it is only at these points that the subdivision surface is not a standard B-spline surface. Four such points are shown for a simple example in Figure 5.58 and it is important to note that the valence of the vertices is retained down through the subdivision. Thus on the limit surface these points are singularities. Such points are normally dealt with by having modified rules for such vertices (Figure 5.57).

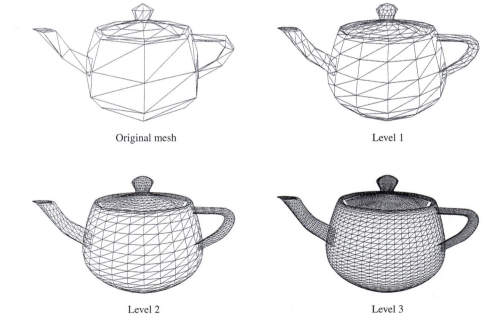

Original mesh

Level 1

Figure 5.59
Mesh refinement using (unmodified) butterfly scheme.

Level 2

Level 3

If we consider the vertices of the coarser mesh as a regular rectangular array then these are also vertices of the finer mesh. New vertices are created on each edge and an additional vertex within each face. The old vertices are retained (albeit moved). For this reason this type of subdivision algorithm is called a vertex insertion algorithm. This distinguishes it from a 'corner cutting' algorithm where old vertices are discarded as the mesh is refined. The subdivision algorithm we used for Bézier patches (Figures 5.47 and 5.60) is a corner-cutting algorithm and, as can be clearly seen in the figure, the mesh shrinks onto the patch. Interpolating schemes may be more useful because they can be used for mesh refinement (Figure 5.59).

Another factor that distinguishes different types of algorithms is whether they are approximating or interpolating. The Catmull-Clark scheme is approximating – the control points specified in M^0 do not lie in the limit surface. An interpolating scheme, on the other hand, has the property that the original control points are part of the limit surface.

An obvious practical enhancement to the basic scheme outlined above is the necessity to retain 'creases' in the limit surface. We require the limit surface to be, in general, a collection of B-spline surfaces which are joined or connected by a crease. Consider a cube as the start mesh. We may require this to converge to a cylinder rather than a sphere. This is commonly achieved by marking certain edges in the control mesh as sharp and modifying the refinement rules when these edges are encountered in the subdivision process. Infinitely sharp creases, where the surface normal is discontinuous across the edge, were first implemented by Hoppe *et al.* (1994). To retain a sharp edge we can change Equation 5.9 to

$$e_j^{i+1} = \frac{v^i + e_j^i}{2}$$

placing the new edge point coincident with the edge from which it has been derived. Consider the simple example of the cube required to converge to a cylinder. Eight edges in the top and bottom surface are marked as sharp, and as the subdivision proceeds, new edge points generated from these marked edges are constrained to lie in the top and bottom planes of the start mesh.

The modified vertex rules depend on the number of sharp edges incident on the vertex. A vertex with a single sharp edge – known as a 'dart' – uses Equation 5.9 unaltered. A vertex with two sharp edges uses:

$$v^{i+1} = \frac{e_j^i + 6v^i + e_k^i}{8}$$

In the cube to cylinder example, two of the three edges incident on each vertex are sharp and the new vertices remain in the top and bottom planes of the start mesh.

A vertex with three or more sharp edges uses:

$$v^{i+1} = v^i$$

This is called a corner and does not move under subdivision.

Thus it is relatively straightforward to implement sharp creases. However, many models will require 'semi-sharp' creases (known in CAD as fillets or blends) which do not exhibit surface normal discontinuity. These are more difficult to implement. The main problem is the proliferation of refinement rules required as a function of the nature of the sharpness required and the number of creases incident on a vertex.

De Rose *et al.* (1998) use a scheme they term hybrid subdivision. A remarkably simple idea, this invokes the application of the set of infinitely sharp rules for the first few steps, followed by the application of the smooth (modified) rules to produce the limit surface. They point out that this leads to surfaces that are sharp at a coarse scale, but smooth at a finer scale. In addition, De Rose *et al.* implement a scheme to vary the sharpness of a crease along its length.

5.9.2   Butterfly subdivision

Another popular subdivision approach is the butterfly scheme (Dyn *et al.*, 1990). This is an interpolating method – the limit surface passes through the M^0 points. This means that it can be used to refine existing models as Figure 5.59 illustrates. Figure 5.60 shows, for comparison, Bézier patch subdivision using the same model. The difference between the interpolating scheme (butterfly) and the approximating method (Bézier subdivision) is perhaps not obvious in this particular example and Figure 5.61 (Colour Plate) shows the butterfly method after three levels of subdivision 'containing' the original mesh. The butterfly scheme as originally proposed deals with triangular meshes rather than quadrilateral meshes

The mask for butterfly subdivision is shown in Figure 5.62. For a mesh where all the vertices have valence 6, the mask computes a new vertex at each existing edge midpoint. Control over the flatness of the surface is available by altering the value of w (Figure 5.63). In this scheme vertices generally have valence 6 (for interior points, 4 for boundary points). For vertices of valence 3, like the apex of the pyramid in Figure 5.63, the surface is not C^1 continuous.

Figure 5.64 shows the nature of the subdivision for three simple solids. Points to note are the behaviour of the surface near the extraordinary points on the pyramid and the emergence of asymmetry in the cube surface. In the latter case the behaviour is due to the fact that in the original mesh the vertices have differing valences. The limit surface for the cube seems to be asymmetrical. For example, if one corner has valence 6 then it must be joined to a corner which can only have valence 4.

To implement a butterfly scheme we can proceed as follows (Figure 5.65(a):

For each edge in the model, add a new vertex as:

- edge defined by vertex $v0[0]$ and $v0[1]$
- edge also defined by the faces $f0[0]$ and $f0[1]$

Figure 5.60
Bézier patch subdivision for comparison with the previous figure.

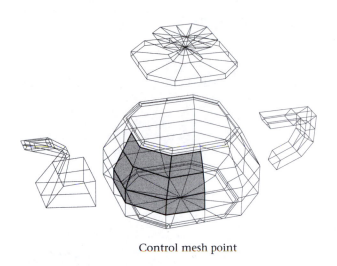

Control mesh point

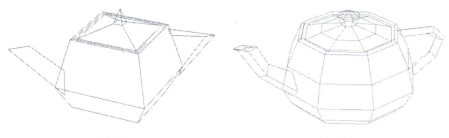

Level 1   Level 2

Level 3   Level 4

- find vertices $v1[0]$ and $v1[1]$ (other edges from $f0[0..1]$ that are not $v0[0..1]$)
- find edges $e[0..3]$ using $v0[0..1]$ and $v1[0..1]$
- find faces $f1[0..3]$ using $e[0..3]$ (other faces from $e[0..3]$ that are not $f0[0..1]$

Figure 5.62
Masks for the Butterfly
subdivision rule.

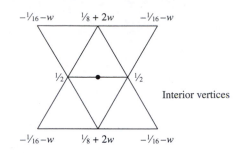

Figure 5.63
Varying *w* in the
(unmodified) Butterfly
scheme.

$w = -1/16$

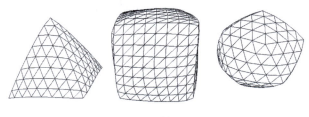

$w = -1/32$

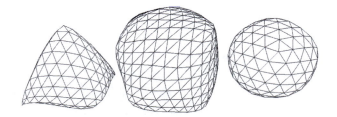

$w = 0$

Figure 5.64
Four levels of sub-division using the (unmodified) Butterfly scheme.

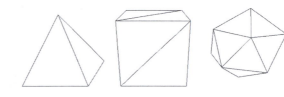

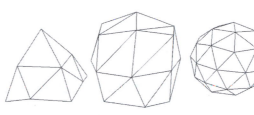

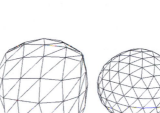

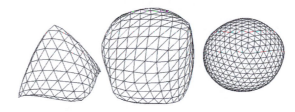

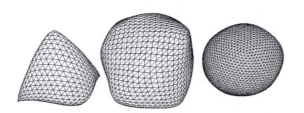

Figure 5.65
Implementing a butterfly
scheme. (a) Adding a new
vertex *v* to an edge.
(b) Convert each face
into four using new edge
vertices.

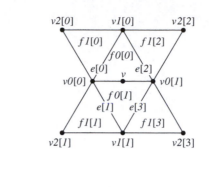

(a)

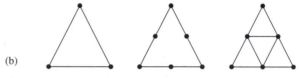

(b)

- find vertices $v2[0..4]$ using the $f1[0..3]$ and $e[0..3]$ (vertices from $f1[0..3]$ that are not from $e[0..3]$)
- add $v0[0..1]$, $v1[0..1]$ and $v2[0..3]$ with their weights to form v

where:

v – the vertex being added and $v0[0..1]$ – the current edge vertices (weight $1/2$)
$v1[0..1]$ – vertices with weight $1/8 + 2w$
$v2[0..3]$ – vertices with weight $-1/16 - w$
$f0[0..1]$ – the two faces sharing the current edge $f1[0..4]$ – the faces connected to $f0[0..1]$

Then each face is converted into four using its edge vertices (Figure 5.65(b)).

The code is as follows:

```
class subdivsurf
{
public:
    subdivsurf()
    {
        divmesh=0; nedges=0; edges=0; edgefaces=0;
    };
    ~subdivsurf() { reset(); };

    int nsubdiv;    // num subdivisions
    mesh* basemesh;        // base mesh
    mesh* divmesh; // basemesh subdivided nsubdiv times

    int nedges;            // number of edges
    int *edges;            // edges array (2*nedges)
    int *edgefaces;        // faces array (2*nedges)
```

```
    void reset();  // reset allocated data
    void subdiv(); // subdiv mesh nsubdiv times

    // finds edge with vertices v1,v2
    int get_edge(int v1,int v2);
    // get valence for vertex v1
    int get_valence(int v1);

    // add all mesh edges to the edges array
    void build_edge_list(mesh *m1);
    // add a single edge to the edges array
    void add_edge(int v1,int v2,int f);

    // add one vertex at m2 for each edge in m1
    void add_vertices(mesh *m1,mesh *m2);
    // add 4 faces in m2 for each face from m1
    void add_faces(mesh *m1,mesh *m2);
};
void subdivsurf::reset()
{
    if (divmesh) delete divmesh;
    if (edges) delete edges;
    if (edgefaces) delete edgefaces;
    divmesh=0;
    edges=0;
    edgefaces=0;
    nedges=0;
}
void subdivsurf::subdiv()
{
    reset();
    if (source==0 || basemesh==0)
            return;

    int i;
    mesh *m1,*m2;
    m1=basemesh->clone();

    // for each subdiv step, subdivide mesh m1 into mesh m2
    for( i=0;i<nsubdiv;i++ )
    {
    // create mesh
    m2=new mesh;
    // lists all edges for mesh m1
    build_edge_list(m1);
    // add one vertex at each edge in mesh m2
    add_vertices(m1,m2);
    // add 3 faces at each original face
```

```
        add_faces(m1,m2);
        // compute mesh normals
        m2->compute_normals();

        // delete mesh m1 and replace it with mesh m2
        delete m1;
        m1=m2;
        }

        // store last subdivided mesh
        divmesh=m1;
}
int subdivsurf::get_edge(int v1,int v2)
{
        // returns index into edges list for edge (v1,v2)
        int i;
        for( i=0;i<nedges;i++ )
                if ((edges[i*2]==v1 && edges[i*2+1]==v2) ||
                        (edges[i*2+1]==v1 && edges[i*2]==v2))
                        break;
        if (i==nedges)
                return -1;
        return i;
}
int subdivsurf::get_valence(int v1)
{
        // returns the number of edges using vertex v1
        int i,count=0;
        for( i=0;i<nedges;i++ )
                if (edges[i*2]==v1 || edges[i*2+1]==v1)
                        count++;
        return count;
}
void subdivsurf::build_edge_list(mesh *m1)
{
        // build the edges list adding all edges from
        // all faces (faces can share edges)
        int i,j;
        for( i=0;i<m1->nf;i++ )
                for( j=0;j<3;j++ )
                        add_edge(
                                m1->faces[i]->vert[j]-m1->vert,
                                m1->faces[i]->vert[(j+1)%3]-m1->vert,
                                i);
}
void subdivsurf::add_edge(int v1,int v2,int f)
```

```
{
    // adds a new edge to the edges list

    int i=get_edge(v1,v2);
    if (i>=0)
            // edge already exists, just store face index
            edgefaces[i*2+1]=f;
    else
    {
    // add two new entries to the lists
    int *tmp;
    tmp=new int [nedges*2+2];
    memcpy(tmp,edges,sizeof(int)*2*nedges);
    delete edges;
    edges=tmp;
    tmp=new int [nedges*2+2];
    memcpy(tmp,edgefaces,sizeof(int)*2*nedges);
    delete edgefaces;
    edgefaces=tmp;

    // store edge and face
    edges[nedges*2]=v1;
    edges[nedges*2+1]=v2;
    edgefaces[nedges*2]=f;
    edgefaces[nedges*2+1]=-1;
    nedges++;
    }
}
void subdivsurf::add_vertices(mesh *m1,mesh *m2)
{
    int a,i,j,k,v0[2],v1[2],v2[4],e[4],f0[2],f1[4],valence[2];

    // alloc vertices for destination mesh m2
    m2->nv=nedges + m1->nv;
    m2->vert=new vector[m2->nv];
    // copy mesh m1 vertices into mesh m2
    memcpy(m2->vert,m1->vert,sizeof(vector)*m1->nv);

    // for all edges from mesh m1
    for( i=0;i<nedges;i++ )
    {
            // place vertex in the center of the edge
            v0[0]=edges[i*2];
            v0[1]=edges[i*2+1];
            m2->vert[m1->nv+i]=
                    (m1->vert[v0[0]]+m1->vert[v0[1]])*0.5f;

            // find the faces sharing this edge
```

```
f0[0]=edgefaces[i*2];
f0[1]=edgefaces[i*2+1];
if (f0[0]==-1 || f0[1]==-1)
        continue;

// compute the two v1 vertices
v1[0]=v1[1]=-1;
for( j=0;j<2;j++ )
        for( k=0;k<3;k++ )
        {
        a=m1->localfaces[f0[j]].vert[k]-m1->vert;
        if (a!=v0[0] && a!=v0[1])
                {
                v1[j]=a;
                break;
                }
        }
// compute the four e edges
e[0]=get_edge(v0[0],v1[0]);
e[1]=get_edge(v0[0],v1[1]);
e[2]=get_edge(v0[1],v1[0]);
e[3]=get_edge(v0[1],v1[1]);
if (e[0]==-1 || e[1]==-1 || e[2]==-1 || e[3]==-1)
        continue;

// compute the four f faces
for( j=0;j<4;j++ )
        if (edgefaces[e[j]*2]!=edgefaces[i*2] &&
                edgefaces[e[j]*2]!=edgefaces[i*2+1])
                f1[j]=edgefaces[e[j]*2];
        else f1[j]=edgefaces[e[j]*2+1];
if (f1[0]==-1 || f1[1]==-1 || f1[2]==-1 || f1[3]==-1)
        continue;

// compute the four v2 vertices
v2[0]=v2[1]=v2[2]=v2[3]=-1;
for( j=0;j<4;j++ )
for( k=0;k<3;k++ )
        {
        a=m1->localfaces[f1[j]].vert[k]-m1->vert;
        if (a!=edges[e[j]*2] && a!=edges[e[j]*2+1])
                {
                v2[j]=a;
                break;
                }
        }
if (v2[0]==-1 || v2[1]==-1 || v2[2]==-1 || v2[3]==-1)
        continue;
```

```
                    // move vertex based on v1 and v2 and subdivfactor
                    m2->vert[m1->nv+i]+=
                            (m1->vert[v1[0]]+m1->vert[v1[1]])*
(1.0f/8.0f+2.0f*flyengine->subdivfactor)+
                            (m1->vert[v2[0]]+m1->vert[v2[1]]+m1->vert
[v2[2]]+m1->vert[v2[3]])*(-1.0f/16.0f-flyengine->subdivfactor);
        }
    }
    void subdivsurf::add_faces(mesh *m1,mesh *m2)
    {
        int i,j,k,e[3];
        float euv[3][2];

        // alloc faces for destination mesh m2
        m2->nf=m1->nf*4;
        m2->localfaces=new face[m2->nf];
        m2->faces=new face *[m2->nf];
        for( i=0;i<m2->nf;i++ )
                m2->faces[i]=&m2->localfaces[i];

        // for all faces in m1
        for( i=j=0;i<m1->nf;i++ )
        {
        // find edges for mesh m1 face i and
        // compute the face edges center texture coordinates
        for( k=0;k<3;k++ )
                {
                e[k]=get_edge(
                        m1->localfaces[i].vert[k]-m1->vert,
                        m1->localfaces[i].vert[(k+1)%3]-m1->vert);
                euv[k][0]=0.5f*(m1->localfaces[i].uv[k][0]+m1->
                localfaces[i].uv[(k+1)%3][0]);
                euv[k][1]=0.5f*(m1->localfaces[i].uv[k][1]+m1->
                localfaces[i].uv[(k+1)%3][1]);
                }

        // create face f1
        m2->localfaces[j]=m1->localfaces[i];
        m2->localfaces[j].vert[0]=&m2->vert[m1->localfaces[i].vert[0]-
        m1->vert];
        m2->localfaces[j].vert[1]=&m2->vert[e[0]+m1->nv];
        m2->localfaces[j].vert[2]=&m2->vert[e[2]+m1->nv];
        m2->localfaces[j].uv[1][0]=euv[0][0];
        m2->localfaces[j].uv[1][1]=euv[0][1];
        m2->localfaces[j].uv[2][0]=euv[2][0];
        m2->localfaces[j].uv[2][1]=euv[2][1];
        j++;
```

```
// create face f2
m2->localfaces[j]=m1->localfaces[i];
m2->localfaces[j].vert[0]=&m2->vert[e[0]+m1->nv];
m2->localfaces[j].vert[1]=&m2->vert[m1->localfaces[i].vert[1]-
m1->vert];
m2->localfaces[j].vert[2]=&m2->vert[e[1]+m1->nv];
m2->localfaces[j].uv[0][0]=euv[0][0];
m2->localfaces[j].uv[0][1]=euv[0][1];
m2->localfaces[j].uv[2][0]=euv[1][0];
m2->localfaces[j].uv[2][1]=euv[1][1];
j++;

// create face f3
m2->localfaces[j]=m1->localfaces[i];
m2->localfaces[j].vert[0]=&m2->vert[e[2]+m1->nv];
m2->localfaces[j].vert[1]=&m2->vert[e[1]+m1->nv];
m2->localfaces[j].vert[2]=&m2->vert[m1->localfaces[i].vert[2]-
m1->vert];
m2->localfaces[j].uv[0][0]=euv[2][0];
m2->localfaces[j].uv[0][1]=euv[2][1];
m2->localfaces[j].uv[1][0]=euv[1][0];
m2->localfaces[j].uv[1][1]=euv[1][1];
j++;

// create face f4
m2->localfaces[j]=m1->localfaces[i];
m2->localfaces[j].vert[0]=&m2->vert[e[0]+m1->nv];
m2->localfaces[j].vert[1]=&m2->vert[e[1]+m1->nv];
m2->localfaces[j].vert[2]=&m2->vert[e[2]+m1->nv];
m2->localfaces[j].uv[0][0]=euv[0][0];
m2->localfaces[j].uv[0][1]=euv[0][1];
m2->localfaces[j].uv[1][0]=euv[1][0];
m2->localfaces[j].uv[1][1]=euv[1][1];
m2->localfaces[j].uv[2][0]=euv[2][0];
m2->localfaces[j].uv[2][1]=euv[2][1];
j++;
}
}
```

(5.9.3)   ## Modified butterfly

Zorrin *et al.* (1996) developed a modification of the butterfly scheme which retained its advantages of interpolation and locality but dealt with the artefacts that the original scheme introduces. Interpolation is potentially important as we have observed in many practical applications. Locality in this context means that the neighbourhood used to define the mask should be as small as possible for computational efficiency.

Zorrin *et al.* distinguish four types of edges which are treated as follows:

- An edge connecting two vertices of valence 6. This uses a modified or extended butterfly mask of 10 points (Figure 5.66).

$$a = 1/2 - w$$
$$b = 1/8 + 2w$$
$$c = -1/16 - w$$
$$d = w$$

- An edge connecting a valence 6 vertex with an extraordinary vertex (valence ≠ 6).

  – for $n \geq 5$ the weights are given by:

  $$s_j = (1/4 + \cos(2\pi j/n) + 1/2\cos(4\pi j/n))/n$$

  – for $n = 3$

  $$s_0 = 5/12 \qquad s_{1,2} = -1/2$$

  – for $n = 4$

  $$s_0 = 3/8 \qquad s_2 = -1/8 \qquad s_{1,3} = 0$$

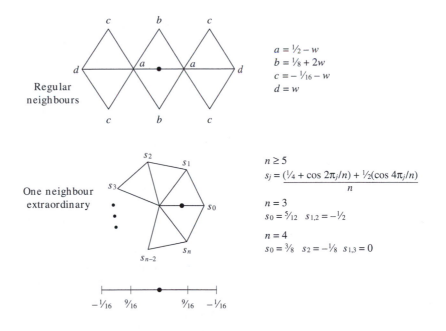

Figure 5.66
Masks for the modified butterfly scheme.

Figure 5.67
The modified butterfly
($w = -1/32$, original, $w = 0$).

- An edge connecting two extraordinary vertices. The average of the two values obtained by applying the appropriate type of the previous scheme according to the nature of each endpoint.
- Boundary edges. The one-dimensional four-point method shown in Figure 5.66 is used.

Figure 5.67 shows the modified rules for $w = -1/32$ and $w = 0$. The creases at the pyramid vertices (valence = 3) are no longer retained.

5.10 Scalability – polygon meshes, patch meshes and subdivision surfaces

All of Chapter 3 was devoted to the economics of polygon meshes. Three topics were examined: the transformation of a high-resolution polygon mesh into a series of lower-resolution models, data compression of vertex information and triangle stripification. It is apparent that both patch meshes and subdivision surfaces 'automatically' generate LOD meshes and we are now in a position to compare these approaches.

Scalability is the general term given to a topic that is becoming increasingly important as graphics processors keep increasing their performance (they now appear to be breaking Moore's law). This is a major problem for games developers because the gap between the latest hardware and that of, say, two or three years ago continually widens. Nevertheless developers need to produce games that both run on old hardware and exploit the quality advantages of the new processors. And, of course, an approach that neatly addresses these issues is to implement geometry that is scalable. For a particular processor the best visual quality possible is then obtained. Although it is possible to scale other aspects of a game – game content itself – possibly scaling the geometry is the most important element of scalability.

Consider in the first instance, polygon mesh LOD vs. subdivision surfaces. The polygon mesh LOD approach starts with a high-resolution mesh and successively generates lower-resolution meshes. The subdivision surface is exactly the opposite, starting with a low-resolution mesh and going to successively higher and higher resolutions, converging in the limit to a smooth surface. Also, subdivision surfaces are lower code complexity than LOD algorithms and they may eventually predominate in real-time rendering. We will now summarise the main points as they relate to scalability issues in the form of a comparison between the three representations.

5.10.1

LOD polygon meshes

- The object is modelled to a degree of accuracy that depends on the number of polygons used. The generality of the representation means that there are no restrictions on the shapes representable and detail is easy to add.
- The database representation of the high-resolution mesh is straightforward.
- Generation of lower-resolution meshes in a way that keeps as close as possible to the original surface is difficult and is generally done offline.
- Pre-processed LOD structures are bi-directional. From the current level we can go to a higher or lower level.

5.10.2

Patch meshes

- Depending on the object this can be an exact representation. There are difficulties in building a mesh because of continuity constraints.
- The database representation is simple – a two-dimensional array – and memory/bandwidth requirements are low.
- Subdivision is fast and, depending on the complexity, can proceed in real time.
- Non-uniform subdivision is possible, which optimises the representation's scalability, but cracking problems must be dealt with.

5.10.3

Subdivision surfaces

- The object is modelled as a low-resolution mesh using software that enables the creator to visualise the limit surface.
- The database representation can be any subdivision level from M^0 upwards. The memory/bandwidth requirements are low. Although the refinement rules are straightforward, the arbitrary topology makes the data structure manipulations difficult. A vertex edge and edge vertex map need to be maintained.
- Subdivision is fast and, depending on the complexity, can proceed in real time.
- Only uniform subdivision is possible.

6 Classic polygon mesh rendering technology

6.1 Coordinate spaces and geometric operations in the graphics pipeline

6.2 Operations carried out in view space

6.3 Algorithmic operations in the graphics pipeline

6.4 Rendering examples

This chapter details all the operations necessary to convert a polygon mesh representation into a shaded object on the screen. It is the case that nowadays a games engine developer is insulated from most of the detail in this chapter by graphics APIs and 3D hardware. However, it is still necessary to have a good detailed knowledge of the underlying techniques, particularly if it is required to implement any effect not available through the API. It also goes without saying that a good knowledge of algorithms, such as interpolative or Gouraud shading, is necessary to understand the limitations and defects inherent in them. The three chapters in this section will thus deal with explaining rendering, mapping and anti-aliasing, as they have developed over the last three decades in off-line rendering software. The chapters in the next section (Real time rendering) look at how the traditional approach to rendering has had to be modified in the games industry to facilitate real-time operation.

The purpose of a rendering pipeline is to take a description of a scene in three-dimensional space and map it into a two-dimensional projection on the view surface – the monitor screen. We can loosely classify the various processes involved in the graphics pipeline by putting them into one of two categories – geometric and algorithmic. Geometric processes involve operations on the vertices of polygons – transforming the vertices from one coordinate space to another or discarding polygons that cannot be seen from the viewpoint, for example. Algorithmic processes involve operations like shading and texture mapping and are considerably more costly than the geometric operations, most of which involve matrix multiplication.

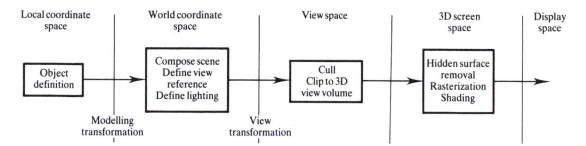

Figure 6.1
A three-dimensional rendering pipeline.

Currently 3D cards support the algorithmic processes and the geometric processes are carried out in the CPU. However, this situation is likely to change in the near future with geometric processes also being implemented in hardware.

A diagram representing the consecutive process in a graphics pipeline is shown in Figure 6.1. From this it can be seen that the overall process is a progression through various three-dimensional spaces – we transform the object representation from space to space. In the final space, which we have called screen space, the rendering operations take place. This space is also three-dimensional for reasons that we will shortly discover.

We shall discover in Chapter 9 that one of the main ways in which the games industry changed the basic pipeline shown in Figure 6.1 was to attend to the high cost of the view space operations for complex scenes. Real-time rendering has focused much on efficiently deciding what elements of a complex scene are contained within the view frustum. Another way in which current games technology differs from classic rendering techniques is the dichotomy between static objects or levels and dynamic objects. This difference is most apparent in lighting where off-line techniques (light maps) are applied to static objects and different techniques are used for dynamic objects. This dichotomy causes problems when the lights themselves are dynamic, requiring special local techniques to update the pre-calculated lighting.

6.1 Coordinate spaces and geometric operations in the graphics pipeline

A useful way of visualising a rendering pipeline is as a series of transformations into different coordinate spaces. These are now listed.

6.1.1 Local or modelling coordinate systems

For ease of modelling it makes sense to store the vertices of a polygon mesh object with respect to some point located in or near the object. For example, we would almost certainly want to locate the origin of a cube at one of the cube vertices, or we would want to make the axis of symmetry of an object generated as a solid of revolution coincident with the z axis. As well as storing the polygon vertices in a coordinate system that is local to the object, we would also store the polygon normal and the vertex normals. When local transformations are applied to the vertices of an object, the corresponding transformations are applied to the associated normals.

6.1.2 World coordinate systems

Once an object has been modelled the next stage is to place it in the scene that we wish to render. All objects that together constitute a scene each have their separate local coordinate systems. The global coordinate system of the scene is known as the 'world coordinate system'. All objects have to be transformed into this common space in order that their relative spatial relationships may be defined. The act of placing an object in a scene defines the transformation required to take the object from local space to world space. If the object is being animated, then the animation system provides a time-varying transformation that takes the object into world space on a frame by frame basis.

The scene is lit in world space. Light sources are specified, and if the shaders within the renderer function in world space then this is the final transformation that the normals of the object have to undergo. The surface attributes of an object – texture, colour and so on – are specified and tuned in this space.

6.1.3 Camera or eye or view coordinate system

The camera, eye or view coordinate system is a space that is used to establish viewing parameters (viewpoint, viewing direction) and a view volume. (A virtual camera is often used as the analogy in viewing systems, but if such an allusion is made we must be careful to distinguish between external camera parameters – its position and the direction it is pointing in – and internal camera parameters or those that affect the nature and size of the image on the film plane. Most rendering systems imitate a camera which in practice would be a perfect pinhole (or lensless) device with a film plane that can be positioned at any distance with respect to the pinhole. However, there are other facilities in computer graphics that cannot be imitated by a camera and because of this the analogy is of limited utility.)

Cameras in games are commonly 'first person', where the game player is the virtual viewer, or 'third person', where the camera is fixed relative to a character (usually an over-the-shoulder view) whose actions are being viewed by the game player. There can be more than one camera in a game with, say, a backwards-looking camera rendering to a separate viewport on the screen. Cameras may be subject to effects in games such as being shaken due to the proximity of the player to an explosion. From this we can see that the camera or view coordinate system in games is effectively an animated object translating and rotating under control of the player and/or the game.

We will now deal with a basic view coordinate system and the transformation from world space to view coordinate space. The reasons that this space exists – after all, we could go directly from world space to screen space – is that certain operations (and specifications) are most conveniently carried out in view space.

We define a viewing system as being the combination of a view coordinate system together with the specification of certain facilities such as a view volume. The simplest or minimum system would consist of the following:

- a viewpoint, C, which establishes the viewer's position in world space; this can be either the origin of the view coordinate system or the centre of projection together with a view direction N;
- a view coordinate system defined with respect to the viewpoint;
- a view plane onto which the two-dimensional image of the scene is projected;
- a view frustum or volume which defines the field of view.

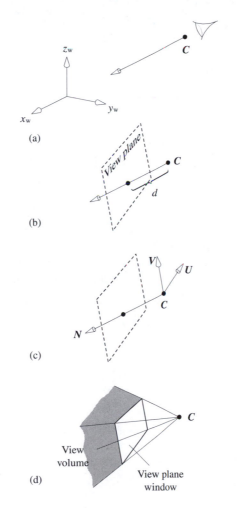

Figure 6.2
The minimum entities required in a practical viewing system. (a) Viewpoint C and viewing direction N. (b) A view plane normal to the viewing direction N positioned d units from C. (c) A view coordinate system with the origin C and UV axes embedded in a plane parallel to the view plane. (d) A view volume defined by the frustum formed by C and the view plane window.

These entities are shown in Figure 6.2. The view coordinate system UVN has N coincident with the viewing direction and V and U lying in a plane parallel to the view plane. We can consider the origin of the system to be the view point C. The view plane containing U and V is of infinite extent and we specify a a view volume or frustum which defines a window in the view plane. It is the contents of this window – the projection of that part of the scene that is contained within the view volume – that finally appears on the screen.

Thus using the virtual camera analogue we have a camera that can be positioned anywhere in world coordinate space, pointed in any direction and rotated about the viewing direction N.

To transform points in world coordinate space we invoke a change of coordinate system transformation and this splits into two components, a translational and a rotational (see Section 1.1.2). Thus:

$$\begin{bmatrix} x_v \\ y_v \\ z_v \\ 1 \end{bmatrix} = T_{view} \begin{bmatrix} x_w \\ y_w \\ z_w \\ 1 \end{bmatrix}$$

where:

$$T_{view} = RT$$

and

$$T = \begin{bmatrix} 1 & 0 & 0 & -C_x \\ 0 & 1 & 0 & -C_y \\ 0 & 0 & 1 & -C_z \\ 0 & 0 & 0 & 1 \end{bmatrix} \qquad R = \begin{bmatrix} U_x & U_y & U_z & 0 \\ V_x & V_y & V_z & 0 \\ N_x & N_y & N_z & 0 \\ 0 & 0 & 0 & 1 \end{bmatrix}$$

The only problem now is specifying a user interface for the system and mapping whatever parameters are used by the interface into U, V and N. A user needs to specify C, N and V. C is easy enough. N, the viewing direction or viewplane normal, can be entered, say, using two angles in a spherical coordinate system (Figure 6.3); this seems reasonably intuitive:

θ the azimuth angle

ϕ the colatitude or elevation angle

Figure 6.3
Specifying the orientation of a vector N using 2 angles ϕ and θ.

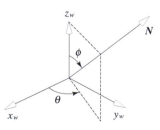

Figure 6.4
The up vector **V** can be calculated from an 'indication' given by **V'**.

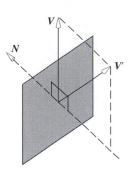

where:

$$\mathbf{N}_x = \sin \phi \cos \theta$$
$$\mathbf{N}_y = \sin \phi \sin \theta$$
$$\mathbf{N}_z = \cos \phi$$

V is more problematic. For example, a user may require 'up' to be the same sense as 'up' in the world coordinate system. However, this cannot be achieved by setting:

$$\mathbf{V} = (0,0,1)$$

because **V** must be perpendicular to **N**. A sensible strategy is to allow a user to specify an approximate orientation for **V**, say **V'** and have the system calculate **V** Figure 6.4 demonstrates this. **V'** is the user-specified up vector. This is projected onto the viewplane:

$$\mathbf{V} = \mathbf{V'} - (\mathbf{V'}.\mathbf{N})\mathbf{N}$$

and normalised. **U** can be specified or not depending on the user's requirements. If **U** is unspecified, it is obtained from:

$$\mathbf{U} = \mathbf{N} \times \mathbf{V}$$

This results in an LH coordinate system, which although somewhat inconsistent, conforms with our intuition of a practical viewing system, which has increasing distances from the viewpoint as increasing values along the view direction axis. Having established the viewing transformation using UVN notation we will now in subsequent sections use (x_v, y_v, z_v) to specify points in the view coordinate system.

In many APIs the following notation is used for the above UVN terminology:

$$\mathbf{V} = \text{VUP (view-up vector)}$$

$$\mathbf{N} = \text{VPN (view plane normal)}$$

$$\mathbf{C} = \text{VRP (view reference point)}$$

In OpenGL, for example, the viewing utility uses a camera point (called an eye point), a 'look at' point and an up vector and in this case we have:

Figure 6.5
A third-person camera uses
a look-at point and a
constant offset vector.

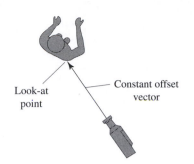

Look-at
point

Constant offset
vector

gluLookAt(eyeX,eyeY,eyeZ,centreX,centreY,centreZ,upX,upY,upZ)

The utility calulates from these parameters the elements of the viewing matrix $\boldsymbol{T}_{\text{view}}$.

$\boldsymbol{U} = \boldsymbol{N} \times$ (upX,upY,upZ)

$\boldsymbol{V} =$ (upX,upY,upZ)

$\boldsymbol{N} =$ (centreX,centreY,centreZ) $-$ (eyeX,eyeY,eyeZ)

$\boldsymbol{C} =$ (eyeX,eyeY,eyeZ)

Controlling a camera in a game depends on both the viewing parameters supplied by the API being used and the application. A third-person camera (Figure 6.5) could be controlled conveniently using the above 'look-at' utility. The look at point becomes a reference coordinate on the character the camera is tracking and the camera point $\boldsymbol{C}$ is obtained by subtracting a constant offset vector from this point. The reference point on the character takes the same low-level animation transformations as the character. Clearly the orientation of the offset vector is easily changed under user control.

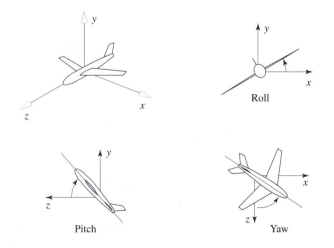

Figure 6.6
3-DOF control of an aircraft
using three angles.

In many applications it is more convenient to calculate T_{view} directly. Consider, for example, a flight simulator being controlled by a joystick. Here the camera would remain fixed to the local coordinate system of the aircraft and would take the same transformations – translation and three rotations specifying roll, pitch and yaw (Figure 6.6). Here we can calculate UVN from the three angles, but it is easier just to concatenate three matrices to obtain R as:

Rotate roll degrees about the *z* axis

Rotate pitch degrees about the *x* axis

Rotate yaw degrees about the *y* axis

Adding the translation from simulation then completes the view matrix. In OpenGL we have:

```
glLoadIdentity();
glRotate(rot.x,1,0,0); // roll
glRotate(rot.y,0,1,0); // pitch
glRotate(rot.z,0,0,1); // yaw
glTranslate(-pos.x,-pos.y,-pos.z);
```

6.2 Operations carried out in view space

As we have explained at the beginning of the chapter, real-time rendering methodologies have concentrated much effort on this stage of the rendering pipeline. The basic principle of the operations in view space is that we do not want to render anything that cannot be seen. In other words, at this stage in the process we want to discard all polygons that lie outside the view volume. In Chapter 9 we return to look at real-time specialisations of this topic and in this section we examine the foundation principles.

6.2.1 Culling or back-face elimination

Culling or back-face elimination is an operation that compares the orientation of complete polygons with the viewpoint or centre of projection and removes those polygons that cannot be seen. If a scene contains only a single convex

Figure 6.7
Culling and hidden space removal. (a) Culling removes complete polygons that cannot be seen. (b) Hidden surface removal deals with the general problem: polygons will partially obscure others.

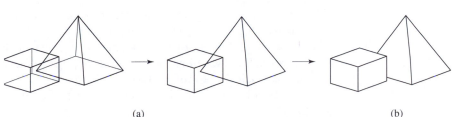

(a)   (b)

Figure 6.8
Culling or back-face elimination. (a) The desired view of the object (back faces shown as dotted lines). (b) A view of the geometry of the culling operation. (c) The culled object.

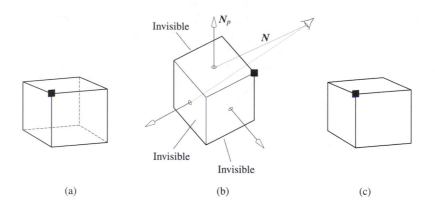

(a)   (b)   (c)

object, then culling generalises to hidden surface removal. A general hidden surface removal algorithm is always required when one polygon partially obscures another (Figure 6.7). On average, half of the polygons in a polyhedron are back-facing and the advantage of this process is that a simple test removes these polygons from consideration by a more expensive hidden surface removal algorithm.

The test for visibility is straightforward and is best carried out in view space. We calculate the outward normal for a polygon (Section 1.2.3) and examine the sign of the dot product of this and the vector from the centre of projection (Figure 6.8). Thus:

visibility = $\mathbf{N}_p.\mathbf{N} > 0$

where

$\mathbf{N}_p$ is the polygon normal

$\mathbf{N}$ is the 'line of sight' vector

6.2.2 The view volume

In Figure 6.2 the view volume was introduced as a semi-infinite pyramid. In many applications this is further constrained to a general view volume which is defined by a view plane window, a near clip plane and a far clip plane, but to simplify matters we will dispense with the near clip plane, which is of limited practical utility, and reconsider a view volume defined only by a view plane window and a far clip plane (Figure 6.9). Note that the far clip plane is a cut-off plane normal to the viewing direction and any objects beyond this cannot be seen. Far clip planes are extremely useful and can be used to cut down the number of polygons that need to be processed when rendering a very complex scene. However, they will in general result in popping effects in a computer game. The standard solution to this disturbance is to use depth-modulated fog to diminish the disturbance as objects 'switch-on' when they suddenly intersect the far clip plane.

Figure 6.9
A practical view volume: the near clip plane is made coincident with the view plane.

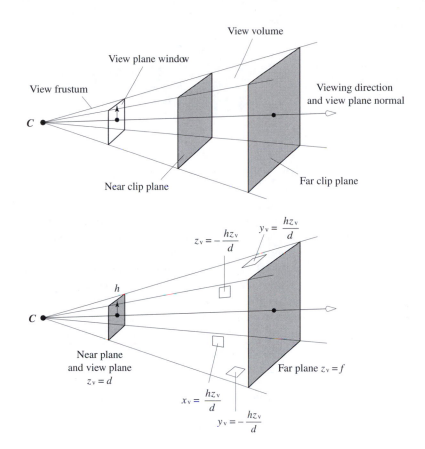

If we further simplify the geometry by specifying a square view plane window of dimension $2h$ arranged symmetrically about the viewing direction, then the four planes defining the sides of the view volume are given by:

$$x_v = \pm \frac{hz_v}{d}$$

$$y_v = \pm \frac{hz_v}{d}$$

We use the view volume to discard polygons that lie outside it and, as Figure 6.10 shows, a polygon either lies completely outside the volume or it straddles it and must be clipped. Clipping against the view volume can be carried out using polygon plane intersection calculations given in Section 1.3.3. Because of the inherent expense of the polygon/view volume comparison and clipping we have to avoid a straightforward or brute force approach and we describe (algorithmic) approaches to this problem in Sections 6.3.1 and 9.5.4.

Figure 6.10
Clipping against a view volume – a routine polygon operation in the pipeline.
(a) Polygons outside the view volume are discarded.
(b) Polygons inside the view volume are retained.
(c) Polygons intersecting a boundary are clipped.

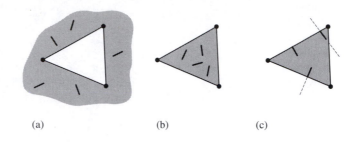

(a)   (b)   (c)

Three-dimensional screen space

The final three-dimensional space in our pipeline we call three-dimensional screen space. In this space we carry out (practical) clipping against the view volume and the rendering processes that we will describe later. Three-dimensional screen space is used because it simplifies both clipping and hidden surface removal – the classic hidden surface removal algorithm being the Z-buffer algorithm which operates by comparing the depth values associated with different objects that project onto the same pixel. Also in this space there is a final transformation to two-dimensional view plane coordinates – sometimes called the perspective divide. (The terms 'screen' and 'view plane' mean slightly different things. Strictly, screen coordinates are derived from view plane coordinates by a device-dependent transformation.)

Because the viewing surface in computer graphics is deemed to be flat we consider the class of projections known as planar geometric projections. Two basic

Figure 6.11
Two points projected onto a plane using parallel and perspective projections.

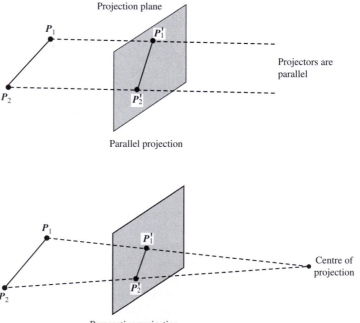

Figure 6.12
In a perspective projection a
distant line is displayed
smaller than a nearer line
the same length.

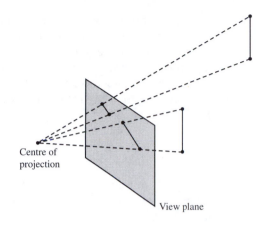

Centre of
projection

View plane

projections, perspective and parallel, are now described. These projections and
the difference in their nature is illustrated in Figure 6.11.

A perspective projection is the more popular or common choice in computer
graphics because it incorporates foreshortening. In a perspective projection relative dimensions are not preserved, and a distant line is displayed smaller than a
nearer line of the same length (Figure 6.12). This effect enables human beings
to perceive depth in a two-dimensional photograph or a stylisation of three-
dimensional reality. A perspective projection is characterised by a point known
as the centre of projection and the projection of three-dimensional points on to
the view plane is the intersection of the lines from each point to the centre of
projection. These lines are called projectors.

Figure 6.13
Deriving a perspective
transformation.

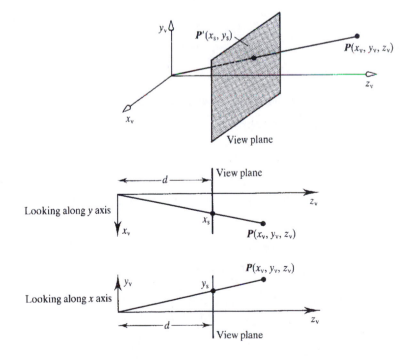

Figure 6.13 shows how a perspective projection is derived. Point P (x_v, y_v, z_v) is a three-dimensional point in the view coordinate system. This point is to be projected onto a view plane normal to the z_v axis and positioned at distance d from the origin of this system. Point P' is the projection of this point in the view plane and has two-dimensional coordinates (x_s, y_s) in a view plane coordinate system with the origin at the intersection of the z_v axis and the viewplane.

Similar triangles give:

$$\frac{x_s}{d} = \frac{x_v}{z_v} \quad \frac{y_s}{d} = \frac{y_v}{z_v}$$

To express this non-linear transformation as a 4×4 matrix we can consider it in two parts – a linear part followed by a non-linear part. Using homogeneous coordinates we have:

$$X = x_v$$
$$Y = y_v$$
$$Z = z_v$$
$$w = z_v / d$$

We can now write

$$\begin{bmatrix} X \\ Y \\ Z \\ w \end{bmatrix} = T_{\text{pers}} \begin{bmatrix} x_v \\ y_v \\ z_v \\ 1 \end{bmatrix}$$

where

$$T_{\text{pers}} = \begin{bmatrix} 1 & 0 & 0 & 0 \\ 0 & 1 & 0 & 0 \\ 0 & 0 & 1 & 0 \\ 0 & 0 & 1/d & 0 \end{bmatrix}$$

Following this with the perspective divide, we have:

$$x_s = X/w$$
$$y_s = Y/w$$
$$z_s = Z/w$$

In a parallel projection, if the view plane is normal to the direction of projection then the projection is orthographic and we have:

$$x_s = x_v \quad y_s = y_v$$

Expressed as a matrix:

$$T_{\text{ort}} = \begin{bmatrix} 1 & 0 & 0 & 0 \\ 0 & 1 & 0 & 0 \\ 0 & 0 & 0 & 0 \\ 0 & 0 & 0 & 1 \end{bmatrix}$$

View volume and depth

We now consider extending the above simple transformations to include the simplified view volume introduced in Figure 6.9. In particular, we discuss in more detail the transformation of the third component of screen space, namely z_s – ignored so far because the derivation of this transformation is somewhat subtle. Now, the bulk of the computation involved in rendering an image takes place in screen space. In screen space polygons are clipped against scan lines and pixels, and hidden surface calculations are performed on these clipped fragments. In order to perform hidden surface calculations (in the Z-buffer algorithm) depth information has to be generated on arbitrary points within the polygon. In practical terms this means, given a line and plane in screen space, being able to intersect the line with the plane, and to interpolate the depth of this intersection point, lying on the line, from the depth of the two end points. This is only a meaningful operation in screen space providing that in moving from eye space to screen space, lines transform into lines and planes transform into planes. It can be shown (Newman and Sproull, 1973) that these conditions are satisfied provided the transformation of z takes the form:

$$z_s = A + B/z_v$$

where A and B are constants. These constants are determined from the following constraints:

(1) Choosing $B < 0$ so that as z_v increases then so does z_s. This preserves our intuitive Euclidean notion of depth. If one point is behind another, then it will have a larger z_v value; if $B < 0$ it will also have a larger z_s value.

(2) An important practical consideration concerning depth is the accuracy to which we store its value. To ensure this is as high as possible we normalise the range of z_s values so that the range $z_v \in [d,f]$ maps into the range $z_s \in [0,1]$

Considering the view volume in Figure 6.9, the full perspective transformation is given by:

$$x_s = d\frac{x_v}{hz_v}, \quad y_s = d\frac{y_v}{hz_v}, \quad z_s = f\frac{(1-d/z_v)}{(f-d)}$$

where the additional constant, h, appearing in the transformation for x_s and y_s, ensures that these values fall in the range $[-1,1]$ over the square screen. Adopting a similar manipulation to Section 6.2.3, we have:

$$X = \frac{d}{h}x_v$$

$$Y = \frac{d}{h}y_v$$

$$Z = \frac{fz_v}{f-d} - \frac{df}{f-d}$$

$$w = z_v$$

giving:

$$\begin{bmatrix} X \\ Y \\ Z \\ w \end{bmatrix} = T_{\text{pers}} \begin{bmatrix} x_v \\ y_v \\ z_v \\ 1 \end{bmatrix}$$

where:

$$T_{\text{pers}} = \begin{bmatrix} d/h & 0 & 0 & 0 \\ 0 & d/h & 0 & 0 \\ 0 & 0 & f/(f-d) & -df/(f-d) \\ 0 & 0 & 1 & 0 \end{bmatrix} \qquad [6.1]$$

We can now express the overall transformation from world space to screen space as a single transformation obtained by concatenating the view and perspective transformation giving:

$$\begin{bmatrix} X \\ Y \\ Z \\ w \end{bmatrix} = T_{\text{pers}} T_{\text{view}} \begin{bmatrix} x_v \\ y_v \\ z_v \\ 1 \end{bmatrix}$$

It is instructive to consider the relationship between z_v and z_s a little more closely; although, as we have seen by construction, they both provide a measure of the depth of a point, interpolating along a line in eye space is not the same as interpolating this line in screen space. Figure 6.14 illustrates this point. Equal intervals in z_v are compared with the corresponding intervals in z_s. As z_v approaches the far clipping plane, z_s approaches 1 more rapidly. Objects in screen space thus get pushed and distorted towards the back of the viewing frustum. This difference can lead to errors when interpolating quantities, other than position, in screen space.

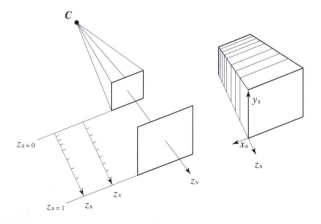

Figure 6.14
Illustrating the distortion in three-dimensional screen space due to the z_v to z_s transformation.

Figure 6.15
Transformation of box and
light rays from eye space to
screen space.

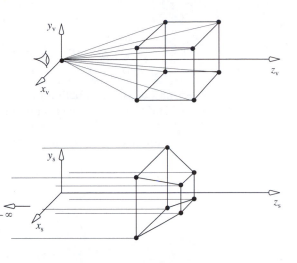

In spite of this difficulty, by its very construction screen space is eminently suited to perform the hidden surface calculation. All rays passing through the viewpoint are now parallel to the z_s axis because the centre of projection has been moved to negative infinity along the z_s axis. This can be seen by putting $z_v = 0$ into the above equation giving $z_s = -\infty$. Making those rays that hit the eye parallel, in screen space, means that hidden surface calculation need only be carried out on those points that have the same (x_s, y_s) coordinates. The test reduces to a simple comparison between z_s values to tell if a point is in front of another. The transformation of a box with one side parallel to the image plane is shown in Figure 6.15. Here, rays from the vertices of the box to the viewpoint become parallel in three-dimensional screen space.

The overall precision required for the screen depth is a function of scene complexity. For most scenes eight bits is insufficient and 16 bits usually suffices. The effects of insufficient precision are easily seen when, for example, a Z-buffer algorithm is used in conjunction with two intersecting objects. If the objects exhibit a curve where they intersect, this will produce aliasing artefacts of increasing severity as the precision of the screen depth is reduced.

Now return to the problem of clipping. It is easily seen from Figure 6.15 that in the homogeneous coordinate representation of screen space the sides of the view volume are parallel. This means that clipping calculations reduce to limit comparisons – we no longer have to substitute points into plane equations. The clipping operations must be performed on the homogeneous coordinates before the perspective divide and translating the definition of the viewing frustum into homogeneous coordinates gives us the clipping limits:

$$-w \leq x \leq w$$
$$-w \leq y \leq w$$
$$0 \leq z \leq w$$

It is instructive also to consider the view space to eye space transformation by splitting equation 6.1 into a product:

$$\boldsymbol{T}_{\text{pers}} = \begin{bmatrix} 1 & 0 & 0 & 0 \\ 0 & 1 & 0 & 0 \\ 0 & 0 & f/(f-d) & -df/(f-d) \\ 0 & 0 & 1 & 0 \end{bmatrix} \begin{bmatrix} d/h & 0 & 0 & 0 \\ 0 & d/h & 0 & 0 \\ 0 & 0 & 1 & 0 \\ 0 & 0 & 0 & 1 \end{bmatrix} = \boldsymbol{T}_{\text{pers2}}\,\boldsymbol{T}_{\text{pers1}}$$

This enables a useful visualisation of the process. The first matrix is a scaling (d/h) in x and y. This effectively converts the view volume from a truncated pyramid with slides sloping at an angle determined by h/d into a regular pyramid with sides sloping at 45° (Figure 6.16). For example, point:

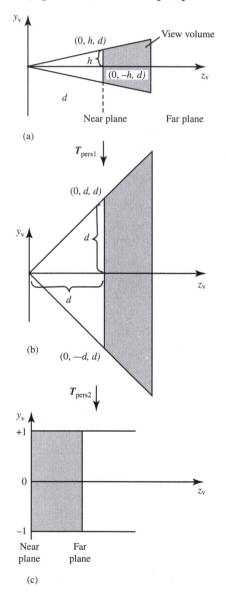

Figure 6.16

Transformation of the view volume into a canonical view volume (a box) using two matrix transformations.

$(0,h,d,1)$ transforms to $(0,d,d,1)$

and point:

$(0,-h,d,1)$ transforms to $(0,-d,d,1)$

The second transformation maps the regular pyramid into a box. The near plane maps into the (x,y) plane and the far plane is mapped into $z = 1$. For example, point:

$(0,d,d,1)$ transforms to $(0,d,0,d)$

which is equivalent to $(0,1,0,1)$.

6.3 Algorithmic operations in the graphics pipeline

We will now describe the algorithmic operations that are required to render a polygon mesh object. We will describe a particular, but common, approach which uses a hidden surface algorithm called the Z-buffer algorithm and which utilises some form of interpolative shading. The advantage of this strategy is that it enables us to fetch individual polygons from the object database in any order. It also means that there is absolutely no upwards limit on scene complexity as far as the polygon count is concerned. The enduring success of this approach is due not only to these factors but also to the visual success of interpolative shading techniques in making the piecewise linear nature of the object almost invisible. Its success is also reflected in its migration into hardware in the form of 3D cards or graphics accelerators. The disadvantage of this approach, which is not without importance, is its inherent inefficiency. Polygons may be rendered to the screen which are subsequently over-written by polygons nearer to the viewer.

In this renderer the processes that we need to perform are rasterisation, or finding the set of pixels onto which a polygon projects, hidden surface removal and shading. We will not consider rasterisation, the final conversion of polygons to pixels, because it is unlikely that any graphics programmer will require knowledge of this low-level technique. To this we add clipping against the view volume, a process that we dealt with briefly as a pure geometric operation in the previous section. In this section we will develop an algorithmic structure that 'encloses' the geometric operation.

As we remarked in the previous section, these processes are mostly carried out in three-dimensional screen space, the innermost loop in the algorithm being a **for each** pixel structure. In other words, the algorithms are known as screen space algorithms. This is certainly not always the case – rendering by ray tracing is mostly a view space algorithm and rendering using the radiosity method is a world space algorithm.

Basic view frustum culling and clipping

We have already considered the principle of culling and clipping in Sections 6.2.1 and 6.2.3 and now we will describe an efficient structure for the task. This section deals with the basic algorithm. View frustum culling in the context of BSP trees and more advanced approaches that use, for example, frame coherence are given in Chapter 9.

In Section 6.2.4 we saw how to determine if a single point was within the view volume. This is an inefficient approach – we need a fast method for evaluating whether an object is wholly outside, wholly inside or straddles the view volume. Clipping has become an extremely important operation with the growth of polygon counts and the demand for real-time rendering. In principle we want to discard as many polygons as possible at an early stage in the rendering pipeline. The two common approaches to avoiding detailed low-level testing are scene management techniques and bounding volumes. (Bounding volumes themselves can be considered a form of scene management.) We will look at using a simple bounding volume – the sphere; other bounding volume techniques for view frustum culling are given in Chapter 9.

It is possible to perform a simple test that will reject objects wholly outside the view volume and accept those wholly within the view volume. This can be achieved by calculating a bounding sphere for an object and testing this against the view volume. The radius of the bounding sphere of an object is a fixed value and this can be pre-calculated and stored as part of the database. When an object is processed by the 3D viewing pipeline, its local coordinate system origin (the bounding sphere we assume is centred on this origin) is also transformed by the pipeline.

If the object is completely outside the view volume it can be discarded; if it is entirely within the view volume it does not need to be clipped. If neither of these conditions applies then it may need to be clipped. We cannot be certain because although the sphere may intersect the view volume the object that it

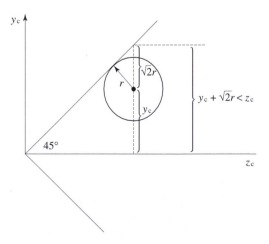

Figure 6.17
Showing one of the conditions for a bounding sphere to lie wholly within the view volume.

contains may not. This problem with bounding objects affects their use through-out computer graphics and it is further examined in Chapter 15 in the context of collision detection.

For a sphere the conditions are easily shown (Figure 6.17) to be:

● completely inside if all following conditions are true

$$z_c > x_c + \sqrt{2}r$$

$$z_c > -x_c + \sqrt{2}r$$

$$z_c > y_c + \sqrt{2}r$$

$$z_c > -y_c + \sqrt{2}r$$

$$z_c > r + n$$

$$z_c > -r + f$$

● completely outside if any of the following conditions apply

$$z_c > x_c - \sqrt{2}r$$

$$z_c > -x_c - \sqrt{2}r$$

$$z_c > y_c - \sqrt{2}r$$

$$z_c > -y_c - \sqrt{2}r$$

$$z_c > -r + n$$

$$z_c > r + f$$

where:

$$\begin{bmatrix} x_c \\ y_c \\ z_c \\ 1 \end{bmatrix} = \begin{bmatrix} d/h & 0 & 0 & 0 \\ 0 & d/h & 0 & 0 \\ 0 & 0 & 1 & 0 \\ 0 & 0 & 0 & 1 \end{bmatrix} \begin{bmatrix} x_v \\ y_v \\ z_v \\ 1 \end{bmatrix}$$

In other words, this operation takes place in the clipping space shown in Figure 6.16.

Objects that need to be clipped can be dealt with by the Sutherland-Hodgman re-entrant polygon clipper (Sutherland *et al.*, 1974). This is easily extended to three dimensions. A polygon is tested against a clip boundary by testing each polygon edge against a single infinite clip boundary. This structure is shown in Figure 6.18.

We consider the innermost loop of the algorithm, where a single edge is being tested against a single clip boundary. In this step the process outputs zero, one or two vertices to add to the list of vertices defining the clipped polygon. Figure 6.19 shows the four possible cases. An edge is defined by vertices **S** and **F**. In the first case the edge is inside the clip boundary and the existing vertex **F** is added to the output list. In the second case the edge crosses the clip boundary and a

Figure 6.18
Sutherland–Hodgman
clipper clips each polygon
against each edge of each
clip rectangle.

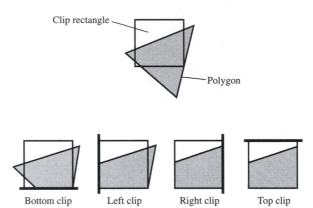

new vertex **I** is calculated and output. The third case shows an edge that is completely outside the clip boundary. This produces no output. (The intersection for the edge that caused the excursion outside is calculated in the previous iteration and the intersection for the edge that causes the incursion inside is calculated in the next iteration.) The final case again produces a new vertex which is added to the output list.

To calculate whether a point or vertex is inside, outside or on the clip boundary we use a dot product test. Figure 6.20 shows a clip boundary **C** with an outward normal $\mathbf{N}_c$ and a line with endpoints **S** and **F**. We represent the line parametrically as:

$$\mathbf{P}(t) = \mathbf{S} + (\mathbf{F} - \mathbf{S})t \qquad [6.2]$$

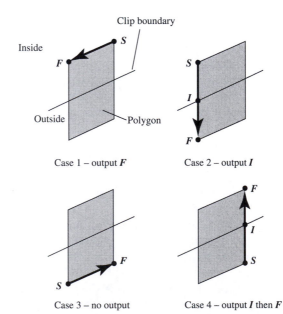

Figure 6.19
Sutherland–Hodgman
clipper – within the polygon
loop each edge of a polygon
is tested against each clip
boundary.

Figure 6.20
Dot product test to determine whether a line is inside or outside a clip boundary.

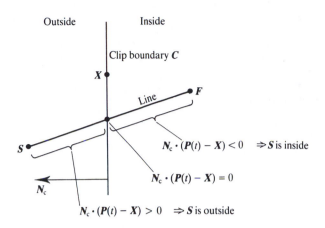

where

$$0 \leq t \leq 1$$

We define an arbitrary point on the clip boundary as X and a vector from X to any point on the line. The dot product of this vector and the normal allows us to distinguish whether a point on the line is outside, inside or on the clip boundary. In the case shown in Figure 6.20:

$$\mathbf{N}_c.(\mathbf{S} - \mathbf{X}) > 0 \Rightarrow \mathbf{S} \text{ is outside the clip region}$$
$$\mathbf{N}_c.(\mathbf{F} - \mathbf{X}) < 0 \Rightarrow \mathbf{F} \text{ is inside the clip region}$$

and

$$\mathbf{N}_c.(\mathbf{P}(t) - \mathbf{X}) = 0$$

defines the point of intersection of the line and the clip boundary. Solving Equation 6.2 for t enables the intersecting vertex to be calculated and added to the output list.

In practice the algorithm is written recursively. As soon as a vertex is output the procedure calls itself with that vertex and no intermediate storage is required for the partially clipped polygon. This structure makes the algorithm eminently suitable for hardware implementation.

6.3.2 Shading pixels

The first quality shading in computer graphics was developed by H. Gouraud (1971). Phong Bui-Tuong (1975) improved on Gouraud's model and Phong shading, as it is universally known, became the *de facto* standard in mainstream 3D graphics. Despite the subsequent development of 'global' techniques, such as ray tracing and radiosity, Phong shading has remained ubiquitous. This is because it enables reality to be mimicked to an acceptable level at reasonable cost.

Currently (2000) 3D cards support Gouraud shading, Phong shading being 5–10 times the cost of Gouraud.

Figure 6.21
Illustrating the difference between local reflection models and shading algorithms. (a) Local reflection models calculate light intensity at any point *P* on the surface of an object. (b) Shading algorithms interpolate pixel values from calculated light intensities at the polygon vertices.

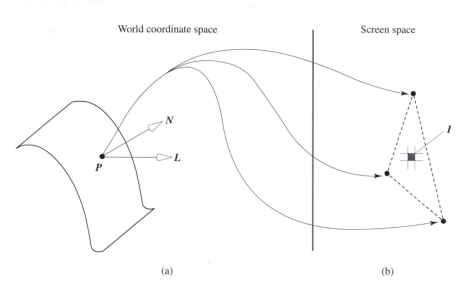

(a)   (b)

There are two separate considerations to shading the pixels onto which a polygon projects. First, we consider how to calculate the light reflected at any point on the surface of an object. Given a theoretical framework that enables us to do this, we can then calculate the light intensity at the pixels onto which the polygon projects. The first consideration we call 'local reflection models' and the second, 'shading algorithms'. The difference is illustrated conceptually in Figure 6.21. For example, one of the easiest approaches to shading – Gouraud shading – applies a local reflection model at each of the vertices to calculate a vertex intensity, then derives a pixel intensity using the same interpolation equations as we used in the previous section to interpolate depth values.

Basically there is a conflict here. We only want to calculate the shade for each pixel onto which the polygon projects. But the reflected light intensity at every point on the surface of a polygon is by definition a world space calculation. We are basing the calculation on the orientation of the surface with respect to a light source both of which are defined in world space. Thus we use a 2D projection of the polygon as the basis of an interpolation scheme that controls the world space calculations of intensity and this is incorrect. Linear interpolation, using equal increments, in screen space does not correspond to how the reflected intensity should vary across the face of the polygon in world space. One of the reasons for this is that we have already performed a (non-affine) perspective transformation to get into screen space. Like many algorithms in 3D computer graphics it produces an acceptable visual result, even using incorrect mathematics. However, this approach does lead to visible artefacts in certain contexts.

Local reflection models

A local reflection model enables the calculation of the reflected light intensity from a point on the surface of an object. The local reflection model used in both

Figure 6.22
(a) A local reflection model calculates intensity at P_b and P_a considering direct illumination only. (b) Any indirect reflected light from A to B or from B to A is not taken into account.

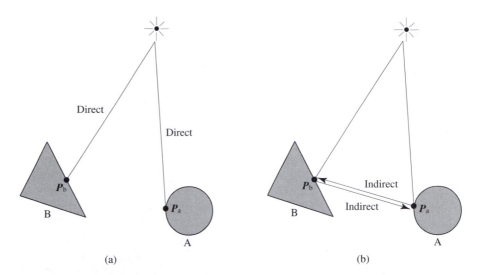

(a)   (b)

Gouraud and Phong shading evaluates the intensity of the reflected light as a function of the orientation of the surface at the point of interest with respect to the position of a point light source and surface properties. We refer to such a model as a local reflection model because it considers only direct illumination. It is as if the object under consideration were an isolated object floating in free space. Interaction with other objects that result in shadows and inter-reflection are not taken into account by local reflection models. This point is emphasised in Figure 6.22.

The physical reflection phenomena that the model simulates are:

- perfect specular reflection;
- imperfect specular reflection;
- perfect diffuse reflection.

These are illustrated in Figure 6.23 for a point light source that is sending an infinitely thin beam of light to a point on a surface. Perfect specular reflection occurs when incident light is reflected, without diverging, in the 'mirror' direction. Imperfect specular reflection is that which occurs when a thin beam of light strikes an imperfect mirror. That is, a surface whose reflecting properties are that of a perfect mirror but only at a microscopic level – because the surface is physically rough. Any area element of such a surface can be considered to be made up of thousands of tiny perfect mirrors all at slightly different orientations. Perfect specular reflection does not occur in practice but we use it in ray tracing models simply because calculating interaction due to imperfect specular reflection is too expensive. A perfect diffuse surface reflects the light equally in all directions and such a surface is usually called matte.

The Phong reflection model considers the reflection from a surface to consist of three components linearly combined:

reflected light = ambient light + diffuse component + specular component

Figure 6.23
The three reflection
phenomena used in
computer graphics. (a)
Perfect specular reflection.
(b) Imperfect specular
reflection. (c) Perfect diffuse
reflection.

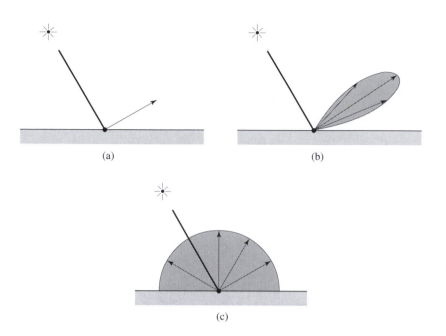

The ambient term is a constant and simulates global or indirect illumination. This term is necessary because parts of a surface that cannot 'see' the light source, but which can be seen by the viewer, need to be lit. Otherwise they would be rendered as black. In reality such lighting comes from global or indirect illumination and simply adding a constant side-steps the complexity of indirect or global illumination calculations.

It is useful to consider what type of surfaces such a model simulates. Linear combination of a diffuse and specular component occurs in polished surfaces such as varnished wood. Specular reflection results from the transparent layer and diffuse reflection from the underlying surface (Figure 6.24). Many different physical types, although not physically the same as a varnished wood, can be approximately simulated by the same model. The veracity of this can be imagined by considering looking at a sample of real varnished wood, shiny plastic and gloss paint. If all contextual clues are removed and the reflected light from each sample exhibited the same spectral distribution, an observer would find it difficult to distinguish amongst the samples.

As well as possessing the limitation of being a local model, this local reflection model is completely empirical or imitative. One of its major defects is that the value of reflected intensity calculated by the model is a function only of the viewing direction and the orientation of the surface with respect to the light source. In practice reflected light intensity exhibits **bi-directional** behaviour. It depends also on the direction of the incident light. This defect has led to much research into physically based reflection models, where an attempt is made to model reflected light by simulating real surface properties. However, the subtle improvements possible by using such models – such as the ability to make surfaces look metallic – have not resulted in the demise of the Phong reflection

Figure 6.24
The 'computer graphics'
surface.

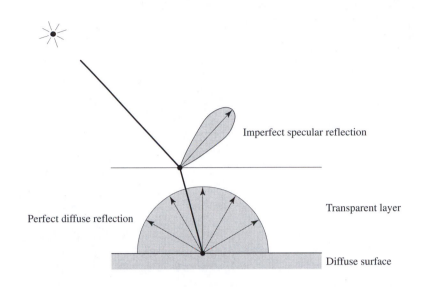

Imperfect specular reflection

Transparent layer

Perfect diffuse reflection

Diffuse surface

model and the main thrust of current research into rendering methods deals with the limitation of 'localness'. Global methods, such as radiosity, result in much more significant improvements to the apparent reality of a scene.

Leaving aside, for a moment, the issue of colour, the physical nature of a surface is simulated by controlling the proportion of the diffuse specular to reflection and we have the reflected light:

$$I = k_a I_a + k_d I_d + k_s I_s$$

where the proportions of the three components, ambient diffuse and specular are controlled by three constants, where:

$$k_a + k_d + k_s = 1$$

Consider I_d. This is evaluated as:

$$I_d = I_i \cos \theta$$

where:

I_i is the intensity of the incident light

θ is the angle between the surface normal at the point of interest and the direction of the light source.

In vector notation

$$I_d = I_i \, (\boldsymbol{L.N})$$

The geometry is shown in Figure 6.25.

Now physically the specular reflection consists of an image of the light source 'smeared' across an area of the surface resulting in what is commonly known as a highlight. A highlight is only seen by a viewer if the viewing direction is near to the mirror direction. We therefore simulate specular reflection by:

Figure 6.25
The Phong diffuse
component.

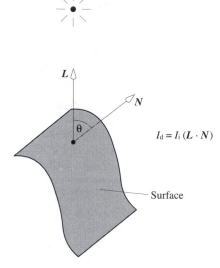

$$I_d = I_i (\boldsymbol{L} \cdot \boldsymbol{N})$$

$$I_s = I_i \cos^n \Omega$$

where:

Ω is the angle between the viewing direction and the mirror direction $\boldsymbol{R}$. n is an index that simulates the degree of imperfection of a surface; when $n = \infty$ the surface is a perfect mirror – all reflected light emerges along the mirror direction. For other values of n an imperfect specular reflector is simulated (Figure 6.23(b))

The geometry of this is shown in Figure 6.26. In vector notation we have:

$$I_s = I_i (\boldsymbol{R}.\boldsymbol{V})^n$$

Bringing these terms together gives:

$$I = k_a I_a + I_i(k_d(\boldsymbol{L}.\boldsymbol{N}) + k_s(\boldsymbol{R}.\boldsymbol{V})^n)$$

The behaviour of this equation is illustrated in Figures 6.27 and 6.28 (Colour Plate). Figure 6.27 shows the light intensity at a single point $\boldsymbol{P}$ as a function of the orientation of the viewing vector $\boldsymbol{V}$. The semicircle is the sum of the constant ambient term and the diffuse term – which is constant for a particular value of $\boldsymbol{N}$. Addition of the specular term gives the profile shown in the figure. As the value of n is increased the specular bump is narrowed. Figure 6.28 (Colour Plate) shows the equation applied to the same object using different values of k_s and k_d and n.

Local reflection models – practical points

A number of practical matters that deal with colour and the simplification of the geometry now need to be explained.

Figure 6.26
The Phong specular
component.

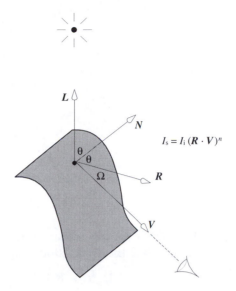

$$I_s = I_i (\boldsymbol{R} \cdot \boldsymbol{V})^n$$

The expense of the above shading equation, which is applied a number of times at every pixel, can be considerably reduced by making geometric simplifications that reduce the calculation time, but which do not affect the quality of the shading. First, if the light source is considered a point source located at infinity, then $\boldsymbol{L}$ is constant over the domain of the scene. Second, we can also place the viewpoint at infinity, making $\boldsymbol{V}$ constant. Of course, for the view and perspective transformation, the viewpoint needs to be firmly located in world space so we end up using a finite viewpoint for the geometric transformations and an infinite one for the shading equation.

Next, the vector $\boldsymbol{R}$ is expensive to calculate and it is easier to define a vector $\boldsymbol{H}$ (halfway) which is the unit normal to a hypothetical surface that is oriented in a direction halfway between the light direction vector $\boldsymbol{L}$ and the viewing vector $\boldsymbol{V}$ (Figure 6.29). It is easily seen that:

$$\boldsymbol{H} = (\boldsymbol{L} + \boldsymbol{V})/2$$

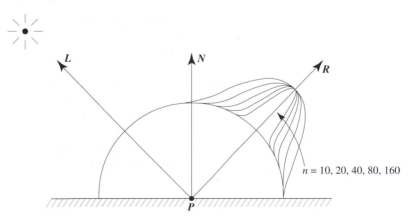

Figure 6.27
The light intensity at point P
as a function of the
orientation of the viewing
vector $\boldsymbol{V}$.

$n = 10, 20, 40, 80, 160$

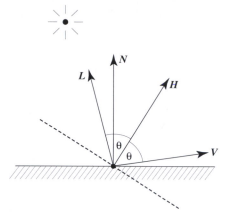

This is the orientation that a surface would require if it were to reflect light maximally along the *V* direction. Our shading equation now becomes

$$I = I_a k_a + I_i(k_d(\boldsymbol{L.N}) + (\boldsymbol{N.H})^n) \tag{6.3}$$

because the term $(\boldsymbol{N.H})$ varies in the same manner as $(\boldsymbol{R.V})$. These simplifications mean that I is now a function only of $\boldsymbol{N}$.

For coloured objects we generate three components of the intensity I_r, I_g and I_b controlling the colour of the objects by appropriate setting of the diffuse reflection coefficients k_{dr}, k_{db} and k_{dg}. In effect the specular highlight is just the reflection of the light source in the surface of the object and we set the proportions of the k_s to match the colour of the light. For a white light, k_s is equal in all three equations. Thus we have:

$$I_r = I_a k_{ar} + I_i(k_{dr}(\boldsymbol{L.N}) + k_s(\boldsymbol{N.H})^n)$$
$$I_g = I_a k_{ag} + I_i(k_{dg}(\boldsymbol{L.N}) + k_s(\boldsymbol{N.H})^n)$$
$$I_b = I_a k_{ab} + I_i(k_{db}(\boldsymbol{L.N}) + k_s(\boldsymbol{N.H})^n)$$

Local reflection models – light source considerations

One of the most limiting approximations in the above model is reducing the light source to a point at infinity. Also, we can see in Figure 6.28 that there is an unsatisfactory confusion concerning the interpretation of the parameter n, which is supposed to give the impression of 'glossiness'. In practice it looks as if we are changing the size of the light source.

A simple directional light (non-point) source is easily modelled and the following was suggested by Warn (1983). In this method a directional light source is modelled in the same way as a specularly reflecting surface, where the light emitted from the source is given by a cosine function raised to a power. Here we assume that for a directional source, the light intensity in a particular direction, given by the angle ϕ is:

$$I_s \cos^m \phi$$

Figure 6.30
Light source represented as a specularly reflecting surface.

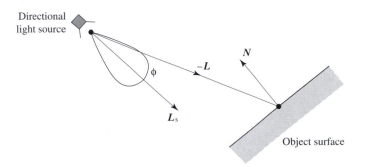

Now ϕ is the angle between $-\boldsymbol{L}$, the direction of the point on the surface that we are considering, and $\boldsymbol{L}_s$, the orientation of the light source (Figure 6.30). The value of I_i that we use in the shading equation is then given by:

$$I_i = I_s(-\boldsymbol{L}.\boldsymbol{L}_s)^m$$

Note that we can no longer consider the vector $\boldsymbol{L}$ constant over the scene.

6.3.3   Interpolative shading techniques

Having dealt with the problem of calculating light intensity at a point, we now consider how to apply such a model to a polygon and calculate the light intensity over its surface. Two classic techniques have emerged – Gouraud and Phong shading. The difference in quality between these two techniques is shown and discussed in the examples in Section 6.4 and we now deal with each separately. Phong interpolation gives the more accurate highlights, as we shall see, and is generally the preferred model. Gouraud shading, on the other hand, is considerably cheaper. Both techniques have been developed both to interpolate information efficiently across the face of a polygon and to diminish the visibility of the polygon edges in the final shaded image. Information is interpolated from values at the vertices of a polygon and the situation is exactly analogous to depth interpolation.

Interpolative shading techniques – Gouraud shading

In Gouraud shading we calculate light intensity, using the local reflection model of the previous section, at the vertices of the polygon and then interpolate between these intensities to find values at projected pixels. To do this we use the bi-linear interpolation equations given in Section 1.4, the property p being the vertex intensity I. The particular surface normals used at a vertex are special normals called vertex normals. If we consider a polygon in isolation then, of course, the vertex normals are all parallel; however, in Gouraud shading we use special normals called vertex normals and it is this device that reduces the visibility of polygon edges. Consider Figure 6.31. Here the vertex normal $\boldsymbol{N}_A$ is calculated by averaging $\boldsymbol{N}_1$, $\boldsymbol{N}_2$, $\boldsymbol{N}_3$ and $\boldsymbol{N}_4$.

Figure 6.31
The vertex normal **N** is the average of the normals N_1, N_2, N_3 and N_4, the normals of the polygon that meet at the vertex.

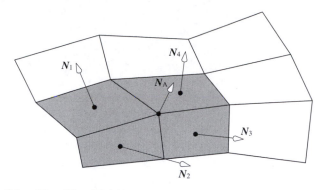

$$N_A = (N_1 + N_2 + N_3 + N_4)/4$$

N_A is then used to calculate an intensity at vertex A that is common to all the polygons that share vertex A.

For computational efficiency the interpolation equations are implemented as incremental calculations. This is particularly important in the case of the third equation, which is evaluated for every pixel. If we define Δx to be the incremental distance along a scan line then ΔI_s, the change in intensity, from one pixel to the next is

$$\Delta I_s = \frac{\Delta x}{x_b - x_a}(I_b - I_a)$$

$$I_{s,n} = I_{s,n-1} + \Delta I_s$$

Because the intensity is only calculated at vertices the method cannot adequately deal with highlights and this is its major disadvantage. The cause of this defect can be understood by examining Figure 6.32(a). We have to bear in mind that the polygon mesh is an approximation to a curved surface. For a particular viewing and light source direction we can have a diffuse component at A and B and a specular highlight confined to some region between them. Clearly if we

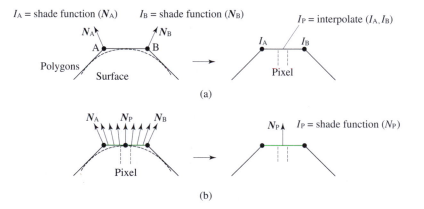

Figure 6.32
Illustrating the difference between Gouraud and Phong shading. (a) Gouraud shading. (b) Phong shading.

are deriving the intensity at pixel P from information at A and B we will not calculate a highlight. This situation is neatly taken care of by interpolating vertex normals rather than intensities as shown in Figure 6.32(b). This approach is known as Phong shading.

Interpolative shading techniques – Phong shading

Here we interpolate vertex normals across the polygon interior and calculate for each polygon pixel projection an interpolated normal. This interpolated normal is then used in the shading equation which is applied for every pixel projection. This has the geometric effect (Figure 6.32) of 'restoring' some curvature to polygonally faceted surfaces.

The price that we pay for this improved model is efficiency. Not only is the vector interpolation three times the cost of intensity interpolation, but each vector has to be normalised and a shading equation calculated for each pixel projection.

Incremental computations can be employed as with intensity interpolation, and the interpolation would be implemented as:

$$N_{sx,n} = N_{sx,n-1} + \Delta N_{sx}$$

$$N_{sy,n} = N_{sy,n-1} + \Delta N_{sy}$$

$$N_{sz,n} = N_{sz,n-1} + \Delta N_{sz}$$

where N_{sx}, N_{sy} and N_{sz} are the components of a general scanline normal vector $\mathbf{N}_s$ and

$$\Delta N_{sx} = \frac{\Delta x}{x_b - x_a} (N_{bx} - N_{ax})$$

$$\Delta N_{sy} = \frac{\Delta x}{x_b - x_a} (N_{by} - N_{ay})$$

$$\Delta N_{sz} = \frac{\Delta x}{x_b - x_a} (N_{bz} - N_{az})$$

Renderer shading options

Most renderers have a hierarchy of shading options where you trade wait time against the quality of the shaded image. This approach also, of course, applies to the addition of shadows and texture. The normal hierarchy is:

(1) **Wireframe** No rendering or shading at all. A wireframe display may be used to position objects in a scene by interacting with the viewing parameters. It is also commonly used in animation systems where an animator may be creating movement of objects in a scene interactively. He or she can

adjust various aspects of the animation and generate a real-time animation sequence in wireframe display mode. In both these applications a full shaded image is obviously not necessary. One practical problem is that using the same overall renderer strategy for wireframe rendering as for shading (that is, independently drawing each polygon) will result in each edge being drawn twice – doubling the draw time for an object.

(2) **Flat shaded polygons** Again a fast option. The single 'true' polygon normal is used, one shade calculated using the Gouraud equation for each polygon, and the shading interpolative process is avoided.

(3) **Gouraud shading** The basic shading option which produces a variation across the face of polygons. Because it cannot deal properly with specular highlights, a Gouraud shading option normally only calculates diffuse reflection.

(4) **Phong shading** The 'standard' quality shading method which, owing to the vector interpolation and the evaluation of a shading equation at every pixel, is 4–5 times slower than Gouraud shading.

(5) **Mixing Phong and Gouraud shading** Consider a diffuse object. Although using Gouraud shading for the object produces a slightly different effect to using Phong shading with the specular reflection coefficient set to zero, the difference is not visually important. This suggests that in a scene consisting of specular and diffuse objects we can use Gouraud shading for the diffuse objects and use Phong shading only for the specular ones. The Gouraud/Phong option then becomes part of the object property data.

These options are compared in some detail in Section 6.4.

Comparison of Gouraud and Phong shading

Gouraud shading is effective for shading surfaces which reflect light diffusely. Specular reflections can be modelled using Gouraud shading, but the shape of the specular highlight produced is dependent on the relative positions of the underlying polygons. The advantage of Gouraud shading is that it is computationally the less expensive of the two models, only requiring the evaluation of the intensity equation at the polygon vertices, and then bi-linear interpolation of these values for each pixel. Phong shading produces highlights which are much less dependent on the underlying polygons. But, more calculations are required involving the interpolation of the surface normal and the evaluation of the intensity function for each pixel. These facts suggest a straightforward approach to speeding up Phong shading by combining Gouraud and Phong shading.

6.3.4 Hidden surface removal

The *de facto* algorithm used for hidden surface removal is, of course, the Z-buffer algorithm. However, just like shadow algorithms it makes sense to study the classic hidden surface removal algorithm. As will become clear, the Z-buffer algorithm has certain serious disadvantages – mainly inefficiency and accuracy – and although it has reigned supreme for at least two decades it may not last forever. It is also the case that there are certain contexts in which alternative approaches are already being used. This is the case with the list priority algorithm, for example, described later. This section, then, will deal with the prominent classic methods, starting with the Z-buffer. An extension of the Z-buffer which is used in conjunction with an octree decomposition of the scene is described in Section 9.9.3.

The major hidden surface removal algorithms are described and classified in an early, but still highly relevant paper by Sutherland *et al.* entitled 'A characterization of ten hidden surface algorithms' (Sutherland *et al.* 1974). In this paper algorithms are characterised as to whether they operate primarily in object space or image (screen) space and the different uses of 'coherence' that the algorithms employ. Coherence is a term used to describe the process where geometrical units, such as areas or scan line segments, instead of single points, are operated on by the hidden surface removal algorithm.

There are many different ways of approaching hidden surface removal. Possibly the most common approaches are scan-line-based systems and Z-buffer-based systems. Other approaches to hidden surface removal such as area subdivision (Warnock, 1969), or depth list schemes (Newell *et al.* 1972) are not particularly popular or are reserved for special purpose applications such as flight simulation. However, we are beginning to see the re-emergence of the depth list algorithms.

The Z-buffer algorithm

The Z-buffer algorithm, developed by Catmull (1975), is as ubiquitous in computer graphics as the Phong reflection model and interpolator, and the combination of these represents the most popular rendering option. Using Sutherland's classification scheme (Sutherland *et al.* 1974), it is an algorithm that operates in image, that is, three-dimensional, screen space.

Pixels in the interior of a polygon are shaded, using an incremental shading scheme, and their depth is evaluated by interpolation from the z values of the polygon vertices after the viewing transformation has been applied. The equations in Section 1.4 are used to interpolate the depth values.

The Z-buffer algorithm is equivalent, for each point (x_s, y_s) to a search through the associated z values of each interior polygon point, to find that point with the minimum z value. This search is conveniently implemented by using a Z-buffer, which holds for a current point (x,y) the smallest z value so far encountered. During the processing of a polygon we either write the intensity of a point (x,y) into the frame buffer, or not, depending on whether the depth z, of the current point, is less than the depth so far encountered as recorded in the Z-buffer.

One of the major advantages of the Z-buffer is that it is independent of object representation form. Although we see it used most often in the context of polygon mesh rendering, it can be used with any representation – all that is required is the ability to calculate a z value for each point on the surface of an object. It can be used in compositing, with separately rendered objects being merged into a multiple object scene using Z-buffer information on each object. A generalisation of this idea embraces the new topic of image-based rendering which we examine in detail in Chapter 19.

The overwhelming advantage of the Z-buffer algorithm is its simplicity of implementation. Its main disadvantage is the amount of memory required for the Z-buffer. The size of the Z-buffer depends on the accuracy to which the depth value of each point (x,y) is to be stored, which is a function of scene complexity; 20–32 bits is usually deemed sufficient (although currently 16 bits is used on low-cost graphics processors) and the scene has to be scaled to this fixed range of z so that accuracy within the scene is maximised. Recall in the previous section that we discussed the compression of z_s values. This means that a pair of distinct points with different z_v values can map into identical z_s values. Note that for frame buffers with less than 24 bits per pixel, say, the Z-buffer will in fact be larger than the frame buffer. In the past, Z-buffers have tended to be part of the main memory of the host processor, but now 3D cards have dedicated Z-buffers.

An interesting use of the Z-buffer is suggested by Foley *et al.* (1989). This involves rendering selected objects but leaving the Z-buffer contents unmodified by such objects. The idea can be applied to interaction where a three-dimensional cursor object can be moved about in a scene. The cursor is the selected object, and when it is rendered in its current position, the Z-buffer is not written to. Nevertheless, the Z-buffer is used to perform hidden surface removal on the object and will move about the scene obscuring some objects and being obscured by others.

Z-buffer and rendering

The Z-buffer imposes no constraints on database organisation (other than those required by the shading interpolation) and in its simplest form can be driven on a polygon by polygon basis, with polygons being presented in any convenient order. This is, of course, the main reason for its implementation in 3D card hardware.

In principle, for each polygon we compute:

(1) the (x,y) value of the interior pixels,

(2) the z depth for each point (x,y), and

(3) the intensity, I, for each point (x,y).

Thus we have three concurrent bi-linear interpolation processes and a triple nested loop. The z values and intensities, I, are available at each vertex and the interpolation scheme for z and I is distributed between the two inner loops of the algorithm.

A by-polygon algorithm with Z-buffer hidden surface removal is as follows:

for *all x,y* **do**
    Z-Buffer[x,y] := maximum_depth

for *each polygon* **do**
    construct an edge list from the polygon edges
    (that is, for each edge, calculate the values
    of x,z and I for each scan line by interpolation
    and store them in the edge list)

    for $y := y_{min}$ **to** y_{max} **do**

        for *each segment in EdgeList[y]* **do**
          get $X_{left}, X_{right}, Z_{left}, Z_{right}, I_{left}, I_{right}$

            for $x := X_{left}$ to X_{right} **do**
            linearly interpolate z and I between
            Z_{left}, Z_{right} *and* I_{left}, I_{right} *respectively*
            if $z < Z\_Buffer[x,y]$ **then**
               Z_Buffer[x,y] := z
               frame_buffer[x,y] := I

The structure of the algorithm reveals the major inefficiency of the method in that shading calculations are performed on hidden pixels which are subsequently overwritten.

If Phong interpolation is used then the final reflection model calculations, which are a function of the interpolated normal, should also appear within the innermost loop; that is, interpolate N rather than I, and replace the last line with:

frame_buffer[x,y] := ShadingFunction(N)

Z-buffer deficiencies

The algorithm exhibits a number of serious problems. First, inefficiency: it results in polygons being rendered which are subsequently overwritten in the frame buffer. This is a problem which can be tolerated or not depending on scene complexity. We deal with this aspect in detail in Section 9.8.

A related problem is the demand made on the speed of the memory itself. This is a problem imposed by the algorithm on the hardware resources. As the demand for increasing spatial resolution increases then so does the demand on the speed of the RAM.

The Z-buffer exhibits a quality problem that results in visual artefacts. As is always the case, visual defects, perhaps tolerable in static imagery, can become quite disturbing when animated. The problem is a consequence of lack of precision (currently 16 bits) which can only be alleviated by increasing the word length. Note also that precision also depends on the distance between the near and far planes (Section 6.2.4), a factor that is, to a certain extent, under control of the programmer. The consequence of lack of precision is rounding errors and for nearly planar polygons a 'random' interchange of priority causing a 'buzzing' effect at the edges. For penetrating polygons the boundary edge 'jaggies' become animated, causing a typical 'crawling' effect.

An important restriction placed on the type of object that can be rendered by a Z-buffer is that transparent objects cannot be dealt with without extra processing. If polygons are sent down the pipeline in any order then a partially transparent polygon may:

(1) be completely covered by an opaque nearer polygon, in which case there is no problem, or

(2) be the nearest polygon, in which case a list of all polygons behind it must be maintained so that an appropriate combination of the transparent polygon and the next nearest can be computed. (The next nearest polygon is not of course known until all polygons are processed.)

In this event, either the 3D card will support translucent polygons, in which case it will alter the order in which you send the polygons, or the programmer has to arrange for the translucent polygons to be depth sorted and sent after the opaque ones.

Scan line Z-buffer

There is a variation of the Z-buffer algorithm for use with scan-line-based renderers, known (not suprisingly) as a scan line Z-buffer. This is simply a Z-buffer which is only one pixel high, and is used to solve the hidden surface problem for a given scan line. It is reinitialised for each new scan line. Its chief advantage lies in the small amount of memory it requires relative to a full-blown Z-buffer; and it is common to see a scan line Z-buffer based program running on systems which do not have sufficient memory to support a full Z-buffer.

Spanning hidden surface removal

A spanning hidden surface removal algorithm attempts, for each scan line, to find 'spans' across which shading can be performed. The hidden surface removal problem is thus solved by dividing the scan line into lengths over which a single surface is dominant. This means that shading calculations are performed only once per pixel, removing the basic inefficiency inherent in the Z-buffer method. Set against this is the problem that spans do not necessarily correspond to polygon segments, making it harder to perform incremental shading calculations (the start values must be calculated at an arbitrary point along a polygon segment, rather than being set to the values at the left-hand edge). The other major drawback is in the increase in complexity of the algorithm itself, as will be seen.

It is generally claimed that spanning algorithms are more efficient than Z-buffer-based algorithms, except for very large numbers of polygons (Foley *et al.*

(1989) and Sutherland *et al.* (1974)). However, since extremely complex scenes are now becoming the norm, it is becoming clear that overall, the Z-buffer is more efficient, unless a very complex shading function is being used.

A spanning scan line algorithm

The basic idea, as has been mentioned, is that rather than solving the hidden surface problem on a pixel by pixel basis using incremental z calculation, the spanning scan line algorithm uses spans along the scan line over which there is no depth conflict. The hidden surface removal process uses coherence in x and deals in units of many pixels. The processing implication is that a sort in x is required for each scan line and the spans have to be evaluated.

The easiest way to see how a scan line algorithm works is to consider the situation in three-dimensional screen space (x_s, y_s, z_s). A scan line algorithm effectively moves a scan line plane, that is a plane parallel to the (x_s, z_s) plane, down the y_s axis. This plane intersects objects in the scene and reduces the hidden surface problem to two-dimensional space (x_s, z_s). Here the intersection of the scan line plane with object polygons become lines (Figure 6.33). These line segments are then compared to solve the hidden surface problem by considering 'spans'. A span is that part of a line segment that is contained between the edge intersections of all active polygons. A span can be considered a coherence unit, within whose extent the hidden surface removal problem is 'constant' and can be solved by depth comparisons at either end of the span. Note that a more complicated approach has to be taken if penetrating polygons are allowed.

It can be seen from this geometric overview that the first stage in a spanning scan line algorithm is to sort the polygon edges by y_s vertex values. This results in an active edge list which is updated as the scan line moves down the y_s axis.

Figure 6.33
A scan line is moved down through the scene producing line segments and spans.

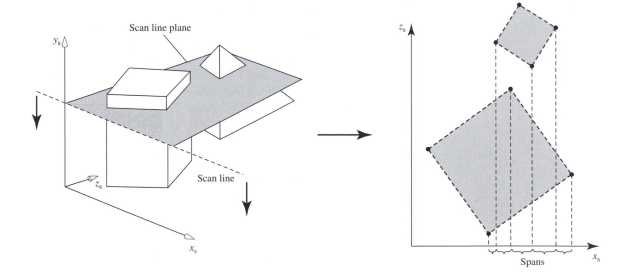

Figure 6.34
Processing spans.

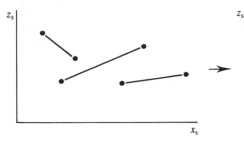

Active line segments produce span boundaries

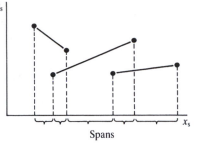

Which are used to subdivide a line

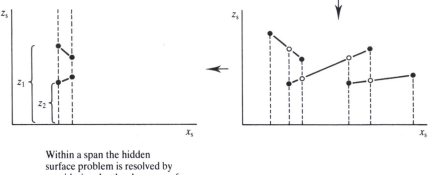

Within a span the hidden
surface problem is resolved by
considering depths along one of
the span boundaries.

If penetrating polygons are not allowed, then each edge intersection with the current scan line specifies a point on the scan line where 'something is changing', and so these collectively define all the span boundary points.

By going through the active edge list in order, it is possible to generate a set of line segments, each of which represents the intersection of the scan line plane with a polygon. These are then sorted in order of increasing x_s.

The innermost loop then processes each span in the current scan line. Active line segments are clipped against span boundaries and are thus subdivided by these boundaries. The depth of each subdivided segment is then evaluated at one of the span boundaries and hidden surface removal is effected by searching within a span for the closest subdivided segment. This process is shown in Figure 6.34.

In pseudo-code the algorithm is:

for *each polygon* **do**

> *Generate and bucket sort in y_s the polygon edge information.*

for *each scanline* **do**

> **for** *each active polygon* **do**

> *Determine the segment or intersection of the*

scan plane and polygon.
Sort these active segments in x_s.

Update the rate of change per scan line of the
shading parameters.

Generate the span boundaries.

for *each span* ***do***

Clip active segments to span boundaries.

Evaluate the depth for all clipped segments
at one of the span boundaries.

Solve the hidden surface problem
for the span with minimum z_s.

Shade the visible clipped line segment.

Update the shading parameters for all
other line segments by the rate of change
per pixel times the span width.

Note that integrating shading information is far more cumbersome than with the Z-buffer. Records of values at the end of clipped line segments have to be kept and updated. This places another scene complexity overhead (along with the absolute number of polygons overhead) on the efficiency and memory requirements of the process.

Depth sorting

An early (and obvious idea) was to sort polygons in depth order according to the value of z_v, the distance of the polygon from the viewpoint. This algorithm is now being used again for pre-computation approaches in complex scenes. Its integration into such methods is described in Section 9.3. If the polygons do not overlap in depth (Figure 6.35.(a)) then the procedure is completed. In general a polygon P will overlap in depth a set of polygons {q} that are above it on the list (Figure 6.35(b)). In this case the members of {q} are compared with P to check that P does *not* obscure any member of {q}. Obscure means an overlap in the (x, y)

Figure 6.35
Illustrating the concept of overlaps in z and (x, y) in the Newell, Newell and Sancha sorting algorithm. (a) Polygons do not overlap in z. (b) Q is nearer than P, giving order QP. Correct order is PQ. (c) Full overlap test required to indicate that P does not obscure Q in (x,y).

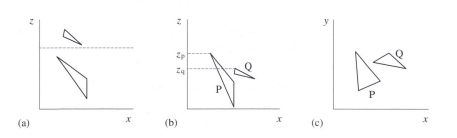

plane. If there exists a polygon Q in {q} that is obscured by P, then Q should have lower priority than P and they are swapped. P does *not* obscure Q is true if any one of the following conditions (listed in order of increasing expense) hold:

(1) A depth minimax test indicates that P and Q do not overlap in depth and Q is closer to the viewpoint than P. A minimax box is what is now known as an AABB – or at least a two-dimensional version of one (Section 15.3) – and is a rectangle enclosing the polygon in the (x,z) plane.

(2) A minimax test in the (x,y) plane indicates that P and Q do not overlap.

(3) All vertices of P are farther from the viewpoint than the plane of Q.

(4) All vertices of Q are closer to the viewpoint than the plane of P.

(5) A full overlap test between P and Q indicates that P and Q do not overlap in x or y (as shown in Figure 6.35(c)).

This basic algorithm needs enhancing to cater for the cases of non-convex objects where P can overlap Q and Q can overlap P. In these cases the plane of one polygon is used to split the other into two. The priority order that emerges from this algorithm is with respect to a specific viewpoint but remains unaltered for a viewpoint moving parallel with the z axis. Note the similarity between this approach and the one described in Section 9.5.2 where the partitioning planes lie in the face of a polygon and in general split other polygons.

6.4 Rendering examples

We complete this chapter with a series of illustrations showing the standard cost/image quality trade-off used in mainstream shading of polygon mesh objects. Low-quality images are used to preview and tune work.

6.4.1 Figure 6.36 (Colour Plate)

An office scene, together with a wireframe visualisation, that has been shaded using the constant ambient term only.

6.4.2 Figure 6.37 (Colour Plate)

The same scene using flat shading. Flat shading shows the polygonal nature of the surfaces due to discontinuities in intensity.

6.4.3 Figure 6.38 (Colour Plate)

The office scene with Gouraud shading.

There are three highly visible defects in shaded imagery that use interpolative techniques. The first always occurs in Gouraud shaded imagery and is called Mach banding. This is almost impossible to reproduce in a text (but is usually visible on a monitor) and we will restrict ourselves to a description. If we consider the light intensity profile across the surface of a polygon mesh object then this will be piecewise linear as shown in Figure 6.39 (Colour Plate). When the surface is viewed on the screen the human visual system sees bands or lines on the surface that correspond to the polygon edges. These do not physically exist but are the response of low-level processing in the retina to the piecewise linear changes in the light intensity. They appear as faint but still discernible bands that appear to exhibit a lighter intensity than the surrounding surface. (They also appear in radiosity images that use Gouraud style interpolation to calculate the final projected image.)

Interpolation defects in Gouraud shading manifest as unwanted changes in light intensity across a surface. This problem is clearly visible in Figure 6.38 on the wall adjacent to the door. Here the discontinuities occur on scan lines as the edges that are being used in the interpolation switch (see Section 1.4 for the interpolation equations used to produce this illustration). This can be solved by subdividing the large polygon into triangles – in other words, we have to sample the geometry more accurately; we cannot necessarily map large flat areas into single polygons without considering the consequences in the renderer.

6.4.4

Figure 6.40 (Colour Plate)

This is the same scene using Phong shading.

A glaring defect in Phong interpolation is demonstrated in this figure. Here the reflected light from the wall light and the image of the light have become separated due to the nature of the interpolation. In this case, to calculate the reflection we have interpolated using equal steps along a scan line in screen space. However, the image of the light appears in a different position because this has been mapped from world space using a perspective projection. In other words, the screen space projection treats as equal pixel units along the wall but these do not correspond to equal length units in world space. This problem, and others that occur when we try to include a light source as part of the scene, is a motivation for excluding lights from rendered scenes. Consider the spherical light. Treating it as a shaded object doesn't quite work. In this case the point light source is inside the surrounding sphere and cannot by definition illuminate it. The light object can only get illumination from the wall light and we can turn up the ambient component for the point light to make it look more like a source.

6.4.5

Figure 6.41 (Colour Plate)

Stylised rendering – called non-photorealistic rendering (or NPR) in the computer graphics world – has been a research topic for a number of years. The motivation is to imitate the stylisations that artists adopt in different media, such as pen and ink work, where, for example, various hatching patterns are employed. In computer games there has been recent interest in imitating the look of film cartoons where cells are painted with opaque colour. In this section we look at a simple look-up table transformation that can approximate this look.

This is an approach that was first reported in Bass (1981) (which appears to have been rediscovered recently (Landers, 2000)) and involves simply using the dot product $N.L$ as an index into a LUT which maps the normal variation of this product over a range of surface normal orientations into a piecewise linear function. If this function is, for example, a step function then only two colour values are stored in the LUT. The final result is then exactly equivalent to per pixel thresholding. However, this expense can be avoided by considering the LUT as a one-dimensional texture map and using texture mapping hardware. Clearly the mapping function stored in the LUT can be adjusted to give different effects.

For a two-value step function we have an object flat shaded with an abrupt transition from a light into a dark region. To complete the cartoon effect we need to draw a dark line around the light region and for this we need silhouette edge detection. The most straightforward way to do this is to calculate the dot product of the two face normals that share an edge with the view vector:

if $(N_1 \cdot V)*(N_2.V) < 0$ then   the edge shared by face$_1$ and face$_2$
                                            is a silhouette edge

This implies at run time we need to examine all edges of an object. This can be facilitated by pre-processing the object data and setting up a list of edges as:

   2 vertex numbers that define the edge
   2 face numbers that define the faces meeting at the edge

We then supply the above faces to the run time processes.

Classic mapping techniques

7.1 Introduction

7.2 Two-dimensional texture maps to polygon mesh objects

7.3 Two-dimensional texture domain to bi-cubic parametric patch objects

7.4 Bump mapping

7.5 Environment or reflection mapping

7.6 Three-dimensional texture domain techniques

7.7 Comparative examples

7.1 Introduction

In this chapter we will look at techniques which store information (usually) in a two-dimensional domain which is used during rendering to simulate textures. The mainstream application is texture mapping but many other applications are described such as reflection mapping to simulate ray tracing. Texture mapping, like much of polygon mesh rendering, has migrated into hardware. This development has also enabled lighting for static objects to be pre-calculated as a special texture map known as a light map. Light map technology is described in detail in Chapter 10. In this chapter we will look at the theory of mapping techniques.

Texture mapping became a highly developed tool in the 1980s and was the technique used to enhance Phong-shaded scenes so that they were more visually interesting, looked more realistic or esoteric. Objects that are rendered using only Phong shading look plastic-like and texture mapping is the obvious way to add interest without much expense.

In mainstream computer graphics, texture mapping developed in parallel with research into global illumination algorithms – ray tracing and radiosity. It was a device that could be used to enhance the visual interest of a scene, rather than its photo-realism, and its main attraction was cheapness – it could be grafted onto a standard rendering method without adding too much to the processing cost. This contrasted to the global illumination methods which used completely different algorithms and were much more expensive than direct reflection models.

Another use of texture mapping that became ubiquitous in the 1980s was to add pseudo-realism to shiny animated objects by causing their surrounding environment to be reflected in them. Thus tumbling logos and titles became chromium and the texture reflected on them moved as the objects moved. This technique – known as environment mapping – can also be used with a real photographed environment and can help to merge a computer-animated object with a real environment. Environment mapping does not accomplish anything that could not be achieved by ray tracing – but it is much more efficient. A more recent use of environment map techniques is in image-based rendering which is discussed in Chapter 19.

As used in computer graphics, 'texture' is a somewhat confusing term and generally does not mean controlling the small-scale geometry of the surface of a computer graphics object – the normal meaning of the word. It is easy to modulate the colour of a shaded object by controlling the value of the three diffuse coefficients and this became the most common object parameter to be controlled by texture mapping. (Colour variations in the physical world are not, of course, generally regarded as texture.) Thus as the rendering proceeds at pixel by pixel level, we pick up values for the Phong diffuse reflection coefficients and the diffuse component (the colour) of the shading changes as a function of the texture map(s). A better term is colour mapping and this appears to be coming into common usage.

This simple pixel-level operation conceals many difficulties and the geometry of texture mapping is not straightforward. As usual we make simplifications that lead to a visually acceptable solution. There are three origins to the difficulties:

(1) We mostly want to use texture mapping with the most popular representation in computer graphics – the polygon mesh representation. This, as we know, is a geometric representation where the object surface is approximated, and this approximation is only defined at the vertices. In a sense we have no surface – only an approximation to one – so how can we physically derive a texture value at a surface point if the surface does not exist?

(2) We want to use, in the main, two-dimensional texture maps because we have an almost endless source of textures that we can derive from frame grabbing the real world, by using two-dimensional paint software or by generating textures procedurally. Thus the mainstream demand is to map a two-dimensional texture onto a surface that is approximated by a polygon mesh. This situation has become consolidated with the advent of cheap texture mapping hardware facilities.

(3) Aliasing problems in texture mapping are usually highly visible. By definition textures usually manifest some kind of coherence or periodicity. Aliasing breaks this up and the resulting mess is usually highly visible. This effect occurs as the periodicity in the texture approaches the pixel resolution.

We now list the possible ways in which certain properties of a computer graphics model can be modulated with variations under control of a texture map. We have listed these in approximate order of their popularity (which also tends to relate to their ease of use or implementation). These are:

(1) **Colour**   As we have already pointed out, this is by far the most common object property that is controlled by a texture map. We simply modulate the diffuse reflection coefficients in the local reflection model with the corresponding colour from the texture map.

(2) **Specular 'colour'**   This technique, known as environment mapping or chrome mapping, is a special case of ray tracing where we use texture map techniques to avoid the expense of full ray tracing. The map is designed so that it looks as if the (specular) object is reflecting the environment or background in which it is placed.

(3) **Normal vector perturbation**   This elegant technique applies a perturbation to the surface normal according to the corresponding value in the map. The technique is known as **bump mapping** and was developed by a famous pioneer of three-dimensional computer graphic techniques – J. Blinn. The device works because the intensity that is returned by a Phong shading equation reduces, if the appropriate simplifications are made to a function of the surface normal at the point currently being shaded. If the surface normal is perturbed then the shading changes and the surface that is rendered looks as if it was textured. We can therefore use a global or general definition for the texture of a surface which is represented in the database as a polygon mesh structure. The games industry has developed a number of efficient algorithms for this classic technique (see, for example, Section 7.4.1).

(4) **Displacement mapping**   Related to the previous technique, this mapping method uses a height field to perturb a surface point along the direction of its surface normal. It is not a convenient technique to implement since the map must perturb the geometry of the model rather than modulate parameters in the shading equation.

(5) **Transparency**   A map is used to control the opacity of a transparent object. A good example is etched glass where a shiny surface is roughened (to cause opacity) with some decorative pattern.

To start with, we will restrict the discussion to two-dimensional texture maps – the most popular and common form – used in conjunction with polygon mesh objects. (Many of the insights detailed in this section are based on descriptions in Heckbert's defining work in this area (Heckbert, 1986).

Mapping a two-dimensional texture map onto the surface of an object then projecting the object into screen space is a two-dimensional to two-dimensional transformation and can thus be viewed as an image warping operation. The most common way to do this is to inverse map – for each pixel we find its corresponding 'pre-image' in texture space (Figure 7.1(b)). However, for reasons that will

Figure 7.1

Two ways of viewing the process of two-dimensional texture mapping.
(a) Forward mapping.
(b) Inverse mapping.

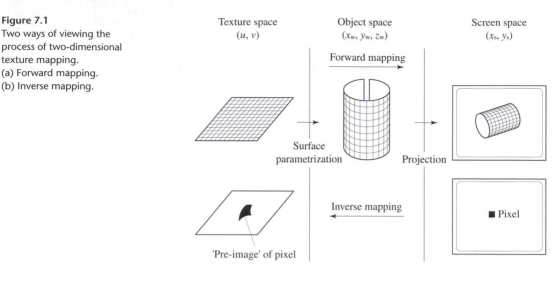

shortly become clear, specifying this overall transformation is not straightforward and we consider initially that texture mapping is a two-stage process that takes us from the two-dimensional texture space into the three-dimensional space of the object and then via the projective transform into two-dimensional screen space (Figure 7.1(a)). The first transformation is known as parametrisation and the second stage is the normal computer graphics projective transformation. The parametrisation associates all points in texture space with points on the object surface.

The real-time implementation of texture mapping is analogous to the way in which lighting (of static objects) is dealt with in games. Part of it is a pre-calculation and part is a real-time (hardware based) operation. The pre-calculation involves associating a (u,v) texture coordinate with each polygon mesh vertex in the object, and the real-time part is reduced to, for each pixel, fetching the corresponding $T(u,v)$ value from the texture map.

7.2 Two-dimensional texture maps to polygon mesh objects

The most popular practical strategy for texture mapping is to associate, during the modelling phase, texture space coordinates (u,v) with polygon vertices. This can, and very often is, set up manually by the artist at the modelling stage. Alternatively it can be calculated using, say, the algorithm described in Section 7.2.2. The task of the rendering engine then is to find the appropriate (u,v) coordinate for pixels internal to each polygon. The main problem comes about because the geometry of a polygon mesh is only defined at the vertices – in other words, there is no analytical parametrisation possible. (If the object has an analytical definition – a cylinder, for example – then we have a parametrisation and the mapping of the texture onto the object surface is trivial.)

There are two main algorithm structures possible in texture mapping, inverse mapping (the more common) and forward mapping. (Heckbert refers to these as screen order and texture order algorithms respectively.) Inverse mapping (Figure 7.1(b)) is where the algorithm is driven from screen space and for every pixel we find by an inverse mapping its 'pre-image' in texture space. For each pixel we find its corresponding (u,v) coordinates. A filtering operation integrates the information contained in the pre-image and assigns the resulting colour to the pixel. This algorithm is advantageous if the texture mapping is to be incorporated into a Z-buffer algorithm where the polygon is rasterised and depth and lighting interpolated on a scan line basis. The square pixel produces a curvilinear quadrilateral as a pre-image.

In forward mapping the algorithm is driven from texture space. This time a square texel in texture space produces a curvilinear quadrilateral in screen space and there is a potential problem due to holes and overlaps in the texture image when it is mapped into screen space. Forward mapping is like considering the texture map as a rubber sheet – stretching it in a way (determined by the parametrisation) so that it sticks on the object surface.

7.2.1   Inverse mapping by bi-linear interpolation

Although forward mapping is easy to understand, in practical algorithms inverse mapping is preferred and we will only consider this strategy for polygon mesh objects. For inverse mapping it is convenient to consider a single (compound) transformation from two-dimensional screen space (x,y) to two-dimensional texture space (u,v). This is just an image warping operation and it can be modelled as a rational linear projective transform:

$$x = \frac{au + bv + c}{gu + hu + i} \qquad y = \frac{du + ev + f}{gu + hv + i} \qquad\qquad [7.1]$$

This is, of course, a non-linear transformation as we would expect.

Alternatively we can write this in homogeneous coordinates as:

$$\begin{bmatrix} x' \\ y' \\ w \end{bmatrix} = \begin{bmatrix} a & b & c \\ d & e & f \\ g & h & i \end{bmatrix} \begin{bmatrix} u' \\ v' \\ q \end{bmatrix}$$

where:

$$(x,y) = (x'/w, y'/w) \quad \text{and} \quad (u,v) = (u'/q, v'/q)$$

This is known as a rational linear transformation. The inverse transform – the one of interest to us in practice is given by:

$$\begin{bmatrix} u' \\ v' \\ q \end{bmatrix} = \begin{bmatrix} A & B & C \\ D & E & F \\ G & H & I \end{bmatrix} \begin{bmatrix} x' \\ y' \\ w \end{bmatrix}$$

$$= \begin{bmatrix} ei - fh & ch - bi & bf - ce \\ fg - di & ai - cg & cd - af \\ dh - eg & bg - ah & ae - bd \end{bmatrix} \begin{bmatrix} x' \\ y' \\ w \end{bmatrix}$$

Now recall that in most practical texture mapping applications we set up, during the modelling phase, an association between polygon mesh vertices and texture map coordinates. So, for example, if we have the association for the four vertices of a quadrilateral we can find the nine coefficients (a,b,c,d,e,f,g,h,i). We thus have the required inverse transform for any point within the polygon. This is done as follows. Return to the first half of Equation 7.1, the equation for x. Note that we can multiply top and bottom by an arbitrary non-zero scalar constant without changing the value of y – in effect we only have 5 degrees of freedom, not 6, and because of this we can, without loss of generality, set $i = 1$. Thus in the overall transformation we only have eight coefficients to determine and our quadrilateral to quadrilateral association will give a set of eight equations in eight unknowns which can be solved by any standard algorithm for linear equations – Gaussian elimination, for example. Although this can be done as a pre-process, we still have to store eight coefficients for each polygon and the inverse transform is relatively expensive. Full details of this procedure are given in Heckbert (1986).

A better practical alternative is to achieve the same effect by bi-linear interpolation in screen space. So we interpolate the texture coordinates at the same time as interpolating lighting and depth. However, we note from the above that it is the homogeneous coordinates (u',v',q) that we have to interpolate, because the u and v do not change linearly with x and y.

Assuming vertex coordinate/texture coordinate for all polygons we consider each vertex to have homogeneous texture coordinates:

$$(u',v',q)$$

where: $u = u'/q$ $v = v'/q$ $q = 1/z$

We interpolate using the normal bi-linear interpolation scheme within the polygon (Section 1.4), using these homogeneous coordinates as vertices to give (u',v',q) for each pixel; then the required texture coordinates are given by:

$$(u,v) = (u'/q,v'/q)$$

Note that this costs two divides per pixel. For the standard incremental implementation of this interpolation process we need three gradients down each edge (in the current edge-pair) and three gradients for the current scan line.

7.2.2

Inverse mapping by using an intermediate surface

The previous method for mapping two-dimensional textures is now undoubtedly the most popular approach. The method we now describe can be used in applications where there is no texture coordinate/vertex coordinate correspondence. Alternatively it can be used as a pre-process to determine this correspondence if this is to be calculated rather than set up manually by an artist.

Two-part texture mapping is a technique that overcomes the surface parametrisation problem in polygon mesh objects by using an 'easy' intermediate surface onto which the texture is initially projected. Introduced by Bier and Sloan, (1986), the method can also be used to implement environment mapping and is thus a method that unifies texture mapping and environment mapping.

The process is known as two-part mapping because the texture is mapped onto an intermediate surface before being mapped onto the object. The intermediate surface is in general non-planar but it possesses an analytic mapping function and the two-dimensional texture is mapped onto this surface without difficulty. Finding the correspondence between the object point and the texture point then becomes a three-dimensional to three-dimensional mapping.

The basis of the method is most easily described as a two-stage forward mapping process (Figure 7.2):

(1) The first stage is a mapping from two-dimensional texture space to a simple three-dimensional intermediate surface such as a cylinder.

$$T(u,v) \rightarrow T'(x_i,y_i,z_i)$$

This is known as the S mapping.

(2) A second stage maps the three-dimensional texture pattern onto the object surface.

$$T'(x_i,y_i,z_i) \rightarrow O(x_w,y_w,z_w)$$

This is referred to as the O mapping.

These combined operations can distort the texture pattern onto the object in a 'natural' way; for example, one variation of the method is a 'shrink wrap' mapping, where the planar texture pattern shrinks onto the object in the manner suggested by the eponym.

For the S mapping Bier describes four intermediate surfaces: a plane at any orientation, the curved surface of a cylinder, the faces of a cube and the surface of a sphere. Although it makes no difference mathematically, it is useful to consider that $T(u,v)$ is mapped onto the interior surfaces of these objects. For example, consider the cylinder. Given a parametric definition of the curved surface of a

Figure 7.2
Two-stage mapping as a forward process. (a) S mapping. (b) O mapping.

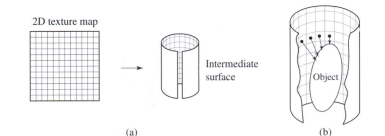

(a)   (b)

cylinder as a set of points (θ,h), we transform the point (u,v) onto the cylinder as follows. We have:

$$S_{\text{cylinder}}: (\theta,h) \rightarrow (u,v)$$

$$= \left(\frac{r}{c} (\theta - \theta_0), \frac{1}{d} (h - h_0) \right)$$

where c and d are scaling factors and θ_0 and h_0 position the texture on the cylinder of radius r.

Various possibilities occur for the O mapping where the texture values for $O(x_w,y_w,z_w)$ are obtained from $T'(x_i,y_i,z_i)$, and these are best considered from a ray tracing point of view. The four O mappings are shown in Figure 7.3 and are:

(1) The intersection of the reflected view ray with the intermediate surface, T'. (This is in fact identical to environment mapping described in Section 7.5. The only difference between the general process of using this O mapping and environment mapping is that the texture pattern that is mapped onto the intermediate surface is a surrounding environment like a room interior.)

(2) The intersection of the surface normal at (x_w,y_w,z_w) with T'.

(3) The intersection of a line through (x_w,y_w,z_w) and the object centroid with T'.

(4) The intersection of the line from (x_w,y_w,z_w) to T' whose orientation is given by the surface normal at (x_i,y_i,z). If the intermediate surface is simply a plane then this is equivalent to considering the texture map to be a slide in a slide projector. A bundle of parallel rays of light from the slide projector impinges on

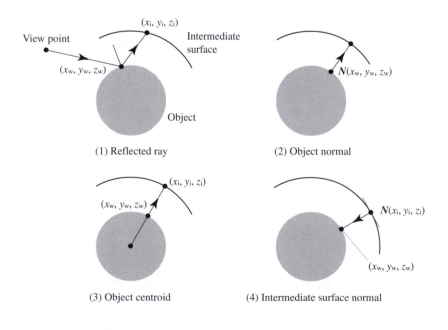

Figure 7.3
The four possible O mappings that map the intermediate surface texture T' onto the object.

(1) Reflected ray

(2) Object normal

(3) Object centroid

(4) Intermediate surface normal

Figure 7.4
Inverse mapping using the shrinkwrap method.

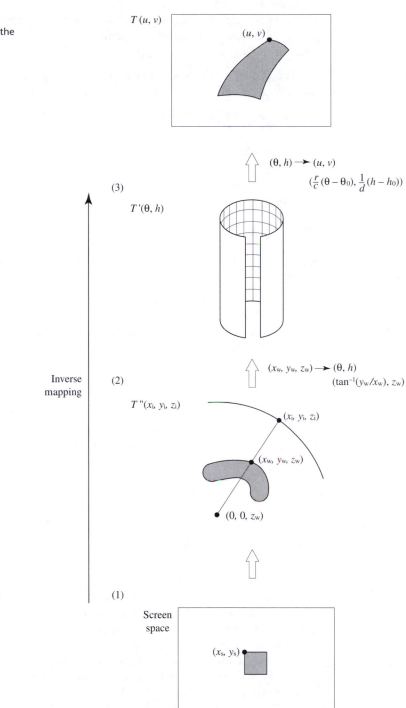

$T(u, v)$

(u, v)

$(\theta, h) \longrightarrow (u, v)$

$(\frac{r}{c}(\theta - \theta_0), \frac{1}{d}(h - h_0))$

(3)

$T'(\theta, h)$

$(x_w, y_w, z_w) \longrightarrow (\theta, h)$

$(\tan^{-1}(y_w/x_w), z_w)$

Inverse mapping

(2)

$T''(x_i, y_i, z_i)$

(x_i, y_i, z_i)

(x_w, y_w, z_w)

$(0, 0, z_w)$

(1)

Screen space

(x_s, y_s)

the object surface. Alternatively it is also equivalent to three-dimensional texture mapping (Section 7.6) where the field is defined by 'extruding' the two-dimensional texture map along an axis normal to the plane of the pattern.

Let us now consider this procedure as an inverse mapping process for the shrink wrap case. We break the process into three stages (Figure 7.4).

(1) Inverse map four pixel points to four points (x_w, y_w, z_w) on the surface of the object.

(2) Apply the O mapping to find the point (θ, h) on the surface of the cylinder. In the shrinkwrap case we simply join the object point to the centre of the cylinder and the intersection of this line with the surface of the cylinder gives us (x_i, y_i, z_i).

$$x_w, y_w, z_w \rightarrow (\theta, h)$$
$$= (\tan^{-1}(y_w/z_w), z_w)$$

(3) Apply the S mapping to find the point (u, v) corresponding to (θ, h).

Figure 7.5 (Colour Plate) shows examples of mapping the same texture onto an object using different intermediate surfaces. The intermediate objects are a plane (equivalently no intermediate surface – the texture map is a plane), a cylinder and a sphere. The simple shape of the vase was chosen to illustrate the different distortions that each intermediate object produces. There are two points that can be made from these illustrations. First, you can choose an intermediate mapping that is appropriate to the shape of the object. A solid of revolution may be best suited, for example, to a cylinder. Second, although the method does not place any constraints on the shape of the object, the final visual effect may be deemed unsatisfactory. Usually what we mean by texture does not involve the texture pattern being subject to large geometric distortions. It is because of this reason that many practical methods are interactive and involve some strategy like pre-distorting the texture map in two-dimensional space until it produces a good result when it is stuck onto the object.

Practical texture mapping

We now look at some simple practical devices used in games. Figure 7.6 (Colour Plate) is an example of an interface for a texture modelling program where an artist can interactively adjust the texture by dragging (u, v) coordinates in texture space. The texture map can be created by any convenient means then a visual association between the texture map and the two-dimensional projection of the object set up in the manner suggested in the illustration. A vertex in the $T(u, v)$ grid is 'tied' to the vertex in world space by the topological equivalence of the two-dimensional and three-dimensional models. Adjusting the (u, v) coordinates then maps $T(u, v)$ onto its equivalent object vertex. Figure 7.7 is another illustration of this approach where a simplified tank model has been texture mapped

Figure 7.7
An example of a tank object texture being created from a photograph of a tank.

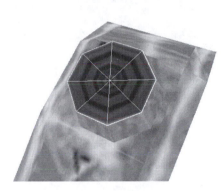

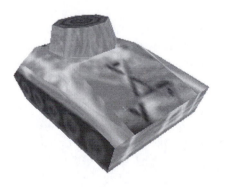

Figure 7.8
Interactive texture mapping
– painting in $T(u,v)$ space.
(a) Texture is painted using
an interactive paint
program. (b) Using the
object's bounding box, the
texture map points are
projected onto the object.
All projectors are parallel to
each other and normal to
the bounding box face.
(c) The object is rendered,
the 'distortion' visualised
and the artist repeats the
cycle if necessary.

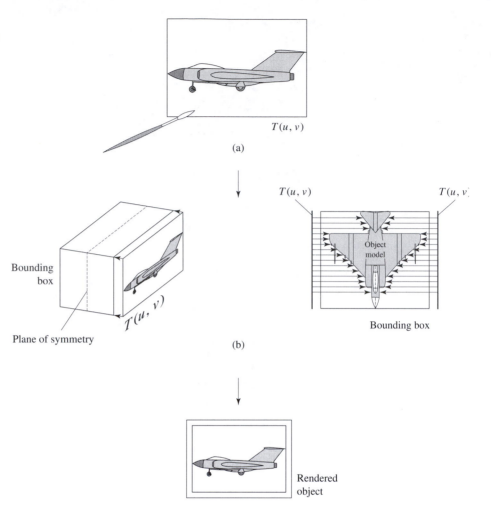

from a photograph of a tank. The illustration attempts to show that the technique can be quite 'free' – the top of the turret of the tank having been constructed by sweeping a radial line of pixels extracted from the wheels in the photograph.

Another useful way of setting up an interactive association between a texture map and an object is shown in Figure 7.8. If an object exhibits a plane of symmetry then $T(u,v)$ can form two faces of a bounding volume and the texture can be projected onto the object as suggested in the figure. An artist can then paint the texture in one window while viewing the three-dimensional texture mapped object in another.

The next illustration (Figure 7.9 Colour Plate) indicates an important practical point, which is that if an object is to receive a number of different texture maps then these should be agglomerated into a single map. Switching textures in and out of texture memory is to be avoided and this is an obvious way to accomplish this goal.

7.3 Two-dimensional texture domain to bi-cubic parametric patch objects

If an object is a quadric or a cubic then surface parametrisation is straightforward. In the previous section we used quadrics as intermediate surfaces exactly for this reason. If the object is a bi-cubic parametric patch, texture mapping is trivial since a parametric patch by definition already possesses (u,v) values everywhere on its surface.

The first use of texture in computer graphics was a method developed by Catmull (1974). This technique applied to bi-cubic parametric patch models; the algorithm subdivides a surface patch in object space, and at the same time executes a corresponding subdivision in texture space. The idea is that the patch subdivision proceeds until it covers a single pixel (a standard patch rendering approach described in detail in Chapter 5). When the patch subdivision process terminates the required texture value(s) for the pixel is obtained from the area enclosed by the current level of subdivision in the texture domain. This is a straightforward technique that is easily implemented as an extension to a bi-cubic patch renderer. A variation of this method was used by Cook (Cook *et al.* 1987) where object surfaces are subdivided into 'micro-polygons' and flat shaded with values from a corresponding subdivision in texture space.

An example of this technique is shown in Figure 7.10 (Colour Plate). Here each patch on the teapot causes subdivision of a single texture map, which is itself a rendered version of the teapot. For each patch, the u,v values from the parameter space subdivision are used to index the texture map whose u,v values also vary between 0 and 1. This scheme is easily altered to, say, map four patches into the entire texture domain by using a scale factor of two in the u,v mapping.

7.4 Bump mapping

Bump mapping, a technique developed by Blinn in 1978, is an elegant device that enables a surface to appear as if it was wrinkled or dimpled without the need to geometrically model these depressions. Instead, the surface normal is angularly perturbed according to information given in a two-dimensional bump map and this 'tricks' a local reflection model, wherein intensity is a function mainly of the surface normal, into producing (apparent) local geometric variations on a smooth surface. The only problem with bump mapping is that because the pits or depressions do not exist in the model, a silhouette edge that appears to pass through a depression will not produce the expected cross-section. In other words, the silhouette edge will follow the original geometry of the model.

It is an important technique because it appears to texture a surface in the normal sense of the word rather than modulating the colour of a flat surface. Figure 7.11 (Colour Plate) shows examples of this technique.

Texturing the surface in the rendering phase, without perturbing the geometry, bypasses serious modelling problems that would otherwise occur. If the object is polygonal the mesh would have to be fine enough to receive the perturbations from the texture map – a serious imposition on the original modelling phase, particularly if the texture is to be an option.

Thus the technique converts a two-dimensional height field $B(u,v)$ called the bump map – which represents some desired surface displacement – into appropriate perturbations of the local surface normal. When this surface normal is used in the shading equation the reflected light calculations vary as if the surface had been displaced.

Consider a point $\boldsymbol{P}(u,v)$ on a (parameterised) surface corresponding to $B(u,v)$. We define the surface normal at the point to be

$$\boldsymbol{N} = \frac{\partial \boldsymbol{P}}{\partial u} \times \frac{\partial \boldsymbol{P}}{\partial v}$$

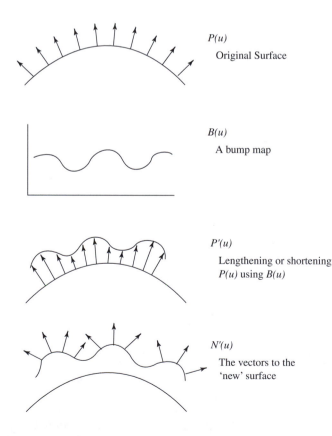

$P(u)$
Original Surface

$B(u)$
A bump map

$P'(u)$
Lengthening or shortening $P(u)$ using $B(u)$

$N'(u)$
The vectors to the 'new' surface

Figure 7.12
A one-dimensional example of the stages involved in bump mapping (after Blinn (1978)).

$$= \boldsymbol{P}_u \times \boldsymbol{P}_v$$

where $\boldsymbol{P}_u$ and $\boldsymbol{P}_v$ are the partial derivatives lying in the tangent plane to the surface at point $\boldsymbol{P}$. What we want to do is to have the same effect as displacing the point $\boldsymbol{P}$ in the direction of the surface normal at that point by an amount $B(u,v)$ – a one-dimensional analogue is shown in Figure 7.12. That is:

$$\boldsymbol{P}'(u,v) = \boldsymbol{P}(u,v) + B(u,v)\boldsymbol{N}$$

Locally the surface would not now be as smooth as it was before because of this displacement and the normal vector $\boldsymbol{N}'$ to the 'new' surface is given by differentiating this equation:

$$\boldsymbol{N}' = \boldsymbol{P}'_u \times \boldsymbol{P}'_v$$
$$\boldsymbol{P}'_u = \boldsymbol{P}_u + B_u\boldsymbol{N} + B(u,v)\boldsymbol{N}_u$$
$$\boldsymbol{P}'_v = \boldsymbol{P}_v + B_v\boldsymbol{N} + B(u,v)\boldsymbol{N}_v$$

If B is small we can ignore the final term in each equation and we have:

$$\boldsymbol{N}' = \boldsymbol{N} + B_u\boldsymbol{N} \times \boldsymbol{P}_v + B_v\boldsymbol{P}_u \times \boldsymbol{N}$$

or

$$\boldsymbol{N}' = \boldsymbol{N} + B_u\boldsymbol{N} \times \boldsymbol{P}_v - B_v\boldsymbol{N} \times \boldsymbol{P}_u$$
$$= \boldsymbol{N} + (B_u\boldsymbol{A} - B_v\boldsymbol{B})$$
$$= \boldsymbol{N} + \boldsymbol{D}$$

Then $\boldsymbol{D}$ is a vector lying in the tangent plane that 'pulls' N into the desired orientation and is calculated from the partial derivatives of the bump map and the two vectors in the tangent plane (Figure 7.13).

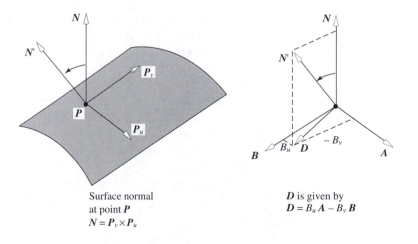

Figure 7.13
Geometric interpretation of bump mapping.

Surface normal
at point P
$N = P_v \times P_u$

D is given by
$D = B_u A - B_v B$

A multi-pass technique for bump mapping

For polygon mesh objects McReynolds and Blythe (1997) define a multi-pass technique that can exploit standard texture mapping hardware facilities. To do this they split the calculation into two components as follows. The final intensity value is proportional to $\mathbf{N'}.\mathbf{L}$ where:

$$\mathbf{N'}.\mathbf{L} = \mathbf{N}.\mathbf{L} + \mathbf{D}.\mathbf{L}$$

The first component is the normal Gouraud component and the second component is found from the differential coefficient of two image projections formed by rendering the surface with the height field as a normal texture map. To do this it is necessary to transform the light vector into tangent space at each vertex of the polygon. This space is defined by $\mathbf{N}$, $\mathbf{B}$ and $\mathbf{T}$ where:

$\mathbf{N}$ is the vertex normal

$\mathbf{T}$ is the direction of increasing u (or v) in the object space coordinate system

$\mathbf{B} = \mathbf{N} \times \mathbf{T}$

The normalised components of these vectors defines the matrix that transforms points into tangent space:

$$\mathbf{L}_{\text{TS}} =: \begin{bmatrix} T_x & T_y & T_z & 0 \\ B_x & B_y & B_z & 0 \\ N_x & N_y & N_z & 0 \\ 0 & 0 & 0 & 1 \end{bmatrix} \mathbf{L}$$

The algorithm is as follows:

(1) The object is rendered using a normal renderer with texture mapping facilities. The texture map used is the bump map or height field.

(2) $\mathbf{T}$ and $\mathbf{B}$ are found at each vertex and the light vector transformed into tangent space.

(3) A second image is created in the same way but now the texture/vertex correspondence is shifted by small amounts in the direction of the X, Y components of $\mathbf{L}_{\text{TS}}$. We now have two image projections where the height field or the bump map has been mapped onto the object and shifted with respect to the surface. If we subtract these two images we get the differential coefficient which is the required term $\mathbf{D}.\mathbf{L}$. (Finding the differential coefficient of an image by subtraction is a standard image processing technique – see, for example, Watt and Policarpo (1998).)

(4) The object is rendered in the normal manner *without* any texture and this component is added to the subtrahend calculated in step 3 to give the final bump mapped image.

Thus we replace the explicit bump mapping calculations with two texture mapped rendering passes, an image subtract, a Gouraud shading pass then an image add to get the final result.

A pre-calculation technique for bump mapping

Tangent space can also be used to facilitate a pre-calculation technique as proposed by Peercy *et al.* (1997). This depends on the fact that the perturbed normal $\mathbf{N}'_{TS}$ in tangent space is a function only of the surface itself and the bump map. Peercy *et al.* define this normal at each vertex in terms of three pre-calculated coefficients.

It can be shown (Peercy *et al.*, 1997) that the perturbed normal vector on tangent space is given by:

$$\mathbf{N}'_{TS} = \frac{a,b,c}{(a^2 + b^2 + c^2)^{1/2}}$$

where:

$$a = -B_u(\mathbf{B}.\mathbf{P}_v)$$
$$b = -(B_v|\mathbf{P}_u| - B_u(\mathbf{T}.\mathbf{P}_v))$$
$$c = |\mathbf{P}_u \times \mathbf{P}_v|$$

For each point in the bump map these points can be pre-computed and a map of perturbed normals is stored for use during rendering instead of the bump map.

Environment or reflection mapping

Originally called reflection mapping and first suggested by Blinn (1977), environment mapping was consolidated into mainline rendering techniques in an important paper in 1986 by Greene. Environment maps are a shortcut to rendering shiny objects that reflect the environment in which they are placed. They can approximate the quality of a ray tracer for specular reflections and do this by reducing the problem of following a reflected view vector to indexing into a two-dimensional map which is no different from a conventional texture map. Thus processing costs that would be incurred in ray tracing programs are regulated to the (off-line) construction of the map(s). In this sense it is a classic partial off-line or pre-calculation technique like pre-sorting for hidden surface removal. An example of a scene and its corresponding (cubic) environment map is shown in Figure 7.24 (Colour Plate).

The disadvantages of environment mapping are:

- It is only (geometrically) correct when the object becomes small with respect to the environment that contains it. This effect is usually not noticeable in the sense that we are not disturbed by 'wrong' reflections in the curved surface of a shiny object. The extent of the problem is shown in Figure 7.25 which shows the same object ray traced and environment mapped.

● An object can only reflect the environment – not itself – and so the technique is 'wrong' for concave objects. Again this can be seen in Figure 7.25 where the reflection of the spout is apparent in the ray traced image.

● A separate map is required for each object in the scene that is to be environment mapped

● In one common form of environment mapping (sphere mapping) a new map is required whenever the viewpoint changes.

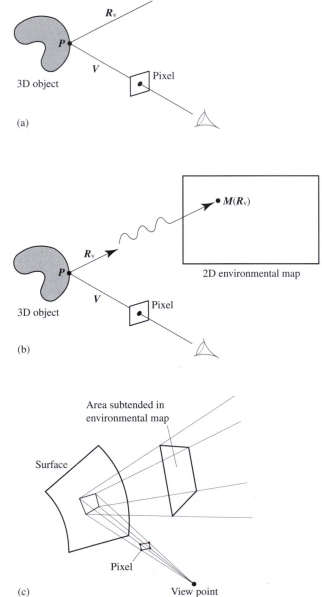

Figure 7.14
Environment mapping
(a) The ray tracing model –
that part of the environment
reflected at point *P* is
determined by reflecting the
view ray R_v. (b) We try to
achieve the same effect as in
(a) by using a function of R_v
to index into a two-
dimensional map. (c) A pixel
subtends a reflection beam.

In this section we will examine three methods of environment mapping which are classified according to the way in which the three-dimensional environment information is mapped into two dimensions. These are cubic, latitude-longitude and sphere mapping. (Latitude-longitude is also a spherical mapping but the term sphere mapping is now applied to the more recent form.) The general principles are shown in Figure 7.14. Figure 7.14(a)) shows the conventional ray tracing paradigm which we replace with the scheme shown in Figure 7.14(b)). This involves mapping the reflected view vector into a two-dimensional environment map. We calculate the reflected view vector as (Section 1.2.5):

$$\mathbf{R}_v = 2(\mathbf{N}.\mathbf{V})\mathbf{N} - \mathbf{V} \tag{7.2}$$

Figure 7.14(c) shows that in practice for a single pixel we should consider the reflection beam, rather than a single vector, and the area subtended by the beam in the map is then filtered for the pixel value. A reflection beam originates either from four pixel corners if we are indexing the map for each pixel, or from polygon vertices if we are using a fast (approximate) scheme. An important point to note here is that the area intersected in the environment map is a function of the curvature of the projected pixel area on the object surface. However, because we are now using texture mapping techniques we can employ pre-filtering anti-aliasing methods (Section 8.7).

In real-time polygon mesh rendering, we can calculate reflected view vectors only at the vertices and use linear interpolation as we do in conventional texture mapping. Because we expect to see fine detail in the resulting image, the quality of this approach depends strongly on the polygon size.

In effect an environment map caches the incident illumination from all directions at a single point in the environment with the object that is to receive the mapping removed from the scene. Reflected illumination at the surface of an object is calculated from this incident illumination by employing the aforementioned geometric approximation – that the size of the object itself can be considered to approach the point.

7.5.1 Cubic mapping

As we have already implied, environment mapping is a two-stage process that involves – as a pre-process – the construction of the map. Cubic mapping is popular because the maps can easily be constructed using a conventional rendering system. The environment map is in practice six maps that form the surfaces of a cube (Figure 7.15). An example of an environment map is shown in Figure 7.24. The viewpoint is fixed at the centre of the object to receive the environment map, and six views are rendered. Consider a viewpoint fixed at the centre of a room. If we consider the room to be empty then these views would contain the four walls and the floor and ceiling. One of the problems of a cubic map is that if we are considering a reflection beam formed by pixel corners, or equivalently by the reflected view vectors at a polygon vertex, the beam can index into more

Figure 7.15
Cubic environment
mapping: the reflection
beam can range over more
than one map.

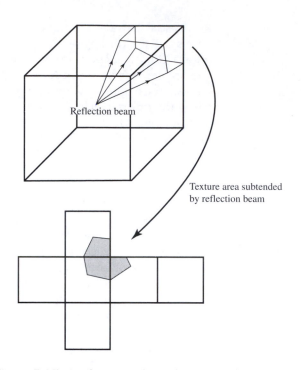

Reflection beam

Texture area subtended
by reflection beam

than one map (Figure 7.15). In that case the polygon can be subdivided so that
each piece is constrained to a single map.

With cubic maps we need an algorithm to determine the mapping from the
three-dimensional view vector into one or more two-dimensional maps. (With
the techniques described in the next section this mapping algorithm is replaced
by a simple calculation.) If we consider that the reflected view vector is in the
same coordinate frame as the environment map cube (the case if the view were
constructed by pointing the (virtual or real) camera along the world axes in both
directions), then the mapping is as follows:

For a single reflection vector:

(1) find the face it intersects – the map number. This involves a simple comparison of the components of the normalised reflected view vector against
the (unit) cube extents which is centred on the origin.

(2) map the components into (u,v) coordinates. For example, a point (x,y,z)
intersecting the face normal to the negative z axis is given by:

$$u = x + 0.5$$
$$v = -z + 0.5$$

for the convention scheme shown in Figure 7.16.

One of the applications of cubic environment maps (or indeed any environment
map method) that became popular in the 1980s is to 'matte' an animated
computer graphics object into a real environment. In that case the environment

Figure 7.16
Cubic environment map
convention.

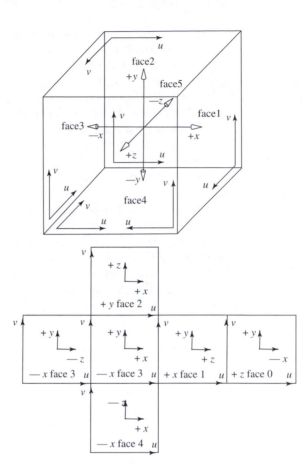

map is constructed from photographs of a real environment and the (specular) computer graphics object can be matted into the scene, and appear to be part of it as it moves and reflects its surroundings.

7.5.2 Sphere mapping

The first use of environment mapping was by Blinn and Newell (1976) wherein a sphere rather than a cube was the basis of the method used. The environment map consisted of a latitude-longitude projection and the reflected view vector was mapped into (u,v) coordinates as:

$$u = \frac{1}{2}\left(1 + \frac{1}{\pi}\tan^{-1}\left(\frac{R_{vy}}{R_{vx}}\right)\right) \quad -\pi < \tan^{-1}() < \pi$$

$$v = \frac{R_{vz} + 1}{2}$$

The main problem with this simple technique is the singularities at the poles. In the polar area small changes in the direction of the reflection vector produce large changes in (u,v) coordinates. As $R_{vz} \to \pm1$, both R_{vx} and $R_{vy} \to 0$ and R_{vy}/R_{vx} becomes ill-defined. Equivalently, as $v \to 1$ or 0 the behaviour of u starts to break down, causing visual disturbances on the surface. This can be ameliorated by modulating the horizontal resolution of the map with $\sin \theta$ (where θ is the elevation angle in polar coordinates.)

An alternative sphere mapping form (Haeberli and Segal (1993) and Miller *et al.* (1998) consists of a circular map which is the orthographic projection of the reflection of the environment as seen in the surface of a perfect mirror sphere (Figure 7.17). Clearly such a map can be generated by ray tracing from the viewplane. (Alternatively a photograph can be taken of a shiny sphere.) Although the map caches the incident illumination at the reference point by using an orthographic projection, it can be used to generate, to within the accuracy of the process, a normal perspective projection.

To generate the map we proceed as follows. We trace a parallel ray bundle – one ray for each texel (u,v) and reflect each ray from the sphere. The point on the sphere at the point hit by the ray from (u,v) is $\boldsymbol{P}$:
where

$$P_x = u \qquad P_y = v$$
$$P_z = (1.0 - P_x^2 - P_y^2)^{1/2}$$

This is also the normal to the sphere at the hit point and we can compute the reflected vector using Equation 7.2.

To index into the map we reflect the view vector from the object (either for each pixel or for each polygon vertex) and calculate the map coordinates as:

$$u = \frac{R_x}{m} + \frac{1}{2}$$

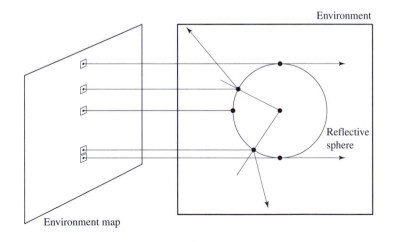

Figure 7.17
Constructing a spherical map by ray tracing from the map texels onto a reflective sphere.

Environment

Reflective sphere

Environment map

$$v = \frac{R_y}{m} + \frac{1}{2}$$

where:

$$m = 2(R_x^2 + R_y^2 + (R_z + 1)^2)^{1/2}$$

7.5.3

Environment mapping: comparative points

Sphere mapping overcomes the main limitation of cubic maps which require, in general, access to a number of the face maps, and is to be preferred when speed is important. However, both types of sphere mapping suffer more from non-uniform sampling than cubic mapping. Refer to Figure 7.18 which attempts to

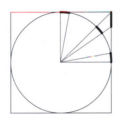

(a)

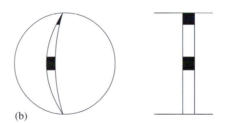

(b)

Figure 7.18
Sampling the surface of a sphere. (a) Cubic perspective: under-sampling at the centre of the map (equator and meridian) compared to the corners. (b) Mercator or latitude–longditude: severe over-sampling at edges of the map in the v direction (poles). (c) Orthographic: severe under-sampling at the edges of the map in the u direction (equator).

(c)

demonstrate this point. In all three cases we consider that the environment map is sampling incoming illumination incident on the surface of the unit sphere centred at the viewpoint. The illustration shows the difference between the areas on the surface of the sphere sampled by a texel in the environment map. Sampling only approaches uniformity when the viewing direction during the rendering phase aligns with the viewing direction from which the map was computed. For this reason this type of spherical mapping is considered to be view dependent and a new map has to be computed when the view direction changes.

7.6 Three-dimensional texture domain techniques

We have seen in preceding sections that there are many difficulties associated with mapping a two-dimensional texture onto the surface of a three-dimensional object. The reasons for this are:

(1) Two-dimensional texture mapping based on a surface coordinate system can produce large variations in the compression of the texture that reflect a corresponding variation in the curvature of the surface.

(2) Attempting to continuously texture map the surface of an object possessing a non-trivial topology can quickly become very awkward. Textural continuity across surface elements that can be of a different type and can connect together in any *ad hoc* manner is problematic to maintain.

Three-dimensional texture mapping neatly circumvents these problems since the only information required to assign a point a texture value is its position in space. Assigning an object a texture just involves evaluating a three-dimensional texture function at the surface points of the object. A fairly obvious requirement of this technique is that the three-dimensional texture field is procedurally generated. Otherwise the memory requirements, particularly if three-dimensional mip-mapping is used, become exorbitant. Also, it is inherently inefficient to construct an entire cubic field of texture when we only require these values at the surface of the object.

Given a point (x,y,z) on the surface of an object, the colour is defined as $T(x,y,z)$, where T is the value of texture field. That is, we simply use the identity mapping (possibly in conjunction with a scaling):

$$u = x \quad v = y \quad w = z$$

where

(u,v,w) is a coordinate in the texture field.

This can be considered analogous to actually sculpting or carving an object out of a block of material. The colour of the object is determined by the intersection of its surface with the texture field. The method was reported simultaneously by Perlin (1985) and Peachey (1985) wherein the term 'solid texture' was coined.

The disadvantage of the technique is that although it eliminates mapping problems, the texture patterns themselves are limited to whatever definition you can think up. This contrasts with a two-dimensional texture map; here any texture can be set up by using, say, a frame grabbed image from a television camera.

7.6.1

Three-dimensional noise

A popular class of procedural texturing techniques all have in common the fact that they use a three-dimensional, or spatial noise function, as a basic modelling primitive. These techniques, the most notable of which is the simulation of turbulence, can produce a surprising variety of realistic, natural-looking texture effects. In this section we will concern ourselves with the issues involved in the algorithmic generation of the basic primitive – solid noise.

Perlin (1985) was the first to suggest this application of noise, defining a function noise() that takes a three-dimensional position as its input and returns a single scalar value. This is called model-directed synthesis – we evaluate the noise function only at the point of interest. Ideally the function should possess the following three properties:

(1) statistical invariance under rotation;

(2) statistical invariance under translation;

(3) a narrow bandpass limit in frequency.

The first two conditions ensure that the noise function is controllable – that is, no matter how we move or orientate the noise function in space, its general appearance is guaranteed to stay the same. The third condition enables us to sample the noise function without aliasing. Whilst an insufficiently sampled noise function may not produce noticeable defects in static images, if used in animation applications, incorrectly sampled noise will produce a shimmering or bubbling effect.

Perlin's method of generating noise is to define an integer lattice, or a set of points in space, situated at locations (i,j,k) where i,j and k are all integers. Each point of the lattice has a random number associated with it. This can be done either by using a simple lookup table or, as Perlin suggests, via a hashing function to save space. The value of the noise function, at a point in space coincident with a lattice point, is just this random number. For points in space not on the lattice – in general (u,v,w) – the noise value can be obtained by linear interpolation from the nearby lattice points. If, using this method, we generate a solid noise function $T(u,v,w)$ then it will tend to exhibit directional (axis aligned) coherences. These can be ameliorated by using cubic interpolation but this is far more expensive and the coherences still tend to be visible. Alternative noise generation methods that eliminate this problem are to be found in Lewis (1989), however, it is worth bearing in mind that the entire solid noise function is sampled by the surface and usually undergoes a transformation (it is modulated, for example, to simulate turbulence) and this in itself may be enough to eliminate the coherences.

Simulating turbulence

A single piece of noise can be put to use to simulate a remarkable number of effects. By far the most versatile of its applications is the use of the so-called turbulence function, as defined by Perlin, which takes a position x and returns a turbulent scalar value. It is written in terms of the progression, a one-dimensional version of which would be defined as:

$$\text{turblence}(x) = \sum_{i=0}^{k} \text{abs}\left(\frac{\text{noise}(2^i x)}{2^i}\right)$$

The summation is truncated at k which is the smallest integer satisfying:

$$\frac{1}{2^{k+1}} < \text{the size of a pixel}$$

The truncation band limits the function, ensuring proper anti-aliasing. Consider the difference between the first two terms in the progression, noise (x) and noise $(2x)/2$. The noise function in the latter term will vary twice as fast as the first – it has twice the frequency – and will contain features that are half the size of the first. Moreover, its contribution to the final value for the turbulence is also scaled by one-half. At each scale of detail the amount of noise added in to the series is proportional to the scale of detail of the noise and inversely proportional to the frequency of the noise. This is self-similarity and is analogous to the self-similarity obtained through fractal subdivision, except that this time the subdivision does not drive displacement, but octaves of noise, producing a function that exhibits the same noisy behaviour over a range of scales. That this function should prove so useful is best seen from the point of view of signal analysis, which tells us that the power spectrum of turbulence() obeys a $1/f$ power law, thereby loosely approximating the $1/f^2$ power law of Brownian motion.

The turbulence function in isolation only represents half the story, however. Rendering the turbulence function directly results in a homogeneous pattern that could not be described as naturalistic. This is due to the fact that most textures that occur naturally contain some non-homogeneous structural features and so cannot be simulated by turbulence alone. Take marble, for example, which has easily distinguished veins of colour running through it that were made turbulent before the marble solidified during an earlier geological era. In the light of this fact we can identify two distinct stages in the process of simulating turbulence:

(1) Representation of the basic, first-order, structural features of a texture through some basic functional form. Typically the function is continuous and contains significant variations in its first derivatives.

(2) Addition of second and higher-order detail by using turbulence to perturb the parameters of the function.

(a)

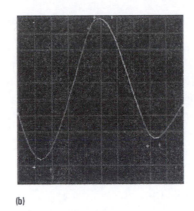

(b)

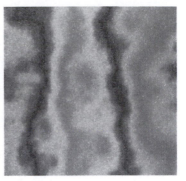

(c)

Figure 7.19
Simulating marble. (a) Unturbulated slice obtained by using the spline shown in (b). (b) Colour spline used to produce (a). (c) Marble section obtained by turbulating the slice shown in (a).

The classic example, as first described by Perlin, is the turbulation of a sine wave to give the appearance of marble. Unperturbed, the colour veins running through the marble are given by a sine wave passing through a colour map. For a sine wave running along the x axis we write:

marble (x) = marble_colour $(\sin(x))$

The colour map marble_colour() maps a scalar input to an intensity. Visualizing this expression, Figure 7.19(a) is a two-dimensional slice of marble rendered with the colour spline given in Figure 7.19(b). Next we add turbulence:

marble(x) = marble_colour $(\sin(x + \text{turbulence}(x))$

to give us Figure 7.19(c), a convincing simulation of marble texture. Figure 7.20 (Colour Plate) shows the effect in three dimensions.

Of course, use of the turbulence function need not be restricted to modulate just the colour of an object. Any parameter that affects the appearance of an object can be turbulated. Oppenheimer (1986) turbulates a sawtooth function to bump map the ridges of bark on a tree. Turbulence can drive the transparency of objects such as clouds. Clouds can be modelled by texturing an opacity map onto a sphere that is concentric with the earth. The opacity map can be created with a paint program; clouds are represented as white blobs with soft edges that fade into complete transparency. These edges become turbulent after perturbation of the texture coordinates. In an extension to his earlier work, Perlin (1989) uses turbulence to volumetrically render regions of space rather than just evaluating texture at the surface of an object. Solid texture is used to modulate the geometry of an object as well as its appearance. Density modulation functions that specify the soft regions of objects are turbulated and rendered using a ray marching algorithm. A variety of applications are described, including erosion, fire and fur.

Three-dimensional texture and animation

The turbulence function can be defined over time as well as space simply by adding an extra dimension that represents time to the noise integer lattice. So the lattice points will now be specified by the indices (i,j,k,l) enabling us to extend the parameter list to noise (x,t) and similarly for turbulence (x,t). Internal to these procedures the time axis is not treated any differently than the three spatial axes.

For example, if we want to simulate fire, the first thing that we do is to try to represent its basic form functionally, that is a 'flame shape'. The completely *ad hoc* nature of this functional sculpting is apparent here. The final form decided on was simply that which, after experimentation, gave the best results. We shall work in two-space due to the expense of the three-dimensional volumetric approach referred to at the end of the last section.

A flame region is defined in the xy plane by the rectangle with minimax coordinates $(-b,0)$, (b,h). Within this region the flame's colour is given by:

$$\text{flame}(x) = (1 - y/h)\ \text{flame\_colour}(\text{abs}(x/b))$$

This is shown schematically in Figure 7.21 (Colour Plate). Flame_colour (x) consists of three separate colour splines that map a scalar value x to a colour vector. Each of the R,G,B splines have a maximum intensity at $x = 0$ which corresponds to the centre of the flame and a fade off to zero intensity at $x = 1$. The green and blue splines go to zero faster than the red. The colour returned by flame_colour() is weighted according to its height from the base of the flame to get an appropriate variation along y. The flame is rendered by applying flame() to colour a rectangular polygon that covers the region of the flames definition. The opacity of the polygon is also textured by using a similar functional construction. Figure 7.21 also shows the turbulated counterpart obtained by introducing the turbulence function thus:

$$\text{flame}\ (x,t) = (1 - y/h)\ \text{flame\_colour}(\text{abs}(x/b) + \text{turbulence}(x,t))$$

To animate the flame we simply render successive slices of noise which are perpendicular to the time axis and equispaced by an amount corresponding to the frame interval. It is as if we are translating the polygon along the time axis. However, mere translation in time is not enough, recognisable detail in the flame, though changing shape with time, remained curiously static in space. This is because there is a general sense of direction associated with a flame, convection sends detail upwards. This was simulated, and immediately gave better results, by moving the polygon down in y as well as through time, as shown in Figure 7.22. The final construction is thus:

$$\text{flame}(x,t) = (1 - y/h)\text{flame\_colour}(\text{abs}(x/b) + \text{turbulence}(x + (0, t\Delta y, 0), t))$$

where Δy is the distance moved in y by the polygon relative to the noise per unit time.

Figure 7.22
Animating turbulence for a
two-dimensional object.

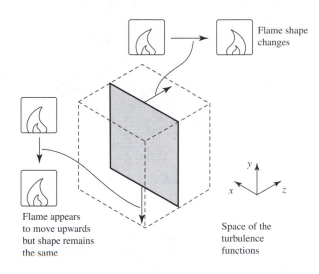

Flame shape
changes

Flame appears
to move upwards
but shape remains
the same

Space of the
turbulence
functions

 7.6.4

Three-dimensional light maps

In principle there is no reason why we cannot have three-dimensional light maps – the practical restriction is the vast memory resources that would be required. In the event that it is possible, we have a method of caching the reflected light at every point in the scene. We use any view-independent rendering method and assign the calculated light intensity at point (x,y,z) in object space to $T(x,y,z)$. It is interesting now to compare our pre-calculation mapping methods.

With environment mapping we cache all the incoming illumination at a **single** point in object space in a two-dimensional map which is labelled by the direction of the incoming light at the point. A reflected view vector is then used to retrieve the reflected light directed towards the user. These are normally used for perfect specular surfaces and give us fast view-dependent effects.

With two-dimensional light maps we cache the reflected light for each surface in the scene in a set of two-dimensional maps. Indexing into these maps during the rendering phase depends on the method that was used to sample three-dimensional object space. We use these to cache view-independent non-dynamic lighting.

With three-dimensional light maps we store reflected light at a point in a three-dimensional structure that represents object space. Three-dimensional light maps are a subset of light fields (Chapter 19).

7.7

Comparative examples

We now look at the effect of adding various mapping techniques to the office scene.

7.7.1

Figure 7.23 (Colour Plate)

The office scene with 'traditional' two-dimensional texture maps. The addition of apparent complexity/'reality'/visual interest of simple textures to a Phong-shaded scene is the reason for its enduring popularity. If anything, the addition of textures makes a scene look less real in the sense that its obvious computer signature is increased.

7.7.2

Figure 7.24 (Colour Plate)

The same scene with shadow and environment mapping (the teapot) added. The resolution on the shadow maps are 256 × 256 and this causes geometric aliasing – as is apparent in the leaf shadow on the wall which has actually broken up (shadow mapping is described in Chapter 11). Note that there is 'interaction' between shadow mapping and environment mapping; the order of operations is important. In this image the environment map was computed before the shadow map and hence the shadow of the teapot does not appear in the reflections of the teapot.

Alternatively we can generate the shadow map (Section 11.2.4) for the whole scene including the teapot then remove it and compute the environment map. The teapot is then reinserted in the scene for the rendering and environment mapping will now include its shadow.

Note also the shadow edge definition. The inadequacies here are due to the spatial resolution of the shadow map which is here 256 × 256 for each component.

7.7.3

Figure 7.25 (Colour Plate)

This is a comparison between generating reflections using environment mapping and ray tracing. The demonstration illustrates the extent of geometric distortion introduced by environment mapping. The 'incorrectness' is a function of the size of the object in the environment – as the object approaches a point the reflections become correct. Another defect of environment mapping is that it does not implement self-reflections – the teapot does not contain a reflection of its spout. When the environment map is generated the object is 'removed' from the scene.

A point worth noting is that in ray tracing it is easy to assign a global specular reflectivity coefficient to as many objects as we require. With environment mapping we have to create a separate map for each object.

Anti-aliasing theory and practice

8.1 Introduction

8.2 Aliases and sampling

8.3 Jagged edges

8.4 Sampling in computer graphics compared with sampling reality

8.5 Sampling and reconstruction

8.6 A simple comparision

8.7 Pre-filtering methods

8.8 Supersampling or post-filtering

8.9 Anti-aliasing in texture mapping

8.10 The Fourier transform of images

Note
This chapter discusses the classical approach to anti-aliasing and requires some understanding of Fourier theory. A brief introduction, sufficient for an intuitive appreciation of this, is given at the end of the chapter.

8.1 Introduction

The final quality of computer graphics imagery depends on many varied factors. Artefacts arise out of modelling and other factors that are a consequence of operations in the particular rendering algorithm that was used to generate the image. For example, consider the many image defects in polygon mesh scenes. We have modelling artefacts sometimes called geometric aliasing – the visibility of piece-wise linearities on the silhouette edge of a polygon mesh object. There are artefacts that emerge from the shading algorithm such as Mach bands and inadequacies due to the interpolation method.

Anti-aliasing is the general term given to methods that deal with discrepancies that arise from undersampling and it is this issue that we deal with in this chapter.

8.2 Aliases and sampling

We first consider the term alias. In theory this refers to a particular image artefact that is mostly visible in texture maps when the periodicity in the texture approaches the dimension of a pixel. This is easily demonstrated and Figure 8.10(a) is the classic example of this effect – an infinite chequerboard. Towards the top of the image the squares reduce then apparently increase in size, cause a glaring visual disturbance. This is due to undersampling. The notion of sampling in computer graphics comes from the fact that we are calculating a single colour or value for each pixel; we are sampling a solution at a discrete point in a solution space. This is a space that is potentially continuous in the sense that, because computer graphics images are generated from abstractions, we can calculate samples anywhere or everywhere in the image plane.

We will now look at a simple one-dimensional example which will relate undersampling, aliases and the notion of spatial frequencies. Consider using a sine wave to represent an information signal (although a sine wave does not contain any information anyway, this does not matter for our purposes). Figure 8.1 shows a sine wave being sampled at different rates (with respect to the

Figure 8.1
Space domain representation of the sampling of a sine wave. (a) Sampling interval is less than one-half the period of the sine wave. (b) Sampling interval is equal to one-half the period of the sine wave. (c) Sampling interval is greater than one-half the period of the sine wave. (d) Sampling interval is much greater than one-half the period of the sine wave.

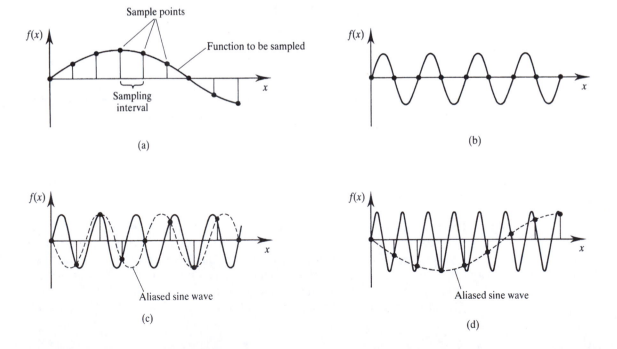

(a) (b) (c) (d)

frequency of the sine wave). Undersampling the sine wave, and reconstructing a continuous signal from the samples (dotted line in the figure), produces an 'alias' of the original signal – another sine wave at a lower frequency than the one being sampled. We can say that this happens because the coherence or regularity of the sampling pattern is interfering with the regularity of the information. To avoid aliasing artefacts we have to sample at an appropriately high frequency with respect to the signal or image information and we normally consider the process of calculating an image function at discrete points in the image plane to be equivalent to sampling.

The defects that arise in computer graphics that are due to insufficient calculations or samples and which are easily modelled by an image plane sampling model are coherent patterns breaking up – the case that we have already discussed – and small fragments that are missed because they fall between two sample points.

Consider the chequerboard example again. Very quickly the pattern units approach the size of a pixel and the pattern 'breaks up'. High spatial frequencies are aliasing as lower ones and forming new visually disturbing coherent patterns. Now consider Figure 8.10(b) where we render the same image onto a view plane with double the resolution of the previous. Aliasing artefacts still appear but at a higher spatial frequency. In theoretical terms we have increased the sampling frequency, but the effect persists except that it happens at a higher spatial

Figure 8.2
Frequency domain representation of the sampling process when $f_s > 2f_{max}$. (a) Frequency spectrum of $f(x)$. (b) Frequency spectrum of the sampling function. (c) Frequency spectrum of the sampled function (convolution of (a) and (b)). (d) Ideal reconstruction filter. (e) Frequency spectrum of the reconstructed $f(x)$.

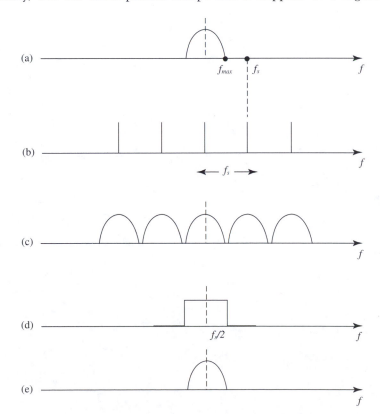

frequency. This demonstrates two important facts. Spatial frequencies in a computer graphics image are unlimited because they originate from a mathematical definition. You cannot get rid of aliases by simply increasing the pixel resolution. The artefacts simply occur at a higher spatial frequency. But they are, of course, less noticeable.

It is impossible to explain the reason for, and the cure for, aliasing in computer graphics without some recourse to Fourier theory. This we now do.

Now the example in Figure 8.1 can be generalised by considering these cases in the frequency domain for an $f(x)$ that contains information, that is, not a pure sine wave. We now have an $f(x)$ that is any general variation in x and may, for example, represent the variation in intensity along a segment of a scan line. The frequency spectrum of $f(x)$ will exhibit some 'envelope' (Figure 8.2(a)) whose limit is the highest frequency component in $f(x)$, say, f_{max}. The frequency spectrum of a sampling function (Figure 8.2(b)) is a series of lines, theoretically extending to infinity, separated by the interval f_s (the sampling frequency). Sampling in the space domain involves multiplying $f(x)$ by the sampling function. The equivalent process in the frequency domain is convolution and the frequency spectrum of the sampling function is convolved with $f(x)$ to produce the frequency spectrum shown in Figure 8.2(c) – the spectrum of the sampled version of $f(x)$. This sampled function is then multiplied by a reconstructing filter to reproduce the original function. A good example of this process, in the time

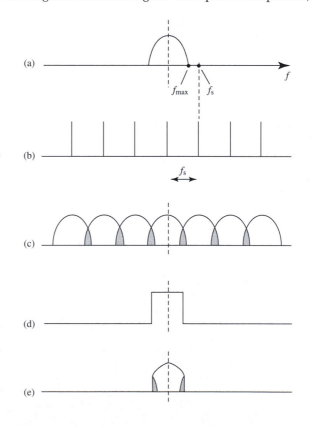

Figure 8.3
Frequency domain representation of the sampling process when $f_s > 2f_{max}$. (a) Frequency spectrum of $f(x)$. (b) Frequency spectrum of the sampling function. (c) Frequency spectrum of the sampled function (convolution of (a) and (b)). (d) Ideal reconstruction filter. (e) Frequency spectrum of the reconstructed $f(x)$.

domain, is a modern telephone network. In its simplest form this involves sampling a speech waveform, encoding and transmitting digital versions of each sample over a communications channel, then reconstructing the original signal from the decoded samples by using a reconstructing filter.

Note that the reconstruction process, which is multiplication in the frequency domain, is convolution in the space domain. In summary, the process in the space domain is multiplication of the original function with the sampled function, followed by convolution of the sampled version of the function with a reconstructing filter.

Now in the above example the condition:

$$f_s > 2f_{max}$$

is true. In the second example (Figure 8.3) we show the same two processes of multiplication and convolution but this time we have:

$$f_s < 2f_{max}$$

Incidentally $f_s/2$ is known as the Nyquist limit. Here the envelopes, representing the information in $f(x)$, overlap. It is as if the spectrum has 'folded' over a line defined by the Nyquist limit (Figure 8.3(e). This folding is an information-destroying process; high frequencies (detail in images) are lost and appear as interference (aliases) in low frequency regions. This is precisely the effect shown in Figure 8.10 where low spatial frequency structures are emerging in high frequency regions.

The sampling theorem extends to two-dimensional frequencies or spatial frequencies. The two-dimensional frequency spectrum of a graphics image in the continuous generation domain is theoretically infinite. Sampling and reconstructing in computer graphics is the process of calculation of a value at the centre of a pixel and then assigning that value to the entire spatial extent of that pixel.

Aliasing artefacts in computer graphics can be reduced by increasing the frequency of the sampling grid (that is, increasing the spatial resolution of the pixel array). There are two drawbacks to this approach: the obvious one that there is both an economic and a technical limit to increasing the spatial resolution of the display (not to mention the computational limits on the cost of the image generation process) and, since the frequency spectrum of computer graphics images can extend to infinity, increasing the sampling frequency does not necessarily solve the problem. When, for example, we applied the increased resolution approach to coherent texture in perspective, we simply shifted the effect up the spatial frequency spectrum.

8.3   Jagged edges

The other familiar defect in computer graphics is the jagged edge. This is produced by the finite size of a (usually) square pixel when a high contrast edge appears in the image. These edges are particularly troublesome in animated images where their movement gives them the appearance of small animated objects and makes them glaringly visible. These defects are easier than texture aliases to get rid of because they do not arise out of the algorithm *per se* – they are simply a consequence of the resolution of the image plane.

Jagged edges are recognised by everyone and described in all computer graphics textbooks, but they are not aliasing defects in the classical sense of an aliased spatial frequency, where a high spatial frequency appears as a disruptive lower one. They are defects produced by the final limiting effect of the display device. We can certainly ameliorate their effect by, for example, calculating an image at a resolution higher than the pixel resolution; in other words, increasing the sampling frequency deals with both aliases and jaggies.

8.4 Sampling in computer graphics compared with sampling reality

Let us now return in more detail to the notion of sampling in the image plane. In image synthesis what we are doing is performing, for each pixel, a number of (sometimes very complicated) operations that eventually calculate, for that pixel, a constant value. Usually we calculate a value at the centre of the pixel and 'spread' that value over the pixel extent.

We assume that in principle this is no different to having a continuous image in the view plane and sampling this with a discrete two-dimensional array of sample points (one for each pixel). We say that this assumption is valid because we can approach such an image by continually increasing the sample resolution and calculating a value for the image at more and more points in the image plane. However, it is important to bear in mind that we do not have access to a continuous image in computer graphics and this limits and conditions our approaches to anti-aliasing measures.

In fact both the terms 'sampling' and 'reconstruction' – another term borrowed from digital signal processing – are used indiscriminately and, we feel, somewhat confusingly in computer graphics and we will now emphasise the difference between an image processing system, where their usage is wholly appropriate, and their somewhat artificial use in computer graphics.

Consider Figure 8.4 which shows a schematic diagram for an image processor and a computer graphics system. In the image processor a sampler converts a two-dimensional continuous image into an array of samples. Some operations are then performed on the digital image and a reconstruction filter converts the processed samples back into an analogue signal.

Not so in image synthesis. Sampling does not exist in the same sense – the operations involved in assigning a value to a pixel depend on the rendering algorithm used and we can only ever calculate the value of an image function at these points.

Reconstruction, in image synthesis, does not mean generating a continuous image from a digital one but may mean, for example, generating a low (pixel) resolution image from an image stored at a higher (undisplayable) resolution. We are not reconstructing an image since a continuous image never existed in

Figure 8.4
Sampling, reconstruction and anti-aliasing in image processing and image synthesis. (a) Image capture and processing. (b) Image synthesis. (c) Anti-aliasing in image capture.

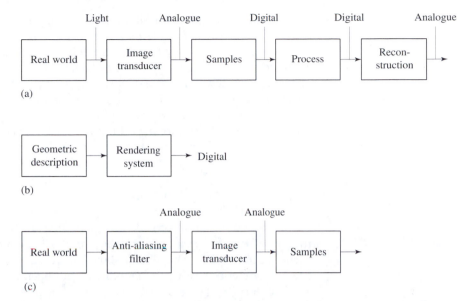

the first place. An appreciation of these differences will avoid confusion. (In reality we do reconstruct a continuous image for display on a computer graphics monitor, but this is done by fixed electronics that operate on the image produced in the framestore by a graphics program. A comprehensive approach to anti-aliasing would need to take the transfer characteristics of the conversion electronics into account but we will not do so in this text.)

To return to the problem of aliasing artefacts, Fourier theory tells us that aliasing occurs because we sample a continuous image (or the equivalent operation in computer graphics) and we do not do this at a high enough resolution to capture the high spatial frequencies or detail in the image. The sampling theorem states that if we wish to sample an image function without loss of information then our (two-dimensional) sampling frequency must be at least twice as high as the highest frequency component in the image.

So what does this mean in terms of practical computer graphics? Just this: if we consider we are sampling a continuous image in the view plane with a grid of square pixels, then the highest frequency that can appear in the image along a scan line is:

$$f = 1/2d$$

where d is the distance between pixel centres.

Having fixed these concepts it is easy to see why anti-aliasing is so difficult in computer graphics. The problem stems from two surprising facts. There is no limit to the value of the high frequencies in computer graphics – we have already discussed this using the example of the infinite chequerboard – and there is no direct way to limit (the technical term is band-limit) these spatial frequencies.

This is easily seen by comparing image synthesis with image capture through a device like a TV camera (Figure 8.4(c). Prior to sampling a continuous image we can pass it through a band-limiting filter (or an anti-aliasing filter). Higher frequencies that cannot be displayed are simply eliminated from the image before it is sampled. We say that the image is pre-filtered. In such systems aliasing problems are simply not allowed to occur.

In image synthesis our scene database exists as a mathematical description or as a set of points connected by edges. Our notion of sampling is inextricably entwined with rendering. We sample by evaluating the projection of the scene at discrete points. We cannot band-limit the image because no image exists – we can only define its existence at the chosen points.

8.5 Sampling and reconstruction

In Figure 8.2 we saw that provided the sampling theory is obeyed then reconstruction of the information from the samples is obtained by using a reconstruction filter in the shape of a box. However, this is a Fourier domain representation and in computer graphics all our operations have to take place in the space domain. Therefore the reconstruction process is convolution in the space or image domain. In computer graphics this implies (usually) filtering a rendered image in some way. If the rendered image was continuous then our reconstruction filter would consist of a sinc function $h(x,y)$ – which is the transform of the Fourier domain equivalent of a circular step function (Figure 8.5). There are, however, practical difficulties associated with this. The filter cannot have unlimited extent – it has to be truncated at some point and the way in which this is done is an important aspect of the design of the filter.

Figure 8.5
Ideal filters in the Fourier and space domains. (a) An ideal low pass (multiplicative) filter $H(u,v)$. (b) The equivalent (convolving) filter $h(x,y)$.

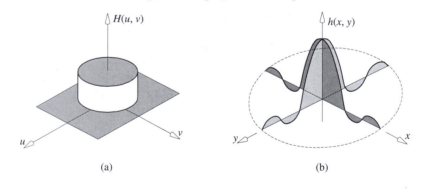

(a)   (b)

8.6 A simple comparison

We will now consider the anti-aliasing options in computer graphics briefly in the form of a comparative overview. Figure 8.6 shows four main approaches.

(1) **Pre-filtering – 'infinite' samples per pixel**   Here we calculate the precise contribution of fragments of projected object structure as it appears in a pixel. This single value is taken as the pixel colour. The practical effect of

Figure 8.6
A comparison of four approaches to calculating a single value for a pixel.

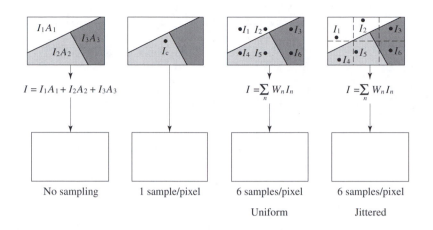

$$I = I_1A_1 + I_2A_2 + I_3A_3 \qquad\qquad I = \sum_n W_n I_n \qquad\qquad I = \sum_n W_n I_n$$

No sampling	1 sample/pixel	6 samples/pixel	6 samples/pixel
		Uniform	Jittered

this approach is simply a reduction of the 'infinite' resolution to the finite resolution of the pixel display. If the physical extent of a pixel is small this is a high quality but totally impractical method. However, note that although this method assumes accurate geometry we assume that the light intensity is constant across any fragment. Effectively what we are doing with this algorithm is pre-filtering – that is, filtering *before* sampling using a box filter.

This is the method which approaches the anti-aliasing filter in Figure 8.6(c). It effectively removes those high frequencies that manifest as sub-pixel detail but because the calculations are continuous it is doing this before sampling.

(2) **No filtering – one sample per pixel**   In the second case we consider only one sample per pixel. This becomes equivalent to the first case if and only if the projection is such that a pixel only ever contains a single geometric structure and all structure boundaries in the projection coincide with pixel edges – impossible constraints in practice. This 'do nothing' approach is extremely common in real-time animation. It is also used as a preview method in off-line production with a final anti-aliased image generated only when a creator is satisfied with the preview.

(3) **Post filtering – *n* uniform samples per pixel**   This is the commonest approach to anti-aliasing and involves rendering a virtual image at *n* times the resolution of the final screen image. This is an approximation to the notion of a continuous image. The final image is produced by sampling the virtual image and reconstructing it by a convolution operation. Both operations are combined into a single operation. The effectiveness of this approach depends on the number of supersamples and the relationship between the image structure within a pixel and the sampling grid point. Note that although we can regard this approach as an approximation to the first case, the samples that relate to the same fragment can now have different intensities.

(4) **Post filtering – stochastic samples**   This approach can be seen as a simple alteration of the previous – instead of uniformly sampling within a pixel we now jitter the samples according to some scheme.

8.7 Pre-filtering methods

The originator of this technique was Catmull (1978). Although Catmull's original algorithm is prohibitively expensive, it has spawned a number of more practical successors.

The algorithm essentially performs sub-pixel geometry in the continuous image generation domain and returns, for each pixel, an intensity which is computed by using the areas of visible sub-pixel fragments as weights in an intensity sum. This is equivalent to convolving the image with a box filter and using the value of the convolution integral at a single point as the final pixel value. (Note that the width of the filter is less than ideal and a wider filter using information from neighbouring regions would give a lower cut-off frequency.) Another way of looking at the method is to say that it is an area sampling method.

We can ask the question: what does performing 'subpixel geometry' mean in practical computer graphics terms? To do this we inevitably have to use a practical approximation. (To reiterate an earlier point, we have no access to a continuous image. In computer graphics we can only define an image at certain points.) This means that the distinction between area sampling techniques and supersampling is somewhat artificial and indeed the A-buffer approach (described shortly), usually categorised as an area sampling technique, could equally well be seen as supersampling.

Catmull's method is incorporated in a scan line renderer. It proceeds by dividing the continuous image generation domain into square pixel extents. An intensity for each square is computed by clipping polygons against the square pixel boundary. If polygon fragments overlap within a square they are sorted in z and clipped against each other to produce visible fragments. A final intensity is computed by multiplying the shade of a polygon by the area of its visible fragment and summing.

The origin of the severe computational overheads inherent in this method is obvious. The original method was so expensive that it was used only in two-dimensional animation applications involving a few largish polygons. Here most pixels are completely covered by a polygon and the recursive clipping process of polygon fragment against polygon fragment is not entered.

Recent developments have involved approximating the sub-pixel fragments with bit masks (Carpenter, 1984) and (Fiume *et al.* 1983). Carpenter (1984) uses this approach with a Z-buffer to produce a technique known as the A-buffer (anti-aliased, area averaged, accumulator buffer). The significant advantage of this approach is that floating point geometry calculations are avoided. Coverage and area weighting is accomplished by using bit-wise logical operators between the bit patterns or masks representing polygon fragments. It is an efficient area sampling technique, where the processing per pixel square will depend on the number of visible fragments.

Another efficient approach to area sampling, due to Abram and Westover (Abram *et al.* 1985), pre-computes contributions to the convolution integral and stores these in lookup tables indexed by the polygon fragments. The method is based on the fact that the way in which a polygon covers a pixel can be approximated by a limited number of cases. The algorithm is embedded in a scan line renderer. The convolution is not restricted to one pixel extent but more correctly extends over, say, a 3 × 3 area. Pixels act as accumulators whose final value is correct when all fragments that can influence its value have been taken into account.

Consider a 3 × 3 pixel area and a 3 × 3 filter kernel (Figure 8.7). A single visible fragment in the centre pixel will contribute to the convolution integral when the filter is centred on each of the nine squares. The nine contributions that such a fragment makes can be pre-computed and stored in a lookup table. The two main stages in the process are:

(1) Find the visible fragments and identify or categorise their shape.

(2) Index a pre-computed lookup table which gives the nine contributions for each shape. A single multiplication of the fragment's intensity by the pre-computed contribution weighting gives the desired result.

Abram assumes that the shapes fall into one of seven categories:

(1) There is no fragment in the pixel.

(2) The fragment completely covers the pixel.

(3) The fragment is trapezoidal and splits the pixel along opposite edges.

(4) The fragment is triangular and splits the pixel along adjacent edges.

(5) The complement of 4) (a pentagonal fragment).

(6) The fragment is an odd shape that can be described by the difference of two or more of the previous types.

(7) The fragment cannot be easily defined by these simple types.

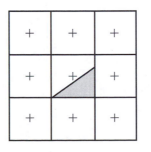

Figure 8.7
A single fragment in the centre pixel will cause contributions to filtering on each of the nine squares.

8.8   Supersampling or post-filtering

Supersampling is the most common from of anti-aliasing and is usually used with polygon mesh rendering. It involves calculating a virtual image at a spatial resolution higher than the pixel resolution and 'averaging down' the high-resolution image to a lower (pixel) resolution. In broad terms, subject to the previous reservations about the use of the term sampling, we are increasing the sampling frequency. The advantage of the method is trivial implementation which needs to be set against the high disadvantage of cost and increased Z-buffer memory. In terms of Fourier theory we can:

(1) Generate a set of samples of $I(x,y)$ at some resolution (higher than the pixel resolution);

(2) Low pass filter this image which we regard as an approximation to a continuous image;

(3) Re-sample the image at the pixel resolution.

Steps 2 and 3 (often confusingly referred to as reconstruction) are carried out simultaneously by convolving a filter with the virtual image and using it as steps

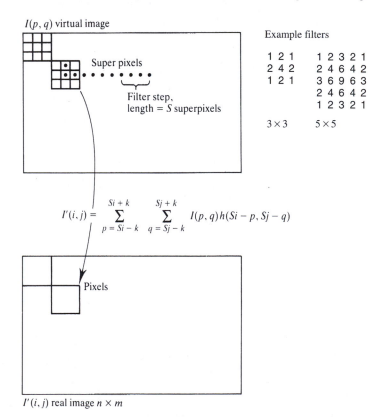

Figure 8.8
'Reducing' a virtual image by convolution.

in the convolution intervals of pixel width. That is, for a 3× virtual image, the filter would be positioned on (super) pixels in the virtual image, using a step length of three superpixels. Figure 8.8 is a representation of the method working and two examples of filters tabulated as weights (note that these are unnormalised – the filter weights must sum to unity). For an (odd) scaling factor S and a filter h of dimension k

$$I'(i,j) = \sum_{P=S_{i-k}}^{S_{i+k}} \sum_{q=S_{j-k}}^{S_{j+k}} I(p,q)h(S_i - p, S_j - q)$$

This method works well with most computer graphics images and is easily integrated into a Z-buffer algorithm. It does not work with images whose spectrum energy does not fall off with increasing frequency. (As we have already mentioned, supersampling is not, in general, a theoretically correct method of anti-aliasing.)

Supersampling methods differ trivially in the value of n and the shape of the filter used. For, say, a medium resolution image of 512×512 it is usually considered adequate to supersample at 2048×2048 ($n = 4$). The high-resolution image can be reduced to the final 512×512 form by averaging and this is equivalent to convolving with a box filter. Better results can be obtained using a shaped filter, a filter whose values vary over the extent of its kernel. There is a considerable body of knowledge on the optimum shape of filters with respect to the nature of the information that they operate on (see, for example, Oppenheimer and Shafer (1975). Most of this work is in digital signal processing and has been carried out with functions of a single variable $f(t)$. Computer graphics has unique problems that are not addressed by conventional digital signal processing techniques. For example, space variant filters are required in texture mapping. Here both the weights of the filter kernel and its shape have to change.

To return to supersampling and shaped filters, Crow (1981) used a Bartlett window, three of which are shown in Table 8.1. Digital convolution is easy to understand and implement but is computationally expensive. A window is centred on a supersample and a weighted sum of products is obtained by multiplying each supersample by the corresponding weight in the filter. The weights can

Table 8.1 Bartlett windows used in post-filtering a supersampled image

3 × 3	5 × 5	7 × 7
1 2 1	1 2 3 2 1	1 2 3 4 3 2 1
2 4 2	2 4 6 4 2	2 4 6 8 6 4 2
1 2 1	3 6 9 6 3	3 6 9 12 9 6 3
	2 4 6 4 2	4 8 12 16 12 8 4
	1 2 3 2 1	3 6 9 12 9 6 3
		2 4 6 8 6 4 2
		1 2 3 4 3 2 1

be adjusted to implement different filter kernels. The digital convolution proceeds by moving the window through n supersamples and computing the next weighted sum of products. Using a 3×3 window means that nine supersamples are involved in the final pixel computation. On the other hand, using the 7×7 window means a computation of 49 integer multiplications. The implication of the computation overheads is obvious. For example, reducing a 2048×2048 supersampled image to 512×512, with a 7×7 filter kernel, requires $512 \times 512 \times 49$ multiplications and additions.

An inevitable side-effect of filtering is blurring. In fact we could say that we trade aliasing artefacts against blurring. This occurs because information is integrated from a number of neighbouring pixels. This means that the choice of the spatial extent of the filter is a compromise. A wide filter has a lower cut-off frequency and will be better at reducing aliasing artefacts. It will, however, blur the image more than a narrower filter which will exhibit a higher cut-off frequency.

Finally, the disadvantages of the technique should be noted. Supersampling is not a suitable method for dealing with very small objects. Also it is a 'global' method – the computation is not context dependent. A scene that exhibited a few large area polygons would be subject to the same computational overheads as one with a large number of small area polygons. The memory requirements are large if the method is to be used with a Z-buffer. The supersampled version of the image has to be created and stored before the filtering process can be applied. This increases the storage requirements of the Z-buffer by a factor of n^2, making it essentially a virtual memory technique.

8.9 Anti-aliasing in texture mapping

The use of an anti-aliasing method is mandatory with texture mapping. This is easily seen by considering an object retreating away from a viewer so that its projection in screen space covers fewer and fewer pixels. As the object size decreases the pre-image of a pixel in texture space will increase, covering a larger area. If we simply point sample at the centre of the pixel and take the value of $T(u,v)$ at the corresponding point in texture space, then grossly incorrect results will follow (Figure 8.9(a),(b) and (c)). An example of this effect is shown in Figure 8.10. Here, as the chequerboard pattern recedes into the distance it begins to break up in a disturbing manner. These problems are highly visible and move when animated. Consider Figure 8.9(b) and (c). Say, for example, that an object projects onto a single pixel and moves in such a way that the pre-image translates across the $T(u,v)$. As the object moves it would switch colour from black to white.

Anti-aliasing in this context, then, means integrating the information over the pixel pre-image and using this value in the shading calculation for the current pixel (Figure 8.9(d)). At best we can only approximate this integral because we have no knowledge of the shape of the quadrilateral, only its four corner points.

Defects are highly noticeable, particularly in texture that exhibits coherence or periodicity, as soon as the predominant spatial frequency in the texture

Figure 8.9
Pixels and pre-images in
$T(u,v)$ space.

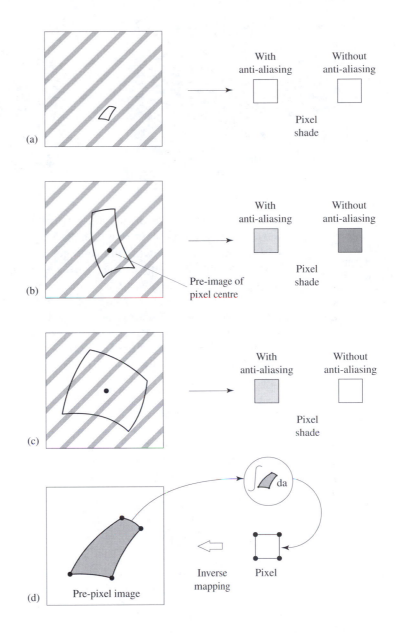

pattern approaches the dimension of a pixel. Artefacts generated by texture mapping are not well handled by the common anti-aliasing method – such as supersampling – and because of this, standard two-dimensional texture mapping procedures usually incorporate a specific anti-aliasing technique. Because of the migration of texture mapping and the vital nature of texture anti-aliasing, there has been a simultaneous development of hardware texture anti-aliasing. This commonly takes the form of 'mip-mapping' which is the topic of this section.

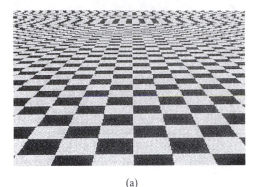
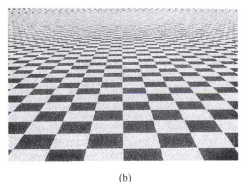

(a)   (b)

Figure 8.10
Aliasing in texture mapping. The pattern in (b) is a supersampled (anti-aliased) version of that in (a). Aliases still occur but appear at a higher spatial frequency.

Anti-aliasing in texture mapping is difficult because, to do it properly, we need to find the pre-image of a pixel and sum weighted values of $T(u,v)$ that fall within the extent of the pre-image to get a single texture intensity for the pixel. Unfortunately, the shape of the pre-image changes from pixel to pixel and this filtering process consequently becomes expensive. Refer again to Figure 8.9. This shows that when we are considering a pixel its pre-image in texture space is, in general, a curvilinear quadrilateral, because the net effect of the texture mapping and perspective mapping is of a non-linear transformation. The figure also shows for the diagonal band texture that unless this operation is performed or approximated, erroneous results will occur. In particular if the texture map is merely sampled at the inverse mapping of the pixel centre then the sampled intensity may be correct if the inverse image size of the pixel is sufficiently small, but in general it will be wrong.

In the context of Figure 8.11(a), anti-aliasing means approximating the integration shown in the figure. The pre-image varies from pixel to pixel and this implies that we must vary the shape of the filter accordingly. This is called anisotropic filtering. An approximate, but visually successful, method ignores

Figure 8.11
Mip-mapping approximations. (a) The pre-image of a pixel is a curvilinear quadrilateral in texture space. (b) A pre-image can be approximated by a square. (c) Compression is required when a pixel maps onto many texels. (d) Magnification is required when a pixel maps onto less than one texel.

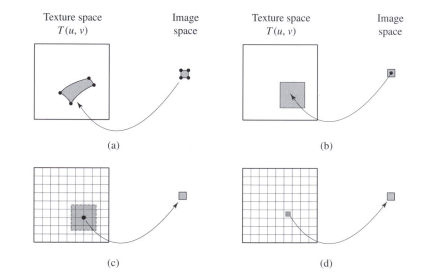

the shape but not the size or extent of the pre-image and **pre-calculates** all the required filtering operations. This is **mip-mapping** invented by Williams (1983) and is the most common anti-aliasing method developed specifically for texture mapping. His method is based on pre-calculation and an assumption that the inverse pixel image is reasonably close to a square. Figure 8.11(b) shows the pixel pre-image approximated by a square. It is this approximation that enables the anti-aliasing or filtering operation to be pre-calculated. In fact there are two problems. The first is more common and is known as compression or minification. This occurs when an object becomes small in screen space and consequently a pixel has a large pre-image in texture space. Figure 8.11(c) shows this situation. Many texture elements (sometimes called 'texels') need to be mapped into a single pixel. The other problem is called magnification. Here, an object becomes very close to the viewer and only part of the object may occupy the whole of screen space, resulting in a pixel pre-images that have less area than one texel (Figure 8.11(d). Mip-mapping deals with compression and some elaboration to mip-mapping is usually required for the magnification problem.

In mip-mapping, instead of a texture domain comprising a single image, Williams uses many images, all derived by averaging down the original image to successively lower resolutions. In other words, they form a set of pre-filtered texture maps. Each image in the sequence is exactly half the resolution of the previous. Figure 8.12 shows an approximation to the idea. An object near to the

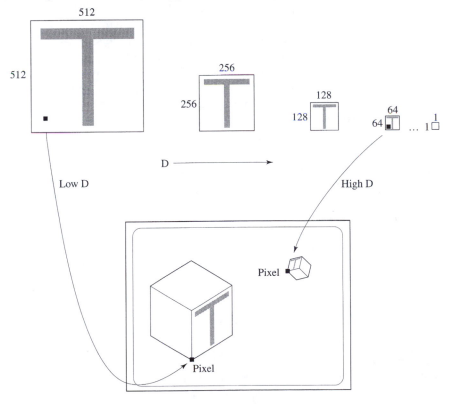

Figure 8.12
Showing the principle of mip-mapping.

viewer, and large in screen space, selects a single texel from a high-resolution map. The same object further away from the viewer and smaller in screen space selects a single texel from a low-resolution map. An appropriate map is selected by a parameter D. Figure 8.13 (Colour Plate) shows the mip-map used in Figure 7.10.

In a low-resolution version of the image each texel represents the average of a number of texels from the previous map. By a suitable choice of D, an image at appropriate resolution is selected and the filtering cost remains constant – the many texels to one pixel cost problem being avoided. The centre of the pixel is mapped into that map determined by D and this single value is used. In this way, the original texture is filtered and to avoid discontinuities between the images at varying resolutions, different levels are also blended. Blending between levels occurs when D is selected.

Williams selects D from:

$$D = \text{max\_of}\left(\left(\left(\frac{\partial u}{\partial x}\right)^2 + \left(\frac{\partial v}{\partial x}\right)^2 \right)^{1/2}, \left(\left(\frac{\partial u}{\partial y}\right)^2 + \left(\frac{\partial v}{\partial y}\right)^2 \right)^{1/2} \right)$$

where ∂u and ∂v are the original dimensions of the pre-image in texture space and $\partial x = \partial y = 1$ for a square pixel (Figure 8.14). Note that this implies a per-pixel algorithm − D is calculated separately for each pixel.

A 'correct' or accurate estimation of D is important. If D is too large then the image will look blurred, too small and aliasing artefacts will still be visible. Detailed practical methods for determining – depending on the mapping context are given in Watt and Watt (1992).

In general, D and T are continuous values and a process known as tri-linear interpolation is used to calculate the result. First, bi-linear interpolation is carried out amongst the texels in the mip-map closest to $T(u,v)$ (Figure 8.15). This process is repeated for the next (coarsest) map in the sequence and the two

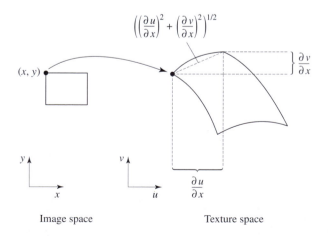

Figure 8.14
William's metric for the selection of **D**.

Image space   Texture space

Figure 8.15
Tri-linear interpolation in
mip-mapping.

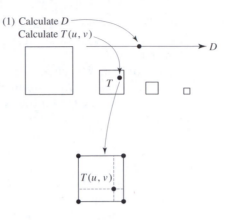

(1) Calculate D
Calculate $T(u, v)$

(2) Bi-linearly interpolate between four texels nearest to $T(u, v)$

(3) Repeat this process for next (coarsest mip-map) and linearly
interpolate the two results

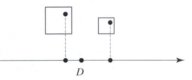

results so obtained are linearly blended according to the value of D. Figure 8.16
(Colour Plate) is a set of comparison images showing the increase in quality
available from mip-mapping. Figure 8.16(a) uses no filtering whatsoever. Figure
8.16(b) uses simple neighbourhood filtering where the four closest pixels are linearly interpolated to give the final value. Figures 8.16(c) and (d) employ mip-
mapping. The first image uses one map and the second linearly interpolates
between two maps (tri-linear interpolation).

In a theoretical sense the magnification problem does not exist. Ideally we
would like mip-maps that can be used at any level of detail, but in practice, storage limitations restrict the highest resolution mask to, say, 512×512 texels. This
problem does not seem to have been addressed in the literature and the following two approaches are supplied by Silicon Graphics for their workstation family. Silicon Graphics suggest two solutions: first, simply extrapolate beyond the
highest resolution mip-map, and second, a more elaborate procedure that
extracts separate texture information into low- and high-frequency components.

Extrapolation is defined as

$$\text{LOD}(+1) = \text{LOD}(0) + (\text{LOD}(0) - \text{LOD}(-1))$$

where LOD (level of detail) represents mip-maps as follows:

LOD(+1) is the extrapolated mip-map
LOD(0) is the highest resolution stored mip-map
LOD(−1) is the next highest resolution stored mip-map

This operation derives an extrapolated mip map of blocks of 4 × 4 pixels over which there is no variation. However, the magnification process preserves edges – hence the name.

Extrapolation works best when high-frequency information is correlated with low-frequency structural information, that is, when the high-frequency information represents edges in the texture. For example, consider that texture pattern is made up of block letters. Extrapolation will blur/magnify the interior of the letters, while keeping the edges sharp.

When high-frequency information is not correlated with low-frequency information, extrapolation causes blurring. This occurs with texture that tends to vary uniformly throughout, for example wood grain. Silicon Graphics suggest separating the low- and high-frequency information and converting a high resolution (unstorable at, say, 2K × 2K) into a 512 × 512 map that stores low frequency or structural information and a 256 × 256 map that stores high-frequency detail. This separation can be achieved accurately using classical filtering techniques. Alternatively a space domain procedure is as follows:

(1) Make a 512 × 512 low-frequency map by simply re-sampling the original 2K × 2K map.

(2) Make the 256 × 256 detail mask as follows:
  (i)   Select a 256 × 256 window from the original map that contains representative high-frequency texture.
  (ii) Re-sample this to 64 × 64 and re-scale to 256 × 256, resulting in a blurred version of the original 256 × 256 map.
  (iii) Subtract the blurred map from the original, adding a bias to make the subtrahend image unsigned. This results in a 256 × 256 high-frequency map.

Now when magnification is required a mix of the 512 × 512 low resolution texture with the high-resolution detail is used.

8.10 The Fourier transform of images

Fourier theory is not used to any extent in computer graphics except in specialised applications such as generating terrain height fields using Fourier synthesis. However, an intuitive understanding of it is vital to understanding the effects of and the cure for image defects due to undersampling.

The Fourier transform is one of the fundamental tools of modern science and engineering and it finds applications in both analogue and digital electronics, where information is represented (usually) as a continuous function of time, and in work associated with computer imagery where the image $I(x,y)$ is represented as an intensity function of two spatial variables.

Calculating the Fourier transform of an image, $I(x,y)$, means that the image is represented as a weighted set of spatial frequencies (or weighted sinusoidally undulating surfaces) and this confers, as far as certain operations are concerned, particular advantages. The individual spatial frequencies are known as basis functions.

Any process that uses the Fourier domain will usually be made up of three main phases. The image is transformed into the Fourier domain. Some operation is performed on this representation of the image and it is then transformed back into its normal representation – known as the space domain. The transformations are called forward and reverse transforms. Fourier transforms are important, and this is reflected in the fact that the algorithms which perform the transformations are implemented in hardware in image processing computers.

There is no information lost in transforming an image into the Fourier domain – the visual information in the image is just represented in a different way. For the non-mathematically minded it is, at first sight, a strange beast. One point in the Fourier domain representation of an image contains information about the entire image. The value of the point tells us how much of a spatial frequency is in the image.

We define the Fourier transform of an image $I(x,y)$:

$$F(u,v) = \frac{1}{2\pi} \iint I(x,y) e^{-j(ux+vy)} dx dy$$

and the reverse transform as:

$$I(x,y) = \frac{1}{2\pi} \iint F(u,v) e^{j(ux+vy)} du dv$$

The Fourier transform is a complex quantity and can be expressed as a real and imaginary part:

$$F(u,v) = \text{Real}(u,v) + j\,\text{Imag}(u,v)$$

and we can represent $F(u,v)$ as two functions known as the amplitude and phase spectrum respectively:

$$|F(u,v)| = (\text{Real}^2(u,v) + \text{Imag}^2(u,v))^{1/2}$$

$$\varphi(u,v) = \tan^{-1}(\text{Imag}(u,v)/\text{Real}(u,v))$$

Now it is important to have an intuitive idea of the nature of the transform and in particular the physical meaning of a spatial frequency. We first consider the easier case of a function of a single variable $I(x)$. If we transform this into the Fourier domain then we have the transform $F(u)$. The amplitude spectrum, $|F(u)|$, specifies a set of sinusoids that when added together produce the original function $I(x)$ and the phase spectrum specifies the phase relationship of each sinusoid (the value of the sinusoid at $x = 0$). That is, each point in $|F(u)|$ specifies the amplitude and frequency of a single sine wave component. Another way of putting it is to say that any function $I(x)$ decomposes into a set of sine wave coefficients. This situation is shown in Figure 8.17. The first part of the figure shows the amplitude spectrum of a single sinusoid which is just a single point (actually

Figure 8.17
One-dimensional Fourier transform. (a) A sine wave maps into a single point. (b) A 'window' of an 'information wave' maps into a frequency spectrum.

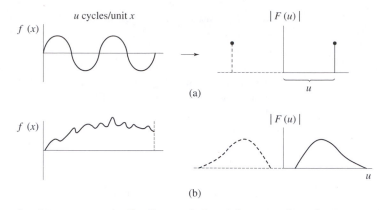

a pair of points symmetrically disposed about the origin) in the Fourier domain. The second example shows a function that contains information – it could be a speech signal. This exhibits a spectrum that has extent in the Fourier domain. The spread from the minimum to the maximum frequency is called the bandwidth.

A 2D function $I(x,y)$ – an image function – decomposes into a set of **spatial** frequencies $|F(u,v)|$. A spatial frequency is a surface – a sinusoidal 'corrugation' whose frequency or rate of undulation is given by the distance of the point (u,v) from the origin:

$$\sqrt{u^2 + v^2}$$

and whose orientation – the angle the peaks and troughs of the corrugation make with the x axis – is given by

$$\tan^{-1}(u/v)$$

A single point $F(u,v)$ tells us how much of that spatial frequency is contained by the image. Figure 8.18 is a two-dimensional analogue of Figure 8.17. Here a sinusoid has spatial extent and maps into a single point (again actually a pair of points) in the Fourier domain. If we now consider an image $I(x,y)$, this maps into a two-dimensional frequency spectrum that is a function of the two variables u and v. Different categories of images exhibit different categories of Fourier transforms, as we shall demonstrate shortly by example. However, most images have Fourier representations with the amplitude characteristic peaking at (0,0) and decreasing with increasing spatial frequency. Images of natural scenes tend to

Figure 8.18
An image made up of a single spatial frequency and its Fourier transform.

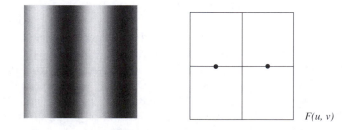

exhibit Fourier representations that contain no coherent structures. Images of man-made scenes generally exhibit coherences in the Fourier domain reflecting the occurrence of coherent structures (roads, buildings, etc.) in the original scene. Computer graphics images often have high energy in high spatial frequency components, reflecting the occurrence of detailed texture in the image.

A property of the Fourier representation that is of importance in image processing is that the circumference of a circle, centred on the origin, specifies a set of spatial frequencies of identical rate of undulation

$$r = \sqrt{u^2 + v^2}$$

having every possible orientation.

We will now look at the nature of the transform qualitatively by examining three different examples of amplitude spectra.

- **Figure 8.19(a)** is an image from nature. It produces a Fourier transform that exhibits virtually no coherences. Despite the fact that there is much line structure manifested in the edges of the leaves, the lines are at every possible orientation and no coherence is visible in the Fourier domain.

(a) Bush

Fourier transform $|F(u, v)|$

(b) Arcos da Lapa
(Rio de Janeiro)

Fourier transform $|F(u, v)|$

Figure 8.19
Fourier transforms of natural and man-made scenes.

● **Figure 8.19(b)** is an image of a man-made scene. There is obvious structure in the Fourier domain that relates to the scene. First, there is the line structure that originates from the tramline discontinuity (top of the arches). Second, there is the discontinuity between the upper and lower arches that manifests as another line in the Fourier domain. There are coherences around the v axis that are due to the horizontal edges of the structure. Because the orientation of these lines is due to the camera perspective, they map into non-vertical lines in the Fourier domain. There is a vertical coherence in the Fourier domain that relates to scan lines in the data collection device and is also due to horizontal discontinuities manifested by the long shadows. The remainder of the contributions in the Fourier domain originate from the natural components in the image such as the texture on the arch walls.

● **Figures 8.20(a) and 8.20(b)** are two man-made textures. The relationships between the coherences of the texture and the structures in the Fourier domain should be clear. In both cases the textures have been overlaid with a leaf – which manifests as a blurry 'off-vertical' line in the Fourier domain.

(a)

Figure 8.20
Fourier transforms of textures.

(b)

What can we conclude from these examples? A very important observation is that information that is 'spread' throughout the space domain separates out in the Fourier domain. In particular, we see that in the second example the coherences in the image structure are reflected in the Fourier domain as lines or spokes that pass through the origin. In the third example, the texture produces components that are strictly localised in the Fourier domain at their predominant spatial frequencies. This property of the Fourier domain is probably the most commonly used and accounts for spatial filtering, where we may want to enhance some spatial frequencies and diminish others to effect particular changes to the image. It is also used in image compression where we encode or quantise the transform of the image, rather than the image itself. This gives us the opportunity to use less information to encode those components of the transform that we know have less 'importance'. This is a powerful approach and it happens that much less information can be used to encode certain parts of the transform without any significant fall in image quality. The original information in the image is reordered in the transform in a way that enables us to make easy judgements about its relative importance in the image domain.

Visibility processing of complex scenes

9.1   Introduction

9.2   Why trees?

9.3   BSP trees

9.4   Bounding volume hierarchies

9.5   BSP trees and polygon objects

9.6   Specialisations for building interior-type environments

9.7   Portals and mirrors

9.8   Advanced view frustum culling

9.9   Exact visibility

9.10 Dynamic objects and visibility

9.1   Introduction

This chapter is concerned with the efficient processing of complex scenes. In the context of computer games this means fast visibility processing and fast collision detection. We will see how to best represent complex scenes that consist of thousands of objects in ways that facilitate these calculations. In Chapter 2 we looked at how to represent individual objects and we will now be concerned with how we impose a secondary data structure on these objects that comprise the scene. From the outset it is important to realise that such a structure subdivides the scene space into partitions and, although these partitions can contain individual objects, more usually the subdivision will continue 'inside' objects. In the limit we may continue the subdivision until partitions contain single polygons. It is easy to see why this is the necessary. When we are processing for visibility an object may intersect the view frustum – part of it is inside and part outside. For a complex object that straddles the view volume we may decide that a partitioning scheme that subdivides the object is necessary. Alternatively in collision detection, if two objects collide, we need to evaluate the point of collision, which in the general case will be a single point in each object. The need for effective scene management is then obvious – we easily have a scene that contains thousands of objects, each of which is made up of thousands of polygons.

With the growth of complexity of scenes has come a realisation that traditional techniques will no longer suffice if real-time performance has to be achieved. The critical areas that have seen new (or rediscovered existing) techniques applied to them are visibility processing and collision detection. (Here we use the term visibility processing rather than hidden surface removal to reflect the emphasis on powerful culling techniques which remove, as far as possible, all those scene elements that are not contained within the view frustum.)

Although a case could be made that the visibility or hidden surface removal problem has, in the form of the Z-buffer, had a solution for more than two decades, with the growth in scene complexity, its inherent inefficiency (described in Chapter 6) becomes more and more problematic. In this chapter we will look at alternative Z-buffer techniques that can be applied to scenes of high complexity. In the main these are combinations of techniques – rather than a single algorithm – some of which may involve a pre-processing phase that evaluates approximate visibility which is then refined dynamically. Many techniques, including some of the ones that we will describe, were researched in the early 1970s, when there was much energetic work being done on the hidden surface problem. With the irresistible rise of the Z-buffer method, this was forgotten and is now being re-examined in the light of modern demands for scenes of sufficiently high complexity to imitate reality.

The main emphasis of the chapter is on organising the scene into a hierarchy. The way in which this can help in visibility processing is fairly obvious. The idea of a scene hierarchy is shown conceptually in Figure 9.1. Note that the nodes can be 'switches' that are set in reaction to a player crossing a threshold from one part of the scene to another (going from indoors to outdoors, for example). Such an enhanced hierarchy needs a secondary record, say a plan in the form of a binary map, which detects when a player crosses a threshold.

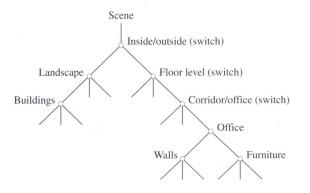

Figure 9.1
The concept of a scene hierarchy.

The kind of hierarchy that is useful to us in scene management must embody spatial occupancy information at each level. In computer graphics object hierarchies are used where a scene will be decomposed, say, into objects, objects into parts, parts into polygons. A reference world space coordinate may be associated with the object at the root of the tree but the information that describes the surface of the object is embedded in polygon vertex lists at the leaf of the tree. In scene management we need to be able to efficiently answer such queries as: is a moving ball object likely to be in collision with any static object in the room? And we want to do this efficiently by descending a tree. This implies that the tree must contain information like: this node, which represents a particular region in space, contains these objects or object parts.

There are two commonly used hierarchies in scene management: BSP trees, which we consider as a generalisations of octrees, and bounding volume trees. In BSP trees and octrees all of space is represented and partitions are categorised as containing an object(s) or empty. With bounding volume trees we enclose clusters of objects and individual objects inside a standard object known as a bounding volume. This may be a sphere or a box, for example. With bounding volume trees we categorise only that space inside the bounding volumes. We can think about the hierarchy as a kind of shape-simplified version of the scene.

The building of a hierarchy implies a pre-processing operation that is only carried out once and has thus no complexity limit imposed on it. This basic strategy has a long history and appears to have been introduced into early flight simulators by Schumaker *et al.* as early as 1969.

Once a tree is built we can descend or traverse it with coordinates of, for example, the view frustum and cull away large parts of the scene early, 'homing in' on those elements that need detailed consideration. We can also apply a hierarchical approach to collision detection. In principle it is no different from view frustum culling if we consider the view frustum to be an object. However, there is one important difference, which is illustrated in Figure 9.2. This shows that 'static' collision detection where we check for interference between a pair of objects once per frame will not in general suffice. At time t_2 we could have already passed through or into an object. The naïve approach of sampling at intervals between the frames simply multiplies the cost. We will return to this problem in Chapter 15.

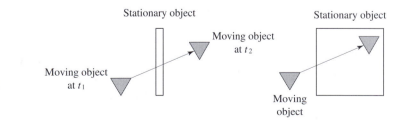

Figure 9.2
'Static' collision detection implies that a moving object can pass through/into a stationary object.

It is the case that bounding volume hierarchies tend to be used in collision detection and spatial subdivision techniques are used in rendering speed-ups and so we deal with BSP trees and octrees in this chapter and bounding volume hierarchies in Chapter 15. Of course, both applications are collision detection – in both cases we are testing to see if two volumes intersect or are disjoint; the only (trivial) difference is that in (broad phase) collision detection we test pairs of bounding volumes whereas in view frustum culling we generally test an exact view volume against a bounding volume.

Let us now look at what we mean by visibility processing in more detail. The key to rendering complex scenes is fast visibility processing and we obviously try to do this by only giving consideration to that part of the scene that is going to be projected into screen space. We try to accomplish this aim by pre-processing to build a secondary data structure which we hope will enable us to deal only with visible sections of the scene. This operation is generally costly and hence cannot be done in real time. This fact immediately raises the main problem of such techniques – they do not deal with dynamic objects (leaving aside the case of a moving view volume and a static scene).

In the chapter there are three interlinked themes which it is useful to overview at this stage. The first is the use of a hierarchy to cull away parts of the scene that do not intersect the view frustum – view frustum culling or VFC. Prior to the need for efficiency in rendering complex scenes VFC was carried out as a routine low-level operation in the graphics pipeline – every polygon of every object in the scene being subject to a separate test against the view volume. This is clearly extremely wasteful for a complex scene where by definition most of the scene will lie outside the view frustum. Also, the second and third requirements were generally implemented by a Z-buffer algorithm which, of course, is the root of the inefficiency of the Z-buffer – it will cause objects to be rendered which are subsequently overwritten by nearer objects. Spatial subdivision techniques enable what we refer to as conservative visibility, the fast determination of potentially visible objects – they do not determine exact visibility.

The second theme is exact visibility determination – culling and clipping and hidden surface removal. Those objects that were not eliminated as a consequence of the spatial partitioning method have to be passed over to a method that determines exact visibility amongst objects – which objects or polygons obscure other objects or polygons. Here we look again at using spatial partitioning, looking at a technique that utilises octrees. This method uses a hierarchy of strategies to exploit the various coherences that exist in scenes. Coherence – a simple concept – just means that an entity is likely to possess attributes similar or identical to a neighbouring entity. Thus the phrase 'exploiting object space coherence' means that we should initially deal with visibility by considering entire objects. The algorithm attempts to exploit object space, image space and temporal coherence.

Finally, we look at how we can exploit the special properties of building interior-type environments to **pre-compute** visibility from any general viewpoint.

9.2 Why trees?

We begin by considering why it is that such scene management techniques function so well with complex scenes. In particular, we introduce a comparison that ignores object representation and concentrates just on scene subdivision. In all cases we build a tree as a pre-process, then descend this tree in real time to find out, for example, if two objects occupy the same spatial partition – and are therefore maybe in collision; or to find out if the space of an object and the view frustum are disjoint, enabling us to eliminate the entire object from further processing. The answer, then, to why trees? should be clear – all of these operations reduce to tree descent or traversal – a fast linear time operation.

9.2.1 Space subdivision hierarchies

Space subdivision or partitioning techniques are methods that consider the whole of object space and label each point in the space according to object occupancy. Thus in a brute force scheme we might divide up all of world space into regular or cubic voxels and label each voxel. Figure 9.3 shows a two-dimensional analogue of a space occupied by three objects. The shaded objects are given a label that is the identity of the object that occupies that space.

The classic example of the use of spatial subdivision in computer graphics is intersection testing in ray tracing. Here, instead of asking the question: does this ray intersect with any objects in the scene? which implies a very expensive intersection test to be carried out on each object, we pose the question: what objects are encountered as we track a ray through voxel space? Since all voxels are labelled, this requires no exhaustive search through the primary data structure for possible intersections and is a much more practical strategy.

Clearly this is very costly in terms of memory consumption and a number of schemes are available that impose a structural organisation on the basic voxel labelling scheme.

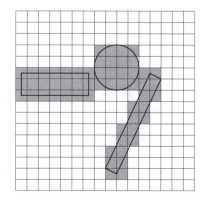

Figure 9.3
A two-dimensional analogue of three objects and their representation.

Octrees

An octree is a data structure that describes how the objects in a scene are distributed throughout the three-dimensional space occupied by the scene. It simply organises the voxels into a hierarchy. The ideas involved in an octree representation can be more easily demonstrated by using a 'quadtree' to represent the occupancy of a two-dimensional region. Figure 9.4 shows a two-dimensional region containing some simple objects together with a quadtree representation of the region and the objects. The tree is created by starting with a square region representing the whole of the occupied space. This region is represented by the node at the top of the tree. (In the three-dimensional case, the region would be a cube.) Because the region is occupied by objects, it is subdivided into four subregions, represented by the four child nodes in the tree. Figure 9.4 indicates the ordering scheme used for the child nodes. (In the three-dimensional case, a region would be subdivided into eight subregions, and the node representing the region would have eight children – hence the term octree.) Any subregion that is occupied by objects is further subdivided until the size of the subregion corresponds to the maximum resolution required of the representation scheme.

Thus, there are two types of terminal node in the tree. Some terminal nodes correspond to subregions that are unoccupied by objects, while others correspond to cells of minimum size that are occupied by part of an object. Note that in the two-dimensional case, we have represented objects by their boundaries and the interior of an object counts as unoccupied space. In the three-dimensional case, objects are represented by their surfaces and we would only subdivide regions that contain parts of the surface.

There are actually two ways in which the octree decomposition of a scene can be used to represent the scene. Firstly, an octree as described above can be used in itself as a complete representation of the objects in the scene. The set of cells occupied by an object constitute the representation of the object. However, for a complex scene, high resolution work would require the decomposition of occupied space into an extremely large number of cells and this technique requires enormous amounts of data storage. A common alternative is to use a standard data structure representation of the objects and to use the octree as a representation of the distribution of the objects in the scene. In this case, a terminal node of a tree representing an occupied region would be represented by a pointer to the data structure for any object intersecting that region. Figure 9.5 illustrates this possibility in the two-dimensional case. Here the region subdivision has stopped as soon as a region is encountered that intersects only one object. A region represented by a terminal node is not necessarily completely occupied by the object associated with that region. The shape of the object within the region would be described by its data structure representation. In the case of a surface model representation of a scene, the 'objects' would be polygons or patches. In general, an occupied region represented by a terminal node could intersect with several polygons and would be represented by a list of pointers into the object data structures.

Figure 9.4
(a) Quadtree representation of a two-dimensional scene at the pixel level. A similar method is used to represent a three-dimensional scene by an octree.
(b) Ordering scheme for child nodes in quadtree illustrations.

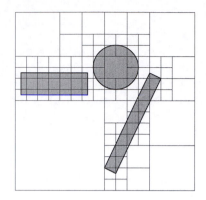

e = empty
r = rod
b = box
c = circle

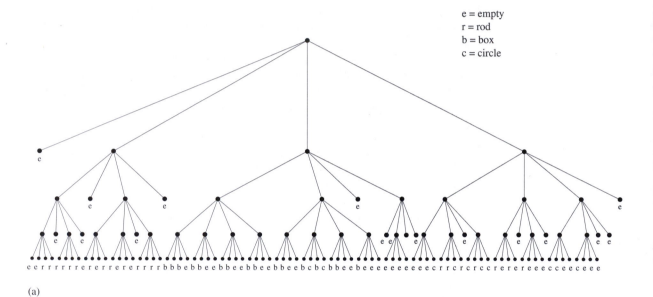

e e r r r r r r e r e r r r e r e r r r b b b e b b e e b b e e b b e e b b e e b c b c b b e e b e e e e e e e e e c r r c r c r c c r e r e r e e e c c e e c e e c e e

(a)

(b)

Figure 9.5
Quadtree representation of a two-dimensional scene down to the level of cells containing at most a single object. Terminal nodes for cells containing objects are represented by a pointer to a data structure representation of the object.

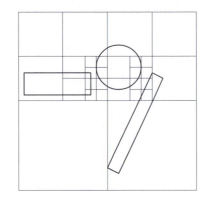

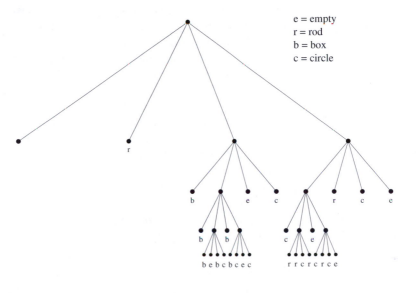

e = empty
r = rod
b = box
c = circle

BSP trees

A binary space partitioning tree, or BSP tree, partitions space by dividing into two parts at each level by using a splitting plane. Figure 9.6 demonstrates the idea in two dimensions. It contains a one-level subdivision of a square region together with the one-level quadtree representation and the corresponding BSP tree. A simple extension to three dimensions enables an octree to be coded as a BSP tree. Each non-terminal node in the BSP tree represents a single partitioning plane that divides occupied space into two. A terminal node represents a region that is not further subdivided and would contain pointers to data structure representations of the objects intersecting that region (again typically one or two).

Figure 9.6
Quadtree and BSP tree representations of a one-level subdivision of a two-dimensional region.

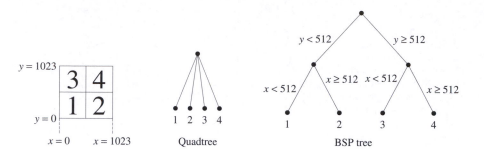

Quadtree   BSP tree

Adaptive subdivision with a BSP tree

When a BSP tree is used to represent a subdivision of space into cubic cells, it shows no significant advantage over a direct data structure encoding of the octree. However, nothing said above requires that the subdivision should be into cubic cells. In fact the idea of a BSP tree was originally introduced in Fuchs (1980) where the planes used to subdivide space could be at any orientation. In Fuchs (1980), the BSP structure was used as an aid to sorting the planes in a scene into a back to front ordering consistent with a given viewpoint. The planes used to subdivide space were the planes defined by the polygons constituting the scene. These planes could lie at any orientation. Thus we can consider BSP trees as generalisations of octrees.

Objects will often be unevenly distributed throughout occupied space. This is particularly the case when the 'objects' are actually patches used to approximate the surfaces of real objects. A single real object will be represented by a large cluster of patches in space and there will be relatively large regions of empty space between objects.

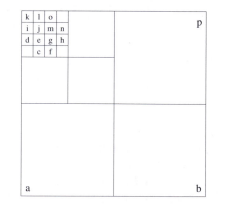

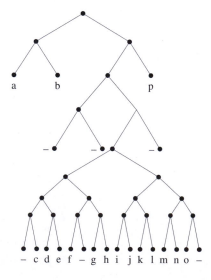

Figure 9.7
Straightforward subdivision of a two-dimensional scene containing 'objects' a–p unevenly distributed throughout the scene. The search path length in the tree for most objects is 8.

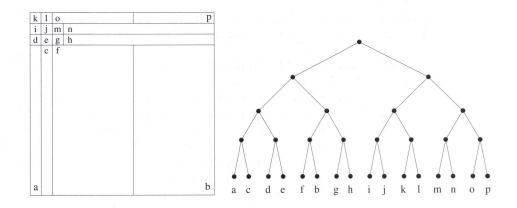

Figure 9.8
Adaptive BSP subdivision of a two-dimensional scene with unevenly distributed objects. The maximum search path length in the BSP is reduced to 4.

We can easily illustrate the idea of adaptive partitioning in two dimensions and give some idea of why it is advantageous. Figures 9.7 and 9.8 show two alternative partitions of a region containing 16 objects labelled 'a' to 'p'. These objects are rather unevenly distributed throughout this region. In Figure 9.7, a straightforward quadtree subdivision has been used and this has been represented by a BSP tree. The maximum depth of this tree is eight, and this would be the maximum length of search required to identify the region in which a given point lies.

In Figure 9.8, adaptive partitioning has been used. At each step, a partitioning line has been chosen that divides the current region in such a way that the region contains equal numbers of objects on either side of the line. This results in a more balanced BSP tree in which the maximum search length is four.

9.4 Bounding volume hierarchies

A bounding volume representation attempts to label the space using partitions that enclose all of the object, the common bounding volumes being spheres, boxes (axis aligned bounding boxes or AABBs) or oriented bounding boxes (OBBs). Originally introduced in ray tracing, bounding volumes were used to speed up intersection testing. Their rationale in this context is that it is quicker to test a ray for intersection against a standard bounding volume such as a box or a sphere. Only if the ray intersects the bounding volume need the expensive ray/object intersection test be applied. However, it is easy to see the obvious drawback of this scheme, which is that if the bounding volume does not tightly enclose the object (consider a sphere enclosing a long thin cylinder object) the likelihood is that the ray/object intersection test will fail, obviating the method. The fastest bounding volume – the sphere – is also potentially an inefficient bounding volume. Bounding volumes are discussed in more detail in Chapter 15.

9.5 BSP trees and polygon objects

9.5.1 BSP trees and hidden surface removal

BSP trees were first introduced to solve the hidden surface removal problem in real time. The original idea depends on having a static scene and a changing viewpoint – the classic flight simulator/computer game application, and it works as a two-phase process. In the first phase a BSP tree of the scene is constructed (once only – which in practice would be an off-line process) and in the second phase the viewpoint is compared with this structure to determine visibility.

BSP trees are not an object representation – although in certain circumstances they can be – but a way of partitioning space so that we can solve certain rendering requirements in an efficient manner. We will look first of all at the simpler issue of determining visibility amongst objects, then see how the principles can be extended to determine polygon visibility within an object.

If our scene consists of convex objects that can be separated by convex regions made up of planes then we can use a recursive divide and conquer strategy to divide up the space. We assume that we have an appropriate strategy for positioning the planes and that the tree is complete when all regions contain only a single object. Figure 9.9 shows the idea. The first plane inserted into the scene space is plane A and this forms the root node and divides the space into two regions each containing a pair of objects. The process continues recursively and the partitioning is represented by a tree. Two branches emanate from a node, representing the negative and positive sides of the plane respectively.

Having constructed a tree we can then determine a visibility ordering for a viewpoint inserted into the scene. Consider Figure 9.9(b) which shows a viewpoint inserted into the scene. We descend the tree from the root node with the viewpoint coordinates to find the leaf node that the viewpoint is in and hence the object 'closest' to the viewpoint. (The precise meaning of 'closest' will become clear shortly.) Starting at the root node we descend the subtree on the side of plane A nearest to the viewpoint, taking us to the node associated with plane B and thenceforth to object 2. Object 3 is the next nearest to the viewpoint and returning to the root node and descending, the remaining ordering is Object 1 followed by object 4 (Figure 9.9(c)).

This gives us a near to far visibility ordering which for this scene is Objects 2, 3, 1 and 4. Alternatively we can just as easily generate a far to near ordering.

In practice this scheme is not particularly useful because most computer graphics applications are made up of scenes where the object complexity (number of polygons per object) is much greater than scene complexity (number of objects per scene) and for the approach to be useful we have to deal with polygons within objects rather than entire objects. Also, there is the problem of positioning the planes – itself a non-trivial problem. If the number of objects is small we can have a separating plane for every pair of objects – a total of n^2 for an n-object scene.

Figure 9.9
BSP operations for a four-object scene.
(a) Constructing a BSP tree.
(b) Descending the tree with the viewpoint coordinates gives the nearest object.
(c) Evaluating a visibility order for all objects.

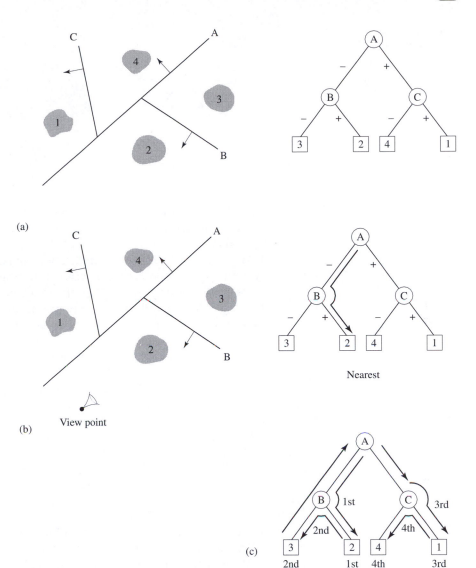

For polygon visibility ordering there is nothing to stop us choosing partitioning planes that contain face polygons. A polygon is selected and used as a root node. All other polygons are tested against the plane containing this polygon and placed on the appropriate descendent branch. Any polygon that crosses the plane of the root polygon is split into two constituents. The process continues recursively until all polygons are contained by a plane or until some other appropriate terminating condition is reached. Obviously the procedure creates more polygons than were originally in the scene but practice has shown that this is usually less than a factor of two.

The process is shown for a simple example in Figure 9.10. The first plane chosen, plane A, containing a polygon from object 1, splits object 3 into two parts.

Figure 9.10
A BSP tree for polygons.

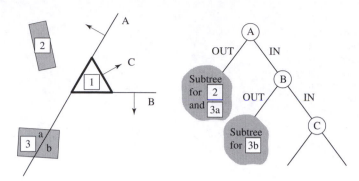

The tree builds up as before and we now use the convention IN/OUT to say which side of a partition an entity lies, since this now has meaning with respect to the polygonal objects.

We will now consider the different ramifications of far to near versus near to far ordering with respect to polygonal objects. Far to near ordering was the original scheme used. Rendering polygons into the frame buffer in this order results in the so-called painter's algorithm – near polygons are written 'on top of' farther ones. This is clearly inefficient as rendered polygons may be subsequently written over. Near to far ordering can also be used but in this case we have to mark in some way the fact that a pixel has been already written to, by using a write mask. There are high potential savings over the far to near ordering – particularly if there are significant lighting calculations per pixel. The easiest way to implement a write mask, within a scan-line rendering strategy, is to maintain a list of pixel spans (groups of consecutive pixels) that have not yet been written to. This is checked and updated as polygon scan conversion proceeds. (For this type of operation the name 'stencil' buffer is now used.) Thus we can exit a process when all pixels have been written to. This is in effect an occlusion culling algorithm – objects that are obscured by closer objects are never processed. (Occlusion algorithms are dealt with in more detail in Section 9.8.3.)

Alternatively we can use the BSP idea in two-dimensional screen space and represent current pixel coverage with a two-dimensional BSP tree representing the areas written to so far. Higher-level strategies can be adopted to avoid rendering completely occluded objects, for example, by comparing their image plane extents with the (already projected) extents of nearer objects.

Thus to generate a visibility order for a polygonal scene we:

(1) descend the tree with viewpoint coordinates;

(2) at each node, we determine whether the viewpoint is in front or behind the node plane;

(3) descend the far side subtree first and output polygons;

(4) descend the near side subtree and output polygons.

This algorithm results in a far to near ordering for the polygons with respect to the current viewpoint position and these can be rendered into the frame buffer in this order. Note that using a BSP tree in conjunction with the painter's algorithm eliminates the classic problem of this algorithm, which is that even if we had a back to front ordering the painter's algorithm will not work for intersecting polygons. The BSP tree overcomes this by splitting such polygons.

If this procedure is used then, as we have already discussed, the algorithm suffers from the same efficiency disadvantage as the Z-buffer – rendered polygons may be subsequently obscured. However, one of the disadvantages of the Z-buffer is immediately overcome. Polygon ordering allows the unlimited use of transparency with no additional effort. Transparent polygons are simply composited according to their transparency value. Thus in summary we can say that if transparency effects are required, choose far to near ordering, but if efficiency is of prime import then near to far ordering should be used in conjunction with a masking scheme.

Note that the in-order tree traversal that produces a visibility ordering is the (sorted) set of *all* the polygons in the scene. Only a small subset of these will finally be handled by the renderer. The rest are discarded by culling and clipping against the view frustum – an operation that can also be performed by BSP tree operations (Section 9.5). Other points worth noting are that the visibility ordering is not directly related to the distance of the polygon from the viewpoint, nor is it related to viewing direction. These somewhat surprising properties are demonstrated in Figures 9.11 and 9.12. In Figure 9.11 the polygons F and N still appear in the visibility ordering even though they cannot be seen from the viewpoint. Figure 9.12 shows that visibility ordering does not depend on the distance of the polygon from the viewpoint. Note that since a visibility ordering implies a tree-traversal – every node in the tree is visited – it does not matter whether the tree is balanced or not. A balanced tree means that subtrees will tend to contain the same number of polygons.

Finally, note that Abrash in his mighty tome *Graphics Programming Black Book* (1997) reports that even with precalculated PVS (potentially visible sets – Section 9.5) using this approach often results in five times as many polygons as are finally visible, resulting in massive overdraws and a reduction in performance, and this led them to consider the back to front painter's algorithm too slow for BSP rendering.

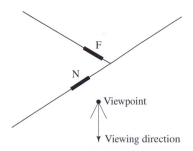

Figure 9.11

A visibility ordering is independent of viewing direction. F and N still appear in the visibility ordering.

Figure 9.12
Visibility ordering does not depend on the distance of the polygon from the viewpoint.

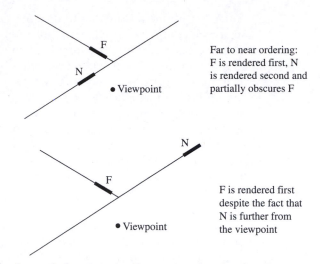

Far to near ordering: F is rendered first, N is rendered second and partially obscures F

F is rendered first despite the fact that N is further from the viewpoint

The code shown below is a simple routine that implements a tree traversal for far to near ordering. For near to far ordering the recursive calls to draw_bsp are reversed.

```
void draw_bsp(bsp_node *n, camera *c)
{
    // x1 is dot product of plane normal and camera look dir
    x1=VecDot(n->normal,c->Z);

    // x2 is the perpendicular distance from the camera point to the
    plane
    // it is the smallest distance from the camera point to the plane
    x2=VecDot(n->normal,c->pos)+n->d0;

    // y is the perpendicular distance divided by x1
    // this gives the distance from the camera point, in the look
    direction,
    // to the plane
    y=x2/x1;

    if(y>0 || fabs(x1)<0.7071) // if plane crosses the look dir line
      {
          if (x2>0) // draw the two children back to front
            {
                draw_bsp(n->child[1],c);
                draw_bsp(n->child[0],c);
            }
      else
        {
            draw_bsp(n->child[0],c);
            draw_bsp(n->child[1],c);
        }
```

```
        }
    else
      {
          if (x2>0) // draws only one node
            draw_bsp(n->child[0],c);
          else
            draw_bsp(n->child[1],c);
      }
  }
```

How to build a BSP tree for a polygon mesh scene

This is a lengthy process that takes place once only or off-line for any given scene. The easiest structure to implement is that of using partition planes that coincide with polygons. The first polygon in the database is read. This determines the root plane, which then categorises every other polygon. All polygons remaining lie on one side of the plane, or the other side, or the plane splits the polygon. The process recurses with each of the two sets of polygons until either a maximum depth is reached, the number of polygons in a leaf node is below a threshold or there is only one polygon at a leaf node. As we have already mentioned, the splitting procedure will make the number of polygons grow – usually by around a factor of two. A simple strategy to minimise splitting is to examine the effect of a potential splitting plane, before it is finally inserted in the tree, by looking at the number of splits it will produce, then selecting that plane which causes the minimum number of splits.

To determine a plane from a polygon we evaluate its coefficients as follows. A plane has the equation:

$$Ax + By + Cz + D = 0 \qquad [9.1]$$

where A, B, C are the coordinate values of its normal vector calculated from any three (non-collinear) vertices.

From Chapter 1 we have that the cross-product of two vectors $\mathbf{V}$ and $\mathbf{W}$ is defined as:

$$\mathbf{X} = \mathbf{V} \times \mathbf{W}$$

$$= (v_2w_3 - v_3w_2)\mathbf{i} + (v_3w_1 - v_1w_3)\mathbf{j} + (v_1w_2 - v_2w_1)\mathbf{k}$$

where $\mathbf{i}$, $\mathbf{j}$ and $\mathbf{k}$ are the standard unit vectors. A, B and C are thus:

$$A = v_2w_3 - v_3w_2$$

$$B = v_3w_1 - v_1w_3$$

$$C = v_1w_2 - v_2w_1$$

D is obtained by substituting a point known to lie on the plane (in other words, a vertex) into Equation 9.1.

Classifying a point with respect to a plane is the foundation of all simple operations that use BSP trees. We simply substitute the point into Equation 9.1. The result will be positive, negative or zero depending on whether the point is on the side of the plane consistent with the direction of the normal vector, is on the other side or lies in the plane. Thus to see if a polygon lies on one side or the other we test each of its vertices in turn. They will result in either all positive, all negative or a mixture which means that the polygon is intersected by the plane. The pair of vertices of edges that cross the plane (from positive to negative and vice versa) are detected as the vertex list is examined and the intersection points are computed by solving the line/plane intersection as follows.

$$t = \frac{Ax_1 + By_1 + Cz_1 + D}{A(x_2 - x_1) + B(y_2 - y_1) + C(z_2 - z_1)}$$

$$x = x_1 + (x_2 - x_1)t$$
$$y = y_1 + (y_2 - y_1)t$$
$$z = z_1 + (z_2 - z_1)t$$

where (x_1, y_1, z_1) and (x_2, y_2, z_2) are the two vertices of the edge that crosses the plane at intersection point (x, y, z).

To save the expense of splitting, an alternative strategy is to build a tree by adding an intersected polygon to both children of the partitioning plane. (More than one leaf can then point to the same polygon.) Then when drawing, lighting or ray-intersecting, we have to flag faces already processed. The following code adopts this strategy.

```
void bsp_node::split()
{
  // if no more planes, return
  if (nplanes==0)
    return;

  int i,p,j;

  // find the plane with best distribution for splitting the current
  node faces
  p=find_split_plane();
  if (p==-1)
    return;

  static_mesh *o=(static_mesh *)elem;
  side=-1;

  // create children
  child[0]=new bsp_node;
  child[1]=new bsp_node;
  child[0]->elem=new static_mesh;
  child[1]->elem=new static_mesh;

  // for each face in node, move it to appropriate children
```

```
            float d1,d2,d3;
            for( i=0;i<o->objmesh->nf;i++ )
              {
              d1=distance(*o->objmesh->faces[i]->vert[0]);
              d2=distance(*o->objmesh->faces[i]->vert[1]);
              d3=distance(*o->objmesh->faces[i]->vert[2]);

              j=find_plane(o->objmesh->faces[i]->normal,o->objmesh->faces[i]-
              >d0);
              if (j==p)
                child[0]->add_face(o->objmesh->faces[i]);
              else
              if (d1>-SMALLF && d2>-SMALLF && d3>-SMALLF)
                child[0]->add_face(o->objmesh->faces[i]);
              else
              if (d1<SMALLF && d2<SMALLF && d3<SMALLF)
                child[1]->add_face(o->objmesh->faces[i]);
              else
                {
                child[0]->add_face(o->objmesh->faces[i]);
                child[1]->add_face(o->objmesh->faces[i]);
                }
              }
        delete o;
        elem=0;
        if (planes) delete planes;
        nplanes=0;
        planes=0;

        for( i=0;i<2;i++ )
        if (child[i]->nplanes)
        {
          child[i]->side=i;
          child[i]->split();
        }
        else
        {
          delete child[i]->elem;
          child[i]->elem=0;
          delete child[i];
          child[i]=0;
        }
}
int bsp_node_max::find_split_plane()
{
    int i,k=-1;
    int n,dif,bestdif=100000,n1,n2,n3;
```

```
        float d1,d2,d3;
        static_mesh *o=(static_mesh *)elem;
        if (o==0) return -1;

        // for each plane in node
        for( i=0;i<nplanes;i++ )
           {
           normal=planes[i].normal;
           d0=planes[i].d0;

           // for each face, check how many faces in each side and cross-
           ing plane
           n1=n2=n3=0;
           for( n=0;n<o->objmesh->nf;n++ )
              {
              d1=distance(*o->objmesh->faces[n]->vert[0]);
              d2=distance(*o->objmesh->faces[n]->vert[1]);
              d3=distance(*o->objmesh->faces[n]->vert[2]);

              if (d1>-SMALLF && d2>-SMALLF && d3>-SMALLF)
                   n1++;
              else
              if (d1<SMALLF && d2<SMALLF && d3<SMALLF)
                   n2++;
              else n3++;
              }
           // if a better balance, store it
           dif=abs(n1-n2)+n3*2;
           if (dif<bestdif)
              {
              bestdif=dif;
              k=i;
              }
           }

        if (k==-1) return -1;

        // return split plane with best balance
        normal=planes[k].normal;
        d0=planes[k].d0;
        return k;
        }
```

9.5.3

Back-face culling

Back-face culling can be a no-cost operation carried out during tree traversal to find a visibility ordering. Whenever the viewpoint is in the OUT half space of the plane of a polygon – that polygon is culled. Thus in Figure 9.13 two poly-

Figure 9.13
Back face culling with a BSP
tree. Only C and D are
culled.

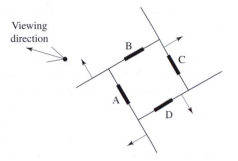

gons are culled. Note again that this operation is independent of the direction
of the viewer. Using a conventional culling operation, where the polygon normal and a line of sight vector from the viewpoint to the polygon are compared,
all four polygons would be culled. In other words, culling with a BSP tree does
not eliminate all the polygons that would be culled by a test involving a line of
sight vector.

9.5.4   **Culling against the view frustum**

As well as hidden surface elimination, a BSP tree can be used to cull polygons
against a view frustum. At a node the view frustum is compared with the partitioning plane and if the appropriate culling condition is fulfilled the entire subtree associated with that node can be eliminated. Consider first a semi-infinite
view frustum (Figure 9.14(a)). In this case we only have to compare the view vector with the normal of the partition plane. The culling condition for a viewpoint
on the positive side of the plane is:

$$\mathbf{N_v}.\mathbf{N_p} \geq \cos^{-1}(\pi/2 - \theta)$$

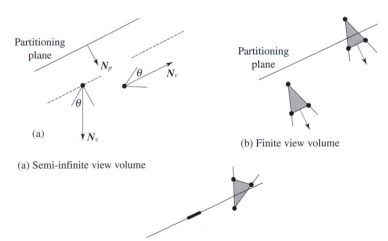

(a) Semi-infinite view volume

(b) Finite view volume

(c) Culling may not remove polygons that lie outside the view volume

Figure 9.14
Culling against the view
frustum. (a) Semi-infinite
view volume. (b) Finite view
volume. (c) Culling may not
remove polygons that lie
outside the view frustum.

The entire contents of the subtree on the negative side of the partition can therefore not be seen. A similar argument persists for viewpoints on the negative side of the plane.

A more powerful culling operation can be performed by considering a finite view volume (Figure 9.14(b)). A finite view volume can be implemented by using a far plane in conjunction with depth-modulated fog. Any polygons farther than the far plane are culled, the fog preventing any disturbing effect occurring when a previously culled polygon 'switches on' when the viewpoint moves towards it. To eliminate subtrees of polygons that cannot intersect the view frustum we check for intersection between the view volume and the partition plane. This reduces to checking that the five vertices return the same sign when injected into Equation 9.1. Note that this culling operation is operating on the partition planes that contain the polygons and it will not remove polygons whose extent is outside the view frustum but whose plane intersects it (Figure 9.14(c)).

This approximation (the use of a far clip plane plus fog) is not entirely satisfactory and more rigorous approaches to the visibility problem are discussed at length in Section 9.6.

The following code implements view frustum culling for interior scenes (no far plane). It also uses PVS which are described in Section 9.5.

```
void draw_bsp(bsp_node *n)
{
  // if n is a leaf, check pvs, draw elements in the leaf and return
  if (n->leaf!=-1)
  {
  int i=c->node->leaf*nleaf + n->leaf;
  if (pvs[i/8]&(1<<(i%8)))
    n->draw();
  return;
  }

  float x1,x2;
  int i;

  // check all five frustum vertices for being in same side of bsp
  // plane
  x1=n->distance(frustum[0]);
  for( i=1;i<5;i++ )
    {
    x2=n->distance(frustum[i]);
    if (x1*x2<=0)
      break;
    }
  // if all in same side, recourse into single node
  if (i==5)
    if (x1>0)
    {
```

```
      if (n->child[0])
        draw_bsp(n->child[0]);
    }
    else
    {
    if (n->child[1])
      draw_bsp(n->child[1]);
    }
    // if frustum crosses the bsp plane, recourse the two children
    else
      if (x1<0)
        {
        if (n->child[1])
          draw_bsp(n->child[1]);
        if (n->child[0])
          draw_bsp(n->child[0]);
        }
      else
        {
        if (n->child[0])
          draw_bsp(n->child[0]);
        if (n->child[1])
          draw_bsp(n->child[1]);
        }
  }
```

9.5.5 Spheres of influence

Consider an event such as an explosion at a point whose influence we decide to limit to a sphere centred on the reference point or the event centre. For example, we may only want to 'paint light' on polygons that are near to the explosion. This is easily implemented by descending the tree from a node only if the distance from the event centre to the partitioning plane is less than the required radius. We use such a facility extensively in Chapters 10 and 12.

9.5.6 BSP trees in practice

The way in which BSP trees are employed in practice depends on the application and/or the scene complexity. Two important choices are: how are subdivision planes chosen and when does the subdivision terminate? A common application is the cell-like scenes found in building interiors and games environments. Here it makes sense to use wall-aligned or axis-aligned partitioning planes so as to partition the environment according to the cell or room structure. After this partitioning is complete we can continue subdividing the space within a room with polygons aligned as appropriate for the room contents. (This important application is developed at length in Section 9.6 where various enhancements to the BSP strategy, which exploit the properties of cell-like scenes, are discussed.)

Partitioning can terminate at room level, object level or objects themselves can be subdivided. If a leaf contains a cluster of polygons, rather than a single face, then this implies a hybrid visibility scheme where the BSP tree is used to quickly cull away objects outside the view frustum and exact visibility within the view frustum is left to a normal rendering process that will use, say, a Z-buffer algorithm for hidden surface removal. Currently this is the most popular strategy and the BSP part of the rendering functions as a fast culling pre-processor to a normal rendering engine.

Another practical point is that we can avoid the additional code complexity of polygon splitting by leaving the polygon whole and 'sending' the entire polygon down each branch node. This strategy can again be adopted in room-type environments where the initial partitions are wall-aligned and do not intersect objects. Object subdivision only occurs well down the tree.

9.5.7 Landscapes and BSP technology

For landscapes the BSP construction procedure must be particularised. Because of the high level of detail in landscapes we cannot use face planes as partitioning planes. However, because the landscape has been built on a regular grid, possibly at varying levels of detail, we can use splitting planes normal to the ground plane making a choice at each level between the plane parallel to the x axis and that parallel to the y axis according to occupancy, as before (Figure 9.15). Thus all splitting planes can only have one of two orientations. By introducing a third orientation – parallel to the ground plane – we can deal with three-dimensional strategy games. We now have rectangular partitions that contain the game objects.

The following code is a recursive function that generates a 2D BSP tree for a set of faces. It first finds the centre of the faces bounding box and uses this as the split plane origin. Then it evaluates the two possible split planes available (perpendicular to x or y) to see which one results in the most balanced split. With

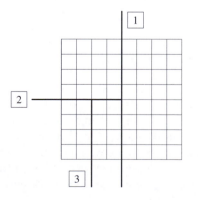

Figure 9.15
Particularisation of BSP partitioning procedure for landscapes.

the selected splitting plane, it creates two children and moves the faces to the children based on their position relative to the splitting plane (faces on the front of the plane are positioned in child 0 and faces on the back in child 1). It then recurses into the two children applying the same algorithm until a max tree depth is reached.

```
void bsp_node::split_landscape(int depth)
{
// if no faces or at maximum tree depth, bail out
static_mesh *o=(static_mesh *)elem;
if (--depth==0 || o==0) return;

int i,j,k=-1;
int dif,bestdif=0xFFFF,n1,n2,n3;
float d1,d2,d3;

// find split plane point
calc_bbox();
vector pos=(bbox.min+bbox.max)/2;

// test two possible split planes (XZ and YZ)
for( i=0;i<2;i++ )
{
  // create split plane
  normal.vec(0,0,0);
  (&normal.x)[i]=1;
  d0=-vec_dot(pos,normal);

  // loop all faces to find best distribution
  n1=n2=n3=0;
  for( j=0;j<o->objmesh->nf;j++ )
  {
    d1=distance(*o->objmesh->faces[j]->vert[0]);
    d2=distance(*o->objmesh->faces[j]->vert[1]);
    d3=distance(*o->objmesh->faces[j]->vert[2]);

    // if on positive side
    if (d1>-SMALLF && d2>-SMALLF && d3>-SMALLF)
      n1++;
    else
    // if on negative side
    if (d1<SMALLF && d2<SMALLF && d3<SMALLF)
      n2++;
    // crossing split plane
    else n3++;
  }
  // if a more equal distribution, store it
  dif=(n1-n2)+n3*2;
  if (dif<bestdif)
```

```
      {
        bestdif=dif;
        k=i;
      }
    }

  if (k==-1) return;

  // create split plane
  normal.vec(0,0,0);
  (&normal.x)[k]=1;
  d0=-vec_dot(pos,normal);

  // alloc children
  child[0]=new bsp_node;
  child[1]=new bsp_node;
  child[0]->elem=new static_mesh;
  child[1]->elem=new static_mesh;

  // loop all faces
  for( i=0;i<o->objmesh->nf;i++ )
     {
     // get distance from each vertex to the split plane
     d1=distance(*o->objmesh->faces[i]->vert[0]);
     d2=distance(*o->objmesh->faces[i]->vert[1]);
     d3=distance(*o->objmesh->faces[i]->vert[2]);

     // if in negative side
     if (d1<SMALLF && d2<SMALLF && d3<SMALLF)
        ((bsp_node_max *)child[1])->add_face(o->objmesh->
        faces[i],0);
     else
     // if in positive side
     if (d1>-SMALLF && d2>-SMALLF && d3>-SMALLF)
        ((bsp_node_max *)child[0])->add_face(o->objmesh->
        faces[i],0);
     else
     {
     // crossing split plane
     child[0]->add_face(o->objmesh->faces[i],0);
     child[1]->add_face(o->objmesh->faces[i],0);
     }
  }
}
// delete parent faces
delete elem;
elem=0;

// recurse into children
child[0]->split_landscape(depth);
child[1]->split_landscape(depth);
}
```

9.6 Specialisations for building interior-type environments

This section concentrates on enhancing BSP strategies to afford greater efficiency. Such enhancements tend to be specific to the scene structure and we use the common example of building-type interiors exploiting the constraints of their cell-like structure.

The first section introduces a simple low-complexity algorithm that can easily be added to a conventional BSP scheme. We then go on to consider the way in which we can exploit portals or doors as an acceleration device that is implemented as a culling and clipping operation. In subsequent sections, portals are further developed to implement the pre-calculation of conservative visibility or potentially visible sets (PVS).

BSP trees exhibit a number of disadvantages and they do not cope well with complex interior models. Unless we have a 'closed door' environment where a viewer can only see the contents of the room that he or she is in, we have to consider the contents of adjacent rooms seen through doors or windows. Having a single BSP tree for all the rooms is inefficient since only a very small proportion of adjacent rooms will be seen through the portals. In other words, BSP trees do not cope well with scenes that exhibit both high complexity and high occlusion. This is sometime called the 'overdraw' problem. We spend time rendering objects in an adjacent room that are eventually overdrawn by a wall.

In Section 9.5.6 we suggested that building interiors imply a simple partitioning strategy for BSP trees. We choose planes that are initially aligned with room walls, before selecting partitions that divide up rooms. We now look at how we can use the partitioning scheme together with the concept of portals to **pre-calculate** only those polygons which are potentially visible to a viewer located in the room. This set of polygons is known as a PVS or potentially visible set.

9.6.1 BSPs and PVS: a simple non-deterministic algorithm

A simple non-deterministic algorithm for building interiors computes potentially visible sets by evaluating a connectivity matrix for every leaf in a BSP tree. It does not explicitly make use of portals as structures that we can use in precomputations of visibility and simply treats them as empty parts of the scene. The connectivity matrix is a binary array that for each leaf defines the visibility of other leaves in the scene with respect to the leaf. If there are N leaves then this has dimensionality N^2. The rendering phase of the process then proceeds as normal – with the view frustum being used with the BSP tree to cull away objects that cannot be seen. When a leaf node is reached its contents are only passed for rendering if the node is connected to the node that contains the viewpoint.

The connectivity matrix is evaluated as follows:

(1) Build the BSP tree as normal.

(2) Go to a random viewpoint in the scene and determine the leaf node that contains the point.

(3) 'Render' the scene from this viewpoint in six mutually orthogonal view directions. The BSP is employed as usual to implement view frustum culling. In this context, 'render' implies using a full cube version of the hemicube algorithm in radiosity (see Watt and Policarpo (1998)) which means that we end up with an image where each polygon has an identity label.

(4) The leaf nodes that contain these polygons, visible from the random viewpoint, are connected to the viewpoint node in the connectivity matrix.

(5) The process is repeated for a large number of sample viewpoints.

For a simple games environment of 9900 triangles and a BSP tree of 1500 leaves, 50 000 sample viewpoints resulted in no errors in a substantial test run. The procedure reduced the number of leaf nodes entered in the BSP tree to around 5 per cent of the number reached without this enhancement. Note that this approach enables us to use a semi-infinite view frustum – we do not need to use a far clip plane as suggested in Section 9.5.4. The code corresponding to this approach is given in Section 9.5.4.

9.7 Portals and mirrors

In the previous section we utilised portals implicitly – they were just empty space or gaps in the wall. In this section we will describe a technique that explicitly uses portals. In its simplest form this does not resolve visibility exactly but is a method for culling (and clipping) objects that cannot possibly be seen from the room that contains the viewpoint. It does not pre-compute potentially visible sets nor use BSPs but is nevertheless a good introduction to portals. The model database is divided into rooms or cells and the visibility problem is then constrained to dealing with the contents of the room that contains the viewpoint and those objects in adjoining rooms which can be seen through portals from the viewpoint room. If the process is carried out dynamically then the method is able to cope with changing environments.

For the viewpoint room, objects can be culled against the view volume as normal. If the primary view volume intersects any portal then a view volume for the adjacent room can be constructed from the viewpoint and the corner points of the portal. The process can be recursive if the adjacent room itself contains portals, intersected by this volume, into a third room and so on. Culling can be carried out in screen space by projecting each portal into the image plane and testing the bounding box of objects in a room against the image plane projection of the portal. If more than one adjoining room is visible through a series of portals then an aggregate cull rectangle is built up in screen space. (Since the image plane will in general be oblique with respect to the walls, a rectangular portal will not project onto a rectangle; but the projection itself can be enclosed in a bounding box.) A simple example for three rooms is shown in plan in Figure 9.16.

Figure 9.16
A 'primary' view volume and two portal view volumes.

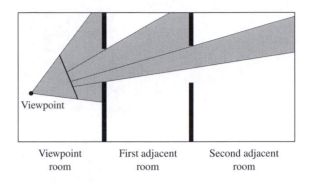

| Viewpoint room | First adjacent room | Second adjacent room |

A rendering algorithm can then proceed as follows:

cull and render the viewpoint room

if a polygon is tagged as a portal **then**
    recurse into the next room, cull and render **until** no more portals are encountered

Note that 'render' in the above outline implies normal Z-buffer rendering. We are only using the portal approach for culling and clipping – the visibility within a room is resolved using standard techniques.

The portal approach is easily extended to mirrors – although there are potential complications. Mirrors are simply tagged as portals except that we recurse into the same room and reflect the room contents (and the view frustum) about the plane of the mirror. However, unless the mirror is contained by an (opaque) wall, objects behind the mirror cannot appear which is an exception to treating them as portals. Also, there is a complication when mirrors overlap in the image plane and if there are mirrors recursively reflecting each other.

The disadvantages of portals is that they are limited in the main to architectural-like scenes where a complex database can be divided into cells separated by opaque boundaries and a limited number of transparent portals. A source of inefficiency in the portal technique is that although we are recursing outwards from the viewpoint through portals, no account is taken of any objects within a room that obscure the portal(s). Each portal is treated as if all of it can be seen from the image plane.

9.7.1   Generalisation of portals

We now look at a deterministic algorithm that combines PVS with BSP trees. The main work in this area is due to Teller and Sequin (1991) and (Funkhouser (1996) who considered scenes where, without loss of generality, all faces were considered to be parallel to the walls – axis-aligned faces. This enables a spatial partitioning with planes coincident or parallel to room walls and floors. (This

Figure 9.17
A diagrammatic overview
of Teller's portal-based PVS
approach.

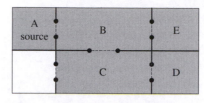

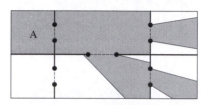

(a) Cells visible from source cell A – cell to cell visibility

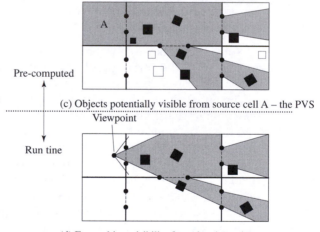

(b) The region potentially visible to a viewer positioned in A
– cell region visibility

(c) Objects potentially visible from source cell A – the PVS

(d) Exact object visibility from the viewpoint

specialisation of a BSP tree is called a k-D tree.) We will consider a two-dimensional analogue of the problem. Extension to three dimensions is not difficult in a environment where the walls are perpendicular.

The key idea of this work is easy to illustrate with a diagrammatic overview and Figure 9.17 attempts to do this as follows: (a) to (c) are pre-computed and (d) is computed dynamically.

(a) is an example of cell to cell visibility. This is the set of cells connected by portals to the source cell A which contains the viewpoint. It is the set of potentially visible cells.

(b) is the space visible to a viewer, positioned anywhere in A, through the portals. This is called cell to region visibility. In general, these are a set of wedges that emanate through each portal in the source cell which narrow as more and more portals are traversed.

(c) All objects that intersect this space are potentially visible from anywhere within the source cell and this is called cell to object visibility. This is the extent of the pre-computation phase.

(d) At run-time a viewpoint and frustum is determined and this defines the sub-set of (c) that intersects with the view frustum. This then gives the eye to object visibility – those objects that can wholly or partially be see through the source cell's portal.

The eye to object visibility set is the final PVS which is input into the normal rendering engine.

Teller *et al.* adopt a subdivision strategy which tends to reflect the cell structure of the environment and when the partitioning terminates they store the portals with a leaf cell together with a pointer to which cell the portal connects. (This operation is equivalent to constructing an adjacency graph with edges representing connectivity and vertices representing cells.) Objects partially and completely inside cell boundaries are also associated with a cell. These associations emerge from the spatial subdivision which operates on contained objects as well as the walls and portals.

Cell to cell visibility is evaluated using 'sightlines' computed through a depth-first search of the cell adjacency graph. A cell is visible from a source cell if a line from the source cell – a sightline – passes unobstructed through a portal sequence to that cell. Teller points out that it is sufficient to consider sightlines originating and terminating on portals and the algorithm strategy is to construct, for each leaf, potential portal sequences that are then tested for the existence of a sightline. Figure 9.18 is a simple example of the principle. If A is the source cell then there exist portal sequences that can be tested for cell to cell visibility. Consider, for example, the sequence [A/B,B/C,C/D]. A sightline for this portal sequence is shown in Figure 9.18(a). The condition for such a sightline to exist is that the set of points L and R, the left and right portal end points with respect to the direction of travel from A to D, must be linearly separable (Figure 9.18(b)). Any sightline is a straightline through all the portals that separates the two sets of points. The linear separability condition is as follows. L and R are linearly separable iff there exists a vector W such that:

$$W.L \geq 0 \qquad \forall L \in L$$

$$W.R \leq 0 \qquad \forall R \in R$$

A deterministic algorithm to determine the existence of W is given in Megido (1983).

As evaluated so far, the cell to cell visibility is a superset of the space visible to any viewer through the source portal. It is the entire space of every cell that can be seen from the source cell and it can be further refined by considering the effect of the portals to represent only that space within each connecting cell that

Figure 9.18
Cell to cell visibility. (a) A simple cell environment and a sightline. (b) The portal sequence [A/B, B/C, C/D]. A sightline S exists if the sets *L* and *R* are linearly separable. (c) Cell to cell visibility from A.

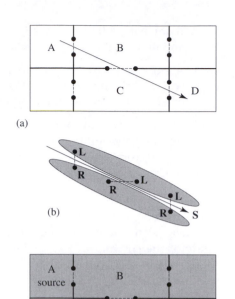

is visible to a viewer positioned anywhere within the source cell. For axially aligned room boundaries all the space in cells that are immediately adjacent to the source cell (portal sequence of one) are visible from the source cell but as the portal sequence becomes longer an observer can see less and less of the distant cells.

Teller approaches this problem by considering the source portal as an area light source and subsequent portals in a sequence as occluders. This leads to a polygon that tracks the visible light through the portal sequence. Figure 9.19(a) shows a simple example; the shaded region in C represents the area visible to an observer in A – the light that reaches C from an area light source on A's portal. In shadow terminology this area in C is the anti-penumbra and the algorithm consists of modifying the anti-penumbra through a portal sequence. Note that the anti-penumbra in the destination cell is bounded by the so-called crossover edges. Figures 9.19(b) and (c) show the regions visible from the source cell A in the example of Figure 9.18 for portal sequences [A/B,B/C] and [A/B,B/C,C/D] (Figure 9.19(c)). The union of these regions gives the entire and exact space visible in cells C and D from A.

Teller refers to the process of determining the region as a 'kind of internal pivoting over the edges and vertices occurring along the portals sequence' and gives

Figure 9.19
The effect of a portal sequence on the visible light from an area scene positional in the source cell portal. (a) Source portal is considered an area light source. (b) Region in C visible from A due to portal sequence [A/B, B/C]. (c) Region in D visible from A due to portal sequence [A/B, B/C, C/D].

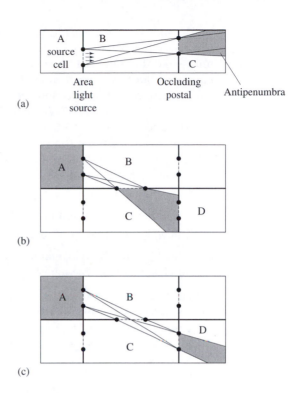

(a)

(b)

(c)

an $O(n)$ complexity algorithm where n is the number of portals in the chain. For rectangular portals in two-dimensional space there are only two vertices to consider. (For portals of arbitrary shape extremal vertices have to be found.) Each portal thus contributes one edge to the polyhedral bound of the illumination volume and for n portals this volume can have at most $2n$ edges.

9.8 Advanced view frustum culling

We have dealt with view frustum culling as one of the many operations that can be performed when the scene complexity is managed by using a BSP tree. We will now look at this important topic in more detail and in more general terms; that is, in the context of general bounding volume hierarchies where a known bounding volume shape is compared with the view frustum. Further details on bounding volumes are given in Chapter 15 and this section should be read in conjunction with that material.

A point we made earlier in the chapter is that VFC can be considered as collision detection where one of the objects is always the same shape – a view volume – and the other is a bounding volume whose shape is known. This enables pairwise strategies that are much faster than the detailed pairwise comparisons required in collision detection when we have to test two arbitrarily shaped objects against each other. We shall also look at how we can exploit coherence in VFC, a technique that has proved of such importance in collision detection.

To recap, we consider the VFC problem as testing an object, or more usually, a bounding volume or bounding volume hierarchy, against the view frustum which is either a rectangular solid or a truncated rectangular pyramid. There are three possible outcomes:

- the volumes are disjoint in which case the object is rejected (trivial rejection);
- the volumes intersect in which case further testing is necessary;
- the object is wholly contained by the frustum in which case the object(s) is rendered (trivial acceptance).

Trivial rejection is established by testing the bounding volume against each of the six planes representing the view frustum. This involves checking the bounding volume vertices against the six view frustum planes. If the volumes intersect then it is important to make use of hierarchy in the further testing. For example, if a node in a BV hierarchy has returned intersection there will one or more planes for which the BV is inside. All the node's children must also, by definition, be inside that plane and a bit pattern needs to be transmitted to all the children indicating which frustum plane(s) need not be tested for.

(9.8.1) Exploiting BV geometry

We now consider how to exploit the geometric properties of the situation using as an example the simple bounding volume of an AABB. If the bounding volume is an AABB then a number of strategies are possible (Assarsson and Möller, 1999). One approach is to effect the comparison in screen space. The AABB can be transformed into view space (Figure 9.20(a)) where by definition it is aligned with the view coordinate system. The AABB and the view frustum can be transformed into three-dimensional screen space (Figure 9.20(b)) and then itself enclosed by a minimum AABB (Figure 9.20(c)). This approach suffers from the fact that trivial rejection does not occur until after the expense of transforming into screen space.

If we restrict ourselves to view space then the trivial rejection test itself can be significantly improved upon in the case of AABBs. A conventional test involves checking each of the eight vertices of the bounding box against each of the six view volume planes, then classifying the result using logical tests. A faster method (suggested by Greene, 1994) is to consider only the two extremal points of the AABB defined with respect to the normal of the plane against which it currently being tested. Thus with respect to the two-dimensional analogue shown in Figure 9.21 we have:

Figure 9.20
VFC and AABBs (after
Assarsson and Möller
(1999)).

(a) AABB transformed to view space

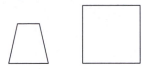

(b) AABB and view frustum in 3D screen space

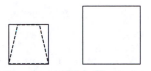

(c) Secondary AABB in 3D screen space

if p_{near} is outside P **then** box is outside P

else if p_{far} is inside **then** box is inside P

else box intersects P

p_{far} is furthest vertex in the direction of the normal and p_{near} the opposite extremal point or the farthest vertex in the negative direction of the normal. Since the box is axis aligned we can find p_{near} and p_{far} by examining the sign of the components of normal vector to the plane. This is done by finding which octant of the AABB the normal vector lies in, then the vertex associated with that octant gives us the required point. Providing the origin is located at the centre of the box then each octant is identified by the signs of the three components. For example:

if $(N_x > 0$ **and** $N_y > 0$ **and** $N_z > 0)$ **then**

p_{far} is the righthand, topmost front vertex of the box

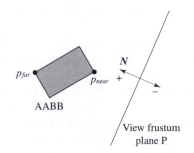

Figure 9.21
AABB view frustum testing.

Figure 9.22
Bounding sphere view
frustum testing.

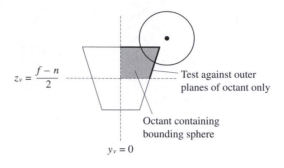

$$z_v = \frac{f - n}{2}$$

Test against outer
planes of octant only

Octant containing
bounding sphere

$y_v = 0$

If the bounding volume is an OBB then the plane normal has to be projected into the box coordinate system given by

$$\mathbf{N_B} = (\mathbf{B^u}.\mathbf{N}, \mathbf{B^v}.\mathbf{N}, \mathbf{B^w}.\mathbf{N})$$

where

$\mathbf{N_B}$ is the plane normal in the box coordinate system and $(\mathbf{B^u}, \mathbf{B^v}, \mathbf{B^w})$ is the OBB frame vector (that is, the vector whose components are the unit axis vector of the OBB axes)

If the object is a sphere then the same algorithm can be used. The near and far points are given by ±radius in the direction of the plane normal.

A particularly fast trivial rejection is possible in the case where the bounding volume is a sphere (Figure 9.22). Here we can divide the view volume into octants using three bisecting planes ($x_v = 0$, $y_v = 0$ and $z_v = (f - n)/2$) and find which octant contains the bounding volume centre. We then need only test against the three outer planes of the view frustum which define that octant as follows:

> if the bounding sphere is outside any of these planes it is completely outside the view frustum (trivial rejection)
>
> if the bounding sphere is inside all of these three planes it is completely inside the view frustum (trivial acceptance)
>
> otherwise it intersects

9.8.2 Exploiting coherence in view frustum culling

The moving elements in a complex scene are either due to a moving view volume, scene objects moving relative to one another or both. In many applications the number of moving objects is low and the viewpoint may change at 'walking pace'. This means that we can exploit frame to frame coherence in VFC. Frame to frame coherence means that, depending on the velocity of the viewpoint, we can expect those parts of a hierarchy that have been culled at time t also to be outside the view frustum at time $t + 1$.

Figure 9.23
Translation and rotation coherence (after Assarsson and Möller (1999)). (a) Translation of the view frustum means that plane P moves away from or towards the BVs by an amount Δ_d in the direction of the plane normal. (b) Rotation about the y axis means that the BV must still be outside the left plane.

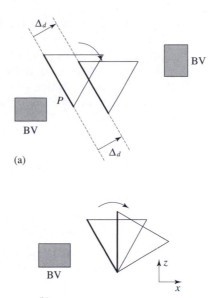

(a)

(b)

Assarsson and Möller take a straightforward approach and implement translation and rotation coherency tests for applications restricted, at any instant, to either translation or rotation about a single axis. For pure translation they observe that between consecutive frames then all BV structures have moved away from or towards a view frustum plane by a fixed amount Δd in the direction of the plane normal (Figure 9.23(a)). This quantity can be computed for each plane in each frame by projecting the translation vector onto the normal for each plane. Then for each BV and view frustum plane it is only necessary compare Δd with the distance between the BV and the plane for the previous frame.

Rotation is similarly handled by calculating the change in the angle of rotation. For example, if a BV was outside the frustum's left plane and the rotation of the view frustum is about the y axis and to the right (Figure 9.23(b)), then the BV will remain outside the frustum (providing also that the angle or rotation is less than 180° – field of view angle)

9.9 Exact visibility

Above, we have dealt with certain aspects of visibility processing; in this section we will return to look at how hidden surface algorithms, described in Chapter 6, can be enhanced to deal better with very complex scenes. As is well known, the *de facto* standard HSR algorithm – the Z-buffer – suffers from significant disadvantages. It is inefficient, it uses large memory resources and because polygons are scan converted into the frame buffer in an arbitrary order it cannot cope with transparency. However, much beloved because of its low complexity, it became an irresistible strategy when memory prices plummeted. Prior to its wholesale adoption there was (in the 1970s) much research into a variety of HSR algorithms. (This is well documented in a famous paper by Sutherland *et al.* (1974) entitled 'A characterisation of ten hidden surface algorithms'.) The demands of games programs has seen a return to some of these algorithms – most commonly priority sorting.

Exact visibility and pre-computation

Dynamic hidden surface removal algorithms, like the Z-buffer, compute exact visibility at run time for a single viewpoint. We have seen that we can speed up the task by using spatial partitioning and divide hidden surface determination

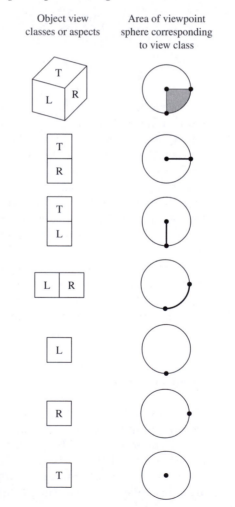

Figure 9.24
Aspects and corresponding viewpoints for three faces of a cube.

into a pre-calculation viewpoint-independent phase followed by a dynamic viewpoint-dependent phase. The purpose of the pre-calculation phase as we described it above was to enable a fast culling of objects at run time. We now consider extending the scope of visibility pre-computation. How far can we go in pre-calculating exact visibility for any viewpoint? If there is no limit on time/complexity then we can pre-compute exact visibility for a single object and this approach has been explored in 3D object recognition. It is instructive to begin by considering this extreme case.

The idea is shown in Figure 9.24 for three faces of a cube. In each of the seven aspects the same faces of the object are visible in a projection from that set of viewpoints that forms a view class. (Different views within a class are related by the coefficients of an affine transformation.) In the example shown, the first view class corresponds to viewpoints lying in an octant of the sphere, the next three to lines and the final three to single points. Thus to render the object from a certain viewpoint we classify the viewpoint according to what area of a sphere surrounding the object the camera point occupies, then select the corresponding faces from the object database. This straightforward approach falls down very quickly as a function of object complexity. If we just consider the six cube faces (instead of three) we now have 8×7 view aspects to consider. In fact it can be shown that the view categories approach space complexity $O(n^9)$, an impossibly large number for an object of any complexity.

9.9.2

Sorting strategies for visibility processing

Sorting graphics entities into depth order was an early and obvious idea. It is simple in principle but the details make it have somewhat high coding complexity. One of the earliest sorting HSR algorithms was the Newell, Newell and Sancha algorithm reported in 1972 and described in Section 6.3.4. As graphics practitioners were then mostly concerned with displaying single polygon mesh objects, the algorithm sorted polygons into depth order, allocating a higher priority to those polygons nearer to the viewpoint. The eventual aim is to scan polygons into the frame buffer in farthest to nearest order (the painter's algorithm). Note that this strategy facilitates transparency calculations.

Bishop *et al.* (1998) describe a strategy that they implement in the games engine NetImmerse. Called hierarchical sorting, the strategy enables sorting to be turned on or off at any node in the scene hierarchy. Each node has a switch that indicates that object's children as 'needing sorting', 'not needing sorting' or 'inheriting' (the sorting mode of the node's parent). Bishop *et al.* illustrate the efficacy of the approach by using a room example (Figure 9.25). The root is the entire room and the two children are the walls and room contents. The root node has sorting turned to 'not needing sorting' because the children are already (permanently) sorted (walls followed by furniture). The walls are drawn first with their node set to inherit ('not needing sorting'). This is because walls can be drawn in any order – they can never obscure each other – providing that they

Figure 9.25
Hierarchical sorting.

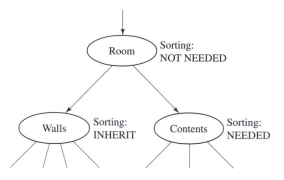

form a box. The room contents have sorting turned to 'needing sorting' because their depth order is a function of the camera position within the room. BSP sub-trees can be embedded in the structure and this facilitates a powerful strategy that enables sorting for, say, moving objects within the room but retains a pre-calculated BSP tree for the objects themselves. Dynamic sorting is thus restricted to the objects and not to polygons within the objects.

9.9.3   Visibility within the view frustum: occlusion culling

We have seen that an efficiency disadvantage of BSP trees in a complex environment relates to the overdraw problem – all polygons that intersect the view frustum are rendered and many polygons will be subsequently obscured. We ameliorate this in the case of portals by considering only view frustums that can be constructed through portals but in that case we are still left with the 'over-draw within a frustum' inefficiency. Also, although portals quickly reject most of the hidden geometry, they can only be applied easily to architectural environments. Algorithms that deal with culling within the view frustum are called occlusion culling algorithms because they cull away objects that are hidden behind objects nearer to the viewpoint.

The principle of occlusion culling is easy to describe but efficient algorithms are complex. Figure 9.26 shows the principle and also the problem which is: how do we select those objects that are likely to be occluders? Like hidden surface removal algorithms, occlusion algorithms can operate in object space or (3D) screen space or a combination of both. Screen space algorithms are simplest and effectively reduce to an overlap and depth test. If an occluder is nearer to the viewpoint than the object being tested and it overlaps it, then the object is occluded. We now look at a selection of algorithms.

The simplest approach is to ignore the problem of choosing potential occluders and render a bounding box projection into the Z-buffer. The object contained by the bounding box can then be culled or not. This is the approach taken in Scott *et al.* (1998) and it suffers from the clear disadvantage that if an object is

Figure 9.26
Occlusion culling.

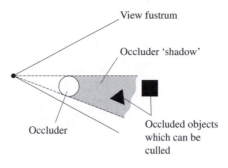

View fustrum

Occluder 'shadow'

Occluder

Occluded objects
which can be
culled

not culled then the time taken to render it into the Z-buffer is lost. Nevertheless
Scott reported a speed-up of between 25 per cent and 100 per cent using this
approach.

An approach due to Coorg and Teller (1997) involves explicit selection of
potential occluders. Of course, the actual occluders are the visible surfaces of the
objects in the current projection and the aim of such algorithms is to estimate,
if possible, a subset of these and use them in an algorithm that culls away
occluded objects. The potential occluders change as the viewpoint changes and
Coorg and Teller pre-process the scene to build a database of potential occluders
which is then indexed in real time by the current viewpoint. They do this by dis-
cretising all possible viewing directions and using a metric for occlusion potential as (Figure 9.27):

$$\frac{-A(\mathbf{N}.\mathbf{V})}{|\mathbf{D}|^2}$$

where:

A is the area of the occluder

$\mathbf{N}$ is the surface normal of the occluder

$\mathbf{V}$ is the view direction vector

$\mathbf{D}$ is the vector from the viewpoint to the centre of the occluder

This enables the set of potential occluders to be selected as the viewpoint moves.

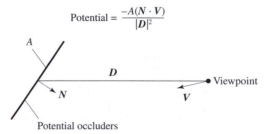

$$\text{Potential} = \frac{-A(N \cdot V)}{|\mathbf{D}|^2}$$

A

D

N

V

Viewpoint

Potential occluders

Figure 9.27
Measuring the potential of a
possible occlude.

Figure 9.28
The plane of the potential occlude and the supporting and separating planes divide the region behind the potential occludes into three qualitatively different volumes (after Coorg and Teller (1997)).

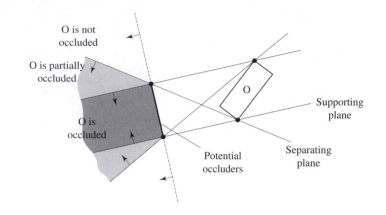

The algorithm works in object space by answering the query: given a viewpoint, a set of potential (convex) occluders and a (convex) occludee, is the occludee visible? The occludee is normally some bounding box of an object. Coorg and Teller answer this by considering the relationship between occluder and occludee as defined by supporting and separating planes. A separating plane of two convex objects is a plane formed by an edge of one object and a vertex of the other such that the objects lie on opposite sides of the plane. A supporting plane is such a plane where the objects lie on the same side. These planes divide the region behind the occluder into three qualitatively distinct volumes as shown in the two-dimensional analogue in Figure 9.28. Only if the viewpoint is contained in the dark shaded region immediately behind the occluder is the occludee invisible. Coorg and Teller use a hybrid method that combines pre-processing and run-time table lookups to compute the planes between two objects. In conjunction with a k-D tree spatial subdivision they report real-time performance and a reduction in rendering load by a factor of 6 to 8 over frustum culling.

Hierarchical occlusion map, or HOM, is the name given to the technique introduced by Zhang *et al.* (1997). Like the previous method, Zhang *et al.* also perform pre-processing to derive an occluder database from the original scene which is indexed at run time using the viewpoint. To build the database they use a similar approach to Coorg and Teller, selecting objects according to their potential to act as occluders from a certain viewpoint. As well as distance and size criteria, they also use temporal coherence. For each frame Zhang *et al.* build an occlusion map in the form of an image pyramid (Chapter 18). The pyramid has 256×256 resolution at level zero and terminates at 4×4. This is, for a particular frame, an overlap map of all the occluders enhanced with opacity information. The occlusion map is used for an efficient overlap test and depth information of the occluder set is maintained in a software (low resolution) depth buffer which Zhang *et al.* construct so as not to rely on the availability of a hardware Z-buffer, or more particularly the ability to read back information from a hardware Z-buffer quickly.

The hierarchical occlusion map is constructed for each frame by rendering the occluders and constructing an image pyramid. At each level of the pyramid an opacity is stored in the occlusion map pixel. This is simply the ratio of the sum of the opaque areas in the pixel to the area of the pixel. Thus for a occluder projection with no holes, the sum of the opaque areas in a pixel at level n is the sum of the opaque pixels at level 0. So if we represent, at level 0, the 100 per cent opacity as white, then as we ascend the hierarchy, the shape will get more and more blocky with the boundary pixels getting darker and darker. The map building, which must take place for each frame, is implemented using texture hardware. The use of this information facilitates an approximate approach if required.

To check an object for occlusion, its screen space bounding rectangle (of its bounding box) is used to index the HOM. If the corners of the bounding rectangle are within an occlusion area in the HOM then the object must be occluded. The level of the HOM indexed is that which possesses a pixel dimension approximately the same size as the bounding rectangle. If the HOM pixel is completely opaque then the test is complete – either the object is occluded or it is not. If the HOM pixel is not completely opaque then we recurse to the next (finer) level, increasing the resolution of the occlusion test each time.

Approximate occlusion culling is implemented by defining an opacity threshold and using this as the test value rather than pure white for 100 per cent opacity. This means that an object may be partially visible but still culled depending on the value of the threshold (the lower the value, the more approximate the culling). This feature can cull away objects that are only visible through small holes in nearer objects, avoiding the expense of rendering them at the penalty of losing their partial visibility.

We will now describe a method that also uses an image pyramid, this time to store depth. This is called Hierarchical Z-buffer Visibility and it is an algorithm developed by Greene *et al.* (1993). At the top of the hierarchy is a conventional octree subdivision of the scene (Section 9.2.2).

The conventional Z-buffer algorithm works in image space and utilises image space coherence in the sense that the depth of a pixel is calculated by incrementing that of the previous pixel. Object space coherence is invoked at the culling stage but all objects inside the view frustum are considered by the Z-buffer algorithm.

The object space coherence is set up by constructing a conventional octree for the scene and using this to guide the rendering strategy. The entire scene – in the form of an octree – is then considered as an object to be rendered. The rendering strategy starts at the root of the tree and applies the following recursively:

- cull – if the current octree cube does not intersect the view frustum then we are done with this node;

- if the cube does intersect the view frustum then the (quadrilateral) projection of the cube is passed down the pipeline and the depth of its faces interpolated and checked against the Z-buffer.

A node of an octree is hidden if all the faces of the cube associated with that node are hidden with respect to the Z-buffer. If such is the case then, of course, all the polygons or complete objects that the cube contains are hidden. If the cube is not completely hidden we proceed with the geometry inside the cube – child nodes or leaf nodes containing polygons. Thus a large number of hidden polygons are culled at the cost of rendering cube faces. So we are imposing a rendering order on the normally arbitrary polygon ordering in the Z-buffer. This strategy deals with the overdraw problem within a view frustum (or a portal).

Greene points out that rendering cubes in itself can be expensive – if the cube being rendered projects onto a large number of pixels – and this consideration leads to further exploiting the normal Z-buffer advantage of image space coherence.

The Z-pyramid is a strategy that attempts to determine complete polygon visibility without pixel by pixel elaboration. A Z-pyramid is an image pyramid (Chapter 18) with the original Z-buffer image at the lowest level. At each level there is a half-resolution Z-buffer, where the z value for a cell is obtained from the largest of the z values of the four cells in the next level down. Maintaining the Z-pyramid involves tracking up the hierarchy in the direction of finer resolution until we encounter a depth that is already as far away as the current depth value. Using the Z-pyramid to test the visibility of a cube face involves finding the finest detail level whose corresponding projection in screen space just covers the projection of the face. Then it is simply a matter of comparing the nearest vertex depth of the face against the value in the Z-pyramid. Using the Z-pyramid to test a complete polygon for visibility is the same except that the screen space bounding box of the polygon is used.

Thus we can say that the algorithm exploits object space coherence by the octree scene subdivision and image space coherence by the Z-pyramid. It is also possible to exploit temporal coherence and carry visibility information over from frame to frame. Temporal coherence is exploited by retaining the visible cubes from the previous frame. For the current frame the polygons within these cubes are rendered first and the cubes marked as such. The algorithm then proceeds as normal. This strategy plays on the usual event that most of the cubes from the previous frame will still be visible – a few will become invisible in the current frame and a few cubes, invisible in the previous frame, will become visible.

9.10 Dynamic objects and visibility

We have already seen in Section 9.7.1 that we can exploit frame coherence for objects moving through a scene and we now come to consider the exact visibility computation for moving objects. If we are not going to consider updating either a spatial subdivision or bounding volume hierarchy, for each frame, to take into account the motion of objects, then we can proceed as follows. We can use the classic Z-buffer algorithm which enables moving objects to be composited into a scene rendered using a BSP tree.

A general approach would proceed by:

(1) BSP rendering the scene and filling the Z-buffer with static polygons' z values. HSR is effectively the painter's algorithm.

(2) rendering moving objects and compositing into the scene using the z values of the moving objects and those of the static objects already in the Z-buffer.

We can deal trivially with dynamic objects by inserting their reference coordinates into the tree but if the object is large and complex its extent may range over several nodes of the tree. If we only consider the node containing the reference point of the object then clearly calculations will be wrong. A solution is to add the object to every BSP node containing the vertices of its bounding box. The efficacy of this will then depend on the bounding efficiency of the box with respect to the object. Some partitions may be marked as containing the object when in fact they do not.

Lighting in games

10.1 Light maps

10.2 Dynamic lighting effects with light maps

10.3 Dynamic lights

10.4 Switchable/destroyable light sources

10.5 Fog maps/volumetric fog

10.6 Lighting case studies

In this chapter we will look at lighting technology in games. The emphasis is mainly on pre-calculated static lighting in the form of light maps because this is the predominant technology currently being used; but we will also look at how light map technology can be modified to deal with moving objects and moving lights. Established effects such as lens flare and missile trails are dealt with in Chapter 19 because we categorise them as two-dimensional (billboard) techniques.

The material in this chapter is based on the following aspects of lighting:

- **Static lights** or lights that do not move. These have their effect on static objects pre-calculated and stored in a light map. They also illuminate dynamic objects on a frame to frame basis.

- **Dynamic lights** move and must therefore have their effect calculated for every frame. They illuminate all objects (static and dynamic) within a sphere of influence.

- **Ambient light**   Each BSP leaf node has an ambient light associated with it. This is calculated as the average of all the light map pixels inside the node.

- **Static objects** are lit by light maps and by dynamic lights. Light maps are updated locally in the region of influence of a dynamic light.

- **Dynamic objects** such as animated meshes, missiles, players, doors, elevators and so on are illuminated by ambient light and point light sources.

Light maps

Light maps are an obvious extension to texture maps that enable lighting to be pre-calculated and stored as a two-dimensional texture map. We sample the reflected light over a surface and store this in a two-dimensional map. Thus shading reduces to indexing into a light map or a light modulated texture map. An advantage of the technique is that there is no restriction on the complexity of the rendering method used in the pre-calculation – we could, for example, use radiosity or any view-independent global illumination method to generate the light maps. Figure 10.1 (Colour Plate) shows a frame rendered using a light map derived from radiosity solution. The original solution took approximately 1 hour to calculate.

In principle, light maps are similar to environment maps (Section 7.5). In environment mapping we cache, in a two-dimensional map, all the illumination incident at a single point in the scene. With light maps we cache the reflected light from every surface in the scene in a set of two-dimensional maps.

If an accurate pre-calculation method is used then we would expect the technique to produce better quality shading and be faster than Gouraud interpolation. The obvious disadvantage of the technique is that for moving objects we can only invoke a very simple lighting environment (diffuse shading with the light source at infinity). A compromise is to use dynamic shading for moving objects and assume that they do not interact, as far as shading is concerned, with static objects shaded with a light map.

Light maps can either be stored separate to texture maps, or the object's texture map can be pre-modulated by the light map (see Section 12.5 for further details on how texture maps and light maps are blended). If the light map is kept as a separate entity then it can be stored at a lower resolution than the texture map because view-independent lighting, except at shadow edges, changes more slowly than texture detail.

If an object is to receive a texture then we can modulate the brightness of the texture during the modelling phase so that it has the same effect as if the (unmodulated) texture colours were injected into, say, a Phong shading equation. This is called surface caching because it stores the final value required for the pixel onto which a surface point projects and because texture caching hardware is used to implement it. If this strategy is employed then the texture mapping transform and the transform that maps light samples on the surface of the object into a light map should be the same.

Light maps were first used in two-pass ray tracing (Arvo and Kirk, 1987) and are also used in Ward's (1994) RADIANCE renderer. Their motivation in these applications was to cache diffuse illumination to enable the implementation of a global illumination model that would work in a reasonable time. Their more recent use in games engines has of course been to facilitate shading in real time.

Light map space selection

The first problem with light maps is how do we sample and store, in a two-dimensional array, the calculated reflected light across the face of a polygon in three-dimensional space. In effect this is the reverse of texture mapping where we need a mapping from two-dimensional space into three-dimensional object space. Another problem concerns economy. For scenes of any complexity it would clearly be uneconomical to construct a light map for each polygon – rather we require many polygons to share a single light map.

Zhukov *et al.* (1998) approach the three-dimensional sampling problem by organising polygons into structure called 'polypacks'. Polygons are projected into the world coordinate planes and collected into polypacks if their angles with a coordinate plane do not exceed some threshold (so that the maximal projection plane is selected for a polygon) and if their extents do not overlap in the projection. The world space coordinate planes are subdivided into square cells (the texels or 'lumels') and back projected onto the polygon. The image of a square cell on a polygon is a parallelogram (whose larger angle <= 102°). These are called patches and are the subdivided polygon elements for which the reflected light is calculated. This scheme thus samples every polygon with almost square elements, storing the result in the light map (Figure 10.2).

These patches form a subdivision of the scene sufficient for the purpose of generating light maps and a single light intensity for each patch can be calculated using whatever algorithm the application demands (for example, Phong shading or radiosity). After this phase is complete there exists a set of (parallelogram shaped) samples for each polygon. These then have to be 'stuffed' into the minimum number of two-dimensional light maps in each coordinate plane. Zhukov *et al.* do this by using a 'first hit decreasing' algorithm which first sorts each polygon group by the number of texels.

Another problem addressed by the authors is that the groups of samples corresponding to a polygon have to be surrounded by 'sand' texels. These are supplementary texels that do not belong to a face group but are used when bi-linear interpolation is used in conjunction with a light map and prevent visual lighting artefacts appearing at the edges of polygons. Thus each texture map consists

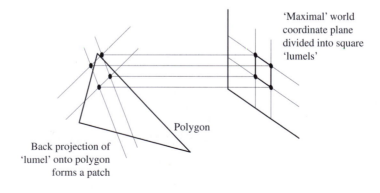

Figure 10.2

Forming a light map in the 'maximal' world coordinate plane.

of a mixture of light texels, sand texels and unoccupied texels. Zhukov *et al.* report that for a scene consisting of 24 000 triangles (700 patches), 14 light maps of 256 × 256 texels were produced which exhibited a breakdown of texels as: 75 per cent light texels, 15 per cent sand texels and 10 per cent unoccupied texels.

10.1.2 Polygon/light map correspondence

Consider now the polygon light map correspondence. A direct scheme for computing light maps for scenes made up of triangles and for which we already have vertex/texture coordinate association is to use this correspondence to derive an affine transformation between texture space and object space and then use this transformation to sample the light across the face of a triangle. The algorithm is then driven from the texture map space (by scan converting the polygon projection in texture space) and for each texel finding its corresponding point or projection on the object surface from:

$$\begin{bmatrix} x \\ y \\ z \end{bmatrix} = \begin{bmatrix} a & b & c \\ d & e & f \\ g & h & i \end{bmatrix} \begin{bmatrix} u \\ v \\ 1 \end{bmatrix}$$

where (x,y,z) is the point on the object corresponding to the texel (u,v). This transformation can be seen as a linear transformation in three-dimensional space with the texture map embedded in the $z = 1$ plane. The coefficients are found from the vertex/texture coordinate correspondence by inverting the U matrix in:

$$\begin{bmatrix} x_0 & x_1 & x_2 \\ y_0 & y_1 & y_2 \\ z_0 & z_1 & z_2 \end{bmatrix} = \begin{bmatrix} a & b & c \\ d & e & f \\ g & h & i \end{bmatrix} \begin{bmatrix} u_0 & u_1 & u_2 \\ v_0 & v_1 & v_2 \\ 1 & 1 & 1 \end{bmatrix}$$

Writing this as:

$X = AU$

we have:

$A = XU^{-1}$

The inverse U^{-1} is guaranteed to exist providing the three points are non-collinear. Note that in terms of our treatment in Chapter 7 this is a forward mapping from texture space to object space. Having derived this correspondence the light map can be 'lit' by scanning through it and evaluating any local reflection model on the polygon.

Rendering using light maps usually implies two passes – a texture map pass followed by a light map pass. This is because in most cases the texture will be tiled and cannot therefore be pre-mixed with light map information. The light map pass causes the values in the map to be blended with the colour already in the frame buffer. Further issues in blending texture maps and light maps are discussed in Section 12.5.

In general, light maps will be constructed at much lower resolution than texture maps. We can only use them correctly in the context of view-independent illumination, in other words diffuse reflection – and this implies that the light intensity changes slowly across a surface. In practice, for games environments, a projected area of a light map pixel of around 1 square metre seems satisfactory.

Finally, note that because of the large size of light map pixels, neighbours in the map exhibit, in general, noticeable differences in intensity. When they are projected onto the scene objects the light map pixel boundaries will be visible (Figure 10.7 – Colour Plate). This can be ameliorated using the same anti-aliasing method as for texture mapping (Section 8.9).

10.1.3   Light map practice

In this section we describe the implementation of a method that seems simpler than that of Section 10.1.1. The method employed divides into two phases. First, we build the light map structure, which means associating each polygon in the scene with light map information. This is done as follows:

(1) For a polygon, find all polygons that are co-planar to it and are also interconnected to it.

(2) Find the AABB for this set of polygons.

(3) Find the face of the bounding box with the largest extent and use this as the light map for the polygon set.

(4) Mark each polygon with a light map index and continue until all faces have a light map.

To limit the number of light maps generated by this approach we need to include a tolerance in the co-planarity test.

The following code assigns values to the game light map. On scene loading the *set_base* function is called once for each light map performing calculations that make the subsequent light map (*u,v*) to object (*x,y,z*) mapping more efficient. The *illum* function is called with the light source point, light radius and light colour. It loops all the light map pixels and computes their position in world space. The illumination value is set simply as proportional to the difference between the radius (*rad*) of the sphere of influence and the distance (*dist*) from the point to the light source – the closer the point is to the light source, the higher the illumination. The reason we use this very basic lighting model is that it enables dynamic lighting effects to be incorporated. That is, because of the ease of implementing a sphere of influence in conjunction with a BSP tree we can use this approach to partially update the light maps in real time.

```
class light_map
{
    vector v0, v1, v2;
    float det;
```

```cpp
        float uv[3][2];
public:
    vector d0, d1, d2;
    int facenum,sizex,sizey;
    unsigned char *bmp;

    light_map(int sx,int sy)
    {
        sizex=sx;
        sizey=sy;
        bmp=new unsigned char [sx*sy*3];
    };
    ~light_map()
    {
        if(bmp) delete bmp;
    };

    void map_point(float u, float v, vector &point);
    void set_base(face *f);
    void illum(vector& pos,vector& color,float rad);
};

void light_map::illum(vector& pos,vector& color,float rad)
{
    vector point;
    int i,j,k;
    float dist;
    unsigned char *uc=bmp;

    for( j=0;j<sizey;j++ )
    for( i=0;i<sizex;i++ )
    {
    point = d0+ d1*((float)i/sizex) + d2*((float)j/sizey);
    dist = (pos-point).length();
    if (dist>rad)
        uc+=3;
    else
        {
        dist=(1.0f-dist/rad)*255.0f;

        k=(int)(color.r*dist)+(int)(*uc);
        *(uc++)=k>255?255:k;

        k=(int)(color.g*dist)+(int)(*uc);
        *(uc++)=k>255?255:k;

        k=(int)(color.b*dist)+(int)(*uc);
        *(uc++)=k>255?255:k;    }
        }
    }
```

```
    }
    void light_map::set_base(face *f)
    {
      v0 = f->vert[0]->pos;
      v1 = f->vert[1]->pos - f->vert[0]->pos;
      v2 = f->vert[2]->pos - f->vert[0]->pos;
      uv[0][0]=f->lmuv[0][0];
      uv[0][1]=f->lmuv[0][1];
      uv[1][0]=f->lmuv[1][0]-f->lmuv[0][0];
      uv[1][1]=f->lmuv[1][1]-f->lmuv[0][1];
      uv[2][0]=f->lmuv[2][0]-f->lmuv[0][0];
      uv[2][1]=f->lmuv[2][1]-f->lmuv[0][1];
      det=uv[1][0]*uv[2][1]-uv[2][0]*uv[1][1];
      vector p1,p2;
      map_point(0.0f,0.0f,d0);
      map_point(1.0f,0.0f,p1);
      map_point(0.0f,1.0f,p2);
      d1=p1-d0;
      d2=p2-d0;
    }
    void light_map::map_point(float u, float v, vector &point)
    {
      u-=uv[0][0];
      v-=uv[0][1];
      point= v0+
         ((u*uv[2][1]-uv[2][0]*v)/det)*v1+
         ((uv[1][0]*v-u*uv[1][1])/det)*v2;
    }
```

10.2   Dynamic lighting effects with light maps

10.2.1   Moving objects – general

Light maps have functioned as one of the classic enabling technologies of computer games, facilitating a high degree of pre-calculation of lighting in an environment. They do, however, suffer from two significant and obvious disadvantages. The first is that their utility decreases as a function of object complexity – the higher the complexity of an object, the greater the number of orientations exhibited by the face planes. The second is that by definition they cannot light dynamic objects. There are many ways in which we can approach dynamic objects, that fall short of classic shading, depending on the application.

As we have described them up to now, light maps are a method of storing precalculated lighting information which can then be accessed and used to shade scenes in real time. They can, however, be *partially* updated in real time thereby facilitating dynamic lights and shadows. The common way of doing this is to restrict the field of influence of the light. If a BSP tree is implemented a sphere of influence can be used, restricting the light/polygon interaction to those polygons within fixed distance from the light source. The BSP tree can then be recursed with the sphere (see Chapter 9) and light object interaction restricted to those faces that lie within the sphere. This idea can be extended to model area sources by using a number of spheres placed with their centres positioned at random points within the emitting surface.

This is shown to effect in Figure 10.3 (Colour Plate) which shows a dark corridor being appropriately illuminated as the door opens from a light source in the adjacent room. This is done by having the light source select a subset of the static objects on a sphere of influence basis. The light maps corresponding to the areas within range of the light source are then updated by using a ray intersect calculation from the selected object to the illuminating source, a ray that either passes through the opening door or collides with it.

Spheres of influence can also be used in dynamic shadow determination. A shadow can only be generated by a light source on a surface that is in the sphere of influence of the light.

10.2.2 Moving (viewer centred) spotlights

A useful effect in many games is a spotlight coincident with the camera. The player can switch on the light and look into dark corners. This is easily implemented by using the camera look direction as a ray and invoking a ray intersection from the viewpoint (Section 1.3). At the point of intersection we define a dynamic spherical light source. This causes the light map to be updated on a sphere of influence basis as we described in the previous section. This is sufficiently efficient for real-time operation but it suffers from two obvious visual discrepancies. First, there is no longitudinal light track from the source. We would normally expect to see this effect with a spotlight. Second, the object on which the spherical light source is placed switches on the basis of a single ray calculation – we are positioning a light with extent as if it was a point source.

10.2.3 Moving objects and ambient light

In this section we consider, for example, the variation of ambient lighting incident on an object as it moves through an environment. Such an object should pick up the quality of the ambient light – changes in colour and intensity – as it moves. For example, a player object should be able to 'hide' in a dark area. This can be implemented by storing an ambient light value with each BSP partition. To do this we can, for each light map pixel, find its position in three-dimensional space and add its value to the corresponding BSP node. The moving object then picks up the ambient light value from the partition that it is currently in.

This is effectively a volumetric light field for ambient lights where the light field elements are the BSP partitions.

10.2.4

Moving objects and Gouraud shading

Current graphics processors offer Gouraud shading where the application passes vertex intensities and hardware performs the bi-linear interpolation.

10.3

Dynamic lights

A self-emitting moving object passing another should cast light. Here we can simply add a constant light, based on the distance from the self-emitting object to the object receiving the light, but this will result in back faces being erroneously lit. This may not be too problematic if the self-emitting object is moving quickly as in the case of a projectile. Alternatively, the self-emitting object can be considered as a point source and classic shading used to light the receiver object. If the receiving object is static – background or level detail – then we can use the sphere of influence approach increasing the (pre-calculated) light level of the selected polygons. This effect is shown in Figure 10.4 (Colour Plate).

10.4

Switchable/destroyable light sources

In implementing switchable or destroyable light sources there is a problem in recalculating the light map if the original values have reached saturation owing to more than one light source having illuminated the same light map pixel. If one of the contributing lights is turned off, what value is to be used to subtract its contribution from the light map?

A possible solution is as follows. For each light map we need a list of the switchable lights that illuminate it. When a light is turned off we loop through all light maps to which this light contributes. This is done by using the light's sphere of influence. Each such light map is restored to contain information from the static contributing sources only, and it is flagged to indicate re-computation. Then the switchable lights that are still turned on are added back into the light maps using the flags.

This process can be extended over several frames, reducing the light source contribution instead of illuminating it. This then simulates a fading light.

10.5

Fog maps/volumetric fog

A technique that fits neatly on the back of light maps is fog maps. Here we simply duplicate the light map's coordinate mapping but store a fog pixel instead of an illumination value. Before we look at the technique in detail we will examine the 'traditional' atmospheric fog effect.

Normal fog is depth modulated and added everywhere to the scene. A common equation used for calculating the fog blending factor, used to mix the scene colour with the fog, is:

$$f = e^{-(z.\text{density})}$$

where z is the eye coordinate distance and density is a constant. The final pixel value is then obtained by blending the penultimate colour with the fog blending factor as:

$$C_{\text{out}} = fC_{\text{in}} + (1 - f)C_{\text{f}} \qquad [10.1]$$

where C_{in} is the penultimate colour and C_{f} is the fog colour – usually white. (Texture blending is described in more detail in Section 12.5.)

A much better and more flexible fog effect can be achieved by considering that the fog itself is an object, say a sphere, which the viewer can be inside or outside. Such an effect is now view dependent and therefore dynamic, and it can be implemented by using the sphere of influence approach we used for dynamic lighting. We call this effect volumetric fog and the enabling technique fog maps.

Fog maps differ from light maps in that they are dynamic and the information may be stored at lower resolution. The blending used is as Equation 10.1 except that now f is the value of the fog map pixel.

A fog sphere is used in conjunction with the BSP tree to find the polygon that it intersects. The resulting effect of the fog is then stored in the light map. When the fog object is rendered the final blending parameter is fetched from the fog map. Although in effect the fog has been painted on whatever surface its sphere intersects as a texture, it is perceived as a three-dimensional object or sphere. In fact, making the sphere of influence larger than the actual fog sphere (so that the fog sphere does not touch any walls) gives the remarkable illusion of a three-dimensional fog ball floating in space.

Fog maps are initialised by inserting a fog sphere into the scene, and finding the polygons enclosed in the sphere of influence. A ray is fired from the camera to the intersected polygons. If the ray does not intersect the fog sphere, then no fog is applied to the fog map, otherwise a value is based on the distance between the two intersections of the ray with the sphere. An image generated using this procedure is shown in Figure 10.5 (Colour Plate).

A 'box' fog object can also be easily implemented which can have the fog density modulated by height. Thus the fog is dense near the base and less dense at the top. An image generated using this procedure is shown in Figure 10.6 (Colour Plate).

10.6 Lighting case studies

Figure 10.7 (Colour Plate) demonstrates the contribution of various options to the final image. A point to note is that we if we elect to consider the light maps and fog maps as dynamic (updateable by dynamic lights) then we cannot use high quality mip-map filtering.

- Figure 10.7(a) Texture map applied with no filtering
- Figure 10.7(b) Texture map applied, with mip-map filtering
- Figure 10.7(c) Light map with no filtering
- Figure 10.7(d) Light map with linear filtering
- Figure 10.7(e) Mip-mapped filtered texture map and filtered light map applied
- Figure 10.7(f) Fog map with linear filtering
- Figure 10.7(g) Mip-mapped filtered texture map with linear filtered, light map, and fog map

Figure 10.8 (Colour Plate) shows the different atmospheres engendered by using different options for dynamic objects.

- Figure 10.8(a) Scene using ambient light only for dynamic object
- Figure 10.8(b) Scene using Gouraud shading for dynamic object
- Figure 10.8(c) Ambient light for dynamic object together with a contribution from the dynamic (missile) object
- Figure 10.8(d) Gouraud shading for the dynamic object together with the missile contribution

10.6.1 Stripifying and lighting a patch model

This example lights an object formed by sweeping a Bézier curve cross-section along a curved spine (lofting). There are two immediate advantages exhibited by the patch representation. First, we can easily create a LOD facility and produce a polygon mesh to whatever resolution is required. This can be implemented dynamically or as a pre-process. At the same time as building the polygon mesh the vertices are arranged into a strip structure as described in Chapter 3. Second, we can effectively separate the lighting resolution from the polygonal resolution – even a very low resolution surface can receive lighting from a light map which has been calculated using the true normal of the original surface at each light map pixel. This effect is demonstrated in Figure 10.9(a) which indicates that the lighting calculations are based on the original surface and then applied to the low resolution mesh. As the figure shows, the true surface normals are effectively transferred onto planar facets as far as the lighting calculations are concerned. This is very similar to the process of vector interpolation in Phong shading. In that case vertex normals are interpolated across the face of the polygons. A subtler effect is demonstrated in Figure 10.9(b) which shows the cross-section of an extruded surface reduced to a rectangle. A point light source directly above the top surface will still illuminate the side surfaces at this resolution. This is a situation which would not occur when using a conventional local reflection

Figure 10.9
(a) Lighting surface resolution independence: the resolution of the lighting can be made independent of the polygonal resolution. (b) Low-resolution polygons are correctly lit even if they cannot see the light source.

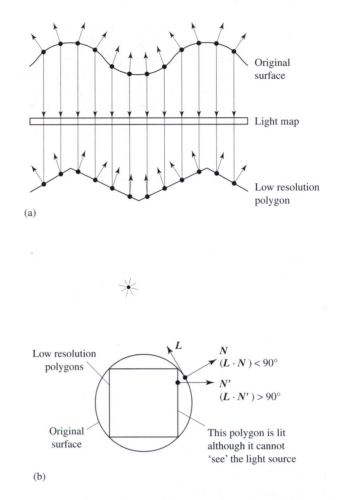

model because the angle between the normal of the side surfaces and the light direction vector L is greater than 90°.

These effects are shown for a rendered object in Figures 5.53 and 5.55 (Colour Plate). Figure 5.55 shows an object which has had its cross-section completely flattened. Nevertheless curvature is 'restored' by the light map which even seems to visually conflict with the straight-line boundary at the base of the arch. Your brain seems unable to accept this straight boundary because of the lighting.

Building a light map for a patch model is much simpler than for a polygon mesh object because, as we point out in Section 7.3, we already have a surface parametrisation – every light map pixel (u,v) can correspond to a patch (u,v). In the code that follows, the light map is computed as follows:

for a light map pixel (x,y) calculate (u,v) coordinates as

$$u = (x + 0.5)/sx \qquad v = (y + 0.5)/sy$$

where (sx,sy) is the light map resolution

Because light map pixels are large (in general, the same scale as a player bounding box projection) it is important to consider the centre of the pixel. Given $Q(u,v)$, we can calculate the corresponding world space point (x,y,z) and the surface normal to the patch at that point. (Calculating the surface normal N at a point on a patch is described in Section 5.5.) This information is then used in a lighting and shadow model and the result assigned to the map.

```
void bezier_loft::build_stripfan()
{
   // allocate new stripfan mesh
   if (sfmesh) delete sfmesh;
   sfmesh=new stripfan_mesh;

   int i,j,k,ns;
   float u,v;
   vector z[2];

   // compute number of vertices in u and v base on curveerr
   // to setup an LOD mesh where each point in the mesh lies in the
   patch surface
   float *pointsu=new float[MAX_CURVE_VERTS];
   int nvu=shape->adaptative_subdiv(flyengine->
   curveerr,pointsu,MAX_CURVE_VERTS);
   float *pointsv=new float[MAX_CURVE_VERTS];
   int nvv=path->adaptative_subdiv(flyengine->
   curveerr,pointsv,MAX_CURVE_VERTS);
   // compute number of strips
   ns=nvu-1;

   // for each strip
   k=0;
   for( i=0;i<ns;i++ )
   {
      // create strip
      sfmesh->add_stripfan(nvv*2,texpic,lm);

      // for each pair of vertices
      for( j=0;j<nvv;j++ )
      {
         // evaluate vertex position, texture and lightmap coordinates

         u=pointsu[i+1];
         v=pointsv[j];
         patch.evaluate(PATCH_EVAL_POINT|PATCH_EVAL_TEXTCOORD,u,v,z);
         sfmesh->vertdata[k].pos=z[0];
         sfmesh->vertdata[k].u=z[1].x;
         sfmesh->vertdata[k].v=z[1].y;
         sfmesh->vertdata[k].ul=z[1].z;
```

```
                sfmesh->vertdata[k].vl=z[1].w;
                k++;

                u=pointsu[i];
                patch.evaluate(PATCH_EVAL_POINT|PATCH_EVAL_TEXTCOORD,u,v,z);
                sfmesh->vertdata[k].pos=z[0];
                sfmesh->vertdata[k].u=z[1].x;
                sfmesh->vertdata[k].v=z[1].y;
                sfmesh->vertdata[k].ul=z[1].z;
                sfmesh->vertdata[k].vl=z[1].w;
                k++;
            }
        }

        delete pointsu;
        delete pointsv;

        if (objmesh) delete objmesh;
        objmesh=sfmesh->build_mesh();
        objmesh->pivotpos=pos;
}

void    bezier_loft::illuminate_patch(vector&   p,float    rad,vector&
color,int shadows)
{
    int i,j,k;
    float dist,u,v;

    // get lightmap applied to patch
    light_map *l=flyengine->lm[lm];
    unsigned char *uc;

    // get light position in patch local coordinates
    vector center=(p-pos)*mat_t,point,dir;
    rad*=rad;

    // for each lightmap pixel in y
    for( j=0;j<l->sizey;j++ )
    {
        uc=&l->bmp[j*l->bytesx];
        v=(j+0.5f)/l->sizey;
        // for each lightmap pixel in x
        for( i=0;i<l->sizex;i++ )
        {
        u=(i+0.5f)/l->sizex;

        // get lightmap pixel position in the patch surface
        patch.evaluate(PATCH_EVAL_POINT,u,v,&point);

        // check if point is inside light radius
```

```
dir=point-center;
dist=dir.x*dir.x+dir.y*dir.y+dir.z*dir.z;
if (dist>rad)
  uc+=3;
else
  {
  // compute lighting factor based on light radius and pixel
  distance
  dist=(1.0f-dist/rad)*255.0f;

  // if shadows required, multiply dot product of patch normal
  and
  // light direction and check for collision
  if (shadows==2)
    {
    vector normal;
    dir.normalize();
    patch.evaluate(PATCH_EVAL_NORMAL,u,v,&normal);
    float dot=-vec_dot(dir,normal);
    flyengine->excludecollision=this;
    if (dot<0.0f ||
      flyengine->collision_test(flyengine->bsp,center,point))
      {
      uc+=3;
      flyengine->excludecollision=0;
      continue;
      }
    flyengine->excludecollision=0;
    dist*=dot;
    }

  // apply colors to lightmap

  k=(int)(color.x*dist)+(int)(*uc);
  *(uc++)=k>255?255:k;

  k=(int)(color.y*dist)+(int)(*uc);
  *(uc++)=k>255?255:k;

  k=(int)(color.z*dist)+(int)(*uc);
  *(uc++)=k>255?255:k;
  }
 }
}
l->lastupdate=flyengine->cur_step;
}
```

Shadows in games

11.1 The nature of shadows

11.2 Classical shadow algorithms

11.3 Shadows in the games

This chapter has three themes. First, we consider the nature of shadows and why it is important to render them in a scene. Second, we consider classical shadow algorithms. Current game algorithms are subsets of these and we can speculate that as hardware marches onwards there will be a demand for higher and higher quality shadows, making a study of such algorithms worthwhile. In this respect it is possible at the moment to implement the shadow volume method, as a multi-pass algorithm (Section 12.3.3), in almost real time. Third, we will look at a fast, approximate and cheap method and possible variations of it. This can be used to generate shadows for dynamic objects in games. For static objects we can include shadows in light maps and this topic is also dealt with.

11.1 The nature of shadows

This chapter deals with the topic of 'geometric' shadows or algorithms that calculate the shape of an area in shadow but only guess at its reflected light intensity. This restriction has long been tolerated in mainstream rendering, the rationale presumably being that it is better to have a shadow with a guessed intensity rather than having no shadow at all.

Shadows, like texture mapping, are commonly handled in classical renderers by using an empirical add-on algorithm. They are pasted into the scene like texture maps. The other parallel with texture maps is that the easiest algorithm to implement computes a map, for each light source in the scene, known as a shadow map. The map is accessed during rendering, just as a texture map is referenced, to find out if a pixel is in shadow or not. Like the Z-buffer algorithm in hidden surface removal, this algorithm is easy to implement and has become a pseudo-standard. Also like the Z-buffer algorithm, it trades simplicity against high memory cost.

Shadows are important in scenes. A scene without shadows looks artificial. They give clues concerning the scene, consolidate spatial relationships between objects and give information on the position of the light source. To compute shadows completely we need knowledge of both their shape and the light intensity inside them. An area of the scene in shadow is not completely bereft of light. It simply cannot see direct illumination, but receives indirect illumination from another nearby object. Thus shadow intensity can only be calculated taking this into account and this means using a global illumination model such as radiosity. In this algorithm shadow areas are treated no differently to any other area in the scene and the shadow intensity is a light intensity, reflected from a surface, like any other. In other words, the shadow solution emerges automatically from the solution, and no separate algorithm has to be invoked.

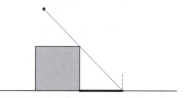

(a) Point light source produces hard-edged shadows ($r = 0$)

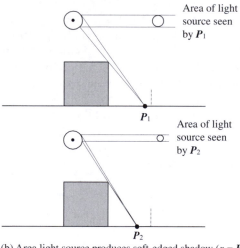

Area of light source seen by P_1

Area of light source seen by P_2

(b) Area light source produces soft-edged shadow ($r = R$)

Figure 11.1
Shadows cast by spherical light sources.

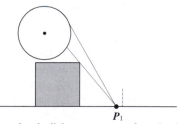

(c) Increasing the light source area softens the shadows more ($r = 2R$)

Shadows are a function of the lighting environment. They can be hard edged or soft edged and contain both an umbra and a penumbra area. The relative size of the umbra/penumbra is a function of the size and the shape of the light source and its distance from the object (Figure 11.1). The umbra is that part of a shadow that is completely cut off from the light source, whereas the penumbra is an area that receives some light from the source. A penumbra surrounds an umbra and there is always a gradual change in intensity from a penumbra to an umbra. In computer graphics, if we are not modelling illumination sources, then we usually consider point light sources at large distances, and assume in the simplest case that objects produce umbrae with sharp edges. This is still only an approximation. Even although light from a large distance produces almost parallel rays, there is still light behind the object due to diffraction and the shadow grades off. This effect also varies over the distance a shadow is thrown. These effects, which determine the quality of a shadow, enable us to infer information concerning the nature of the light source and they are clearly important to us as human beings perceiving a three-dimensional environment. For example, the shadows that we see outdoors depend on the time of day and whether the sky is overcast or not.

(11.1.1)

Properties of shadows used in computer graphics

A number of aspects of shadows are exploited in the computer generation of the phenomenon. These are:

- A shadow from polygon A that falls on polygon B due to a point light source can be calculated by projecting polygon A onto the plane that contains polygon B. The position of the point light source is used as the centre of projection.

- No shadows are seen if the viewpoint is coincident with the (single) light source. An equivalent form of this statement is that shadows can be considered to be areas hidden from the light source, implying that modified hidden surface algorithms can be used to solve the shadow problem.

- If the light source, or sources, are point sources then there is no penumbra to calculate and the shadow has a hard edge.

- For static scenes shadows are fixed and do not change as the viewpoint changes. If the relative positions of objects and light sources change, the shadows have to be re-calculated. This places a high overhead on three-dimensional animation where shadows are important for depth and movement perception.

Because of the high computational overheads, shadows have been regarded in much the same way as texture mapping – as a quality add-on. They have not been viewed as a necessity and compared with shading algorithms there has been little consideration of the quality of shadows. Most shadow generation algorithms produce hard-edge point light source shadows and most algorithms deal only with polygon mesh models.

Simple shadows on a ground plane

An extremely simple method of generating shadows is reported by Blinn (1988). It suffices for single object scenes throwing shadows on a flat ground plane. The method simply involves drawing the projection of the object on the ground plane. It is thus restricted to single-object scenes, or multi-object scenes where objects are sufficiently isolated so as not to cast shadows on each other. The ground plane projection is easily obtained from a linear transformation and the projected polygon can be scanned into a Z-buffer as part of an initialisation procedure at an appropriate (dark) intensity.

If the usual illumination approximation is made – single point source at an infinite distance – then we have parallel light rays in a direction $L = (x_l, y_l, z_l)$ as shown in Figure 11.2. Any point on the object $P = (x_p, y_p, z_p)$ will cast a shadow at $S = (x_{sw}, y_{sw}, 0)$. Considering the geometry in the figure, we have:

$$S = P - \alpha L$$

and given that $z_{sw} = 0$, we have:

$$0 = z_p - \alpha z_l$$
$$\alpha = z_p / z_l$$

and

$$x_{sw} = x_p - (z_p / z_l)\, x_l$$
$$y_{sw} = y_p - (z_p / z_l)\, y_l$$

As a homogeneous transformation this is

$$
\begin{bmatrix} x_{sw} \\ y_{sw} \\ 0 \\ 1 \end{bmatrix}
=
\begin{bmatrix}
1 & 0 & -x_l/z_l & 0 \\
1 & 0 & -y_l/z_l & 0 \\
0 & 0 & 0 & 0 \\
0 & 0 & 0 & 1
\end{bmatrix}
\begin{bmatrix} x_p \\ y_p \\ z_p \\ 1 \end{bmatrix}
$$

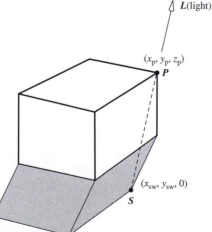

Figure 11.2
Ground plane shadows for single objects.

Note from this that it is just as easy to generate shadows on a vertical back or side plane. Blinn also shows how to extend this idea to handle light sources that are at a finite distance from the object.

This type of approximate shadow (on a flat ground plane) is beloved by traditional animators and its use certainly enhances movement in three-dimensional computer animation.

11.2 Classical shadow algorithms

Unlike hidden surface removal algorithms, where one or two algorithms now predominate and other methods are used only in special cases, no popular candidate has emerged as the top shadow algorithm. In fact, shadow computation is a rather neglected area of computer graphics. What follows, therefore, is a brief description of four major approaches.

11.2.1 Shadow algorithms: projecting polygons/scan line

This approach was developed by Appel (1968) and Bouknight and Kelley (1970). Adding shadows to a scan line algorithm requires a pre-processing stage that builds up a secondary data structure which links all polygons that may shadow a given polygon. Shadow pairs – a polygon together with the polygon that it can possibly shadow – are detected by projecting all polygons onto a sphere centred at the light source. Polygon pairs that cannot interact are detected and discarded. This is an important step because for a scene containing n polygons the number of possible projected shadows is $n(n-1)$.

The algorithm processes the secondary data structure simultaneously with a normal scan conversion process to determine if any shadows fall on the polygon that generated the visible scan line segment under consideration. If no shadow polygon(s) exist then the scan line algorithm proceeds as normal. For a current polygon, if a shadow polygon exists then using the light source as a centre of projection, the shadow is generated by projecting onto the plane that contains the current polygon. Normal scan conversion then proceeds simultaneously with a process that determines whether a current pixel is in shadow or not. Three possibilities now occur:

(1) The shadow polygon does not cover the generated scan line segment and the situation is identical to an algorithm without shadows.
(2) Shadow polygon(s) completely cover the visible scan line segment and the scan conversion process proceeds but the pixel intensity is modulated by an amount that depends on the number of shadows that are covering the segment. For a single light source the segment is either in shadow or not.
(3) A shadow polygon partially covers the visible scan line segment. In this case the segment is subdivided and the process is applied recursively until a solution is obtained.

Figure 11.3
Polygons that receive a shadow from another polygon are linked in a secondary data structure. Scan line segments are now delineated by both viewpoint projection boundaries and shadow boundaries.

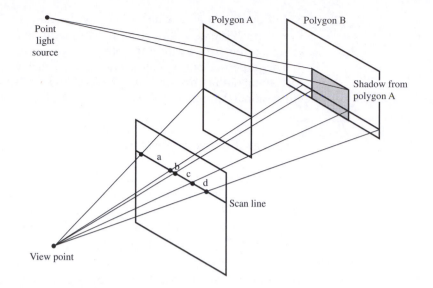

A representation of these possibilities is shown in Figure 11.3. These are, in order along the scan line:

(a) Polygon A is visible, therefore it is rendered.

(b) Polygon B is visible and is rendered.

(c) Polygon B is shadowed by polygon A and is rendered at an appropriately reduced intensity.

(d) Polygon B is visible and is rendered.

11.2.2 Shadow algorithms: shadow volumes

The shadow volume approach was originally developed by Crow (1977) and subsequently extended by others. In particular Brotman and Badler (1984) used the idea as a basis for generating 'soft' shadows – that is, shadows produced by a distributed light source.

A shadow volume is the invisible volume of space swept out by the shadow of an object. It is the infinite volume defined by lines emanating from a point light source through vertices in the object. Figure 11.4 conveys the idea of a shadow volume. A finite shadow volume is obtained by considering the intersection of the infinite volume with the view volume. The shadow volume is computed by first evaluating the contour or silhouette edge of the object, as seen from the light source. The contour edge of a simple object is shown in Figure 11.4(a). A contour edge of an object is the edge made up of one or more connected edges of polygons belonging to the object. A contour edge separates those polygons that can see the light source from those that cannot.

Figure 11.4
Illustrating the formation of a shadow volume. (a) Silhouette edge of an object. (b) Finite shadow volume defined by a silhouette edge polygon, a point light source and a view volume.

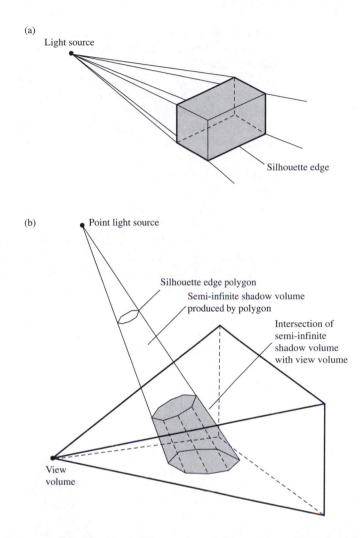

Polygons defined by the light source and the contour edges define the bounding surface of the shadow volume as shown in Figure 11.4(b). Thus each object, considered in conjunction with a point light source, generates a shadow volume object that is made up of a set of shadow polygons. Note that these shadow polygons are 'invisible' and should not be confused with the visible shadow polygons described in the next section. These shadow polygons are themselves used to determine shadows – they are not rendered.

To determine the shadow volume we would proceed as follows. For a polygon mesh object, by definition, the silhouette edge must be made up of edges of connected polygons. Thus a useful pre-processing strategy is to store connectivity data in the form of: for each polygon store a list of all the connected faces. The silhouette edge can then be determined by culling the back faces of the shadowing object from the light source as a viewpoint and then finding the edges that join the culled and not culled faces. For every vertex in the silhouette edge list we can then generate 'extension' edges that need to be clipped against the view frustum. These are then used to build up the shadow volume polygons.

This scheme can be integrated into a number of hidden surface removal algorithms and the polygons that define the shadow volume are processed along with the object polygons except that they are considered invisible. A distinction is made between 'front-facing' polygons and 'back-facing' polygons and the relationship between shadow polygons labelled in this way and object polygons is examined. A point on an object is deemed to be in shadow if it is behind a front-facing shadow polygon and in front of a back-facing polygon. That is, if it is contained within a shadow volume. Thus a front-facing shadow polygon puts anything behind it in shadow and a back-facing shadow polygon cancels the effect of a front-facing one.

As it stands, the algorithm is most easily integrated with a depth priority hidden surface removal algorithm. Consider the operation of the algorithm for a particular pixel. We consider a vector or ray from the viewpoint through the pixel and look at the relationship between real polygons and shadow polygons along this vector. For a pixel a counter is maintained. This is initialised to 1 if the viewpoint is already in shadow, 0 otherwise. As we descend the depth-sorted list of polygons, the counter is incremented when a front-facing polygon is passed and decremented when a back-facing polygon is passed. The value of this counter tells us, when we encounter a real polygon, whether we are inside a shadow volume. This is shown schematically in Figure 11.5.

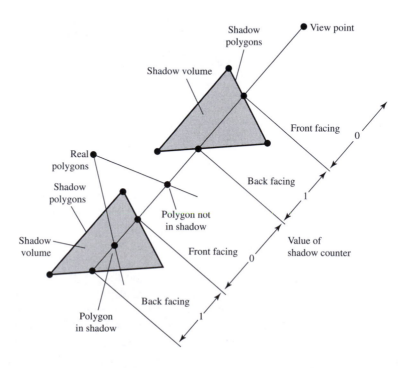

Figure 11.5
Front-facing and back-facing shadow polygons and the shadow counter value.

Brotman and Badler use an enhanced Z-buffer algorithm and this approach has two significant advantages:

(1) the benefits of the Z-buffer rendering approach are retained, and

(2) their method is able to compute soft shadows or umbra/penumbra effects.

The price to be paid for using a shadow volume approach in conjunction with a Z-buffer is memory cost. The Z-buffer has to be extended such that each pixel location is a record of five fields. As shadow polygons are 'rendered' they modify counters in a pixel record and a decision can be made as to whether a point is in shadow or not.

Soft shadows are computed by modelling distributed light sources as arrays of point sources and linearly combining computations due to each point source.

The original shadow volume approach places heavy constraints on the database environment; the most serious restriction is that objects must be convex polyhedrons. Bergeron (1986) developed a general version of Crow's algorithm that overcomes these restrictions and allows concave objects and penetrating polygons. In general, its cost is a function of the shadowing object's complexity.

Finally, a multi-pass version of this algorithm is given in Section 12.3.3. This can achieve real-time performance.

11.2.3 Shadow algorithms: Derivation of shadow polygons from light source transformations

This approach was developed by Atherton *et al.* (1978) and relies on the fact that applying hidden surface removal to a view from the light source produces polygons or parts of polygons that are in shadow. It also relies on the object space polygon clipping algorithm (to produce shadow polygons that are parts of existing polygons) by Weiler and Atherton (1977).

A claimed advantage of this approach is that it operates in object space. This means that it is possible to extract numerical information on shadows from the algorithm. This finds applications, for example, in architectural CAD.

The algorithm enhances the object data structure with shadow polygons to produce a 'complete shadow data file'. This can then be used to produce any view of the object with shadows. It is thus a good approach in generating animated sequences where the virtual camera changes position, but the relative position of the object and the light source remain unchanged. The working of the algorithm is shown for a simple example in Figure 11.6. A single shadow polygon is shown for clarity. Referring to Figure 11.6, the first step in the algorithm is to apply a transformation such that the object or scene is viewed from the light source position. Hidden surface removal then produces visible polygons, that is, polygons that are visible to the light source and are therefore not in shadow. These are either complete or clipped, as the illustration implies. This polygon set can then be combined with the original object polygons, providing

Figure 11.6
Derivation of shadow
polygons from
transformations. (a) Simple
polygonal object in
modelling coordinate
system. (b) Plan view
showing the position of the
light source. (c) Hidden
surface removal from the
light source as a viewpoint.
(d) Visible polygons from (c)
transformed back into
modelling coordinate
systems. (e) Parts (a) and (d)
merged to produce a
database that contains
shadow polygons. (f) Part
(e) can produce any view of
the object with shadows.

(a)

(b)

(c)

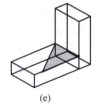

(d)

(e)

(f)

both data sets are in the same coordinate system. The process of combining these sets results in a complete shadow data file – the original polygon set enhanced by shadow polygons for a particular light source. Transforming the database to the required viewpoint and applying hidden surface removal will then result in an image with shadows. This algorithm exploits the fact that shadow polygons are viewpoint independent. Essentially the scene is processed twice for hidden surface removal: once using the light source as a viewpoint, which produces the shadow polygons, and once using normal hidden surface removal (from any viewpoint).

(11.2.4) ## Shadow algorithms: shadow Z-buffer

Possibly the simplest approach to the shadow computation, and one that is easily integrated into a Z-buffer based renderer, is the shadow Z-buffer developed by Williams (1978). This technique requires a separate shadow Z-buffer for each light source and in its basic form is only suitable for a scene illuminated by a single light source. Alternatively a single shadow Z-buffer could be used for many light sources and the algorithm executed for each light source, but this would be somewhat inefficient and slow.

The algorithm is a two-step process. A scene is 'rendered' and depth information stored into the shadow Z-buffer using the light source as a viewpoint. No intensities are calculated. This computes a 'depth image' from the light source, of those polygons that are visible to the light source.

The second step is to render the scene using a Z-buffer algorithm. This process is enhanced as follows: if a point is visible, a coordinate transformation is used to map (x,y,z), the coordinates of the point in three-dimensional screen space (from the viewpoint) to (x',y',z'), the coordinates of the point in screen space from the light point as a coordinate origin. The (x',y') are used to index the shadow Z-buffer and the corresponding depth value is compared with z'. If z' is greater than the value stored in the shadow Z-buffer for that point, then a surface is nearer to the light source than the point under consideration and the point is in shadow, thus a shadow 'intensity' is used, otherwise the point is rendered as normal. An example of shadow maps is shown in Figure 7.24 (Colour Plate). Note that in this particular example we have generated six shadow maps. This will enable us to render a view of the room from a viewpoint situated anywhere within the scene.

Apart from extending the high memory requirements of the Z-buffer hidden surface removal algorithm, the algorithm also extends its inefficiency. Shadow calculations are performed for surfaces that may be subsequently 'overwritten' – just as shading calculations are.

11.3 Shadows in games

11.3.1 Adding shadows to a light map

Shadows can be pre-computed for static light sources and added to the light map. The normal basic computer graphics shadow model is used. In this model we calculate the geometry of the shadow but not the reflected light intensity in the area of the shadow. This is easily done by ray casting using the BSP tree (as in Section 9.5.5). The point light source is considered as a sphere of influence. Only points within the sphere of influence are considered. For each point (x,y,z) corresponding to a light map pixel we use the BSP tree to cast a ray to the light source (considered as a point). Any reported obstruction between the point and the light source means that the point is in shadow and the light intensity in the corresponding light map pixel is reduced.

Note that this is an arbitrary reduction – we have no way of knowing what the reflected light in a shadow area should be without using a global illumination algorithm. The light received and reflected in a shadow area by definition originates from the surface of another object in the scene; it is indirect illumination.

Figures 11.7(a) to 11.7(e) (Colour Plate) are a series of images of the same scene illustrating the various contributions that make up light map shadows. They are as follows:

- Figure 11.7(a) This shows the light map applied with the shadow calculation incorporated
- Figure 11.7(b) As the previous image but this time texture filtering is applied
- Figure 11.7(c) Shows the texture map applied
- Figure 11.7(d) The texture map blended with the image in Figure 11.7(a)
- Figure 11.7(e) The texture map blended with the image in Figured 11.7(b)

Using the sphere of influence method to generate shadows is in a sense the inverse of the method used to generate 'light shadows' in the door sequence shown in Figure 10.3. Light map shadows are generated by invoking a ray intersection test from every light map pixel (that is, from the scene corresponding to the light map pixel) towards the source and **reducing** the stored light if they intersect an object. In the door sequence the light map pixels that are within the sphere of influence are selected and have their stored light **increased** if the ray fired towards the light source is not obstructed by the door.

11.3.2 Soft shadows

If this method is used as described then it will generate hard-edged shadows. Hard-edged shadows only occur for point light sources. However, the method can easily be extended to generate soft-edged shadows from area light sources.

Again we can use the sphere of influence but this time for a series of samples placed on the emitting surface. That is, we consider the area light source to consist of a series of point light sources randomly placed on its surface.

We can proceed as follows:

if a face is an emitter **then**

> choose a value for the number of samples as a function of the area of the light

> **for** each sample

>> compute a random point in the face and place a light sphere there

>> compute the shadow as before by BSP ray intersect from the light map pixel to the (random) light source point

As we have seen, to a certain extent, texture filtering will blur hard-edged shadows but it is always the case that soft shadows rendered by sampling over a light source area will produce better results, as the following sequence (Colour Plate) shows:

- Figure 11.8(a) No soft shadows, no texture filtering
- Figure 11.8(b) Soft shadows, no texture filtering
- Figure 11.8(c) No soft shadows, texture filtering
- Figure 11.8(d) Soft shadows, texture filtering

11.3.3 Fast shadows for dynamic objects

The simplest and fastest approach to generating shadows is to use a texture map blended with the existing image in the frame buffer. This implies that the shadow is of constant shape and size and the texture map can be something like a blurred circle. Although this is the coarsest of approximations it is, nevertheless, better than having no shadows at all and in the example we give (car racing), it certainly assists in interpreting the height of the car when it leaves the ground.

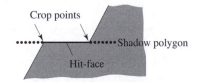
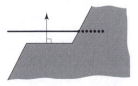

Figure 11.9
Simple arbitrary shape, constant shape shadow options (see also Figure 11.10 Colour Plate).

(a) Option 1 – using Z_{equal} – shadow polygon coincident with hit face but artifacts and cropping occurs

(b) Option 2 – displace shadow polygon above the hit face and use $Z_{less\ than\ equal}$ – shadow polygon still (partially) cropped

Figure 11.9 continued

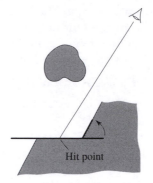

(c) Option 3 – no Z buffer comparison – requires
a ray intersection from camera to hit point.
Shadow is only drawn if there are no intervening
objects in the path of the ray

The algorithm is as follows:

Fire a single ray from the light source through the origin of the shadow-casting object. The intersect of this ray with the first surface identifies the receiving surface and gives a hit point or reference point for the shadow.

The shadow map then becomes a square (say) polygon and is blended into the frame buffer using the appropriate blending function (Section 12.2.2). The depth comparison is used because there may be an object closer to the view-point which obscures part of the shadow.

Although this is an extremely simple procedure it throws up certain subtleties and three options are possible which we will now consider. These are illustrated conceptually in a diagram (Figure 11.9) and their visual effect is shown in Figure 11.10 (Colour Plate).

Consider Figure 11.9 which shows these options as the interaction of a shadow and the receiving surface. The first option shows the shadow coincident with the face plane of the receiving surface (the face that contains the hit point). If we blend into the existing render using a Z_{equal} operator for the depth comparison (Section 12.2.1), then the shadow will only appear on the polygon which contains the hit point. Thus the visual effect is a circle cropped by a polygon edge (Figure 11.10(a)). However, this is not the only problem. Because of Z-buffer inaccuracies the use of the Z_{equal} operator results in an undesirable coherent noise pattern.

The second option shows the shadow displaced along the surface normal of the receiving surface (Figure 11.9(b)) by a small amount to avoid the Z-buffer artefacts just described. The depth comparison is now $Z_{less\ than\ or\ equal}$. Although the artefacts disappear, as Figure 11.10(b) shows, the shadow will now float above the face, producing artefacts depending on the underlying geometry.

Possibly the best option is not to use a depth comparison and use a ray inter-sect to check if there are object(s) obscuring the shadow (Figure 11.9(c)). This results in a binary decision (the shadow is mapped or not). Floating still occurs (shown on the left of Figure 11.10(c)) but this is anyway only visible when the underlying face falls away very sharply from the hit face.

The following procedure implements the simple shadow method for a light always positioned directly overhead the object:

```
void shadow::reposition(bsp_object *obj)
{
    // ray intersect down from object position
    hit=flyengine->collision_bsp(
        flyengine->bsp,obj->pos,
        obj->pos+vector(0,0,-BIG),
        TYPE_STATIC_MESH);
    if(hit)
        {
        // if receiving surface is found, position shadow object there
        pos=flyengine->hitip;
        // align shadow object with face normal
        align_z(flyengine->hitmesh->faces[flyengine->hitface]->normal);
        }
}
void shadow::draw()
{
    // are any objects between shadow and camera (note this is a
    binary decision
    // either it is drawn or not)
    if (flyengine->collision_test(
        flyengine->bsp,pos,flyengine->cam->pos,TYPE_STATIC_MESH))
        return;
    if(hit)
    {
        // draw texture mapped shadow polygon
    }
}
```

We can ameliorate the shape approximation disadvantage by extending the above procedure to fire a ray, from the light source, through each vertex. The hit points of these rays on the receiving surface then define a polygon which approximates the shape the shadow can take and this is then blended into the frame buffer as before. The shape approximation occurs because the shadow does not necessarily become coincident with the receiving object surface. The nature of these errors should be clear from Figure 11.11.

Clearly only those vertices that can see the light source should be processed and this can be implemented by testing the dot product of the face normal with the light direction vector.

Obviously the expense of this approach is a function of object complexity and yet another option would be to use the vertices of a bounding box rather

Figure 11.11
Shooting rays from the light source through object vertices to define a shadow polygon.

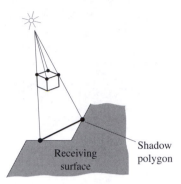

Receiving
surface

Shadow
polygon

than the entire vertex set. The method is made more efficient by applying the same procedure to the vertices of a bounding volume or box.

An example of this method for the car game is shown in Figure 11.12 (Colour Plate). In this example five bounding boxes were used (car body plus four wheels). Note that in this application the lower surface of the bounding box should be positioned sufficiently clear of the ground so that it does not go into the landscape. Also note that because the five bounding boxes are processed separately they will generate shadow polygons that may separate and overlap (as the illustration shows) depending on the nature of the receiving surface.

The method can easily be extended to generate the more complex shadow that results from multiple light sources. We could consider all those light sources within a sphere of influence centred on the car. It then becomes a multi-pass algorithm (see Chapter 12). A practical disadvantage of this approach is that a separate object (the bounding box) must be modelled along with the object and, as we have discussed, this may not be the same as the true bounding box used in collision detection.

Finally, the efficacy of all these approximate approaches depends on the nature of the shadowing and receiving objects. The artefacts generated by the approximations may be unacceptable.

The following code implements the bounding box method:

```
void shadow::reposition(bsp_object *obj)
{
   // ray intersect down from object position
   hit=flyengine->collision_bsp(
       flyengine->bsp,obj->pos,
       obj->pos+vector(0,0,-BIG),
       TYPE_STATIC_MESH);
   if(hit)
   {
      // if receiving surface is found, position shadow object there
      pos=flyengine->hitip;

      // allocate ground vertex array
```

```
if (vert) { delete vert;      vert=0; }
vert=new vector[bbmesh->nv];

// for all bbmesh vertices
vector p1,p2;
for( int i=0;i<bbmesh->nv;i++ )
{
   // compute ray intersection points rotating the bbox using
   // current object rotation matrix
   p1=p2=obj->pos+objmesh->vert[i]*obj->mat;
   p2.z-=flyengine->bboxdiag;
   // ray intersect the vertex ray with the level
   if (flyengine->collision_bsp(flyengine->bsp,p1,p2,TYPE_
   STATIC_MESH))
      vert[i]=flyengine->hitip;
   else
      {
      // if any vertex does not intersect, remove shadow com-
      pletely
      hit=0;
   break;
      }
   }
}
}
void shadow::draw()
{
  // are any objects between shadow and camera (note this is a
  binary decision
  // either it is drawn or not)
  if (flyengine->collision_test(
    flyengine->bsp,pos,flyengine->cam->pos,TYPE_STATIC_MESH))
    return;
  if(hit)
  {
    // draw bounding box shadow mesh
  }
}
```

Multi-pass rendering

12.1   Introduction

12.2   Multi-pass functionality

12.3   Multi-pass algorithms

12.4   Multi-pass sampling approaches

12.5   Multi-texture

12.6   Multi-texture example

12.1   Introduction

Multi-pass rendering is a technique that builds up a final rendered image from a 'combination' of the results of a set of separate rendering passes. The potential benefits are speed and lower algorithm complexity. Combining images means, in general, performing a linear or non-linear pixel by pixel operation which may commonly be exemplified by masking an image with a binary (mask) image or by blending two images together. That speed and complexity gains can be made from such an approach is perhaps not obvious, or even possible with every algorithm, and we will approach the topic through examples or case studies.

Its popularity in games rendering is motivated by supporting hardware facilities and its speed advantage in games application stems from the fact that many dynamic effects are achievable by changing one or more of the passes, leaving the others unaltered.

Multi-pass rendering can be best categorised as an approach that uses what is essentially a 'by polygon' Z-buffer rendering pipeline enhanced with increased functionality and extra image buffers. The approach enables many algorithms that have previously been implemented as object space geometric methods to be constructed as many passes through the Z-buffer pipeline, with each pass using, for example, a functional interaction with the previous pass. Perhaps the best examples of the complexity advantage that accrues in the method is the shadow volume algorithm and back to front sorting of transparent polygons.

Multi-pass rendering is used in conjunction with a normal Z-buffer approach and we begin by defining the common extra utilities that are used to facilitate the

346

approach. This is based mainly on the OpenGL architecture and some of the example algorithm descriptions are taken from examples in McReynolds and Blythe (1998). Further details of the OpenGL architecture are given in Woo *et al.* (1997).

12.2 Multi-pass functionality

12.2.1 Combining rendered images

Compositing images was first introduced into three-dimensional graphics in 1984 (Porter and Duff, 1984; Duff, 1985) and this came from a realisation that images whose Z value had been retained could be combined or merged by using their depth values. Thus separate elements, separately rendered, could be brought together to make up a scene. This system was built around a pixel representation RGBαZ, the α $(0 < \alpha < 1)$ channel being used to specify the area of the pixel covered by the scene element that projected onto the pixel. The use of the α channel effectively extends area anti-aliasing across the compositing of images. Of course this parameter is not normally calculated by a basic Z-buffer renderer and because of this, the method is only suitable when used in conjunction with the A-buffer hidden surface removal method (Carpenter, 1984), an anti-aliased extension to the Z-buffer or some other 'sub-pixel' rendering program.

In this system composites are built up by using a binary operator that combines two sub-images:

$$c = f \textbf{ op } b$$

For example, consider the operator Z$_{min}$. We may have two sub-images, say of single objects, that have been rendered separately, the Z values of each pixel in the final rendering contained in the Z channel. Compositing in this context means effecting hidden surface removal between the objects and is defined as:

$$RGB_c = (\textbf{if } Z_f < Z_b \textbf{ then } RGB_f \textbf{ else } RGB_b)$$

$$Z_c = \min(Z_f, Z_b)$$

for each pixel.

The operator **over** is defined as:

$$RGB_c = RGB_f + (1 - \alpha_f)RGB_b$$

$$\alpha_c = \alpha_f + (1 - \alpha_f)\alpha_b$$

This means that as α_f decreases, more of RGB$_b$ is present in the pixel.

The compositing operator **comp** combines both the above operators. This evaluates pixel results when Z values at the corners of pixels are different between RGB$_f$ and RGB$_b$. Z$_f$ is compared with Z$_b$ at each of the four corners. There are 16 possible outcomes to this and if the Z values are not the same at the four corners, then the pixel is said to be confused. Linear interpolation along the edges takes place and a fraction β computed (the area of the pixel of which f is in front of b). We then have the comp operator:

$$RGB_c = \beta(f \textbf{ over } b) + (1 - \beta)(b \textbf{ over } f)$$

Blending (OpenGL)

Alpha blending in OpenGL is implemented between the RGBα image already in the frame buffer (confusingly called the destination) and the incoming RGBα image (called the source). Various operations are possible. A common example of using blending is the avoidance of the 'popping' effect when a LOD model is switched to another level. Unless the LOD scheme being used is continuous (Chapter 3) the effect of the switch will be visually obvious. The solution is to set the existing image as $RGB(1 - \alpha)$ and the incoming image that is now using the new object level as $RGB\alpha$. α can then be allowed to vary from 0 to 1 over a few frames.

A general blending equation can be written as:

$$(R,G,B,\alpha)_{new} = (R,G,B,\alpha)_{source} * blend_{source} + (R,G,B, \alpha)_{dest} * blend_{dest}$$

In computer games the following options can be used (Table 12.1):

Table 12.1 Applications of blending

Application	$blend_{source}$	$blend_{dest}$
Standard render	$(\alpha,\alpha,\alpha,\alpha)_{source}$	$(1 - \alpha, 1 - \alpha, 1 - \alpha, 1 - \alpha)_{source}$
Haloes and explosions	$(1,1,1,1)$	$(1,1,1,1)$
Shadows and hitmarks	$(0,0,0,0)$	$(1 - R, 1 - B, 1 - G, 1 - \alpha)_{source}$
Light maps	$(0,0,0,0)$	$(R,G,B,\alpha)_{source}$
Fogmaps	$(\alpha,\alpha,\alpha,\alpha)_{source}$	$(1 - \alpha, 1 - \alpha, 1 - \alpha, 1 - \alpha)_{source}$

- **Standard render** This facilitates the rendering of opaque and transparent objects in the conventional manner.

- **Haloes, explosions and so on** This effectively adds the current colour to the colour already in the frame buffer (which may cause saturation). This is precisely the effect required for self-emitting objects, causing them to glow.

- **Shadow maps and hitmarks** This eliminates (multiplies by zero) the source colour and modulates the colour already in the frame buffer by $1 -$ shadow map colour. For example, if we have areas which are completely white in a black and white shadow map these will result in a completely black shadow. Completely black areas in the map have no effect on the frame buffer colour.

- **Light maps** These are in effect the inverse of shadow maps (shadows are the diminution of light due to an obstruction). The colour in the light map modulates the colour in the frame buffer. For example, a completely white light map will not alter the frame buffer whereas a completely black light map will black out the pixels.

- **Fogmaps** The fog colour is given by the RGB values and the fog density is given by the α value.

This is just a selection of possible applications of this powerful and flexible utility.

Z-buffer (OpenGL)

In multi-pass rendering the Z-buffer requires increased functionality beyond its basic 'if statement' implementation. In OpenGL this takes the form of a generalisation of the depth comparison to the six relational operators plus 'never' and 'always' passes, together with the ability to separate depth testing and Z-value updating. That is, the depth test becomes:

if $Z_{incoming}$ **op** Z_{stored}

where:

op is $<, \leq, >, \geq, =, \neq$

Accumulation buffer (OpenGL)

With the decreasing cost of memory and the popularity of the OpenGL the use of accumulation buffers has become common. An accumulation buffer, as the name implies, is used to store the current result of the compositing, which you may not want to be visible, by using the frame buffer as an accumulator. Each pixel in the accumulation buffer consists of RGB and α values. The accumulation buffer will already contain an image and the operation of transferring into the accumulation buffer allows options between the already stored image and the incoming image.

An accumulation buffer accumulates rendered images and the standard operations are addition and multiplication combined into an 'add with weight' operation. In practice, an accumulation buffer may have higher precision than a screen buffer to diminish the effect of rounding errors. The use of an accumulator buffer enables the effect of particular single-pass algorithms to be obtained by a number of passes. After the passes are complete the final result in the accumulation buffer is transferred into the screen buffer.

Currently OpenGL does not support the Porter and Duff compositing operations and only allows simple additive combinations between the incoming image and that already in the accumulation buffer. The same effect has to be achieved by computing pre-multiplied values in another image buffer before transferring into the accumulation buffer.

The OpenGL specification works with two parameters *op* specifying the nature of the operation or how a floating point value *value* is to be used as:

accum	reads RGBα values from a selected buffer, multiplies them by *value* and adds the result to the value already in the accumulation buffer
load	as *accum* but replaces the existing value in the accumulation buffer
add	adds *value* to RGBα values in the accumulation buffer
mult	scales RGBα values in the accumulation buffer by *value*

Stencil buffer (OpenGL)

As the name implies, the stencil buffer is an array of the same dimensionality as the frame or image buffer and is used to control whether an image fragment continues towards the frame buffer or not. (The analogy, of course, is paint applied through a stencil – the paint can only be brushed onto the underlying surface through holes in the stencil.) It appears to have been first introduced by Brotman and Badler (1984) in the guise of an enhanced Z-buffer. Like the Z-buffer, it effectively enables/disables writing into the frame buffer.

Effectively two operations are involved in the stencil test: whether the image fragment associated with a pixel is passed onwards and how the stencil buffer is updated by the result of both the stencil test and the depth test. The depth test is applied immediately after the stencil test and only if both succeed does the image fragment pass into the frame buffer. Thus there are three possible outcomes:

(1) The stencil test fails, in which case the colour and depth for the pixel remain unchanged. The stencil buffer is updated according to the stencil operation pre-set for this condition.

(2) The stencil test succeeds and the depth test fails. Again the colour and depth for the pixel remain unchanged and the stencil buffer is updated according to the stencil operation pre-set for this condition.

(3) The stencil test succeeds and the depth test succeeds. The colour and depth for the pixel are given the new values and the stencil buffer is updated according to the stencil operation pre-set for this condition.

The stencil test applies one of the following conditions

> always fails
>
> always passes
>
> passes **if** (ref & $mask$) **op** ($stencil$ & $mask$)
>
> where
>
>> **op** is $<, \leq, >, \geq, =, \neq$
>>
>> ref is the reference value for the test
>>
>> $mask$ is a bit mask that is ANDed with both the reference value and the stencil value

The value in the stencil buffer is updated as:

> keep – keeps the current value
>
> zero – sets to zero
>
> replace – sets to ref
>
> increment – increments the value by 1
>
> decrement – decrements the value by 1
>
> invert – bitwise inverts the value

12.3 Multi-pass algorithms

12.3.1 Back to front transparency

The effect of multiple transparent surfaces would be easy to implement if it was possible to render the transparent surfaces in back to front order. Simple blending is all that is required. We use:

$$C = tC_f + (1- t)C_b \qquad (0 \le t \le 1)$$

where

> t is a linear transparency factor
>
> and $Z_f < Z_b$ (that is, I_f is a pixel from a polygon nearer to the viewer)

to blend two images in a sequence of depth-sorted transparent polygons. (Note that no refractive effects are implemented by this simple empirical approach. The further object pixels are incorporated into the calculation without the warping that would be caused by the refractive effect of the transparent nearer object.) The problem is, of course, that Z-buffering does not produce a list of sorted pixels. Sorting polygons suffers from well-known geometric problems such as intersecting surfaces and the fact that a correct sort order may not exist. If it is possible to sort the transparent polygons then a rendering order becomes:

(1) Render opaque object normally (depth testing and updates enabled).

(2) Sort the transparent polygons.

(3) Render the transparent polygons in order with blending and depth testing enabled; and with depth updates disabled. This enables the transparent polygons to be correctly composited into the scene if they happen to be behind an opaque object

Back to front transparency 'without sorting' can be implemented as an iterative multi-pass approach as reported by Diefenbach (1996). We describe the approach as 'without sorting' because it avoids the traditional approach of considering each polygon as a single entity and sorting them into an ordered list although, of course, the effect is the same. The algorithm requires two Z-buffers with selectable relational operators which are used to iterate through the transparent polygons until all pixels covered by a transparent object have been dealt with.

The two Z-buffers, which we will refer to as $Z_{previous}$ and $Z_{current}$, require their functionality set as follows:

> $Z_{previous}$ less than
>
> $Z_{current}$ greater than

The Z test is then configured as:

> pass if the depth is closer than that recorded in $Z_{previous}$ and further than that in $Z_{current}$ with $Z_{current}$ being updated.

Consider the ith iteration. The first operation swaps the buffers (together with their functionality). $Z_{previous}$ now contains the depth image of the transparent pixels found in the $(i-1)$th iteration. The current iteration then finds transparent pixels furthest from the viewer but closer than those found in the previous iteration. The order of the operations is as follows:

Initialise $Z_{previous}$ to Z_{min} and $Z_{current}$ to Z_{max}

Set $Z_{current}$ function to *less than* and render opaque objects using this $Z_{current}$

Set $Z_{previous}$ to *greater than*

repeat

Swap Z-buffers (and their functionality), enable $Z_{current}$ for updating, disable rendering

Loop through transparent surfaces

Draw a surface identifier into the stencil buffer

Enable rendering, disable Z-buffering

Loop through the transparent surfaces

Render (blend) pixels that belong to a surface whose identifier is present in the stencil buffer

until nothing is rendered

Thus the algorithm deals with the transparent objects by finding all those pixels that are furthest away, second furthest away, and so on (effectively a back to front pixel sort) until all the pixels covered by transparent objects have been dealt with. At each iteration two passes are made through the transparent surfaces. The first pass configures the stencil buffer but does not write into the frame buffer. In the second pass a transparent polygon is rendered only into those pixels tagged in the stencil buffer in the first pass. Since each rendering pass will, in general, render into different pixels contributions from any (or potentially all) transparent polygons, the stencil buffer needs to be tagged with a transparent object identifier.

12.3.2 Planar reflections

One of the simplest and most popular algorithms that can be implemented using a multi-pass approach is the calculation of reflections in a planar surface such as a two-dimensional mirror. We need two rendering passes, one for the scene as normal and one for its reflected version. The reflected scene is evaluated either by reflecting the objects about the plane containing the mirror, or by reflecting the viewpoint (Figure 12.1 Colour Plate) – both methods are identical in effect. If there are many objects in the scene then clearly it is better to reflect the viewpoint – a single point – than apply a reflection transformation to every object vertex.

The algorithms in outline are:

(1) render the reflected scene excluding the mirror object;

(2) create a stencil mask for the mirror;

(3) render the scene as normal using the stencil mask to prevent the appropriate parts of the reflected scene being overwritten;

or:

(1) render the entire scene excluding the mirror object

(2) create a stencil mask for the mirror

(3) render the reflected scene into the mirror area using the stencil mask.

For the popular option of reflecting a game object in a shiny floor (xy plane) the reflection matrix is given by:

$$R_z = \begin{bmatrix} 1 & 0 & 0 & 0 \\ 0 & 1 & 0 & 0 \\ 0 & 0 & -1 & 0 \\ 0 & 0 & 0 & 1 \end{bmatrix}$$

Note that if the floor is 'infinite' there is no masking to be done, and the method reduces to two conventional rendering passes:

(1) Reflect the objects and render.

(2) Blend in a transparent texture for the floor – floors are rarely a perfect mirror surface.

(3) Render the (unreflected) objects as normal.

In the event that the mirror has any arbitrary orientation in world space we proceed as follows:

(1) Compute the inverse of the mirror's modelling transformation M_M^{-1}.

(2) Assuming the mirror was defined in its own local space in one of the coordinate planes (say the (xy) plane), transform the object(s) into mirror space and reflect.

(3) Transform back into world space using M_M.

Thus the overall transformation is given by:

$$M_M R_z M_M^{-1}$$

The details of the above two algorithm outlines differ and are as follows:

● **Rendering reflected scene first**

(1) Render the reflected scene excluding the mirror object as normal (stencil test off, depth test enabled).

(2) Clear the stencil and depth buffers and render the mirror polygon into the stencil buffer and into the depth buffer. The frame buffer is disabled.

(3) Render the scene from the normal viewpoint with the stencil test enabled. The mirror's depth values enables mirror pixels to be overwritten with objects between the viewer and the mirror. The stencil test prevents visible mirror pixels that contain the reflected view being overwritten.

- **Rendering normal view first**

(1) Render the scene excluding the mirror object (stencil test off, depth test enabled).

(2) Clear the stencil and depth buffers and render the mirror polygon into the stencil buffer and into the depth buffer. The stencil buffer is set to draw only when the depth test passes. We now have at this stage a mirror mask with visible mirror polygons tagged.

(3) Draw the mirror into the Z-buffer using the stencil mask so that the visible mirror pixels are reset to maximum depth (we are going to reflect the scene about the mirror plane).

(4) Reflect the scene and render using stencil testing.

The second structure can easily be extended to handle multiple planar mirror by:

(1) render the scene excluding **all** the mirror objects

(2) **for** each mirror

        proceed as before with steps 2, 3 and 4

        5) reset stencil buffer to zero for use by next mirror

We should also consider the shortcomings of the algorithm. First, by definition, it can only deal with planar reflections. Although it can be extended to cope with inter-reflections, it cannot be used for curved surfaces in this form. So here we are losing the generality of the ray tracing algorithm. Second, in the form outlined above we assume that the reflecting surface is 'infinite' like a floor or that it is a mirror against a wall. If the planar reflecting surface or mirror has objects positioned behind it then in rendering the reflected view we have to split the scene so that these objects are not rendered in the reflected view. This requires us to find the plane containing the mirror and then use it as a clip plane to cull away all objects behind the plane when rendering the reflected view. Note also that this does not deal with recursive reflections that occur, for example, between two mirrors positioned on parallel walls.

Diefenbach (1996) describes a recursive version of the above approach that implements recursive reflections. This exploits the **increment** stencil buffer operation and enables the buffer to be used not only as a mask but also as a recursive counter. He chooses zero as a stencil rendering area, and at each recursive level increments all stencil values by one, which sets the rendering area in the previous level of recursion to one and the mirror area in the current level is drawn setting its stencil values to zero. This corresponds to the images you see in inter-reflecting mirrors as the scene shrinks into itself and marches towards infinity.

Thus one of the distinguishing factors of these kinds of algorithms is that they lose the generality of 'classic' rendering algorithms, having an efficient and simple structure only for special cases.

A source of inefficiency in this particular example comes from the fact that the rendering passes involve calculations for pixels that are subsequently discarded by the masking operation. In other words, we are calculating information that does not contribute to the final value of a pixel. For a multi-mirror scene that facilitates recursive reflections, the real-time performance will quickly degenerate as a function of the number of mirrors and recursive depth allowed. In general, the pixel fill rate of a graphics pipeline (Mpixels/sec) is reduced by a factor of N (the number of rendering passes) and if a majority of the passes are not contributing information then we are certainly trading efficiency against complexity. It should be noted, however, that the multi-pass approach may still be considerably faster than the single-pass alternative, which in the case of reflections would be ray tracing.

12.3.3 Multi-pass shadow volumes

In Chapter 11 we looked at fast, but inaccurate, shadow algorithms for computer games. We saw that the *de facto* standard in off-line rendering tends to be the shadow Z-buffer algorithm and pointed out the disadvantages of this low complexity technique. Apart from these, in dynamic environments it is possessed of the significant disadvantage that whenever an object moves, the entire shadow map (or maps) must be recalculated. The advantage of the shadow volume approach is that it permits recalculation of shadows from only those objects that are moving – the dynamic shadowing objects. If it can achieve real-time performance it is thus a suitable algorithm for games.

A multi-pass algorithm (McReynolds and Blythe, 1998) enables the shadow volume approach to be integrated with a Z-buffer algorithm, as we now describe. Here the stencil buffer is used as an array of pixel counters indicating whether the object polygons are inside the shadow volume or not. The algorithm consists of four rendering passes:

(1) Render the scene as if it was entirely in shadow (ambient light only).

(2) Render front-facing shadow volume polygons to determine if any object polygons are behind them.

(3) Render back-facing shadow volume polygons to determine if any objects from the second pass are in front of them.

(4) Render the scene again, overwriting the results of the first pass with polygons that are not in shadow.

The detailed algorithm is:

(1) Enable the frame buffer, Z-buffer and depth testing.

(2) Turn off the light source and render the scene with ambient illumination. This pass will form the shadow areas in the final scene, with the areas not in shadow being overwritten by the second rendering pass.

(3) Calculate the shadow volume polygons.

(4) Disable the frame buffer and the Z-buffer for writing, leaving depth testing enabled.

(5) Initialise the stencil buffer to zero or 1 depending on whether the viewpoint is outside or inside the shadow volume.

(6) Set the stencil function to **always pass** and the stencil operation to **increment if the depth test passes**.

(7) Enable back-face culling.

(8) Render the shadow volume. The effect of this pass is to increment the stencil buffer for a pixel if there is an object polygon behind the shadow polygon.

(9) Enable front-face culling.

(10) Set the stencil operation to **decrement if the depth test passes**.

(11) Render the shadow volume. The effect of this pass is to decrement the stencil buffer for a pixel if there is an object polygon in front of the shadow polygon. The stencil buffer now holds a positive value for all pixels that lie within the shadow volume.

(12) Set the stencil function to **equality with zero**.

(13) Render the scene – pixels not in shadow are now normally lit.

(12.3.4) Multi-pass shadow volumes – implementation

The following code is an example implementation of the shadow volume algorithm. Note that the shadow volume computation for the car object is more involved than that for the walking player. The walking player is a single object but the car is considered as five objects each producing a shadow volume.

Also, the car only casts shadows from a single (sun) source whereas the player casts shadows from the closest light interacting with him, dynamic (missile, headlight, etc.) or static (fixed scene lights with pre-computed lighting)).

```
void mesh::draw_shadow_volume(vector& lightdir)
{
    static vector v[8];

    // sets no texture
    tc->use(-1);

    // set up stencil state
    glEnableClientState(GL_VERTEX_ARRAY);
    glEnable(GL_STENCIL_TEST);
    glStencilFunc(GL_ALWAYS,0,~0);
    glColorMask(GL_FALSE,GL_FALSE,GL_FALSE,GL_FALSE);
    glDepthMask(GL_FALSE);

    // for each face, if face is frontfacing the light
    // draw its shadow volume using the lightdir
    for( int i=0;i<nf;i++ )
    if (vec_dot(localfaces[i].normal,lightdir)>0)
        {
        // compute shadow volume quad strips vertices
        v[0]=*localfaces[i].vert[0];
        v[1]=v[0]-lightdir;
        v[2]=*localfaces[i].vert[1];
        v[3]=v[2]-lightdir;
        v[4]=*localfaces[i].vert[2];
        v[5]=v[4]-lightdir;
        v[6]=v[0];
        v[7]=v[1];
        glVertexPointer(3,GL_FLOAT,sizeof(vector),v);

        // draw front faces incrementing stencil buffer
        glStencilOp(GL_KEEP,GL_KEEP,GL_INCR);
        glCullFace(GL_BACK);
        glDrawArrays(GL_QUAD_STRIP,0,8);

        // draw back faces decrementing stencil buffer
        glStencilOp(GL_KEEP,GL_KEEP,GL_DECR);
        glCullFace(GL_FRONT);
        glDrawArrays(GL_QUAD_STRIP,0,8);
        }

    // restore render state
    glDisableClientState(GL_VERTEX_ARRAY);
    glStencilOp(GL_KEEP,GL_KEEP,GL_KEEP);
    glDisable(GL_STENCIL_TEST);
    glCullFace(GL_BACK);
    glColorMask(GL_TRUE,GL_TRUE,GL_TRUE,GL_TRUE);
    glDepthMask(GL_TRUE);
}
```

```
void car::draw_stencil_shadow(vector& lightpos)
{
  // compute light direction
  vector lightdir=lightpos-pos;
  lightdir.normalize();
  lightdir*=flyengine->shadowdepth;

  // set current car pos and rotation
  glPushMatrix();
  glTranslatef(pos.x,pos.y,pos.z);
  glMultMatrixf((float *)&mat);

  // draw body shadow
  carmesh->draw_shadow_volume(lightdir);

  // draw back right wheel shadow
  glPushMatrix();
  glTranslatef(wheelposbk.x,wheelposbk.y,wheelposbk.z);
  wheelmesh->draw_shadow_volume(lightdir);
  glPopMatrix();

  // draw back left wheel shadow
  glPushMatrix();
  glTranslatef(-wheelposbk.x,wheelposbk.y,wheelposbk.z);
  wheelmesh->draw_shadow_volume(lightdir);
  glPopMatrix();

  // compute front wheel rotation
  static mat4x4 m;
  m.set_rotation(-wheelrot,vector(0,1,0));
  lightdir=lightdir*m;

  // draw front right wheel shadow
  glPushMatrix();
  glTranslatef(wheelposft.x,wheelposft.y,wheelposft.z);
  glRotatef(wheelrot,0,1,0);
  wheelmesh->draw_shadow_volume(lightdir);
  glPopMatrix();

  // draw front left wheel shadow
  glPushMatrix();
  glTranslatef(-wheelposft.x,wheelposft.y,wheelposft.z);
  glRotatef(wheelrot,0,1,0);
  wheelmesh->draw_shadow_volume(lightdir);
  glPopMatrix();

  glPopMatrix();
}
```

```
void person::draw_shadow_volume()
{
  // find the light closest to the player
  int i,mini=-1;
  float f,minf=BIG;
  vector lp;
  for( i=0;i<dynlights.nlights;i++ )
    {
      f=(dynlights.pos[i]-pos).length();
      if (f<minf)
      {
        minf=f;
        mini=i;
      }
    }

  // if there is a light near the player
  // draw the stencil shadow from this light
  if (mini!=-1)
    {
      // compute shadow direction
      lp=dynlights.pos[mini]-pos;
      lp.z+=height/2;
      lp=lp*mat_t;
      lp.normalize();

      // multiply direction by maximum shadow depth
      // (size of shadow volume)
      lp*=flyengine->shadowdepth;

      // set player position and rotation
      glPushMatrix();
      glTranslatef(pos.x,pos.y,pos.z-height/2);
      glMultMatrixf((float *)&mat);

      // draw player and weapon shadows
      p_anim[cur_anim]->draw_shadow_volume(lp);
      w_anim[cur_anim]->draw_shadow_volume(lp);

      glPopMatrix();
    }
}
```

```
// set a 2d camera in screen coordinates
flyengine->start_text_mode();

// set stencil operation
glEnable(GL_STENCIL_TEST);
glStencilFunc(GL_NOTEQUAL,0,~0);
glStencilOp(GL_KEEP,GL_KEEP,GL_KEEP);

// set blend mode and shadow color
glBlendFunc(GL_ZERO, GL_SRC_COLOR);
glColor3fv(&flyengine->shadowcolor.x);

// draw single quad over all the screen
// with shadow colour setting the stencil operation to
//draw only on pixels with stencil value>0

glRecti(0, 0, screen_sx, screen_sy);
glDisable(GL_STENCIL_TEST);
```

(12.3.5) Light objects

An alternative to updating light maps using a sphere of influence to implement dynamic lights (Section 10.3) is to treat the light as an object or volume and subject it to a multi-pass rendering device.

Many games employ the idea of lighting as an object, say, for example, a sphere or a cone to simulate a headlight, that modulates the surface of objects with which it interacts. In this method we trade off shading operations against the introduction of an extra object entity – the light object – on which only geometric operations are performed.

Consider Figure 12.2. This shows a spherical light object that intersects a planar surface. The light object is invisible and has the effect of modulating the RGB values on the area of intersection between the sphere and the surface to be lit. In the example we define four areas on the surface of the sphere as follows:

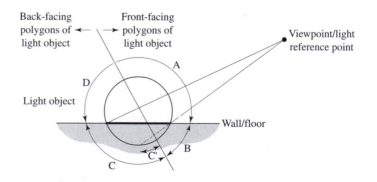

Figure 12.2
A spherical light object intersecting a static planar surface.

A and B are front facing.

C and D are back facing and C′ is that part of C obscured by B.

B and C are behind the wall and have Z values greater than the corresponding current Z-buffer values, which contain the depth values for the wall object.

A and D have Z values smaller than the corresponding current Z-buffer values.

We can see from this that modulating the intersect area can be achieved by blending the wall pixels with those faces of C that are not obscured by B. This suggests the following algorithm:

(1) Render the scene, omitting the light object.

(2) Activate the stencil buffer (pixels turn on a mask in the stencil buffer, the frame buffer is not written to).

(3) Invert the Z-buffer test (pixels must now have a Z value *greater* than the current value to be drawn).

(4) Render the light object using back-face culling which implies that only A and B are processed. This creates a mask with the projected area of B; A is discarded by the inverted Z-buffer test.

(5) Render the light object into the frame buffer using front-face culling at pixels not masked out by the stencil buffer. D is discarded by the inverted Z-buffer test, leaving C – C′ the required intersection which modulates the intensity of the existing pixel values.

12.4 Multi-pass sampling approaches

The following techniques describe how a multi-pass approach can be used to implement supersampling and jittered sampling techniques which are used for various anti-aliasing effects.

The easiest approach to anti-aliasing is supersampling which means generating a virtual image, at n times the resolution of the final image, then reducing this to the final image by using a filter (Chapter 8). The same effect can be obtained by jittering the viewport and generating n images and accumulating these with the appropriate weighting value which is a function of the jitter value. In Figure 12.3, to generate the four images that are required to sample each pixel four times we displace the view window through a $1/2$ pixel distance horizontally and vertically. To find this displacement we only have to calculate the size of the viewport in pixel units. (Note that this cannot be implemented using the simple viewing system given in Chapter 6, which assumes that the view window is always centred on the line through the viewpoint.)

To create a motion blurred image it is only necessary to accumulate a series of images rendered while the moving objects in the scene change their position over time. Exactly analogous to the spatial anti-aliasing example, we are now

Figure 12.3
Multi-pass supersampling.
(a) Aliased image (1
sample/pixel). (b) A one
component/pass of the anti-
aliased image (four
samples/pixel or four
passes). For this pass the
viewpoint is moved up and
to the left by $\frac{1}{2}$ pixel
dimension.

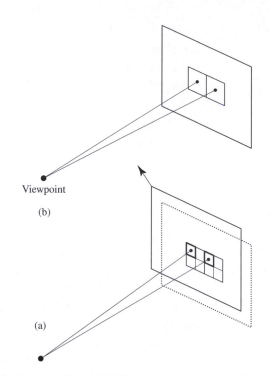

Viewpoint

(b)

(a)

anti-aliasing in the time domain. There are two approaches to motion blur. We can display a single image by averaging N images built up in the accumulation buffer. Alternatively we can display an image for every calculated image by averaging over a window of N frames moving in time. To do this we accumulate N images initially. At the next step the frame that was accumulated $N-1$ frames ago is re-rendered and subtracted from the accumulation buffer. Then the contents of the accumulation buffer are displayed. Thus after the initial sequence is generated, each time a frame is displayed two frames have to be rendered – the $(N-1)$th and the current.

Simulating depth of field is achieved (approximately) by jittering both the view window, as was done for anti-aliasing, and the viewpoint. Depth of field is the effect seen in a photograph where, depending on the lens and aperture setting, objects a certain distance from the camera are in focus whereas others nearer and farther are out of focus and blurred. Jittering the view window makes all objects out of focus and jittering the viewpoint at the same time ensures that objects in the equivalent of the focal plane remain in focus. The idea is shown in Figure 12.4. A plane of perfect focus is decided on. Viewport jitter values and viewpoint perturbations are chosen so that a common rectangle is maintained in the plane of perfect focus. The overall transformation applied to the view frustum is a shear and translation. Again this facility cannot be implemented using the simple view frustum in Section ** which does not admit shear projections.

Soft shadows are easily created by accumulating N passes and changing the position of a point light source between passes to simulate sampling of an area

Figure 12.4
Simulating depth of field by shearing the view frustum and translating the viewpoint.

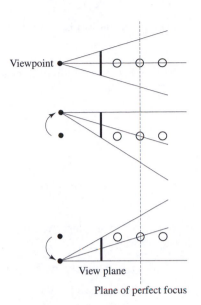

source. Clearly this approach will also enable shadows from separate light sources to be rendered.

12.5 Multi-texture

Multi-texture is the name given to a hardware facility for combining texture maps. Its utility does not originate from the combination facility *per se* but from the fact that the way in which the component maps are combined can be modified in real time. For example, we may implement the common combination of texture map, light map and fog map as shown schematically in Figure 12.5. In this example the texture map may remain unchanged from frame to frame while the light map may be (partially) updated by a dynamic light and the fog map by the moving camera. Although mult-texture can be achieved by separate passes, the term usually refers to a hardware facility that enables the effect of a texture multi-pass to be achieved in a single pass.

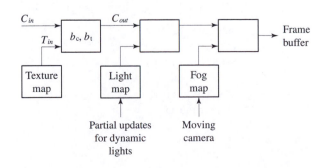

Figure 12.5
Schematic diagram of multi-texture.

A general equation for blending multi-texture components is given by:

$$C_{out} = b_c C_{in} + b_t T_{in}$$

where b_c and b_t are the blending factors for which the usual options are:

b_c/b_t	1
b_c/b_t	0
b_t	C_{in}
b_c	T_{in}
b_t	$1 - C_{in}$
b_c	$1 - T_{in}$

For example, to implement fog blending (Section 10.5) we would use the following settings:

C_{in}	C_{in} (penultimate stage pixel)
b_c	f (fog map pixel)
b_t	$(1 - f)$
T_{in}`	1 (fog colour = white)

Multi-texture hardware effectively enables different texture maps to be drawn 'simultaneously'. For each stage the source texture maps and blending mode are specified prior to drawing a polygon. The texture coordinate vertex correspondence can be different for each phase so in the event that we are using different coordinates for the light map and texture map, this is specified and handled by the hardware.

12.5.1 A comparison of multi-pass/multi-texture rendering

We can render using either a multi-texture or a multi-pass approach. In multi-pass rendering we have to draw the object as many times as necessary, whereas in multi-texture approaches we draw the object once with several textures. The latter approach is, of course, faster as the following pseudo-code demonstrates:

Multi-pass	Multi-texture
Select(texture)	Select(texture,lightmap,fogmap,. . .)
Draw(object)	Draw(object)
Select(lightmap)	
Draw(object)	
Select(fogmap)	
Draw(object)	
. . .	

12.6 Multi-texture example

12.6.1 Detail modulation

This is a simple example of a pass that may be added to the standard passes. It superimposes a 'grain' on an existing texture. In effect it modulates the texture colour with a grey scale detail map (Figure 12.6(a) – Colour Plate) . The detail texture is drawn after the texture pass but before the light map pass and it uses the same blending mode as a light map. The detail map can be scaled so that it tiles at a higher rate than the texture matrix. The following simple example (Colour Plate) demonstrates the idea:

- Figure 12.6(a) shows a simple detail map made up of a random dark pattern on a white background.
- Figure 12.6(b) shows a scene using conventional texture – no detail phase added.
- Figure 12.6(c) shows the detail only added to the previous image.
- Figure 12.6(d) shows the previous image using tri-linear filtering. Compared to the previous image we can see that for deep mip-map levels the detail turns to almost solid white (as we would expect).
- Figure 12.6(e) shows the scene with detail added and should be compared with Figure 12.6(b).

12.6.2 View-dependent detail light maps

This example demonstrates the real utility of a multi-texture pipeline which is to make simple realtime alterations to the way in which the maps are combined and/or which maps are combined, to achieve a fairly complex effect.

A light map caches reflected light on all surfaces in a scene due to all light sources. As a viewer moves around a scene the view-independent object shading is obtained from the light map. The two significant advantages of the light map are that it enables lighting to be pre-calculated and for view-independent lighting – diffuse – the light map texels can be large. In other words, the light map caches low frequency reflected light and it is view independent. A technique which appears to have been pioneered by Quake3 developers extends this concept to include high frequency detail.

The motivation for this development is the need for an economical scheme that caches high frequency information or small perturbations in the surface. The traditional computer graphics approach to this problem is to use bump mapping which causes a surface normal to be perturbed according to information in a bump map (see Section 7.4). The interaction of the perturbed surface normal with the lighting model makes it appear that the surface itself is exhibiting small three-dimensional texture detail. (This, of course, is the reason for the popularity of the technique. It enables high frequency surface detail to be rendered without modelling the geometry.)

A multi-pass scheme which produces the same effect, confusingly also known as bump mapping, is achieved by calculating a series of high frequency light maps that cache the light reflected from the surface detail into a number of different view directions. Ideally we would want to cache the reflected light from all directions but this can be restricted, without loss of generality, to say four viewing directions with the view vector at an elevation of 45° in each case. Now the three-dimensionality of the detail must be apparent as the viewer moves around with respect to the surface and this is achieved during a multi-pass render by calculating the dot product between the current viewing direction and each of the 45° pre-calculation view vectors and using the resulting value as a blend factor for the four maps.

Thus in a multi-texture pipeline all that has to be done dynamically as the camera moves is to calculate the viewing direction/bump map angle dot products and use these to blend the bump maps.

12.6.3 Multi-texture as a complete lighting model

The advent of multi-texture hardware has meant that routine rendering can be implemented entirely as a set of map blending operations. We can summarise the situation in Table 12.2.

Table 12.2 Map blending operations

Lighting phenomenon	Map used	View dependent/ view independent	Pre-calculated or updated
Object colour	Texture	Independent	Pre-modelled
Object texture	Bump	Dependent	Pre-calculated
Object diffuse reflection	Light	Independent	Pre-calculated
Object shadows	Light	Independent	Pre-calculated
Moving lights	Light	Independent	Update light map by constraining influence
Object specular reflection	Specular map Gloss map	Dependent	Pre-modelled
Object/ environment specular reflection	Environment	Dependent	Pre-calculated

A general lighting equation may then be written as:

C = fog*(texture map*(light map) + specular map + environment map)

where for simplicity we consider only the operators + and *.

In the event that the bump mapping implementation described in Section 12.6.2 is used, then the light map term expands to:

((((Light map + bump1) + bump2) + bump3) + bump4)

Here the light map/texture map operator is * and this darkens or lightens the texture map appropriate to the result of the lighting calculations cached in the light map. Specular maps, on the other hand, are added to the current result. That this should be so is easily seen by referring to Equation 6.3 for the Phong local reflection model where the diffuse and specular components are added together. The diffuse component is:

$$I_i\, k_d(\boldsymbol{L}.\boldsymbol{N})$$

Here k_d, the diffuse reflection coefficient, is equivalent to the texture map and $I_i\,(\boldsymbol{L}.\boldsymbol{N})$ is of course the reflected intensity cached in the light map. The specular term is replaced in its entirety by a specular map which is indexed by the reflected view vector.

In the above equations there is a hierarchy implied by the parentheses. Obviously fog should be factored with the result of all previous operations since it uniformly affects all images. Other options are not so clear cut and may require experimentation. For example, adding the light specular map to the product of the light and texture map:

(texture map*light map) + specular map

may cause the specular detail to be too bright (appearing emissive) in regions which are also in shadow. In which event

(texture map + specular map)*light map

may be a better option. This problem originates from the fact that we may be using the light map to cache direct reflection and shadows. The normal Phong method adds shadow areas onto the image *after* the full equation has been applied.

Motion control – kinematic

13.1   Introduction

13.2   Pre-scripting animation – linear interpolation and elapsed time

13.3   Pre-scripted animation – interpolation problems

13.4   Pre-scripted animation – explicit scripting

13.5   Interpolation of rotation

13.6   Using quaternions to represent rotation

13.7   The camera as an animated object

13.8   Particle animation

13.9   Particle animation and computer games

13.10   Articulated structures

13.1   Introduction

Computer animation is about controlling or specifying the motion of objects. The classic problem of an off-line computer animation is 'insufficient animator leverage', which means that the animator has to (tediously) specify all motion in great detail. Consider, for example, the workload involved in the Pixar production *Toy Story* where the main character contained 700 DOFs (including the facial animation controls). The game industry has to a certain extent bypassed this problem by employing motion capture but, of course, this has the serious limitation that the game can only contain pre-recorded sequences.

This problem can be addressed by viewing motion control as a hierarchy and Figure 17.1 shows on the left-hand side 'traditional' low-level computer animation as a two-level hierarchy, the animator using kinematic controls operating directly on the geometry of the model. A significant development was physically based animation which used dynamic simulation to script the motion, and later approaches have produced behavioural and AI levels. The top levels tend to use high-level languages to specify the behaviour of the objects and, like most good ideas, using scripting languages has a long history.

One view of the evolution of computer animation is that these early high-level developments eventually faded away as the demand for more and more detailed motion behaviour meant that (off-line) animators have had to operate at the kinetic level because higher-level tools for many contexts have proved up to now too difficult to develop. For example, despite much research effort, low-level kinematic techniques are still used for human characters. The development of higher levels has been motivated by the need to specify how characters interact with each other or to environmental stimuli rather than the detailed motion of their geometry. This has led to new scripting models which are in effect specialised high-level languages.

We will follow this evolution of motion control by dealing, in separate chapters, with these topics:

Kinematic animation of objects

User interaction basics to control motion

Dynamic simulation

Collision detection

AI techniques

Computer games are computer animations controlled in real time by the game player. At the moment, animations are either pre-scripted or pre-prepared in some way, motion capture being perhaps the commonest method, or they are calculated in real time using simple dynamics (Chapter 14). With pre-scripted sequences the user interaction is responsible for selecting particular animations and perhaps directions. Thus a human-like character may be made to walk or run in a particular direction.

Now consider player/animation control. In conventional computer animation an animator designs a sequence using some interface that enables scripting of the character(s) in the animation. In a computer game the player interacts with pre-prepared animation. The player is presented with animation sequences, the nature of which depend on user input. Thus a standard game loop has the simple structure:

read_input()

move_objects()

render()

where move_objects() implies the selection of a particular pre-calculated sequence or a call to a dynamic simulation.

One of the commonest high-level control structures that facilitates this combination is known as branching loop animation. Here a set of pre-prepared sequences are available, all of which start and finish at a neutral position. The player chooses, through the input device, which of these to execute. This kind of control is apparent in many fighting games where a 'natural' neutral animation would be a punch stance. Such characters may have different sequences for different parts of the body so that, for example, a punch sequence can be run at the same time as a jump sequence. The two actions are combined rather than have the punch starting after the jump has finished.

Many games exhibit 'behavioural signatures' that are a consequence of this type of player interaction with prepared sequences. The ideal set-up for any action-type game would be for the program to react to player input and calculate character action on the basis of a physical model. Providing hardware resources are available, it is better to simulate physical worlds by using known physical laws than to store a set of visual simulations. The latter course is inherently limiting.

13.2   Pre-scripting animation – linear interpolation and elapsed time

Pre-scripted sequences can be prepared either by the (expensive) route of motion capture or by using well-developed computer animation techniques such as interpolation between pre-specified key positions. The simplest approach to moving rigid bodies is to use linear interpolation – the disadvantage of which is well known. Consider the simple problem of the bouncing ball. If we use three keys – the start position, the end position and the zenith with simple linear interpolation, then the resulting trajectory will be unrealistic (Figure 13.1). Nonlinear interpolation can be implemented by using curves as described in Section 5.6.3. This is more general but is far more expensive if the interpolation is to be carried out in real time

Consider, as a simple example of linear interpolation, the animation of a door which is to open and close when a player comes into contact with it.

We can use linear interpolation on the vertices, defining the door closed, door open and door closed as the keyframe sequence. However, because in games applications we cannot guarantee a fixed frame time, the interpolation must be set up to take into account the non-uniform time interval. The following structure calculates the position of a vertex at time t:

elapsed_time = t_0 time at which door begins to open

IN THE RENDER LOOP INCLUDE

    elapsed time = elapsed time + dt

    where dt = time to generate last frame

      for each vertex i in model

$$V_i^t = (V_i^{\text{finish}} - V_i^{\text{start}}) \frac{\text{elapsed\_time} - t_0}{\text{length\_of\_animation}}$$

Now consider a common type of door made up of four triangles all moving outwards from the centre. In this case we would simply treat the four-part door as a single object with 12 vertices rather than consider each part as a single rigid body. The animation is then completely defined by two vertex lists, one for the

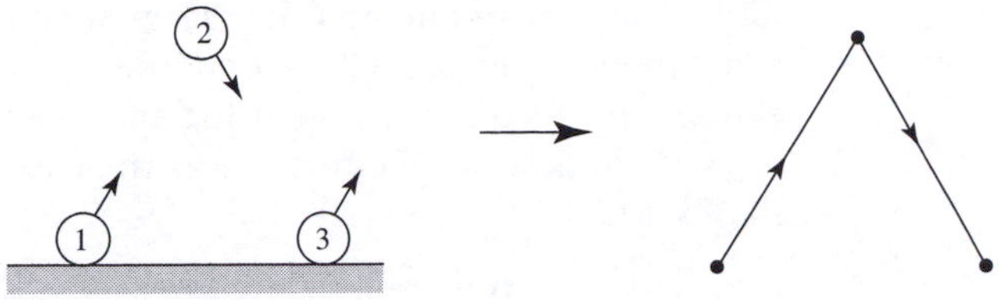

Figure 13.1

Linear interpolation will produce an unrealistic trajectory for a bouncing ball specified at three key positions.

initial and one for the final position. Because the object then changes shape (albeit in a simple way by moving parts relative to one another) this is sometimes know as vertex morphing. A more elaborate example is shown in Figure 13.2 (Colour Plate) where much manual effort has to be expended to model the separate keys and tune the interpolation – the main motivation for using motion capture is, of course, to avoid this labour.

Yet another problem is connected with the magnitude of the elapsed time. If this is too small, say less than 10 ms, then the action may become too fast and we may concatenate two or more frames into a single frame. On the other hand, if the elapsed time is too large (say, greater than 1 s) then processing a simulation may result in an enormous positional shift. And anyway the game may be

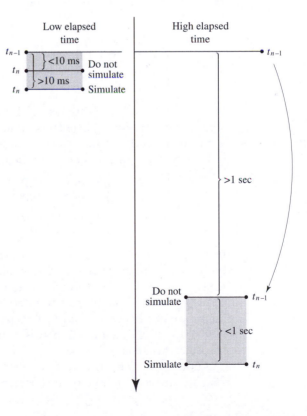

Figure 13.3

Elapsed time must be between 10 ms and 1 s. High and low elapsed times are dealt with differently.

unplayable at this rate. In this case we effectively pause the game by deleting the time interval (Figure 13.3). Yet another reason for defining a valid range for the elapsed time is that if we are using an integer for this parameter, then small values will result in large errors. If t_n is the current frame time and t_{n-1} the previous then we have:

t_n := current time in ms

$dt := t_n - t_{n-1}$ (elapsed time)

if $dt < 10$ **then** return

$t_n := t_{n-1}$

if $dt > 1000$ **then** return

simulate

Note the difference in the definition of the elapsed time in each case (shown shaded in the figure).

13.3   Pre-scripted animation – interpolation problems

If we restrict ourselves to considering position then we emplace an object as a function of time in the scene using a 4×4 modelling transformation $\boldsymbol{M}$ of the form:

$$\boldsymbol{M}(t) = \begin{bmatrix} 0 & 0 & 0 & t_x(t) \\ 0 & 0 & 0 & t_y(t) \\ 0 & 0 & 0 & t_z(t) \\ 0 & 0 & 0 & 1 \end{bmatrix}$$

So it seems that interpolation from keys is straightforward and indeed it is for simple cases. However, there are a number of problems. Usually we want to animate an object that exhibits some rotation as it translates along a path. We cannot apply the same interpolation scheme to:

$$\boldsymbol{M}(t) = \begin{bmatrix} a_{11}(t) & a_{12}(t) & a_{13}(t) & t_x(t) \\ a_{21}(t) & a_{22}(t) & a_{23}(t) & t_y(t) \\ a_{31}(t) & a_{32}(t) & a_{33}(t) & t_z(t) \\ 0 & 0 & 0 & 1 \end{bmatrix}$$

because the matrix elements $a_{11}, \ldots, a_{33}$ are not independent. We do not want the body to change shape and so the sub-matrix $\boldsymbol{A}$ must remain orthonormal at all times – the column vectors must be unit vectors and form a perpendicular triple. Thus positional elements can be interpolated independently but rotational elements cannot. If we attempt to linearly interpolate between nine pairs of elements $a_{11}, \ldots, a_{33}$ then the in-between matrices $\boldsymbol{A}_i$ will not be orthonormal and the object will change shape.

Another problem arises from the fact that the kinematics of the motion (the velocity and acceleration) of the body and the geometry of the path are specified by the same entity – the transformation matrix $\boldsymbol{M}(t)$. In general, an artist will require control so that the kinematics of the body along the path can be modified – we should be able to specify a path and change the velocity along the path after the path is established..

Yet another problem emerges from the specifics of the interpolation scheme. It may be that the nature of the path between keys is not what the artist requires; in particular, depending on the number of keys specified, unwanted excursion may occur. Also, if B-spline (Section 5.6.3) interpolation is used there is the problem of the locality of influence of the keys which are the knot points in the B-spline curve. It may be that the animator requires to change the path in a way that is not possible by changing the position of a single key and requires the insertion of new keys. These disadvantages suggest an alternative approach where the animator explicitly specifies the curves for path and motion along a path rather than presenting a set of keys to an interpolation scheme whose behaviour is 'mysterious'.

⟨13.4⟩ ## Pre-scripted animation – explicit scripting

The technique described in this section was developed for off-line animation. It is, however, suitable for pre-scripted games animation in contexts where motion capture is not to be used, and we give a typical example later in the section. The animation control or script is conveniently stored as a set of parametric curves.

For more complex movement other than simple translation we need to specify arbitrary paths through three-dimensional space. We also have to consider that the motion along the path may be more complex than a step function where we instantaneously start and stop an object that travels with uniform velocity. This method splits into two phases – the off-line generation of the curves (the editor) and the method required to access the script curves and play the animation in real time.

An obvious idea is to use cubic parametric curves as a script form (Chapter 5). Such a curve can be used as a path over which the reference point or origin of the object is to move. These can be easily edited and stored for future use. The best approach, called the double interpolant method, is to use two curves, one for the path of the object through space and one for its motion characteristic along the path. Then an artist can alter one characteristic independently of the other.

The animation is then stored as two Bézier curves – one for the path and one for the motion characteristic. In real time the renderer accesses these curves and generates translation and rotation matrices to move the object through space.

An interface possibility is shown in Figure 13.4. The path characteristic is visualised and altered in three windows that are the projections of the curve in the xy, yz and xz planes. The path itself can be shown embedded in the scene with three-dimensional interpretative clues coming from the position of other objects in the scene and vertical lines drawn from the curve to the xy plane. The

Figure 13.4
Motion specification for
rigid body animation – an
interface specification.

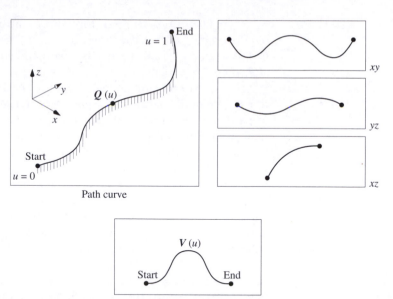

Path curve

Motion curve

animator sets up the path curve $Q(u)$, applies a velocity curve $V(u)$ and views the
resulting animation, editing either or both characteristics if necessary.

Generating the animation from these characteristics means deriving the
position of the object at equal intervals in time along the path characteristic.
This is shown in principle in Figure 13.5. The steps are:

(1) For a frame at time t find the distance s corresponding to the frame time t
from $V(u)$.

(2) Measure s units along the path characteristic $Q(u)$ to find the corresponding
value for u.

(3) Substitute this value of u into the equations for $Q(u)$ to find the position of
the object (x,y,z).

(4) Render the object in this position.

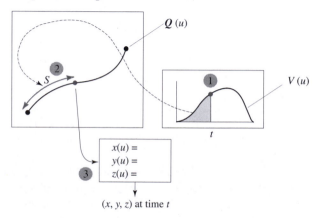

Figure 13.5
Finding the object position
(x, y, z) at time t.

Figure 13.6
Intervals of equal parametric
length (outline arrowheads)
do not correspond to equal
intervals of arclength (black
arrowheads).

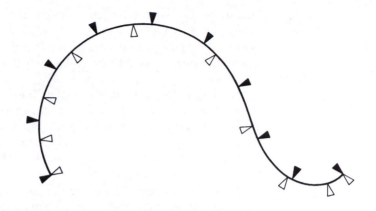

This simple process hides a subsidiary problem called reparametrization. V is parameterised in terms of u, that is:

$$V(u) = (t,s)$$

where $t = T(u)$ and $s = S(u)$

Given the frame time t_f we have to find the value of u such that $t_f = T(u)$. We then substitute this value of u into $s = S(u)$ and 'plot' this distance on the path characteristic $Q(u)$. Here we have exactly the same problem. The path characteristic is parametrised in terms of u, not s. The significance of this problem is demonstrated graphically in Figure 13.6 which compares equal arclength intervals with equal intervals in the curve parameter. The general problem of reparametrisation in both cases involves inverting the two equations:

$$u = T^{-1}(t) \text{ and } u = Q^{-1}(s)$$

An approximate method that given t or s finds a close value of u is accumulated chord length. Shown in principle in Figure 13.7 the algorithm is:

(1) Construct a table of accumulated chord lengths by taking some small interval in u and calculating the distances $l_1, l_2, l_3, \ldots$ and inserting in the table l_1, $(l_1 + l_2)$, $(l_1 + l_2 + l_3), \ldots$ the accumulated lengths.

(2) To find the value of u corresponding to s, say, to within the accuracy of this method, we take the nearest entry in the table to s.

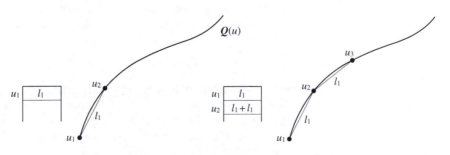

Figure 13.7
Accumulated chord-length
approximation.

This simple approach does not address many of the requirements of a practical system, but it is a good basic method from which context-dependent enhancements can be grown. In particular, it can form the basis for both a scripting system and an interactive interface. We briefly describe some of the more important omissions.

The first is that if we freely change $V(u)$, then the total time taken for the object to travel along the curve will, in general, change. We may, for example, make the object accelerate more quickly from rest, shortening the time taken to travel along the path. Many animations, however, have to fit into an exact time slot and a more normal situation would involve changing $V(u)$ under the constraint that the travel time remains fixed.

The consequences of ignoring the arclength parametrisation problem are many and varied and we now give a simple example where a race track has been modelled as a multi-segment Bézier curve along which a car is to track.

Consider the car pursuit example introduced in Section 16.5. Here we have an object (in the illustrations a sphere) tracking along a Bézier curve. If arclength parametrisation is not implemented then the object being pursued exhibits non-uniform velocity along the path. For a simple pursuit strategy, the varying velocity causes the pursuit vehicle to oscillate and circle about the path as Figure 13.8 (Colour Plate) clearly shows. If the forward velocity of the car is constant then this situation will occur when the object speed is less than that of the pursuing vehicle, which will tend to overshoot the target point. This problem can be ameliorated by invoking a more involved pursuit algorithm, such as, for example, making the magnitude of the pursuit velocity proportional to the separation current separation distance, but clearly it is important in any application to deal with the arclength parametrisation problem in the first instance.

13.5 Interpolation of rotation

In rigid body animation we usually want to be able to deal with both translation and rotation. An object moves through space and changes its orientation in the process. To do this we need to parametrise rotation. (We distinguish between rotation and orientation as: orientation is specified by a normal vector embedded in an object; rotation is specified by an axis and an angle.) The traditional method is to use Euler angles where rotation is represented by using angles with respect to three mutually perpendicular axes. In many engineering applications – aeronautics, for example – these are known as roll, pitch and yaw angles. We can thus write down a rotation as:

$$R(\theta_1, \theta_2, \theta_3)$$

Euler angles are implemented by using a transformation matrix – one matrix for each Euler angle – as introduced in Chapter 1. A general rotation is thus effected by the product of the three matrices. As we saw in Chapter 1, to effect a rotation we specify three rotation matrices, noting that rotation matrices are not com-

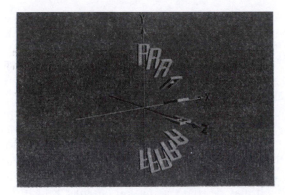

Figure 13.9
Euler angle parametrisation. (a) A single x-roll of π. (b) A y-roll of π followed by a z-roll of π.

mutative and the nature of the rotation depends on the order in which they are applied. However, leaving that problem aside, we will now see that more significant difficulties for an animator occur if rotation is parametrised in this way.

We now consider a simple example. Figure 13.9 shows a letter **R** moving from an initial to a final position. In both cases the start and final positions are the same but the path in between these is substantially different. In the first case a single rotation about the x axis of 180° has been applied. In the second case two rotations of 180° about the y and z axis are applied simultaneously. The single rotation results in the character moving in a two-dimensional plane without 'twisting' while in the latter case the character follows a completely different path through space, twisting about an axis through the character as it translates. What are we to conclude from this? There are two important implications. If an animator requires a certain path from one position and orientation to another, then in general all three Euler angles must be controlled in a manner that will give the desired effect. Return to Figure 13.9. The examples here were generated by the following two sequences:

$$R(0,0,0),\ldots,R(\pi t,0,0),\ldots,R(\pi,0,0) \qquad t \in [0,1]$$

for the first route, and

$$R(0,0,0),\ldots,R(0,\pi t,\pi t),\ldots,R(0,\pi,\pi)$$

for the second route. Examining in particular the second case, we could conclude that it would be practically unworkable to expect an animator to translate an idea involving an object twisting through space into a particular movement specified by Euler angles.

The same consideration applies to interpolation: if an animator specifies keys how is the interpolation to proceed? In fact, there exists an infinity of ways of getting from one key to another in the parameter space of Euler angles. Clearly there is a need for an understood rotation from one key to the other. This single rotation may not be what the animator desires, but it is better than the alternative situation where no unique rotation is available.

Euler's theorem tells us that it is possible to get from one orientation to another by a single steady rotation. In particular, it states that for two orientations O and O' there exists an axis l and an angle θ such that O undergoes rotation to O' when rotated θ about l. And we can interpret Figure 13.9 in the light of this – the first example being the single axis rotation that takes us from the start to the stop position. But that was a special case and easy to visualise; in general, for two orientations O and O', how do we find or specify this motion? This problem is solved by using quaternions.

There is another potentially important consideration in the above interpolation scheme of Euler angles. We separated motion and path in the explicitly scripted animation method because we considered that an animator would, in general, require control of the motion an object exhibited along a path separate to the specification of the path in space. The same consideration is likely to apply in specifying rotation – it may be that the motion (angular velocity) that results from linearly interpolating Euler angles is not what the animator requires.

13.6

Using quaternions to represent rotation

A useful introductory notion concerning quaternions is to consider them as an operator, like a matrix, that changes one vector into another, but where the infinite choice of matrix elements is removed. Instead of specifying the nine elements of a matrix we define four real numbers. We begin by looking at angular displacement of a vector rotating a vector by θ about an axis $\boldsymbol{n}$.

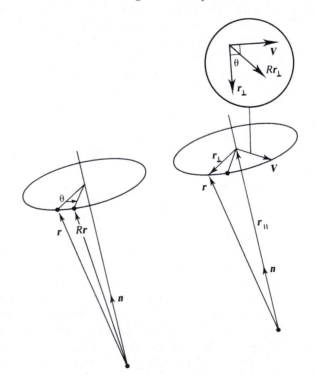

Figure 13.10
Angular displacement (θ, $\boldsymbol{n}$)
of $\boldsymbol{r}$.

We define rotation as an angular displacement given by $(\theta, \boldsymbol{n})$ of an amount θ about an axis $\boldsymbol{n}$. That is, instead of specifying rotation as $R(\theta_1, \theta_2, \theta_3)$ we write $R(\theta, \boldsymbol{n})$. Consider the angular displacement acting on a vector $\boldsymbol{r}$ taking it to position $R\boldsymbol{r}$ as shown in Figure 13.10.

The problem can be decomposed by resolving $\boldsymbol{r}$ into components parallel to $\boldsymbol{n}$, which by definition remains unchanged after rotation, and perpendicular to $\boldsymbol{n}$ in the plane passing through $\boldsymbol{r}$ and $R\boldsymbol{r}$.

$$r_\parallel = (\boldsymbol{n}.\boldsymbol{r})\boldsymbol{n}$$

$$r_\perp = \boldsymbol{r} - (\boldsymbol{n}.\boldsymbol{r})\boldsymbol{n}$$

$r_\perp$ is rotated into position $R r_\perp$. We construct a vector perpendicular to $r_\perp$ and lying in the plane. In order to evaluate this rotation, we write:

$$\boldsymbol{V} = \boldsymbol{n} \times r_\perp = \boldsymbol{n} \times \boldsymbol{r}$$

so

$$R r_\perp = (\cos \theta)\, r_\perp + (\sin \theta)\boldsymbol{V}$$

hence

$$R\boldsymbol{r} = R r_\parallel + R r_\perp$$
$$= R r_\parallel + (\cos \theta) r_\perp + (\sin \theta)\boldsymbol{V}$$
$$= (\boldsymbol{n}.\boldsymbol{r})\boldsymbol{n} + \cos \theta (\boldsymbol{r} - (\boldsymbol{n}.\boldsymbol{r})\boldsymbol{n}) + (\sin \theta)\boldsymbol{n} \times \boldsymbol{r}$$
$$= (\cos \theta)\boldsymbol{r} + (1 - \cos \theta)\boldsymbol{n}(\boldsymbol{n}.\boldsymbol{r}) + (\sin \theta)\boldsymbol{n} \times \boldsymbol{r} \qquad [17.1]$$

We will now show that rotating the vector $\boldsymbol{r}$ by the angular displacement can be achieved by a quaternion transformation. That is, we apply a quaternion like a matrix to change a vector.

We begin by noting that to effect such an operation we only need four real numbers (this compares with the nine elements in a matrix). We require:

● the change of length of the vector;
● the plane of the rotation (which can be defined by two angles from two axes);
● the angle of the rotation.

In other words, we need a representation that only possesses the four degrees of freedom required according to Euler's theorem. For this we will use **unit** quaternions. As the name implies, quaternions are 'four-vectors' and can be considered as a generalisation of complex numbers with s as the real or scalar part and x, y, z as the imaginary part:

$$q = s + x\boldsymbol{i} + y\boldsymbol{j} + z\boldsymbol{k}$$
$$= (s, \boldsymbol{v})$$

Here we can note their similarity to a two-dimensional complex number that can be used to specify a point or vector in two-dimensional space. A quaternion can specify a point in four-dimensional space and if $s = 0$ a point or vector in three-dimensional space. In this context they are used to represent a vector plus rotation. $\boldsymbol{i}$, $\boldsymbol{j}$, and $\boldsymbol{k}$ are unit quaternions and are equivalent to unit vectors in a vector system; however, they obey different combination rules:

$$\boldsymbol{i}^2 = \boldsymbol{j}^2 = \boldsymbol{k}^2 = \boldsymbol{ijk} = -1, \; \boldsymbol{ij} = \boldsymbol{k}, \; \boldsymbol{ji} = -\boldsymbol{k}$$

Using these we can derive addition and multiplication rules each of which yields a quaternion:

Addition:

$$q + q' = (s + s', \boldsymbol{v} + \boldsymbol{v}')$$

Multiplication:

$$qq' = (ss' - \boldsymbol{v}.\boldsymbol{v}', \; \boldsymbol{v} \times \boldsymbol{v}' + s\boldsymbol{v}' + s'\boldsymbol{v})$$

The conjugate of the quaternion

$$q = (s, \boldsymbol{v})$$

is

$$\bar{q} = (s, -\boldsymbol{v})$$

and the product of the quaternion with its conjugate defines its magnitude

$$q\bar{q} = s^2 + \left|\boldsymbol{v}^2\right| = q^2$$

If

$$\left|q\right| = 1$$

then q is called a unit quaternion. The set of all unit quaternions forms a unit sphere in four-dimensional space and unit quaternions play an important part in specifying general rotations.

It can be shown that if

$$q = (s, \boldsymbol{v})$$

then there exists a $\boldsymbol{v}'$ and a $\theta \in [-\pi, \pi]$ such that

$$q = (\cos \theta, \boldsymbol{v}' \sin \theta)$$

and if q is a unit quaternion then

$$q = (\cos \theta, \sin \theta \, \boldsymbol{n}) \hspace{3cm} \text{Proposition [13.1]}$$

where $\left|\boldsymbol{n}\right| = 1$.

We now consider operating on a vector $\boldsymbol{r}$ in Figure 13.10 by using quaternions. $\boldsymbol{r}$ is defined as the quaternion $p = (0, \boldsymbol{r})$ and we define the operation as:

$$R_q(p) = qpq^{-1}$$

That is, it is proposed to rotate the vector r by expressing it as a quaternion, multiplying it on the left by q and on the right by q^{-1}. This guarantees that the result will be a quaternion of the form $(0,v)$, in other words a vector. q is defined to be a unit quaternion (s,v). It is easily shown that:

$$R_q(p) = (0,(s^2 - v.v)r + 2v(v.r) + 2s(v \times r))$$

Using Proposition 13.1 and substituting gives

$$R_q(p) = (0,(\cos^2\theta - \sin^2\theta)r + 2\sin^2\theta\, n(n.r) + 2\cos\theta\sin\theta\,(n \times r))$$

$$= (0, r\cos2\theta + (1 - \cos2\theta)\, n(n.r) + \sin2\theta\,(n \times r))$$

Now compare this with Equation 13.1. You will notice that aside from a factor of 2 appearing in the angle they are identical in form. What can we conclude from this? The act of rotating a vector r by an angular displacement (θ,n) is the same as taking this angular displacement, 'lifting' it into quaternion space, by representing it as the unit quaternion

$$(\cos(\theta/2), \sin(\theta/2)\, n)$$

and performing the operation $q()q^{-1}$ on the quaternion $(0,r)$. We could therefore parametrise orientation in terms of the four parameters

$$\cos(\theta/2), \sin(\theta/2)\, n_x, \sin(\theta/2)\, n_y, \sin(\theta/2)\, n_z$$

using quaternion algebra to manipulate the components.

Let us now return to our example of Figure 13.9 to see how this works in practice. The first single x-roll of π is represented by the quaternion

$$(\cos(\pi/2), \sin(\pi/2)(1,0,0)) = (0,(1,0,0))$$

Similarly a y-roll of π and a z-roll of π are given by $(0,(0,1,0))$ and $(0,(0,0,1))$ respectively. Now the effect of a y-roll of π followed by a z-roll of π can be represented by the single quaternion formed by multiplying these two quaternions together:

$$(0,(0,1,0))\,(0,(0,0,1)) = (0,(0,1,0) \times (0,0,1))$$

$$= (0,(1,0,0))$$

which is identically the single x-roll of π.

We conclude this section by noting that quaternions are used exclusively to represent orientation – they can be used to represent translation but combining rotation and translation into a scheme analogous to homogeneous coordinates is not straightforward.

Interpolating quaternions

Given the superiority of quaternion parametrisation over Euler angle parametrisation, this section covers the issue of of interpolating rotation in quaternion space. Consider an animator sitting at a workstation and interactively setting up a sequence of key orientations by whatever method is appropriate. This is usually done with the principal rotation operations, but now the restrictions that were placed on the animator when using Euler angles, namely using a fixed number of principal rotations in a fixed order for each key, can be removed. In general, each key will be represented as a single rotation matrix. This sequence of matrices will then be converted into a sequence of quaternions. Interpolation between key quaternions is performed and this produces a sequence of in-between quaternions, which are then converted back into rotation matrices. The matrices are then applied to the object. The fact that a quaternion interpolation is being used is transparent to the animator.

Moving in and out of quaternion space

The implementation of such a scheme requires us to move into and out of quaternion space, that is, to go from a general rotation matrix to a quaternion and vice versa. Now to rotate a vector p with the quaternion q we use the operation

$$q(0,p)q^{-1}$$

where q is the quaternion:

$$(\cos(\theta/2), \sin(\theta/2)\,n) = (s,(x,y,z))$$

It can be shown that this is exactly equivalent to applying the following rotation matrix to the vector

$$M = \begin{bmatrix} 1-2(y^2 + z^2) & 2xy - 2sz & 2sy + 2xz & 0 \\ 2xy + 2sz & 1-2(x^2 + z^2) & -2sx + 2yz & 0 \\ -2sy + 2xz & 2sx + 2yz & 1-2(x^2 + y^2) & 0 \\ 0 & 0 & 0 & 1 \end{bmatrix}$$

By these means, then, we can move from quaternion space to rotation matrices.

The inverse mapping, from a rotation matrix to a quaternion, is as follows. All that is required is to convert a general rotation matrix:

$$\begin{bmatrix} M_{00} & M_{01} & M_{02} & M_{03} \\ M_{10} & M_{11} & M_{12} & M_{13} \\ M_{20} & M_{21} & M_{22} & M_{23} \\ M_{30} & M_{31} & M_{32} & M_{33} \end{bmatrix}$$

where $M_{03} = M_{13} = M_{23} = M_{30} = M_{31} = M_{32} = 0$ and $M_{33} = 1$, into the matrix format directly above. Given a general rotation matrix, the first thing to do is to examine the sum of its diagonal components M_{ii}, which is:

$$4 - 4(x^2 + y^2 + z^2)$$

Since the quaternion corresponding to the rotation matrix is of unit magnitude we have:

$$s^2 + x^2 + y^2 + z^2 = 1$$

and:

$$4 - 4(x^2 + y^2 + z^2) = 4 - 4(1 - s^2) = 4s^2$$

Thus for a 4×4 homogeneous matrix we have:

$$s = \pm \frac{1}{2} \sqrt{M_{00} + M_{11} + M_{22} + M_{33}}$$

and

$$x = \frac{M_{21} - M_{12}}{4s}$$

$$y = \frac{M_{02} - M_{20}}{4s}$$

$$z = \frac{M_{10} - M_{01}}{4s}$$

13.6.3 Spherical linear interpolation (*slerp*)

Having outlined our scheme we now discuss how to interpolate in quaternion space. Since a rotation maps onto a quaternion of unit magnitude, the entire group of rotations maps onto the surface of the four-dimensional unit hypersphere in quaternion space. Curves interpolating through key orientations should therefore lie on the surface of this sphere. Consider the simplest case of interpolating between just two key quaternions. A naïve, straightforward linear interpo-

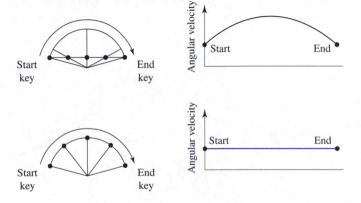

Figure 13.11
A two-dimensional analogy showing the difference between simple linear interpolation and simple spherical linear interpolation (*slerp*).

lation between the two keys results in a motion that speeds up in the middle. An analogy of this process in a two-dimensional plane is shown in Figure 13.11, which shows that the path on the surface of the sphere yielded by linear interpolation gives unequal angles and causes a speed-up in angular velocity.

This is because we are not moving along the surface of the hypersphere but cutting across it. In order to ensure a steady rotation we must employ spherical linear interpolation (or *slerp*), where we move along an arc of the geodesic that passes through the two keys.

The formula for spherical linear interpolation is easy to derive geometrically. Consider the two-dimensional case of two vectors A and B separated by angle Ω and vector P which makes an angle θ with A as shown in Figure 13.12. P is derived from spherical interpolation between A and B and we write

$$P = \alpha A + \beta B$$

Trivially we can solve for α and β given

$$|P| = 1$$
$$A.B = \cos \Omega$$
$$A.P = \cos \theta$$

to give

$$P = A \, \frac{\sin(\Omega - \theta)}{\sin \Omega} + B \, \frac{\sin \theta}{\sin \Omega}$$

Spherical linear interpolation between two unit quaternions q_1 and q_2, where

$$q_1.q_2 = \cos \Omega$$

is obtained by generalising the above to four dimensions and replacing θ by Ωu where $u \in [0,1]$. We write

$$\text{slerp}(q_1, q_2, u) = q_1 \, \frac{\sin(1 - u)\Omega}{\sin \Omega} + q_2 \, \frac{\sin \Omega u}{\sin \Omega}$$

Now given any two key quaternions, p and q, there exist two possible arcs along which one can move, corresponding to alternative starting directions on

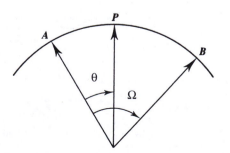

Figure 13.12
Spherical linear
interpolation.

the geodesic that connects them. One of them goes around the long way and this is the one that we wish to avoid. Naïvely one might assume that this reduces to either spherically interpolating between p and q by the angle Ω, where

$$p.q = \cos \Omega$$

or interpolating in the opposite direction by the angle $2\pi - \Omega$. This, however, will not produce the desired effect. The reason for this is that the topology of the hypersphere of orientation is not just a straightforward extension of the three-dimensional Euclidean sphere. To appreciate this, it is sufficient to consider the fact that every rotation has two representations in quaternion space, namely q and $-q$; that is, the effect of q and $-q$ is the same. That this is so is due to the fact that algebraically the operator $q()q^{-1}$ has exactly the same effect as $(-q)()(-q)^{-1}$. Thus points diametrically opposed represent the same rotation. Because of this topological oddity, care must be taken when determining the shortest arc. A strategy that works is to choose either interpolating between the quaternion pair p and q or the pair p and $-q$. Given two key orientations p and q find the magnitude of their difference, that is $(p-q).(p-q)$, and compare this to the magnitude of the difference when the second key is negated, that is $(p + q).(p + q)$. If the former is smaller then we are already moving along the smaller arc and nothing needs to be done. If, however, the second is smallest, then we replace q by $-q$ and proceed. These considerations are shown schematically in Figure 13.13.

So far we have described the spherical equivalent of linear interpolation between two key orientations, and, just as was the case for linear interpolation, spherical linear interpolation between more than two key orientations will produce jerky, sharply changing motion across the keys. The situation is summarised in Figure 13.14 as a three-dimensional analogy which shows that the curve on the surface of the sphere is not continuous through the keys. Also shown in this figure is the angular velocity which is not constant and discontinuous at the keys. The angular velocity can be made constant across all frames by assigning to each interval between keys a number of frames proportional to the magnitude of the interval. That is, we calculate the magnitude of the angle θ between a pair of keys q_t and q_{t+1} as:

$$\cos \theta = q_i . q_{i+1}$$

Figure 13.13
Shortest arc determination
on quaternion hypersphere.

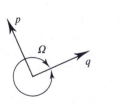

Incorrect

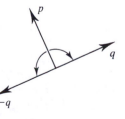

Correct

Figure 13.14
A three-dimensional analogy of using slerp to interpolate between four keys.

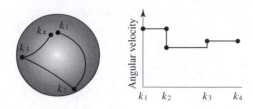

where the inner product of two quaternions $q = (s, \mathbf{v})$ and $q' = (s', \mathbf{v}')$ is defined as:

$$q.q' = ss' + \mathbf{v}.\mathbf{v}'$$

Curing the path continuity is more difficult. What is required for higher-order continuity is the spherical equivalent of the cubic spline. Unfortunately, because we are now working on the surface of a four-dimensional hypersphere, the problem is far more complex than constructing splines in three-dimensional Euclidean space. Duff (1986) and Shoemake (1987) have all tackled this problem.

Finally, we mention a potential difficulty when applying quaternions. Quaternion interpolation is indiscriminate in that it does not prefer any one direction to any other. Interpolating between two keys produces a move that depends on the orientations of the keys and nothing else. This is inconvenient when choreographing the virtual camera. Normally when moving a camera the film plane is always required to be upright – this is usually specified by an 'up' vector. By its very nature, the notion of a preferred direction cannot easily be built into the quaternion representation, and if it is used in this context the camera up vector may have to be reset or some other fix employed. (Roll of the camera is, of course, used in certain contexts.)

13.7 The camera as an animated object

Any or all of the external camera parameters can be animated but the most common type of camera animation is surely that employed in first-person computer games and similar applications where a camera flies through a mostly static environment under user interface control – the so-called 'walk through' or 'flyby'. Here the user is controlling the viewpoint, and usually a (two degrees of freedom) viewing direction. Interpolation is usually required between consecutive interface samples that form the keys and the most important constraint is to keep the camera up vector up; normally no orientation about the view direction vector is tolerated. (The only time the camera rolls about the view direction in first-person games is when you die.)

Another common application is where the viewpoint is under user control but the camera always points to an object of interest which can be static or itself moving. A common example of this is the (confusingly called) third-person computer games where the camera is tied to (say) the head of the character, via an 'invisible' rigid link. Instead of seeing the environment through the eyes of the character the user sees over the character's shoulder. In this case the view direction vector is derived from the character. The viewpoint effectively moves over a part of the surface of a sphere centred on the character. If quaternion interpolation is used in this application then the up vector has to be reset after an interpolation.

13.8 Particle animation

Particle animation is a classic technique that was invented almost two decades ago. It has found wide acceptance and is still a popular tool. The basic idea is that certain (natural) phenomena can be simulated by scripting the movement of and rendering a large population of individual particles. A particle is usually a primitive whose geometrical extent is small or zero – that is, many particles can project into a single pixel extent – but which possesses certain fixed attributes such as colour. Each particle is scripted and the idea is that rendering a population of particles from frame to frame produces a sort of cloud object that can grow, shrink, move, change shape and so on. An animation may involve literally tens or hundreds of thousands of particles and supplying an individual script for each one is out of the question. Rather, a general script is provided for each particle with in-built random behaviour which produces the requisite differences for each particle as the position, say, of the particle evolves over time. Different phenomena are modelled by using particle general scripts and varying the attribute of the particle such as colour. For example, in simulating a firework the basic particle script may be a parabola. Parameters that would be varied for each particle may include the start point of the parabola, its shape parameters, the colour of the particle as a function of its position along its parabolic path and its lifetime (extinction) along the path.

Thus the dynamic behaviour of the particles and their appearance, as a function of time, can be merged into the same script. Stochastic processes can be used to control both these aspects of particle behaviour. The overall result is an animated object such as a cloud which changes shape as the scripts for the thousands of particles that make up its overall shape are obeyed. The pioneer in this field is Reeves, who published a paper in 1983 that used particle sets to model 'fuzzy' objects such as fire and clouds. Other people have used his idea to model, for example, the behaviour of water in fountains, in waterfalls and in the spray of breaking waves.

Reeves describes the generation of a frame in an animation sequence as a process of five steps:

(1) New particles are generated and injected into the current system.

(2) Each new particle is assigned its individual attributes.

(3) Any particles that have exceeded their lifetime are extinguished.

(4) The current particles are moved according to their scripts.

(5) The current particles are rendered.

The instantaneous population of a particle cloud is controlled or scripted by an application-dependent stochastic process. For example, the number of particles generated at a particular time t can be derived from:

$$N(t) = M(t) + \text{rand}(r)V(t)$$

where $M(t)$ is the mean number of particles perturbed by a random variable of variance V. The time dependency of this equation can be used to control the overall growth (or contraction) in cloud size. Reeves used a linear time dependency with constant variance in the examples given, but he points out that the control can incorporate quadratic, cubic or even stochastic variations. The number of particles can also be related to the screen size of the object – a mechanism that allows the amount of computation undertaken to relate to the final size of the object.

Although this mechanism will clearly contribute something to shape evolution of the cloud, this is also determined by individual particle scripts. The combination of these two scripting mechanisms was used to animate phenomena such as an expanding wall of fire used in the motion picture *Star Trek II: The Wrath of Khan*, and has been used to simulate multicoloured fireworks. Individual particle scripting is based on the following attributes:

(1) initial position;

(2) initial velocity and direction;

(3) initial size;

(4) initial transparency;

(5) shape;

(6) lifetime.

Velocity and lifetime scripts can be based on dynamic constraints. An explosion, for example, may cause a particle to be ejected upwards and then pulled down under the influence of gravity. Associated with both the attribute script and the population script is a 'generation shape' – a geometric region about the origin of the particle cloud into which 'newly born' particles are placed. For example, an exploding firework might have a spherical generation shape. Figure 13.15 is an example of part of an animation sequence produced using these techniques.

Although the applications Reeves described are generally growing phenomena, where the population of the particle cloud tends to increase, the method is general enough to model phenomena where, say, the population remains constant, while the shape of the cloud perturbs or where the population decreases or implodes. As we have already pointed out, the final object appearance is determined from the net effect of individually rendering all the particles. Rendering is carried out by simply treating each particle as a single light source and using the final value of the appearance parameters.

In a later paper, Reeves and Blau (1985) further develop particle systems. Moving away from using particles to model amorphous and continually changing shapes, they use them as 'volume filling' primitives to generate solid shapes whose form then remains generally constant, but which have the ability to

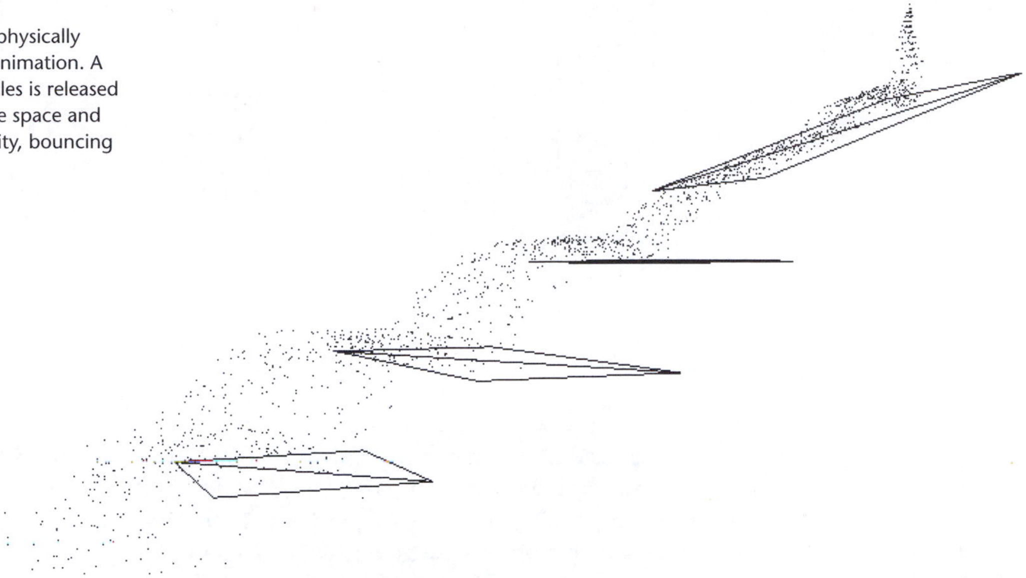

Figure 13.15
An example of physically based particle animation. A stream of particles is released at the top of the space and falls under gravity, bouncing off each step.

change shape in such situations as blades of grass moving in the wind. These techniques were used in the film *The Adventures of Andre and Wally B.* to generate the three-dimensional background images of a forest and grass.

The primary significance of particle systems in this context is not their ability to model shape-changing objects, but rather the property of 'database amplification' – the ability of a simple database to describe the general characteristics of an object that can then be modelled to the required level of detail. Objects are modelled with a resulting complexity that is far higher than that obtainable by conventional techniques. For example, in a forest scene, Reeves states that typically well over a million particles will be generated from basic tree descriptions.

13.9 Particle animation and computer games

A common extension of particle animation alluded to in the previous section is to associate geometric entities with a particle, using particle animation to control the movement of such primitives. The best example of this is an explosion, where the fragments of the explosion move under a particle script. This is the example that we will develop in this section.

Two ways of implementing populations are shown in Figure 13.16. The first uses a linear array where each element is a particle class. The process can be viewed as a window which moves downwards through the particle array. The length of the array represents the lifetime of the population. The particles inside the window comprise the current population. (Note that the birth rate and death rate need not be equal or constant.) A better structure is shown in Figure 13.16(b). This circular structure has an infinite lifetime required in applications where a very long particle display is required – say, for example, a missile trail.

Figure 13.16
Two ways of implementing
a particle population.

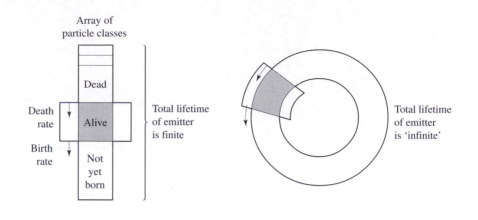

Using particle effects in conjunction with a BSP structure (and collision detection) raises an obvious problem. The realism of effects that use particles depends on employing a large number of particles. If the particles are simply implemented as separate objects – which is what we generally do in off-line computer graphics applications – then there will be a processing explosion with particles moving within the BSP structure and individual collision detection. This is clearly wasteful as, by definition, groups of particles will tend to cluster and processing them individually does not exploit this spatial coherence. The other alternative is to consider a group of particles as a single object and process only the emitter (for visibility and collision detection). This clearly has the disadvantage that if the emitter becomes invisible then all the particles become invisible. It is easy to imagine applications where we will require partial visibility of a particle set.

In the example we now describe, all particle behaviour is inherited from the emitter which has assigned:

Emitting directions (a cone whose solid angle can vary)

Initial velocity

Bump/bounce factor

Friction

Colour

Transparency

Radius

Gravity

Texture map (A particle is always rendered as a square parallel to the view plane which then receives a texture map with a transparent background.)

Three frames in a particle explosion are shown in Figure 13.17 (Colour Plate). This is a fairly standard implementation of a particle system based on a single emitter.

The code proceeds as follows:

Render each of the particles

Update each of the particles using the same elapsed time for each and the pre-set dynamic properties. In the explosion example the particles initially move outwards from the explosion centre then fall under the influence of gravity. Update also implies kill the particles whose lifetime has been exceeded and generate new particles if required by the application.

```
void particle_system::draw()
{
  // draw all particles alive at this time
  if (part)
  {
    int i;
    for( i=part0;i<part1;i++ )
      part[i].draw();
  }
}
int particle_system::step(int dt)
{
  // if particle array has not been allocated, allocate it
  if (part==0)
    {
    part=new color_particle[totpart];
    part0=part1=0;
    }
  else
    {
    // for each particle alive
    int i;
    for( i=part0;i<part1;i++ )
      {
      // move particle based on current properties
      part[i].step(dt);
      // if life is negative, increment death index
      if (part[i].life<0)
        part0++;
      else
      // if life last is less then fade time, fade it out
      if (part[i].life<fadetime)
        part[i].transp=(float)part[i].life/fadetime;
      }
    }
  // compute total number of particles born in the timestep
  float rnd;
```

```
int i,tot;
i=source->life-life;
if (i>emmtime) i=emmtime;
tot=totpart*i/emmtime-part1;

// generate 'tot' new particles
for( i=0;i<tot;i++ )
   {
   // set all newly created particle properties
   rnd=FRAND;
   part[part1].life=source->life-emmtime;
   part[part1].col_flag=col_flag_new;
   part[part1].texture=texture_new;
   part[part1].radius=0.0f;
   part[part1].size=radius_new;
   part[part1].color=color_new+colorvar_new*rnd;
   part[part1].pos=pos;
   if (ax==0 && ay==0)
      part[part1].vel=FRAND*X+FRAND*Y+FRAND*Z;
   else part[part1].vel=FRAND*ax*X+FRAND*ay*Y+Z;
   part[part1].vel.normalize();
   part[part1].vel*=speed_new+speed_var*rnd;
   part[part1].bump=bump_new;
   part[part1].friction=friction_new;
   part[part1].force.vec(0.0f,0.0f,-gravity_new);
   part[part1].transp=1.0f;
   part[part1].mass=1.0f;
   part1++;
   }
   life-=dt;
   return 0;
}
```

An explosion of an object can also be modelled by breaking an object down into separate parts then scripting the motion of these parts by using the particle motion – the local coordinate origin of the part is tied to the particle. This gives a much better visual effect than exploding the object using its polygons as fragments. It is important that the user sees identifiable parts in the explosion animation.

13.10 Articulated structures

Articulated structures are most commonly dealt with by acquiring a script to control the structure from motion capture. Motion capture technology is outside the scope of this text and we will simply deal with how articulated structures can be scripted without recourse to motion capture. The aim of this section is to give a feel for the difficulties involved and to introduce the concepts of forward and inverse kinematics rather than give solutions. It is the case, however, that if the games industry is going to develop into new and more complex genres then it must embrace more general control of articulated structures; control that enables *any* movement required by a higher-level game process, such as an AI module, to be executed in real time. Pre-recorded motion capture will not suffice in such applications.

Scripting of movement of quadruped or biped models in computer animation has, for some time, been an energetically pursued research topic. The computer models are known as articulated structures and most approaches to movement control in animation have attempted to extend techniques developed in the industrial robotics field. Just as interpolation was the first idea to be applied to rigid body animation, parametrising the movement of links or limbs in an articulated structure using robotic methodology seemed the way to proceed. Although this is perhaps an obvious approach, it has not proved very fruitful. One problem is that robot control is itself a research area – by no means have all the problems been solved in that field. Probably a more important reason is that the techniques required to control the precise mechanical movements of an industrial robot do not make a comfortable and creative environment in which an animator can script the freer, more complex and subtler movements of a human or an animal. (This is a general problem in computer graphics that we have discussed elsewhere. Despite the exotic claims of the software developers, artists tend to be constrained by the nature of the interface tools supplied. Rather than have their creative abilities expanded by the medium they are usually shrunk.) Yet another reason is that animal structures are not rigid and the links themselves deform as illustrated in Figure 13.18. In fact, the most successful articulated structure animation to date – *Jurassic Park* – used an *ad hoc* technique to represent or to derive the motion. Let us look briefly at these techniques. This will give an appreciation of the difficulty of the problem faced by the animators in *Jurassic Park* and the efficacy of their solution.

Figure 13.18
Spine flexion in a horse and a cheetah (after Gray (1968)).

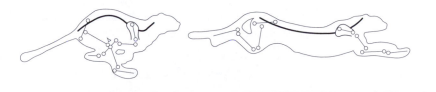

Figure 13.19
A simple articulated
structure and its hierarchical
representation.

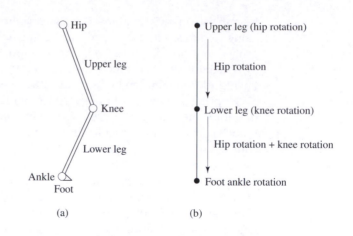

(a)   (b)

First – what is an articulated structure? It is simply a set of rigid objects, or links, connected to each other by joints which enable the various parts of the structure to move, in some way, with respect to each other. Consider a simple example – a single human leg. We might model this as represented in Figure 13.19(a) using two links connecting three joints – the hip joint, the knee joint and the ankle joint. Simplistically we could constrain movement to the plane containing the joints and allow the link between the hip and the knee to rotate, between certain limits, about the hip joint and allow the link between the ankle and the knee to rotate about the knee joint (and, of course, we know that this link can only rotate in one direction). The rotation of the foot about the ankle joint is more complicated since the foot itself is an articulated structure. Given such a structure, how do we begin to specify a script for, say, the way the leg structure is to behave to execute a walk action? There are two major approaches to this problem, both of which come out of robotics – **forward kinematics** and **inverse kinematics**.

Forward kinematics is a somewhat tedious low-level approach where the animator has to explicitly specify all the motions of every part of the articulated structure. Like any low-level approach, the amount of work that has to be done by the animator is a function of the complexity of the structure. The articulated structure is considered as a hierarchy of nodes (Figure 13.19(b)) with an associated transformation which moves the link connected to the node in some way. We could animate such a structure by using curves to specify the transformation values as a function of time. Instead of having just a single path characteristic which moves a reference point for a rigid body, we may now have many characteristics each moving one part of the structure. An important point is that each node in the hierarchy inherits the movement of all the nodes above it. The hip rotation in the example causes the lower leg as well as the upper leg to rotate. The following considerations are apparent:

● **Hip joint**   This is the 'top' joint in the structure and needs to be given global movement. In our simple walk this is just translation.

- **Hip knee link rotation about the hip joint** We can specify the rotation as an angular function of time. If we leave everything below this link fixed then we have a stiff-legged walk (politely known as a compass gait but possibly more familiar as the 'goose step').
- **Knee ankle link rotation about the knee joint** To relax the goose step into a natural walk we specify rotation about the knee joint.

And so on. To achieve the desired movement the animator starts at the top of the hierarchy and works downwards, explicitly applying a script at every point. The evolution of a script is shown in Figure 13.20. Applying the top script would result in a goose step. The second script – knee rotation – allows the lower leg to bend. Applying both these scripts would result in a walk where the foot was always at right angles to the lower leg. This leads us into the ankle script.

Even in this simple example problems begin to accrue. It is not to difficult to see that when we come to script the foot, we cannot tolerate the hip joint moving in a straight line parallel to the floor. This would cause the foot to penetrate the floor. We have to apply some vertical displacement to the hip as a function of time, and so on. And we are considering a very simple example – a walk action. How do we extend this technique for a complex articulated structure that has to execute a fight sequence rather than make a repetitive walk cycle?

Inverse kinematics, on the other hand, is a more high-level approach. Here an animator might specify something like: walk slowly from point A to point B. And the inverse kinematics technique works out a precise script for all the parts of the structure so that the whole body will perform the desired action. More precisely, inverse kinematics means that only the required position of the end (or ends) of the structure are specified. The animator does not indicate how each separate part of the articulated structure is to move, only that the ends of it move in the desired way. The idea comes from robotics where we mostly want the end effector of a robot arm to take up precise positions and perform certain actions. The inverse kinematics then works out the attitude that all the other joints in the structure have to take up so that the end effector is positioned as required. However, herein lurks the problem. As the articulated structure becomes more and more complex, the inverse kinematics solution becomes more and more difficult to work out. Also, inverse kinematics does not, generally, leave much scope for the animator to inject 'character' into the movements, which is after all the art of animation. The inverse kinematics functions as a black box into which is input the desired movement of the ends of the structure and the detailed movement of the entire structure is controlled by the inverse kinematics method. An animator makes character with movement. Forward kinematics is more flexible in this respect, but if we are dealing with a complex model there is much expense. Figure 13.21 (Colour Plate) shows a simple character executing a somewhat flamboyant gait that was animated using forward kinematics.

Thus we have two 'formal' approaches to scripting an articulated structure. Inverse kinematics enables us to specify a script by listing the consecutive positions of the end points of the hierarchy – the position of the hands or feet as a

Figure 13.20
Evolution of a script for a leg.

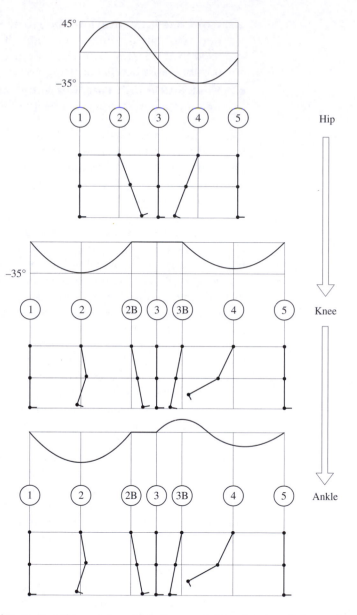

function of time. But the way in which the complete structure behaves is a function of the method used to solve the inverse kinematic equations and the animator has no control over the 'global' behaviour of the structure. Alternatively, if the structure is complex it may be impossible to implement an inverse kinematics solution anyway. On the other hand, forwards kinematics enables the complete structure to be explicitly scripted but at the expense of inordinate labour, except for very simple structures. Any refinements have to be made by starting at the top of the hierarchy again and working downwards.

Figure 13.22
An allegory of a forward kinematics script – four examples of dance notations. *Source*: Tufte, E.R. (1994) *Envisioning Information*, Cheshire, Conn.: Graphics Press.

An illustrative example from the world of dance nicely illustrates this gulf. Figure 13.22 shows an allegory of a forwards kinematics script – in this case for a dance movement. Different notations are used to try to describe the movements of the human body, considering it as an articulated structure, that are required to execute a certain movement in dance. In each illustration an attempt is made to describe the individual movements of each part of the human body that is involved in the expression of the dance movement.

The second example, Figure 13.23, simply gives a script for emplacement of the feet as a function of time. The footprints occur at equal time subdivisions of the music. This is an analogy of an inverse kinematics script. Only the positions of the end points of the hierarchy are specified. The reader of the script can move his or her body in a large number of different ways, all of which fit the footprint script. This is in fact one of the difficulties encountered in implementing an inverse kinematics solution for a structure – there are a large number of possible solutions. Note also that this script specifies part of a complete dance sequence whereas the previous illustration only specifies a single gesture, nicely illustrating the fact that we end up with a low-level script in forward kinematics and a high-level script in inverse kinematics.

In the high-level script the gestural movements of all parts of the body except the feet are left up to the interpretation of the dancer. Again this highlights the difference in artistic flexibility between the two approaches when computer animation is concerned. With forward kinematics the animator has complete freedom over the movement of any part of the structure – the problem is how the movement required by the animator is going to be imposed on the model. What is going to be the nature of the interface that facilitates the ideas of the artist? Using inverse kinematics the animator specifies 'footprints' but unfortunately the model being driven by this script does not possess the interpretation of a human being and the overall movement of the structure depends on the inverse kinematics solution. The same footprints produce the same body movements.

We now illustrate the distinction between forward and inverse kinematics more formally using as an example the simplest articulated structure possible –

Figure 13.23
An allegory of an inverse
kinematics script. *Source*:
Tufte, E.R. (1994) *Envisioning
Information*, Cheshire,
Conn.: Graphics Press.

a two-link machine where one link is fixed and each link moves in the plane of
the paper (Figure 13.24). In forward kinematics we explicitly specify the motion
of all the joints. All the joints are linked and the motion of the end effector
(hands or feet in the case of an animal figure) is determined by the accumulation of all transformations that lead to the end effector. We say that:

$$\boldsymbol{X} = f(\Theta)$$

where $\boldsymbol{X}$ is the motion of the end effector and Θ is a state vector specifying the
position, orientation and rotation of all joints in the system. In the case of the
simple two-link mechanism we have:

$$\boldsymbol{X} = (l_1 \cos \theta_1 + l_2 \cos (\theta_1 + \theta_2), l_1 \sin \theta_1 + l_2 \sin (\theta_1 + \theta_2))$$

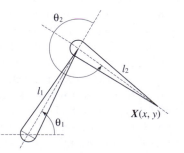

Figure 13.24
A two-link structure.

but this expression is irrelevant in the sense that to control or animate such an arm using forward kinematics we would simply specify:

$$\Theta = (\theta_1, \theta_2)$$

and the model would have applied to it the two angles which would result in the movement X.

In inverse kinematics we specify the position of the end effector and the algorithm has to evaluate the required Θ given X. We have:

$$\Theta = f^{-1}(X)$$

and in our simple example we can obtain from simple trigonometry:

$$\theta_2 = \frac{\cos^{-1}(x^2 + y^2 - l_1{}^2 - l_2{}^2)}{2l_1 l_2}$$

$$\theta_1 = \tan^{-1}\frac{-(l_2 \sin \theta_2)x + (l_1 + l_2 \cos \theta_2)y}{(l_2 \sin \theta_2)y + (l_1 + l_2 \cos \theta_2)x}$$

Now as the complexity of the structure increases the inverse kinematics solution becomes more and more difficult. Quickly the situation develops where many configurations satisfy the required end effector movement. In the simple two-link mechanism, for example, it is easy to see that there are two link configurations possible for each position X, one with the interlink joint above the end effector the other with it below. The attitude or state of this mechanism is specified by two angles (degrees of freedom) and we can easily foresee that as a structure becomes more complex it becomes increasingly difficult to derive an expression of the form $\Theta = f^{-1}(X)$. Thus with forward kinematics the animator has to handle more and more transformations while in inverse kinematics a solution may not be possible except for reasonably simple mechanisms. A human body possesses more than 200 degrees of freedom. An inverse kinematics solution for this is practically impossible and a forward kinematics script is inordinately complicated. A way forward is to invest such models with prewritten forward kinematic scripts for common gestures such as walking, running, grasping, and so on. An animator then creates by putting together a sequence from prewritten parts.

In animating the dinosaurs in *Jurassic Park*, ILM used neither of these approaches, and in the time-honoured tradition of efficacious innovations, came up with a much simpler solution than those offered by the literature of articulated computer graphics animation. Their approach was to drive the models with a low-level forwards kinematics script but they bypassed the script complexity problem by creating a script semi-automatically. They effectively enabled stop-motion animators to input their expertise directly into the computer. The stop-motion animators moved their models in the normal way and the computer sampled the motion, producing a script for the computer models. ILM describe their technique in the following way:

The system is precise, fast, compact, and easy to use. It lets traditional stop-motion animators produce animation on a computer without requiring them to learn complex software. The working environment is very similar to the traditional environment but without the nuisances of lights, a camera and delicate foam-latex skin. The resulting animation lacks the artefacts of stop-motion animation, the ops and jerkiness, and yet retains the intentional subtleties and hard stops that computer animation often lacks.

The general idea is not original. For many years it has been possible to train industrial robots by having a human operator hold the robot's hand, taking it through the actions that the robot is eventually going to perform in the stead of the human operator. Spot welding and paint spraying in the car industry are good examples of the application of this technique. Movements of all the joints in the robot's articulated structure are then read from sensors and from these a script derived to control the robot. Future invocations of the motion sequence involved in a task can then be endlessly and perfectly repeated – indeed the robot will go on reproducing the sequence perfectly even if something else has gone wrong and a car is not present.

In *Jurassic Park* robots were already available because the stop-motion animators had already built 'animatronic' models in anticipation of the film being produced by stop-motion techniques. These were then used, in reverse as it were, by the stop-motion animators, to produce a script for the computer models. Figure 13.25 shows a stop motion animator working out the movements for the dinosaur wrestling with the car scene. The models now, instead of being clothed and filmed one frame at a time, are turned into an input device from which a script is derived.

Figure 13.25
A stop-motion animator using a (real) model fitted with transducers from which a script is derived for a (virtual) computer model. (*Source*: Magid, R. *'After Jurassic Park'*, American Cinematographer, December 1993).

This, of course, is similar to motion capture which involves fixing motion-tracking devices to the appropriate positions of the actor's body and deriving a kinematic script in this way from the real movements of the actor. This approach is particularly popular in the games industry. The requirements of the animation in games is somewhat less demanding in the sense that all that is required is certain sequences in response to user interaction events. It is natural and economic to use motion capture in this context to record the original motion scripts for the computer models.

In games, motion capture and inverse kinematics exhibit inadequacies that are mutually exclusive in this sense. Motion capture can only, in its basic form, provide a utility that is the same as pre-scripted animation – it cannot easily adapt in real time as game action changes. Inverse kinematics provides a new solution each time an end effector is moved and appears to overcome the disadvantages of motion capture. However, as we have seen, inverse kinematics solutions are difficult. In addition, it is almost certain that inverse kinematics will not provide a 'good' or 'best practice' solution. In the case of human motion it will not necessarily produce convincing motion. For example, a human reaching to grasp an object will produce a more direct motion of elbow and shoulder joint motion than an inverse kinematics solution. 'Best practice constraints' often exist in applications and will not emerge from an inverse kinematics solution. A goalkeeper, for example, always attempts to move in such a way to try to position his body behind an incoming ball – and does not simply outstretch his arms towards it. It is unlikely that inverse kinematics will prove useful unless such constraints are incorporated.

Control by dynamic simulation

14.1   Dynamics in off-line animation – the famous example

14.2   Initial value problems vs. boundary value problems

14.3   Topic areas

14.4   Motivations for dynamic simulations

14.5   Basic classical theory for particles

14.6   Basic classical theory for rigid bodies

14.7   The practicalities of dynamic simulations

14.8   Numerical integration

14.1   Dynamics in off-line animation – the famous example

Luxo Jr., an animated short produced by John Lasseter of Pixar in 1987, was possibly the first computer graphics animation that was perceived to have motion and appeal comparable in quality to that of traditional animators. The skills of John Lasseter imbued a desk lamp with some of the anthropomorphic behaviour reminiscent of Disney-type cartoons. The motion in *Luxo Jr.* was produced by keyframing, where the animator specifies the state of the articulated structure as a key and the global motion of the structure as a spline curve. Although it is not 100 per cent explicit control, where the animator specifies the entire state of every frame, he or she has a high degree of control. And the fact that the title of Lasseter's presentation to SIGGRAPH '87 was 'Principles of traditional animation applied to 3D computer animation' reinforces this observation.

In 1988 Witkin and Kass presented a paper in which they demonstrated that a higher-level motion control technique, based on dynamic simulation, could be used to animate *Luxo Jr.* and commented on their motivation as follows:

> Although *Luxo Jr.* showed us that the team of animator, keyframe system, and renderer can be a powerful one, the responsibility defining the motion remains almost entirely with the animator. Some aspects of animation – personality and appeal, for example – will surely be left to the animator's

artistry and skill for a long time to come. However, many of the principles of animation are concerned with making the character's motion look *real* at a basic mechanical level that ought to admit to formal physical treatment . . . Moreover, simple changes to the goals of the motion or to the physical model give rise to interesting variations on the basic motion. For example, doubling (or quadrupling) the mass of *Luxo Jr.* creates amusingly exaggerated motion in which the base looks heavy.

In other words, what they are saying that this type of computer animation can benefit by higher-level motion control. Beyond performing rudimentary interpolation for in-between frames a program can be set up to interpret scripts such as 'jump from A to B'. The dynamic simulation will then produce motion that is accurate and therefore realistic.

The interest in the use of dynamic simulation in computer games is motivated by the desire for realistic motion. Unfortunately, classical dynamics is not a toolbox that can easily be exploited in many, if not most, applications of interest to the computer games community. The main reason for this is that accessible classical dynamics tends to deal with single-state unconstrained models. This is fine for 'asteroids' but not for human motion, to give an obvious example. If we consider a single limb – a leg – then we see that a walking motion involves changes of state of the leg from 'stance' to 'flight'. Motion of animal skeletons also involves constrained dynamics, which means that objects cannot move freely under the influence of applied forces.

Thus the future use of dynamics in games is likely to involve 'application difficulties' rather than the exploitation of classical dynamics and numerical integration – both much-studied techniques. Application difficulties means any or all of the following (which are not necessarily separable):

- defining a simulation loop for the problem, which implies deriving the equations;

- integrating constraints into the simulation

- controlling the simulation – user-controlled dynamic simulations run continuously under the control of a higher-level process/interface.

14.2 Initial value problems vs. boundary value problems

In most current applications dynamic simulation models initial value problems – you set a simulation going using initial values and step forward in time. The classic simple example is the projectile flying through the air. You have no control over how/where the simulation finishes. It is likely in the future that boundary value problems will also be of interest. The development of AI will in games will no doubt lead to a demand for dynamic boundary value problems. For example, say a higher-level process wants to know what is the velocity and angle of the kick required from the player in possession of the ball to hit the crossbar, and for the rebound to be headable by another player in the vicinity of the goal. This is a difficult problem and in most applications straightforward inverse dynamic solutions will not be available.

14.3 Topic areas

There are (possibly) three main areas of dynamics that are relevant to computer games. These are:

(1) The motion of an unconstrained rigid body. This means using the equations of classical dynamics to describe how an undeformable object moves. (Unconstrained in this context does not mean that the object is not subject to such constraints as gravity which keeps it on the ground, but that it can be modelled as a single entity and is not part of a system of connected bodies or components.) A rocket is a simple example of an unconstrained rigid body. Currently this appears to be the main use of physics in computer games. To be able to model even quite simple situations we need to develop equations that take into account the fact that rigid bodies can rotate as well as translate

(2) The motion of constrained rigid bodies. This is the study of systems that are made up of components that constrain each other in some way. An animal skeleton, for example, is a complex structure where each component is geometrically constrained by its connection to adjacent components. This is a much more demanding field and in the case of skeletons a kinematic approach is often taken. (Kinematics is the study of the motion of bodies without regard to the forces that produced the motion. Scripting an animation for a skeleton using motion capture data is an example of a kinematics approach.) The difficulty with constrained rigid bodies is obvious: setting up an analysis that satisfies both Newton's laws and the geometric constraints.

(3) Numerical solutions to ODEs. The class of ODEs of interest in dynamics are equations of the form:

$$\dot{x} = f(x,t)$$

This is a well worked out area, but needs to be understood. Different methods exhibit different accuracies and speed.

The absolute minimum expertise required to consider using dynamic theory in computer games is a familiarity with Newton/Euler equations. These deal with the general motion of a rigid body which consists of both rotation and translation. These equations apply not only to unconstrained motion but to the motions of 'links' in constrained structures. For example, if we are considering the dynamics of a kick initiated by, say, applying a torque at the knee joint, then we have to use an equation that relates the applied torque to the angular acceleration and the constant of proportionality – the moment of inertia of the lower leg.

As well as acquiring a knowledge of classical dynamics, other topics need to be studied if useful simulations are to result. Most classical dynamics texts deal with single-state problems – the motion of a compound pendulum may be studied in detail but not what happens in a system after the pendulum collides with another object. Interaction between objects is obviously an important aspect of future simulations. Another important topic is the control of the application of forces and torques. If we model a football player as a linked structure controlled by the application of torques to the joints, then how do we inject torques and forces into the structure?

14.4 Motivations for dynamic simulations

Some considerations in simulating dynamics in computer games are:

- **Dynamic simulations work**   One of the most significant events of the twentieth century – the moon landing – owed much to dynamic simulations.

- **Simulations 'capture' complexity**   'Complex' behaviour will emerge 'automatically' from dynamic simulations. Two familiar examples:

  - the increase in the angular velocity of a spinning ice skater due to the reduction in the moment of inertia as the skater becomes 'thinner';

  - a child gaining height on a swing by kicking out and contracting his or her legs at the appropriate height and injecting rotational energy into the system.

In both these cases a simple dynamic model will produce the expected results when the mass redistribution occurs.

- **Why do it if you can fake it?**   Faking does not lead to a development of reusable expertise. Solutions that look right are developed for particular contexts. Development of dynamics expertise means it can be used in any application. It may be required in the future as game complexity increases.

  Somewhat similar to motion capture in this respect, faked dynamics can only produce animation that has already 'been seen' by the programmer. In the future, if agents such as virtual humans are going to interact with a virtual environment in an unconstrained manner, then only an encapsulation of the dynamic behaviour of the agent will result in the desired generality.

- **Plausibility vs. game play**   The plausibility issue is obvious but an accurate simulation may make a boring game. It may be that the designer wants dynamics plus 'extra natural' behaviour to occur from time to time in the game. Simulations can easily incorporate implausible behaviour if required.

- **The granularity of the system**   This will, of course, determine complexity. A good example of this point is car racing games. Here the nature of the detail of the simulation depends on the nature of the game. If a game was developed that enabled the user to compete, say, against the gg (accelerometer) records of Senna on particular F1 tracks then the quality of the simulation would have to be that of an advanced vehicle simulator. This would mean simulating all the dynamic elements and modelling the car as a suspended mass. The interactions would have to include tyre behaviour, suspension modelling, aerodynamics and so on, and all accelerations – longitudinal, yaw and lateral – would have to be accounted for.

● **Granularity of the interactions** Complexity resides in both the object and its interaction (with other objects and the environment). For example, it is easy to calculate if a car is going to roll in a steady-state turn due to centrifugal force. All you need is the mass and C of G of the car, its speed and the turn radius. However, in reality family cars rarely overturn because of this. Roll-overs usually occur when a car in a skid hits an obstacle – a so-called trip roll-over and a much more difficult situation to simulate. In other words, feasibility.

● **Feasibility** The difficulty or feasibility of a simulation depends on the inherent complexity of the system being simulated. Examples of 'easy' simulations are golf and flight simulators. Difficult simulations are F1 cars and human beings.

14.5 Basic classical theory for particles

The basic familiar law of motion, Newton's Second Law, is:

$$\boldsymbol{F} = m\boldsymbol{a}$$

and this is easiest to consider in the context of a particle or a point mass. $\boldsymbol{F}$ is a three-dimensional vector, as is $\boldsymbol{a}$, the acceleration that the point undergoes. A point mass is a simple abstraction that can be used to model simple behaviour – we can assume that a rigid body that has extent behaves like a particle because we consider its mass concentrated at a single point – the centre of mass. A point mass can only undergo translation under the application of a force.

Newton's Second Law can also be written as:

$$\boldsymbol{F} = m\dot{\boldsymbol{v}} = m\ddot{\boldsymbol{x}}$$

where $\boldsymbol{v}$ is the velocity and $\boldsymbol{x}$ the position of the particle. This leads to a method that finds, by integration, the position of the particle at time $t + dt$ given its position at time t as:

$$\boldsymbol{v}(t + dt) = \boldsymbol{v}(t) + \frac{\boldsymbol{F}}{m}\, dt$$

$$\boldsymbol{x}(t + dt) = \boldsymbol{x}(t) + \boldsymbol{v}(t)dt + \frac{1}{2}\frac{\boldsymbol{F}}{m}\, dt^2$$

$$= \mathbf{x}(t) + \frac{1}{2}(\mathbf{v}(t) + \mathbf{v}(t + dt))dt$$

In practice we would have three equations, one for each dimension:

$$x(t + dt) = x(t) + \frac{1}{2}(v_x(t) + v_x(t + dt))dt$$

$$y(t + dt) = x(t) + \frac{1}{2}(v_y(t) + v_y(t + dt))dt$$

$$z(t + dt) = x(t) + \frac{1}{2}(v_z(t) + v_z(t + dt))dt$$

This method is called Euler's method and it is generally too inaccurate for practical applications. Its inaccuracy is a function of the step length dt (see Section 14.8 for more details).

For a given $\mathbf{v}(0)$ and a constant $\mathbf{F}$ the above will always produce the same particle motion and in most applications of interest $\mathbf{F}$ is a function of time. Also, we may have more than one force acting on the body and in that case we simply calculate the net force using vector addition. If the mass of the body changes as it travels, the case of a vehicle burning fuel, for example, then the second law is expressed as:

$$\mathbf{F} = \frac{d(m.\mathbf{v})}{dt}$$

As a simple example, consider a cannon-ball being fired from the mouth of a cannon (or any ball/projectile problem). This could be modelled using the above equations. The cannon-ball is acted on by two forces – the constant acceleration due to gravity and an air resistance force that acts opposite to the velocity and is a function (quadratic) of the velocity and the square of the cross-sectional area of the ball. A simulation would be provided with the initial (muzzle) velocity and the inclination of the barrel and Newton's Second Law used to compute the arc of the missile. What we have achieved here is a simulation where at each time step the program computes continuous behaviour as a function of time.

(14.5.1)

The nature of forces

Only in very simple cases can we proceed by considering an object as a point mass or equivalently as a lumped mass undergoing acceleration upon application of a force. The way in which an object moves in the modelled environment depends on the model itself, its constraints and the nature of the force. Common examples of the different types of forces used in dynamic simulation are:

- Acceleration due to gravity is a constant downwards force on a body proportional to its mass and acting on the centre of mass.

- A damping force which is opposite and proportional to the body's velocity and resists its motion. Damping forces remove energy from the body, dissipating heat. A viscous damping force is linearly proportional to velocity and a quadratic force is proportional to the square of speed. Air resistance is approximately quadratic if we ignore effects due to the disturbance of the air.

- Elastic springs, which can connect two bodies with a force proportional to the displacement of the string from its rest length (Hooke's law).

- Bodies can possess geometric constraints which can be considered as (constraint) forces. A simple pendulum exhibits a 'point to nail' constraint. These forces adapt to maintain the geometric constraints regardless of the force applied to the body. Points on a clock pendulum can only move along the circumference of a circle irrespective of where the impulse force, which the pendulum receives to keep it in motion, is applied.

14.6 Basic classical theory for rigid bodies

14.6.1 Linear and angular momentum and centre of mass

To perform the simulation we use the concept of linear and angular momentum. Momentum is an important concept that enables many dynamic calculations. In particular, momentum is conserved – once acquired, it cannot change unless a force or a torque is applied. This conservation theory is used in particular in collision calculations. Another important concept is the centre of mass. The total linear momentum of a system is the same as if the entire mass were concentrated at the centre of mass. A good example of this is a shell which explodes in flight. The centre of mass of the shell, which now consists of fragments moving away from the explosion centre, continues in motion unaffected by the explosion – that is, as if the shell were still whole.

Forces applied at the centre of mass cause a change in linear momentum and those applied elsewhere are torques and cause a change in angular momentum. We have:

$$\boldsymbol{M}(t) = m\boldsymbol{v}(t) \qquad\qquad \boldsymbol{v}(t) = \boldsymbol{M}(t)/m$$

$$\dot{\boldsymbol{M}}(t) = m\dot{\boldsymbol{v}}(t) = m\boldsymbol{a}(t) = \boldsymbol{F}(t)$$

that is, the rate of change of momentum equals the applied force.

Similarly we can define angular momentum as

$$\boldsymbol{L}(t) = \boldsymbol{I}(t)\boldsymbol{\omega}(t) \qquad\qquad \boldsymbol{\omega}(t) = \boldsymbol{I}^{-1}(t)\boldsymbol{L}(t)$$

$$\dot{\boldsymbol{L}}(t) = \boldsymbol{I}(t)\dot{\boldsymbol{\omega}}(t) = \boldsymbol{I}(t)\boldsymbol{\alpha}(t) = \boldsymbol{\tau}(t)$$

which says that the rate of change of angular momentum is equal to the applied torque. Note that linear velocity and angular velocity are both linearly related to linear and angular momentum. The difference in the case of angular velocity is that the constant of proportionality is a tensor (we can consider that a tensor is a 3×3 matrix) $\boldsymbol{I}$ whereas with linear velocity it is a scalar (mass). This is because the 'resistance' to angularly accelerating a body depends on its mass distribution about the rotation axis. This dependence is parametrised by the inertia tensor $\boldsymbol{I}$.

The conservation of momentum applies to the sum of linear and angular momentum. These can change as long as their total remains the same. A spinning ball hitting the ground changes its direction of spin and some angular momentum will convert to linear momentum.

(14.6.2)

World frame and body frame

In the dynamics of rigid bodies – entities that can only undergo translation and rotation – we have to set up two coordinate systems; one is called the inertial frame known in computer graphics as the world coordinate system and the other, which is embedded in the rigid body and moves with it, is called the body frame (Figure 14.1). We need to perform our simulation in world space, because we need to specify the position of the body and also how the body may be interacting with other entities. However, certain body constants are specified in body space which we locate with the centre of mass of the body as the origin. The orientation of the body is specified by the orientation of the body frame in world space.

Figure 14.1
Inertial frame and body frame.

Inertial frame
is fixed

Body frame is rigidly attached
to the moving object

(14.6.3)

Orientation of a rigid body

An unconstrained rigid body moving in three-dimensional space possesses 6 DOF – it can translate and rotate. Translation is easily specified by a position vector in world space; rotation is more difficult. To specify the rotation of a rigid body we use the body frame. Since any two coordinate systems are related by a translation and a rotation, we can specify the current position of the body coordinate system – the position of the centre of mass – in world space as $\boldsymbol{x}(t)$ and the rotation of the body system as $\boldsymbol{R}(t)$ where:

$$\mathbf{R}(t) = \begin{bmatrix} r_{xx} & r_{yx} & r_{zx} \\ r_{xy} & r_{yy} & r_{zy} \\ r_{xz} & r_{yz} & r_{zz} \end{bmatrix}$$

The physical meaning of $\mathbf{R}(t)$ is that the columns give the direction of each body space axis in world space. Consider, for example, the body space x axis $(1,0,0)$. In world space this vector has the direction:

$$\mathbf{R}(t) \begin{bmatrix} 1 \\ 0 \\ 0 \end{bmatrix} = \begin{bmatrix} r_{xx} \\ r_{xy} \\ r_{xz} \end{bmatrix}$$

Thus the columns of $\mathbf{R}(t)$ specify three mutually perpendicular vectors which are the axes of the body space coordinate system.

Matrix $\mathbf{R}$ is an orthogonal matrix which means that all of its columns are of unit length and are mutually perpendicular vectors. It has the properties:

$|\mathbf{R}| = 1$ \qquad the determinant is equal to $+1$

$\mathbf{R}^{-1} = \mathbf{R}^{\mathrm{T}}$ \qquad the inverse is equal to the transpose

Now if we consider any point $\mathbf{r}_{\text{body}}$ on the rigid body, its position $\mathbf{r}$ in world space is given by rotating it about the body space origin and translating it by $\mathbf{x}$.

$$\mathbf{r}(t) = \mathbf{R}(t)\mathbf{r}_{\text{body}} + \mathbf{x}(t)$$

Thus $\mathbf{x}(t)$ locates the position of the centre of mass of the body at time t in world space and $\mathbf{R}$ specifies the orientation of the body frame (the orientation of the body) with respect to the world frame.

14.6.4 Angular velocity

We now consider the concept of angular velocity and the part it plays in the general equations of motion for a rigid body by considering how we define the rate of change of a vector $\mathbf{r}_{\text{body}}$, embedded in the rigid body in world space. An observer fixed in the body system sees no change whatever, but an observer in the world system sees a vector translating and rotating about an axis which itself continually changes. We define this axis by the angular velocity vector $\boldsymbol{\omega}(t)$ (Figure 14.2). This is a vector that passes through the centre of mass whose direction defines an axis of rotation and whose magnitude defines a rate of rotation (in radians/sec) about that axis. We can consider any fixed point in the body and

Figure 14.2
Motion of a rigid body consists of angular and translational components.

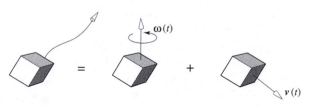

Figure 14.3
The rate of change of *r* is
$\boldsymbol{\omega} \times \boldsymbol{r}$.

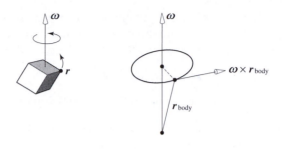

define this using a vector $\boldsymbol{r}_{\text{body}}$ in the body frame (Figure 14.3). The tip of $\boldsymbol{r}_{\text{body}}$ rotates at a speed determined by $|\boldsymbol{\omega}|$ and the radius of the circle shown. The instantaneous direction of the tip of $\boldsymbol{r}_{\text{body}}$ is given by $\boldsymbol{\omega} \times \boldsymbol{r}_{\text{body}}$ and we define the rate of change of $\boldsymbol{r}_{\text{body}}$ as:

$$\dot{\boldsymbol{r}}_{\text{body}}(t) = \boldsymbol{\omega}(t) \times \boldsymbol{r}_{\text{body}}(t)$$

This is the velocity of any point in the body that is due only to the angular velocity or spin of the body. That is, it is independent of the linear velocity $\boldsymbol{v}(t)$. Now we return to the concept that the position and orientation of the rigid body is defined by $\boldsymbol{x}(t)$ and $\boldsymbol{R}(t)$ and find the relationship between $\boldsymbol{\omega}(t)$ and $\dot{\boldsymbol{R}}(t)$. Bear in mind that our simulation is going to output an evolving $\boldsymbol{x}(t)$ and $\boldsymbol{R}(t)$ which we finally require to generate the frames of the animation and so we need to find the relationship between angular acceleration (induced by torque) and $\boldsymbol{R}(t)$ just as in the case of translation we need the relationship between linear acceleration (induced by force) and position as a function of time.

Consider the previous equation again. This is a general result that says that the rate of change of any vector is the cross-product of the vector with the angular velocity vector. Now $\boldsymbol{R}$ can be considered as a group of three mutually orthogonal vectors which form the directions of the axes of body space and to differentiate $\boldsymbol{R}$ we simply need to apply this operation separately to each of these vectors:

$$\dot{\boldsymbol{R}}(t) = \left[\boldsymbol{\omega}(t) \times \begin{bmatrix} r_{xx} \\ r_{xy} \\ r_{xz} \end{bmatrix} \ \boldsymbol{\omega}(t) \times \begin{bmatrix} r_{yx} \\ r_{yy} \\ r_{yz} \end{bmatrix} \ \boldsymbol{\omega}(t) \times \begin{bmatrix} r_{zx} \\ r_{zy} \\ r_{zz} \end{bmatrix} \right] = \boldsymbol{\omega}(t)^{*}\boldsymbol{R}(t) \qquad [14.1]$$

Now consider writing the equation for the position of a point on a rigid body in world space as:

$$\boldsymbol{r}(t) = \boldsymbol{x}(t) + \boldsymbol{R}(t)\boldsymbol{r}_{\text{body}}$$

where $\boldsymbol{r}_{\text{body}}$ and $\boldsymbol{r}$ are the position vectors of the particle in body space and world space respectively. Differentiating we have:

$$\dot{\boldsymbol{r}}(t) = \dot{\boldsymbol{x}}(t) + \dot{\boldsymbol{R}}(t)\boldsymbol{r}_{\text{body}}$$

which gives us the means to express the velocity in world space as the sum of two components – a linear component $v(t)$ and a component relating to the angular velocity vector. We derive this expression as follows:

$$\dot{r}(t) = v(t) + \omega(t)^*R(t)r_{\text{body}}$$

where the operator $*$ implies Equation 14.1. Thus:

$$\dot{r}(t) = v(t) + \omega(t)^*(R(t)r_{\text{body}} + x(t) - x(t))$$
$$= v(t) + \omega(t)^*(r(t) - x(t))$$
$$= v(t) + \omega(t) \times (r(t) - x(t))$$

and this finally expresses the velocity of a point r on a rigid body in world space as the sum of the linear velocity of a reference point (the centre of mass in our case) x on the body and an angular velocity component.

14.6.5

Rigid bodies – forces and torques

A particle can only admit translation. When a motive force is applied to bodies with extent, the movement induced can consist of both translation and rotation. It is obvious that an unconstrained long thin cylinder will tumble through space if a force is applied to it other than at the centre of mass. We describe such a force as a torque τ.

Torque differs from force in that its magnitude depends on the relationship between its point of application and the centre of mass of the body. If we apply force F to a body where the point of application in the body has position vector r then torque is defined as:

$$\tau = (r - x) \times F$$

where x is the position vector of the centre of mass.

We now consider any motive as a force F (or a number of forces which combine to produce F), which acts on the centre of mass and induces motion as if it was a particle, and a torque τ which induces rotation about a particular axis. The body translates and rotates through space. Consider applying two equal forces to a symmetric body at equal distances from its centre of mass. In the absence of any geometric constraints the body undergoes translation (Figure 14.4). If we now move one of the points of application of the forces the body both translates and rotates. (An important point that emerges from this example is that although the same net force is applied in both cases, in the rotating case the body has acquired a higher kinetic energy at time $t + dt$ because it has acquired both a linear and an angular velocity.) Other possibilities are shown in the figure, which also demonstrates the effect of more than one applied force.

To incorporate this intuitive motion into physical laws we need first to specify how the mass of a body is distributed about its centre of mass. This information enables us to treat the body as a single entity – a single mass concentrated at its centre of mass.

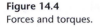

Figure 14.4
Forces and torques.

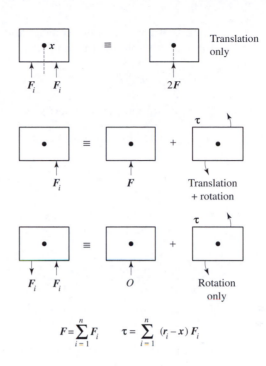

$$F = \sum_{i=1}^{n} F_i \qquad \tau = \sum_{i=1}^{n} (r_i - x)\, F_i$$

14.6.6

The inertia tensor

To simulate an unconstrained rigid body we need three physical constants that describe the nature of the mass of the body: its magnitude, the centre of mass/gravity and a 3×3 matrix known as the inertia tensor. As we have already defined, $\boldsymbol{I}$, the inertia tensor, is the constant of proportionality between angular momentum and angular velocity and it describes how the mass is distributed about the centre of mass. The information contained in the inertia tensor is constant providing its elements are defined in the body system. The only complication is that our simulation takes place always in world space and so we need a transformation from body space to world space.

For symmetrical bodies the inertia tensor contains just three non-zero (diagonal) elements and these are the three moments of inertia – one about each axis. Considering a rigid body as an infinity of particles, a moment of inertia is just the sum of the masses of each particle weighted by the square of the perpendicular distance to each axis:

$$I_x = \int (y^2 + z^2)\, dm$$
$$I_y = \int (x^2 + z^2)\, dm$$
$$I_z = \int (x^2 + y^2)\, dm$$

Note that dm is a mass element and for bodies of homogeneous material the integral is a volume integral:

$$\mathbf{I} = \iiint \rho()\,dxdydz$$

Examples of moment of inertia for symmetric homogeneous rigid bodies are:

- a sphere of radius r and mass m

$$I_x = I_y = I_z = \frac{2}{5}\,mr^2$$

- a cylinder of radius r and height h where the z axis is coincident with the long axis of the cylinder

$$I_x = I_y = \frac{1}{4}\,m(r^2 + \frac{1}{3}\,h^2)$$

$$I_z = \frac{1}{2}\,mr^2$$

- a rectangular box of sides a, b and c where the axes x, y and z are along sides a, b and c respectively

$$I_x = \frac{1}{12}\,m(a^2 + b^2)$$

$$I_y = \frac{1}{12}\,m(a^2 + c^2)$$

$$I_z = \frac{1}{12}\,m(a^2 + d^2)$$

The box formulation is useful because a common approximation to a polygonal object in computer graphics is its bounding box. The mass m is given by some default density multiplied by the volume and the centre of mass is the centre of the box. If we calculate moments of inertia of a polyhedron using a bounding volume then the degree of approximation depends on how tightly the volume fits the object.

Moments of inertia are a simple concept to imagine. Consider a long thin rod which can rotate about its centre with two sliding weights that are always symmetrically disposed about its centre. If we apply a torque to the end of the rod then it is intuitively obvious that the 'resistance to angular acceleration' – the inertia – will depend on how close the weights are to the ends of the rod. The system will be easier to accelerate if the weights are close to the centre – a fact well known by spinning ice skaters who increase their angular velocity by reducing their moment of inertia about their body's perpendicular axis.

If the body is not symmetric then the products of inertia are also required for a complete specification of the mass distribution for a dynamic model. These are:

$$I_{xy} = \int xy \, dm$$

$$I_{xz} = \int xz \, dm$$

$$I_{yz} = \int yz \, dm$$

It is easily shown that these go to zero for a symmetric body. If we consider the balls on the rod example and move the balls such that they are no longer symmetrically disposed about the centre point, then two of the products of inertia become non-zero. In mechanical engineering a rotating mass with non-zero products of inertia is unbalanced and results in vibration – the reason why your washing machine executes a dance when in the spin part of the cycle.

All of these are arranged into a 3 × 3 matrix known as the inertial tensor:

$$\boldsymbol{I} = \begin{bmatrix} I_x & -I_{xy} & -I_{xz} \\ -I_{xy} & I_y & -I_{yz} \\ -I_{xz} & -I_{yz} & I_z \end{bmatrix}$$

and we re-emphasise that $\boldsymbol{I}$ is constant providing the integrations are performed in the body coordinate system that is rigidly attached to the object and moves with it. This makes $\boldsymbol{I}$ an invariant description of the object which is calculated once only. The inertia tensor can be transformed under rotation to any coordinate system and to transform it into world coordinate space – the simulation space – it can be shown that:

$$\boldsymbol{I}(t) = \boldsymbol{R}(t)\boldsymbol{I}_{\text{body}}\boldsymbol{R}(t)^{\text{T}}$$

where the notation emphasises that $\boldsymbol{I}$ now varies as a function of time because $\boldsymbol{R}(t)$ varies with time. We will also require:

$$\boldsymbol{I}^{-1}(t) = \boldsymbol{R}(t) \, \boldsymbol{I}_{\text{body}}^{-1}\boldsymbol{R}(t)^{\text{T}}$$

There is, for any arbitrary-shaped object, a special coordinate system for which $\boldsymbol{I}$ is diagonalised – the products of inertia are zero. This is known as the principal axis and the diagonal elements of $\boldsymbol{I}$ as the principal moments of inertia. It makes sense then to choose this as a body coordinate system. To find the principal axis we rotationally transform the inertia tensor to a frame in which it is diagonalized. This is done by finding the eigenvectors $\boldsymbol{E}$ and the associated eigenvalues (see *Numerical Recipes in C* (Press *et al.*, 1988)).

14.6.7

Collision response

Collision response in a dynamic simulation is a state that enables one part of the simulation to transform into another. We may consider two cars moving under the dynamic simulation; they collide, a collision response calculation is executed and a new simulation begins with initial values output from the collision response mechanism.

The nature of the collision response calculations is strictly application dependent. The application may not admit collisions; for example, in path planning, an object may have to move from a source to a destination without colliding. When objects are allowed to collide the reaction depends on the nature of the objects and the calculations involved are properly part of the overall dynamic simulation, although we need to introduce a new theory or model to deal with special cases.

The clear distinction is between elastic collisions, where the bodies do not permanently deform and where there is no loss of kinetic energy, and inelastic collisions where they do. Inelastic collisions and the deformations caused by them are more difficult to deal with and in this case energy is dissipated in the collision. Classical dynamics treats the problem by considering a large impulsive force or reaction, $\boldsymbol{P}$, acting for a very short period of time – the duration of the collision. Consider Figure 14.5 which shows two spheres moving along a line joining their centres. We have:

$$m_1(\boldsymbol{v}_1^{\text{after}} - \boldsymbol{v}_1) = -\boldsymbol{P}$$

$$m_2(\boldsymbol{v}_2^{\text{after}} - \boldsymbol{v}_2) = \boldsymbol{P}$$

where

$\boldsymbol{P}$ is the impulse force

$\boldsymbol{v}_1$ and $\boldsymbol{v}_2$ are the velocities of the spheres before impact

$\boldsymbol{v}_1^{\text{after}}$ and $\boldsymbol{v}_2^{\text{after}}$ and are the velocities of the spheres after impact

thus

$$m_1\boldsymbol{v}_1^{\text{after}} + m_2\boldsymbol{v}_2^{\text{after}} = m_1\boldsymbol{v}_1 + m_2\boldsymbol{v}_2$$

which we might have deduced anyway since there is no external force acting on the system.

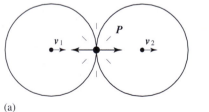

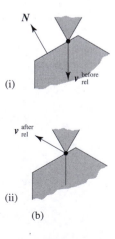

Figure 14.5
(a) Two spheres colliding.
(b) Vertex face collision for polyhedra. (i) A vertex face contact. (ii) $e = 1$. The relative velocity in the direction of $\boldsymbol{N}$ is reversed. The relative velocity perpendicular to $\boldsymbol{N}$ remains the same.

We define:

$$\boldsymbol{v}_{\text{rel}}^{\text{before}} = \boldsymbol{v}_1 - \boldsymbol{v}_2$$

as the speed of approach, and

$$\boldsymbol{v}_{\text{rel}}^{\text{after}} = \boldsymbol{v}_1^{\text{after}} - \boldsymbol{v}_2^{\text{after}}$$

as the speed of separation, and hypothesise that these are connected by a coefficient of restitution e:

$$\boldsymbol{v}_{\text{rel}}^{\text{after}} = -e\boldsymbol{v}_{\text{rel}}^{\text{before}}$$

where

if $e = 0$ then $\boldsymbol{v}_1^{\text{after}} = \boldsymbol{v}_2^{\text{after}}$ there is no rebound – an inelastic collision

if $e = 1$ then $\boldsymbol{v}_1^{\text{after}} = \boldsymbol{v}_2$ and $\boldsymbol{v}_2^{\text{after}} = \boldsymbol{v}_1$ the spheres exchange velocities – a perfectly elastic collision.

Now consider polyhedra colliding. For simplicity we will only consider one mode of contact – a vertex colliding with a face. (In practice we can, of course, have two faces or two vertices colliding.) In this case the surface of contact is the face of one of the colliding bodies and we can define a normal $\boldsymbol{N}$ to this surface of contact. We then consider what happens to the component of the relative velocity in the direction of $\boldsymbol{N}$. If $e = 1$ (Figure 14.5(b)) then the component in the direction of $\boldsymbol{N}$ is reversed and the relative velocity perpendicular to $\boldsymbol{N}$ remains unchanged. For the case $0 \leq e \leq 1$ the relative velocity in the direction of $\boldsymbol{N}$ is reduced.

In general, we must consider that rigid bodies in motion are both translating and rotating and we can define the velocity of the point of contact $\boldsymbol{Q}$ immediately after the time of the collision as:

$$\boldsymbol{V}_A^{\text{after}} = \boldsymbol{v}_A^{\text{after}} + (\boldsymbol{\omega}_A^{\text{after}} \times \boldsymbol{r}_A)$$

where $\boldsymbol{\omega}_A^{\text{after}}$ is the angular velocity of body A after impact and $\boldsymbol{r}_A$ the distance from the point of contact to the centre of gravity of A.

We now return to consider the nature of the impulse force $\boldsymbol{P}$ in more detail. As we have already mentioned, $\boldsymbol{P}$ is an entity that acts over a very short time interval:

$$\boldsymbol{P} = \int_{\Delta t} \boldsymbol{F} dt$$

The effect of $\boldsymbol{P}$ is to produce an instantaneous change in velocity and it has the units of momentum. If we denote the magnitude of $\boldsymbol{P}$ as p we can write:

$$\boldsymbol{V}_A^{\text{after}} = \boldsymbol{V}_A^{\text{before}} + \frac{p\boldsymbol{N}}{m_A}$$

where m_A is the mass of body A, and

$$\boldsymbol{\omega}_A^{\text{after}} + \boldsymbol{\omega}_A^{\text{before}} \; \boldsymbol{I}_A^{-1}(\boldsymbol{r}_A \times p\boldsymbol{N})$$

Similar expressions can be obtained for body B. Deriving the relative velocities as a function of p and the equations for the velocity and angular velocity of A and B, and using the previous equation yields:

$$p = \frac{-(1 - e)\boldsymbol{V}_{\text{rel}}^{\text{before}}}{\dfrac{1}{m_A} + \dfrac{1}{m_B} + \boldsymbol{N} . (\boldsymbol{I}_A^{-1}(\boldsymbol{r}_A \times \boldsymbol{N})) \times \boldsymbol{r}_A + \boldsymbol{N} . (\boldsymbol{I}_B^{-1}(\boldsymbol{r}_B \times \boldsymbol{N})) \times \boldsymbol{r}_B}$$

If a moving body collides with a large mass static body, which we can assume does not move at all, then $1/m$ can be set to zero and $\boldsymbol{I}$ is a zero matrix.

(14.7)

The practicalities of dynamic simulations

A dynamic simulation will contain the following components:

- A module that controls the injection of the forces and torques that move the objects. This depends on the application and may take input from a higher-level controller such as an AI module and/or a user interface. The output from this module is a set of time varying forces and torques (Chapter 16).

- The low-level dynamics module – the equations that control the motion of the objects in the environment. These depend on the nature of the objects and the environment.

- A module that performs the numerical integration

(14.7.1)

A general dynamics module

Now that we have defined all the necessary equations that specify the motion of an unconstrained body in space, it is straightforward to set up a simulation. We maintain a state vector for the body as:

$$\boldsymbol{S}(t) = [\boldsymbol{x}(t), \boldsymbol{R}(t), \boldsymbol{M}(t), \boldsymbol{L}(t)]$$

where, to remind ourselves:

x is the current position

R is the current rotation matrix specifying the orientation of the body frame with respect to the world frame

M is the current linear momentum

L is the current angular momentum

and this evolves in time as the simulation proceeds. We calculate $S(t + dt)$ by calculating and integrating the differential state vector

$$\frac{d}{dt} S(t) = [v(t),\ \omega{}^{\star}R(t),\ F(t),\ \tau(t)]$$

In most cases it is not necessary to store M; for linear velocity, since $v = M/m$ we can integrate it directly. However, in many situations we may need to change momentum: new forces may be introduced or there may be an exchange of linear and angular momentum. We store angular momentum because we compute angular velocity from it.

The steps of the simulation are as follows:

(1) **Determine/compute/get from input and sum individual sources and torques**

$F(t),\ \tau(t)$

(2) **Integration**

Update position

$x(t + dt) = x(t) + dt v(t)$

Update orientation

$R(t + dt) = R(t) + dt \omega(t)\ {}^{\star}R(t)$

Update momentum

$M(t + dt) = M(t) + dt F(t)$

$L(t + dt) = L(t) + dt \tau(t)$

(3) **Calculate those quantities that depend on the integrated values (auxiliaries)**

$v(t + dt) = M(t + dt)/m$

$\omega(t + dt) = I^{-1}(t)L(t + dt)$

$I^{-1}(t + dt) = R(t + dt)\ I^{-1}_{body}(t)R(t + dt)^{T}$

(4) **Go to (1)**

This is a general simulation of an unconstrained rigid body subject to both applied forces and torque. It has to be particularised with the application dependencies that will supply initial conditions and applied forces and torques. Nevertheless we now have a tool where the application complexities are effectively separated from the simulation.

A potential problem with $\boldsymbol{R}(t)$ (and one of the motivations for using quaternions (see Chapter 13) to represent orientation) is that numerical drift will cause the matrix to drift out of orthogonality. A rotation matrix drifting out of orthogonality may cause problems in a computer graphics simulation – the transformation is no longer pure rotation. At each frame of the simulation $\boldsymbol{R}(t)$ will be applied to the polygon vertices as part of the rendering process and this may cause the object to skew and scale noticeably.

If there is more than one object in the game then we will maintain a separate simulation for each body. We could view these as independent modules which are executed in (simulated) parallel, exchanging momentum when they collide. After a collision each module has its initial values rest by the collision response calculations.

Finally, in practice we cannot use such a simple integration scheme. Errors quickly accumulate and in practice we must make a more intelligent choice for dt other than a fixed step (Section 14.8).

14.7.2   Determining exact collision time

Integrated into the above scheme will be a collision detection (Chapter 15) determination and a collision response calculation. If a collision is detected then a collision response calculation is initiated and we have to consider a subtlety involving the time of collision.

The usual model for collision detection is to advance from state $\boldsymbol{S}(t)$ to state $\boldsymbol{S}(t + dt)$ where dt is some step size and assume that if there were no collisions at time t and also none at time $t + dt$ then none occurred in between. The weakness of this approach with respect to fast-moving objects and 'thin' static ones is obvious. The other problem is that, in general, a collision will always be detected after objects have passed into each other. This means that the time of collision is inaccurate. Some help is given by adaptive stepsize integrators but these can cause large variations in frame rate.

If impulse dynamics is being used, the exact time of collision is required and this has to be done by controlling the integrator in such a way that it goes back in time then steps forward so that a state is simulated with the objects just colliding. Consider that we have just deteced a collision because we have found, say, a vertex of polygon P inside polygon Q (Figure 15.12). This means that the exact collision has occurred sometime between t and $t + dt$. The integrator control algorithm is as follows:

Find the shortest distance from vertex P and the edges of Q – d_{in} (conventionally negative)

Get the state at time t and repeat this process – d_{out} (positive)

$$t_e = t + dt \frac{d_{out}}{d_{out} - d_{in}}$$

The integrator is used to compute $x(t_e)$ and this gives a new interpenetration point d'

if d' is positive {t_e is too early} **then** recurse in the interval $[t_e, t + dt]$

if d' is negative {t_e is too late} **then** recurse in the interval $[t, t_e]$

terminate recursion when $|d'| <$ tolerance

The practical problem with this process is cost. Whenever a collision is detected, a single time step in the simulation is replaced by however many steps are required to position the simulation at the current time.

(14.7.3)

Application dependencies

The structure of a simulation will also follow from the application. For example, an 'asteroids' application that consists of N objects moving around in the environment might be as follows:

(1) Collision detection – a minimum distance tracking algorithm (Chapter 15) is suitable for this application. From this we can determine a maximum time for evolving the system before we need to check for collision. The collision detection module can maintain an estimated time of collision for each pair of close objects. The pair that has minimum time defines the safe time interval.

(2) Move the objects – evolve the system forward within this time interval, moving each object according to its equations of motion. Note that each object can be moved independent of the others and so this phase is completely parallelisable.

(3) At the end of this interval we check the critical pair of objects for collision. If they have collided the collision response module is entered and new initial paths computed for the colliding objects.

(14.7.4)

Simple examples

Dynamic simulation for a projectile

This is a simple initial value problem – a gun firing a projectile or a footballer kicking a ball (if no spin is implemented). The initial values are kicked into the simulation which then proceeds.

initial values – position, elevation and muzzle velocity – given/input

$x(0) = x_{gun}$

$y(0) = y_{gun}$

$z(0) = z_{gun}$

$v_x(0) = \boldsymbol{v}(0) \cos \theta_i$

$v_y(0) = \boldsymbol{v}(0) \sin \theta_i$

assume without loss of generality that the projectile is travelling in the xy plane $v_z(t) = 0$ for all t

$\theta(0) = \theta_i$

assume air resistance $\boldsymbol{F}_{air}(t) = f(|\boldsymbol{v}(t)^2|)\boldsymbol{v}_{unit} = f(v_x^2 + v_y^2)\boldsymbol{v}_{unit}$

where $f = A\rho k$ and

A is the cross-sectional area

ρ is the air density

k is the drag coefficient

simulation loop

update position

$\boldsymbol{x}(t + dt) = \boldsymbol{x}(t) + dt\boldsymbol{v}(t)$

update velocity components

$v_x(t + dt) = v_x(t) - dt\left(\dfrac{\boldsymbol{F}_{air}(t)}{m} \cos\theta(t)\right)$

$v_y(t + dt) = v_y(t) - dt\left(g + \dfrac{\boldsymbol{F}_{air}(t)}{m} \sin\theta(t)\right)$

Auxiliaries

$\boldsymbol{F}_{air}(t + dt) = f(v_x^2(t + dt) + v_y^2(t + dt))$

$\theta(t + dt) = \tan^{-1}(v_x(t + dt)/v_y(t + dt))$

(Note that in this example there are no new forces being injected and we have integrated the velocity directly.)

Kinematic solution for the same problem

The purpose of this section is to demonstrate the relative ease of the simulation compared to the kinematic solution.

The projectile problem is, of course, an initial value problem that can be solved kinematically and if we ignore, for simplicity, the air resistance, we have:

$\boldsymbol{F}_y = -mg$

thus at time $t = 0$ we have:

$$\ddot{x} = 0 \qquad \ddot{y} = -g \qquad \ddot{z} = 0$$

and integrating gives:

$$\dot{x} = c_1 \qquad \dot{y} = -gt + c_2 \qquad \dot{z} = c_3$$

Without loss of generality we can orient our coordinate system so that the ball travels in the xy plane, and define:

$$\dot{x}_{|t=0} = v_0 \cos \theta \qquad \dot{y}_{|t=0} = v_0 \sin \theta \qquad \dot{z}_{|t=0} = 0$$

where v_0 is the magnitude of the initial velocity and θ its angle. Thus:

$$c_1 = v_0 \cos \theta \qquad c_2 = v_0 \sin \theta \qquad c_3 = 0$$

and integrating again gives

$$x = v_0 \cos \theta t + c_4 \qquad y = -\frac{gt^2}{2} + v_0 \sin \theta t + c_5 \qquad z = c_6$$

and since:

$$x(0) = 0 \qquad y(0) = 0 \qquad z(0) = 0$$

we have finally the kinematic equations of the motion:

$$x = v_0 \cos \theta t \qquad y = -\frac{gt^2}{2} + v_0 \sin \theta t \qquad z = 0$$

which is of course a parabola in the xy plane.

Kicked football

This is just a generalisation of the previous problem except that now the projectile/ball can have a spin imparted to it. We shall assume the ball is stationary originally and ignore all aerodynamics apart from air resistance and lift due to spin.

If the kick is also part of a simulation we can use the collision response equation to calculate $\boldsymbol{v}(0)$ and $\boldsymbol{\omega}(0)$. Here we assume the impulse dynamics model which is that there is an instantaneous change in velocity without a change in position and that the ball starts from a stationary position with a finite velocity. Thus the simulation for the ball begins, just as for the projectile, with a non-zero $\boldsymbol{v}(0)$.

(In reality the gun/kicked ball problems are also connected. Muzzle velocities of guns are determined by firing a bullet, at close range, into a 'ballistic pendulum', then calculating the velocity of the bullet from the angle through which the pendulum swings.)

The simulation is exactly the same as before except that now we have an angular momentum and the ball spins. If we leave the simulation as it is then the path the ball takes will be no different from the path without spin – as if the ball was kicked so that F passes through the centre. In practice, spin affects the trajectory of a ball because there is a lift due to the turbulence created by the spin. The air pressure is less on the side of the ball that is moving less quickly through the air. This lift force is a function of the angular velocity (direction of the spin) and the relative velocity between the ball and the wind ($\boldsymbol{v}$ for no wind or still air).

So we add a positive force to the equation for $\boldsymbol{v}$.

$$\boldsymbol{F}_{\text{lift}} = f(|\boldsymbol{v}|^2)\ (\boldsymbol{\omega} \times \boldsymbol{v})/(|\ (\boldsymbol{\omega} \times \boldsymbol{v}|)$$

where $f = A\rho k$ and A and ρ are as before and k is a lift coefficient that depends on $|\omega|$

Using quasi-statics

Classical dynamics usually studies single-state problems. Games scenarios try to imitate real life where most interesting problems are multi-state. Consider a racing car simulation. In a perfect simulation we use the same simulator – the same set of equations – whether the car is travelling with four wheels on the ground or tumbling through the air. However, it may be that we want to use a different simulator for different states as a complexity-reducing tool. It is not the case that a complete simulation covering every state is not available, just that considering the problem as different states leads to a simpler overall solution. We may have different granularities for different states; when the car is tumbling through the

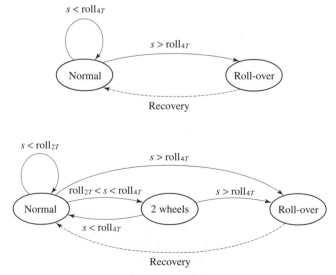

Figure 14.6
Multi-state problems as
state transition diagrams.

air we may want to terminate the action with an explosion. In this case we can consider the problem as a multi-state model and use a simple test to indicate when a transition should occur from one simulator to another.

Figure 14.6 shows a simple example of a car. The forward normal driving under user control passes to a roll-over module when the roll-over condition is exceeded. The roll-over may terminate the action or return to the normal driving mode. Presumably the roll-over module would not be under user control. A more complex framework results if we consider an intermediate state where the car is driven on two wheels. Clearly there are now four transitions possible between the three states. Also, in the intermediate state stunt driving is possible, indicated by the loop.

Many state transitions can be handled by quasi-statics which just means using equilibrium rules at any time instant as if the dynamic model were a static structure. We will look at the simple example of roll-over in a car. The program states are, for example, the current position, which gives the current road condition (flat, incline, decline or banked) and the current attitude of the car: travelling ahead in a straight line, turning or (catastrophically) overturned.

An approximate dynamic simulation can be very simple and consist of a vehicle which has the axles rigidly attached to the car body; in other words, no suspension. This gives us a simulation of just three equations, which control the car's behaviour, and whether or not it is about to overturn. These are:

$$\sum_i \boldsymbol{F}_\mathrm{f} = m\boldsymbol{a}_\mathrm{c}$$

$$\sum_i \boldsymbol{F}_\mathrm{p} = 0$$

$$\sum_i M = 0$$

where

$\boldsymbol{F}_\mathrm{f}$ is the tractive force applied at the surface on which the car travels in the direction of the linear acceleration

$\boldsymbol{F}_\mathrm{p}$ is the force perpendicular to the tractive force

M represents the moments of all forces about the mass centre (non-bold to distinguish it from the linear momentum)

Note that the car moves forward or slows down by the tractive force which acts as a frictional force between the road surface and the tyres. The engine or the brakes only supply power to the wheels. Thus for a car accelerating in a straight line on a flat surface we have (Figure 14.7(b))

$$\boldsymbol{F}_\mathrm{t} = m\boldsymbol{a}_\mathrm{c}$$

$$mg = \boldsymbol{R}_\mathrm{r} + \boldsymbol{R}_\mathrm{f}$$

$$\boldsymbol{F}_\mathrm{t}h + \boldsymbol{R}_\mathrm{f}l_1 = \boldsymbol{R}_\mathrm{r}l_2$$

The last equation implies an anti-clockwise moment which tends to lift the front wheels off the ground. For a normal car we assume that the weight is sufficient

Figure 14.7
Forces for quasi-static calculations for a vehicle. (a) Vehicle coordinate system (Society of Automotive Engineers Inc.). (b) Forward motion in a straight line. (c) Steady state turning. (d) Steady state banked turning compared to (c). F_s decreases, R_i and R_o increase.

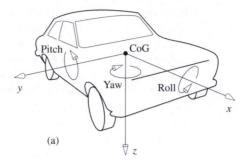

(a)

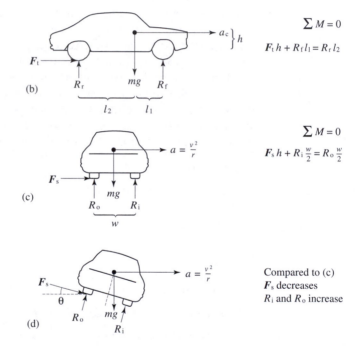

(b)

$$\sum M = 0$$

$$F_t h + R_f l_1 = R_r l_2$$

(c)

$$\sum M = 0$$

$$F_s h + R_i \frac{w}{2} = R_o \frac{w}{2}$$

(d)

Compared to (c)
F_s decreases
R_i and R_o increase

to keep it on the road (although the front end will move up for a real car with suspension). In a drag-racing car, however, because of the position of the centre of gravity and of course $|F_t|$, it is easy to cause the front wheels to lift off the ground ($R_f = 0$).

An important point that should be mentioned here is that we have in this trivial simulation **implicitly** implemented a constraint by *not* implementing any wheel slip whatever the magnitude of the tractive force – we assume that the coefficient of friction between the tyres and the road surface is such that slippage will not occur.

We now consider the forces of the car travelling around a bend on a surface (Figure 14.7(c)). In a steady state turn the vehicle will now be subject to a centripetal acceleration of v^2/r directed towards the centre of a circle whose circumference forms the bend. This is manifested in a sideways frictional force $\boldsymbol{F}_s$ between the tyres and the road and using the same three equations as before we have:

$$\boldsymbol{F}_s = m\,\frac{v^2}{r}$$

$$mg = \boldsymbol{R}_o + \boldsymbol{R}_i$$

$$\boldsymbol{F}_s h + \boldsymbol{R}_i\,\frac{w}{2} = \boldsymbol{R}_o\,\frac{w}{2}$$

This implies that $\boldsymbol{R}_o$ is greater than $\boldsymbol{R}_i$ and if v and r are such that $\boldsymbol{R}_i$ goes to zero then the car overturns.

A banked road, of course, ameliorates the situation – indeed that is its *raison d'être* and we now have (Figure 14.7(d)):

$$\boldsymbol{F}_s \cos\theta = m\,\frac{v^2}{r}$$

$$mg + \boldsymbol{F}_s \sin\theta = (\boldsymbol{R}_o + \boldsymbol{R}_i)\cos\theta$$

$$\boldsymbol{F}_s h + \boldsymbol{R}_i\,\frac{w}{2} = \boldsymbol{R}_o\,\frac{w}{2}$$

The effect of banking is to decrease $\boldsymbol{F}_s$ and to increase both wheel reaction forces, thus reducing the roll-over tendency. The reaction forces now have a horizontal component which assists in producing the required acceleration, reducing the friction force.

Now to return to an earlier point which is that the granularity and thus the accuracy of the simulation depends on its application. In this context it is instructive now to examine the deficiencies in the above simulation.

Consider the roll-over calculation. In practice, a car would have suspension and in a turn this causes lateral shift in the centre of gravity of the suspended mass. In this case the suspension characteristics and the roll rate (the angular velocity about the x axis) have to be considered. Furthermore, even if these factors are taken into account the calculations are 'quasi-static': they assume the car is executing a steady turn and there is no angular acceleration (yaw) about the vertical z axis through the CoG. Quasi-static calculations cannot, for example, model the transient behaviour of the inner wheels lifting off the ground and returning because of interactions between suspension components; they simply determine for the current condition a roll-over threshold. Thus in such a simulation, once the threshold had been reached by the driver, there is no possibility of recovery – the car rolls. In practice, this kind of roll-over rarely occurs for family cars because a driver will not steer the car into a steady-state turn that will cause roll-over. The driver makes transient adjustments to the steering all the time and roll-over in a family car usually occurs when a car slides and strikes an obstruction – a so-called tripped roll-over. This occurrence is far more difficult to model.

Apart from the non-implementation of suspension, another critical factor is the physics of the tyres and the tyre–road surface interaction. The entire behaviour of the car is determined by the contact forces between the four tyres and the road surface. If the vehicle is not travelling in a straight line then the lateral forces developed can cause the tyres to slip or skid. The characteristics of tyres, temperature, wear and inflation pressure, change as the car is driven and are, of course, critically important in F1 car racing.

Aerodynamic effects, although easily modelled at low speeds as a simple braking function proportional to the square of the speed, become increasingly complex at high speeds where the shape of the car needs to be taken into account.

Thus this simple example demonstrates that accurate dynamic simulations can be extremely complex and are properly a part of mechanical engineering design rather than computer graphics. A would-be animator usually resorts to a simplified simulation both in terms of those aspects modelled and the accuracy of the modelling.

Pre-calculated vs. on-line simulation

One of the main speed-up tools of real time rendering is pre-calculation, the best example being the use of BSP trees in conjunction with PVS. There is no reason why the same philosophy cannot be applied in dynamic simulation and, just as in real-time rendering, a mix between off-line and on-line calculations are likely to result.

In any simulation we have to set up the equations for the physical system in advance and the efficacy of the simulation depends ultimately on how accurately our equations represent the system. If we have an application where all the inputs are predictable then we can solve the system in advance, either analytically or by running an off-line simulation, storing the results and using the pre-calculated solution on-line.

The use of pre-calculated data is likely to be most feasible for increasing the granularity of a basic simulation. An example of this might be the use of tyre behaviour data under a variety of different conditions.

Space time constraints

We will now return to the example we began with, *Luxo Jr.* In the previous sections we have given examples of dynamic simulation. This type of simulation is known as an initial value problem or forward simulation. The user inputs initial value(s) – albeit continuously in the case of computer games – and the motion is then completely determined by the equations used to perform the simulation. This is adequate for the simple examples above, but certainly for most types of off-line animation and perhaps interactive animation in the future, greater control is required. Animators are more likely to specify motion for a dynamic simulation that makes it a two-point boundary value problem. Such problems are far more difficult to solve. In such animation the animator wants to specify that the ball is to be kicked by the player, execute physically based motion in flight, and land at a particular point. Because of the computational requirements such simulations are currently constrained to be off-line.

The success of the early classic computer animations, such as *Luxo Jr.*, was due to the artistry of the animator who specified and tuned the motion. The role of the computer in such productions was to interpolate and render, the animator retaining complete control over the motion. In this section we will describe the basis of important developments whose aim is to enable the animator to exploit the realistic motion that results from dynamic simulation without the loss of control that the use of initial value systems implies.

Witkin and Kass (1988) introduced the concept of space time constraints, using as an example a (planar) model of *Luxo Jr.* parametrized by four joint angles and translation (Figure 14.8). These parameters, and only these, would be controlled by an animator using a conventional animation system. The aim of the study was to enable a physically based animation together with high-level control by allowing the animator to specify:

- *What* the character has to do, for instance 'jump from here to there'

- *How* the motion should be performed, for instance 'don't waste energy' or 'come down hard enough to spatter whatever you land upon'

- What the character's *physical structure* is – what the pieces are shaped like, what they weigh, how they are connected etc.

- What physical resources are available to the character to accomplish the desired motion, for instance the character's muscles...a floor to push off from etc.

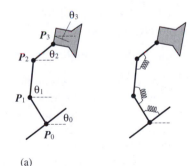

(a)

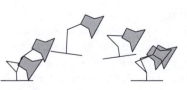

(b)

Figure 14.8
Witkin and Kass's simulation of *Luxo Jr.* (Based on an illustration in Witkin and Kass (1988).) A planar model constructed of rigid links and frictionless joints. (b) The simulation of a jump.

Commenting on the success of their approach, Witkins and Kass state:

> . . . making a Luxo lamp execute a convincing jump just by telling it where to start and end. The results...show that such properties as anticipation, follow-through, squash and stretch, and timing indeed emerge from a bare description of the motion's purpose and the physical context in which it occurs.

Such motion subtleties, developed as part of the animator's art by Disney animators in the 1930s, are precisely the effects that John Lasseter manually built into the original animation. The potential of the approach is not only to give the animator control over a physically based animation but to engender a higher-level motion control, leaving the physical model to take care of its own detailed movements.

The solution to such a problem is then a set of five motion curves – one for translation and four for the joint angles. These are a function both of time and of the positional constraints given by the animator or which emerge from some higher-level scripting control – hence the term space time constraints.

A solution is enabled by introducing an objective function which is minimised together with the constraints, which in this case comprise the initial and final pose and position. The framework of the solution algorithm is then: find the set of joint angle motion curves that minimises the objective function subject to the constraints. The forces in the system are 'muscle' forces, the contact force between the floor and the base and gravity. Muscles are simulated by three angular springs joining the links at each joint, where the spring force is given by:

$$\boldsymbol{F}_i = k_i(\varphi_i - \rho_i)$$

where

k_i is the spring stiffness

φ_i is the joint angle

ρ_i is the rest angle

Both the stiffness and rest angle are allowed to vary. The springs are used to build the objective function which optimises the motion's mechanical efficiency by ensuring that minimum power is consumed by the muscles at each time step, where muscle power is the product of the muscle force and the joint's angular velocity. The key point here is that the system solves for the character's motion and time-varying muscle force over the entire interval of interest rather than progressing sequentially through time. The system works by accepting space time constraints as input, then searching for a solution that, say, minimises the power consumed by the muscles.

This example demonstrates both the potential of the approach and its limitations. Essentially this is a simple model. The complexity growth of the problem is severe for 'creatures' that we would like to animate and more recent research on space time constraints has concentrated on addressing this problem.

14.8 Numerical integration

In our development of a dynamic simulator we used Euler integration. Unfortunately, although simple, this method is too inaccurate to be used in practice. Accurate dynamic simulation requires a rudimentary knowledge of numerical integration techniques and in this section we present a series of methods starting with Euler integration. If your application requires an accurate simulation, a knowledge of such techniques is mandatory. We simply present an outline here; implementation details are to be found in Press *et al.* (1988). The methods appear in order of increasing accuracy (and computational expense). We start by looking at the nature of inaccuracy in Euler integration and use this as a basis from which to derive more accurate methods.

14.8.1 Euler method and errors

The simulations that we considered are first-order initial value problems of the type:

$$dx/dt = f(x,t)$$

Euler integration uses a simple difference to step forward in time:

$$x_{i+1} = x_i + \Delta t f(x,t)$$
$$= x_i + h f(x,t)$$

We decide on a value for h, substitute the initial value at $t = 0$ and evaluate a solution. The extent of the inaccuracy can be seen from a simple example:

$$dx/dt + x^2 = 0 \qquad x(0) = 1$$

which for 10 steps at $h = 0.1$ gives 0.462878, compared with the exact value calculated from the analytical solution:

$$x = 1/(1 + t)$$

of 0.5.

The nature of the error can be seen by examining Figure 14.9 which shows Euler solutions for:

$$dx/dt = x^2 t e^{-t} \qquad x(0) = 0.91$$

for values of $h = 0.05$, 0.025 and 0.0125. The complete set of all solutions is represented by a vector field in the (x,t) plane and for a particular initial value, the solution is represented by the curve which is everywhere tangential to the field lines. Thus the vector field and a particular initial value determines the exact solution curve. We can now see why the Euler method can never be correct. If we consider discrete points then we construct a piecewise linear solution curve which can only be approximately tangential to the vector field between the

Figure 14.9
The Euler-method solutions
of $dx/dt = x^2te^{-t}$ for
$h = 0.05$, 0.025 and 0.0125.
From James, G., Burley, D.,
Clements, D., Dyke, P.,
Searl, J. and Wright, J.
(1996) Modern Engineering
Mathematics, 2nd edn,
Addison-Wesley, Harlow

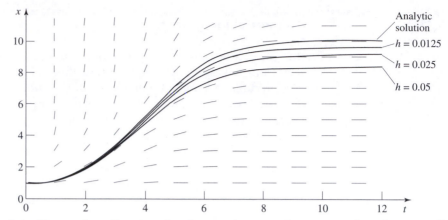

points. If we reduce the step size then we increase the accuracy but there is still an error and the solution curve always drifts away from the analytic solution because the next point is constructed from the previous point which is itself in error.

The error can be quantified by using the Taylor series expansion which is an infinite series giving the value at the end of a step in terms of the value at the beginning. The Taylor series expansion for $x(t)$ is:

$$x(t + h) = x(t) + h\frac{dx}{dt}(t) + \frac{h^2}{2!}\frac{d^2x}{dt^2}(t) + \frac{h^3}{3!}\frac{d^3x}{dt^3} + \ldots$$

truncating this after the second term and representing the truncated terms by $O(h^2)$, we have:

$$x(t + h) = x(t) + h\frac{dx}{dt}(t) + O(h^2)$$

If we return to our Euler scheme and write:

$$X(t + h) = x(t) + hf(x,t)$$

where we now use upper case X to denote a numerical approximation, we have, combining the previous two equations:

$$X(t + h) = x(t + h) + O(h^2)$$

and this equation states that the truncation error in a single step is $O(h^2)$. However, the error in a complete solution is an accumulation of all the single step errors. Say we want to compute:

$$X(t_0 + T)$$

This will require T/h steps where each step acquires an error of $O(h^2)$ resulting in a total error of:

$$(T/h)\, O(h^2)$$

which means that the total error is linear in h, or halving the step size in an Euler solution halves the error in the solution. The single step error and the total error are known as the local and global error respectively. Finally we simplify the notation and quote the general Euler formula as:

$$X_{n+1} = X_n + hF_n$$

14.8.2

Multi-step methods – Adams–Bashforth

The first improvement that we can make to the accuracy of the Euler method is to consider a Taylor series expansion truncating after the first three terms:

$$x(t + h) = x(t) + h\frac{dx}{dt}(t) + \frac{h^2}{2!}\frac{d^2x}{dt^2}(t) + O(h^3) \qquad [14.2]$$

and we can show as before that any method based on this formula will have a local error $O(h^3)$. However we now require an analytic expression for:

$$\frac{d^2x}{dt^2}(t)$$

A way around this problem leads to the family of methods known as Adams–Bashforth. We first write the Taylor series expansion for the function dx/dt for increments of $-h$:

$$\frac{dx}{dt}(t - h) = \frac{dx}{dt}(t) - h\frac{d^2x}{dt^2} + \frac{h^2}{2!}\frac{d^3x}{dt^3} - O(h^3)$$

or writing only the first two terms and rearranging gives:

$$h\frac{d^2x}{dt^2}(t) = \frac{dx}{dt}(t) - \frac{dx}{dt}(t - h) + O(h^2)$$

substituting this into Equation 14.2 gives

$$x(t + h) = x(t) + \frac{h}{2}\left(3\frac{dx}{dt}(t) - \frac{dx}{dt}(t - h)\right) + O(h^3)$$

This can be written as:

$$X_{n+1} = X_n + \frac{1}{2}h(3F_n - F_{n-1})$$

which is the second-order Adams–Bashforth method. The first four members of this family are:

$$X_{n+1} = X_n + hF_n$$

$$X_{n+1} = X_n + \frac{1}{2}h(3F_n - F_{n-1})$$

$$X_{n+1} = X_n + \frac{1}{12}h(23F_n - 16F_{n-1} + 5F_{n-2})$$

$$X_{n+1} = X_n + \frac{1}{24} h(55F_n - 59F_{n-1} + 37F_{n-2} - 9F_{n-3})$$

where we can note that the first-order formula is identical to the Euler formula. These are called multi-step methods because they involve values of the derivative of the dependent variable at more than one value of the independent variable. This, of course, raises the problem of how do we start them off and we have to use one method to start the computation and another for the main computation. For the second-order formula we could use the first-order formula for the first step.

14.8.3 Predictor–corrector

This method is best demonstrated geometrically. It can be shown, again using Taylor's series, that it is a second-order method. Its disadvantage is that two evaluations are required for each step but it is 'self starting' – no special procedure is necessary to start the computation. The first evaluation results in the predicted value and this is then used to make a more accurate calculation – the corrected value. The predicted value can use the Euler formula:

predicted value: $X_{n+1}^P = X_n + hF_n$

$$= X_n + hf(t_n, X_n)$$

This is then used in the corrected formula as:

corrected value $X_{n+1} = X_n + \frac{1}{2} h(f(t_n, X_n) + f(t_{n+1}, X_{n+1}^P))$

The method is most easily conceptualised graphically. Consider Figure 14.10 which shows that the corrected value is arrived at by taking the average of the gradient at t_n and t_{n+1}.

In algorithmic terms we:

march forward to from point A to point B by using the gradient at A. This determines the intercept with the t_{n+1} ordinate:

$$d_1 = hf(t_n, X_n)$$

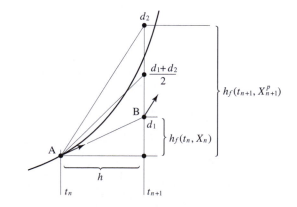

Figure 14.10
Prediction–corrector
method.

we return to point A and use the gradient from point B to determine the intercept with the t_{n+1} ordinate:

$$d_2 = h\, f(t_{n+1}, X_{n+1}^P)$$

The intercept we require is then given by the average

$$(d_1 + d_2)/2$$

Effectively we are assuming that the average gradient over the interval is equal to the average of the gradients at each end of the interval. This contrasts with the Euler method which assumes that the average gradient over the interval is equal to the gradient at the start. The difference between the Euler step and the predictor–corrector step is then

$$(d_2 - d_1)/2$$

Runge–Kutta

Runge–Kutta methods are also self-starting and can be seen as an extension of the predictor–corrector approach of averaging gradients. This time the interval $t_{n+1} - t_n$ is subdivided and more gradients are used. The formula for a fourth-order Runge–Kutta is:

$$d_1 = hf(t_n, X_n)$$

$$d_2 = hf(t_n + \frac{1}{2}h, X_n + \frac{1}{2}d_1)$$

$$d_3 = hf(t_n + \frac{1}{2}h, X_n + \frac{1}{2}d_2)$$

$$d_4 = hf(t_n + h, X_n + d_3)$$

$$X_{n+1} = X_n + \frac{1}{6}(d_1 + 2d_2 + 2d_3 + d_4)$$

Figure 14.11 shows a geometric visualisation of the formula as:

(1) March forward to point B using the gradient at A.
(2) Return to A. March forward to point C using the gradient at point B.
(3) Return to A. March forward to point D using the gradient at point C.
(4) Return to A. March forward to point E using the gradient at point D.

Adaptive step size

All of the foregoing methods have used equal steps. It is clear that step size is critical in real-time applications and one way to increase the accuracy of the Euler method, while retaining its inherent simplicity and low cost, is to adopt a

Figure 14.11
A visualisation of the fourth-order Runge–Kutta method.

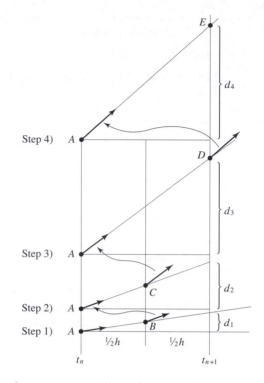

method where the step size is allowed to vary. This means that we continually monitor the truncation error and adjust h up or down so that the magnitude of the error is within some predefined limit. The easiest way to monitor error is to obtain an estimate from 'step doubling'. That is, we compute a solution for a step X_1 using a single step of h and a solution X_2 using two steps $h/2$. We then propose that the difference between the two solutions:

$$\Delta = |X_1 - X_2| = O(h^2)$$

is a good estimate of the truncation error and implement a change in the step length:

$$\left(\frac{E}{\Delta}\right)^{1/2} h$$

where E is the predefined maximum tolerable error. We are now performing three evaluations per step and, compared with the double-step solution, this implies 1.5 times extra computation as the overhead for the truncation error monitoring.

If we apply the same method to the fourth-order Runge–Kutta then 11 evaluations are required per step (3×4 derivatives minus one common derivative $-d_1$) for both the single and double-step evaluation. Thus the extra computation for error monitoring with fourth-order Runge–Kutta is 1.375 times extra computation per step.

Collision detection

15.1   Broad phase/narrow phase algorithms

15.2   Bounding volume hierarchies

15.3   Broad phase collision detection with AABBs

15.4   Broad phase collision detection with OBBs

15.5   Broad phase collision detection with local or object spatial partitioning

15.6   Narrow phase collision detection

15.7   Single phase approaches

Introduction

In this chapter we will deal with the important topic of collision detection. Its importance, and the amount of research that has been carried out on this topic, make it deserve a chapter to itself. One of the main emphases of collision detection, and the reason why the material runs to a whole chapter, compared to the small coverage of collision response, is the need for efficiency. In a simple simulation a collision detection check has to be carried out for every time step – an operation whose cost increases steeply with scene complexity.

Collision detection is used in two main contexts – it detects any collision between objects which an application allows to collide and it is used in path planning where an animation agent may need to be sent along a path that keeps it maximally clear of other objects. Although much theoretical research is devoted to the N independently moving objects problem, the common scenario in both games and VR is one or a few moving objects in a static environment.

The phrase tends to be applied loosely to any of the following:

- detecting the occurrence of a collision between two objects;

- detecting a collision occurrence and the point of contact to some degree of accuracy;

- detecting the point of contact and modelling a response.

The first two operations are geometric and the third requires a dynamic model, as we saw in the previous chapter.

A simple taxonomy of the field can be drawn up in terms of the way in which the testing is divided up; in particular, whether or not we attempt an early or easy test that eliminates as many objects as possible. The taxonomy is:

- **Broad phase/narrow phase algorithms**
  - **Broad phase** (cull away pairs of objects that cannot possibly collide)
    A broad phase procedure can use one or a combination of:
    Games rules or context
    Spatial partitioning in world space
    Spatial partitioning in local space
    Bounding volumes (spheres, AABBs and OBBs) and bounding volume hierarchies
  - **Narrow phase** (applies accurate collision detection)
    Polyhedron/polyhedron testing
    Lin-Canny closest feature tracking
    Separating planes
  - **Methods that serve either phase**
    Bounding volume hierarchies
    Spatial partitioning in local space
    Z-buffer

- **Single phase methods**
  - Using a single partitioning method for the entire process (Hubbard's sphere trees, for example)
  - Using the popular BSP tree partitioning scheme (for both rendering and collision detection)

- **Strategies**

  All algorithms that claim real-time performance use one or more of the following strategies:

  Exploit spatial/temporal coherence – objects tend to occupy the same region of space from one frame to another.

  Pre-calculation – there is considerable investment in a pre-calculation or off-line phase. (This has a long history in real-time graphics. Early flight simulators (1969) used list priority algorithms for hidden surface removal.) Of course, by definition, spatial partitioning and bounding volumes involve some degree of pre-calculation.

Collision detection is currently a very active research area and no universally popular algorithm has emerged. In this respect it is somewhat reminiscent of the research activity in hidden surface removal algorithms in the 1970s, prior to the adoption of the Z-buffer algorithm as the *de facto* standard, which happened as soon as memory availability facilitated this.

Much of the research in collision detection addresses the 'N-body' problem – the worst-case scenario of N unconstrained objects all moving around a scene. However, complexity deriving from a large value of N may not be as important a scenario as complexity that derives from the intra-object complexity. For example, Held *et al.* (1995) describe a research project at the Boeing Aircraft Co. where a proposed VR system is required to check for collision between a moving object – a virtual hand (5000–10 000) polygons, say – and a set of static obstacles (of say 5–10 million polygons) at 20 fps.

In games applications, of course, there are context-dependent constraints which can be exploited to reduce the cost of a general approach. Such strategies result in either particularisations of the general approach or game-specific algorithms.

In what follows we shall consider algorithms for convex polyhedra only. Procedures for non-convex polyhedra are uncommon at the moment and most approach the inherent difficulties by breaking the object into a set of convex polyhedra. A comprehensive survey of algorithms that deal with other representations is given in Lin and Gottschalk (1998).

The most popular approach to solving the general case is the use of a broad phase/narrow phase strategy where bounding volumes, or some other scheme such as spatial partitioning, is used to cull away pairs that cannot collide. This is followed by a narrow phase calculation that determines whether unculled pairs collide and finds the intersection to within some degree of accuracy. Culling strategies are important in real-time rendering of complex scenes. Here, view frustum culling is a process wherein objects or parts of the scene are eliminated from the rendering pipeline if they do not intersect the view frustum. View frustum culling is in effect no different from culling in collision detection, except that one of the objects – the view frustum – is of fixed shape.

A selection of common bounding volumes are shown as two-dimensional analogies in Figure 15.1 from which it is easily seen that they exhibit different 'bounding efficiencies' – the amount of empty space that is inside the bounding volume (BV) but outside the object. The rationale for bounding volumes is that

Figure 15.1
Bounding volumes (2D analogue).

| Sphere | Axis aligned AABB | Oriented regtangaloid OBB | Discrete orientation polytope k-dop ($k = 8$ in this example) |

testing for an intersection between two pairs of bounding volumes is far quicker than testing between two objects. However, this advantage is obviated if an expensive test is entered, because the BVs intersect, despite the objects themselves not intersecting.

Collision detection is a problem whose expense is a quadratic function of the number of moving objects in the scene and their complexity (average number of faces per object). This is easy to see for the standard approach to collision detection – a broad phase followed by a narrow phase. A naïve broad phase algorithm has complexity $O(N^2/2)$ – the exact number of comparisons that have to be made is:

$$\frac{N^2 - N}{2}$$

Within this process an exact collision calculation for polyhedra will typically have complexity $O(n^2)$ where n is the number of faces per object.

We can compare this with a ray tracing intersection test – a much simpler collision detection problem. Here, the equivalent broad phase checks for intersection between a known object – the current ray – and the object bounding volumes and has complexity $O(N)$. The narrow phase in ray tracing – finding the ray/polygon intersection – has complexity $O(n)$. The other association that collision detection has to ray tracing is the extensive use of bounding volumes. When checking for collision between a pair of bounded objects we first invoke a (fast) intersection test between the objects' bounding volumes. If the bounding volumes do not collide then the objects cannot. Bounding volume checks are possibly the most popular approach to the broad phase of two-phase algorithms.

Another source of computational expense is what Hubbard (1993) refers to as the 'fixed-timestep weakness' combining with the 'all pairs weakness'. The fixed-timestep weakness is simply the application of an all-pairs algorithm at equal intervals in time – a wasteful approach unless the environment is going to produce a collision for each time interval. What is required is a sampling interval that is inversely proportional to the likelihood of collision.

Apart from the expense, there are other difficulties associated with temporal sampling. If the simulated velocity of objects is high with respect to the sampling rate for collision detection then objects can pass through each other without a collision being detected. In general, a collision will not be detected at the instant an impact occurs but at some time later when the colliding objects have moved into each others space. Some strategy is then necessary to determine the impact point; say, moving one of the objects back along its path (Section 14.7.2).

15.1 Broad phase/narrow phase algorithms

The most common approach at the moment, this structure tries to cull away pairs of moving objects that cannot possibly collide, leaving exact collision detection to be applied to the remaining pairs that survive the culling process. An important advantage of this strategy is that the choice of algorithm for each phase can be made independently. In this section we will look briefly at broad phase strategies. Many broad phase strategies exist – the use of time coherence, spatial partitioning or using spatial coherence, bounding volumes or any combination of these.

A direct method of exploiting time coherence is given by Hubbard (1993) where four-dimensional space-time bounding volumes are associated with an object. Hubbard shows that the four-dimensional object swept out by a three-dimensional moving object, moving with any motion from a start point, is a 'parabolic horn'. This is based on the contention that given a start position $x(0)$, an initial velocity $\dot{x}(0)$ and a bound on the magnitude of the acceleration, then the position of the object at time t is predicted to lie within the parabolic horn. Consider, for simplicity, that the moving object is a point:

given a scalar f

$$\left| \ddot{x}(t) \right| \leq f \qquad\qquad 0 \leq t \leq T$$

then it can be shown that

$$\left| x(t) - (x(0) + \dot{x}(0)t) \right| \leq \frac{f}{2} t^2 \qquad 0 \leq t \leq T$$

A geometric interpretation of this inequality is that at time t, the object is within a distance $\dfrac{f}{2} t^2$ from the point $x(0) + \dot{x}(0)t$. Thus a bound on the position of the object at time t is a sphere of radius $\dfrac{f}{2} t^2$ centred at $x(0) + \dot{x}(0)t$. A two-dimenional analogue is shown in Figure 15.2 where the parabolic horn is a function of (x,y,t). For a three-dimensional object in three-dimensional space, the horn is four-dimensional – a function of (x,y,z,t).

To simplify the intersection check, Hubbard bounds this with a four-dimensional trapezoid. The broad phase is based on calculating the earliest time that a collision can occur for any pair of objects and doing no further collision

Figure 15.2
A 3D 'parabolic horn' for a particle moving in 2D space.

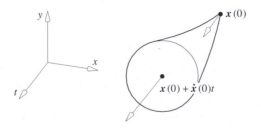

detection checking until that time has been reached. (The motivation of the work was collision detection for VR which must function in real time.) If two objects are to collide at some future time t then their space time bounds must intersect at some time $t' \leq t$ because the space time bounds are conservative in four-dimensional space just as bounding volumes are in three-dimensional space. The detection algorithm computes the earliest t' over all pairs of objects. This approach by definition ameliorates the constant timestep weakness and Hubbard also addresses the all-pairs weakness in the intersection test. If the path of the object(s) is known then a simpler bounding volume can be used to bound the space that the object occupies over a time interval. Whether there is prior knowledge of object motion is a function of the application.

Spatial coherency is most easily exploited by dividing the scene space up into unit cells. For interactive computer animation where the moving objects remain on the ground, the cells become a two-dimensional grid. Potential collisions are found by examining a cell to see if it contains more than one object. The problem with this simple approach is the optimal choice for the size of a cell and the algorithm is only really suitable for an environment where all the objects are more or less the same size.

The obvious enhancement to uniform spatial subdivision is to use an octree partitioning. To check for potential colliding pairs, the tree is descended and only those regions that contain more than one object are examined. In effect, the octree eliminates testing pairs of objects which are distant from each other. However, because objects are moving, the octree must be updated at each timestep. This can result in significant extra computation. Whether spatial partitioning is worthwhile or not depends on the number of objects N and the time taken to update the partitioning scheme. Testing for all pairs is approximately

$O(\frac{N^2}{2})$ and if we define $s(N)$ to be the number of pairs tested for exact collision

when we use spatial partitioning as a broad phase culling strategy then we have:

$$s(N)t_{exact} + t_{update} < \frac{N^2}{2} t_{exact}$$

where t_{exact} is the time for an exact collision detection

t_{update} is the time to update the spatial partitioning scheme

giving that the average number of exact collision tests per frame should be:

$$s(N) < \frac{N^2}{2} - \frac{t_{update}}{t_{exact}}$$

Another possible approach is to maintain, for each object, a list of nearest neighbours based on some distance threshold. This strategy can also admit an adaptive timestep. Cohen *et al.* (1995) maintain potential collision pairs that are in close proximity by sorting axis-aligned bounding boxes or AABBs.

The use of bounding boxes in broad phase collision detection is extremely common and four types of volumes are used (Figure 15.1): spheres, AABBs (bounding boxes aligned with the coordinate axis), OBBs (bounding boxes whose orientation 'best suits' the object they are bounding) and discrete orientation polytopes (objects made up of pairs of parallel planes). Spheres are easy but suffer from the disadvantage that their 'bounding efficiency' may be low. A bounding sphere for a long thin object is mainly empty space and most broad phase intersections would subsequently fail the narrow phase checks for such an object.

AABBs also result in low complexity and are generally more efficient at bounding objects than spheres but they have to be updated as an object moves. If a rotational component is involved in the movement then the efficiency of the bounding box will vary. OBBs on the other hand are defined with respect to the object and can be pre-computed, either algorithmically or manually, during modelling and do not change. OBBs can be set up for a particular object by considering the vertices as a set of points and applying a multivariate statistical technique known as principal component analysis (full details are given in Gottschalk *et al.* (1996).

The efficiency of bounding volumes can be quantified by employing a cost function first proposed by Weghorst *et al.* (1984) to analyse the effectiveness of hierarchical methods in ray tracing. This is:

$$T = N_v C_v + N_p C_p$$

where

T is the total cost of testing for interference between two large models represented by OBB trees

N_v is the number of bounding volume pair overlap tests

C_v is the cost of the bounding volume tests

N_p is the number of primitive pair tests

C_p is the cost of primitive pair tests

The idea of a tight bounding volume is to lower N_p as far as possible but this is usually at the expense of C_v. C_v for spheres and AABBs is much lower than that for OBBs. Also, collision detection differs from ray tracing in that we are in general comparing two complex objects. (In ray tracing one object is always a ray.) Gottschalk *et al.* (1996) point out that the overall cost depends on the relative placements of the models; when they are far apart sphere trees and AABB trees tend to cost less than OBB trees. They conclude that for large models in close proximity:

● C_v is one order higher than that for sphere trees and AABB trees.

● N_v and N_p for OBB trees are asymptotically lower than those for sphere and AABB trees.

Bounding volume hierarchies

A hierarchy in collision detection is either a spatial partitioning scheme, for example an octree or a BSP tree, or it is a hierarchy of bounding volumes (Figure 15.3). Another distinguishing factor is that some hierarchies terminate at object level and some continue to subdivide objects – we partition the space occupied by the object itself. This could be termed intra-object spatial partitioning to distinguish it from inter-object partitioning where, as we have seen, octrees are a common example. The most common approach seems to be to use a hierarchy down to the level of the object for fast culling as a broad phase then use a narrow phase within the leaves of the tree. Intra-object partitioning schemes are motivated by narrow phase speed-up. However, they can result in a single phase strategy where effectively we combine inter- and intra-object schemes into one partitioning. An example of this approach is given later. Thus hierarchical partitioning schemes can answer the question 'do a pair of objects intersect?' either at an object level or at a level of individual primitives within the object, as we shall see.

A problem with hierarchies is updating them for moving objects. In most applications we have one or a few moving objects of some complexity moving within a scene. If the moving object is represented by a bounding volume hierarchy then this has to be updated as the object translates and rotates. This is problematic for trees based on AABBs which by definition have to be recalculated as the object rotates.

In the previous section we considered the efficiency of single bounding volumes; when these are arranged into a hierarchy certain other considerations are important. For example, for a particular granularity in an application, how many

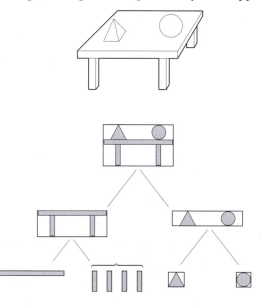

Figure 15.3
BV hierarchy.

levels are in the tree? The cost of traversing a tree depends on the number of levels and to get the same answer from a collision query different trees may have to be descended to different depths. Because OBBs, for example, bound more tightly than sphere trees and AABB trees, we would expect to descend fewer levels to process a query for two objects in close proximity.

Other considerations can be seen by returning to Figure 15.3. These are: apart from the choice of the BV, how do we effect the subdivision? Do we use a binary or a n-ary tree (search expense per node vs. tree depth). Another important point can be seen from the figure, which is at each subdivision level the new BV shrinks within the subdivision space – the hierarchy shrinking onto the object surface within the constraints of the shape of the BV. This is distinct from spatial subdivision schemes which simply divide up **all** space.

Another potential advantage of bounding volume hierarchies is that they could be used in conjunction with articulated structures. If a bounding volume is associated with each link in the structure then changes at the bottom of the hierarchy can be propagated up to the root and the bounding volume at each node appropriately adjusted.

15.3 Broad phase collision detection with AABBs

AABBs can be used as hierarchies or simply to enclose single objects. They are the basis of I-Collide (Cohen *et al.*, 1995), which involves using AABBs in conjunction with coordinate sorting. The simplicity of the approach derives from the fact that it is a dimension-reducing strategy – the tests operate in one-dimensional space. This straightforward idea is shown in principle in Figure 15.4 where it is easily seen that a pair of AABBs can overlap if and only if their extents overlap in each of the axes. The minimax coordinates of each AABB are maintained in a sorted list. Coherence is exploited because the new sorted lists are obtained by updating the previous, and this is manifested in the number of exchanges required to obtain the new list. The worst case here will be $O(N^2)$.

AABB overlap checking can proceed by sweeping through the sorted list – a so-called sort and sweep approach. The sorted list for each axis contains the box extents or intervals $[s_i, e_i]$ and an active list of extents is maintained as the sweep

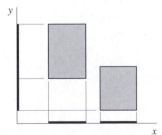

Figure 15.4
AABBs overlap iff their axis
extents overlap on each axis.

Figure 15.5
Sweep and prime scheme
for processing extents along
a single coordinates axis.

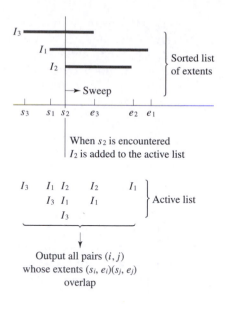

proceeds. When an s_i is encountered the interval identity is added to the list and all the current members of the list are output as overlapping with object i. When the corresponding e_i is met, the interval is removed. Thus in Figure 15.5, when s_2 is encountered I_2 is added to the active list.

Assuming the sorted list does not change much between updates, a sifting sort can be used to reorder the list. A sifting sort moves elements towards the beginning of the list until a smaller element is encountered. Thus we start with the second element, compare it with the first and swap if necessary. Then the third element is examined and moved towards the beginning if it is smaller than the current first or second. This reordering requires $O(N + c)$ where c is the number of swaps.

Using this approach in three dimensions clearly needs careful consideration. The performance of the sort algorithm can easily approach $O(N^2)$ when box extents cluster along an axis. This may occur in a football game, for example, if this method was used. But in that context we would reduce the test to two dimensions rather than one dimension and use circles, say.

AABBs trade simplicity and fast intersection against updating cost and bounding efficiency. Each time an object is rotated, either the boxes have to be recomputed from the new vertex positions, or else we can apply the object transformations to the eight box vertices and describe a new bounding box around these. The latter is quicker but will in general reduce the bounding efficiency. Hubbard (1996) reports that in an experiment involving 500 000 random rotations of a unit cube, its bounding box increased in volume by a factor of 3.4 on average and 4.7 in the worst case.

OBB trees

OBBs, as we have discussed, were originally employed in ray tracing and their motivation was to enable a tight fit around the enclosed object. In fact, there is little difference in principle between collision detection and intersection testing in ray tracing, if we consider a ray to be a geometric entity or object. With OBB trees the tightness of fit implies that we need to descend the tree to fewer levels when testing for collision, than if the hierarchy consisted of spheres or AABBs.

The following treatment of OBBs is based on the work of Gottchalk *et al.* (1996) who appeared to be the first to consider them for this application.

Building an OBB tree

To build an OBB tree we need an algorithm that recursively partitions the object polygons down to a desired level of accuracy and a procedure, which for a cluster of polygons, finds the OBB. We begin with the latter problem.

For a set of (triangular) polygons Gottchalk *et al.* find the mean and the covariance matrix of the vertices. This means that we consider the cloud of points representing the vertices as a trivariate probability distribution that can then be parameterised by a mean and covariances. In general, the points will form into a cluster which can be represented by an ellipsoid. The problem is then to find the 'best' bounding box for the ellipsoid. Clearly the extremal points are one constraint but it is not immediately obvious, given the other constraint – that the box is a rectangular solid, what its best orientation is. That is, the orientation that encloses the points most tightly. Representing the points as a probability distribution enables us to find the orientation by a simple analytical procedure. This is defined as the mean:

$$M = \frac{1}{3n} \sum_{i=1}^{n} p^i + q^i + r^i$$

where

p^i q^i and r^i are the vertices of the ith triangle

n is the number of triangles in the partition

The 3×3 covariance matrix is defined as:

$$C_{jk} = \frac{1}{3n} \sum_{i=1}^{n} (p_j^i - M_j)(p_k^i - M_k) + (q_j^i - M_j)(q_k^i - M_k) + (r_j^i - M_j)(r_k^i - M_k) \quad 1 \leq j, k \leq 3$$

where the superscript i is the triangle index as before and the subscripts j and k represent the (x, y, z) components of the points.

The covariance martrix is a 3×3 symmetric matrix – the diagonals give the components of the mean and the off-diagonal elements specify the orientation

Figure 15.6
Principal component analysis
in 2D space.

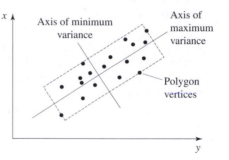

of the ellipsoidal probability distribution function. The eigenvectors of this matrix yield a basis or coordinate axes parallel to the faces of the OBB, which are then found from the extreme points. This technique is known in multivariate statistics as principal component analysis (PCA). The idea is shown in Figure 15.6 which shows a projection of a set of vertices into the x, y plane. PCA yields the axes shown (which in the two-dimensional space of the diagram are the axes of maximum and minimum variance).

A problem with this approach is that if the surface represented by the vertices is not convex, then interior points can influence the orientation of the bounding box. This is an undesirable consequence of the method – the faces of the bounding box should not line up with internal features. The idea of the bounding volume is that it 'shrinks' onto the object as tightly as possible. It cannot do this if it is influenced by the geometry of concavities. Gottchalk *et al.* address this problem by finding the convex hull of the vertices, then sampling this to obtain a new set of points from which an OBB is obtained as before.

The OBB computation can then be ordered into a recursive algorithm that determines a tree or hierarchy. This is done by fitting an OBB to the entire scene and recursively partitioning this into two halves using a plane orthogonal to one of its axes. This produces two new partitions which each have a new OBB fitted to them. The subdivision is first tried by partitioning the plane orthogonal to the longest axis at the mean vertex point. Figure 15.7 shows a two-dimensional analogue of the process.

Figure 15.7
A 2D analogue of the OBB
tree building process.
Clusters of polygons are
bound and (recursively)
partitioned and bound.

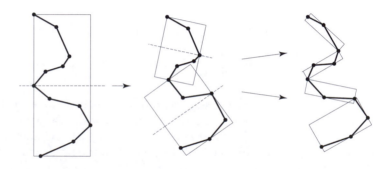

Broad phase collision detection with OBBs

In this section we describe a method that uses a hierarchy of OBBs. The root of the hierarchy contains the object itself and the leaves contain one or more polygons. It is thus an intra-object spatial partitioning and the trees for two objects are descended if their roots intersect. In this way broad phase collision detection is implemented down to whatever level of detail is represented at the leaves of the tree. Because of the tighter bounding efficiency of OBB trees it is likely that fewer levels of the tree need to be traversed to process a collision query.

Although overlap checking with AABBs involves only straightforward one-dimensional limit checks, checking OBBs for overlap is reportedly faster (Gottschalk *et al.*, 1996) and we will now describe how this works.

A naïve algorithm for checking for interference between two OBBs would require an edge-face test from each. In other words, we would test the edges of one box for penetration against the faces of the other and vice versa. This would result in 12 edges × 6 faces × 2 boxes = 144 edge-face tests. Gottchalk *et al.* develop the following strategy. First, consider Figure 15.8 which shows two OBBs projected onto an (arbitrary) axis. It is clear from this that if the intervals of the projected vertices do not overlap then the boxes cannot overlap. The axis is then a separating axis because it is oriented in such a way as to produce disjoint intervals from disjoint OBBs. If the intervals do overlap then the OBBs may or may not be disjoint and a further test is necessary.

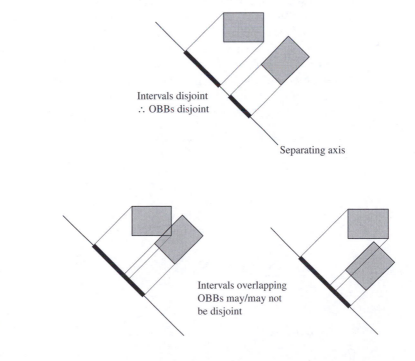

Intervals disjoint
∴ OBBs disjoint

Separating axis

Intervals overlapping
OBBs may/may not
be disjoint

Figure 15.8
Projecting OBBs onto an axis. If the intervals are disjoint, the axis is a separating axis. Checking for disjoint OBBs involves searching for a separating axis.

Figure 15.9
L is an axis being tested to
see if it is a separating axis.
The 'radius' of each OBB is
projected onto *L*. For
separation: *D.L* > r_A + r_B.

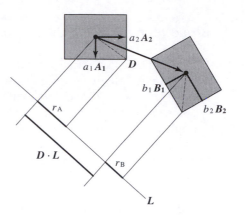

Now consider that if the OBBs are disjoint they can be (possibly) separated by a plane that contains one of their faces. It is less obvious that if they are disjoint but cannot be separated by a face plane, they can be separated by a plane parallel to an edge from each box. This means that the OBBs are disjoint if there exists a separating axis orthogonal to a face from either OBB, or orthogonal to a face from each. Thus to test for separation it is sufficient to test 15 potential axes (three face orientations from each box plus nine pairwise edge combinations). Positive interference will thus require 15 tests and if the OBBs do not intersect this will take on average 7.5 tests to determine this.

Testing for the existence of a separating axis, *L*, proceeds as follows. Refer to Figure 15.9 and note that the placement (but not the orientation) of the axis is immaterial; we assume that it passes through the centre of the box A, although for clarity it is shown outside the box. Up to 15 *L*s are chosen according to the geometry of the boxes involved in the comparison, as we have explained. If the axes of box A are the unit vectors A_1, A_2 and A_3 and the half dimensions of A are a_1, a_2 and a_3, then we have the projected length of the 'radius' of the box:

$$r_A = a_1 A_1.L + a_2 A_2.L + a_3 A_3.L$$

$$= \sum_{i=1}^{3} |a_i A_i.L|$$

A similar expression exists for r_B of box B. If *D* is the translation of B relative to A, then we have that the intervals are disjoint if:

$$D.L > \sum_{i=1}^{3} |a_i A_i.L| + \sum_{i=1}^{3} |b_i A_i.L|$$

or

$$D.L > r_A + r_B$$

Since the 15 potential separating axes are defined with respect to one of the objects, they move with the object and the intervals themselves have a velocity associated with them. If we assume, for simplicity, that the object moves in a straight line with constant velocity between frames, the velocity of the interval corresponding to that object is easily calculated and we can find out if, for any time between the frames, the moving object is likely to collide with a static one that it is currently being compared to.

15.4.1 k-dop trees

K-dops are a generalisation of AABBs. Now, as we have discussed, bounding volumes are in practice used in the form of hierarchies. The efficiency of a bounding volume that is organised into a tree structure is then expressed as: how far do we need to descend the tree to resolve a collision query? We would, in general, have to descend the AABB tree to a greater depth to resolve a query between two objects, than if the objects were bound with OBB trees. Gottchalk *et al.* define a convergence criterion for low curvature surfaces and show that if bounding a surface to within a certain tightness takes $O(m)$ OBBS then $O(m^2)$ AABBs or spheres will be required. The rationale, then, for the generalisation of AABBs into k-dops was to increase the bounding efficiency of AABBs and at the same time retain their relative advantage over OBBs, which is simpler and faster overlap testing Klosowski *et al.*, 1998).

As Figure 15.1 shows, k-dops are constructed by 'cutting off the corners' of AABBs. For example, a 14-dop is constructed for an object by finding the maximum and minimum coordinate values along each of the seven axes – the three principal axes $(x, y$ and $z)$ and the four diagonals through the cube centred on the origin and defined by the vectors $(1,1,1)$, $(1,-1,1)$, $(1,1,-1)$ and $(1,-1,-1)$. Thus the value of k is the number of half spaces defined by the facets of the bounding volume and the higher the value of k, the more empty space is chopped off the AABB.

A problem with k-dop is that because they are generalisations of AABBs they have to be updated when the contained object rotates. Klowowski *et al.* simply generalise the approximate technique for AABBs (Section 15.3) and rotate the vertices of the original k-dop, then bound these vertices with a new k-dop.

15.5 Broad phase collision detection with local or object spatial partitioning

We have already mentioned that the significant disadvantage of spatial partitioning is that the scheme has to be updated as the objects move and the cost of updating can negate their efficiency savings. Garcia-Alonso *et al.* (1995) employ local spatial partitioning for the object itself. In principle the same as bounding volume hierarchies, they use a one-level subdivision for each object. An object is enclosed in a box called a container and this is divided into voxels which point

Figure 15.10
Object is embedded in a
local partitioned space
(called a container). The
containers are embedded in
AABBs. In this example only
the AABBs overlap.

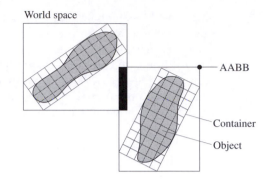

to object polygons. Each object possesses its own voxelised container which
receives the same transformations as the object; in other words, the voxels are
aligned with the local frame of the object. Effectively the container is the same
as an OBB root, but instead of being split up into a hierarchy it is subdivided uniformly.

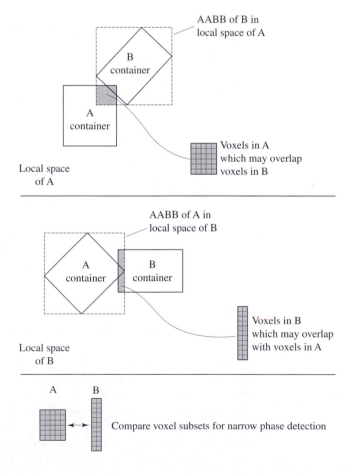

Figure 15.11
Determining voxel
interference by transforming
into each local space.

A broad phase/narrow phase strategy is invoked by enclosing the containers in AABBs as shown in Figure 15.10. The bounding inefficiency of the AABB reduces the efficiency of the container overlap test whenever the containers are subject to rotation. A potential collision detected by AABB overlap then causes the containers to be tested for overlap. In the example shown, only the AABBs overlap. Clearly there are many occurrences of AABB and container overlap without any object overlap taking place.

The progress of the algorithm for two objects A and B is as follows:

Test the AABBs for overlap in world coordinate space. If an overlap is detected, continue.

Compute the AABB of object A in the local coordinate system of B and that of object B in the local coordinate system of A. This is done by computing the inverse transformation matrices of both A and B in world space T_{AW}^{-1} and T_{BW}^{-1}. The transformation from the local system of A into that of B is then given by $T_{AW}T_{BW}^{-1}$.

Find those voxels that overlap in A's frame and those that overlap in B's frame (Figure 15.11).

For each voxel in the set of A: check against each voxel in the set of B.

15.6 Narrow phase collision detection

15.6.1 Pairs of convex polyhedra – exact collision detection

In this section we will describe a common straightforward exact collision detection algorithm using the constraint that the objects must be convex polyhedra. (In principle, concave polyhedra can be decomposed into collections of convex ones.) The algorithm is due to Moore and Wilhelms (1988).

Three tests are applied and the success of any of these implies that a collision has occurred. Consider two polyhedra P and Q. First, all the vertices of Q are checked to see if they are contained by P and vice versa (Figure 15.12). Second, the edges of Q are tested for penetration against the faces of P and vice versa (Figure 15.12). Finally, there is a test for the infrequent case of two (identical) polyhedra moving through each other with faces perfectly aligned. This is done by considering the centroid of each face of Q and using the same test as for vertex inclusion. We could surmise that most polyhedron/polyhedron collisions are going to be detected by the first test and many systems implement this check only.

Consider the first test: each vertex of Q has to be checked against every face of P and a collision is detected if any vertex is on the inward side of all the faces of P. Thus for each vertex v_i of Q and for each face j of P the dot product:

$$(v_i - u_j).n_j$$

Figure 15.12
Collision detection tests for
convex polyhedra. (a) Any
vertex of Q contained in P.
(b) any edge of Q penetrates
a face of P.

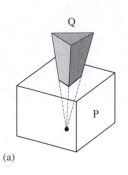

(a)

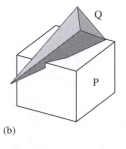

(b)

is evaluated, where $\boldsymbol{u}_j$ is any vertex of face j and $\boldsymbol{n}_j$ is its (outwards) normal
(Figure 15.13). If this dot product is negative then the vertex $\boldsymbol{v}_i$ is on the inwards
side of face j.

The second test proceeds by first calculating for any edge $(\boldsymbol{v}_i, \boldsymbol{v}_j)$ of Q the intersections of the edge with the (infinite) planes containing the faces of P. For any

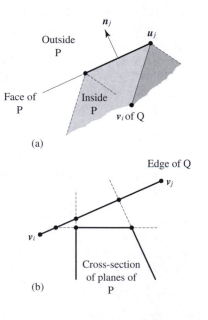

Figure 15.13
Notation for collision
detection tests for convex
polyhedra. (a) Notation for
a vertex of Q contained by
P test. (b) Notation for an
edge of Q cutting a face
of P.

plane k of P an edge of Q intersects it if the perpendicular distance from each vertex to the plane changes sign. The intersection point x can then be calculated as:

$$d_i = (v_i - u_k).n_k$$

$$d_j = (v_j - u_k).n_k$$

$$t = \frac{|d_i|}{|d_i| + |d_j|}$$

$$x = v_i + t(v_j - v_i)$$

This gives, in general, a number of intersection points along the edge. Those for which $t \notin [0,1]$ are discarded and the remainder are sorted into order of their t values. These form a sequence of potential intersections, where two consecutive points may be an 'entry' and 'exit' point of the edge through object P. To check for intersection, Moore and Wilhelms use the midpoint of each pair of such points, substituting this value into the first test.

Lin-Canny closest features algorithm

This classic narrow phase algorithm (Lin, 1993) identifies the closest features between a pair of objects. Clearly, tracking closest features enables a culling strategy. In addition, it exploits coherence by searching for the current closest pair from the position of the previous closest pair. If the situation has not changed since the last invocation then the algorithm confirms this in (near) constant time and the feature pairs are 'tracked'. In other words, the features are cached and the search for the current nearest pair starts from the previous.

Overall, the algorithm operates in 'near constant time'. Mirtich (1997) points out that this is slightly misleading and gives the example of a satellite/Earth simulation where the earth is represented by an N-facet sphere. Here, we can consider the closest feature pair circumnavigating the globe. For one orbit of the satellite on the equator, $O(\sqrt{N})$ Earth features are encountered by the satellite. More work has to be done per unit time if the satellite speeds up or the resolution of the Earth model increases. However, if the satellite falls towards the Earth the algorithm operates in constant time. Thus the algorithm complexity depends on how the objects move with respect to each other and the object resolutions. However, in practice Mirtich reports that slowdown is negligible when polyhedral models of spheres with a few hundred facets are replaced with polyhedral models with over 20 000 facets.

The algorithm works by first pre-processing convex polyhedra to find their Voronoi regions. Consider the Voronoi regions for a two-dimensional example – the polygon in Figure 15.14. A polygon has only two types of features – edges and vertices. The Voronoi region of a feature F is the set of points which are closer to F than to any other feature of the polygon. The Voronoi region for an edge is delineated by the two lines emanating from the vertices that form the

Figure 15.14
Voronoi regions for a polygon.

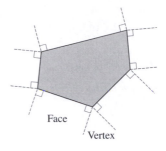

edge, and for a vertex by the two lines belonging to the Voronoi regions for the edges that share the vertex. Polyhedra possess three feature types – vertices, edges and faces, and the boundaries between Voronoi regions are planes. These planes that bound the region need to be recorded as a data structure associated with the feature together with a pointer into the adjacent Voronoi region that shares the planes. These structures are built in a pre-processing phase.

The main part of the algorithm searches for closest points P_A and P_B between a pair of features on two objects, then confirms or otherwise that the candidate pair found in the search are indeed the closest pair. This assertion is confirmed by checking that each point lies within the Voronoi region of the other feature. Figure 15.15 shows two polygons A and B; the point P_A lies within the Voronoi region of F_{B1} (a face of B) and P_B lies within F_{A1} (a vertex of A) and so P_A, P_B are a closest pair.

Since the points each belong to a feature, finding the closest distance splits into six categories of calculation: vertex–vertex, vertex–edge, vertex–face, edge–edge, edge–face and face–face. (The last category is degenerate and has to be dealt with algorithmically.) For example, the vertex–edge calculation is given by:

Figure 15.15
Applicability criteria.

$$P_E = V_{E1} + \min\left(1, \max\left(0, \frac{(V - V_{E1}).\boldsymbol{E}}{|\boldsymbol{E}|^2}\right)\right)\boldsymbol{E}$$

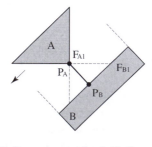

P_A, P_B are closest points in F_{A1} F_{B1}
$P_A \in v(F_{B1})$ $P_B \in v(F_{A1})$
$\therefore$ F_{A1}, F_{B1} are closest features

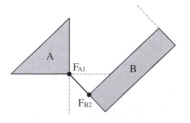

$P_A \notin v(F_{B1})$
Now F_{A1}, F_{B2} are closest
features

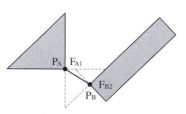

$P_A \in v(F_{B2})$ $P_B \in v(F_{A1})$
$\therefore$ F_{A1}, F_{B2} are closest
features

Figure 15.16
An example of a 3D Voronoi region – the prism associated with edge E. If P_A passes through plane E_1, V_1 must be the next feature of B.

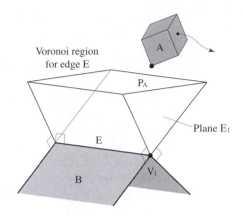

where

P_E is the nearest point on the edge E to the vertex V

$\boldsymbol{E} = V_{E2} - V_{E1}$

V_{E2} and V_{E1} are the vertices defining the edge

Now return to Figure 15.15 and consider polygon A translating as shown. P_A is no longer in the Voronoi associated with the feature F_{B1} and has in fact moved into the region associated with F_{B2}. This means that a point on F_{B1} can no longer form a closest pair with P_A and the new feature pair is F_{A1}, F_{B2}. We know that we must now consider the pair F_{A1}, F_{B2} from the adjacency information stored as part of the Voronoi region associated with F_{A1}. Thus the algorithm tracks pairs of closest features and evaluates closest points to facilitate this. When the closest point distance falls below a small threshold we assume that a collision has occurred.

The confirmation that a point P_A lies within the Voronoi region of feature F_B is called an applicability criterion and three categories are possible: point-vertex, point-edge and point-face. A three-dimensional example of the point-edge criterion is shown in Figure 15.16. The Voronoi region for the edge E is a prism with two planes perpendicular to the edge and two planes perpendicular to each face sharing the edge. If P_A is inside this region then the test succeeds. If the test fails then P_A has moved outside the region by passing through one of the planes. We can find which plane this is by testing the bounding planes of the Voronoi region in order. The plane identity tells us the next feature to be considered as forming a new pair with F_A. For example, if P_A fails the test for plane E_1 then it now must be nearer to vertex V_1 and the algorithm is called recursively with this new feature and P_A tested against its Voronoi region.

15.6.3

Separating planes

This approach relies on finding a separating plane between the two polyhedra. (A separating plane approach can also be applied to curved (non-polygonal) surfaces.) It can be shown that a separating plane exists between two disjoint or contacting convex polyhedra which embeds one of the faces of one of the polyhedra, or embeds an edge from each (the same criteria as were used to determine if OBBs are disjoint). In this case the significance of using a plane attached to a face is that it can be used to exploit coherence. The plane receives the same motion as the object face to which it is attached and can be used in the next frame as a potential separator. To verify if a plane in the previous invocation is still a separator has complexity $O(n)$, where n is the total number of vertices in both polyhedra and a new plane is obtained without any extra computation. If the new plane is no longer a separator then either the objects have inter-penetrated or they are still disjoint and a new plane must be found. This is the approach taken by Baraff (1990) who finds a new plane by 'exhaustive search'. Presumably this means testing each face of the polyhedra to see if it is a new separator.

The actual point of contact (or inter-penetration) is easily determined using this method because it must occur on the most recent separating plane. This is shown for a simple example in Figure 15.17. As moving object B translates towards (static) object A we retain the same separator. When this plane penetrates object A a new separator is found and for this example this is the 'final' separator which contains the point of contact or the inter-penetration. To find the point of contact we compare only those faces, edges or vertices that are coincident with the separating plane. This comparison can be made efficient by caching information found during the determination of the final separator.

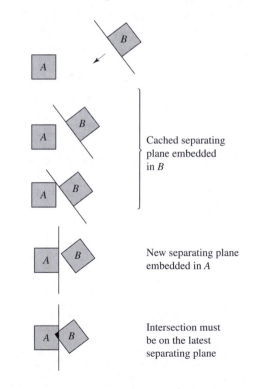

Figure 15.17
Exploiting coherence by
caching a separating plane
embedded in one of the
objects.

15.7

Single phase approaches

15.7.1

BSP trees

The attraction of using BSP trees for single phase collision detection is that this partitioning suffices for both real-time rendering and collision detection. For the simple cases outlined, the additional code complexity required to incorporate collision detection in a BSP renderer is low.

We begin by looking at a simple example – ray casting in first-person shooter games. This is a good example of the way in which collision detection is simplified by the game context. The question is: if I continue in my current direction, which (static) objects will I hit? If a scene is partitioned with a BSP tree then we can easily find the first intersection between a ray and an object. This test is used not only for virtual collision detection between objects but also in dynamic light calculations (Chapter 10) and shadow calculations (Chapter 11).

A ray intersect test with a BSP tree has low code complexity, as the following example demonstrates.

```
call bsp_intersect(bsp root node,start,end)

bsp_intersect(node,p1,p2)
{
if (node is leaf) rayintersect(leaf objects)
clasify p1 (+/-)
clasify p2 (+/-)
if (p1 and p2 are +) bsp_intersect(+ child)
else
if (p1 and p2 are -) bsp_intersect(- child)
else
{
bsp_intersect(- child);
bsp_intersect(+ child);
}
}
```

This code will return all the intersects along the ray and we have to get the nearest from the set. An efficiency enhancement is:

```
call bsp_intersect(bsp root node,start,end)

bsp_intersect(node,p1,p2)
{
if (node is leaf) rayintersetc(leaf objects)
clasify p1 (+/-)
clasify p2 (+/-)
if (p1 and p2 are +)
   bsp_intersect(+ child)
```

```
else
if (p1 and p2 are -)
  bsp_intersect(- child)
else
{
if (p1 is +)
  {
  bsp_intersect(+ child);
  bsp_intersect(- child);
  }
else
  {
  bsp_intersect(- child);
  bsp_intersect(+ child);
  }
}
}
```

This will always examine the half of the current ray segment nearer to the start of the ray p1 and guarantees that the first intersection encountered is the required point. Effectively the ray is split into segments along its length by the partitioning planes.

15.7.2 Local or object spatial partitioning – BSP tree merging

If we have a local BSP tree for each object then checking for intersection is a tree-merging operation in a common space. This is intuitively obvious; each tree partitions the space of the object and to check for overlap or intersection we merge the representations of the two spaces – equivalent to merging the space itself. Naylor *et al.* (1990) in fact generalise the concept to perform Boolean set operations, the foundation of CSG application; however, for collision detection we are only interested in the set operation intersection – is there a common space or overlap shared by each object?

The concept of tree merging to determine intersection is easily demonstrated using a simple example. Consider the two objects in Figure 15.18. Each has a simple three-node BSP tree where three partitioning planes, lying in the object faces, enclose the space occupied by the object. This is the subset of all space that is on the negative side of the three planes. We ask the question: is any part of object 2 inside object 1? To answer this, we merge the trees by using object 1's planes to partition object 2's space. Examination of the merged tree yields the result that the fragment D_2 is in the subspace which is the interior of object 1.

For collision detection, the key concept for BSP tree merging is that of the tree as a bounding volume that 'shrinks' onto the object. Figure 15.19 shows a simple object 'enclosed' initially by three partitioning planes. As the number of planes is increased the bounding volume enclosed by the planes approximates the

Figure 15.18
A simple example of BSP tree merging to determine intersection.

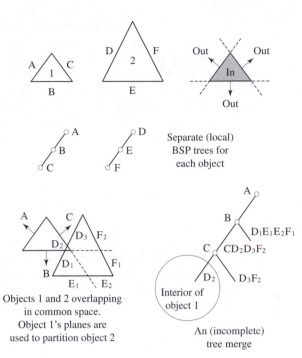

Separate (local) BSP trees for each object

Objects 1 and 2 overlapping in common space. Object 1's planes are used to partition object 2

Interior of object 1

An (incomplete) tree merge

Figure 15.19
The concept of partitioning planes as a shrinking bounding volume enabling a multi-resolution representation of the bounding volume.

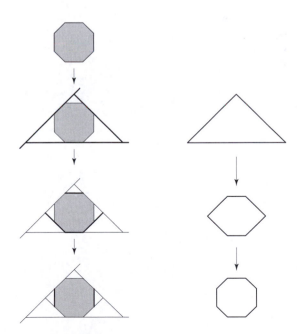

object better. Eventually the bounding volume and the object will coincide (for a convex object). In other words, the BSP tree enables us to access bounding volumes by going from a low to a higher resolution. If the bounding volumes for a pair of objects intersect at some resolution then the objects themselves may intersect. We can find out if the objects intersect by tree merging. As the merging process proceeds, pairs of tree regions are compared to determine whether they intersect or not. If they do not intersect then the associated subtrees are never compared. This process homes in on the region of intersection and enables us to determine whether an intersection has occurred and the region in which it has occurred.

15.7.3 Sphere/polyhedron specialisations

Collision detection can be simplified if we can always consider a standard object. This approach is commonly used in a games application to detect collisions between spherically bound moving objects and polygonal static objects. We can either consider the sphere as a bounding volume and invoke a narrow phase test or, as is common, make no distinction, as far as collision detection is concerned, between the sphere and the object – the sphere becomes the object for collision detection.

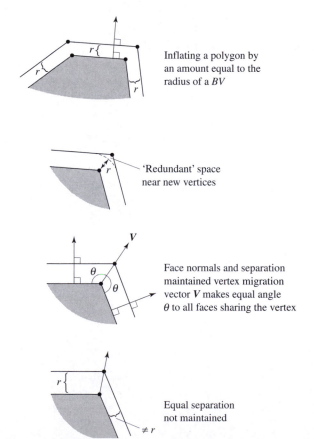

Inflating a polygon by an amount equal to the radius of a *BV*

'Redundant' space near new vertices

Face normals and separation maintained vertex migration vector **V** makes equal angle θ to all faces sharing the vertex

Equal separation not maintained

Figure 15.20
'Inflating' a polyhedron.

Exploiting special case geometry is used in view frustum culling (VFC) which can also be considered a form of collision detection. Here we compared bounding objects with the view frustum which has the known shape of a truncated pyramid and trivially reject (no collision), trivially accept (object entirely within the view frustum) or further investigate if the bounding volume intersects the frustum.

Consider the simple case of a spherical moving object. We can reduce the sphere/polygon object test to a point (the centre of the sphere) object test by 'inflating' the object equally all directions by an amount equal to the radius of the sphere. Figure 15.20 shows the idea from which it can be seen that certain inaccuracies near the polygon vertices will ensue. However, if the sphere is used as a bounding volume the outcome of this test is always conservative. The object must be inflated so that the new faces are parallel to the old faces and at distance, r, equal to the radius of the sphere.

The problem is how to inflate the object. Clearly we must move all faces outward so that in their new position they are parallel to the corresponding original face, and we want to do this by moving the vertex. This is easy for a special object like a view frustum but more difficult to do efficiently for a general polygon mesh object. For each vertex we would like to define a new vertex by displacing the original vertex along a displacement vector. The necessary condition for the displacement vector is that it should subtend equal angles to all faces that contribute. If this condition is not met then the faces in the inflated object will not be maintained at equal distances (Figure 15.20). In many cases the vertex normal will satisfy this condition. However, it is easy to construct a counterexample. Figure 15.21 shows an object constructed by slicing a regular pyramid in half. The vertex normal at the apex, formed from the face normals shown, will not subtend equal angles to all four faces. A better approach is to calculate the dot products of the vertex normal and contributing face normals and use the average of this angle to define the direction of the displacement vector.

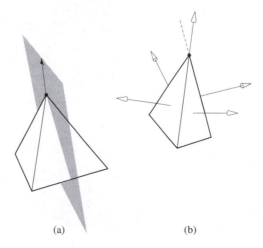

Figure 15.21
An example where the vertex normal does not subtend equal angles to the face normals. (a) Pyramid vertex normal is vertical. (b) Half pyramid vertex makes an angle of 53° to sloping faces and 82° to vertical face.

(a) (b)

15.7.4

Using a depth buffer

A low complexity algorithm that could be used for both broad and narrow phase approaches is to rasterise polygons into a Z-buffer. Consider a depth buffer that can store two depth values, a maximum and a minimum depth. An algorithm that detects collision between A and B is:

Rasterise A into the depth buffer

Rasterise B:

$\qquad$ **if** $(Z_{min} \leq Z_B \leq Z_{max})$ **then** collision on that pixel

$\qquad\qquad$ **if** $Z_B \geq Z_{Bmax}$ **then** $Z_{Bmax} = Z_B$

$\qquad\qquad\qquad$ max_penetration = [i,j]

This gives the pixel at which the maximum penetration occurred and its depth.

15.7.5

Hubbard's time-critical sphere tree algorithm – a single phase approach

Hierarchies are used in two distinct ways in collision detection algorithms. They can be used to represent the entire space of the environment – using octrees, for example, or each object can have a hierarchy associated with it. The potential advantage of an object hierarchy is that it enables a unified approach – we can build a single phase algorithm that detects collisions to an accuracy that depends on how far we have descended the hierarchy. This enables what Hubbard (1996) calls time-critical collision detection where in interactive computer animation the accuracy is determined by the time available for the calculation. This approach – a hierarchical representation of an object surface – is, of course, the

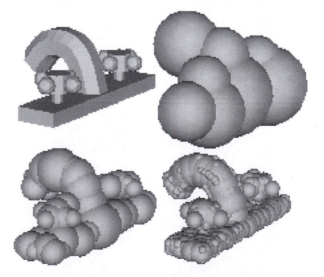

Figure 15.22
An example of three levels in the construction of a sphere tree. *Source*: Hubbard, P.M., *ACM Transactions on Graphics*, 15:3, July 1996, reprinted with permission from ACM Publications.

same as the level of detail approach for polygons. However, in this context a LOD hierarchy comprising polygons is not convenient for collision detection and Hubbard uses a sphere tree for fast determination of intersection. The topmost level of a sphere hierarchy is the bounding sphere from the object and as we descend smaller and smaller spheres 'shrink' onto the surface, as is evident in Figure 15.22. Hubbard states that two important requirements of the sphere tree are that the (off-line) building process should be automatic and each level in the hierarchy must fit the object as tightly as possible. (Note that the requirements of the process are somewhat different from using a hierarchical bounding volume in ray tracing. Ray tracing, by definition, is a two-phase process – we must have a narrow phase which evaluates exactly the intersection between a ray and

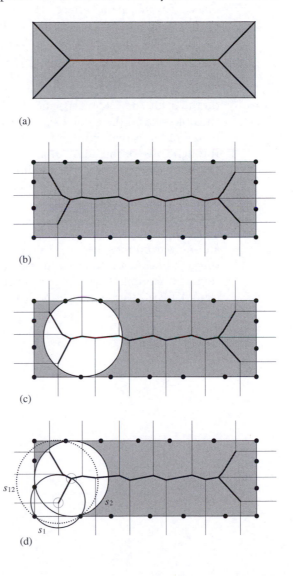

(a)

(b)

(c)

(d)

Figure 15.23
A two-dimensional analogy of Hubbard's scheme for building sphere trees (based on illustrations in Hubbard (1996)). (a) Medial axis of a polygon (bold lines). (b) Deriving an approximation of the medial axis by 'populating' the edges with points and finding the associated Voronoi regions. (c) Each Voronoi vertex is the centre of a circle that passes through three points. (d) Merging the two circles s_1 and s_2.

a polygon. It may be sufficient in ray tracing to build hierarchies that simply enclose parts of the object. For example, a table may be represented by just five bounding volumes. In collision detection we need to compare spheres at any level in the hierarchy for intersection and the spheres must intersect and range over the surface of an object, as Figure 15.22 clearly shows.)

To obtain such a tree is not straightforward and we will simply overview the process using a two-dimensional analogy – full details of the algorithm are given in Hubbard (1996). Hubbard first derives a medial axis surface from the object and then uses this surface to place the spheres. A medial axis for a two-dimensional object is shown in Figure 15.23(a). Sometimes called a skeleton, a medial axis is the locus of points equidistant from its sides. In the case of an object it would be a surface. The medial axis is approximated by building a Voronoi diagram for a set of points P that are assigned to the surface of the object. Figure 15.23(b) shows a set of points on the shape and their associated Voronoi regions. A Voronoi region for a point is defined as that region of space closer to that point than to any other of the points and so for a set of points on the surface of the object the Voronoi cells must have faces lying approximately on the medial axis. More specifically, the vertices of the Voronoi cells interior to the object lie on the medial axis. As shown in Figure 15.23(c), each such vertex by definition is the centre of a circle (sphere in three dimensions) which passes through three of the points (four points in three dimensions) and these circles (spheres) are the basis of the building of the hierarchy.

The complete set of such spheres tightly enclose the surface of the object and form the leaves of the hierarchy, which is now built by reducing the number of spheres occupying each level using a merging operation. The process is shown as a two-dimensional analogy again in Figure 15.23(d). Two spheres, S_1 and S_2, are merged into a sphere S_{12} using an algorithm that ensures S_{ab} either passes through or contains the forming points for S_1 and S_2. Hubbard treats this operation as a minimisation problem by choosing the minimum cost merger – the candidate pair whose merger most preserves the level's tightness.

Interactive control

16.1   Interaction and animation

16.2   Controller module

16.3   User–object interaction – 6 DOF control with simple damping

16.4   User–object animation – a four-key car simulation

16.5   Object–object interaction

16.6   Camera–object interaction

16.7   Objects with simple autonomous behaviour

16.8   User–scene interaction

16.1 Interaction and animation

As we have discussed in the introduction, computer games animation is a combination of user interaction and either pre-scripted animation or dynamic simulation. Controlling the movement of objects in a game implies using classical computer animation techniques to impart realistic motion to computer graphics objects. It also implies designing the interaction of objects in a game in a way that imparts autocracy to objects, such as enemies, that are not under player control. In this chapter we look at basic techniques for controlling user/object and object/object interaction. The issue of autonomous objects controlled by more elaborate (AI) technology is dealt with in the next chapter.

16.2 Controller module

Up to the advent of dynamic simulation, computer animation was controlled by a kinematics 'script', the only variation being the way in which the script was implemented and derived. The basic premise is that we cannot start or stop a motion in an animation instantaneously. Traditional animators handled this problem manually, calling their technique 'easing in' and 'easing out'. Computer

Figure 16.1
Explicit scripting – path and
motion splines.

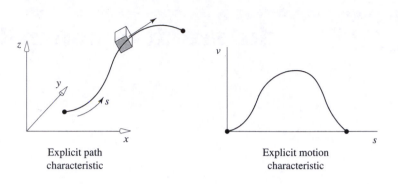

Explicit path
characteristic

Explicit motion
characteristic

animators use the same basic idea but use tools to achieve the same effect. For
example, we may explicitly script the motion of an unconstrained rigid body
through space by developing a path characteristic – a three-dimensional space
curve and a motion characteristic (Figure 16.1) which describes the velocity of
the object at each point on the path. The system then generates frames in the
animation from these characteristics. Motion capture is in effect an identical

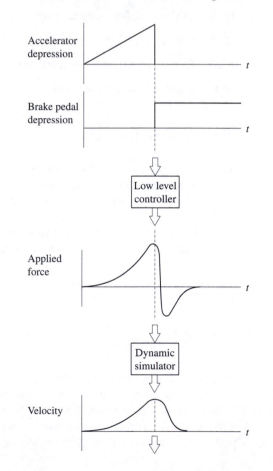

Figure 16.2
Controllers and simulators.

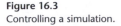

Figure 16.3
Controlling a simulation.

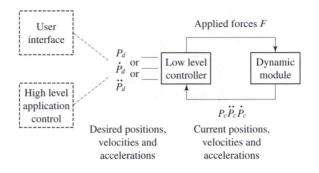

technique. The difference now is that instead of the animator having to guess or develop how a body should accelerate or decelerate, data is collected directly from real motion and applied to the computer graphics object.

In a dynamic simulation we are not normally too interested in simulations where we apply a single force and torque to a simulation as in the case of a projectile. These are situations where an initial impulse is applied and the body moves forward in time subject only to that impulse. In many cases we wish to continually apply forces and torques under the control of some higher-level process. We have to cause a body to move in a way desired by the high-level controller/interface and these forces are derived by the low-level controller. Say, for example, we required a vehicle to respond in the normal way to an accelerator pedal that is depressed then allowed to rise immediately followed by an application of the brakes (Figure 16.2). The controller has to produce applied forces which will result in the required motion by deriving these from the pedal interface. The conversion from pedal positions to applied force is designed to imitate the characteristics of the physical system that are being simulated. In the case of an accelerator pedal the response depends on the depression and the engine characteristics. The deceleration produced by the braking system similarly depends on the foot pressure and the efficiency of the braking system.

This is generalised in Figure 16.3 where we see that the input to the low-level controller consists of a desired position or velocity or acceleration. This produces an applied force which is input to the dynamic simulator. The current positions, velocities and accelerations are fed back to the controller from the dynamic module, and the controller calculates an applied force which is a function of the desired position, velocity or acceleration and the current values of these parameters.

We can consider the two curves, applied force and velocity, as time histories of the system over a simulation interval. From this we can see that the applied force characteristic depends on values built into the controller and the velocity characteristic depends on the applied force, the equations set up in the dynamic simulator and (importantly) the characteristics of the numerical integrator used by the dynamic simulator.

A simple but effective scheme is proportional control:

$$a_c = k_1(v_t - v_l)$$

where:

v_t is the target speed given by the position of the accelerator pedal, or set to zero if the brakes are applied.

v_i is the current speed

k_1 is a vehicle-dependent constant (or variable) for acceleration and braking

This basic control has to be enhanced by a limit factor, since as a first-order approximation, the acceleration available, for example from a car, is a function of engine HP and is inversely proportional to v_i. That is:

$$0 \leq \boldsymbol{a}_c \leq \frac{k_2}{v_i} \qquad k_2 = \frac{550\text{HP}}{m}$$

where HP is the engine horse power and m is the mass of the vehicle.

Now the critical point about the above theory is that it employs feedback. It uses the difference between the current output state and the desired state as an error which drives the simulation. In the example, as the error decreases the acceleration output from the controller decreases accordingly.

Whether we would use this type of control depends on the application. In a car game where a user is operating real pedals and controlling a real steering wheel, we would require some form of proportional control for the pedals, otherwise the car would attain the target velocity as soon as the pedal depression was sampled by the application. Also, an AI module controlling a movable game object would also need to input to the dynamic simulation via a controller. On the other hand, if we are using the keyboard then a simple time pressed calculation will normally suffice:

if keypressed **then** vel = acc *dt

We will now look at interaction techniques using a number of case studies as examples

16.3 User–object interaction – 6 DOF control with simple damping

A very common user interaction mode is a 6 DOF control required to control the orientation of a spaceship, for example. The spaceship moves under control of a velocity vector whose current magnitude specifies the speed and whose orientation specifies the attitude of the craft.

As well as calculating the increments in orientation and speed and applying them, we need to decide how we are going to interpret key presses. For simplicity, we will consider controlling an object constrained to move in a straight line. Three examples are shown in Figure 16.4. These are:

(1) **Step function** When the control key is pressed the velocity instantaneously attains a constant velocity (infinite acceleration); when it is released the velocity immediately returns to zero

Figure 16.4
Simple key press modes.

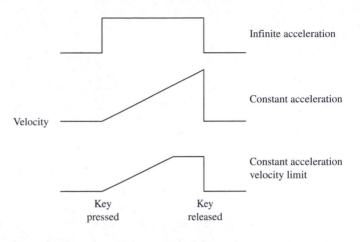

Figure 16.4
Simple key press modes.

Infinite acceleration

Constant acceleration

Constant acceleration
velocity limit

Velocity

Key
pressed

Key
released

(2) **Constant acceleration, no maximum velocity** When the key is pressed the velocity increases linearly; when released the velocity immediately returns to zero

(3) **Constant acceleration and deceleration – maximum velocity** When the key is pressed the velocity linearly increases until it reaches a constant value; when released it linearly decreases.

If we consider the distance increment in each case then we have:

(1) distance = distance + $V_{constant}dt$

(2) $V_{current} = V_{previous} + fdt$

distance = $V_{previous}dt + \frac{1}{2}(V_{current} + V_{previous})dt$

(3) **if** key_pressed **then**

   if $V_{current} < V_{max}$ **then** as (2)
   else   as (1)

  if key_released **then**

    if $V_{current} > 0$ **then** as (2) with negative acceleration

where

  dt is the time from the elapsed time

  f is a (constant) acceleration

To control a body such as a spaceship (Figure 16.5), consider the velocity vector to be represented (redundantly) as a magnitude and three orientation angles:

$(|V|, \theta_x, \theta_y, \theta_z)$

Figure 16.5
A convention for 6 DOF user
control.

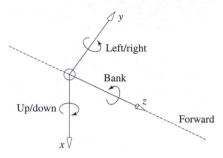

The representation is redundant because we only need two angles to specify the direction of a vector; but of course we prefer to use three to give an easy (three-pair) key interface of up/down, left/right and bank (Figure 16.5). In other words, we require four pairs of keys to control each of the parameters positively or negatively. We have:

> **for** each frame
>> sample rotation keys and update θ_x, θ_y and θ_z
>>
>> sample speed key and update $|\boldsymbol{V}|$
>>
>> calculate V_x, V_y, and V_z and update position of object

To maintain an existing orientation and decelerate a ship to rest we can use:

> **while** $|\boldsymbol{V}| > 0$
>> $\boldsymbol{V}_{\text{unit}} = \boldsymbol{V}/|\boldsymbol{V}|$
>>
>> Decrease $|\boldsymbol{V}|$ by some pre-specified amount
>>
>> $\boldsymbol{V} = \boldsymbol{V}_{\text{unit}} * |\boldsymbol{V}|$
>>
>> Update position of the object

To include damping in the rotational acceleration and deceleration we can define a rotational velocity vector:

$$\boldsymbol{R} = \left(\frac{d\theta_x}{dt}, \frac{d\theta_y}{dt}, \frac{d\theta_z}{dt} \right)$$

and the following code implements rotation with acceleration and deceleration:

```
my_object::step( int dt )
{
  if (up_key_pressed)
    rotvel.x += rotaccel*dt;
  if (down_key_pressed)
    rotvel.x -= rotaccel*dt;
  if (left_key_pressed)
    rotvel.y += rotaccel*dt;
```

```
if (right_key_pressed)
   rotvel.y -= rotaccel*dt;

if (bank_left_key_pressed)
   rotvel.z += rotaccel*dt;
if (bank_right_key_pressed)
   rotvel.z -= rotaccel*dt;

len=rotvel.length();
if (len > 0)        // if rotating
   {
   rotvel /= len;          // normalize rotation vector
   len -= dt * rotdamp;    // apply damping
   if (len < 0)            // crop at zero
      len = 0;
   else
   if (len > rotmaxvel)    // crop at max rotation velocity
      len = rotmaxvel;
   rotvel *= len;          // restore rotation vector
   rotate(rotvel*dt);      // apply rotation to object local system
   }
}
```

16.4 User–object animation – a four-key car simulation

This example shows how a simple car simulation is easily built from Newton's second law and Euler integration as described in Chapter 14. The user interface – the simplest possible – consists of the up and down arrow for forward acceleration and braking and the left and right arrow for steering. Key press control requires both steering and velocity to be continually damped, as we described in the previous section

The car tracks around a bend in the normal manner. Before entering the bend the velocity is parallel to the forward (z) axis of the local coordinate system of the car. After leaving the bend the same condition pertains. As the car is travelling around the bend there will be a (diminishing) angle between the horizontal component of the velocity vector and the car z axis. A superposition image is shown in Figure 16.6 (Colour Plate) which shows this motion. The vertical component of the velocity vector is effected by the landscape and if the car leaves the ground then gravity is applied to that component. The local y axis of the car always rotates so as to align with the current landscape normal.

The algorithm is as follows:

Calculate the magnitude of the velocity vector, normalise it and apply a maximum velocity constraint

Project the velocity vector into the car's local coordinate system and damp each component with an individual damping factor

Rebuild the velocity vector

Calculate the number of revolutions of the wheel for the time increment *dt* (based on forward motion only)

Rotate the body of the car about its vertical (*y*) axis

Apply the velocity and move the car

Check for ground collision – if no collision apply gravity to the vertical velocity component. If collision then align the car with the landscape normal

```cpp
int car::step(int dt)
{
  // if no contact, apply gravity
  if (!contactobj)
    vel.z-=gravity*dt;
  // if moving
  float len=vel.length();
  if (len>0.01f)
  {
    // normalize velocity
    vel/=len;
    if (len>maxvel)
      len=maxvel;

    // project velocity in car local axes
    vector v;
    v.x=vec_dot(vel,X)*len;
    v.y=vec_dot(vel,Y)*len;
    v.z=vec_dot(vel,Z)*len;

    // apply damping to individual axes
    // X for sliding and Z for breaking
    for( int i=0;i<3;i++ )
      if (v[i]>=0.0f)
        {
        v[i]-=veldamp[i]*dt;
        if (v[i]<0.0) v[i]=0.0f;
        }
      else
        {
        v[i]+=veldamp[i]*dt;
        if (v[i]>0.0) v[i]=0.0f;
        }

    // restore velocity vector from axes components
    vel=v.x*X + v.y*Y + v.z*Z;

    // compute wheel roll based on forward motion and wheel radius
    wheelrollft+=v.z*dt/(M_2Pi*wheelradiusft)*360.0f;
```

```
wheelrollft=(float)fmod(wheelrollft,360);
wheelrollbk+=v.z*dt/(M_2Pi*wheelradiusbk)*360.0f;
wheelrollbk=(float)fmod(wheelrollbk,360);

// rotate car body based on forward motion and steering angle
if in
//contact
if (contactobj)
   rotate(-wheelrot*v.z*dt/carwheelrot,Y);

// move by applying velocity and force
flyengine->excludecollision=this;
particle::step(dt);
flyengine->excludecollision=0;
life=0;
}

// apply damping to the steering
if (wheelrot>=0.0f)
   {
   wheelrot-=wheelrotdamp*dt;
   if (wheelrot<0.0f)
      wheelrot=0.0f;
   if (wheelrot>wheelmaxrot)
      wheelrot=wheelmaxrot;
   }
else
   {
   wheelrot+=wheelrotdamp*dt;
   if (wheelrot>0.0f)
      wheelrot=0.0f;
   if (wheelrot<-wheelmaxrot)
      wheelrot=-wheelmaxrot;
   }

// ray intersect collision detection to check for ground contact
vector p=pos-carheight*Y,ip;
flyengine->excludecollision=this;
contactobj=flyengine->collision_bsp(flyengine->bsp,pos,p,ip,contact
facenum);
flyengine->excludecollision=0;

// if in contact
if (contactobj)
{
   // position the car at a fixed distance from the ground
   pos=ip+(carheight-0.1f)*Y;
   // align car with ground
   rotate(Y,contactobj->faces[contactfacenum]->normal,0.1f*dt);
```

```
        }
      return 1;
    }
    void car::check_keys(int dt)
    {
      unsigned char *diks=directx->diks;
      if (diks[0xcb]&0x80)       // left arrow
        wheelrot+=wheelrotvel*dt;

      if (diks[0xcd]&0x80)       // right arrow
        wheelrot-=wheelrotvel*dt;

      if (contactobj) // cannot move unless in contact with the ground
      {
      if (diks[0xc8]&0x80)        // up arrow
        vel-=Z*(accel*dt);

      if (diks[0xd0]&0x80)        // down arrow
        vel+=Z*(accel*dt);
      }
    }
```

16.5 Object–object Interaction

The simple car simulation of the previous section can easily be enhanced to include other cars. Consider a robot car that follows a rabbit (or any object) which is tracking around a Bézier curve. (This example was also used in Section 13.4 to illustrate the problem of maintaining a uniform velocity for the rabbit with respect to the Bézier path.) The pursuit car is the same as the user-controlled car introduced in the previous section except that the input to the car simulation now outputs from the pursuit algorithm rather than coming from user-controlled keys. The simple pursuit strategy consists of maintaining the forward (z) component of the velocity constant and turning right or left depending on which side of $\mathbf{V_z}$ the target vector $\mathbf{T}$ is located (Figure 16.7).

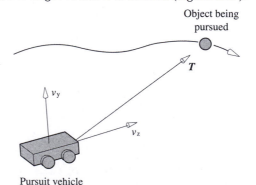

Figure 16.7
Vectors used in pursuit strategy.

Turning is implemented by activating a turn if the angle between T and V_z exceeds a threshold:

if $(V_z \cdot T) > \cos(\theta_{\text{threshold}})$ **then** turn

The turn direction is determined comparing V_y and the cross-product between T and V_z:

if $V_y * (V_z \times T) > 0$ **then** turn right **else** turn left

```
void car::check_robot_keys(int dt)
{
  if (track==0 || contactobj==0)
    return;

  vector P,T,V;
  float len,dot;

  // get position of rabbit
  curtracktime=(curtracktime+dt)%totaltracktime;
  track->interpolate((float)curtracktime/totaltracktime,&P.x);
  T=P-pos;
  len=T.length();
  T/=len;
  dot=vec_dot(T,Z);
  if (dot<0.996) // 0.996=cos(8)
    {
    V.cross(T,Z);
    if (vec_dot(V,Y)>0)
      wheelrot+=wheelrotvel*dt; // rotate right
    else
      wheelrot-=wheelrotvel*dt; // rotate left
    }

  vel-=Z*(accel*dt); // move forward
}
```

16.6 Camera–object interaction

A good example of camera–object interaction is a ship death. For normal ship movement the camera is fixed relative to the ship and moves with it. When a ship is killed the following sequence can ensue:

(1) The camera is stopped at the kill position so that the death sequence is observable.

(2) The player loses control of the ship and a transition is made to a dynamic simulation, the ship moving under the influence of gravity and the forces applied by the projectile that caused the kill.

(3) The first collision that occurs causes the ship to explode, the camera remaining stationary to observe the explosion.

(4) The player reappears at the start position and the camera repositions accordingly.

Objects with simple autonomous behaviour

Enemy objects are distinguished by not being under user control. Thus they have to be scripted, with respect to user objects, so that they behave in a way that results in good game play. One obvious way to consider their behaviour is as independent entities with rudimentary perception. The following two examples demonstrate this. These are two extremely simple but typical examples; in the next chapter we look into autonomous behaviour in greater depth.

Turret gun

The turret gun is a static object with a movable gun barrel. Its behaviour is categorised as follows:

The gun is activated at its first render.

The gun looks for enemies within a bounding sphere.

If an enemy is within its bounding sphere then the dot product of the target direction and the current muzzle direction is calculated.

The gun tries to move its muzzle to align with the target direction. However, it possesses a pre-set maximum angular velocity and this may not be possible. If the target is within a predefined angular tolerance (say, 5°) then a projectile is fired.

```
int turret::step(int dt)
{
    // not activated yet by a render
    if (active!=2) return 0;
    // if no shield, explode and die
    if (shield<0.0f)
        {
        life=-1; // die
        if (exp)
            exp->do_explode(pos,Z,-1); // explode
        return 0;
        }
    // look around for enemy
```

```
enemy=0;
enemydist=lookrange;
flyengine->apply_bsp(flyengine->bsp,pos,lookrange,this,turret_find);

// if enemy found
if (enemy)
{
   // get enemy direction and try to align cannon
   vector dir=pos-enemy->pos;
   dir.normalize();
   tubels.rotate(tubels.Z,dir,rotvel*dt);

   // if cannon is inside fire angle threshold
   if (g && vec_dot(dir,tubels.Z)>fireang)
      // if cannon still has bullets
      if (g->firecount)
         // fire
         g->fire(this,-1);
}

return 0;
}
```

(16.7.2)

Robot flying object

This object is similar to the turret gun except it possesses the ability to move. It is thus animated like any other moving object and its motion is based on elapsed time. We can also give it a rudimentary vision detection and make it look for an enemy within a bounding sphere and a pre-set field of view angle. As before, the device is only activated at the first render. The action is best represented by a state transition diagram (Figure 16.8). This shows the following motion states:

- **Looking for an enemy** In this state the robot is continually looking around and can detect objects that lie in both its field of view and its bounding sphere.

- **Tracking the enemy** When an enemy is found the robot rotates into the target direction and fires when it is within a pre-set angular threshold. At the same time it must continually invoke a ray intersect collision detection test because the player can move into a position where he or she is hidden from the robot.

- **Move to last known position** If the player becomes hidden then a state transition occurs and the robot moves to the last known position, then back to the initial state.

Figure 16.8
State transition for robot
motion.

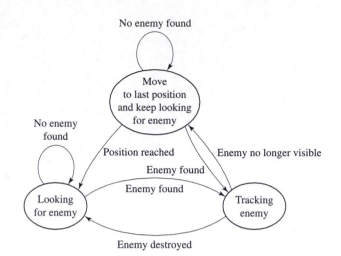

```cpp
int robot::step(int dt)
{
  // if not activated by a render, return
  if (active!=2)
    return 0;

  // if no shield left, die and explode
  if (shield<0)
  {
    life=-1; // die
    if (exp)
      exp->do_explode(pos,Z,-1); // explode
    return 0;
  }

  vector dir;
  float dist;

  // if enemy, test if enemy is still visible or is dead
  if (enemy)
  {
    flyengine->excludecollision=enemy;
    if (((ship *)enemy)->flag2 ||
      (((ship *)enemy)->flag3&SHIP_FLAG3_INVISIBLE) ||
      flyengine->test_collision(flyengine->bsp,pos,enemy->pos))
      {
      flag=((ship *)enemy)->flag2?0:2;
      enemy=0;
      }
    flyengine->excludecollision=0;
  }
```

```
// if no enemy, look around for further possible enemies
if (enemy==0)
  {
  enemydist=lookrange;
  flyengine->apply_bsp(flyengine->bsp,pos,lookrange,this,
  robot_find);
  }
if (enemy)
{
  // compute enemy distance and direction vector
  enemylastpos=enemy->pos;
  dir=pos-enemylastpos;
  dist=dir.length();
  dir/=dist;

  // try to face the enemy and align with floor
  rotate(Z,dir,rotvel*dt); // try to face enemy
  rotate(Y,vector(0,0,1),rotvel*(dt>>2)); //try to align with
floor

  // if in gun range, fire
  if (g && vec_dot(dir,Z)>fireang)
    // if bullets available
    if (g->firecount)
      // fire
      g->fire(this,-1);

  // if not too close, move behind the enemy
  if (dist>mindist)
    {
    flag=1; // moving
    enemylastpos+=enemy->Z*mindist;
    }
  else flag=0; // stay still
}
if (flag) // move in direction of enemy's last position
  {
  dir=enemylastpos-pos;
  dist=dir.length();
  if (dist<0.1f)
    flag=0;

  else
    {
    vel=dir*(maxvel/dist);
    flyengine->stepobj=this;
    particle::step(dt);
    force.null();
```

```
                    life=1;
                    }
                }
            return 1;
        }
```

User–scene interaction

A common user–scene interaction is a three-dimensional selection. This is used in three-dimensional strategy games which impart a better feel than the original two-dimensional games. The user clicks on the two-dimensional screen coordinate occupied by the object to be selected and the utility must find the identity of the object. This reduces to finding the ray that leaves the camera and intersects the object and we can do this as follows:

(1) Transform the clicked pixel into normalised field of view coordinates:

$$x_v = 2x_s/s_x - 1$$

$$y_v = 1 - 2y_s/s_y$$

$$z_v = C_z$$

where

(x_s, y_s) is the clicked pixel coordinate

(s_x, s_y) is the screen resolution

(2) Find the direction D of the ray from C the camera position to this point (Figure 16.9)

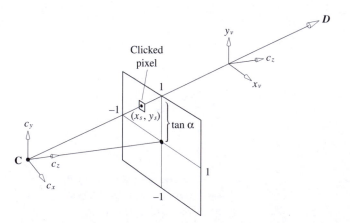

Figure 16.9
3D user selection: finding the ray that passes through a selected pixel.

$$\boldsymbol{D} = (x,y,z)$$

where

$$x = x_v \tan(\alpha) \text{ / aspect ratio}$$

$$y = y_v \tan(\alpha)$$

$$z = C_z$$

α is half the field of view angle

(3) Use the ray with origin $\boldsymbol{C}$ and direction $\boldsymbol{D}$ to ray intersect the BSP tree. A simple implementation of user–scene interaction is as follows:

```
POINT point;
GetCursorPos(&point);
ScreenToClient(hwnd,&point);

float xv=-1+((float)point.x/(flyengine->SCREEN_SX/2));
float yv=1-((float)point.y/(flyengine->SCREEN_SY/2));

dir =   (float)tan(flyengine->camangle/2*flyengine->aspect*PiOver180)
*xv*X + (float)tan(flyengine->camangle/2*PiOver180)*yv*Y - Z;
if (flyengine->collision_bsp(flyengine->bsp,pos,pos+dir*flyengine->
                  viewmaxdist))
     {
       // use collision information
     }
```

Finally note that there is a function in OpenGL for mapping from world space to screen space and vice versa:

gluProject (world to screen) and gluUnProject (screen to world)

Behaviour and AI

17.1   Established approaches and architectures

17.2   Agents and hierarchies

17.3   Examples of agent architectures

17.4   Cognitive modelling and situation calculus

17.5   The role of sensing – vision as an example

17.6   Learning architectures

Introduction

In this chapter we will look at the difficulty of building behaviour into a game which is of sufficient complexity that to the player it appears to imitate human opponents. We are most interested in games involving game-controlled human or human-like characters and the solution most suggested for this is to use AI technology. In other words, characters, or agents as we will subsequently call them, are given the ability to react autonomously to environmental stimuli and communicate with other agents in the game to act as a multi-agent system or team.

The chapter is very definitely not a treatise on how to use AI in games. This is a very large and currently very fluid topic. Rather the aim is to give a feel for the potential of AI technology in terms of the benefits it can bring to both game development and game content. The chapter is more of a debate about the potential of AI in games – a hard treatment of the subject would require a book in its own right. In particular, we try to demonstrate the power of AI techniques as high-level design tools which may lead to game content that would be inordinately difficult to achieve using conventional programming techniques. We will do this by looking at examples both from the gaming and academic worlds. Although it is not the only potential application of AI technology, we will concentrate on how we can develop game characters or 'bots'. Other mainstream applications of AI in games – A-life, genetic algorithms, path planning and so on – are not covered.

Up to now we have been concerned with low-level motion – given that an object is to move from point A to point B, how do we motivate the actions of the character to achieve this? We now come to discuss the difficult and generally unsolved area of high-level motion control – how do we know at a point in the game to issue the command to the character: move from point A to point B? We tend to use the term behaviour to emphasise that we are now concerned with how a character behaves rather than how the geometry is controlled to execute a behaviour or motion.

As we have already discussed, human-character computer games are conventionally designed by using pre-calculated sequences which are selected during the game by user intersection. What we are now considering is not how these low-level sequences are generated (the topic of previous chapters in this section) but how they are selected and controlled. We do this by assuming that we already have a low-level module that is capable of appropriately interpreting any high-level commands from an AI module; although as we noted in Chapter 13 the problems associated with the low-level animation of human agents are themselves certainly not all solved.

The motivation of the use of AI technology comes from the demand for apparently intelligent computer-controlled characters or opponents that are autonomous. It is possibly the case that the success of multi-player deathmatch games reflects the fact that intelligent autonomous computer characters of sufficient quality to sustain user interest in a single player game have not yet emerged. In the future games that contain such characters will be inherently more interesting and engaging. Characters may be opponents, helpers/advisers or just onlookers but they need to have a conceptual understanding of the game world and be able to perceive changes in it if they are to react in a human-like manner.

It is difficult to define AI in such contexts. We know that we can build complexity into agents by conventional techniques using imperative programming languages so where exactly do such techniques end and AI methods begin? The answer is a matter of opinion. AI methods are programs like any other; it is simply the case that the program writer constructs the programs by using AI models and by defining rules for the agents and their interactions. The motivation is that this is a better and more robust way of injecting the required complexity than by writing a program in terms of reactions to all predicted events. And in imperative programming in general it is not obvious how to go about constructing such a system. In this way it may be possible to produce agent actions that would (perhaps) have been unpredictable. It is this unpredictability that is at the root of interesting and apparently complex behaviour, and this is done by facilitating (apparently) autonomous interaction between the agent and the environment and between agents. This is called 'emergent' behaviour. It means behaviour that emerges from a program which does not apparently contain explicit instructions that specify the behaviour.

Animation of human-like characters must eventually be derived from processes that decide upon the behaviour of agents. The animation becomes the result of the behaviour. An important emphasis here is the separation of the

Figure 17.1
Hierarchies in
motion/behaviour control.

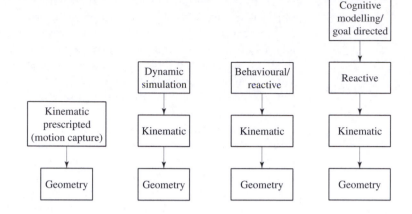

levels in the motion control hierarchy (Figure 17.1). The existence of two levels at the top of the hierarchy on the right is after a definition by Funge *et al.* (1999). The role and difference between these levels is subtle and will hopefully become clear during the course of the chapter.

An obvious advantage for game development is that the separation of an animation from the behaviour that motivates it means that development tools should eventually be possible that enable, say, a football manager to design the AI of a football game or a fighter pilot to design air combat game play.

In what follows we will be reviewing two main approaches to implementing behaviour. The established approaches – mainly based on variations of the finite state machine (FSM) model – are generally pre-programmed. The game programmer attempts to define the behaviour of the agent by building an FSM which can be viewed simplistically as a lookup table. At run-time, input to the FSM determines the behaviour. Newer approaches are goal based. Instead of trying to account for all possible modes of behaviour, the programmer defines goals and ways in which these can be achieved. At run-time the program looks for a solution that achieves the required goal. The motivation for the latter approach is that complex behaviours are easier to set up in this way. The penalty is that the run-time computational cost is much higher. However, with more and more processor time being freed from graphics production, this consideration will matter less in the future.

These two approaches are termed deterministic and (perhaps confusingly) non-deterministic. In the deterministic case, the programmer determines exactly what is going to happen and writes high-level code accordingly. Non-deterministic, on the other hand, simply means that the behaviour is determined at run time. It is non-deterministic from the programmer's point of view; because of the layers of complexity involved, he or she cannot predict exactly what is going to happen. However, we are still driving a Von Neumann machine and behind the scenes tree-searching strategies determine exactly what is going to happen.

17.1 Established approaches and architectures

Most games behave according to rules explicitly coded in an imperative programming language in the form of constructs like **if** statements. Woodcock (1999) categorises this as rule-based AI and lists the following reasons for its inertia in games development:

(1) Rule-based approaches are familiar, taking their principle from comfortable programming paradigms.

(2) Rule-based designs are generally predictable and hence easy to test (although this in turn leads to one of the biggest complaints on the part of players – predictability of game AI).

(3) Most developers lack any training in, or knowledge of, the more exotic AI technologies and thus don't turn to them when deadlines loom.

17.1.1 Finite state machines (FSMs)

Rule-based AI can be modelled as a finite state machine. A finite state machine is a box with inputs and outputs as shown in Figure 17.2. Each state is characterised by identical inputs and outputs and states occur only in pre-determined sequences. In this case the inputs are the game situations, which the machine recognises, and the outputs are the actions. Although such models can be made complex by putting in more and more rules, they are to a greater or lesser extent predictable as far as the player is concerned.

Let us now look at FSMs in more detail. Processors at the hardware level can be modelled by considering them as a Von Neumann machine which is a collection of functional units: arithmetic, memory and I/O processors all of which are organised by a control unit. Such a hardware model is not particularly useful for our purposes and FSMs model the behaviour of the hardware in a more accessible manner. A processor can be in an (almost) infinite number of states, where any one state is just a snapshot of all variable parts of the machine at any instant. Thus we model the machine as a memory representing the current-state, next-state logic which samples the inputs and the current state and then decides what the next state should be. Equivalently we can model a problem or game or agent as an FSM and conveniently represent the problem world as a state transition diagram. Figure 17.2(b) (which is the simple robot example of Figure 16.8 duplicated here) shows such a diagram categorising the behaviour of the robot as an entity that at any instant is in a certain state and can only move to another state when a particular event occurs.

In an imperative language we can build an FSM using a plethora of **if** statements and/or **case** statements. However, as our problem becomes more and more complex, it may not be the most convenient way to express or implement the problem. That is not to say that an AI language can ever make our computer

Figure 17.2
General model of a finite
state machine.

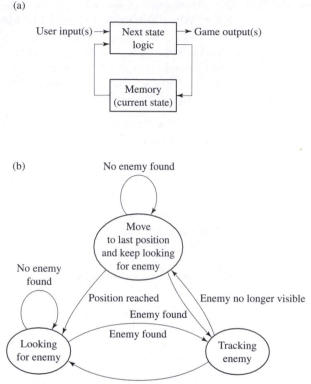

(a)

User input(s) → Next state logic → Game output(s)

Memory (current state)

(b)

No enemy found

Move to last position and keep looking for enemy

No enemy found

Position reached

Enemy no longer visible

Enemy found

Enemy found

Looking for enemy

Tracking enemy

Enemy destroyed

more than an FSM, just that we may be able to deal with problems that are inordinately difficult to implement in an imperative language.

Let us look at this point in more detail. We see that we have (at least) 3 models for the behaviour of a FSM:

● A graphical representation in the form of a state transition diagram;

● A collection of statements in an imperative language;

● A collection of hardware units comprising a memory and combinatorial logic.

The point here is that the first two representations are in effect one-to-one mappings of the third – the hardware – and from this flows the inherent limitation in building complex behaviour using an FSM. In practice, if we want to go about building an FSM, then there are established design procedures that enable us to set about the task in a methodical manner, remove redundancies and so on. However, the individual design phase involves us in setting up a complete representation of the FSM (in the form of a state transition diagram, say). It is this stage – requiring the designer to have a complete low-level internal representation of the problem – that probably limits the complexity of the behaviour that can be built using an FSM.

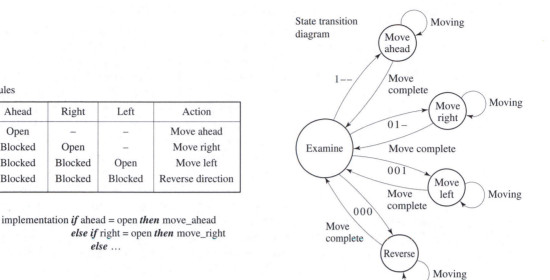

Rules

Ahead	Right	Left	Action
Open	–	–	Move ahead
Blocked	Open	–	Move right
Blocked	Blocked	Open	Move left
Blocked	Blocked	Blocked	Reverse direction

implementation *if* ahead = open *then* move_ahead
else if right = open *then* move_right
else …

Figure 17.3
Three representations of the mouse moving problem.

We now consider a simple example – a mouse running through a maze. The mouse examines the possibilities at each step by looking ahead, right and left. We may decide to implement the following rules:

Ahead	**Right**	**Left**	**Action**
Open	–	–	Move ahead
Blocked	Open	–	Move right
Blocked	Blocked	Open	Move left
Blocked	Blocked	Blocked	Reverse direction

These are shown as a state transition diagram in Figure 17.3. The actions require further elaboration because the precise movement in two-dimensional space expressed as an increment in *x* and *y* depends on the current direction. Each of these can themselves be elaborated with an FSM and this demonstrates the notion of a hierarchical FSM. Such rules are then transformed into appropriate code – a combination of **if** and **case** statements. We can note that the exact behaviour of the mouse will be a function of the maze itself and the order in which the rules are implemented in an **if then else** construct. That is the implementation defaults to the first possible action it encounters in the **if then else** chain in the event that more than one action is available.

Fuzzy state machines (FuSM)

If we observe the behaviour of an FSM as a black box with inputs and outputs then we see that it generates a specific output for a particular input. (And we must not forget that the current state is also an input in this view.) Now if we consider that for a particular input we can generate any one of a set of particular outputs, then we have an FuSM. The actual output may be chosen randomly or some other more complex weighting function may be involved. This model can implement unpredictable behaviour in the sense that each time a game is played a different behaviour results. The game is no longer deterministic, which means that for consecutive plays, if the user controlled the interface in exactly the same way each time, then the observed game events would be identical. An aspect of intelligent behaviour is unpredictability but we should take care to note that, of course, it is only a single manifestation of intelligence, and perhaps an attribute of lesser import.

In the maze example we could implement a simple FuSM by storing the possible move directions, then randomly selecting one of them, instead of taking the first available direction.

We could implement more 'realistic or expressive' behaviour as refinements to this basic behaviour. For example, consider the effect of the mouse leaving droppings as it travels back from a dead end so that they are never re-explored.

From this trivial example we can now begin to see how an autonomous agent can be built from an FSM. The inputs to the FSM are provided by (pseudo) sensors which provide the agent with information on its environment. In the mouse example it has the ability to examine the state of the maze at each step and such information causes a state transition in the FSM which invokes an output. The output affects the world – the mouse moves and may leave a dropping.

The mouse is an example of easily implementable behaviour. However, the truth about FSMs is that as the behaviour becomes more and more complex, so does the difficulty of constructing the rules that will produce the behaviour. To illustrate this, we consider that a single classic rule for navigating a maze – always turn left and only turn right if forced to do so – would have produced a convincing behaviour had we thought of it in the first place.

One observation we make about the SOAR system in Section 17.3 is that its inherent difficulty is the generation of the rules. Laird and Jones (1998) describe a (military) simulation using SOAR which has 5200 rules. Rules have to refer to both the current state of the world and what went on before.

17.2 Agents and hierarchies

Arthur Koestler in his book *The Ghost in the Machine* (1967) famously remarked that 'wherever there is life , it must be hierarchically organised'. We have already seen how the problem of controlling a software robot can be viewed as a hierarchy and in this section we will see how a hierarchical approach persists.

Agent is a generic term in AI to describe software that perceives a world, thinks, then effects actions on the world. The world may be real – in the case of robotics – or virtual in the case of games. Virtual worlds are forgiving compared to real worlds and the significant problems in robotics – the demanding electromechanics and vision difficulties – are removed in virtual worlds. There is no electromechanics and the computer vision problem is ameliorated in virtual worlds as we describe in Section 17.5.

In computer games an agent will usually be a character – an opponent or maybe an adviser. We can look upon an agent in a game as a separate software entity – an autonomous agent – communicating with the game world via a (sensor) input link and an output link. The game character sees the game world, through (say) a synthetic vision facility and acts on the world according to its AI, moving virtual objects, avoiding obstacles, and so on. Thus it can be seen as a module whose decision cycle is executed in (simulated) parallel with the game cycle. A game that contains many agents is like many processors all executing in parallel.

The second action in the decision cycle – thinks – is that which defines the nature and effectiveness of the agent and we first look at the attributes an agent may possess. One of the problems with this new field is the profileration of terminology, and we will look at three categorisations due to Russel and Norvig (1995), called:

- reflex or reactive agent;
- reflex or reactive agent with internal state;
- goal-based agent.

Van Lent and Laird (1999) term these reactive, context specific and flexible respectively and off-line computer graphics has tended to lump all categories together under the generic term of behavioural animation.

Perhaps it doesn't need emphasising that software agents, as we have described them, are a reflection of the current technology. That is, they take input from, and output to, the game world only (considering, that is, the monitor screen as part of the game world rather than the real world.) This is likely to change in the future, and indeed other modalities are already implemented in research institutions.

Perhaps the most predictable extension is for a software agent to link with both the real and the virtual world. In a turn-based game a software opponent could interact with a player by observing his or her facial expressions and listening to and reacting to what he or she says as well as basing play on the state of the board. In games such as poker, for example, it is vital to interpret the behaviour of opponents outside of their card play. The sensor link to the agent would require computer vision and speech recognition and the agent's AI would require natural language processing so that it could interpret dialogue and respond to it.

In the ALIVE project (Maes *et al.*, 1995) human and autonomous software agents inhabit the same virtual world, allowing the humans to interact with the virtual characters:

> The ALIVE system consists of different virtual worlds between which the user can switch by pressing a virtual button. Each world is inhabited by dif-

ferent agents: one world is inhabited by a Puppet, a second one by a Hamster and Predator and a third one by a Dog. The Puppet follows the user around and tries to hold the user's hand. It also imitates some of the actions of the user (sitting down, jumping etc.). It will be sent away when the user points away and will come back when the user waves. The Puppet employs facial expressions to convey its internal state. For example, it pouts when the user sends it away, smiles when the user motions to it to come back. It giggles when the user touches its belly.

17.2.1 Reflex or reactive agent

This is the simplest type of game agent which reacts to a situation according to rules of the form:

> **if** condition **then** action

An example would be a character that opened fire when an enemy is in sight/range. However, if the enemy moves out of sight it has no capacity to remember that an enemy exists. A reactive agent simply searches its rule database for a rule whose condition matches the perceived state of the world and performs the appropriate action. A reflex or reactive agent can be implemented using an FSM.

17.2.2 Reflex agent with internal state

A simple reflex agent reacts to the current situation with no memory of past events. Its entire knowledge of the world is derived from its sensor at the instant its decision cycle is activated. The first facility that we may consider that extends its powers is a memory; an agent needs to remember past events. The agent sees a rock behind which an enemy has moved in the previous frame...

17.2.3 Goal-based agents

Technically we say that a reactive agent is an entity that immediately maps percepts into actions. (A percept is the unit of information supplied to the agent as input.) A reactive agent only considers current percepts – it has no memory. Such an agent is extremely limited. We can extend rules to deal with the past as well as the present, but this complicates even more the construction of the appropriate rules.

A better approach is to use a description of the world which is based on current percepts with the important qualification that this can be updated. Thus as the new percepts arrive and actions result from these, the description of the world changes. This is the basis of the situation calculus approach described in Section 17.4.

Goal-based agents consider the consequence of actions, rather than simply reacting to the current state of the world. The agent has to consider what will happen if it performs action X. Thus the agent needs to have knowledge or be supplied with goals and strategies that can operate on the current world state to see if and how these goals can be reached. For example, search strategies and path planning strategies are algorithms that result in action sequences that try to achieve the agents' goals.

Funge *et al.* (1999) argue that a general model of any system requires a reasoning level above the behavioural or reactive level. This is built up by the designer who gives knowledge to the agents by defining a set of axioms that constitute the way in which agents interact with each other and the environment. Characters possess knowledge concerning their goals and how they may be achieved. The system's behaviour becomes *emergent* – it arises out of the interaction of the agent's behavioural rules. It is not reactive in the sense that hard-wired program statements produce a reaction to all possible environmental events. Such a model is an explicit statement of how a designer expects the world to behave. It is the emergent approach that may produce behaviour he or she did not anticipate. An important point here is that there may be overlap between a behavioural level and a reasoning level and the separation of the top two levels in the motion control hierarchy (Figure 17.1) is an over-simplification.

17.3   Examples of agent architectures

In this section we will look at examples of systems that exhibit the properties we have just described. We first start with reactive systems and use the term behavioural animation because that is how they were originally categorised in the computer graphics literature. In computer graphics reactive or behavioural animation has been used to generate group or social behaviour between rudimentary entities: schooling in fish, flocking behaviour in birds and stampeding in animal herds are three common examples.

Behavioural animation in computer graphics can be seen, in many of its manifestations, as an elaboration of particle animation. Usually we set up a kind of rudimentary 'sociological' model involving the behaviour of a population of entities (or a single entity). The significant difference between behavioural and particle animation is that in behavioural animation each entity is allocated a set of rules that govern its behaviour as a function of its relationship (usually spatial) to neighbouring entities.

The early and influential example of a behavioural model was developed by Reynolds (1987) to simulate the flocking phenomenon in birds and fishes. Here, each bird or fish possessed a set of rules that governed its behaviour with respect to neighbouring members of the group which was controlled by supplying global direction vectors. This basic idea was used to great effect in the Disney production *The Lion King* (1994) where a stampede sequence was controlled in this way.

Reynolds points out that flocking behaviour consists of two opposing factors – a desire to stay close to the flock and a desire to avoid collision within the flock. He simulated this behaviour as three rules, which in order of decreasing precedence are:

(1) Collision avoidance: avoid collisions with nearby flock mates.

(2) Velocity matching: attempt to match the velocity of nearby flock mates.

(3) Flock centring: attempt to stay close to nearby flock mates.

The behaviour of the model is summarised by Reynolds as follows:

> The flocking model described gives birds an eagerness to participate in an acceptable approximation of flock-like motion. Birds released near one another begin to flock together cavorting and jostling for position. The birds stay near one another (flock centring) but always maintain prudent separation from their neighbours (collision avoidance), and the flock becomes quickly 'polarised' – its members heading in approximately the same direction at approximately the same speed (velocity matching); when they change direction they do it in synchronisation. Solitary birds and smaller flocks join to become larger flocks, and in the presence of external obstacles, larger flocks can be split into smaller flocks.

From the pioneering work of Reynolds we now look at a more recent ambitious system of behavioural animation. This work by Tu and Terzopoulos (1994), simulating the behaviour of fish, is a self-animating system where the models are equipped with rudimentary vision, a physics-based locomotion capacity that reacts with hydrodynamic forces to simulate swimming behaviour and a set of behavioural rules. This appears to be the first attempt in computer animation to integrate all these aspects into one system.

The autonomous model that makes up each fish is made up of different levels of abstraction. Internal to the fish body is an 'animate spring-mass system'. This is a set of 23 nodes interconnected by 91 springs – some of the springs also serving as contractile muscles. The position of the nodes control the shape of the fish. The fish swims like a real fish by contracting its muscles – decreasing the rest length of a muscle spring. The characteristic swinging of the tail, for example, is set up by contracting muscles on one side of the body while simultaneously relaxing muscles on the other side. An equation is set up for each node, relating the mass and acceleration of the node together with the forces exerted, through the springs, from all other nodes to the external hydrodynamic force. These equations are solved at each time step to give the overall movement of the nodes. Thus the basis of this part of the model is a cloud of nodal points moving forward through the water and at the same time moving with respect to each other. Motion is initiated by motion controllers which translate a desired action, such as swimming ahead or turning, into detailed muscle actions.

To these nodes is coupled the control points of a parametric surface which models the skin of the fish. This results in a deformable body whose deformation is controlled by the underlying physical model. Additionally controlling the orientation of fins gives pitch, yaw and roll control to the basic motion. To this model, which successfully imitates fish locomotion to a high level of fidelity, is added a behaviour system to which is input information from a rudimentary visual perception and a temperature sensor. The visual sensor extracts such information as the colour, size, distance and identity of objects that enter its field of view.

The behavioural aspect is implemented as a set of routines that generate the appropriate actions to control the muscles. These are selected by an intention generator which selects a behaviour based on the sensory information, the fish's current mental state and its habits. Habits are represented as parameters and the mental state by variables. A state such as hunger is incremented by time and decremented when a fish eats a food particle. The behavioural routines simulate such activities as avoid-static-obstacle, avoid-fish, eat-food, mate, escape, school, and so on. A representation of information flow in a fish model is shown in Figure 17.4.

We now look at a game example of a goal-based agent architecture – the SOAR model described by Van Lent and Laird (1999). Lent and Laird call their agent architecture a flexible agent which has a choice of high-level tactics that specify goals and a choice of lower-level behaviours which implement the tactics.

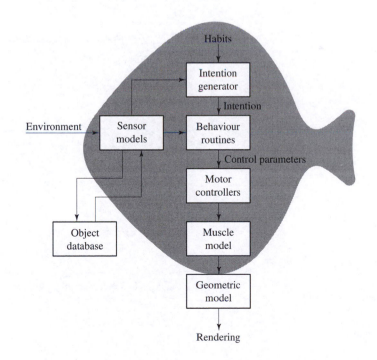

Figure 17.4
Information flow in the artificial fish (after Tu and Terzopoulos (1994)).

The SOAR architecture consists of:

● a set of user written **if-then** rules;

● an input link which transfers game world knowledge into the AI – sensor information;

● a working memory which contains intermediate data structures and a stack of current goals;

● an output link over which SOAR acts on the game world.

If all the rule's conditions are matched by sensor information, a rule is activated and actions may include updating state information in the memory, proposing new goals, selecting from proposed goals and using commands to act on the world. Much of the flexibility of the agents' behaviour derives from the ways in which the goals are structured into the inevitable hierarchy. Knowledge is invested in the agent by a hierarchy of operators (Figure 17.5). As the hierarchy is descended the behaviour becomes more and more specific. The top level represents the goals and a leaf of the hierarchy a primitive action. The second level represents tactics used to achieve the goal and lower levels represent behaviours and sub-behaviours. The implementation handles up to 10 agents at 5 decision

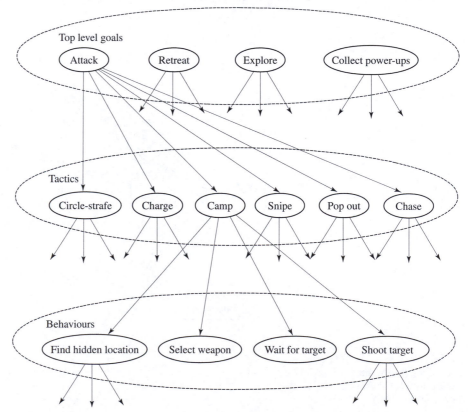

Figure 17.5
SOAR operator hierarchy for a Quake II type game (based on an illustration by Lent and Laird (1999))

cycles/second for each agent. In any given decision cycle one operator can be active at each level of the hierarchy and an operator is chosen on the basis of the selection conditions. All potential operators with matching selection conditions are considered.

Theoretically SOAR is known as a production system. A production system is based (again) on **if then** statements – if a condition is satisfied an action is performed. It differs crucially from a simple reaction system in the following way. In a simple reaction system even if the percept matches more than one rule – only one rule/action is selected; either the one that is first encountered by the system or by a random selection. This contrasts with production systems where more than one rule is triggered at the same time which requires a decision procedure to select the 'best' rule in the circumstances. The system is presented with a new percept and for each cycle through the system we can identify three phases. First, we identify the subset of rules that match the percept. This is followed by a conflict resolution phase which decides which rules should be executed. The final phase executes the actions of the selected rules.

Lent and Jones (1998) give the following example from an air combat simulation. Suppose an aircraft is currently intercepting an enemy plane and two rules are proposed: the intercepting craft should fire a missile and the intercepting craft should invoke a defensive manoeuvre (because the enemy may have already fired a missile). These proposed actions will themselves be tested by another rule which recognises that both these actions have been proposed but decides that because the first priority is to destroy the enemy the fire missile wins over the defensive manoeuvre.

This type of architecture is often compared to the (presumed) organisation of the human brain. Here we suppose that we have a knowledge base containing percepts known as the short-term memory and a long-term memory which contains the productions.

One of the motivations for the study was to develop an AI engine design with a knowledge base that was not specific to a particular game but to a particular genre. The engine then requires a small amount of context-dependent information to be added for a particular game.

Lent and Laird report that a simple agent for Quake II was developed that used just 15 operators in a three-level hierarchy to battle human opponents. They remark that while this does not result in an expert player it is sufficient to beat beginners easily and provides a challenging opponent for intermediate players.

17.3.1 Top down vs. bottom up

An important observation that can be made from these examples is that the SOAR system could be considered a top-down approach whereas the artificial fish and flocking examples are bottom-up approaches. In the top-down example the developer has complete knowledge of how he or she wants the agent to behave. This is perhaps conceived hierarchically just as the final structure is hierarchical. Thus the designer can at the outset build in engaging and interesting behaviour – he or she creates the creature.

In a bottom-up approach we argue that we can have high-level behaviour emerging from the interaction of low-level mechanisms. The designer creates the low-level entities and the behaviour emerges from their interaction with each other and their environment. Anyone who has seen Reynolds' flocking simulations would agree with this argument. Apparently complex and realistic behaviour emerges from populations of agents programmed with simple reactive rules, and this is the reason for the enduring popularity of the method.

Bottom-up methods offer a designer a different kind of control where the effectiveness of the emergent behaviour is a function of the ingenuity of the low-level units and the interaction rules. Behaviour may emerge which is satisfyingly complex and which satisfies the game application, and the programming effort may be much less than explicit high-level design. However, Woodcock (1999) states that A-life techniques used to control non-player characters (NPCs) in Ultima ONLINE were to some extent compromised in the interests of gameplay. (A-life are computer programs which in some way facilitate the evolution of a population. Ultima ONLINE uses A-life to control the spawning, migration and other activities of wildlife NPCs.)

Perhaps all we can conclude at the moment is that it is too early to make firm conclusions on the different approaches.

17.4 Cognitive modelling and situation calculus

In the previous section we informally introduced the notion of agents of varying complexity and gave examples of implementations. The implementations were context-dependent architectures built using conventional software. One of the ways of looking at the difficulties of such AI technology is to recognise that imperative programming languages, manifested as **if** and **case** statements, are representations of propositional logic.

Propositional logic is limited in the way in which it can represent knowledge about a virtual world and in this section we look at a variation of first-order logic or first-order predicate calculus. We can introduce first-order logic by stating that it deals with facts, objects and relations. This contrasts with propositional logic which can deal only with facts. As always in this chapter, we intend only to give the reader a feel for the technology and the interested reader is directed to the references.

The motivation for using first-order predicate calculus is defined by Russell and Norvig as:

> . . . any system that makes decisions on the basis of past percepts (events perceived in the past) can be re-written to use instead a set of sentences about the current world state, providing that these sentences are updated as each new percept arrives and each action is done.

Funge *et al.* (1999) employ *situation calculus* (a form of first-order logic) to model a system consisting of agents interacting with each other and the environment. In this section we will give a very informal introduction to the topic and use a demonstration developed by Funge. This is to apply the approach to an obvious example that could easily have been programmed using an imperative language – a simple environment where we can easily deduce the interaction between an agent and its environment. The aim is not to deliver an exhaustive treatment of this topic but to give a feel for the style and relevance of the approach using an easy example. The notation we use is that of Funge.

Situation calculus, as the name implies, is a construct that enables us to describe a changing world or environment as a sequence of situations or states. In animation a situation is just all the world or information we need to render a frame – the position and pose of the objects in the frame and so on. A transition is made from state to state by an *action*.

In what follows we use the following convention:

Negation (NOT)	$\neg P$
Conjunction (AND)	$P \wedge Q$
Disjunction (OR)	$P \vee Q$
Implication (IF)	$P \Rightarrow Q$
Equivalence (IFF)	$P \Leftrightarrow Q$
Universal (ALL)	$\forall x\, [P(x)]$
Existential (EXISTS)	$\exists x\, [P(x)]$

Actions or operations change situations and situation calculus enhances first-order logic to deal with events that change as time passes. Consider the simple block example in Figure 17.6. We can define our goal as:

initial state | **goal state**
on_top(B,A)∧on_top(A,table) | on_top(B,table)∧on_top(A, table)

These predicates, which can take only the values true or false, are enhanced by introducing a situation variable *s*. The above is then rewritten as:

on_top(B,A,s_0)∧on_top(A,table,s_0)

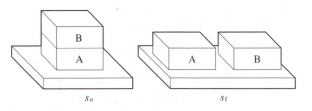

Figure 17.6
A simple two-situation example.

where s_0 is the initial situation, and:

$\exists s_f \, [\text{on\_top}(B,\text{table},s_f)]$

where s_f is the goal or final situation. This states that there exists a state s_f in which B is on top of the table.

on_top() is an example of a fluent, a property of a situation that can change (or flow) from state to state. Fluents can only be changed by actions, so that state s' results from state s when an action is performed:

$s' = \text{result}(\text{action},s)$

In other words, the result of an action is a new situation. In our simple example we could write:

$s_{i+1} = \text{result}(\text{move\_block}(x), s_i)$

Actions are defined by stating their effects, for example

$\forall s \forall x [\neg \text{on\_top}(x,\text{table},s) \Rightarrow \text{on\_top}(x,\text{table},\text{result}(\text{move\_block}(x),s))]$

which states that:

for all situations s and all objects x:

if x is not on top of the table in situation s then x is on top of the new state

result(move_block(x),s).

We now return to the simple two-dimensional world of a mouse moving through a maze. The situations are represented by the maze on which is displayed the position of the mouse in consecutive frames and a transition is made from frame to frame by the mouse moving (N, S, E or W). A single step made by the mouse is then the only action that takes place.

In Figure 17.7 we see that the actions that make the transition from frame to frame are:

result(move(forward), s_0) = s_1

result(move(turn(right)), s_1) = s_2

result(move(forward), s_2) = s_3

As well as actions we require **pre-condition axioms** – to define whether an action is possible or not. They specify what state the world should be in if an action is to be carried out. For example, we may specify that the mouse can only move to an adjacent cell if it does not contain an obstacle, the cell is within the maze (not out of range) and it has not already been visited. Thus to define:

possible(move(d),s)

we need a function like

adjacent(position(s),d)

Figure 17.7
4 situations linked by four actions (after an illustration by Russ 1995).

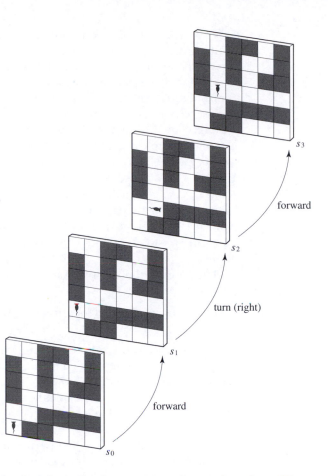

which checks that the cell c does not contain an obstacle and has not been visited before. This is done by a predicate:

free(c) $\Leftrightarrow$ in_range(c) $\wedge\neg$ occupied(c)

which states that c must be in range and not occupied. We also need a fluent:

visited(s)

which is defined recursively and returns a list of all the cells visited. We can then state

possible(move(d),s) $\Leftrightarrow \exists c\ c =$ adjacent(position(s),d) $\wedge$ free(c) $\wedge$ $c \notin$ visited(s)

Axioms that describe how the world changes due to an action are called effect axioms. We need these to state changes in a situation that are a consequence of actions. This is obvious. What may be less obvious is that we also need frame axioms to state what does not change. (Frame – after the term in animation where the background remains constant (usually) with animated characters moving about in the foreground.) If an agent is holding an object in frame s and does not release it we need to state that the agent will be holding it in frame s'. Similarly if the agent does not possess an object in frame s and does not *get* an object, the agent will not be holding one in frame s'. Taken together, effect axioms and frame axioms provide a complete description of what happens when a transition is made from frame s to s'. Combining these axioms enables us to write successor state axioms which, for each predicate, list all the ways in which it can become true and all the ways in which it can become false.

Frame axioms quickly proliferate when situation calculus is used to define a system and this is known as the frame problem. Situation calculus is based on first-order logic and does not admit such 'intuitive assumptions' as: a property does not change if it has not been operated on by an action. Rather we must track each property explicitly from frame to frame. The frame problem can be avoided if we assume a 'closed' world where effect axioms define *all* ways in which the world can change. In this case, effect axioms become successor state axioms.

Returning to the mouse example, we have the following successor state axioms for position:

$$Possible(a,s) \Rightarrow (position(do(a,s)) = p' \Leftrightarrow (\exists d \ a = move(d) \land p' \ adjacent(position(s),d))$$
$$\lor(\neg \exists d \ a = move(d) \land p' = position(s)))$$

which states that if the action is possible then the position after a move is p'. p' is defined as the position which for a direction d is a cell adjacent to the current position, or we have a dead end and the mouse cannot move any further.

Other hurdles, such as the qualification problem and the ramification problem, have to be overcome in any practical application of situation calculus and details of the relevance of these can be found in Funge *et al.* (1999).

All such definitions describing a world are specified in a high-level Prolog-type language. At run-time the system searches for a set of situations that result in the goal. The implementation can be seen as a tree with each node being a situation and each branch an action. The root of the tree is the initial situation and the system invokes a tree-searching strategy to find the solution. A rule-based approach can also be represented as a tree and as we have already remarked, this has to be set up by the programmer. Using situation calculus the programmer describes the world and the goal and the system searches for a solution.

Funge *et al.* (1999) use a language called CML (Cognitive Modelling Language) to produce a number of undersea animations (populated by politically correct mermaids). One mode of behaviour is described as:

> The undersea animations revolve around pursuit and evasion behaviours. The sharks try to eat the merpeople and the merpeople try to use the superior reasoning abilities we give them to avoid such a fate...For example, consider the problem of trying to come up with a plan to hide from a predator. A traditional planning approach will be able to perform a search of various paths according to criteria such as. . . Unfortunately, this kind of planning is expensive and therefore cannot be done over large distances. By using the control structures of CML, we can encode various heuristic knowledge to

help overcome this limitation. For example . . . if the current position is good enough then stay where you are; otherwise search the area around you (the expensive planning part); otherwise check out the obstacles (hidden positions are more likely near obstacles); if all else fails panic and go in random direction . . . the following CML procedure implements the above heuristic:

choose testcurentPosn()

    or search(i)

    or testObstacles(i)

    or panic(i)

17.5 The role of sensing – vision as an example

The AI of an agent communicates with the game world via an input and output link. The output link is no different from a conventional game – it handles the movement of the agent, the acquisition of objects and so on. The input link is of greater interest and in this section we deal with some aspects of this facility.

An agent in a system reacts to an environment and stimuli either automatically or intuitively, controlled by a reactive layer, or it makes a more considered decision based on reasoning supplied by a higher-level layer. Either way, it has to gather information about its surroundings. The vision system in animals is an important high-bandwidth sensing channel and we now consider as an example of an agent's perception a synthetic vision system.

Synthetic computer vision means using computer vision techniques to extract world information from the agent's viewpoint.

At first sight this may seem unnecessary. In any computer simulation, at every frame we have complete knowledge of the environment – the disposition of all objects in an environment is known for all instants in the execution of a program. Why then should we consider apparently complicating matters by giving a synthetic computer vision system to agent(s) in the game? The answer is simply this. It may be the most efficient way of transmitting environmental information of interest to each agent. We can use the engine itself to render the scene from the characters viewpoint exploiting existing efficient utilities to, cull away information too far away to be of interest, for example.

Also, we note that many of the problems that beset 'real' computer vision either do not exist in its synthetic manifestation or they can easily be overcome. For example, the classic problem of computer vision – noise – does not exist in rendered imagery and we can bypass the shape recognition problem by rendering a 'dangerous' or a 'desirable' object in a unique colour. Extraction of three-dimensional information – perhaps the most difficult problem of computer vision – is also solved because we can, in principle, associate a depth buffer with each agent's rendered image.

It may also be the case that a synthetic computer vision solution will scale better in a multi-agent environment. It is likely to be easier to equip each agent with a computer vision facility than to have a master facility broadcasting information of interest to each agent in turn. A subtle point is the believability of the agent. An agent should only possess a vision facility that is consistent with its character – it should have a realistic field of view, for example, and should not be able to see around corners. Possibly the easiest way to implement such realistic vision facilities for agents in a game, particularly if they are going to be sufficiently fine grained to feed into an AI architecture, is actually to give synthetic vision to the agent.

In this respect Lent and Laird point out that the intelligent agent, to be realistic, should only have access to information available to the human player, and no additional information should be given to it. (They point out that a common complaint about game AI is that agents are allowed to cheat by using game information not available to the human player.)

In their study of Quake II opponents, they send sensor information about opponents to the AI engine only if three requirements are met:

● The opponent is in the agent's sight range (a circle based on the agents current position).

● The opponent is in the agent's field of view.

● The agent must have a clear line of sight from its current position to the opponent.

It provides a 'natural' sensing facility for cognitive modelling: 'if you can see the object then move towards it; if it is partially visible then move around the obstacle, if it is not visible look around…'

At a reactive level it is possible to replace, for example, path planning procedures with simple reactive behaviour. A good example of this is given by Blumberg (1996) who develops what he calls a motion energy approach for obstacle avoidance. The approach was inspired by research into bee navigation. It appears that bees flying down a corridor determine their line of flight so as to balance the 'motion energy' in their right and left eyes. Blumberg simply divides the agent's rendered image in half, computes for each pixel a difference term by subtracting consecutive frames, and derives a steering direction as:

$$\text{bearing} = k \left(\sum_{\text{left}} I_\Delta(i,j) - \sum_{\text{right}} I_\Delta(i,j) \right)$$

where

$I_\Delta(i,j)$ is the difference between the value of a pixel between two consecutive frames

k is a gain constant

This of course falls down if an agent is moving normal to a wall.

Learning architectures

From the very earliest days of AI research, learning has figured strongly. The motivation is obvious: if a task seems inordinately difficult to encode in a conventional programming language – recognising handwriting, for example – can we teach an AI architecture to accomplish the task?

Learning can be approached in many and diverse ways. For example, it can be accomplished by explaining experience, training by correcting mistakes (the basic neural net strategy) or by simulating evolution (genetic algorithms), to name but three common approaches.

Explaining experience or explanation-based learning (EBL) generalises from past experience. Its motivation is the speed-up of execution time – a vital requirement in games. A simple but effective idea, it simply means that if the architecture is presented with the same or similar input conditions it does not have to devote the same effort to evaluation because it can remember what it has done before. Because the motivation for EBL is efficiency, it follows that if there is going to be a speed-up in the system it must expect to see occurrences of the same input conditions in the future as it experienced in the past. Otherwise rules will be added to the system, making it larger, and because these new rules still have to be evaluated it will be slower. The SOAR architecture described in Section 17.3 uses EBL. Known as 'chunking', SOAR learns by finding the sequence of conditions that lead to a particular conclusion. It then proposes a new rule or chunk, which proposes the same conclusion given the same conditions.

An obvious application of learning in computer animation is that a computer character can be made more challenging by observing the tactics or behaviour of its human opponent and adjusting its responses accordingly. The synthetic opponent can then gradually adapt its play to the human player's style.

Learning raises certain practical difficulties for real-time processing. Most AI learning architectures – the most common being neural nets – need a supervised or training phase. They cannot learn in the first instance without being presented with a training phase together with the corresponding set of correct responses. In computer games, if this phase is confined to the game development period, with the game being subsequently frozen, then this obviates the potential of the architecture – being able to adapt to individual players. (Unless, that is, the architecture can learn in real time.)

As a final example we will look at classic neural net technology developing a treatment for an extremely simple device – the perceptron. The rationale for presenting this material is not that it necessarily has immediate applications in computer games but that it introduces the important concepts of:

- training and supervision;
- decision making;
- notion of a percept as a single point in multi-dimensional space which can be handled in linear mathematics

Learning and neural nets

Neural nets is the term given to practical implementation of devices that in their simplest form implement linear discriminant functions 'automatically' from a training phase. It is a device, almost always simulated by a program running on a normal processor, that adjusts its structure as it is presented with patterns in a training or supervised phase. Neural nets have applications in many areas of computer science, and we will consider their use in pattern recognition where they were originally known as multi-layer perceptrons.

A pattern in this context can be any n-dimensional vector representing a percept. It could be an image – an array of pixels – in a vision system, or an array of values representing sampled speech. Either way, we consider the percept as a single point in n-dimensional hyperspace. Just as a point in three-dimensional space can represent a percept with three values, a point in n-dimensional space can be used to represent an image of n pixels. A linear discriminant function is a formula that enables us to discriminate between two sets of such points. Each set of points represents a category. So in a computer vision example we may have a set of points representing all the images formed by object A and a set representing object B. The device would be required to output a one or a zero, say, depending on whether it 'sees' A or B. In what follows we generally refer to a percept as a pattern and note that although this suggests an image, any set of values – any perceptual mode – can be represented by a set of numbers. For example, we may have a synthetic opponent which has to make a fire/do not fire decision based on an n-dimensional vector which contains a variety of percept information concerning its human opponent.

The term **neural nets** is perhaps as inappropriate as one that emerged in the 1950s describing early computers as 'giant brains'. It is not just the scale of a human neural network that is unachievable artificially – around 100 billion neurons, – where each individual element may be connected to thousands of others; the complexity of the tasks it performs are inimitable and our knowledge of how human neural nets function is sadly extremely limited. Artificial neurons are extremely simple devices that can be interconnected to form large networks. The size of the network and the number of interconnections make its behaviour difficult to model or predict. However, this fact does not imply that the network is somehow more than the sum of its parts, as the term 'neural net' tends to imply.

In the context of this section a neural net is a system formed by interconnecting a number of simple devices together. The interconnections are fixed but the weight or influence of each connection is variable. Nodes in a network have N inputs and produce a single output. The N inputs can be the components of an N-dimensional pattern vector. An interconnection joins the output of a node to one of the inputs of a node in the next layer. This simple structure is shown in Figure 17.8. It consists of a set of nodes forming an input layer, a set of nodes forming an output layer and a set of intermediate nodes curiously known as hidden layers. The insert shows the set-up in more detail. At each node j we have a

Figure 17.8
Neural net: convention for interconnections.

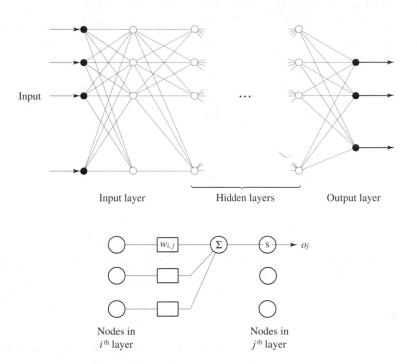

single input I_j which is the sum of the weighted outputs from all the nodes i in the previous layer. This is then operated on by the 'sigmoid' function S to provide the output O_j. The output from the sigmoid unit varies continuously, but not linearly, as the input changes, in a manner that will be explained. We can observe that each node in a layer is presented with the same pattern – the output from the previous layer. However, the input to each node is weighted differently according to how the weights, which are contained in its input line, are adjusted.

Such a network is **trainable**. This means that we can present the device with a number of patterns in a training set and adjust the weights in the network until all the patterns in the training set are correctly categorised. We then suppose that if pattern classes are well represented by the training set, the machine will function well in the future when it is not being supervised – the operating phase. We 'evolve' a decision function by a kind of trial and error method. The machine adjusts its internal structure to effect the correct classification during the training phase.

Consider Figure 17.9, which shows a machine that is to recognise handwritten As and Es. We train the machine by showing it examples from each category. The machine 'sees' these examples as single points in its sensor measurement space (shown in the figure as two-dimensional space). The complete set of points from each category form (hopefully) into clusters and the machine constructs a boundary between these sets. All of its sensor space is then labelled as

Figure 17.9
Training and operating phase for a machine that distinguishes between As and Es.

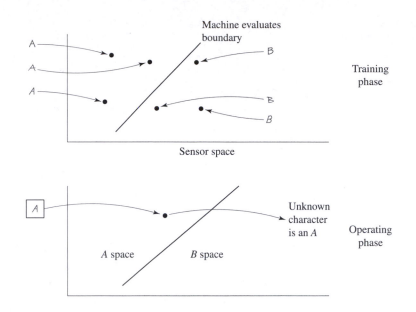

category A or category B. In the operating phase any pattern will fall into one of these labelled categories and can therefore be 'recognised'. Note that the success of such schemes depends critically on the training sets being sufficiently representative of all As and Es. If this is not so, a pattern A will fall into the space categorised as E and vice versa.

The important attribute of neural nets is that they can be trained to deal with pattern classes that are not linearly separable (Figure 17.14). Consider a machine that is to recognise or categorise images that represent hand-written characters. During the training phase it was presented with typical examples of each character and these fell into particular regions in n-dimensional space which the device partitioned and labelled. Linear separability means that these regions can be separated and labelled using hyperplanes. Many if not most practical pattern recognition classes are not linearly separable and because of this it is extremely difficult or even impossible to write a program to recognise, for example, hand-written characters.

Research into such machines has an interesting history. There was much excitement in the late 1950s and early 1960s centred around a device called a **perceptron** that could be trained on linearly separable training sets. In fact, a mathematical proof was developed which demonstrated that a solution would converge after a finite number of iterations in the training phase. It was also known that to deal with training sets that were not linearly separable the perceptron had to be extended into a multi-layer device – a so-called multi-layer perceptron or MLP. The stumbling block then was the lack of effective training algorithms for such devices. Renewed interest in MLPs emerged in 1986 with the popularisation of a training algorithm, known as the **delta rule for learning**

by back propagation, which was originally developed in 1974. This, together with hardware developments and a plethora of potential applications, has caused a resurgence of interest in the field.

The individual element in an MLP is a perceptron for two linearly separable pattern classes and it is with this device that we begin.

17.6.2 Perceptron for two linearly separable pattern classes

This is a simple device that uses a (fixed increment) training algorithm to evolve a linear discriminant function between two linearly separable pattern classes. The device takes as input the pattern vector x. Each input is weighted by a weight coefficient w_i and is fed into a summing device (Figure 17.10). Thus the device implements the linear decision function

$$d(x) = \sum_{i=1}^{N} w_i x_i + w_{N+1}$$

and this is a hyperplane in feature or measurement space whose orientation is determined by the first N coefficients of the weight vector w and whose distance from the origin is set by w_{N+1}. This sum is then tested by an element, called an activation element, to determine its sign and assign the pattern class to which x belongs, depending on whether it is greater or less than zero.

The training algorithm is, for linearly separable categories, guaranteed to find a separating hyperplane and it is known as the **fixed increment correction rule**. The algorithm is more easily stated if we redefine the pattern vector x. We do this by augmenting x with an $(N+1)$th component of unity:

Augmented pattern vector $= y = x_1, x_2, \ldots, x_N, 1$

The weighting of the pattern vector can then be written as a dot product:

$$d(y) = w^T y$$

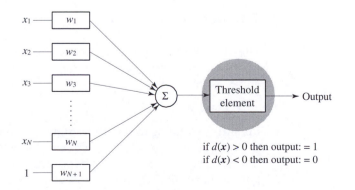

Figure 17.10
Perceptron model for two linearly separable pattern classes.

if $d(x) > 0$ then output: $= 1$
if $d(x) < 0$ then output: $= 0$

where:

$$\mathbf{w} = (w_1, w_2, \ldots, w_N, w_{N+1})^T$$

is called the weight vector.

The algorithm proceeds by presenting the training set (a sample from one class followed by a sample from the other), adjusting $\mathbf{w}$ if the current iteration results in an erroneous classification and stopping when a loop through the algorithm results in 100 per cent correct classification.

Consider a training set consisting of augmented pattern vectors that are known to belong to either category ω_1 or ω_2. The algorithm is:

Assign arbitrary values to $\mathbf{w}$ (say small random numbers)

(k is the iteration number)
repeat

    for each pattern $\mathbf{y}$ in the training set

        evaluate $d^k(y)$
        if $d^k(y) \leq 0$ **and** $\mathbf{y} \in \omega_1$
        then $\mathbf{w}^{k+1} := \mathbf{w}^k + \delta\mathbf{y}$
            an_error := TRUE

        if $d^k(\mathbf{y}) \geq 0$ **and** $\mathbf{y} \in \omega_2$
        then $\mathbf{w}^{k+1} := \mathbf{w}^k - \delta\mathbf{y}$
            an_error := TRUE

    until NOT(an_error)

In this algorithm δ is a fixed number in the range $0, \ldots, 1$. Thus when an complete iteration through the training sets has occurred without any adjustment to $\mathbf{w}$, the process halts and a decision function has been found. Geometrically this process is equivalent to placing a hyperplane in N-dimensional hyperspace. The hyperplane forms the boundary between the two categories and dichotomises the measurement space. Pattern vectors lying on one side of the plane belong to one category and those on the other side belong to the other.

17.6.3   Perceptron for *n* categories

The two-category approach can be extended to a multi-category problem in which we try to find weight vectors W_i, one per category, such that for all categories except $i = j$:

$$\mathbf{w}_j^T\mathbf{y} > \mathbf{w}_i^T\mathbf{y}$$

for all $\mathbf{y}$s belonging to the jth training set. Now we no longer have the geometric concept of a separating hyperplane, but we still have only one weight vector per class. We now have the general structure shown in Figure 17.11 where we have a maximum selector instead of a threshold element. In practical recogni-

Figure 17.11
The structure of a worst case piecewise linear machine. Each category box contains R weight vectors rather than one.

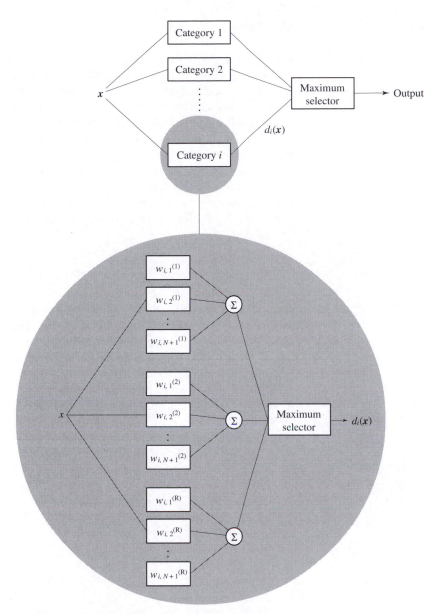

tion problems the disposition of category clusters in measurement space may be such that we require many weight vectors per category, as shown in the expanded part of the figure. Here each set of category weight vectors is implementing a collection of R hyperplanes or a single piecewise linear hyperplane per category. However, with this extension many problems arise. For example, to design a training algorithm we need to know how many weight vectors to use for each category – too few may be chosen for some classes and too many for others.

MLP feed-forward neural nets

For our purposes a neural net or an MLP is just a device that implements the multi-category structure of Figure 17.11 by extending the two-category perceptron in such a way that the one weight vector per class constraint is avoided and where the difficulties associated with a training algorithm for the Figure 17.11 structure are also avoided. It does this by having a number of layers made up of nodes, each of which contains a two-category perceptron; hence the name multi-layer perceptron.

The basic device used as a node in the MLP is the two-category perceptron except that the activation element, which in the case of the simple perceptron for two pattern classes outputs a −1 or a +1, is changed so that it produces a value between 0 and 1 that depends on $d(\mathbf{x})$. This is called a **sigmoid** function and is modelled by:

$$S(I_j) = \frac{1}{1 + \exp(-(I_j + \boldsymbol{\theta}_j)/\boldsymbol{\theta}_0)}$$

where I_j is the input to the sigmoid unit after it has been weighted and summed by the weights associated with the jth layer. The form of the function $S(I)$ is shown in Figure 17.12. θ_j is an offset threshold and $S(I)$ gives a high response (but not 1) for any value of $I > \theta_j$ and a low value (but not 0) for a value of $I < \theta_j$. θ_0 is a shape parameter for the function. The reasons for the use of a continuous function are somewhat involved and they emerge out of the mathematical model that the back propagation training rule is based on.

Now we can define I_j the input pattern to every node in layer j, in terms of the output from the previous layer i:

$$I_j = \sum_i w_{ij} O_i$$

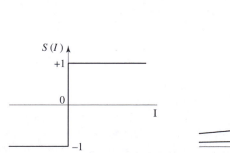

$S(I)$ for the simple two-class perceptron

(a)

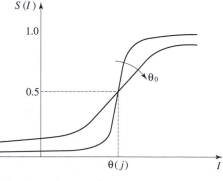

(b)

Figure 17.12
The sigmoid function $S(I)$.

Figure 17.13
Two examples of category clusters that cannot be separated by a single decision function of a single-layer perceptron.

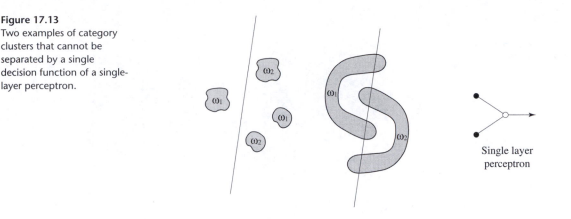

Single layer
perceptron

giving

$$O_j = S(I_j) = \frac{1}{1 + \exp(-(\sum_i w_{ij}O_i + \theta_j)/\theta_o)}$$

We now develop an intuitive justification for MLPs and look at the shape of the hyperplane decision surfaces that can be implemented by them. Consider again the single layer perceptron. We have seen that this implements a single hyperplane and can thus only be used to discriminate between linearly separable pattern classes. In most practical pattern recognition tasks we cannot seem to invent a feature or measurement space in which pattern classes map into clusters that are linearly separable. Figure 17.13 shows two examples of pattern classes in two-dimensional space that cannot be separated by a single line. In one case the pattern clusters 'break' in feature space and in the other case the clusters 'mesh' into one another.

Consider now extending the single-layer perceptron to two layers as shown in Figure 17.14. With the two perceptrons in the first layer we can implement two lines and position these anywhere in measurement space. Say for the example in Figure 17.14(a) we position these as shown. If the first-layer perceptrons output a 1 or 0 depending on whether the pattern falls on the positive or negative side of the decision function or line, then the inputs feeding the single perceptron in the second layer are 01, 10 and 11. Thus the perceptron in the second layer simply has to distinguish between an input of two 1's and an input of a single 1. Note that we still cannot fit a decision function for the case in Figure 17.14(b).

If we extend the number of nodes in the first layer we can implement a decision function that consists of a piecewise linear line, but this is still not sufficient for the case of the meshing categories. For example, Figure 17.15 shows a possible outcome of extending the number of nodes in the input layer to three. Separation is still not possible. In fact, what we need for this case is a piecewise linear line that is not restricted to being convex.

Figure 17.14
Two-layer perceptron can distinguish between classes in (a) but not in (b).

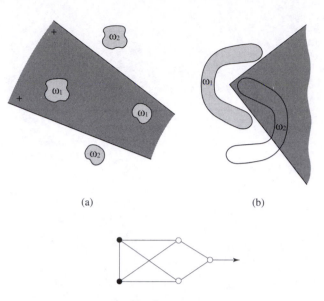

(a)   (b)

Two-layer perceptron

We can do this by extending the number of layers to three. Again, if we consider our simple two-dimensional meshed category example, Figure 17.16 shows that discrimination can be achieved in this case by using two sets of convex piecewise linear lines, one of three segments and one of two segments. Thus by increasing the number of nodes in the first layer to five, we can implement these. We are now dividing the space into three regions and the second layer makes a decision that the pattern belongs to ω_2 if it falls in either of the shaded regions bounded by the component convex piecewise linear functions. Thus we can use a three-layer perceptron to simulate or approximate non-linear, non-convex decision functions.

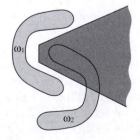

Figure 17.15
Increasing the number of nodes cannot deal with this case.

Two-layer perceptron

Figure 17.16
A three-layer perceptron can implement a non-convex piecewise linear decision function.

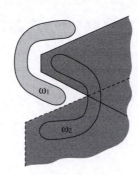

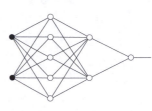

Three-layer perceptron

17.6.5

Back propagation algorithm

The back propagation algorithm is used for the training phase of an MLP feed-forward neural net. It is best described initially in words. In general terms it is controlled in much the same way as the fixed increment correction rule. That is, we have to adjust the weights associated with each node in such a way that the error between the actual output and the desired output is minimised. The back propagation algorithm, however, does this by calculating the error derivatives of the weights. In other words, it calculates how the error is affected for incremental changes in each weight. It can be considered as two phases:

Phase 1

Set all weights to small arbitrary (say random) values.

Input a pattern vector y which will produce an output vector O at the output nodes.

The output vector O is compared with the desired output and a vector of error terms (the deltas of the algorithm's name) is generated.

Phase 2

We work back through the network, passing error signals backwards from layer to layer (hence the name of the algorithm) by using an error term derived for each node to influence the weight changes that are made to all weights that are connected to the node. That is, for each node in the layer or level currently being considered, we adjust all the weights that feed into that node.

Two-dimensional techniques

18.1   Image pyramids

18.2   Wavelet transform

18.3   Image transforms and basis matrices

18.4   Wavelets and computer games

18.5   Image metamorphosis – morphing

We only have to look at the spectacular success of image processing software in popular media (graphic design, video post-processing and so on) to see that many desirable effects could be implemented in games using the same simple procedures. Image processing is a technology that has been in existence since the 1960s and there is a plethora of techniques available. However, PC hardware has evolved along the lines that all we will ever want to do is send millions of polygons to be rendered, and this does not allow efficient access to the frame buffer so that pixel-based operation can be performed. Image processing can only be implemented efficiently if it is an operation that employs the same operation for all pixels. At the moment we cannot fetch individual pixels into an application program and operate on them without incurring an unacceptable time penalty. Thus in this chapter we will confine our treatment to just two potentially useful algorithms – wavelet compression for animation sequences and spline-based morphing. (The more popular morphing approaches are pixel based and currently impractical.)

We begin by introducing the topic of image pyramids, which have already been employed in mip-maps, occlusion maps and hierarchical Z-buffer representation.

18.1   Image pyramids

Image pyramids are image transforms where multiple copies of an image at different resolutions are formed. In the text we have used them for mip-maps

Low-pass pyramid

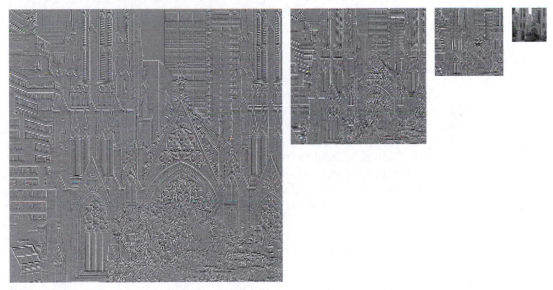

Band-pass pyramid

Figure 18.1
Image domain pyramids
(compare with Figure 18.3).

(Chapter 7), occlusion maps and hierarchical Z-buffer representation. Other applications of image pyramids are in image communication, where the resolution transmitted is appropriate to the needs of the receiver, and multi-resolution painting systems, where a user can edit or alter an image at any desired resolution level. An image pyramid consists of an image at the bottom of the pyramid which is the highest or limiting resolution together with copies at lower and lower resolution. In this chapter we will introduce a special kind of image pyramid, called a wavelet transform, which is one of the simplest and most effective tools that can be used to compress animation sequences.

We start by describing three types of image pyramid, a low pass pyramid, a bandpass pyramid and a wavelet pyramid. Examples of the first two are shown in Figure 18.1. A low pass image consists of the finest resolution image, followed by a half-resolution version, followed by a quarter-resolution version, and so on. Each version is formed from the previous by an averaging process. The top of the image is a single pixel which is the average of the entire image. In a low pass pyramid each image is 'independent' and we simply select an image appropriate to current use by indexing into the required resolution level. A mip-map is the best example of this type of image transform. Here a texture map is stored in this way and when the texture is to be mapped onto the object, a metric that relates to the screen size or projection of the object is used to select a map at the appropriate resolution level. Objects far away from the user would select a small or coarse resolution map.

In a bandpass pyramid the top of the pyramid is again a single pixel – the average of the entire image. Every other level contains detail imagery required to generate the image at a desired resolution level n from the previous resolution level $n-1$. Thus to generate a 4×4 image from the top of the pyramid we assign the final average value to all four pixels and add the detail stored at the second level of the pyramid. Now we cannot index into any level for the required image; we have to generate an image at the required level by starting at the top and working down in this way. The pyramid only stores at each level the information required to go from a coarse level n to a finer level $n-1$. A bandpass image is generated by averaging down to the next (coarser) level. For example, if we have m $\times$ m pixels in the highest resolution image we generate an averaged version at (m/2) $\times$ (m/2). This averaged image is then 'expanded' back to m $\times$ m and subtracted from the original to form the detail image.

The third type of image pyramid is the wavelet transform. It can be thought of as a type of bandpass pyramid, but one that stores separate detail images for horizontal, vertical and diagonal information. It is somewhat more complicated to discuss and we shall devote an entire section to it. We shall begin by comparing a wavelet approach with Fourier techniques, introduced in Chapter 8.

18.2 Wavelet transform

The Fourier transform finds its main application in classical image processing and in image compression in the guise of the DCT. With the inexorable growth of image traffic on the Internet and the use of imagery in CD-ROM-based multimedia, its use as a standard tool in JPEG is surely its most common application. Outside of providing a theoretical base for anti-aliasing, it does not find many applications in computer graphics. The wavelet transform is being increasingly used in computer graphics and it may well become as standard a tool in computer graphics as the Fourier transform is in image processing. We will begin by looking at an inherent disadvantage of the Fourier transform as an image transform. It is this disadvantage that is addressed by the wavelet transform and the removal of this drawback may open up many applications in computer graphics.

In a Fourier transform, a single point in the Fourier domain contains information from everywhere in the image. It specifies the amount or strength of that particular spatial frequency that exists in the image. Considered in the image domain, a single spatial frequency is a sinusoidal 'corrugation' that exists over the entire image space. The existence of a strong high-frequency component, for example, means that there are edges in the image – we know their orientation relates to the orientation of the spatial frequency but the frequency domain information does not tell us where they exist in the image. In fact we do not even know if the edge information is constrained to one particular area of the image or if it dispersed over the entire image as a texture pattern. Technically we say that the Fourier basis functions have infinite support. Practically this fact has important ramifications. In image compression, for example, we can invoke a lossy compression by retaining only part of the Fourier domain. The loss in information is manifested across the entire image as blurring. In other words, image compression using the Fourier transform is independent of image context. This is in many cases a disadvantage. Often what is needed in image compression is a scheme that retains detail where required and compresses non-significant areas of the image.

Wavelets, on the other hand, have compact or finite support and they enable different parts of the image to be represented at different resolutions. They can be used in image compression where parts of the image are represented by a quantity of information – the wavelet coefficients – that is appropriate for the nature of the image. Busy parts of the image are represented using more information than that used for smooth parts.

Wavelet transforms are more difficult to understand than Fourier transforms and we will approach them informally by describing how a transform is performed, then working backwards to intuitively deduce the attributes of the process. The particular transform of interest to us is called the standard decomposition and the basis functions used are called Haar bases, which are rectangular waves.

First, we show a wavelet transform of a stylised image (Figure 18.2 – a square against a background) and of a real image. In the stylised image the absolute amplitude of the wavelet transform coefficients is indicated and from this simple example we can make the following observations:

(1) The number of pixels in the transform is equal to the number of pixels in the image.

(2) The transform has a recursive structure (shown to three resolution levels in the figure) based on quadrants, where each top-left quadrant contains a copy of itself at half the resolution of the copy one level up. The final bottom-left quadrant contains a copy of the image at 1/8 resolution of the original.

(3) At each level the three quadrants which are not subdivided contain edge information, and if we consider the wavelet bases as edge detectors then

Figure 18.2
A wavelet transform of an image (see next figure for a real image). (a) Original image; (b) wavelet transform.

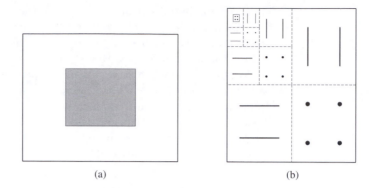

(a)　　　　　　　　　　　　　　(b)

these respond maximally to horizontal, vertical and diagonal edges. They are, however, not just simple edge detectors but functions that respond to differential information concentrated in different parts of the image and existing at different scales.

The same transform is shown in Figure 18.3 for a real image.

Figure 18.3
A wavelet decomposition (first three levels). The original image is shown in Figure 18.1(a).

Figure 18.4
Decomposition and
reconstruction in a wavelet
transform.

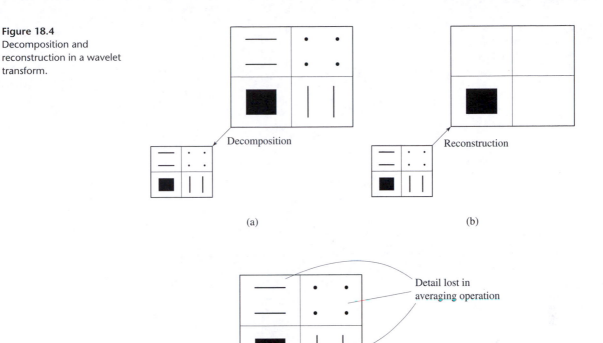

(a) (b)

Detail lost in
averaging operation

Image averaged to
$^1/_2$ previous resolution

(c)

We could consider the generation of a transform as a recursive process where we
generate lower and lower resolution copies of itself. This is called decomposition
and is illustrated conceptually in Figure 18.4(a). The reverse of the process is
called reconstruction (Figure 18.4(b)). In decomposition, at each step in the
recursion we generate an image averaged to 1/2 its previous resolution together
with three copies of 'detail' lost in the averaging operation (Figure 18.4(c)).

Now to generate the transform in this way we can use an algorithm that alter-
nates between operations on rows and operations on columns. The algorithm is
extremely simple:

(1) Perform an averaging and differencing operation on each row of the image
(we will explain exactly what is meant by 'averaging and differencing' in a
moment).

(2) Perform an averaging and differencing operation on each column of the
result of (1).

(3) Repeat this process recursively on the bottom left-hand quadrant of the
result of (2).

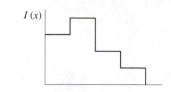

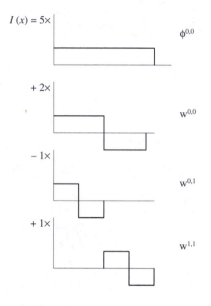

You can see from the illustration that this produces a series of intermediate images where the original image appears at lower and lower resolution in the bottom left-hand quadrant. Eventually it shrinks to a single pixel that contains the average of the entire image. This is called a non-standard decomposition. An alternative method is the standard decomposition and this corresponds to the transform that would be obtained using the basis functions shown in Figure 18.5.

We now need to explain what is meant by averaging and differencing and we will consider this process using simple examples in 1D space. Consider the sequence:

    6 8 4 2

which may be the intensity values of four pixels along a scan line (Figure 18.5). Averaging this 1D image means forming, at each resolution level (or each level of the recursion), the average of consecutive pairs. That is:

6 8 4 2
  7   3
     5

Averaging, by definition, involves a loss of detail information – in image terms it is a blurring operation – and at each level in the process we retain the lost detail in the form of detail coefficients. We now have:

Resolution level	Average	Detail coefficients
4	6 8 4 2	
2	7 3	−1 1
1	5	2

In this case our wavelet transform is the final average together with the detail coefficients – the wavelet transform for the sequence 6 8 4 2 is:

5 2 −1 1

and, for example, to reconstruct from this information the average image at resolution level 2, we have:

7(= 5 + (2)) 3 (= 5 − (−2))

That is, to reconstruct from level n the average image at level $n − 1$ we construct two intensity values at level $n − 1$ by adding and subtracting the detail coefficients to the value at level n. Thus the wavelet transform for an entire image consists of a single pixel representing the average of the entire image together with the complete hierarchy of detail coefficients. This form immediately emphasises its potential in image compression because the detail coefficients are usually very small in magnitude and can be stored in a lossy form with little reduction in image quality.

Let us now use this same example and introduce some formalistics which will give us some insight into the nature of the basis functions. We write the wavelet transform

5 2 −1 1

as

$$I(x) = 5\phi^{0,0}(x) + 2w^{0,0}(x) - w^{1,0}(x) + w^{1,1}(x)$$
$$= b^{0,0}\phi^{0,0}(x) + c^{0,0}w^{0,0}(x) + c^{1,0}w^{1,0}(x) + c^{1,1}w^{1,1}(x)$$

a graphical interpretation of which is given in Figure 18.5. We can see that the function $I(x)$ is built from a scaling function $\phi^{0,0}(x)$, wavelet coefficients $c^{a,b}$ and wavelets $w^{a,b}$. The indices (a,b) on the wavelets refer to the level of the wavelet and its position. As the index a increases, the wavelet base of support halves and the number of wavelets, at this level doubles. These are the Haar basis wavelets, which are step functions taking the values +1 and −1, specifically:

Figure 18.6
Compares basic vectors for DCT and wavelets (a) Basis vectors for the DCT; (b) basis vectors for the Haar transform.

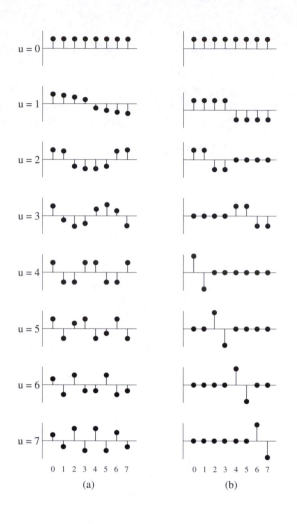

$$W(x) = \begin{cases} 1 & 0 \leq x < 1/2 \\ -1 & 1/2 \leq x < 1 \\ 0 & \text{otherwise} \end{cases}$$

The translated and scaled wavelet basis functions are then defined as:

$$w^{a,b}(x) = w(2^b x - a) \qquad a = 0, \ldots, 2^b - 1$$

From Figure 18.6 can be seen the origin of the term 'wavelet'. The basis functions have only local extent. They are in every case a single rectangular waveform, which for a given 'frequency' differ in that they are all translates of each other. They are wavelets rather than waves. A wavelet can be any basis function that satisfies certain requirements, which are that it must be oscillatory and that it must decay quickly to zero in both the positive and negative direction. The rectangular wave is the simplest possible manifestation of these requirements.

18.3

Image transforms and basis matrices

We have looked fairly informally at two image transforms – the Fourier transform and the wavelet transform (using the Haar basis). In all such transforms we can consider that we are performing the same general process, only differing by the basis functions that we use. We could write a transform in general terms as:

$$T(u,v) = \sum_{x=0}^{M-1} \sum_{y=0}^{N-1} I(x,y)b(x,y,u,v)$$

where

$b(x,y,u,v)$ is the kernel of the transformation that contains the basis functions

The value of each component in the transform is the 'strength' or amount of each basis function in $I(x,y)$. For a particular value of (u,v) in the transform domain we calculate this by multiplying each sample of $I(x,y)$ by the equivalent sample in the basis function, summing and averaging. In the one-dimensional case we can therefore define a set of basis vectors, the components of which form the product with the image samples. This is shown in Figure 18.6 for the Haar transform (the basis functions for the Fourier transform are complex). Also shown for comparison are the functions for the DCT – used in JPEG image compression. The number of basis vectors is equal to the number of components in

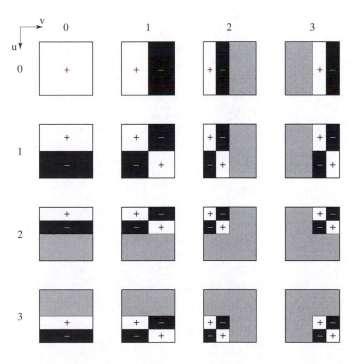

Figure 18.7
Basis functions or basis 'images' for the two-dimensional Haar wavelet.

each vector – in the illustration, eight. The important concept of an image transform as a general process that can select any one of a number of basis functions or vectors then becomes clear. In the case of the two-dimensional transform the basis vectors become basis matrices or basis images. Shown in Figure 18.7 are the 8×8 basis images for the DCT and the Haar/wavelet transform. Note that the Haar/wavelet image only contains three values, 1, 0 and -1.

18.4 Wavelets and computer games

Wavelets can be exploited in computer games in many areas. The quadtree structure means that if the image exhibits varying resolution – and in practice most images do – then for the same storage cost it is possible to store a much higher resolution image. Such a facility can be used to great effect in 3D strategy games where user zooming is a routine operation. A normal image structure, of course, exhibits a 'zoom limit' beyond which blocking occurs, whereas with a wavelet structure a user can be presented with an 'infinite zoom'.

They can be used in standard image compression of pre-prepared 'start-up' animation sequences and in animated textures. Standard texture mapping of three-dimensional objects is easily extended to animated textures – the map index simply becomes a function of time. A common example of this usage is water maps where the reality and interest of the water surface is clearly enhanced by the use of an animated texture.

The third possibility of a wavelet transform is that it can be used to implement a multi-resolution interactive paint system wherein an artist can operate on the same image at different resolutions. Coarse changes can be made to one part of the image and fine changes to some other part. Such a system can operate directly on the compressed structure – there is no need to decompress and recompress the image prior to and after an editing operation. This concept was introduced by Berman *et al.* (1994) and further developed by Perlin and Velho (1995).

In this section we describe a simple scheme that uses a pruned or sparse quadtree to represent the wavelet transform of the image. This is done by first calculating the normal wavelet transform – where every leaf in the quadtree is a pixel from the final image. We then prune or crop the tree according to some quality threshold.

The wavelet decomposition is constructed using the non-standard Haar wavelet basis. A simple recursive procedure decomposes into wavelets and another reconstructs. At any node we decompose using:

$$b_1 = (a_1 + a_2 + a_3 + a_4)/4$$

$$b_2 = (a_1 - a_2 + a_3 - a_4)/4$$

$$b_3 = (a_1 + a_2 - a_3 - a_4)/4$$

$$b_4 = (a_1 - a_2 - a_3 + a_4)/4$$

Figure 18.8
Convention used in non-standard Haar wavelet transform.

Decomposition

b_1	b_2
b_3	b_4

Reconstruction

a_1	a_2
a_3	a_4

$b_1 = (a_1 + a_2 + a_3 + a_4)/4$
$b_2 = (a_1 - a_2 + a_3 - a_4)/4$
$b_3 = (a_1 + a_2 - a_3 - a_4)/4$
$b_4 = (a_1 - a_2 - a_3 + a_4)/4$

$a_1 = (b_1 + b_2 + b_3 + b_4)/4$
$a_2 = (b_1 - b_2 + b_3 - b_4)/4$
$a_3 = (b_1 + b_2 - b_3 - b_4)/4$
$a_4 = (b_1 - b_2 - b_3 + b_4)/4$

Reconstruction is effected by:

$$a_1 = (b_1 + b_2 + b_3 + b_4)/4$$
$$a_2 = (b_1 - b_2 + b_3 - b_4)/4$$
$$a_3 = (b_1 + b_2 - b_3 - b_4)/4$$
$$a_4 = (b_1 - b_2 - b_3 + b_4)/4$$

The convention used is shown in Figure 18.8. After the application of the recursive decomposition procedure we have a full quadtree representation where every leaf in the quadtree is a single pixel from the image. We can then crop the tree simply by applying a quality threshold that measures the difference between the detail coefficients at each node by:

if $abs(b_2) + abs(b_2) + abs(b_3) + abs(b_4) <$ threshold

then collapse the node into a single pixel

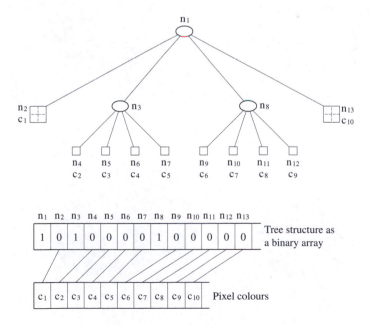

	n_1	n_2	n_3	n_4	n_5	n_6	n_7	n_8	n_9	n_{10}	n_{11}	n_{12}	n_{13}	
	1	0	1	0	0	0	0	1	0	0	0	0	0	Tree structure as a binary array

c_1	c_2	c_3	c_4	c_5	c_6	c_7	c_8	c_9	c_{10}	Pixel colours

Figure 18.9
Storing a sparse quadtree.

Note that we can only collapse a node if **all** four child nodes have been collapsed. A small section of the resulting sparse quadtree is shown in Figure 18.9. A not unimportant aspect of this approach is the way in which this information is stored. An efficient scheme is shown in Figure 18.9 which shows a small part of the tree. The structure of the tree is stored as a binary array, a node being represented by 1 and the child nodes by 0. Coincident with the 0s in the structure array is an array of pixel values which for a colour image would consist of RGB elements.

Figure 18.10 shows two frames from a rotating teapot animation where each frame has been subject to this scheme. The figure demonstrates that a simple modification of the basic scheme will result in a significant improvement in image quality. This modification is that each colour array element is a set of four colours representing the colour of the corners of the square in the original image. Gouraud shading is then used over the square resulting in the improved images shown in the figure. The other implication of this modification is that there is now no need to build the tree down to pixel level – the lowest level of detail possible in the structure is a 2×2 pixel square.

Figure 18.10
Each set of three images is a frame from a compressed animation sequence of a rotating teapot. The first image in each set shows the subdivision products, the second shows these flat shaded and the third shows them Gouraud shaded.

The following code implements the scheme

Node definition:

```
class pwm_node
{
public:
    char b2,b3,b4;
    pwm_node *child[4];

    pwm_node()
    {
        child[0]=child[1]=child[2]=child[3]=0;
    };
    ~pwm_node()
    {
        if(child[0]) delete child[0];
        if(child[1]) delete child[1];
        if(child[2]) delete child[2];
        if(child[3]) delete child[3];
    }
};
```

Tree pruning:

```
void pwm_tree::compress(pwm_node **node,int factor)
{
    int i;
    // compress all children
    for( i=0;i<4;i++ )
        if ((*node)->child[i])
            compress(&(*node)->child[i],factor);

    // if all children have been collapsed
    for( i=0;i<4;i++ )
        if ((*node)->child[i])
            break;

    if (i==4)
    {
        // if quality threshold is satisfied
        if  (abs((*node)->d1)+abs((*node)->d2)+abs((*node)->d3)<factor)
        {
            // collapse node;
            delete *node;
            *node=0;
            numnodes-;
            numleaf-=3;
        }
    }
}
```

Transforming to wavelets:

```
sx - image pixels in x
sy - image pixels in y
wx - minimum kernel pixels in x
wy - minimum kernel pixels in y

void pwm::to_wavelet(unsigned char *data,unsigned char *wdata)
{
   unsigned char *tmp=new unsigned char[sx*sy];

   memcpy(tmp,data,sx*sy);
   memcpy(wdata,tmp,sx*sy);

   int ssx=sx/2,ssy=sy/2,i,j;
   short a1,a2,a3,a4;
   while(ssx>=wx && ssy>=wy)
   {
      for( j=0;j<ssy;j++ )
         for( i=0;i<ssx;i++ )
         {
         a1=tmp[j*2*sx+i*2];
         a2=tmp[j*2*sx+i*2+1];
         a3=tmp[(j*2+1)*sx+i*2];
         a4=tmp[(j*2+1)*sx+i*2+1];
         wdata[j*sx+i]=(a1+a2+a3+a4)/4;
         wdata[j*sx+i+ssx]=(a1-a2+a3-a4)/4;
         wdata[(j+ssy)*sx+i]=(a1+a2-a3-a4)/4;
         wdata[(j+ssy)*sx+i+ssx]=(a1-a2-a3+a4)/4;
         }
      memcpy(tmp,wdata,sx*sy);

      ssx/=2;
      ssy/=2;
   }
   delete tmp;
}
```

Transforming from wavelets:

```
sx - image pixels in x
sy - image pixels in y
wx - minimum kernel pixels in x
wy - minimum kernel pixels in y

void pwm::from_wavelet(unsigned char *wdata,unsigned char *data)
{
   unsigned char *tmp=new unsigned char[sx*sy];

   memcpy(tmp,wdata,sx*sy);
```

```
        memcpy(data,tmp,sx*sy);

        int ssx=wx,ssy=wy,i,j;
        short b1,b2,b3,b4,b;

        while(ssx<sx && ssy<sy)
        {
            for( j=0;j<ssy;j++ )
                for( i=0;i<ssx;i++ )
                {
                b1=tmp[j*sx+i];
                b2=(char)tmp[j*sx+i+ssx];
                b3=(char)tmp[(j+ssy)*sx+i];
                b4=(char)tmp[(j+ssy)*sx+i+ssx];
                b=a+b+c+d;
                data[j*2*sx+i*2]=b>255?255:b<0?0:b;
                b=a-b+c-d;
                data[j*2*sx+i*2+1]=b>255?255:b<0?0:b;
                b=a+b-c-d;
                data[(j*2+1)*sx+i*2]=b>255?255:b<0?0:b;
                b=a-b-c+d;
                data[(j*2+1)*sx+i*2+1]=b>255?255:b<0?0:b;
                }

            memcpy(tmp,data,sx*sy);

            ssx*=2;
            ssy*=2;
        }

        delete tmp;
}
```

18.5

Image metamorphosis – morphing

Morphing appeared to be an overnight discovery. It was found that by using a method that was locked into two-dimensional space, a remarkable illusion of three-dimensional shape change could be created. This meant that it could be used as a post-production technique in films of reality and in this way it effectively bypassed the problems that would arise if three-dimensional graphics techniques were used in this context. It is in reality a two-dimensional image processing technique, but produces an effect that appears to have originated by filming an actual scene. (Although three-dimensional morphing techniques are used, where three-dimensional objects change into other objects, most morphing is a two-dimensional process.) Morphing is used to produce a new sequence from two sets of already moving sequences. Examples of morphing abound in TV commercials, music videos and films.

Figure 18.11
An illustration from D'arcy Thompson's *On Growth and Form.*

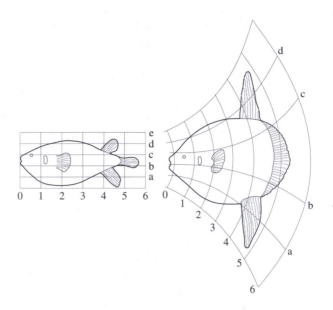

An early illustration of the idea can be found in a classic book by D'arcy Thompson entitled *On Growth and Form* (1961). In this publication he made the observation that certain fish species could be mapped into others using a non-linear transformation that was based on the warping of a coordinate system. In fact, as the reproduction shows (Figure 18.11) he proposed a model that underlies most of the approaches that are in use today.

Morphing is a classic example of the replacement, by a computer implementation, of more rudimentary techniques employed by film makers for many years. The most common is the cross-dissolve, used, for example, to great effect in 1941 in *The Wolfman*. In a cross-dissolve one image sequence is faded out while another is simultaneously faded in. (In fact cross-dissolving is a component of most morphing techniques.)

Another traditional technique used by film makers to accomplish a metamorphosis is stop motion animation, in which the subject is progressively transformed (by make-up or whatever) and photographed one frame at a time. As can be imagined, this device requires much skill and patience.

We can define morphing loosely to be the production of a set of frames that shows one object transforming into another. It has some overlap with the term in-betweening in animation, where a set of in-between frames are generated from two key frames. We define the term warping or self-morphing to mean that we warp between two frames of the same object in different attitudes. This has an important application in facial animation. Thus morphing means a transformation from one object to another, both objects usually being startlingly different. Warping means transformation between two attitudes of the same object. Alternatively we could simply take an object and warp it into some (grotesque) attitude that it could not possess in reality. This is often done in newspapers where a celebrity's or politician's face is twisted to better match the perception that the caricaturist has of him or her.

In morphing two-dimensional images we usually use film or video images of reality. The metamorphosis occurs in the two-dimensional domain. Although all of the operations are locked into two-dimensional space, the idea of two-dimensional morphing is to give the illusion of the source object changing into the target object as if the metamorphosis had actually been filmed. Currently most morphing is of this type.

This was employed to great effect by ILM (Industrial Light and Magic – the special effects division of Lucasfilms) in the 1988 film *Indiana Jones and the Last Crusade* to depict the untimely demise of the villain. Believing he has found the grail, he drinks, only to find that it is the wrong cup. He ages in seconds and dies, shrivelling horribly in the process. Two-dimensional morphing was used in conjunction with three increasingly grotesque masks to produce this sequence.

Three-dimensional morphing is a technique that consists of utilising three-dimensional graphics techniques to effect shape transformations in a three-dimensional graphics domain. By definition, in three-dimensional morphing we can only deal with computer graphics objects. That is, either abstract models or models of reality that have been converted into a computer graphics object. The problem with this type of morphing, used with a real object, is complexity. To retain the illusion of reality the real object, if it is, for example, an animal, must be represented by an extremely complex computer graphics object. This then raises the problem of choreographing the deformation of such an object.

Although both two-dimensional and three-dimensional morphing create an animated sequence – the transformation of one object into another – most morphing is carried out between two sequences of live action rather than between two still images. The source and target are moving sequences rather than still frames. A classic example of this is the Michael Jackson video *Black and White* (produced by Pacific Data Images) where dancers are morphed into each other and Jackson turns into and out of a black panther while moving. Also, in this sequence the morphs were staggered so that different parts of each dancer changed at different times.

18.5.1 ### Morphing two-dimensional images

Morphing between two-dimensional images of three-dimensional reality is the most common kind of shape metamorphosis. We effect a shape transformation from source image to target image, producing a sequence of intermediate images. A much-used example of a morph sequence is to use two facial images, say a man and a woman, or a baby and an old man. The early intermediate images will look like the source image and the later images will resemble the target image. The metric of the quality of the morph is that the intermediate images should look lifelike. In the case of facial images the intermediates should look like real people (Figure 18.12).

We can describe the complete process of two-dimensional morphing as the sequential application of two sub-processes – image warping followed by a

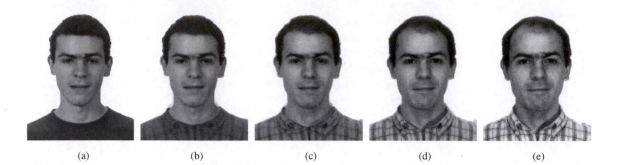

(a)   (b)   (c)   (d)   (e)

Figure 18.12
An author ages during the
production of his book.

colour transformation. Image warping is the process of mapping a pixel in the source image to a (generally different) pixel in the target image, without changing the value of the pixel:

$$S(x,y) \rightarrow T(x',y')$$

where

$$S = T \text{ and } (x',y') = \text{warp}(x,y)$$

warp is an image-warping function that will be derived from an algorithm (rather than a mathematical function). Implied in this process is the ability to generate a sequence of intermediate images.

A colour transformation is where we change the colour of a pixel without changing its coordinates

$$S(x,y) \rightarrow T(x,y)$$

For example, we can specify the traditional cross-dissolve by the following:

$$I(x,y,t) = F_1(x,y,t) \, S(x,y) + F_2(x,y,t) \, T(x,y)$$

where

for $t = 0$ (the first image in the sequence)

$$F_1(x,y,0) = 1, \qquad F_2(x,y,0) = 0$$

for $t = 1$ (the final image in the sequence)

$$F_1(x,y,1) = 0 \qquad F_2(x,y,1) = 1$$

for all t

$$F_1(x,y,t) + F_2(x,y,t) = 1$$

A linear cross-dissolve would be specified by

$$F_1(x,y,t) = 1 - t \text{ and } F_2(x,y,t) = t$$

The overall process can be accomplished by first applying an image warping followed by a colour transformation such as the above linear cross-dissolve. The warping is bi-directional, the source warping towards the target and vice versa.

Figure 18.13
Forming a morph sequence
by shape warping followed
by cross-dissolving.

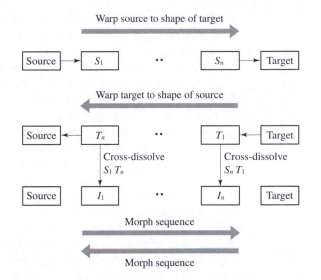

This produces two sets of images which are cross-dissolved into a single sequence. Figure 18.13 shows how a morph sequence is manufactured. We realise a single frame in a morph sequence by cross-dissolving between a pair of shape-warped images. For example, the first frame in a sequence showing a morph from source to target would consist of cross-dissolving between S_1 and T_n. For $n = 0..10$, we have an 11-frame sequence and S_1 would consist of a 10 per cent deformation of source towards target. T_9 would be a 90 per cent deformation of target towards source.

We will now describe in detail the operation of a classic image warping algorithm. The simple process of cross-dissolve does not require further explanation.

Morphing algorithms usually have two components:

(1) They need a mechanism whereby a user can establish correspondence between the two images. A common way to do this, for example, is to mark the silhouette edge of the object of interest in one image into the corresponding feature in the other. This specifies a sparse correspondence between the images.

(2) From this sparse correspondence the algorithm has to determine a dense (pixel) correspondence which is the warp transform.

18.5.2 Two-spline mesh warping

This classic algorithm was developed by Douglas Smythe at ILM. The algorithm was used to produce sequences in the films *Willow*, *Indiana Jones and The Last Crusade* and *The Abyss*.

The sparse correspondence is supplied by the user who specifies a grid of points in the source and target images. Splines are fitted through these points and the user has the visual concept of a spline mesh. Mesh elements are shaped by the user to specify the nature of the warp for each part of the image. Effectively the user selects a patch in the source image and sets a distortion for that patch in the destination image. A rectangular topology is imposed on the grid and the meshes must be topologically equivalent.

The meshes can be thought of as two coordinate systems and the morphing as a transformation from one coordinate system to the other. For a complete morph sequence we require a source mesh G_s, a destination mesh G_T and a set of *in-between* meshes – one for each frame in the morph sequence. Consider the in-between mesh G_{Ii}. The ith warp in a sequence is achieved by distorting the source image S using G_s and G_{Ii}, then G_T and G_{Ii}. The set of in-between grids is obtained by some kind of interpolation – for example, linear. Alternatively the interpolation can be positionally dependent, making it possible to have some parts of the object change at different rates to other parts.

The algorithm utilises a two-pass transform technique. This makes for both efficiency and reduction in complexity. We will describe the implementation of the algorithm in terms of such a structure but the warp process does not, of course, depend on being implemented as a two-pass process.

At any point in the morph sequence we have to generate two frames and cross-dissolve. Thus the basic algorithm is a procedure that accepts as input one image and two grids. At this stage we can simplify the convention and consider two grids G_1 and G_2 (Figure 18.14(a)). In practice this procedure would be called twice for the ith frame with parameters:

$$(G_1, G_2) = (G_s, G_{Ii}) \text{ and } (G_1, G_2) = (G_T, G_{Ii})$$

Figure 18.14(a) shows two grids superimposed with the transform conceptualised as a migration of the points G_1 into the points G_2. Note that the points on the edge of each grid are constrained to remain at the edge. Because of the rectangular topology, correspondence can be established between the points.

The first, or horizontal, pass of the two-pass implementation provides an intermediate grid. This intermediate grid is used by the two-pass structure and it is that set of points having the y coordinate of G_1 and the x coordinate of G_2 (Figure 18.14(b)). We then fit a vertical spline through the column of points in the intermediate grid and G_1 (Chapter 5). Thus we have two sets of vertical splines, one set for G_1 and one set for G_{12} the intermediate grid. These two sets are used to control the distortion in the first pass or the horizontal warp.

This is achieved by, for each scan line, finding the x intercepts with the vertical splines through G_1 and G_{12} (Figure 18.14(c)), From these intercepts a pixel-mapping function for the current scan line is derived. Figure 18.15 shows the intercepts plotted on an x and y axis, producing a set of points through which a spline is fitted. This spline provides a row or scan line mapping function and a complete row of pixels is mapped from source to an intermediate image that contains the result of the first pass. Note that there is a separate mapping function for each scan line. At this stage, in common with any other two-pass transform, all the x coordinates of the output image are now correct and this image is used as input to the second pass.

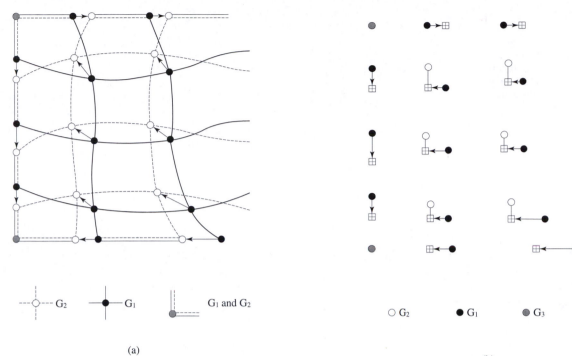

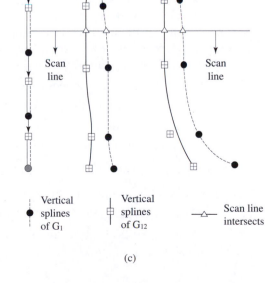

Figure 18.14
(a) Two grids G_1 and G_2. (b) The formation of an 'intermediate' mesh G_{12}. (c) Splines are fitted through columns of G_1 and G_{12} and finding the x intersects of each scan line with these two sets of vertical splines.

Figure 18.15
Building a mapping
function. (a) Scan line
intercepts; (b) a spline fitted
to the points in (a); (c) (b) is
used to map a row from the
input image to the output
image from the first pass.

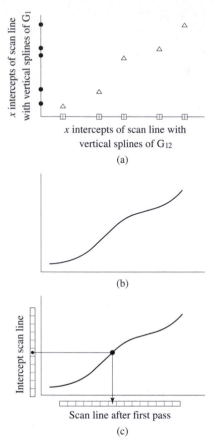

The second pass is completely analogous to the first pass and performs a vertical warp. This time we fit horizontal spines through G_{12} and G_2. These splines are now sampled vertically for each pixel boundary, creating two sets of y intercepts. A spline is fitted and a y mapping function is realised. This is used to perform the vertical warp which completes the entire transform.

The overall process can be summarised as:

> for the ith frame in the sequence
>> derive the in-between grid G_{Ii} by interpolation from G_S and G_T
>> warp the source towards the target using G_S and G_{Ii} producing G_1
>> warp the target towards the source using G_T and G_{Ii} producing G_2

The warp process itself, between G_1 and G_2, can be summarised as:

> First pass (rows or horizontal warp)
>> create G_1 vertical splines and find x intercepts
>> create G_{12} vertical splines and find x intercepts
>> for each scan line find the x mapping function and warp in x

Second pass (columns or vertical warp)

create G_{12} horizontal splines and find y intercepts

create G_2 horizontal splines and find y intercepts

for each pixel boundary or column find the y mapping function and warp in y

Image-based rendering

19.1 Introduction

19.2 Reuse of previously rendered imagery – two-dimensional techniques

19.3 Varying rendering resources

19.4 Using depth information

19.5 View interpolation

19.6 Four-dimentional techniques – the Lumigraph or light field rendering approach

19.7 Photo-modelling and IBR

19.1 Introduction

A new field with many diverse approaches, image-based rendering is difficult to categorise. The motivation for the name is that most of the techniques are based on two-dimensional imagery, but this is not always the case and the way in which the imagery is used varies widely amongst methods. A more accurate common thread that runs through all the methods is pre-calculation. All methods make cost gains by pre-calculating a representation of the scene from which images are derived at run-time. IBR has mostly been studied for the common case of static scenes and a moving viewpoint, but applications for dynamic scenes have been developed.

There is, however, no debate concerning the goal of IBR, which is to decouple rendering time from scene complexity so that the quality of imagery, for a given frame time constraint, in applications like computer games and virtual reality, can be improved over conventionally rendered scenes where all the geometry is reinserted into the graphics pipeline whenever a change is made to the viewpoint. It has emerged simultaneously with LOD approaches (Chapter 3) and scene management techniques (Chapter 9) as an effective means of tackling the dependency of rendering time on scene complexity.

19.2 Reuse of previously rendered imagery – two-dimensional techniques

We begin by considering methods that rely on the concept of frame coherence and reuse already rendered imagery in some way. Also, as the title of the section implies, we are going to consider techniques that are essentially two-dimensional. Although the general topic of image-based rendering, of course, itself implies two-dimensional techniques, there has be some use of the depth information associated with the image, as we shall see in future sections. The distinction is that with techniques which we categorise as two-dimensional we do not operate with detailed depth values, for example a value per pixel. We may only have a single depth value associated with the image entity, as is implied by visibility ordering in image layers (Section 19.3.2).

A useful model of an image-based renderer is to consider a required image being generated from a source or reference image – rendered in the normal way – by warping the reference image in image space (Figure 19.1). In this section we shall consider simple techniques based on texture mapping that can exploit the hardware facilities available on current 3D graphics cards. The novel approach here is that we consider rendered objects in the scene as texture maps, consider a texture map as a three-dimensional entity and pass it through the graphics pipeline. The common application of such techniques is in systems where a viewer moves through a static environment.

Figure 19.1
IBR as a process that produces a final image by warping.

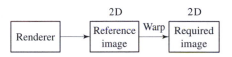

To a greater or lesser extent all such techniques involve some approximation compared to the projections that are computed using conventional techniques, and an important part of such methods is determining when it is valid to reuse previously generated imagery and when new images must be generated.

19.2.1 Planar impostors or sprites

The simplest and most common technique that could go under the name of image based rendering is the billboard. Billboard is the name given to a technique where a texture map is considered as a three-dimensional entity and placed in the scene, rather than as a map that controls the colour over the surface of an object. It is a simple technique that utilises a two-dimensional image in a three-dimensional scene by rotating the plane of the image so that it is normal to its viewing direction (the line from the viewpoint to its position). The idea is illustrated in Figure 19.2. Probably the most common example of this is the image of a tree which is approximately cylindrically symmetric. Such objects

Figure 19.2
Providing the viewing
direction is approximately
parallel to the ground plane,
objects like trees can be
represented as a billboard
and rotated about their y
axis so that they are
oriented normal to the $\boldsymbol{L}_{os}$
vector.

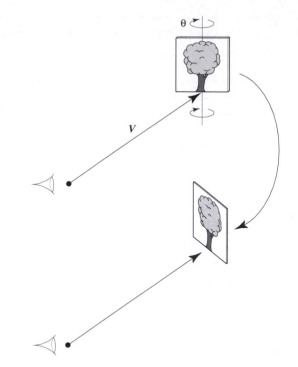

are impossible to render in real time and the visual effect of this trick is quite convincing providing the view vector is close to the horizontal plane in scene space. The original two-dimensional nature of the object is hardly noticeable in the two-dimensional projection, presumably because we do not have an accurate internal notion of what the projection of a tree should look like anyway. The billboard is in effect a two-dimensional object which is rotated about its y axis (for examples like the tree) through an angle which makes it normal to the view direction and translated to the appropriate position in the scene. The background texels in the billboard are set to transparent.

The modelling rotation for the billboard is given as:

$$\theta = \cos^{-1}(\boldsymbol{V}.\boldsymbol{B}_n)$$

where:

$\boldsymbol{B}_n$ is the normal vector of the billboard, say $(0,0,1)$

$\boldsymbol{V}$ is the viewing direction vector

Given θ and the required translation we can then construct a modelling transformation for the geometry of the billboard and transform it. Of course, this simple example will only work if the viewing direction is parallel or approximately parallel to the ground plane. When this is not true the two-dimensional nature of the billboard will be apparent.

Effectively a billboard is an object in its own right – it is a two-dimensional entity inserted into the scene. Impostors are generalisations of this idea. The idea is that because of the inherent coherence in consecutive frames in a moving viewpoint sequence, the same impostor can be reused over a number of frames until an error measure exceeds some threshold. Such impostors are sometimes qualified by the adjective dynamic to distinguish them from pre-calculated object images that are not updated. A planar sprite is used as a texture map in a normal rendering engine. We use the adjective planar to indicate that no depth information is associated with the sprite – just as there is no depth associated with a texture map (although we retain depth information at the vertices of the rectangle that contains the sprite). The normal (perspective) texture mapping in the renderer takes care of warping the sprite as the viewpoint changes.

There are many different possible ways in which sprites can be incorporated into a rendering sequence. Schaufler's method (Schaufler and Sturzlinger, 1996) is typical, and for generating an impostor from an object model it proceeds as follows. The object is enclosed in a bounding box which is projected onto the image plane, resulting in the determination of the object's rectangular extent in screen space – for that particular view. The plane of the impostor is chosen to be that which is normal to the view plane normal and passes through the centre of the bounding box. The rectangular extent in screen space is initialised to transparent and the object rendered into it. This is then treated as a texture map and placed in the texture memory. When the scene is rendered the object is treated as a transparent polygon and texture mapped. Note that texture mapping takes into account the current view transformation and thus the impostor is warped slightly from frame to frame. Those pixels covered by the transparent pixels are unaffected in value or z depth. For the opaque pixels the impostor is treated as a normal polygon and the Z-buffer updated with its depth.

In Maciel and Shirley (1995), 'view-dependent impostors' are pre-calculated – one for each face of the object's bounding box. Space around the object is then divided into viewpoint regions by frustums formed by the bounding box faces and its centre. If an impostor is elected as an appropriate representation then whatever region the current viewpoint is in determines the impostor used.

⟨19.2.2⟩ ## Calculating the validity of planar impostors

As we have implied, the use of impostors requires an error metric to be calculated to quantify the validity of the impostor. Impostors become invalid because we do not use depth information. At some viewpoint away from the viewpoint from which the impostor was generated, the impostor is perceived for what it is – a flat image embedded in three-dimensional space – and the illusion is destroyed.

The magnitude of the error depends on the depth variation in the region of the scene represented by the impostor, the distance of the region from the viewpoint and the movement of the viewpoint away from the reference position from which the impostor was rendered. (The distance factor can be gainfully

Figure 19.3
Angular discrepancy of an
impostor image (after Shade
et al. (1996)).

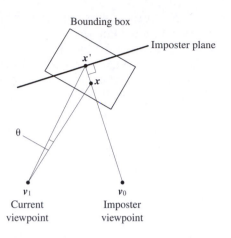

exploited by using lower resolution impostors for distant objects and grouping
more than one object into clusters.) For changing viewpoint applications the
validity has to be dynamically evaluated and new impostors generated as
required.

Shade *et al.* (1996) use a simple metric based on angular discrepancy. Figure
19.3 shows a two-dimensional view of an object bounding box with the plane of
the impostor shown in bold. v_0 is the viewpoint for the impostor rendering and
v_1 is the current viewpoint. x is a point or object vertex which coincides with x'
in the impostor view. Whenever the viewpoint changes from v_0, x and x' subtend an angle θ and Shade *et al.* calculate an error metric which is the maximum
angle over all points x.

Schaufler's error metric (Schaufler and Sturzlinger, 1996) is based on angular
discrepancy related to pixel size and the consideration of two worst cases. First,
consider the angular discrepancy due to translation of the viewpoint parallel to
the impostor plane (Figure 19.4(a)). This is at a maximum when the viewpoint

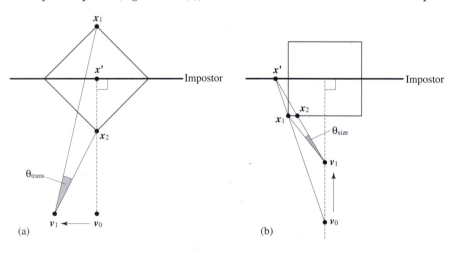

Figure 19.4
Schaufler's worst-case
angular discrepancy metric
(after Schaufler (1996)).
(a) Translation of viewpoint
parallel to an impostor.
(b) Translation of viewpoint
towards an impostor plane.

moves normal to a diagonal of a cube enclosing the bounding box with the impostor plane coincident with the other diagonal. When the viewpoint moves to v_1 the points x', x_1 and x_2 should be seen as separate points. The angular discrepancy due to this component of viewpoint movement is then given by the angle θ_{trans} between the vectors v_1x_1 and v_1x_2. As long as this is less than the angle subtended by a pixel at the viewpoint, this error can be tolerated. For a viewpoint moving towards the object we consider the construction in Figure 19.4(b)). Here the worst case is the corner of the front face of the cube. When the viewpoint moves in to v_1 the points x_1 and x_2 should be seen as separate and the angular discrepancy is given as θ_{size}. An impostor can then be used as:

use_imposter := $(\theta_{trans} < \theta_{screen})$ **or** $(\theta_{size} < \theta_{screen})$

where

$$\theta_{screen} = \frac{\text{field of view}}{\text{screen resolution}}$$

The simplest way to use impostors is to incorporate them as texture maps in a normal rendering scheme exploiting texture mapping hardware.

So far we have said nothing about what makes up an impostor and the assumption has been that we generate an image from an object model. Shade *et al.* (1996) generalise this concept in a scheme called Hierarchical Image Caching and generate impostors from the entire contents of nodes in a BSP tree of the scene, combining the benefits of this powerful scene partitioning method with the use of pre-rendered imagery. Thus, for example, distant objects that require infrequent updates can be grouped into clusters and a single impostor generated for the cluster. The algorithm thus operates on and exploits the hierarchy of the scene representation. Objects may be split over different leaf nodes and this leads to the situation of a single object possessing more than one impostor. This causes visual artefacts and Shade *et al.* minimise this by ensuring that the BSP partitioning strategy splits as few objects as possible and by 'inflating' the geometry slightly in leaf regions so that the impostors overlap to eliminate gaps in the final image that may otherwise appear.

19.2.3 Billboards and lighting effects

Billboards are commonly used in lighting effects in computer games and we will now describe techniques to construct and emplace a billboard object that is used to simulate laser fire. The object, shown in Figure 19.5 (Colour Plate), was built of two cross-sectional planes that are maintained orthogonal to each other. To a certain extent this solves the two-dimensional problem that is common to all billboards. First, half of a longitudinal cross-section was painted and reflected to produce a full cross-section. A line of pixels in this (64×128) image was then rotated to produce the other cross-section. This object is blended into the frame buffer: with the fire added to the current frame buffer and with the black background having no effect.

Figure 19.6
Positioning the missile
billboard wrt to C_p for two
positions M_p.

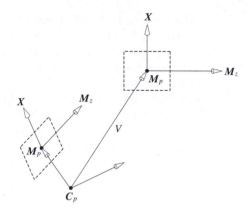

The key to making the object appear three-dimensional is to rotate it about its current position so that the longitudinal cross-section is normal to the plane containing the camera point, the current position of the fire object and the vector joining them. The spatial relationship of the camera point and direction and the current position of the fire and its direction are constantly changing as we assume in general that the vessel that fired the weapon can immediately change direction before the fire has struck home.

This orientation of the billboard is calculated as follows. First, we evaluate V (Figure 19.6)

$$V = C_p - M_p$$

the vector containing the current positions of both the camera and the fire object. Then X is a vector normal to V and M_z given as:

$$X = V \times M_z$$

where M_z is the direction of fire (the missile Z axis).

We embed the longitudinal cross-section in the plane containing X and M_z. This then ensures that, irrespective of the constantly changing spatial relationship between the fire and the viewer, the viewer always sees the billboard cross-sections oriented exactly as if they were the cross-sections of a three-dimensional object representing the fire.

The following code accomplishes the above operations:

```
V = missile.pos - cam.pos;
X.cross(V,missile.Z);
X.normalize();
X = X * 0.5f;

V1 = missile.pos - sizetexture*(missile.Z+X);
V2 = missile.pos + sizetexture*(missile.Z-X);
V3 = missile.pos + sizetexture*(missile.Z+X);
V4 = missile.pos - sizetexture*(missile.Z-X);
```

V1,V2, V3 and V4 are the vertices of the billboard in global space and `size-texture` gives the size of the billboard.

The other common lighting effect simulated by billboards is lens flare. This is caused by a (real) camera lens when it is directed towards a light source. Figure 19.7 (Colour Plate) shows the basis of the idea. The characteristic flare pattern is the billboard which blends into the frame buffer as described in Section 12.6.3. We can modulate both the size of the flare pattern and its transparency as a function of distance. As the viewer gets further away from the light source, the flare pattern can be made larger and less transparent. An important point concerning lens flare is that a viewer either sees the complete pattern or no effect – you never see a partial flare pattern. This implies a ray intersect calculation from the viewpoint to the centre of the light source.

19.3 Varying rendering resources

19.3.1 Priority rendering

An important technique that has been used in conjunction with 2D imagery is the allocation of different amounts of rendering resources to different parts of the image.

An influential (hardware) approach is due to Regan and Pose (1994). They allocated different frame rates to objects in the scene as a function of their distance from the viewpoint. This was called priority rendering because it combined the environment map approach with updating the scene at different rates. They use a six-view cubic environment map as the basic pre-computed solution. In addition, a multiple display memory is used for image composition and on-the-fly alterations to the scene are combined with pre-rendered imagery.

The method is a hybrid of a conventional graphics pipeline approach with an image-based approach. It depends on dividing the scene into a priority hierarchy. Objects are allocated a priority depending on their closeness to the current position of the viewer, and their allocation of rendering resources and update time are determined accordingly. The scene is pre-rendered as environment maps and, if the viewer remains stationary, no changes are made to the environment map. As the viewer changes position the new environment map from the new viewpoint is rendered according to the priority scheme.

Regan *et al.* utilise multiple display memories to implement priority rendering where each display memory is updated at a different rate according to the information it contains. If a memory contains part of the scene that is being approached by a user then it has to be updated, whereas a memory that contains information far away from the current user position can remain as it is. Thus overall, different parts of the scene are updated at different rates – hence priority rendering. Regan *et al.* use memories operating at 60, 30, 15, 7.5 and 3.75 frames per second. Rendering power is directed to those parts of the scene that need it most. At any instant the objects in a scene would be organised into display memories according to their current distance from the user. Simplistically the occupancy of the memories might be arranged as concentric circles emanating from the current position of the user. Dynamically assigning each object to an appropriate display memory involves a calculation which is carried out with respect to a bounding sphere. In the end this factor must impose an upper bound on scene complexity and Regan *et al.* report a test experiment with a test scene of only 1000 objects. Alternatively objects have to be grouped into a hierarchy and dealt with through a secondary data structure, as is done in some speed-up approaches to conventional ray tracing.

19.3.2   Image layering

Lengyel and Snyder (1997) generalised the concept of impostors and variable application of rendering resources, calling their technique 'coherent image layers'. The technique can be seen as representing the information to be rendered as a collection of sprites or sprite layers all at different depths, and each layer is managed independently. Effectively the image is a discrete version of three-dimensional screen space where instead of having a separate depth associated with each pixel we have a separate depth associated with each layer.

Here the motivation is to simplify the warping process and devote rendering resources to different parts of the image according to need, expressed as different spatial and/or temporal sampling rates. The technique also deals with objects moving with respect to each other. This is done by dividing the image into layers. (This is, of course, an old idea; since the 1930s cartoon production has been optimised by dividing the image into layers which are worked on independently and composed into a final film.) Thus fast-moving foreground objects can be allocated more resources than slow-moving background objects.

Another key idea of Lengyel and Snyder's work is that any layer can itself be decomposed into a number of components. The layer approach is taken into the shading itself and different resources given to different components in the shading. A moving object may consist of a diffuse layer plus a highlight layer plus a shadow layer. Each component produces an image stream and a stream of two-dimensional transformations representing its translation and warping in image space. Sprites may be represented at different resolutions to the screen resolution and may be updated at different rates. Thus sprites have different resolution in *both* space and time.

A sprite in the context of this work is now an 'independent' entity rather than being a texture map tied to an object by the normal vertex/texture coordinate association. It is also a pure two-dimensional object – not a two-dimensional part (a texture map) of a three-dimensional object. Thus as a sprite moves the appropriate warping has to be calculated.

In effect the traditional rendering pipeline is split into 'parallel' segments each representing a different part of the image (Figure 19.8). Different quality setting can be applied to each layer, which manifests in different frame rates and

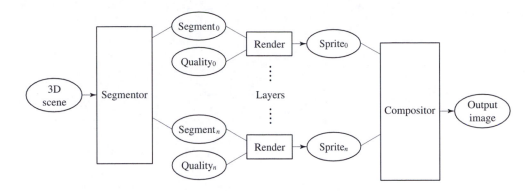

different resolutions for each layer. The layers are then combined in the compositor with transparency or alpha in depth order.

A sprite is created as a rectangular entity by establishing a sprite rendering transform A such that the projection of the object in the sprite domain fits tightly in a bounding box. This is so that points within the sprite do not sample non-object space. The transform A is an affine transform that maps the sprite onto the screen and is determined as follows. If we consider a point in screen space p_s then we have:

$$p_s = T_p$$

where p is the equivalent object point in world space and T is the concatenation of the modelling, viewing and projection transformations

We require an A such that (Figure 19.9):

$$p_s = A^{-1}ATp$$
$$= Aq$$

where q is a point in sprite coordinates and where

$$A = \begin{bmatrix} a & b & t_x \\ c & d & t_y \end{bmatrix}$$

Thus an affine transformation is used to achieve an equivalent warp that would occur due to a conventional transformation T.

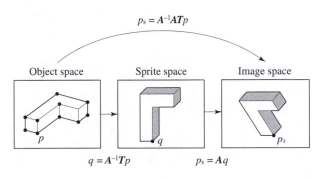

Figure 19.9
The sprite rendering
transform A.

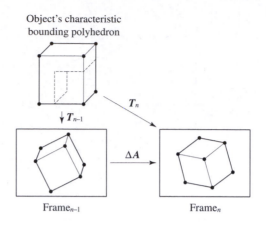

The transform **A** – a 2 × 3 matrix – is updated as an object undergoes rigid motion and provides the warp necessary to change the shape of the sprite in screen space due to the object motion. This is achieved by transforming the points of a characteristic polyhedron (Figure 19.10), representing the object into screen space for two consecutive time intervals using T_{n-1} and T_n and finding the six unknown coefficients for **A**. Full details of this procedure are given in Lengyel and Snyder (1997).

Calculating the validity of layers

As any sequence proceeds, the reusability of the layers needs to be monitored. In Section 19.2.2 we described a simple geometric measure for the validity of sprites. With image layers Lengyel and Snyder develop more elaborate criteria based upon geometric, photometric and sampling considerations. The geometric and photometric tests measure the difference between the image due to the layer or sprite and what the image should be if it was conventionally rendered.

A geometric error metric (Lengyel and Snyder call the metrics fiducials) is calculated from:

$$F_{Geometric} = \max_i \left\| P_i - \boldsymbol{A}p_i' \right\|$$

where $\boldsymbol{A}p_i'$ is a set of characteristic points in the layer in the current frame warped into their position from the previous frame and p_i the position the points actually occupy. (These are always transformed by **T**, the modelling, viewing and perspective transform, in order to calculate the warp. This sounds like a circular argument but finding **A** (previous section) involves a best fit procedure. Remember that the warp is being used to approximate the transformation **T**.) Thus a threshold can be set and the layer considered for re-rendering if this is exceeded.

For changes due to relative motion between the light source and the object represented by the layer, the angular change in **L**, the light direction vector for the object, can be computed.

Finally, a metric associated with the magnification/minification of the layer has to be computed. If the relative movement between a viewer and object is such that layer samples are stretched or compressed then the layer may need to be re-rendered. This operation is similar to determining the depth parameter in mip-mapping and in this case can be computed from the 2×2 sub-matrix of the affine transform.

After a frame is complete a regulator considers resource allocation for the next frame. This can be done either on a 'budget-filling' basis where the scene quality is maximised or on a threshold basis where the error thresholds are set to the highest level the user can tolerate (freeing rendering resources for other tasks). The allocation is made by evaluating the error criteria and estimating the rendering cost per layer based on the fraction of the rendering budget consumed by a particular layer. Layers can then be sorted in a benefit cost order and re-rendered or warped by the regulator.

Ordering layers in depth

So far nothing has been said about the depth of layers – the compositor requires depth information to be able to generate a final image from the separate layers. Because the method is designed to handle moving objects, the depth order of layers can change and the approach is to maintain a sorted list of layers which is dynamically updated. The renderer produces hidden surface eliminated images within a layer and a special algorithm deals with the relative visibility of the layers as indivisible entities. A Kd tree (Chapter 15) is used in conjunction with convex polyhedra that bound the geometry of the layer and an incremental algorithm (fully described in (Snyder (1998))) is employed to deal with occlusion without splitting.

19.4 Using depth information

19.4.1 Three-dimensional warping

As we have already mentioned, the main disadvantage of planar sprites is that they cannot produce motion parallax and they produce a warp that is constrained by a threshold beyond which their planar nature is perceived.

We now come to consider the use of depth information which is, of course, readily available in synthetic imagery. Although the techniques are now going to use the third dimension, we still regard them as image-based techniques in the sense that we are still going to use, as source or reference, rendered imagery albeit augmented with depth information.

Consider, first, what depth information we might employ. The three commonest forms in order of their storage requirements are: using layers or sprites with depth information (previous section), using a complete (unsegmented) image with the associated Z-buffer (in other words, one depth value per pixel) and a layered depth image or LDI (Section 19.4.2). An LDI is a single view of a scene with multiple pixels along each line of sight. The amount of storage that LDIs require is a function of depth complexity, the average number of surfaces that project onto a pixel.

We begin by considering images complete with depth information per pixel – the normal state of affairs for conventionally synthesised imagery. It is intuitively obvious that we should be able to generate or extrapolate an image at a new viewpoint from the reference image providing that the new viewpoint is close to the reference viewpoint. We can define the pixel motion in image space as the warp;

$$I(x,y) \rightarrow I(x',y')$$

which implies that a reference pixel will move to a new destination. (This is a simple statement of the problem which ignores important practical problems that we shall address later.) If we assume that the change in the viewpoint is specified by a rotation $\boldsymbol{R} = [r_{ij}]$ followed by a translation $\boldsymbol{T} = (\Delta x, \Delta y, \Delta z)^T$ of the view coordinate system (in world coordinate space) and that the internal parameters of the viewing system/camera do not change – the focal length is set to unity – then the warp is specified by:

$$x' = \frac{(r_{11}x + r_{12}y + r_{13})Z(x,y) + \Delta x}{(r_{31}x + r_{32}y + r_{33})Z(x,y) + \Delta z}$$

[19.1]

$$y' = \frac{(r_{21}x + r_{22}y + r_{23})Z(x,y) + \Delta y}{(r_{31}x + r_{32}y + r_{33})Z(x,y) + \Delta z}$$

where:

$Z(x,y)$ is the depth of the point $\boldsymbol{p}$ of which (x,y) is the projection.

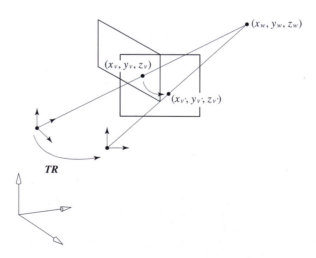

Figure 19.11
A three-dimensional warp is calculated from rotation $\boldsymbol{R}$ and translation $\boldsymbol{T}$ applied to the view coordinate system.

Figure 19.12
Problems in image warping.
(a) Image folding: more
than one pixel in the
reference view maps into a
single pixel in the
extrapolated view. (b) Holes:
information occluded in the
reference view is required in
the extrapolated view. (c)
Holes: the projected area of
a surface increases in the
extrapolated view because
its normal rotates towards
the viewing direction. (d)
See Colour Plate section.

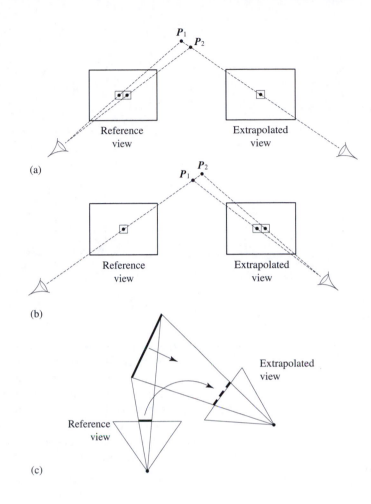

This follows from:

$$x' = \frac{x_{v'}}{z_{v'}} \qquad y' = \frac{y_{v'}}{z_{v'}}$$

where: $(x_{v'}, y_{v'}, z_{v'})$ are the coordinates of the point $\boldsymbol{p}$ in the new viewing system. A visualisation of this process is shown in Figure 19.11

We now consider the problems that occur with this process. The first is called image folding or topological folding and occurs when more than one pixel in the reference image maps into position (x', y') in the extrapolated image (Figure 19.12(a)). The straightforward way to resolve this problem is to calculate $Z(x', y')$ from $Z(x, y)$ but this requires an additional rational expression and an extra Z-buffer to store the results.

Figure 19.13
The viewpoint translates to the left so that the projection of the new viewpoint in the image plane of the reference view coordinate system is to the left of the reference view window. The correct processing order of the reference pixels is from right to left.

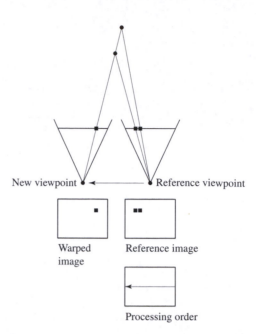

New viewpoint — Reference viewpoint

Warped image   Reference image

Processing order

McMillan (1995) has developed an algorithm that specifies a unique evaluation order for computing the warp function such that surfaces are drawn in a back to front order thus enabling a simple painter's algorithm to resolve this visibility problem. The intuitive justification for this algorithm can be seen by considering a simple special case shown in Figure 19.13. In this case the viewpoint has moved to the left so that its projection in the image plane of the reference view coordinate system is outside and to the left of the reference view window. This fact tells us that the order that we need to access pixels in the reference is

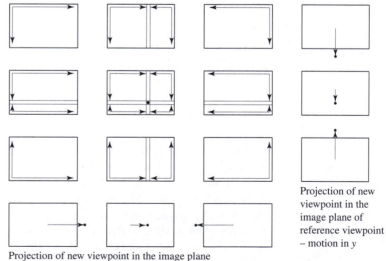

Figure 19.14
A visualisation of McMillan's priority algorithm indicating the correct processing order as a function of viewpoint motion for nine cases (after McMillan (1995)).

Projection of new viewpoint in the image plane of the reference viewpoint – motion in x

Projection of new viewpoint in the image plane of reference viewpoint – motion in y

from right to left. This then resolves the problem – the leftmost pixel in the reference overwriting the right pixel in the warped image. McMillan shows that the accessing or enumeration order of the reference image can be reduced to nine cases depending on the position of the projection of the new viewpoint in the reference coordinate system. These are shown in Figure 19.14. The general case, where the new viewpoint stays within the reference view window, divides the image into quadrants. An algorithm structure that utilises this method to resolve depth problems in the many-to-one case is thus:

(1) Calculate the projection of the new viewpoint in the reference coordinate system.

(2) Determine the enumeration order (one out of the nine cases shown in Figure 19.14) depending on the projected point.

(3) Warp the reference image by applying Equation 19.1 and writing the result into the frame buffer.

The second problem produced by image warping is caused when occluded areas in the reference image 'need' to become visible in the extrapolated image (Figure 19.12(b)) producing holes in the extrapolated image. As the figure demonstrates, holes and folds are in a sense the inverse of each other, but where as a deterministic solution exists for folds no theoretical solution exists for holes, and a heuristic needs to be adopted – we cannot recover information that was not there in the first place. However, it is easy to detect where holes occur. They are simply unassigned pixels in the extrapolated image and this enables the problem to be localised; the most common solution is to fill them in with colours from neighbouring pixels. The extent of the holes problem depends on the difference between the reference and extrapolated viewpoints and it can be ameliorated by considering more than one reference image, calculating an extrapolated image from each and compositing the result. Clearly if a sufficient number of reference images are used then the hole problem will be eliminated and there is no need for a local solution which may insert erroneous information.

A more subtle reason for unassigned pixels in the extrapolated image is apparent if we consider surfaces whose normal rotates towards the view direction in the new view system (Figure 19.12(c)). The projected area of such a surface into the extrapolated image plane will be greater than its projection in the reference image plane and for a one-to-one forward mapping holes will be produced. This suggests that we must take a rigorous approach to reconstruction in the interpolated image. Mark *et al.* (1997) suggest calculating the appropriate dimension of a reconstruction kernel, for each reference pixel, as a function of the viewpoint motion but they point out that this leads to a cost per pixel that is greater than the warp cost. This metric is commonly known as splat size and its calculation is not straightforward for a single reference image with Z depth only for visible pixels. (A method that stores multiple depth values for a pixel is dealt with in the next section.)

These effects of these problems on an image are shown in Figure 19.12(d)) (Colour Plate). The first two images show a simple scene and the corresponding

Z-buffer image. The next image shows the artefacts due to translation (only). In this case these are holes caused by missing information and image folding. The next image shows artefacts due to rotation (only) – holes caused by increasing the projected area of surfaces. Note how these form coherent patterns. The final image shows artefacts caused by both rotation and translation.

Finally, we note that view-dependent illumination effects will not in general be handled correctly with this simple approach. However, as we have already noted in image warping, we must have reference images whose viewpoint is close to the required viewpoint and this means that the problem should not be severe.

19.4.2 Layered depth images (LDIs)

Many of the problems encountered in the previous section disappear if our source imagery is in the form of an LDI (Shade *et al.*, 1998). In particular, we can resolve the problem of holes where we require information in the extrapolated image in areas occluded in the source or reference image. An LDI is a three-dimensional data structure that relates to a particular viewpoint and which samples, for each pixel, all the surfaces and their depth values intersected by the ray through that pixel (Figure 19.15). (In practice, we require a number of LDIs to represent a scene and so can consider a scene representation to be four-dimensional – or the same dimensionality as the light field in Section 19.6). Thus each pixel is associated with an array of information with a number of elements or layers that is determined by the number of surfaces intersected. Each element contains a colour, surface normal and depth for surface. Clearly this representa-

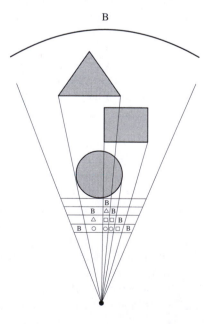

Figure 19.15
A representation of a layered depth image (LDI).

tion requires much more storage than an image plus Z-buffer but this require-ment grows only linearly with depth complexity.

In their work Shade *et al.* suggest two methods for pre-calculating LDIs for synthetic imagery. First, they suggest warping *n* images rendered from different viewpoints into a single viewpoint. During the warping process, if more than one pixel maps into a single LDI pixel then the depth values associated with each source view are compared and enable the layers to be sorted in depth order. This technique is used in the application described in the next section.

An alternative approach which facilitates a more rigorous sampling of the scene is to use a modified ray tracer. This can be done simplistically by initiating a ray for each pixel from the LDI viewpoint and allowing the rays to penetrate the object (rather than being reflected or refracted). Each hit is then recorded as a new depth pixel in the LDI. All of the scene can be considered by pre-calculating six LDIs each of which consists of a 90° frustum centred on the reference viewpoint. Shade *et al.* point out that this sampling scheme is not uniform with respect to a hemisphere of directions centred on the viewpoint. Neighbouring pixel rays project a smaller area onto the image plane as a function of the angle between the image plane nor-mal and the ray direction and they weight the ray direction by the cosine of that angle. Thus each ray has four coordinates, two pixel coordinates and two angles for the ray direction. The algorithm structure to calculate the LDIs is then:

(1) For each pixel, modify the direction and cast the ray into the scene.

(2) For each hit: if the intersected object lies within the LDI frustum it is repro-jected through the LDI viewpoint.

(3) If the new hit is within a tolerance of an existing depth pixel the colour of the new sample is averaged with the existing one; otherwise a new depth pixel is created.

During the rendering phase, an incremental warp can be applied to each layer in back to front order and images are alpha blended into the frame buffer without the need for Z sorting. McMillan's algorithm (see Section 19.4.1) is used to ensure that the pixels are selected for warping in the correct order according to the projection of the output camera in the LDI's system.

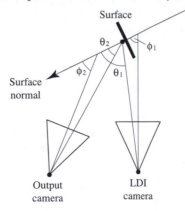

Figure 19.16
Parameters used in splat size computation (after Shade *et al.* (1998)).

To enable splat size computation, Shade *et al.* use the following formula (Figure 19.16):

$$size = \frac{d_1^2 \cos \theta_2 \, res_2 \, \tan \dfrac{fov_1}{2}}{d_2^2 \cos \theta_1 \, res_1 \, \tan \dfrac{fov_2}{2}}$$

where

size is the dimension of a square kernel (in practice this is rounded to 1,3,5 or 7)

The angles θ are approximated as the angles ϕ, where ϕ is the angle between the surface normal and the z axis of the camera system.

fov is the field of view of a camera

res = $w*h$ (the width and height of the LDI)

19.4.3 Portal imagery with LDIs

In Chapter 9 we looked at a rendering speed-up technique called portal rendering where a view from a room through a portal was computed. A natural extension to this technique is to use a rendered portal image as a texture map. If we only compute a single portal image then this is of course no different from a billboard and suffers from the same problem – the portal image will look like a photograph stuck on the doorway as we move away from the viewpoint of the reference image. Clearly we can store a set of portal images, perhaps using the constraint that the set of viewpoints used are constrained to be at one height, but this results in popping. Alternatively we can consider warping a (smaller) set of images to arrive at an approximation for the required view.

Rafferty *et al.* (1998) take the latter approach but use an LDI approach to avoid the visibility problems and work that occur with warping. Effectively the LDI is used to store the information obtained by rendering a number of portal views (13 per portal in this case). Consider Figure 19.17. Each contribution by a portal image to the central LDI is calculated by warping the portal image to the

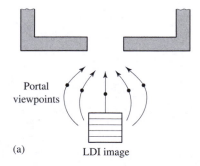

Figure 19.17
(a) An LDI for a central viewpoint is constructed from a set of portal images.

Portal viewpoints

(a)

LDI image

Figure 19.17 *continued* (b) Constructing an LDI image for a viewpoint (after Rafferty *et al.* (1998)).

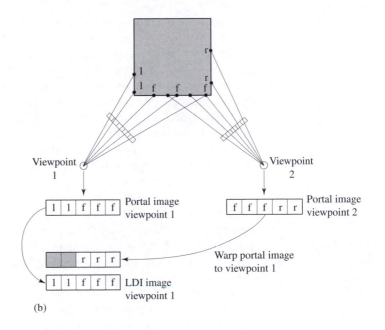

(b)

LDI viewpoint. The LDI then functions as a pre-calculation facility, storing information and decisions that would otherwise have to be calculated (in real time) during the warping process. The algorithm used is as follows:

Render the set of 13 portal images (Figure 19.17(a))

Set up an empty LDI structure with view parameters of the central view

for each portal image

  warp to the LDI viewpoint

  for each pixel in the LDI

    if the portal pixel is at a similar depth resolve the conflict

    else add the pixel into the LDI at the new depth

19.5 View interpolation

View interpolation techniques can be regarded as a subset of 3D warping methods. Instead of extrapolating an image from a reference image, they interpolate a pair of reference images. However, to do this, three-dimensional calculations are necessary. In the light of our earlier two-dimensional/three-dimensional categorisation they could be considered a two-dimensional technique but we have decided to emphasise the interpolation aspect and categorise them separately.

Chen and Williams (1993) were the first to implement view interpolation for a walkthrough application. This was achieved by pre-computing a set of reference images representing an interior – in this case a virtual museum. Frames required in a walkthrough were interpolated at run-time from these reference frames. The interpolation was achieved by storing a 'warp script' that specifies the pixel motion between reference frames. This is a dense set of motion vectors that relates a pixel in the source image to a pixel in the destination image. The simplest example of a motion field is that due to a camera translating parallel to its image plane. In that case the motion field is a set of parallel vectors – one for each pixel – with a direction opposite to the camera motion and having a magnitude proportional to the depth of the pixel. This pixel by pixel correspondence can be determined for each pair of images since the three-dimensional (image space) coordinates of each pixel are known, as is the camera or viewpoint motion. The determination of warp scripts is a pre-processing step and an interior is finally represented by a set of reference images together with a warp script relating every adjacent pair. For a large scene that requires a number of varied walkthroughs the total storage requirement may be very large; however, any derived or interpolated view only requires the appropriate pair of reference images and the warp script.

At run-time a view or set of views between two reference images is then reduced to linear interpolation. Each pixel in both the source and destination image is moved along its motion vector by the amount given by linearly interpolating the image coordinates (Figure 19.18). This gives a pair of interpolated images. These can be composited, and using a pair of images in this way reduces the hole problem. Chen and Williams fill in remaining holes with a procedure that uses the colour local to the hole. Overlaps are resolved by using a Z-buffer to determine the nearest surface, the z values being linearly interpolated along with the (x,y) coordinates. Finally, note that linear interpolation of the motion vectors produces a warp which will not be exactly the same as that produced if the camera was moved into the desired position. The method is only exact from

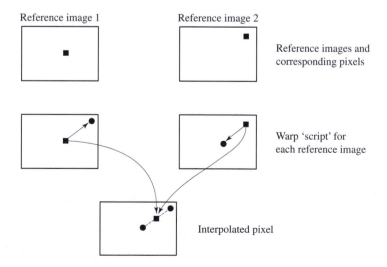

Reference image 1

Reference image 2

Reference images and corresponding pixels

Warp 'script' for each reference image

Interpolated pixel

Figure 19.18
Simple view interpretation: a single pair of corresponding pixels define a path in image space from which an interpolated view can be constructed.

the special case of a camera translating parallel to its image plane. Chen and Williams point out that a better approximation can be obtained by quadratic or cubic interpolation in the image plane.

View morphing

Up to now we have considered techniques that deal with a moving viewpoint and static scenes. In a development that they call view morphing, Seitz and Dyer (1996) address the problem of generating in-between images where non-rigid transformations have occurred. They do this by addressing the approximation implicit in the previous section and distinguish between 'valid' and 'non-valid' in-between views.

View interpolation by warping a reference image into an extrapolated image proceeds in two-dimensional image plane space. A warping operation is just that – it changes the shape of the two-dimensional projection of objects. Clearly the interpolation should proceed so that the projected shape of the objects in the

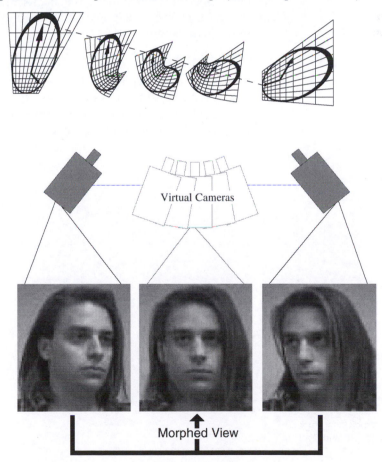

Figure 19.19
Distinguishing between valid and invalid view interpolation. In (a), using a standard (morphing) approach of linear interpolation produces gross shape deformation (this does not matter if we are morphing between two different objects – it becomes part of the effect). (b) The interpolated (or morphed) view is consistent with object shape. (Courtesey of Steve Seitz).

reference projection is consistent with their real three-dimensional shape. In other words, the interpolated view must be equivalent to a view that would be generated in the normal way (either using a camera or a conventional graphics pipeline) by changing the viewpoint from the reference viewpoint to that of the interpolated view. A 'non-valid' view means that the interpolated view does not preserve the object shape. If this condition does not hold then the interpolated views will correspond to an object whose shape is distorting in real three-dimensional space. This is exactly what happens in conventional image morphing between two shapes. 'Impossible', non-existent or arbitrary shapes occur as in-between images because the motivation here is to appear to change one object into an entirely different one. The distinction between valid and invalid view interpolation is shown in Figure 19.19.

An example where linear interpolation of images produces valid interpolated views is the case where the image planes remain parallel (Figure 19.20). Physically this situation would occur if a camera was allowed to move parallel to its image plane (and optionally zoom in and out). If we let the combined viewing and perspective transformations (Chapter 6) be V_0 and V_1 for the two reference images then the transformation for an in-between image can be obtained by linear interpolation:

$$V_i = (1 - s) V_0 + s V_1$$

If we consider a pair of corresponding points in the reference images P_0 and P_1 which are projections of world space point P, then it is easily shown (see Seitz and Dyer) that the projection of point P from the intermediate (interpolated) viewpoint is given by linear interpolation:

$$P_i = P_0(1 - s) + P_1 s$$
$$= V_i P$$

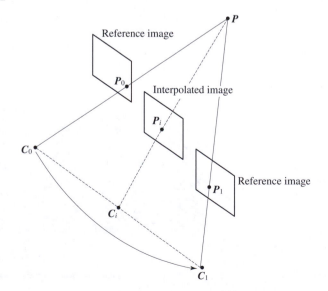

Figure 19.20
Moving the camera from C_0 to C_1 (and zooming) means that the image planes remain parallel and P_i can be linearly interpolated from P_0 and P_1 (after Seitz and Dyer (1996)).

In other words, linear interpolation of pixels along a path determined by pixel correspondence in two reference images is exactly equivalent to projecting the scene point that resulted in these pixels through a viewing and projective transformation given by an intermediate camera position, providing parallel views are maintained. In other words, using the transformation V_i which would be obtained if V_0 and V_1 were linearly interpolated. Note also that we are interpolating views that would correspond to those obtained if we had moved the camera in a straight line from C_0 to C_1. In other words the interpolated view corresponds to the camera position:

$$C_i = (sC_x, sC_y, 0)$$

If we have reference views that are not related in this way then the interpolation has to be preceded (and followed) by an extra transformation. This is the general situation where the image planes of the reference views and the image plane of the required or interpolated view have no parallel relationship. The first transformation, which Seitz and Dyer call a 'prewarp', warps the reference images so that they appear to have been taken by a camera moving in a plane parallel to its image plane. The pixel interpolation, or morphing, can then be performed as in the previous paragraph and the result of this is postwarped to form the final interpolated view, which is the view required from the virtual camera position. A simple geometric illustration of the process is shown in Figure 19.21. Here R_0 and R_1 are the references images. Prewarping these to R_0' and R_1' respectively means that we can now linearly interpolate these rectified images to produce R_i'. This is then postwarped to produce the required R_i. An important consequence of this method is that although the warp operation is image based we require knowledge of the viewpoints involved to effect the pre and post-warp transfor-

Figure 19.21
Prewarping reference images, interpolating and postwarping in view interpolation (after Seitz and Dyer (1996)).

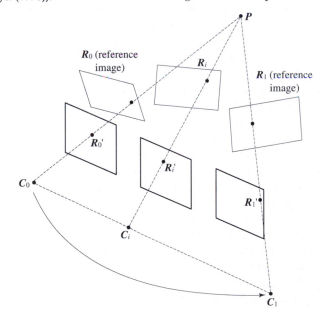

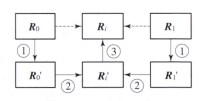

Three-step transformation sequence

mations. Again this has ramifications for the context in which the method is used, implying that in the case of photographic imagery we have to record or recover the camera viewpoints.

The prewarping and postwarping transformations are derived as follows. First it can be shown that any two perspective views that share the same centre of projection are related by a planar projective transformation – a 3×3 matrix obtained from the combined viewing perspective transformation V. Thus R_0 and R_1 are related to R_0' and R_1' by two such matrices T_0 and T_1. The procedure is thus as follows:

(1) Prewarp R_0 and R_1 using T_0^{-1} and T_1^{-1} to produce R_0' and R_1'

(2) Interpolate to calculate R_i', C_i and T_i.

(3) Apply T_i to R_i' to give image R_i.

19.6 Four-dimensional techniques – the Lumigraph or light field rendering approach

Up to now we have considered systems that have used a single image or a small number of reference images from which a required image is generated. We have looked at two-dimensional techniques and methods where depth information has been used – three-dimensional warping. Some of these methods involve pre-calculation of a special form of rendered imagery (LDIs), others post-process a conventionally rendered image. We now come to a method that is an almost total pre-calculation technique. Any scene of any complexity can have its lighting pre-calculated and we can then display any view of the scene in constant time. It is an approach that bears some relationship to environment mapping. An environment map caches all the light rays that arrive at a single point in the scene – the source or reference point for the environment map. By placing an object at that point we can (approximately) determine those light rays that arrive at the surface of the object by indexing into the map. This scheme can be extended so that we store in effect an environment map for every sampled point in the scene. That is, for each point in the scene we have knowledge of all light rays arriving at that point. We can now place an object at any point in the scene and calculate the reflected light. The advantage of this approach is that we now minimise most of the problems related to three-dimensional warping at the cost of storing a vast amount of data. (Tens of megabytes are required even for simple objects and the large storage requirements means that, at the moment, this technique is impracticable.)

A light field is a similar approach. For each and every point of a region in the scene in which we wish to reconstruct a view we pre-calculate and store or cache the radiance in every direction at that point. This representation is called a light field or Lumigraph (Levoy and Hanrahan, 1996 and Gortler et al, 1996) and we construct for a region of free space by which is meant a region free of occluders. The importance of free space is that it reduces the light field from a five-

Figure 19.22
Light field rendering using parallel plane representation for rays. (a) Parametrisation of a ray using parallel planes. (b) Pairs of planes positioned on the face of a bounding cube can represent all the radiance information due to an object. (c) Reconstruction for a single pixel $I(x,y)$.

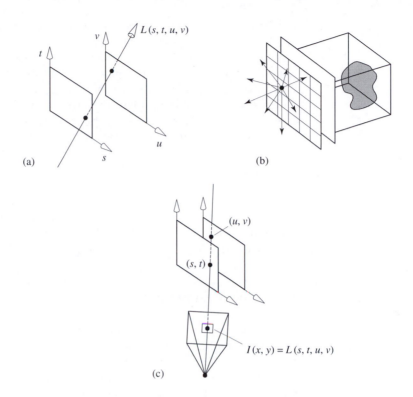

dimensional to a four-dimensional function. In general, for every point (x,y,z) in scene space we have light rays travelling in every direction (parametrised by two angles), giving a five-dimensional function. In occluder-free space we can assume (unless there is atmospheric interaction) that the radiance along a ray is constant. The two 'free space scenes' of interest to us are: viewing an object from anywhere outside its convex hull and viewing an environment such as a room from somewhere within its (empty) interior.

The set of rays in any region in space can be parametrised by their intersection with two parallel planes and this is the most convenient representation for a light field (Figure 19.22(a)). The planes can be positioned anywhere. For example, we can position a pair of planes parallel to each face of a cube enclosing an object and capture all the radiance information due to the object (Figure 19.22(b)). Reconstruction of any view of the object then consists of, for each pixel in the view plane, casting a ray through the plane pair and assigning $L(s,t,u,v)$ to that pixel (Figure 19.22(c)). The reconstruction is essentially a re-sampling process and unlike the methods described in previous sections it is a linear operation.

Light fields are easily constructed from rendered imagery. A light field for a single pair of parallel planes placed near an object can be created by moving the camera in equal increments in the (s,t) plane to generate a series of sheared perspective projections. Each camera point (s,t) then specifies a bundle of rays arriving from every direction in the frustum bounded by the (u,v) extent. It could be argued that we are simply pre-calculating every view of the object that we require at run-time; however, two factors mitigate this brute force approach. First, the resolution in the (s,t) plane can be substantially lower than the resolution in the (u,v) plane. If we consider a point on the surface of the object coincidence, say, with the (u,v) plane then the (s,t) plane contains the reflected light in every direction (constrained by the (s,t) plane extent). By definition the radiance at a single point on the surface of an object varies slowly with direction and a low sampling frequency in the (s,t) plane will capture this variation. A higher sampling frequency is required to calculate the variation as a function of position on the surface of the object. Second, there is substantial coherence exhibited by a light field. Levoy and Hanrahan (1996) report a compression ratio of 118:1 for a 402 MB light field and conclude that given this magnitude of compression the simple (linear) resampling scheme together with simplicity advantages over other IBR methods make light fields a viable proposition.

19.7 Photo-modelling and IBR

Another distinguishing factor in IBR approaches is whether they work only with computer graphics imagery (where depth information is available) or whether they use photographs as the source imagery. Photography has the potential to solve the other major problem with scene complexity – the modelling cost. Real-world detail, whose richness and complexity elude even the most elaborate photo-realistic renderers, is easily captured by conventional photographic means. The idea is to use IBR techniques to manipulate the photographs so that they can be used to generate an image from a viewpoint different from the camera viewpoint.

Photographs have always been used in texture mapping and this classical tool is still finding new applications in areas which demand an impression of realism that would be unobtainable from conventional modelling techniques, except at great expense. A good example is facial animation where a photograph of a face is wrapped onto a computer graphics model or structure. The photo-map provides the fine level of detail, necessary for convincing and realistic expressions, and the underlying three-dimensional model is used as a basis for controlling the animation.

In building geometric representations from photographs, many of the problems that are encountered are traditionally part of the computer vision area but the goals are different. Geometric information recovered from a scene in a computer vision context usually has some single goal, such as collision avoidance in robot navigation or object recognition, and we are usually concerned in some way with reducing the information that impinges on the low-level sensor. We are generally interested in recovering the shape of an object without regard to such irrelevant information as texture; although we may use such information as a device for extracting the required geometry, we are not interested in it *per se*.

In modelling a scene in detail, it is precisely the details such as texture that we are interested in as well as the pure geometry.

Consider first the device of using photography to assist in modelling. Currently available commercial photo-modelling software concentrates on extracting pure geometry using a high degree of manual intervention. Common approaches use a pre-calibrated camera, knowledge of the position of the camera for each shot and a sufficient number of shots to capture the structure of the building, say, that is being modelled. Extracting the edges from the shots of the building enables a wireframe model to be constructed. This is usually done semi-automatically with an operator corresponding edges in the different projections. It is exactly equivalent to the shape from stereo problem using feature correspondence except that now we use a human being instead of a correspondence establishing algorithm. We may end up performing a large amount of manual work on the projections, as much work as would be entailed in using a conventional CAD package to construct the building. The obvious potential advantage is that photo-modelling offers the possibility of automatically extracting the rich visual detail of the scene as well as the geometry.

It is interesting to note that in modelling from photographs approaches, the computer graphics community has side-stepped the most difficult problems that are researched in computer vision by embracing some degree of manual intervention. For example, the classical problem of correspondence between images projected from different viewpoints is solved by having an operator manually establish a degree of correspondence between frames which can enable the success of algorithms that establish detailed pixel by pixel correspondence. In computer vision such approaches do not seem to be considered. Perhaps this is due to well-established traditional attitudes in computer vision which has tended to see the imitation of human capabilities as an ultimate goal as well as constraints from applications.

Using photo-modelling to capture detail has some problems. One is that the information we obtain may contain light source and view-dependent phenomena such as shadows and specular reflections. These would have to be removed before the imagery could be used to generate the simulated environment from any viewpoint. Another problem of significance is that we may need to warp detail in a photograph to fit the geometric model. This may involve expanding a very small area of an image. Consider, for example, a photograph – taken from the ground – of a high building with a detailed facade. Important detail information near the top of the building may be mapped into a small area due to the projective distortion. In fact this problem is identical to view interpolation.

Let us now consider the use of photo-modelling without attempting to extract the geometry. We simply keep the collected images as two-dimensional projections and use these to calculate new two-dimensional projections. We never attempt to recover three-dimensional geometry of the scene (although it is necessary to consider the three-dimensional information concerning the projections). This is a form of image-based rendering and it has something of a history.

Consider a virtual walk through an art gallery or museum. The quality requirements are obvious. The user needs to experience the subtle lighting conditions designed to best view the exhibits. These must be reproduced and sufficient detail must be visible in the paintings. A standard computer graphics approach may result in using a (view-independent) radiosity solution for the rendering together with (photographic) texture maps for the paintings. The radiosity approach, where the expensive rendering calculations are performed once only to give a view-independent solution, may suffice in many contexts in virtual reality, but it is not a general solution for scenes that contain complex geometrical detail. Radiosity rendered scene has to be divided up into as large elements as possible to facilitate a solution and there is always a high cost for detailed scene geometry.

This kind of application – virtual tours around buildings and the like – has already emerged with the bulk storage freedom offered by videodisk and CD-ROM. The inherent disadvantage of most approaches is that they do not offer continuous movement or walkthrough but discrete views selected by a user's position as he or she (interactively) navigates around the building. They are akin to an interactive catalogue and require the user to navigate in discrete steps from one position to the other as determined by the points from which the photographic images were taken. The user 'hops' from viewpoint to viewpoint.

An early example of a videodisk implementation is the 'Movie Map' developed in 1980 (Lippman, 1980). In this early example the streets of Aspen were filmed at 10-foot intervals. To invoke a walkthrough, a viewer retrieved selected views from two videodisk players. To record the environment four cameras were

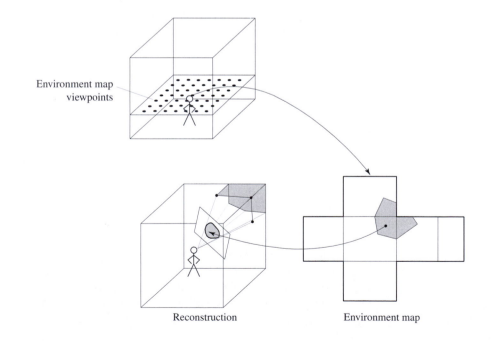

Figure 19.23
Compositing a user projection from an environment map.

Reconstruction   Environment map

used at every viewpoint – thus enabling the viewer to pan to the left and right. The example demonstrates the trade-off implicit in this approach – because all reconstructed views are pre-stored, the recording is limited to discrete viewpoints.

An obvious computer graphics approach is to use environment maps – originally developed in rendering to enable a surrounding environment to be reflected in a shiny object (see Chapter 7). In image-based rendering we simply replace the shiny object with a virtual viewer. Consider a user positioned at a point from which a six-view (cubic) environment map has been constructed (either photographically or synthetically). If we make the approximation that the user's eyes are always positioned exactly at the environment map's viewpoint, then we can compose any view-direction-dependent projection demanded by the user changing his or her direction of gaze by sampling the appropriate environment maps. This idea is shown schematically in Figure 19.23. Thus we have, for a stationary viewer coincidentally positioned at the environment map viewpoint, achieved our goal of a view-independent solution. We have decoupled the viewing direction from the rendering pipeline. Composing a new view now consists of sampling environment maps and the scene complexity problem has been bound by the resolution of the precomputed or photographed maps.

The highest demand on an image generator used in immersive virtual reality comes from head movements (we need to compute at 60 frames per second to avoid the head latency effect) and if we can devise a method where the rendering cost is almost independent of head movement this would be a great step forward. However, the environment map suggestion only works for a stationary viewer. We would need a set of maps for each position that the viewer could be in. Can we extend the environment map approach to cope with complete walkthroughs? Using the constraint that in a walkthrough the eyes of the user are always at a constant height, we could construct a number of environment maps whose viewpoints were situated at the lattice points of a coarse grid in a plane, parallel to the ground plane and positioned at eye height. For any user position, could we compose, to some degree of accuracy, a user projection by using information from the environment maps at the four adjacent lattice points? The quality of the final projections are going to depend on the resolution of the maps and the number of maps taken in a room – the resolution of the eye plane lattice. The map resolution will determine detailed quality of the projection and the number of maps its geometric accuracy.

To be able to emulate the flexibility of using a traditional graphics pipeline approach, by using photographs (or pre-rendered environment maps), either we have to use a brute force approach and collect sufficient views compatible with the required 'resolution' of our walkthrough, or we have to try to obtain new views from the existing ones.

Currently, viewing from cylindrical panoramas is being established as a popular facility on PC-based equipment (see Section 19.7.1). This involves collecting the component images by moving a camera in a semi-constrained manner –

rotating it in a horizontal plane. The computer is used merely to 'stitch' the component images into a continuous panorama – no attempt is made to recover depth information.

This system can be seen as the beginning of a development that may eventually result in being able to capture all the information in a scene by walking around with a video camera, resulting in a three-dimensional photograph of the scene. We could see such a development as merging the separate stages of modelling and rendering, as there is now no distinction between them. The virtual viewer can then be immersed in a photographic quality environment and have the freedom to move around in it without having his or her movement restricted to the excursions of the camera.

19.7.1 Image-based rendering using photographic panoramas

Developed in 1994, Apple Computer's QuickTime VR is a classic example of using a photographic panorama as a pre-stored virtual environment. A cylindrical panorama is chosen for this system because it does not require any special equipment beyond a standard camera and a tripod with some accessories. As for reprojection – a cylindrical map has the advantage that it only curves in one direction, thus making the necessary warping to produce the desired planar projection fast. The basic disadvantage of the cylindrical map – the restricted vertical field of view – can be overcome by using an alternative cubic or spherical map, but both of these involve a more difficult photographic collection process and the sphere is more difficult to warp. The inherent viewing disadvantage of the cylinder depends on the application. For example, in architectural visualisation it may be a serious drawback.

Figure 19.24 (Colour Plate) is an illustration of the system. A user takes a series of normal photographs, using a camera rotating on a tripod, which are then 'stitched' together to form a cylindrical panoramic image. A viewer positions himself at the viewpoint and looks at a portion of the cylindrical surface. The reprojection of the selected part of the cylinder onto a (planar) view surface involves a simple image warping operation which, in conjunction with other speed-up strategies, operates in real time on a standard PC. A viewer can continuously pan in the horizontal direction and the vertical direction to within the vertical field of view limit.

Currently restricted to monocular imagery, it is interesting to note that one of the most lauded aspects of virtual reality – three-dimensionality and immersion – has been for the moment ignored. It may be that in the immediate future monocular non-immersive imagery, which does not require expensive stereo viewing facilities and which concentrates on reproducing a visually complex environment, will predominate in the popularisation of virtual reality facilities.

Compositing panoramas

Compositing environment maps with synthetic imagery is straightforward. For example, to construct a cylindrical panorama we map viewspace coordinates (x,y,z) onto a cylindrical viewing surface (θ,h) as:

$$\theta = \tan^{-1}(x/z) \qquad h = y/(x^2 + z^2)^{1/2}$$

Constructing a cylindrical panorama from photographs involves a number of practical points. Instead of having three-dimensional coordinates we now have photographs. The above equations can still be used, substituting the focal length of the lens for z and calculating x and y from the coordinates in the photograph plane and the lens parameters. This is equivalent to considering the scene as a picture of itself – all objects in the scene are considered to be at the same depth.

Another inherent advantage of a cylindrical panorama is that after the overlapping planar photographs are mapped into cylindrical coordinates (just as if we had a cylindrical film plane in the camera), the construction of the complete panorama can be achieved by translation only – implying that it is straightforward to automate the process. The separate images are moved over one another until a match is achieved – a process sometimes called 'stitching'. As well as translating the component images, the photographs may have to be processed to correct for exposure differences that would otherwise leave a visible vertical boundary in the panorama.

The overall process can now be seen as a warping of the scene onto a cylindrical viewing surface followed by the inverse warping to re-obtain a planar projection from the panorama. From the user's point of view the cylinder enables both an easy image collection model and a natural model for viewing in the sense that we normally view an environment from a fixed height – eye level – and look around and up and down.

20 Multi-player game technology

20.1   Introduction

20.2   Definitions

20.3   Implementation of multi-player games

20.4   The origin and nature of problems in multi-player games

20.5   Reducing the information in messages

20.6   Multi-player implementation using client–server

20.1 Introduction

Multi-player games are games that are played by two or more people on a network. Each player controls one or more games objects and the effect of this action has to be communicated to all other players. The goal of any multi-player game should be that the playability of the game is maintained despite the communication delay. In other words, delays should be, as far as possible, invisible to the players. An associated problem is the reliability of the communication. A designer has to deal with the effects of delays and the fact that the information may be lost or reordered in transit. Thus, to be more precise about the goal, we want to achieve the reliable transfer of the minimum amount of information required to maintain playability. In this respect we will look at the difficulties that 'delay intolerant' games such as first person shooter games throw up and how to deal with them.

Many interacting factors are involved in information transfer in multi-player games:

● how much information is sent to each player and the bandwidth of the channel?

● how many players are currently logged onto the game (many systems do not scale linearly)?

● what is the required reliability of the information?

● what is the network architecture?

Designers are faced with a complex system exhibiting many behaviours over which they have no control and for which they must design solutions. All problems faced by designers stem from the fact that network communication is effectively a channel with a bandwidth that varies from instant to instant.

The first true multi-player game did not face the same problems because it was implemented on a mainframe with the players participating via a dumb terminal. This was MUD, developed by Bartle and Trubshaw in 1978 (Burka, 1995). Nowadays the multi-player model is that of distributed processors in the form of PCs running some application that not only performs the same role as a single-player game but communicates with other players over the Internet.

Multi-player systems introduce the possibility of new genres. For example, we have cooperative types where a player is part of a computer opponent. Alternatively we can have 'deathmatch'-type games where players play against each other and usually the one with more 'kills' wins. An extension of this type of game is to have teams of players competing against each other.

20.2 Definitions

The terms associated with multi-player games are:

- **Packet**   This is just the technical term for a message. Any information is divided up into packets – the indivisible unit that is sent on its journey over the Internet. It is necessary to divide information up in this way because the Internet is not a dedicated channel – unlike the channel you set up when you send a fax, for example. Packets can be interrupted if they 'collide' with another packet and have to be re-sent. The longer the packet is, the greater the probability of collision.

- **Protocol**   This is the data format standard that the packet is embedded in. It also embodies the organisation of the message transfer: acknowledgement, error recovery and so on. TCP and UDP are the two common protocols. TCP guarantees a message; UDP does not initiate resends of dropped information and will thus incur a lower latency.

- **Lag or latency**   This is the technical term for the delay between when a message is sent by a source and when it is received at a destination. Delays are the source of most problems in multi-player games. Network latencies may range from under a millisecond for a local area network (LAN) up to hundreds of milliseconds for a wide area network (WAN). (Note that anyway there is an insurmountable speed of light limitation implicit in WAN transfers which for inter-continental transfers can be tens of msecs.) If we consider network delays of, say, 100–200 msecs then this implies a latency in frame times of between 5 and 10. The variability or jitter in the latency can also cause problems. Players can become used to a constant lag, but variation in the length of the delay can be far more disturbing because it causes jerkiness.

- **Bandwidth**   This is the maximum rate at which information can be transferred from a source to a destination. It is important to bear in mind that this is a separate entity to latency. We can have a high bandwidth link which transfers information very quickly but for which there is a delay before the reception of a message.

20.3 Implementation of multi-player games

Multi-player games can be implemented by the application setting up and sending the messages (known in network jargon as packets), or more commonly by using an API such as DirectPlay, which does this for you. Such an application acts as an interface between the games application and the Internet, handling the transmission and reception of messages and the player management.

The ideal framework for a multi-player application can be reduced to the following main processes:

For each of my frames

(1) Receive messages from all other players in the game, updating their status.

(2) Process these messages with game logic.

(3) Send messages updating my status to all other players.

(4) Render the frame; go to (1).

Depending on the player activity step 3 may result in updates being generated (say) every 30 msecs. All problems in multi-player games emerge from the (unpredictable) network transmission delays involved in processes 1 and 3. These delays scale quadratically, for the simplest mode of operation (peer to peer), as the number of players increases, and this difficulty is probably the main reason for the slow growth of multi-player games compared to the phenomenal growth of single-player games. Another problem with network delays is that they are inversely proportional to reliability. The more reliable the protocol, the longer the delay – guaranteeing delivery implies acknowledgement and error recovery.

The main modes used for managing multi-player games are 'client–server' and peer to peer (Figure 20.1). A client–server system is also known as a logical star configuration. A single computer – the server – collects messages from all players and stores these in a single database. Players or clients only send messages to, or receive messages from, the server.

From a player's point of view the following activities are facilitated by the management system:

(1) Player requests to join an existing game or start a new one.

(2) Player receives game application and/or level data.

Figure 20.1
Management modes in
multi-player games.

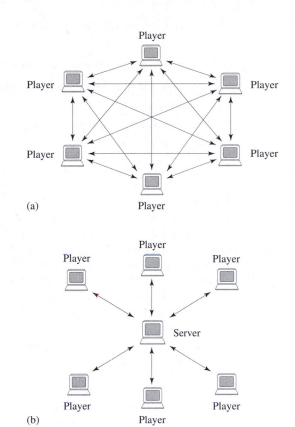

(a)

(b)

(3) Player starts the game and begins to play.

(4) Player exits the session

Client–server types have a separate server application which is, in general, different from the application being executed by each of the players. For example, a server application will not have to render the imagery. This enables the server application to act as an arbitrator, preventing, for example, users creating alterations to game code that make their game invincible. The disadvantage of this scheme is fairly obvious: as more and more players join the game, the delay perceived by any one of them increases and there will be an upper limit on the total number of players who can participate. Another consideration of client–server mode is that the player needs a good connection to the server in order to get his or her simulation running smoothly. If you want to be the best player, all you need to do is create the server running in your machine. This way your 'ping' or round trip time (ping is the time taken for a message to go to a destination and for the recipient to send back an acknowledgement) to the server will be 0 and you will feel that it will be easy to 'kill' all other players (they will all have a lower update rate).

As far as game events are concerned, a client–server mode can function as follows:

(1) The server collects messages from the clients and issues acknowledgements.

(2) The server applies the command on its application and issues acknowledgement.

(3) On receipt of an acknowledgement the client applies the commands contained in the message.

Clearly this implies a delay between the player issuing the command and its visual consequence appearing on the screen. This may or may not be tolerable, depending on the application. One solution is to render the effects of a command immediately but in a different style from that of a verified command.

Note that if there were no problems with lag and bandwidth a client–server mode would provide the ideal solution to multi-player game implementation. We would simply run a single application on the server which would issue all the necessary rendering information for all players.

Peer to peer mode (Figure 20.1) requires no server application to be developed. The communication is handled by an application embedded in the game itself and each player maintains his or her own complete copy of the game database. Here we are replacing the problem of a potential bottleneck in the server with more connections and messages. If there are n players in the game then a single change made by one player needs to be communicated to the other $(n - 1)$ players; and if all players make changes – the general situation at any instant in a game – then $n(n - 1)$ messages need to be sent.

A protocol that reduces the number of connections required by peer to peer is broadcast. A player sends out a single message and all other players read it. Also, a player joining a game does not have to establish $(n - 1)$ connections but merely has to know which broadcast channel to listen to. Multicast is a subset of broadcast which allows arbitrary-sized groups to be serviced by a single source transmission, providing one-to-many communication as seen from a single source. Some internet service providers support multicast but none support broadcast.

The idea of peer to peer is that a player appears to be modifying a common database. In reality, each player is running his or her own complete copy of the data with modifications being distributed to all players. Peer to peer is simpler than client–server and only requires an application to be able to send, receive and process messages.

20.4 The origin and nature of problems in multi-player games

20.4.1 Origins of delays

Although we normally associate lag with Internet delays, there is an inherent lag associated with a client–server communication which needs to be taken into account in any quantitative assessment of latency. In this section we will look at the origin of this, following a treatment in Blow (1998). Blow points out that there is an inherent latency in single-player games which is increased by a client–server connection *even* if the connection is ideal, that is, there is zero communication delay between the client and the server. For a standard game loop of:

```
read_input()
move_objects()
render()
```

if we consider that if there is an even distribution of input events in time, then on average an event will occur halfway through the render time (assuming for simplicity that this consumes all of the cycle). There is then an inherent delay in the game between the user pressing a key and the effect appearing on the screen of 1.5c (where c is the loop time). Blow defines the 0.5c delay between a key press and its processing by the application as the 'influence' time and the 1.0 render time as the 'observation' lag.

Now consider a client connected to a server with a cycle time of s. The server cycle time is different from the client time because the server does not have to render the game, although, as we shall see, it has to perform game play management functions. The delays now accumulate as follows:

Client presses a key	0.5c influence lag
Client sends message to server	0.5s influence lag
Server cycle	1.0s
Server sends message to client	0.5c influence lag
Client sees effect on screen	1.0c observation lag

This makes a total of 2.0c + 1.5s and, assuming for simplicity that c and s are equal at 50 ms (20 frames per second), we have a total delay of 175 ms with a standard deviation of 22 ms.

To be added to this are modem and network delays. Modem delays are predictable and add a further latency and variability; network delays are not so predictable and substantially increase both the latency and the variability. The Internet delays can add between 100 and 200 ms and a variability of 50 ms on

Figure 20.2
Effect of an Internet lag and timing variability.
(a) modem only.
(b) internet.

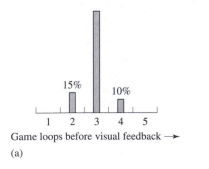

(a)

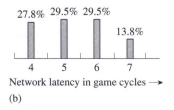

(b)

average. Figure 20.2 (b) shows client statistics collected from trials of a game played at random times over a five-day period. Apart from the inherent communication delay on the Internet, second-order factors add to the problem – the number of bytes transmitted is greatly increased from the game layer by other layers in the message protocol system, including overheads from DirectPlay (Section 20.6.1). Messages may have to be carefully managed to minimise timing variability. Blow points out that even although it may appear to be a good idea to transmit a variable number of messages per frame depending on what is currently happening in the game, this leads to latency variability or jitter. Sending two consecutive messages with a latency of 20 ms, for example, means the first arrives after 20 ms and the second after 40 ms, resulting in an average latency of 30 ms and a standard deviation of 10 ms. Sending four consecutive messages means the average is 50 ms deviating by 22 ms.

20.4.2   Semantics of delays, message loss and reordering

Positional update delays

Problems arise out of delays in the reception of messages. These are due to limited bandwidth and network delays – known as lag or latency. Delays are caused by both network delays and the bulk of information in the message. The latter is the responsibility of the games application and we look at ways in which this can be approached in Section 20.5. Reducing latency on the network itself is a general problem and is usually inversely related to reliability. Decreasing network delays implies decreasing the reliability. Protocols that do not require acknowledgement will function faster but there is no guarantee that all messages will arrive.

A delay can occur on a high bandwidth link in the form of a wait time. In general, a lower bandwidth with little delay is preferable to a high bandwidth link with a delay because the latter will result in greater latency jitter on average. The bandwidth determines the number of updates per second that can be sent to the other players. For example, say you have a bandwidth that allows you to update your position to other players at 30 positions per second, and this comes with a 2 s delay. This is certainly worse than a lower bandwidth of, say, 10 positions per second and a very short delay. Delays in positional updates result in you perceiving the player in the past. You may kill him but he will not die. In such a situation each player perceives a different simulation.

A common example is missile tracking. If you fire a homing missile at an opponent, in your simulation you might see the missile tracking the player and hitting it. However, because in your opponent's simulation the firing was delayed, and his position was not the position you saw him at, in his simulation the missile will track him on a different path and may not hit him.

In peer to peer simulation we can deal with this problem by having players send the message 'I have been killed' rather than the owner of the missile sending the message 'I have killed you'. Consider A and B both firing at C simultaneously. C makes the decision that it has been hit and broadcasts to all other players. In other words, the decision making is distributed. In effect the game states are partitioned – each player can only change the state of the game by updating the state of an object under his or her control. Each player then communicates the changes he or she makes to all other players. In the client–server mode the server application can make the decision.

Thus if all state updates are distributed to every player at the frame rate then every game application will be consistent. Delays prevent this from happening. Of course it is possible to solve most problems by having a (dedicated) low-latency game network and such commercial enterprises exist; but the conventional wisdom is that the real growth of multi-player games will be on the Internet. An early example of a (peer to peer) dedicated game network is Amaze (Bergland and Cheriton, 1985). Bergland and Cheriton called their application, running on a LAN of Sun workstations, a 'distributed implementation consisting of a single program executed in multiple parallel instantiations, one at each player's workstation'. Despite the advantage of such a network they still used dead reckoning (see Section 20.5.2) and this was the first multi-player game to use this method.

Thus multi-player games cope with positional delays in effect by allowing asynchronism to develop in each user's view of the game. Synchronism is only currently possible on LANs and is not necessarily a critical requirement in games applications. (Synchronous views are, however, important in certain VR applications which require, for example, precise cooperative manipulation of objects.)

Acquisition of object

When a player acquires an object whose acquisition implies removal of the object from the game, the communication delay can mean that a competing player can also get the object before it is removed from his simulation. This causes the object to be possessed by both players and thus duplicated.

This problem clearly occurs on peer to peer sessions and is solved by a client–server system where the server will allocate the object to one of the players and refuse it to the other. To solve this using peer to peer mode would require a message to be sent to all players requesting information on the availability of the object and this of course causes more delay.

Smoothness of play

The two different management modes have ramifications for the 'smoothness' of the simulation. On client–server-based games a fast connection to the server is the only factor involved in achieving a smooth game play. Having a slow or delayed server connection will disrupt the smoothness of play as every action has to be processed by the server application before it can happen in the user's game.

Using a peer to peer mode, your simulation will always run smoothly (provided, of course, that sufficient local processor power is available) but your perception of the action of the other players in the game will be jumpy as a function of the delay between you and them.

Packet loss

It is not guaranteed that all messages will be received. Some messages are mandatory, others are not; it depends on the game rules. Positional updates are not, for example, mandatory. If a player misses a positional update from another player then hopefully he or she will receive the next. Messages such as 'I have been killed' are mandatory and need to be confirmed and re-sent if confirmation is not received within a time limit.

Message reordering

It is not guaranteed that messages will be received in the order in which they were sent. The consequences of reordering, if not accounted for, can be catastrophic in some applications. Some messages, much as positional updates, will simply create undesirable visual defects on player movement. Others may cause the receiving application to crash. TCP, for example, is an order-preserving guaranteed-delivery protocol. This should not be used in applications where units in the message data are logically independent, because if a message is dropped, all other data is held up until it is recovered.

20.5 Reducing the information in messages

20.5.1 Data compression

Clearly there is a need, whatever mode of communication is used, to reduce the amount of information sent per unit time. This can be done using standard data compression approaches or by more elaborate context-dependent devices such as a dead-reckoning algorithm.

Consider the former. With most information we can coarsen the accuracy and also send changes between the current value of an entity and the previous. For example, with position updates, we can send the difference between the current position and the previous rather than the absolute value. If we decide that an accuracy of 1 in 256 is sufficient in this context then we require just three bytes to update an (x,y,z) position. Sending the difference between consecutive 'blocks' of information output by a moving system is the basis of data compression in many applications. In particular, it is one of the techniques used in video image compression, where the difference between consecutive frames is calculated and even operated on for further compression. However, we have to bear in mind that we cannot send difference information indefinitely. If the receiver reconstructs a sender's position by adding differences together then eventually the absolute value calculated by the receiver will drift away from the sender's actual absolute value because of the accumulation of errors. Also, it is clear that such schemes cannot operate without reliable protocols.

Finally, information in the message can also be reduced by sending only command information, as we describe next. If a games application can tolerate a 'player delay' then all games can be synchronised. Each player runs his or her game at full speed and each sees the same game, albeit running delayed by a small time interval. This is not the same as a network delay but is a delay between the instant of a key press and its effect. In other words, the delay is used to 'hide' the network lag. Whether the delay between player action and its visual effect is tolerable depends on the application. Each player sends a message that contains his or her game interface or control information together with a time stamp indicating when the commands should be executed. Each player application has a command buffer into which his or her own commands, and those received from other players, are inserted. The message can also contain the number of commands issued so far, so that a receiver knows whether a command is out of order or missing and is able to inform the sender of the latter occurrence.

20.5.2 Predictive methods

Predictive methods reduce bandwidth requirements using messages containing typically position, velocity and acceleration, which are transmitted at a frequency less than the frame rate. Extrapolation is used by the receiver to move the sender's object from this information. The most common method is a dead-reckoning algorithm. Effectively dead reckoning is an agreement between players to use the same extrapolation technique to control the behaviour of all objects owned or controlled by opponents. One of the first multi-player computer games to use dead reckoning was Amaze (Bergland and Cheriton, 1985), and a dead-reckoning approach was proposed by Blau *et al.* (1992) for networked virtual environments. It was formalised in 1993 as a protocol in DIS (Distributed Simulator Networking, IEEE Standard 1278). DIS was used for a variety of combat vehicle simulators such as trucks, helicopters, ships and soldiers.

In this approach a player controls his or her own objects – player objects – and the objects controlled by other players are known as ghosts. A player uses the game application to control his or her objects – the live objects – and a dead-reckoning algorithm to control the ghost objects. If player A sends his current velocity and position to player B then no further information need be sent until player A changes his velocity. Player B uses dead reckoning to update the position of the (ghost) object of player A. (In fact, position, velocity and acceleration information are transmitted and a second-order model is used to predict the object location.) Clearly the main factor involved here is: how far we should allow any game to diverge under control of extrapolation algorithms before updating?

This situation continues until player A decides that his velocity has changed by an amount sufficiently significant to send a message to B. He makes this decision by running the same dead-reckoning algorithm on his live object and measuring the deviation between his actual position and the position calculated by applying the dead reckoning. This is shown in Figure 20.3, which

Figure 20.3
Two players' views of a
game using dead-reckoning.

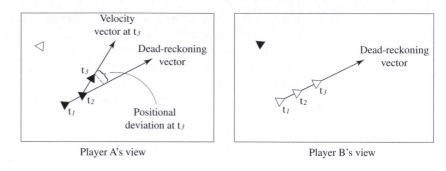

Player A's view   Player B's view

▲ = Live object   △ = Ghost

also emphasises that each player sees object(s) under his control and ghost objects. Thus all players simulate all their competitors' live entities in a game to a level of accuracy determined by the dead-reckoning algorithm. The process is known mathematically as extrapolation – finding points beyond a given set of points. This contrasts with interpolation – finding new points between existing ones, used extensively in animation (see Chapter 13). Figure 20.4 shows how input commands from player A are handled by the system. The diagram is from player A's point of view; of course player B 'sees' a similar organisation.

The magnitude of the error that develops in a dead-reckoning method depends on the speed at which the objects move compared with the rate at which positional updates are received, and because of this not all game applications are suitable for dead reckoning. As we have mentioned, the idea originated in military vehicle simulation where in general we can assume that if we have a current velocity vector then its rate of change is going to be small. Fast-moving vehicles, such as aircraft, tend to continue in straight lines or execute large radius turning motions. On the other hand, a first-person shooter game, where

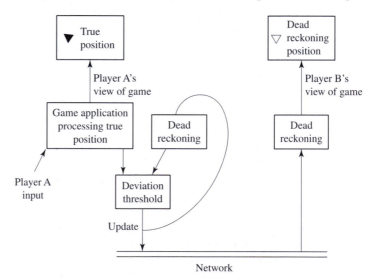

Figure 20.4
Processing user input from
Player A's point of view.

a slow-moving player can suddenly execute a 180° turn, may be less suitable for this approach.

The trade-off in dead-reckoning methods is between accuracy and number of messages sent. A large deviation threshold will cause jerky movement in ghosts when a new message is sent and dead-reckoned positions are suddenly updated. A small deviation will cause more messages to be sent. Jerkiness can be ameliorated by using smoothing algorithms.

A dead-reckoning algorithm only treats the players as active entities. This suffices for enclosing environments or terrains that are immutable. But what happens if a bridge is destroyed by player A so that player B cannot pass over it? This is a passive entity that can change and needs to send an 'I am destroyed' message to all other players.

As we have mentioned, dead-reckoning algorithms are sensitive to sudden changes in velocity acceleration. A predictive method that relies only on positional updates (and thus demands smaller packets) was introduced by Singhal and Cheriton (1994), who point out that object position changes least rapidly (compared with velocity and acceleration) and must be continuous. Like the dead-reckoning scheme, the source application transmits a positional update whenever there is a certain deviation between the true position of the source's object and a tracked position. Object tracking is carried out by fitting a curve to position updates. The idea is demonstrated in Figure 20.5 which shows at t_0, the current time, a deviation between the displayed position and the position just received. The tracking curve is udpated to include the current position, giving a path for the object in the future. This predicted path is then used to derive a

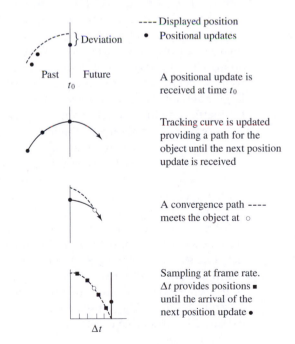

Figure 20.5
Deriving a future path for a remote object from previous position updates.

Figure 20.6
First-order vs. second-order
tracking according to θ.

smooth convergence path for the displayed position. This convergence curve can be sampled at the frame rate and provides a non-jerky correction for the displayed position. The convergence period is chosen to be long enough to eliminate jerkiness in the correction and short enough to be complete before the arrival of the next update.

Two interpolation techniques are used for the tracking curve, based on the angle between the last three updates. If this is angle is small, first-order tracking is used; if large then second-order tracking is applied (Figure 20.6). Since the tracking step involves previous positions, a delayed update can be moved back to the time given by its time stamp. In this manner, receivers subject to different latencies will produce approximately the same tracking of the source object.

20.5.3 Consistency

Above, we mentioned that most of the problems we have encountered can be resolved if we assume that it is practical to run a single application to which all players send commands and from which all players receive dynamic rendering information. This idea has been researched for some time in shared or distributed virtual reality applications (DVEs) and in these contexts a more elaborate approach to message information reduction, other than the low-level measures we have described, is used. A large amount of this research is in the area of very large-scale military simulations involving thousands of participants that simulate battle scenarios. Another application area of DVEs is teleconferencing.

Currently the only main differences between computer games and DVEs is the scale of the hardware used and the communication and input devices used by the participants. Otherwise the same concepts are shared by both applications. The information content of games updates at the moment tends to be restricted to positional updates and simple state alterations (I am in position X and have just been killed). DVEs on the other hand exchange a variety of information: audio, video, graphics objects, and so on. It is interesting to conjecture that the availability of network technologies that will support thousands of participants will undoubtedly lead to new game genres and modalities of play.

Up to now the discussion has proceeded on the basis that all players need to receive all messages sent out by other players. We will now look at relaxing this constraint. The methods used to achieve this aim are all fairly similar in their workings but they have taken a variety of names: interest management, rele-

Figure 20.7
Range and relevance.

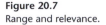

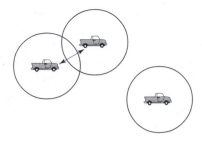

Figure 20.7
Range and relevance.

vance filtering, data distribution management, and so on. Perhaps the best term is relevance filtering, which, as the name implies, is a mechanism whereby participants receive only relevant information. The most obvious relevance criterion is range – an object need only receive information concerning changes in the state of the environment that is within a certain range of it – region of interest (Figure 20.7). Different objects may have different ranges. In military simulation the range of interest of a tank may be tens of kilometres but that of a foot soldier hundreds of metres. A range of interest specification may be based on parameters other than geographical range: consider a radar tracking device or an audio sensor. The same object may have different ranges of interest: an aural range could be smaller than a visual range, for example. Ranges of interest can be dynamic: in an internal environment they may be bounded by the room dimensions. All of these can be used to reduce the message traffic in an 'every participant receives all updates' model.

These approaches have much in common with collision detection methods (Chapter 15) where the idea was to maintain and track pairs of potential collidees. In relevance filtering the range of interest is analogous to the bounding volume.

Van Hook *et al.* (1994) use relevance filtering in conjunction with multicast transmission to selectively route only relevant data to receivers and examine two approaches – grid-based filtering and object-based filtering. In grid-based filtering (here note the similarity to spatial partitioning in collision detection), multicast addresses are associated with cells defined by a square grid system that is overlaid on the environment (in this case, terrain). Updates are received by a participant only from a set of surrounding cells, this set being continuously updated as the participant object moves. Just as in collision detection, the size of the grid cells is critical to the efficacy of the scheme.

An alternative approach Van Hook *et al.* term object-based filtering. Here, a relevancy test is made on behalf of an object by examining the environment in its vicinity. This is a finer-grained test than grid-based filtering and results in greater traffic reduction.

Lea *et al.* (1999) refer to the problem of many users sharing and interacting in a common world database as distributed consistency – the common space must be seen consistently by all users. In distributed virtual worlds the users are known as avatars. Lea *et al.* tackle the problem of scalability by carefully defining the notion of consistency to embrace different levels or degrees of accuracy. In effect the consistency requirement is reduced by partitioning the database. This is done by defining, for each user, an 'aura' – a sphere of interest centred on the user object. Only if the auras of two objects intersect is a communication link established between them. (This is the same as object-based filtering as we described previously.) If two objects intersect in this way then consistency has to be enforced. Traffic is then further reduced by the following data categorisation:

- static data – data which never changes;

- dynamic data, which changes but whose current value, as seen by a receiver, can be out of date;

- dynamic data, which changes but which must always be up to date.

To exploit this categorisation Lea *et al.* make use of object proxies in the form of a software cache. When an object A is within the aura of another object B it creates a proxy for itself and gives it to object B. B then uses the proxy as if it was the remote object and queries and operations are performed on the proxy. In giving its proxy, object A informs object B how the cached information is updated. For static data objects B always uses the initially cached values. For the second category – dynamic data that can be out of date – the currently cached value is returned and the proxy periodically requests the correct value. A request from objects B for vital dynamic data results in the cache requesting data from the remote object.

20.6   Multi-player implementation using client–server

We now consider an example application protocol for game play in a client–server deathmatch game. The protocol is clearly game dependent but conforms to the general client–server sequence given in Section 20.3. In what follows, 'you' refers to a client originating an action.

- **Player movement**   client motion is not synchronised. When a client moves, the positional updates are sent to the server. The server then broadcasts these updates to all other players. When the other players receive the updates the originating client will already be in a different position.

- **You fire a projectile**   a message is sent to the server but no projectile is added to your simulation until the message is received back from the server indicating that the projectile has been added to the server simulation.

- **An explosion damages your ship in the server simulation**   A message is sent to all clients informing them of the damage value. When received by the clients, the ship's shield is set to non-transparent in the clients' games to indicate the damage and the ship's shield effect is subtracted from the damage value. Thus the missile might not hit you in your simulation, but if it hits you in the server simulation, you receive the damage. The 'missile fire' message from the server will be delayed when transmitted to you and also your position is delayed when informed to the server, so the server simulation might not be exactly the same as your simulation. As your ping to the server gets better, your simulation will more closely approximate the server simulation.

- **A player's shield becomes less than zero in the server simulation**
  The server sends a message indicating the dead player and the identity of the client that receives credit for the kill. The client simulations create the ship explosion when this message is received and add points to the appropriate score. You lose control of your ship and see it from the position at which you died, falling down. When it collides with an object it explodes; another message is generated and broadcast to the clients' games and an explosion is created in the appropriate position.

The power-up behaviour on a client–server implementation can be as follows:

- **In a single-player game** The power-up rotates and illuminates the scene around it. If the single-player ship is closer than the power-up radius then the ship receives the power-up. If the power-up life has expired it is moved to another (random) position.

- **In a server simulation** All players' distances are checked to see if anyone is within the power-up radius. If such a situation exists then the closest player is given the power-up and the power-up life is set to -1. A message indicating which player has received the power-up is broadcast to all players. If the power-up life is less than zero, the server chooses another (random) position for it and sends to all players a message with the new power-up position.

- **In a client simulation** The power-up rotates and illuminates just as for a single-player simulation. If a message is received informing the client that a power-up position has been received, it is moved and its lifetime reset. The 'power-up taken' message cannot be sent only to the player getting it, but must be broadcast to all players. (In the case of an invisible power-up you must see the other player ship as transparent.)

20.6.1 Interfacing with the network

Clearly it is easiest to implement multi-player games using an operating system API such as DirectPlay. This gives a single interface to the Internet and enables you to avoid the low-level programming associated with setting up and handling messages. DirectPlay does not completely specify the networking model for a game; it is simply a high-level object that provides an easy interface for developers. The services it provides are:

- Session management – management and organisation of the game session
- Player management – management and organisation of the players
- Group management – management and organisation of a group of players
- Message management – management and organisation of the messages
- Lobby management – management and organisation of the game set-up and session choice.

We will now look at the utilities necessary to implement the simplest possible server application for a client–server application.

In what follows, the engine class directX handles all DirectPlay utilites with a few member functions. The aim here is to expose the methods that send and receive messages, connect to a game and create a game. To initialize the directX class, we call the global function *init_directx()* passing a window handle and application instance handle.

```
init_directx(hWnd,hInst);
```

The *directx* global variable will be available for use.

We must use the *free_directx()* function to release the class and all its allocated data.

```
free_directx();
```

The multi-player protocol used is TCP/UDP and to initialise it, we call the *init_multiplayer()* member function from the directX class.

```
directx->init_multiplayer();
```

To close multi-player mode, we use the *free_multiplayer()* member function.

```
directx->free_multiplayer();
```

After TCP/IP is initialised, we can create a new game (you will be the server) or join a game (you will be the client).

To create a new game we use:

```
directx->create_game(gameID,"game_name");
```

To join an already created game we use:

```
dxplay_games *games = directx->enum_games(gameID);
```

The *games* pointer has information on all available games for the specific *gameID*. We choose one (*n*) and join with:

```
directx->join_game(games->game_guid[n],"player_name");
```

To broadcast messages to all other players, we use:

```
directx->send_message(data,data_len);
```

To send messages to a specific player, use:

```
directx->send_message(data,data_len,player_id);
```

To send guaranteed messages (if message is not confirmed by the receiver, it is re-sent until confirmation is received), use:

```
directx->send_message_garanteeded(data,data_len);
```

or

```
directx->send_message_garanteeded(data,data_len,player_id);
```

The engine loops on receiving all multi-player messages, and passes them to the active plugins. Each plugin will be able to process the multi-player messages on the *fly_message* exported dll function.

The following is example code for the simplest possible server program:

```
main()
{
flyengine=new flyEngine();
init_directx(0,0);
if (flyengine->open_fly_file("mylevel")
   {
   directx->init_multiplayer();
   directx->create_game(&FLYGUID,"mygame");
   run();
   directx->free_multiplayer();
   }
free_directx();
delete flyengine;
}

void run()
{
   int dt,T0=timeGetTime();
   while(1)
   {
   // quit if ESC is pressed
   if (_kbhit())
     if (27==_getch())
       break;

   // finds of elapsed time dt in ms
   flyengine->cur_time=timeGetTime();
   dt=flyengine->cur_time-T0;
   T0=flyengine->cur_time;
   if (dt<1 || dt>1000)
     continue;
```

```
        // steps the scene dt ms
        flyengine->step(dt);
    }
}
```

The following is an example code of a multi-player message processing for the ship game protocol given in Section 20.6:

```
__declspec( dllexport )
int fly_message(int msg,int param,void *data)
{
    switch(msg)
    {
    case FLYM_MPMESSAGE:
        // process message
        mp_message(param,(mp_msg *)data);
        // return 0 indicating message has been processed and
        // needs not to be passed to next plugin
        return 0;
    ...
    other messages
    ...
    }
    return 1;
}
void mp_message(int from,mp_msg *msg)
{
    switch( msg->type )
        {
        case FLYMP_MSG_POS:
            {
            mp_data *data=(mp_data *)&msg->type;
            ship *s=(ship *)directx->players[from].data;
            if (from>0)
                {
                s->remove_from_bsp();
                s->pos=data->pos;
                s->vel=data->vel;
                s->Y=data->Y;
                s->Z=data->Z;
                s->X.cross(s->Y,s->Z);
                s->flag=data->flag&0xffff;
                s->points=data->flag>>16;
                s->update_mat();
                s->add_to_bsp();
                }
```

```
    if (from>=0 && ((data->flag&0xf)!=0xf))
      {
      if (s->g[data->flag&0xf])
         s->g[data->flag&0xf]->fire(s,s->player);
      if (data->flag&0x10)
         s->speedboost=s->speedboost0;
      else s->speedboost=0;
      }
    }
    break;
case FLYMP_MSG_DAMAGE:
    {
    mp_data2 *data=(mp_data2 *)&msg->type;
    ship *s=(ship *)directx->players[from].data;
    s->force+=data->v;
    s->strength-=data->f;
    s->lasthittime=flyengine->cur_time;
    s->lasthitfrom=from;
    if (from==0)
       flyengine->filter.x+=data->f>1.0f?1.0f:data->f;
    }
    break;
case FLYMP_MSG_KILL:
    {
    mp_data *data=(mp_data *)&msg->type;
    ship *s=(ship *)directx->players[from].data;
    s->flag2=s->exptime;
    s->newpos=data->Y;
    s->expcam.pos=s->pos;
    s->expcam.node=s->node;
    *((local_system *)&s->expcam)=*((local_system *)s);
    int i;
    for( i=0;i<directx->nplayers;i++ )
      if (directx->players[i].dpid==data->flag)
         break;
    if (from==i)
      if (i==0)
      {
      ((ship *)flyengine->cam)->points—;
      flyengine->set_status_msg(
         "YOU COMMITTED SUICIDE",
         directx->players[i].name);
      }
      else
      flyengine->set_status_msg(
```

```
                      "%s COMMITTED SUICIDE",
                      directx->players[i].name);
                else
                if (i==0)
                {
                ((ship *)flyengine->cam)->points++;
                flyengine->set_status_msg("YOU KILLED %s",
                    directx->players[from].name);
                }
                else
                if (from==0)
                    flyengine->set_status_msg(
                        "%s KILLED YOU",
                            directx->players[i].name);
                else
                    flyengine->set_status_msg(
                        "%s KILLED %s",
                            directx->players[i].name,
                            directx->players[from].name);
            }
            break;
        case FLYMP_MSG_EXPLODE:
            {
            mp_data *data=(mp_data *)&msg->type;
            ship *s=(ship *)directx->players[from].data;
            if (s->exp)
                s->exp->do_explode(data->pos,data->Z,from);
            s->flag2—;
            s->remove_from_bsp();
            }
            break;
        case FLYMP_MSG_JOIN:
            {
            player_data *data=(player_data *)&msg->type;
            ship *s=(ship *)flyengine->cam->clone();
            s->player=directx->add_player(data->name,data->dpid,s);
            flyengine->set_status_msg("%s   HAS   JOINED   THE   GAME",
                    data->name);
            flyengine->activate(s,(directx->mpmode==FLYMP_SERVER));
            if (directx->mpmode==FLYMP_SERVER)
            {
            powerup *p=0;
            while( p=(powerup *)flyengine->
                get_next_active_object(p,TYPE_POWERUP) )
                {
```

```
            static mp_data d;
            d.type=FLYMP_MSG_POWERUPMOVE;
            d.dpid=DPID_SERVERPLAYER;
            d.flag=p->valuetype;
            d.pos=p->pos;
            directx->send_message_guaranteed(
               &d,sizeof(mp_data),data->dpid);
         }
      }
   }
   break;
case FLYMP_MSG_QUIT:
   {
   player_data *data=(player_data *)&msg->type;
   if (from<directx->nplayers)
      {
      flyengine->set_status_msg(
         "%s HAS LEFT THE GAME",
         directx->players[from].name);
      bsp_object *obj=
         (bsp_object *)directx->remove_player(from);
      for( int i=from;i<directx->nplayers;i++ )
         ((ship *)directx->players[i].data)->player=i;
      if (obj) obj->life=-1;
      }
   }
   break;
case FLYMP_MSG_POWERUPMOVE:
   {
   mp_data *data=(mp_data *)&msg->type;
   powerup *p=0;
   while(p=(powerup *)flyengine->
      get_next_active_object(p,TYPE_POWERUP))
      if (p->valuetype==(int)data->flag)
         break;
   if (p)
      {
      p->pos=data->pos;
      p->life=p->source->life;
      }
   }
   break;
case FLYMP_MSG_POWERUPGET:
   {
   mp_data *data=(mp_data *)&msg->type;
```

```
            powerup *p=0;
            while(p=(powerup *)flyengine->
              get_next_active_object(p,TYPE_POWERUP))
              if (p->valuetype==(int)data->flag)
                break;
              if (p)
              p->powerup_get((ship *)directx->players[from].data);
            }
            break;
        }
    }
}
```

21 Engine architecture

21.1 Game programming in C++

21.2 Managing and evolving complexity in games

21.3 Engine design and architecture

21.4 Fly3D software architecture

21.1 Game programming in C++

This chapter starts with brief introduction to C++ intended for those who already possess a good facility with C. We then overview the engine architecture, leaving the details to Chapter 22. Its emphasis is on those aspects of C++, that are useful in games. We start with definitions of new features that are included in C++, then move on to games applications.

C has been the programming language used in games for a long time and most games are still written in C because of its speed and portability. With the advent of standard C++ definitions, C++ now possesses all the speed and portability of pure C in addition to those features that can be used to advantage game programming. Thus it is becoming the *de facto* standard for modern games.

The conventional wisdom is that C++ is slower than C but this will only occur if sufficient care is not taken in the coding.

Those C++ definitions that are useful in game are as follows.

21.1.1 Classes

C++ classes are basically C structures with embedded code as member functions. Using classes to specify program objects enables all the code that deals with the object to be included within it. This is a more organised approach and makes the object blocks easier to manage and reuse.

An example of the conversion of C to C++ representation is:

C

```
struct vector
{
   float x,y,z;
};
void normalize(struct vector &v)
{
   float len=sqrt(v.x*v.x + v.y*v.y + v.z*v.z);
   if (len>0)
      { v.x/=len; v.y/=len; v.z/=len; }
}
```

C++

```
class vector
{
public:
   float x,y,z;
   void normalize();
};
void vector::normalize()
{
   float len=sqrt(x*x + y*y + z*z);
   if (len>0)
      { x/=len; y/=len; z/=len; }
}
```

21.1.2

Constructors

A constructor is a method called when an instance of the class is allocated. Usually, members are initialised in the constructor. The constructor method must have the same name as the class it is from. The class may have more than one constructor if each of them has different parameters.

Examples of some constructors for the above vector class are:

```
class vector
{
public:
   float x,y,z;

   vector()
   { ; };   // uninitialised

   vector(float f1,float f2,float f3)
   { x=f1; y=f2; z=f3; }; // initialised by 3 floats

   vector(float f)
```

```
        { x=y=z=f; }; // initialised by 1 float
        vector(vector &v)
        { *this=v; }; // initialised by another vector
};
...
{
vector v1;
vector v2(0.0f);
vector v3(0.0f,0.0f,1.0f);
vector v4(v2);
}
```

21.1.3

Destructors

The destructor is a method called when the class is to be released. Usually, you must check for any data that was allocated by the object, and free it. The destructor is called when the class variable is deleted or gets out of scope. The destructor has the same name as the class, but with a '~' character at the beginning.

```
class A
{
public:
    char *data;

    A() { data=0; }
    ~A() { if (data) delete data; };

    void allocate_data(int i)
    {
    if (data) delete data;
    data=new char[i];
    };
};
```

21.1.4

Inheritance

Inheritance is the most important feature of C++ and is the ability to create a new class by derivation from one or more already existing classes. All properties and methods of the original classes are maintained and new properties and methods can be included. In this way you can create a base object and use this base code to create new objects that include the base object as a part of it.

For example, a plane can be defined as deriving from a vector (the plane normal) by adding a single float, the plane distance to the origin. This would be:

```
class plane : public vector
{
public:
```

```
    float d;
    float distance_to(vector &p);
};
float plane::distance_to(vector &p)
{
    // return the distance from point p to the plane
    return x*p.x + y*p.y + z*p.z - d;
}
```

21.1.5 Virtual functions

A virtual function is a member function that you expect to be redefined in derived classes. If you define a function in a class as virtual, any class deriving from it may have a new implementation for the function. When calling the virtual function from a class pointer (even from a base class pointer), the function that will be executed is the one defined at allocation time. If your class does not implement the function, the base class version will be used.

```
class A
{
    A() { printf("A constructor\n");
    virtual ~A() { printf("A destructor\n");

    virtual void print() { printf("A print"); };
};
class B : public A
{
    B() { printf("B constructor\n");
    virtual ~B() { printf("B destructor\n");
};
class C : public A
{
    C() { printf("C constructor\n");
    virtual ~C() { printf("C destructor\n");

    virtual void print() { printf("C print"); };
};
...
{
    A *a;
    B b;
    C c;
    a=&b;
    a->print();
    a=&c;
    a->print();
}
```

will print out:

```
A constructor
B constructor
A constructor
C constructor
A print
C print
C destructor
A destructor
B destructor
A destructor
```

21.1.6 Operators

When a new class is defined operators must also be defined in order to be used. For example, consider the following definitions of two operators for the vector class:

```cpp
inline vector operator +(vector &v1,vector2 &v2)
{
   vector v;
   v.x = v1.x + v2.x;
   v.y = v1.y + v2.y;
   v.z = v1.z + v2.z;
   return v;
}

inline operator *=(vector &v1,float f)
{
   v1.x *= f;
   v1.y *= f;
   v1.z *= f;
}
```

This would be used in the following context

```cpp
{
   vector v1,v2(2,2,2),v3(3,3,3);
   float f=0.2f;
   v1=v2+v3;
   v1*=f;
}
```

will set v1 to (1,1,1).

The operators that can be redefined in this way are:

+	-	++	--	*	/	%
^	&	|	~	!	<	>
=	+=	-=	*=	/=	%=	^=
&=	|=	<<	>>	>>=	<<=	==
!=	<=	>=	&&	||	->*	->
,	()	[]	new	delete	new[]	delete[]

Care must be taken when using operators like:

```
+, -, *, /, %, |, &, ^, and ~
```

as they return values. If the data being operated on is large (a 4 × 4 matrix, for example), the operators will execute slowly as new copies of temporary data will be created in the process. The following code shows this inefficiency problem.

```
class A
{
public:
   int value;
   A(int i=0)
   {
   value=i;
   printf("constructor %i\n",i);
   };
};
A operator +(A a1,A a2)
{
   return A(a1.value+a2.value);
}
...
{
   A a1(3)
   A a2(4);
   A a3=a1+a2;
}
```

will print out:

```
constructor 3
constructor 4
constructor 0
constructor 7
```

The output '0' is the temporary class allocated by the operator that produces the inefficiency – this will be large for large objects.

Templates

Templates are mechanisms for generating functions and classes based on type parameters (templates are sometimes called 'parametrised types'). By using templates, you can design a single class that operates on data of many types, instead of having to create a separate class for each type.

For example, to create a type-safe function that returns the minimum of two parameters without using templates, you would have to write a set of overloaded functions as:

```
// min for ints
int min( int a, int b )
   return ( a < b ) ? a : b;
// min for longs
long min( long a, long b )
   return ( a < b ) ? a : b;
// min for chars
char min( char a, char b )
   return ( a < b ) ? a : b;
//etc...
```

By using templates, you can reduce this duplication to a single function template:

```
template <class T> T min( T a, T b )
   return ( a < b ) ? a : b;
```

Templates can significantly reduce source code size and increase code flexibility without reducing type safety.

Public/private/protected

This facility must be used wisely. The following contrasting examples are taken from Pedri (1999).

He considers the following code.

```
class Point3D{
  public:
    float&        GetX()              { return x; }
    const float&  GetX() const        { return x; }
    float&        GetY()              { return y; }
    const float&  GetY() const        { return y; }
    float&        GetZ()              { return z; }
    const float&  GetZ() const        { return z; }
  private:
    float x, y, z;
};
```

and points out that making accessors for a basic structure like this provides no benefit. Making the accessors inline will make their use as fast as direct access. But then the class would have to be used as follows:

```
Point3D p1, p2;
float dist = sqrt(
     p1.GetX()*p2.GetX() +
     p1.GetY()*p2.GetY() +
     p1.GetZ()*p2.GetZ());
```

instead of:

```
float dist = sqrt(p1.x*p2.x + p1.y*p2.y + p1.z*p2.z);
```

Pedri (1999) states that the only time protected data should be used is when you don't want the users of the class either to know about the data or to modify the data directly.

21.2 Managing and evolving complexity in games

The main factors involved in building an engine to be used by different games are:

- different facilities required by different genres: at what level should the facilities offered by the engine be established?

- different optimisations possible in different games: this has a bearing on the first factor;

- the continual evolution of hardware making software functions redundant: the useful life of the engine may be shortened by new hardware;

- the effort devoted to games development software which may not necessarily be highly reuseable, such as level-building tools and editing facilities for artists.

21.2.1 Game structure

In the example, game complexity is embedded in the game engine and the plug-ins. For a simple first-person shooter game with player and effects easily controlled by simple physics, most of the game programming effort is contained in the engine. For more complicated games the complexity shifts into the plug-ins with the engine relegated to producing the animation. Thus at the outset the decision is made to build a simple engine that will be able to deal with any game structure.

21.3 Engine design and architecture

The purpose of this chapter is to describe the main design choices that were made in the implementation and the reasons for them. Full details on how to use the engine are given in Chapter 22.

Engine architecture design factors are motivated by many requirements. The predominant ones are efficiency of image generation, quality of image generation and the provision of a development platform.

The example engine is based on BSP technology as described in Chapter 9. Although BSP management was originally developed for first-person shooter games it is a general and versatile scene management methodology and will admit many applications, as the examples will demonstrate. As we describe in Chapter 15, different applications will use different partitioning methods to build the BSP object and these options are embedded in the plug-in that converts the model into the tree.

The implemented applications are examples of common games genres and include:

- First person shooter game (ship and walking person)

- Car racing and pursuit game

- Three-dimensional strategy game.

BSP technology is also versatile enough to facilitate combinations of the scene types that support these games, as we describe in Chapter 15. These are:

- **Closed environments** BSP planes are made coincident with the faces and every BSP partition is categorised as **in** or **out**.

- **Landscapes** Partition planes are normal to the ground plane and BSP partitions contain groups of faces.

- **3D strategy games partitions** This is an extension of the previous and includes a third partition plane orientation which defines BSP partitions to be rectangular solids which contain games objects for selection and so on.

- **Combinations** It is possible to implement environments which will contain combinations of these scene types. A type-separating plane dichotomises the different scene within a single tree. A common example might be the traversal from a landscape into a closed environment or vice versa. In this case the two types of environment are merged into a single BSP tree by having, as the root node, the plane that separates the environments. The tree is then built by applying the different building utilities to each side of the tree.

The applicability of BSP technology depends, of course, on the nature of the game application. A popular genre – football games – may or may not be beneficially implemented as a BSP tree depending on the relative complexity of the landscape vs. the players. If the stadium is complex then the landscape approach can be used. If, however, the complexity of the 22 players – dynamic objects – is much greater than the landscape, BSP technology will not be optimal.

In general, BSP technology is best in applications with large complex static meshes and its inherent advantages reduce as the number and complexity of the dynamic objects increases. It is also supreme in applications which require collision detection with the static mesh.

Game development is facilitated by building the environment or level using a modelling utility or editor, then writing plug-ins to define different behaviours, both visual and dynamic, for the game objects. Ideally new plug-ins should be developed to create a unique game but several sample plug-ins are given (Section 21.4.1) which can be edited (source code) or have their behaviour altered by changing the parameter values.

The normal advantages of plug-ins pertain. The front-end has no knowledge of the nature of the plug-ins and is not recompiled when new plug-ins are added. It sees the plug-ins as a group of BSP objects which are new classes, defined by the user, and derived from the BSP base class.

Dynamic objects are handled with their reference position defaulting to particle behaviour.

21.4 Fly3D software architecture

The design reflects the motivation of ease of game development in two main ways. First, all behaviours are embedded in plug-ins. This means that the engine and front-ends are separate and distinct from the game application. The engine becomes a tool used by the game developer who needs to know little about the detailed engine behaviour (precise ways in which scene management or collision detection, for example, is implemented).

Second, inheritance in C++ is heavily exploited. The engine only knows about *bsp_objects* and many new classes can easily be created in a plug-in that inherits the *bsp_object* properties and behaviours. Many different objects that share a common behaviour can be implemented as a base object which specifies the behaviour once only (this aspect is described in more detail in Chapter 22).

The flyEngine is a .lib file that needs to be to be linked with all front-ends, plug-ins and utilities. It includes a global pointer where all access to the engine should be directed:

flyEngine *flyEngine;

The classes defined in the flyEngine.lib file are:

```
class vector;          // standard x,y,z 3d vector
class mat4x4;          // 4x4 matrix to represent rotations, trans-
                       // lations and scales
class boundbox;        // axis aligned bound box
class plane;           // 3d plane
```

```
class vertex;          // 3d vertex
class face;            // 3d face
class local_system;    / local system defined by 3 axis perpendicular
                          vectors
class base_object;     // the base class for all objects to derive
                          from
class sound;           // raw sound data
class mesh;            // 3d mesh with faces, vertices ...
class anim_mesh;       // animated 3d mesh with 3d vertex morphing
class stripfan_mesh;   // mesh specified as strips and fans
class bezier_curve;    // bezier curve with any dimension
class bezier_patch;    // bezier patch with any size in u and v
class particle;        // point particle in 3d space
class bsp_node;        // node from the bsp tree
class bsp_object;      // object inside one bsp node (all plug-ins
                          derive from this class)
class static_mesh;     // object containing faces in a leaf bsp node
                          (derived from bsp_object)
class light_map;       // bitmap for caching light
class light_map_pic;   // collection of bitmaps for caching light
class light_vertex;    // hardware vertex light info
class class_desc;      // describe fly plug-in classes
class flydll;          // handles one dll plug-in
class flydllgroup;     // group of fly plug-ins
class directX;         // directx wrapper
class picture;         // a 24 or 32 bits/pixel bitmap
class console;         // console with text input and command
                          interpreter
class flyEngine;       // the main interface
class directX;         // interface for sound, input and multiplayer
```

The engine class includes all the scene objects, textures, models, sounds and curves. It is the main interface, with several functions which interact with the simulation data.

One fly level or scene(.fly files) is composed of the following items, all included in the flyEngine class:

- a BSP tree (BSP nodes, faces, vertices) representing the static scene or level:

```
// vertex array for static bsp faces
int nvert;
vector *vert;

// faces array for static bsp
int nfaces;
face *faces;

// the bsp tree
bsp_node *bsp;
```

- an array of pictures to be used as texture maps:

```
int npiclib;
picture *piclib[MAX_PICTURES];
```

- object meshes, sounds and curves stored as linked lists:

```
// linked list of model objects
mesh *model_obj0;

// linked list of sound objects
sound *sound_obj0;

// linked list of curve objects
bezier_curve *bezier_curve0;
```

- the group of plug-ins used:

```
// group of active plugins
flydllgroup dll;
```

a linked list of stock *bsp objects*. These are objects that can be cloned and activated during the execution of the game. Activation means adding the object to the BSP tree and to the list of active objects.

```
// linked list of stock script objects
bsp_object *stock_obj0;
```

a linked list of active *bsp objects*:

```
// linked list of active objects
bsp_object *active_obj0;
```

Plug-ins

The fly3d plug-ins are *dll* files that define new classes derived from the engine *bsp_object* class. In this way we can create a *dll* that implements a new *bsp_object* to be used in the simulation. The new object will be able to give new behaviour to new virtual functions defined by the *bsp_object* that requires different behaviour. Common reimplemented functions are the *draw*, *step* and *ray_intersect* virtual functions.

The *bsp_object* class is derived from a particle, and so it behaves as a particle. It includes several properties that are common to all plug-ins, such as *position*, *vel*, *force*, *mass*, *bump*, *friction* and *radius*. If no custom behaviour is defined in new implementations for the object virtual step function, it will move and collide as a particle, using its current *vel* and *force* parameters.

The following plug-ins are supplied:

gamelib.dll

sound	implements 3D sound
particle_system	particle emitter (Chapter 13) and population
sphere	procedural strip fan sphere object

shadow	simple texture mapped shadow (Chapter 11)
explode	a group of other objects (particle system, sound, sphere, lights etc.) When an explosion occurs all the objects are activated at once
subdiv_mesh	subdivision surface mesh object
cartoon_mesh	cartoon rendered mesh object
fao_mesh	animated (vertex morphed) mesh object
dpblend_sphere	dot product texture blend sphere

lights.dll

light	a dynamic light source
spotlight	a dynamic spotlight (Chapter 10)
spritelight	implements haloes and billboard type lighting
meshlight	a 3D object that implements a non-point source – a light object with shape and extent.

bezobj.dll (Chapter 5)

bezier_extrude	an extruded Bézier curve object
bezier_loft	a lofted Bézier curve object

volfog.dll (Chapter 10)

fogsphere	a spherical fog volume
fogbox	a box fog volume

panorama.dll

panorama	implements a texture mapped panorama-box created from six images

viewport.dll (Chapter 6)

viewport	implements a camera position and a viewport

weapon.dll

gun	can include any of the other objects in the dll. It is a container for the projectiles and includes parameters for different behaviour
hit_mark	paints marks due to an explosion onto objects
mine	implements a static object which is triggered by nearby objects
laser	billboard-based projectile (Chapter 19) that simulates a laser gun
missile	mesh projectile that travels until it collides, when it then explodes

menu.dll

menu_group	a group of menu items
menu_item	selectable menu item
menu_camera	camera that can be set to view the group and select menu items

ship.dll

ship	a mesh object that behaves as a flying spaceship

turret	implements a static gun with azimuth and elevation control
robot	ship enemy that attempts to track and destroy
power_up	a resource of special abilities collected by the player (visibility, missiles etc.)
container	mesh that enables a power-up after being destroyed

walk.dll

person	person mesh
jump_pad	pad that applies forces to any player moving on top of it
birth_pad	pad for player regeneration (spawn)
gib	player body part used on death sequence

car.dll

camera	implements a camera that can be targeted to any car. The targeted car is under user control and the camera also gathers user input for this car
car	car
sun	sun object

One fly3d plug-in can implement any number of *bsp_objects* derived classes. Each class can include any number of custom properties. The properties can be of predefined types like int, float, vector, color, string, picture, mesh, sound, curve, pointer to another stock or active *bsp_object,* and so on.

Plug-ins may draw, enumerate objects or do both. The set of draw plug-ins effectively draw into depth-ordered layers which are composited into the frame buffer. For example the **panorma.dll** draws the background but is not added to the BSP tree (as it is outside the level). The **gamelib.dll** draws nothing in its layer but enumerates several objects like sound, particle system, shadow, etc., that will draw themselves when inside the frustum of a requested **bsp_draw** call. The **walk.dll** plug-in implements objects (a walking person, jump-pad, etc.) and to draw its layer, it calls a **bsp–draw** from the player's point of view (this will create a frustum and all game objects inside it will be requested to draw themselves). The **viewport.dll** enumerates an object (the viewport) but this object is not added to the BSP tree as it has no representation in 3D space. Its layer creates a small window and calls a **bsp_draw** from a specific game object (like a missile if implementing a missile camera).

The advantage of this organisation is the ability to define (and clone game) objects easily by defining their update and draw functions. From the rendering point of view it effectively combines a BSP rendering strategy with a layered approach. The plug-ins are associated with the layers which can be blended into the frame buffer using different blend modes.

As an example of a game action element, consider the plug-in dependency for the following case. We require a missile that has sound fixed to it, whose exhaust paints light on nearby objects as it travels and explodes using a particle explosion, also with the appropriate sound. The missile is also to emit smoke. The plug-ins for this set-up are shown in Figure 21.1. The light plug-in instance used by the missile causes the light map(s) within the sphere of influence of the

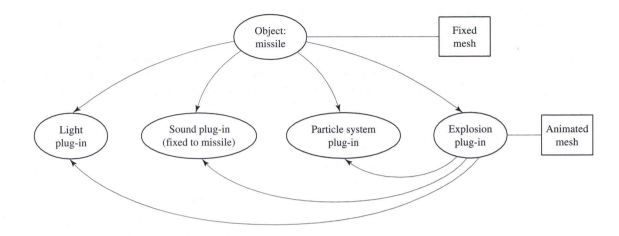

Figure 21.1
An example of plug-in
dependency.

missile light to be recomputed. Sound is fixed to the missile and travels with it. Smoke is modelled and emitted by the travelling missile by simulation in a particle system. The missile 'carries' the explosion and when it is destroyed, this explosion is cloned into the missile position in the BSP tree – effectively replacing it. The activation of the explosion may itself use sound instances and an animated mesh.

bsp_object virtual functions

The *bsp_object* class defines several virtual functions that should be reimplemented in order to define your own behaviours. If these are not implemented then the object will behave as a particle.

```
virtual void init();
```

This function is called for all objects after scene loading is completed. At this point you should initialise all data that your object requires.

```
virtual int step(int dt);
```

dt is the elapsed time from the last frame and your object should be updated using this time. If the object has moved in this time you must return TRUE. Returning will not reposition the object in the BSP tree.

```
virtual bsp_object *clone();
```

the clone function must return a new instance of the object with the same parameter settings as the original. It is used to duplicate objects.

```
virtual mesh *get_mesh();
```

If the object has a mesh representation then this function should return its current mesh object. If a mesh is returned by this function then drawing, ray intersection and collision will be handled internally.

```
virtual void draw();
```

You must draw the object mesh representation and this function is called by the BSP draw for all objects within the view frustum which have not been culled by the PVS. If not implemented a *get_mesh* will be called and if it returns a mesh that mesh will be drawn, otherwise no drawing will take place for this object.

```
virtual mesh *ray_intersect(vector& ro,vector& rd,vector& ip,float&
dist,int &facenum,float rad=0.0f);
```

For special objects that require special ray intersection routines. If not implemented, a *get_mesh* will be called and if it returns a mesh the ray intersection will be done with the mesh. Otherwise no collision detection will occur.

```
virtual int get_custom_param_desc(int i,param_desc *pd);
```

Here you should return the description of all external parameters that your object implements.

```
virtual int message(vector& p,float rad,int msg,int param,void *data);
```

This is a general object message procedure. Here you should process all messages directed to the object; for example, dynamic illumination or any other custom game message.

21.4.2   Fly3D front-ends and main rendering operations performed in each frame

Front-ends are applications created using the flyEngine lib that open a scene and loop through the simulation. The *fly.exe*, *flyEditor.exe*, *fly.ocx* and *flyserv.exe* are all examples of fly3d front-ends. They are responsible for creating and initialising a render if needed (the server front-end is an example of a front-end without a render) and loading the plug-ins.

The main loop in a front-end is as follows (Section 13.1):

```
// compute elapsed time since last frame in ms (dt)
T1=current time
dt=T1-T0
if dt < 10 return
T0=T1
if dt>1000 return
// simulate dt ms
call flyengine->step(dt)
```

dt is the time interval for the next frame and in the step function, the following order of operations are performed:

```
// get input state (keyboard and mouse)
directx->get_input();
// restores all light maps changed in last frame.
```

```
for each active object
  if object life is < 0
      destroy object removing it from BSP tree and active object
        list
    else
      call object->step(dt)
        if this returns true reposition object in BSP tree as it
          may have changed nodes
// update all light maps that were changed in this frame (this
  operation, of course, is
// necessary only for hardware assisted rendering because the maps
  have been cached into the
// hardware
// send a message to all the plug-ins informing them of the
  sumulation step
dll.send_message(FLYM_UPDATESCENE,dt,0);
// if in multi-player mode, process all multi-player messages
// messages like connect/disconnect and server quit are processed
  by the engine and
// custom multi-player messages are passed on to the plug-ins
check_multiplayer();
```

A more expanded version of the comments embedded in the code above is:

(1) The current states of the mouse and keyboard are sampled – the user's interaction with the game

(2) All light maps that were changed in the previous frame due to the influence of a dynamic light are restored to their original values. This is illumination due to static lighting only – the pre-calculated lighting for the level.

(3) All fog maps that were changed in the previous frame are cleared. Fog maps change because of the influence of the fog volumes. The view frustum may intersect the fog volumes as it moves. If such is the case (because either the player is inside the fog volume or is looking through a fog volume) then the fog map pixels need to be updated.

(4) The next operation in the sequence is to process dynamic objects.
    for each active object in active object linked list:

```
if object life<0 delete the object
else
increment cur_step variable
call object step function
if object step function returns true (moved), reposition it in
the bsp
```

Each object implements its own step function through the *bsp_object:step* virtual function. (The standard behaviour of the *bsp_object::step* function is to move as a particle. Objects in general move in different ways and have their behaviour defined in their own step function.

(5) Increment *cur_frame* variable – the frame counter.

(6) At this stage light maps may have been changed by an object step function; and all light maps that have been changed in the frame are updated to the texture manager.

(7) Similarly for fog maps: for all fog maps that have been changed in the frame are updated to the texture manager.

(8) The FLYM_UPDATESCENE message is sent to all loaded plug-ins. This message tells the plug-ins to update their state and render their layer if needed. For example, the *panorama* plug-in will render the background at this stage. The plug-in implementing a game may render the scene from the player's viewpoint. A plug-in implementing viewports may render the scene from a missile camera's point of view and a plug-in that implements a 2D interface may draw its display at this stage.

The next two processes are multiplayer operations

(9) If *multiplayer* is on, *check_multiplayer* is called to process the multiplayer messages. It queries the number of available messages in the message queue and loops through this list. For each message acquired; if it is a system message (player joined, player quit etc.) it processes it. A custom message – one which is defined by the game application – is passed onto the plug-ins through the plug-in fly_message exported funtion. The plug-ins will respond (or not) to the message according to the application.

(10) If *multiplayer* is on and running on a client, the elapsed time since the last player position was sent to the server is checked. If this is greater than the mpdelay variable it sends a FLYM_MPUPDATE message to the plugins. When the plug-ins receive this message they send positional updates for the objects they control to the server. The server then broadcasts this information to all other players. (For a LAN network the value set in mpdelay can be low, for example 25ms.)

(11) The console step function is called and the console state is updated. The console will be rendered (if it is visible), will add or remove lines if it is closing down, or opening. This is the final rendering operation (the console is superimposed on all other visuals).

Finally note that if we are in server mode, no render is defined so no input and light map operations will be executed.

It is apparent in the above that there is no reference to any rendering activity. BSP rendering occurs when the plug-ins process the update scene message. Some may effect a render and others may not. For example, *weapon.dll* effects no render. *Ship.dll* on the other hand effects a (BSP) render of the entire scene using the current ship position as the camera position. Another example is *viewport.dll* which can implement, for example, a back-facing camera or a missile camera. This selects a small viewpoint, sets the camera to the required position and effects a BSP render.

⟨21.4.3⟩

Collision detection

The following functions from the flyEngine should be used for collision detection:

```
int   collision_bsp(bsp_node   *n,vector&   p1,vector&   p2,int   elem-
type=0,float rad=0.0f);
    int   collision_test(bsp_node   *n,vector&   p1,vector&   p2,int   elem-
type=0,float rad=0.0f);
```

The *collision_test* returns 0 if no collision is found between $p1$ and $p2$ and 1 if a collision is found (not the closest collision). The *collision_bsp* returns the closest collision from p_1 to p_2.

If the *elem* type is specified, only objects with the specified type will be intersected (-1 for only the BSP faces). If *radius* is >0, the collision will be tested for a sphere with the specified radius.

The distinction of usage between a nearest collision and the detection of any collision is as follows. A moving object always needs the nearest collision for correct impact calculation. On the other hand, a robot tracking a player simply needs to know if the player is still visible from his or her viewpoint, in which case an 'any' collision will suffice.

Information about the collision is returned in the flyEngine class members:

```
// ray intersection data
bsp_object *hitobj; // bsp_object intersected
mesh *hitmesh;      // mesh from the bsp_objects intersected
int hitface;        // face from mesh intersected
vector hitip;       // intersection point in global coordinates
```

⟨21.4.4⟩

Stock and active object list

All objects defined in a *.fly* file are loaded into the stock objects linked list when a *open_fly_file* command is executed. When saving a *.fly* file, all object properties in the stock objects linked list are saved to the file.

Any stock object can be activated (cloned and added to the bsp) using the following command from the *flyEngine* class:

```
void activate(bsp_object *stockobj,int flag=1);
```

This will make a clone of the stock object (using the *clone() bsp_object* virtual function) and add it to the end of the active object linked list. If flag is true, the object is also added to the bsp.

Every object in the active object linked list will have its *step()* function called for every frame and may be selected for drawing if in the current view frustum and not culled by the PVS.

21.4.5   Sphere of influence

Spheres of influence are used for many operations in the engine. They allow fast selection of all objects in a sphere positioned anywhere in the bsp. A callback function is used, and a call is made for each *bsp_object* included inside the specified sphere of influence.

```
// recourse bsp calling a custom callback function
   void apply_bsp(bsp_node *n,vector& p,float rad,void *data,void
(*func)(void *data,bsp_object *e));
```

The callback function should be something like this:

```
void apply_bsp_callback(void *data,bsp_object *e)
{
// ...
}
```

21.4.6   Communicating between objects and plug-ins

Plug-ins are groups of objects and there are two types of messages used for communication between them – object messages and plug-in messages. Object messages are processed in the *message() bsp_object* virtual function. Plug-in messages are processed in the dll exported *fly_message()* function.

The following functions are used for sending messages:

```
void flyEngine::send_bsp_message(bsp_node *n,vector& p,float rad,int
msg,int param,void *data);
   int flydll::send_message(int msg,int param,void *data);
```

The *send_message()* function sends the message to all plug-in dlls in the current scene calling the *fly_message()* exported function of all dlls. The *send_bsp_message()* sends a message to all *bsp_object* derived classes included in the specified sphere of influence.

21.4.7   Camera and scene drawing

Each plug-in dll will receive a FLYM_UPDATESCENE message every frame. At this point it might draw over the frame buffer if needed. Usually, one plug-in will draw the scene from the player's perspective, but other plug-ins like the viewport may also draw the scene from other objects perspectives for implementing missile cameras and rear cameras. The code will be:

```
flyengine->set_camera(camobj);
flyengine->draw_bsp();
```

Text output

The following functions are used for text output. When entering text mode, a 2D mode is selected for the render. This way we can use 2D calls to draw text textured faces to represent the letters.

```
// text output functions
void start_text_mode();                              // sets 2d mode
void end_text_mode();                                // ends 2d mode
void draw_text(int x,int y,char *text);              // draw text
void draw_text_center(int x,int y,char *text);       // draw centered
                                                     text

virtual void set_status_msg(char *fmt, ...);         // outputs    to
                                                     console
```

Drawing the status of a game, for example, would be as follows:

```
flyengine->start_text_mode();

char str[64];
sprintf(str,"FPS:%i   N:%i",   flyengine->frame_rate,flyengine->node-
    drawcount);
flyengine->draw_text( 0,0, str );

flyengine->end_text_mode();
```

Rendering API

The source code has been written using OpenGL. All rendering is done inside the object *draw()* virtual function as already explained. New objects created on plugins should implement the *bsp_object* function *draw()*. In it you must place the appropriate calls required for drawing your object (see Section 22.3.7 for more details). A simple example for drawing a mesh inside a newly created object would be:

```
void my_object::draw()
{
    // Draw with OpenGL

    glPushMatrix();
    glTranslatef(pos.x,pos.y,pos.z);

    glBlendFunc(GL_ONE, GL_ONE);
    my_mesh->draw();
    glBlendFunc(GL_SRC_ALPHA, GL_ONE_MINUS_SRC_ALPHA);

    glPopMatrix();
}
```

A detailed treatment of programming in OpenGL is outside the scope of this text. A summary of each set of operations in the code above is:

Setting the current rendering matrix to position the object in global coordinates

```
glPushMatrix();
glTranslatef(pos.x,pos.y,pos.z);
```

Set the blending mode required for this object

```
glBlendFunc(GL_ONE, GL_ONE);
```

Draw the object mesh

```
my_mesh->draw();
```

Restore the blending mode

```
glBlendFunc(GL_SRC_ALPHA, GL_ONE_MINUS_SRC_ALPHA);
```

Restore rendering matrix

```
glPopMatrix();
```

Fly3D SDK reference

22.1 Introduction

22.2 Globals reference

22.3 Objects reference

Introduction

This is the reference manual for the Fly3D engine. All classes are defined in the Fly3D.dll dynamic link library. Front ends, plug-ins and utilities must link to this DLL in order to use the classes by using the Fly3D.h/Fly3D.lib files.

An on-line version of this reference manual is included in the CD-ROM and this includes hyperlinks between the pages, making navigation easier.

Globals reference index

Constants   618–20
macros   620
variables   620–21
functions   621

Objects reference index

anim_mesh   622–4
base_object   625
bezier_curve   626–9
bezier_patch   630–35
boundbox   636–7
bsp_node   638
bsp_object   639–45
class_desc   646–7
console   648–51
directX   652–8
face   659–61

fly_pak	662–5
fly_pak_util	666
flydll	667
flydllgroup	668–72
flyEngine	673–94
light_map	695–8
light_map_pic	699–700
light_vertex	701–2
local_system	703–4
mat4×4	705–6
mesh	707–11
mp_games	712
mp_msg	713
param_desc	714–5
particle	716–7
picture	718–21
plane	722
player_data	723
render	724–6
renderGL	727–9
sound	730–31
static_mesh	732–3
stripfan_mesh	734–6
textcache	737–40
textcacheGL	741–4
vector	745–8

22.2 Globals reference

Defined Constants

Constant	Value
FLYMP_GUARANTEED	0×80000000
FLYMP_BROWSETIME	2000
FLYMP_PLAYERDATASIZE	40
FLYMP_MAXPLAYERS	16
FLYMP_MAXSERVICES	16
FLYMP_MAXGAMES	16
FLYMP_MSG_JOIN	9171|FLYMP_GUARANTEED
FLYMP_MSG_QUIT	9172|FLYMP_GUARANTEED
FLYMP_MSG_FLYFILE	9173|FLYMP_GUARANTEED
FLYMP_NOMP	0
FLYMP_CLIENT	1
FLYMP_SERVER	2

FRAND	(((rand()%10000)−5000)/5000.0f)
FABSRAND	((rand()%10000)/10000.0f)
SMALL	1.0e−4f
BIG	1.0e+10f
M_Pi2	1.570796326795f
M_Pi	3.14159265359f
M_2Pi	6.28318530718f
PiOver180	1.74532925199433E−002f
PiUnder180	5.72957795130823E+001f
FP_ONE_BITS	0×3F800000
MAX_ELEMDRAW	16384
MAX_LIGHTMAP	8192
MAX_PICTURES	1024
MAX_VERT	4096
MAX_HWLIGHTS	4
MAX_TEXTURE_UNITS	4
MAX_LATEDRAW_LAYERS	8
NUM_DEFAULT_PARAM	12
FLYM_INITSCENE	1002
FLYM_UPDATESCENE	1003
FLYM_DRAWSCENE	1002
FLYM_DRAWTEXT	1003
FLYM_CLOSESCENE	1004
FLYM_MPMESSAGE	1005
FLYM_MPUPDATE	1006
FLYOBJM_CHANGEPARAM	2000
FLYOBJM_ILLUM	2001
FLYOBJM_STATICILLUM	2002
FLYOBJM_DYNILLUM	2003
FLYOBJM_DAMAGE	2004
FLYAPPID_NONE	0
FLYAPPID_FLY	1
FLYAPPID_FLYEDITOR	2
FLYAPPID_LIGHTBSP	3
FLYAPPID_FLYSERV	4
FLYAPPID_FLYOCX	5
FLYAPPID_VIEWBSPGL	6
TYPE_STATIC_MESH	−1
MAPPING_NUM	4
MAPPING_OPTIONS	16
MAPPING_TEXTURE	1
MAPPING_DETAIL	2
MAPPING_LIGHTMAP	4
MAPPING_FOGMAP	8
MESHCN_IMPLODE	1

MESHCN_FACENORM	2
MESHCN_VERTNORM	4
MESHCN_BBOX	8
MESH_EDGES	16
PATCH_EVAL_POINT	1
PATCH_EVAL_TEXTCOORD	2
PATCH_EVAL_NORMAL	4
CONSOLE_MAX_LINES	128
CONSOLE_COL	40
CONSOLE_LIN	30
FONTS_IMG_SIZE	128
FONTS_SIZE	16
FONTS_NUM	8

Defined macros

Macro	Definition
vec_dot(v1,v2)	((v1).x*(v2).x+(v1).y*(v2).y+(v1).z*(v2).z)
ISZERO(a)	((a)>−SMALL && (a)<SMALL)
FP_BITS(fp)	(*(DWORD *)&(fp))
FP_ABS_BITS(fp)	(FP_BITS(fp)&0x7FFFFFFF)
FP_SIGN_BIT(fp)	(FP_BITS(fp)&0x80000000)

Global variables

flyEngine *flyengine
Interface with engine core.

directX *directx
Interface with direct input, direct sound and direct play.

textcache *tc
Interface with texture cache (load, selection and update of textures)

render *rend
Interface with the current selected render.

GUID FLYGUID
The Fly3D application GUID

int screen_sx

int screen_sy
Render screen size in pixels

HWND hFlyWndMain
Front-end window handle

HINSTANCE hFlyInstance
Front-end instance handle

int textinterp
Flag turning texture filter on/off

int mipmap
Flag turning mip-map on/off

int ntextureunits
Number of available hardware texture units for multi-texture.

int nhwlights
Number of hardware lights available.

int numvideomodes
Number of available fullscreen video modes in *videomodes* array.

int selvideomode
Current selected fullscreen video mode from *videomodes* array.

DEVMODE *videomodes
The fullscreen video modes array.

int fullscreen
Fullscreen flag (FALSE for window mode).

int bitdepth
Current bit render depth (16, 24 or 32).

RECT winrect
The window rectangle while in window mode.

Global functions

void init_directx(HWND hWnd,HINSTANCE hInst)
Initializes the *directx* global variable. It must be called by the frontend before using direct input, direct sound and direct play.

void free_directx()
Frees the *directx* global variable.

void init_render(int type,HWND hwnd)
Initializes the render global variable. It must be called by the frontend before rendering.

void free_render()
Frees the *render* global variable.

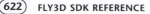

22.3

Objects reference

class anim_mesh : public mesh

Definition

```
class anim_mesh : public mesh
{
   public:
   int nframes,texpic;
   vector *ao_vert;
   vector *ao_bbox;
   int nstripfan,nstripfanvert,*stripfancount,*stripfanvert;
   vertex *vertdata;

   anim_mesh()
   {
      ao_vert=0;
      ao_bbox=0;
      nframes=0;
      nstripfan=0;
      nstripfanvert=0;
      stripfancount=0;
      stripfanvert=0;
      vertdata=0;
      texpic=-1;
   }

   void reset();
   void compute_bbox();
   int load_fao(char *name);
   void set_key(float key);
   void set_key(int key);
   void draw();

   virtual ~anim_mesh()
   { reset(); };
};
```

Data members

Member	Type	Description
nframes	int	number of key frames in animation
texpic	int	the texture picture applied to the mesh
ao_vert	vector *	keyframe vertices (nv*sizeof(vector)*nframes)
ao_bbox	vector *	keyframe bounding boxes (nframes*2*sizeof(vector))
nstripfan	int	number of strips/fans
nstripfanvert	int	number of vertices in strip/fan vertex array

stripfancount	int *	strip/fan vertex count array (nstripfan*sizeof(int))
stripfanvert	int *	vertex indices into ao_vert (nstripfanvert*sizeof*(int))
vertdata	vertex *	strip/fan vertex array (nstripfanvert*sizeof(vertex))

Remarks

This class implements an animated mesh. The mesh animation is defined by keyframes and each keyframe is made up of an array of vertex positions. The mesh can be represented by a group of strip/fans or just the separate triangles. The complete mesh must have a single texture and to interpolate the animation, use the *set_key* function.

Methods

anim_mesh::compute_bbox

Prototype
```
void compute_bbox()
```
Parameters
None
Return value
None
Remarks

This function computes the bounding boxes for all keyframes and stores them in the *ao_bbox* array.

anim_mesh::draw

Prototype
```
void draw()
```
Parameters
None
Return value
None
Remarks

This function draws the animated mesh at its current animation frame. If the mesh was created/loaded with strips/fans, they are used for faster drawing. If no strip/fan information is available, separate triangles are drawn.

anim_mesh::load_fao

Prototype
```
int load_fao(char *name)
```
Parameters

Parameter	Type	Description
name	char *	filename for .fao file

Return value
None

Remarks
This function loads a .fao animated mesh file into the class. All keyframes and textures are loaded and bounding boxes and normals calculated. If a .fao object includes strip/fans they are also loaded.

anim_mesh::reset

Prototype
```
void reset()
```

Parameters
None

Return value
None

Remarks
This function resets the mesh and frees all allocated resources.

anim_mesh::set_key

Prototype
```
void set_key(int key)
void set_key(float key)
```

Parameters

Parameter	Type	Description
key	int	integer key frame (0–numframes)
key	float	float key frame (0–1.0)

Return value
None

Remarks
These functions are used to set the current animation key. The integer version of the function is faster, but can only set the mesh to one of the predefined keyframes. The float version linearly interpolates the two closest key frames to generate a smooth animation between keyframes.

class base_object

Definition

```
class base_object
{
  public:
  char name[32];
  char long_name[32];
  base_object *next_obj;

  base_object()
  { next_obj=0; name[0]=long_name[0]=0; };

  virtual ~base_object()
  { ; };
};
```

Data members

Member	Type	Description
name	char[]	object small name
long_name	char[]	object long name
next_obj	base_object *	next object in the linked list

Remarks

This class is the base class for all objects. Several other classes from the engine derive from this class. It holds the object name and pointer to next object in the specific object linked list.

class bezier_curve : public base_object

Definition

```
class bezier_curve : public base_object
{
   public:
   float *p;
   int np,ns,dim;
   vector pivot;

   bezier_curve()
   { p=0; reset(); };
   virtual ~bezier_curve()
   { reset(); };

   void reset();
   void set_dim(int ndim);
   void add_point(float *f);
   void evaluate(float u,float *f);
   void evaluate_tangent(float u,float *f);
   int adaptative_subdiv(float maxerror,float *points,int maxpoints);
   int load_bez(char *file);
   float length();
};
```

Data members

Member	Type	Description
p	float *	array of points (np*dim floats)
np	int	number of points in array
ns	int	number of curve segments
dim	int	dimension for each point
pivot	vector	position in 3D space for the centre of the curve

Remarks

This class implements a Bézier curve of any dimension (1D, 2D, 3D, etc. . .).

The curve and tangent can be evaluated at any point, and the curve can be adaptively subdivided until the curve error is less than a maximum error factor.

Methods

bezier_curve::adaptative_subdiv

Prototype

```
void adaptative_subdiv(float maxerror,float *points,int maxpoints)
```

Parameters

Parameter	Type	Description
maxerror	float	the curve maximum error
points	float *	pointer to an array of floats to receive the sub-divided points
maxpoints	int	the total number of floats in the points array

Return value
None

Remarks
This function recursively subdivides the Bézier curve adaptatively. It subdivides segments that the midpoint distance to the actual curve is greater than the *maxerror* value.

At the end of the subdivision, the points array will have the curve points (each point a float from 0.0 to 1.0) at which to interpolate the curve to get the actual adaptively subdivided curve.

bezier_curve::add_point

Prototype
```
void add_point(float *f)
```

Parameters

Parameter	Type	Description
f	float *	pointer to first coordinate of the new point to add

Return Value
None

Remarks
This method adds a new point to the Bézier curve.

The number of floats pointed to by the parameter *f* must be equal to the curve dimensionality (*dim*).

bezier_curve::evaluate

Prototype
```
void evaluate(float u,float *f)
```

Parameters

Parameter	Type	Description
u	float	value from 0.0 to 1.0 specifying the position in the curve to be evaluated
f	float *	pointer where to write the evaluated point

Return value
None

Remarks
This function evaluates a Bézier curve point at the specified position.

bezier_curve::evaluate_tangent

Prototype
```
void evaluate_tangent(float u,float *f)
```

Parameters

Parameter	Type	Description
u	float	value from 0 to 1 specifying position in the curve to be evaluated
f	float *	pointer where to write the evaluated curve tangent

Return value
None

Remarks
This function evaluates a Bezier curve tangent at the specified position.

bezier_curve::length

Prototype
```
float length()
```

Parameters
None

Return value
Returns the aproximate length for the Bézier curve.

Remarks
The curve is subdivided into small line segments (equal parametric intervals) and the sum of the length of all line segments is returned.

bezier_curve::load_bez

Prototype
```
int load_bez(char *file)
```

Parameters

Parameter	Type	Description
file	char *	filename for a text .bez curve to load

Return value

Returns 0 if file not found or reading error, otherwise loading occurred.

Remarks

This method loads a Bézier curve from a text .bez file.

bezier_curve::reset

Prototype
```
void reset()
```

Parameters

None

Return value

None

Remarks

Frees all data allocated for the curve control points and resets the curve to empty (no control points).

bezier_curve::set_dim

Prototype
```
void set_dim(int ndim)
```

Parameters

Parameter	Type	Description
ndim	int	new dim value

Return value

None

Remarks

This function sets the number of coordinates in each point of the curve. Setting *ndim* to 3 will make a curve in 3D space.

class bezier_patch : public base_object

Definition

```
class bezier_patch : public base_object
{
public:
    int mode; //2 for quadratic and 3 for cubic
    vector*p; //the surface control points
    vector*t; //the surface texture control points
    int np,    //num points
       npu,    //num points in u dir
       npv,    //num points in v dir
       nsu,    //num segments in u dir
       nsv,    //numsegments in u dir

  int levelu,levelv; //subdivision level in u and v
  int nvertu,nvertv; //surface num vertices in u and v
  int texpic,lm;       //texture and lightmap
  vector*surf;    //discretized surface
  vector pivot;       //the pivot position

  void reset();
  int load_pch(char*file);
  void build_loft(bezier_curve*shape,bezier_curve*path,int
texture,int lightmap,float tileu,float tilev);
  void evaluate(int evaltype,float u,float v,float v,vector*dest);
  void build surface();
  void illuminate(vector& p,float rad,vector& color,int shadows);
  void draw(int nleveldrop=0);
mesh*build_mesh();
    bezier_patch()     { p=0; reset(); };
    ~bezier_patch()     { reset(); };
};
```

Data members

Member	Type	Description
mode	int	Bézier patch mode: 3 for quadratic 4 for cubic
pivot	vector	pivot position
p	vector *	the patch control points array
t	vector *	the patch control points texture coordinates array (x,y) for texture map coordinates (z,w) for lightmap texture coordinates
np	int	number of points in control points array

npu	int	number of points in u dir
npv	int	number of points in v dir
nsu	int	number of segments in u dir
nsv	int	number of segments in v dir
levelu	int	subdivision level u
levelv	int	subdivision level v
nvertu	int	number of discretized vertices in u dir nvertu = (1<<levelu)+1
nvertv	int	number of discretized vertices in v dir nvertv = (1<<levelv)+1
texpic	int	texture applied to the patch (–1 for none)
lm	int	light_map applied to the patch (–1 for none)
surf	vector*	discretized surface points 2 vectors per entry (point and texture coordinates) size = 2*sizeof(vector)*nvertu*nvertv

Remarks

This class implements a Bézier patch. The patch can have any number of segments in u and v directions. The patch is made of several connected cubic or quadratic Bézier patches (*nsu* is the number of patches in the *u* dir and *nsv* in the *v* dir).

For quadratic patches:
nsu = (spu22)/2
nsv = (spv22)/2

For cubic patches:
nsu = (spu21)/2
nsv = (spv21)/2

The surface is discretized based on the subdivision level. The number of vertices in u and v dir are:
nvertu = (1<<levelu)*nsu+1
nvertv = (1<<levelv)*nsv+1

At run-time, the surface car be drawn at any level of detail up to its current selected level. The draw function includes a parameter that represents the number of levels of detail to drop on draw. The number of vertices skipped (col/row draw loop increment) on each direction is:

nvertskip = (1<<nleveldrop)

Methods

bezier_patch::build_loft

Prototype
```
void build_loft(bezier_curve *shape,bezier_curve *path,int
texture,int lightmap,float tileu,float tilev)
```

Parameters

Parameter	Type	Description
shape	bezier_curve *	shape curve
path	bezier_curve *	path curve
texture	int	the texture map
lightmap	int	the light map
tileu	float	texture map tile in u dir
tilev	float	texture map tile in v dir

Return value
  None

Remarks
  This function builds the patch for a shape/path pair of Bézier curves.

bezier_patch::build_mesh

Prototype
```
mesh*build_mesh();
```

Parameters
  None

Return value
  Returns the mesh object representing the patch. Must be deleted by caller when not in need any more.

Remarks
  This function generates a mesh object equivalent to the discretised patch surface. It is used for collision detection with the patch.

bezier_patch::build_surface

Prototype
```
void build_surface();
```

Parameters
  None

Return value
  None

Remarks
  This function discretises the patch into the *surf* array. It finds an independent subdivision level to use in u and v based on the flyengine curve error factor.

bezier_patch::draw

Prototype
```
void draw(int nleveldrop=0);
```

Parameters

Parameter	Type	Description
nleveldrop	int	number of levels of detail to drop on draw (0 for full detail)

Return value
None

Remarks
This function draws the patch using triangle strips. The current patch level of detail can be dropped by the *nleveldrop* parameter.

bezier_patch::evaluate

Prototype
```
void evaluate(int evaltype,float u,float v,vector*dest)
```

Parameters

Parameter	Type	Description
evaltype	int	bit field specifying what to evaluate: bit 1 (1) – point (PATCH_EVAL_POINT) bit 2 (2) – texture coordinates (PATCH_EVAL_TEXTCOORD) bit 3 (4) – normal (PATCH_EVAL_NORMAL)
u	float	u coordinate
v	float	v coordinate
dest	vector*	buffer where to write evaluated data

Return value
None

Remarks
This function evaluates the Bézier patch to obtain a point in the patch surface. The u and v parameters must be in the range 0.0 to 1.0.

bezier_patch::evaluate_normal

Prototype
```
void evaluate_normal(float u,float v,vector& normal)
```

Parameters

Parameter	Type	Description
u	float	u coordinate
v	float	v coordinate
normal	vector&	the returned evaluated normal

Return value
None

Remarks
This function evaluates the Bézier patch to obtain the normal at any point in the patch surface. The u and v parameters must be in the range 0.0 to 1.0.

bezier_patch::evaluate_textcoords

Prototype
```
void evaluate_textcoords(float u,float v,vector& textcoords)
```

Parameters

Parameter	Type	Description
u	float	u position (0−1.0)
v	float	v position (0−1.0)
textcoords	vector&	the returned evaluated texture coordinate

Return value
None

Remarks
This function is used to evaluate texture coordinates anywhere on the patch surface.

bezier_patch::illuminate

Prototype
```
void illuminate(vector& p,float rad,vector& color,int shadows);
```

Parameters

Parameter	Type	Description
p	vector&	light points
rad	float	light radius
color	vector&	light color
shadows	int	shadows flag:
		0 – no shadows
		1 – shadows from specific object (shadow_obj)
		2 – shadows from any object

Return value
   None

Remarks
   This function illuminates the patch light_map pixels based on the light position, radius and colour. Shadows can be computed for a specific object or all objects using the *shadows* flag.

bezier_patch::load_pch

Prototype
```
int load_pch(char *file)
```
Parameters

Parameter	Type	Description
file	char *	filename for a .pch file to load

Return value
   Returns TRUE if loading was OK, FALSE on any error.

Remarks
   This function loads the patch from a text file in the .pch format.

bezier_patch::reset

Prototype
```
void reset()
```
Parameters
   None

Return value
   None

Remarks
   This function frees all data allocated by the patch.

boundbox

Definition
```
class boundbox
{
  public:
  vector min,max;

  void reset()

  {
    min.vec(BIG,BIG,BIG);
    max.vec(-BIG,-BIG,-BIG);
  };
  void add_point(vector &p);
  void add_point(float x,float y,float z);
  int ray_intersect(vector& ro,vector& rd,float& tnear,float& tfar);
};
```

Data members

Member	Type	Description
min	vector	minimum corner of bounding box
max	vector	maximum corner of bounding box

Remarks

This class implements an axis-aligned bounding box (AABB). The *min* vector specifies the minimum coordinates for the AABB and *max* the maximum coordinates.

Methods

boundbox::add_point

Prototype
```
void add_point(vector &p)
void add_point(float x,float y,float z)
```

Parameters

Parameter	Type	Description
p	vector&	point to add
x	float	x coord. of point to add
y	float	y coord. of point to add
z	float	z coord. of point to add

Return value
   None

Remarks
   This method enlarges the bounding box in order for it to contain the specified point. When creating a bounding box for a mesh, call the *reset* method and loop calling this function with all mesh vertices.

boundbox::ray_intersect

Prototype
```
int ray_intersect(vector& ro,vector& rd,float& tnear,float& tfar)
```

Parameters

Parameter	Type	Description
ro	vector&	ray origin
rd	vector&	ray direction
tnear	float&	returns near collision distance
tfar	float&	returns far collision distance

Return value
   Returns 0 if no collision is found, otherwise a collision was found.

Remarks
   This method computes a ray intersection with the bounding box.
   If a collision is found, the *tnear* and *tfar* parameters will be set to the distance from the ray origin where the ray intersected the bounding box.

boundbox::reset

Prototype
```
void reset()
```

Parameters
   None

Return value
   None

Remarks
   This method resets the bounding box by setting the *min* vector to (−BIG,−BIG,−BIG) and the *max* vector to (−BIG,−BIG,−BIG).
   Use this method before calling the *add_point* method when creating a new bounding box.

class bsp_node : public plane

Definition

```
class bsp_node : public plane
{
   public:
   bsp_node *child[2];
   bsp_object *elem, **last_elem;
   int leaf;
   vector color;

   bsp_node()
   { child[0]=child[1]=0; elem=0; leaf=-1; last_elem=&elem; };

   virtual ~bsp_node();
};
```

Data members

Member	Type	Description
child	char[] *	the two children
elem	bsp_object *	linked list of elements in node (if this is a leaf node)
last_elem	bsp_object **	pointer to last element in *elem* linked list
leaf	int	leaf index (−1 if not a leaf node)
color	vector	ambient colour of node (if this is a leaf node)

Remarks

This class implements a bsp tree node. All nodes at the end of the tree are considered leaves and they include a linked list of elements (Fly3D plug-in objects) inside the node and node ambient colour.

class bsp_object : public base_object, particle, local_system

Definition

```
class bsp_object : public base_object, particle, local_system
{
  public:
  int type;
  int active;
  vector rot;
  bsp_object *next_elem;
  bsp_object *source;
  bsp_node *node;

  bsp_object()
  { node=0; col_flag=0; source=0; next_elem=0; type=0; };

  void add_to_bsp();
  void remove_from_bsp();
  virtual int step(int dt)
  { return particle::step(dt); };

  virtual bsp_object *clone()
  { return 0; };

  virtual mesh *get_mesh()
  { return 0; };

  virtual void init()
  { ; };

  int get_param_desc(int i,param_desc *pd);

  virtual int get_custom_param_desc(int i,param_desc *pd)
  { return 0; };

  virtual  mesh  *ray_intersect(vector&  ro,vector&  rd,vector&
ip,float& dist,int &facenum,float rad=0.0f);

  virtual  int  message(vector& p,float  rad,int  msg,int  param,void
*data)
  { return 0; };

  virtual void draw();
  void load_default_params(fly_pak *file,char *sec);
  void load_params(fly_pak *file,char *sec);
  void save_params(char *file,char *sec);

  virtual ~bsp_object()
  { if (node) remove_from_bsp(); };
};
```

Data members

Member	Type	Description
type	int	the object type (Fly3D plug-in type)
active	int	active flag (FALSE for inactive, TRUE activate on start-up)
latedraw	int	last frame of the object that was drawn
rot	vector	object rotation
next_elem	bsp_object *	next element in object's node linked list
source	bsp_object *	the object this one was cloned from (NULL if original object)
node	bsp_node *	the bsp_node the object is in

Remarks

This class implements a bsp_object. All objects created in Fly3D plug-ins must derive from this class. It is the base class for all objects that will be included in the bsp. New object behaviour is implemented by subclassing the class and implementing its virtual functions.

Methods

bsp_object::add_to_bsp

Prototype
```
void add_to_bsp()
```

Parameters
   None

Return value
   None

Remarks

This function adds the current object to the bsp tree. The current object position in 3D world space (*pos*) is used to find the bsp node the object is in and the object is added to that node's elements linked list.

bsp_object::clone

Prototype
```
virtual bsp_object *clone()
```

Parameters
   None

Return value

It must return a new class with the same parameters as the current class.

Remarks

This virtual function is used to clone the object. It must be implemented by all subclasses or no object will be created.

bsp_object::draw

Prototype
```
virtual void draw()
```

Parameters

None

Return value

None

Remarks

This virtual function is used for drawing the object and derived classes should implement it when needed.

Its default behaviour is to call the *get_mesh* function and if a mesh is returned it calls the mesh draw function. So, if neither this function nor *get_mesh* is implemented the object will not be drawn.

bsp_object::get_custom_param_desc

Prototype
```
virtual int get_custom_param_desc(int i,param_desc *pd)
```

Parameters

Parameter	Type	Description
i	int	parameter index
pd	param_desc *	parameter desc to be filled

Return value

If *pd* = 0, the number of custom parameters.

Remarks

This virtual function must be implemented by all subclasses. It returns the number of parameters the object has and each parameter description.

When called with *pd* = 0, it must return the number of parameters. When *pd* <> 0, it fill the description variable *pd* with information on the parameter index *i*.

bsp_object::get_mesh

Prototype
```
virtual mesh *get_mesh()
```

Parameters
    None

Return value
    Returns a mesh representation for the object or NULL if none exists.

Remarks
    This virtual function is used for querying the mesh representation of the object and derived classes should implement it when needed. If this function is implemented, the default *draw, ray_intersect* and *ray_intersect_test* will use it and they do not need to be defined in the derived class.
    Its default behaviour is to return 0.

bsp_object::get_param_desc

Prototype
    `int get_param_desc(int i,param_desc *pd)`

Parameters

Parameter	Type	Description
i	int	parameter index
pd	param_desc *	parameter desc to be filled

Return value
    If *pd* = 0, the number of custom parameters.

Remarks
    This function implements the object standard parameters. All subclasses must have these 12 parameters:
    pos, vel, force, rot, life, colflag, mass, radius, bump, friction, active, latedraw

bsp_object::init

Prototype
    `virtual void init()`

Parameters
    None

Return value
    None

Remarks
    This virtual function is called on object initialisation. In it you can do whatever initialisation your object needs.
    Its default behaviour is to do nothing.

bsp_object::load_default_params

Prototype
```
void load_default_params(fly_pak *file,char *sec)
```
Parameters

Parameter	Type	Description
file	flly_pak *	.fly file
sec	char *	section

Return value
None

Remarks
This function loads all default parameters from a .fly file.

bsp_object::load_params

Prototype
```
void load_params(fly_pak *file,char *sec)
```
Parameters

Parameter	Type	Description
file	fly_pak *	.fly file
sec	char *	section

Return value
None

Remarks
This function loads the object parameters from a .fly file.

bsp_object::message

Prototype
```
virtual int message(vector& p,float rad,int msg,int param,void *data)
```
Parameters

Parameter	Type	Description
p	vector&	position
rad	float	radius
msg	int	type
param	int	parameter
data	void *	general pointer parameter

Return value
Returns 0 for passing the message on, <>0 for stopping message.

Remarks
This virtual function processes messages for the object. It must be implemented if the object needs to receive any messages. Returning 0 will let the

message pass on to next object that is in its radius; returning <>0 will stop the message and return the value to the caller immediately.

bsp_object::ray_intersect

Prototype
```
virtual mesh *ray_intersect(vector& ro,vector& rd,vector& ip,float&
dist,int& facenum,float rad=0.0f)
```
Parameters

Parameter	Type	Description
ro	vector&	ray origin
rd	vector&	ray direction
ip	vector&	intersection point
dist	float&	intersection distance
facenum	int&	intersected face index
rad	float	collision radius

Return value
Returns the intersected mesh or NULL for no intersection.

Remarks
This virtual function implements a ray intersection with the object. It should return the closest collision.

Its default behaviour is to call *get_mesh* and if it returns a mesh, call the mesh *ray_intersect*.

bsp_object::ray_intersect_test

Prototype
virtual int ray_intersect_test(vector& ro,vector& rd,float rad=0.0f)

Parameters

Parameter	Type	Description
ro	vector&	ray origin
rd	vector&	ray_direction
rad	float	radius of collision

Return value
Returns TRUE on any intersection, FALSE for no intersection.

Remarks
This virtual function implements the ray intersection test with the object. It should return the first collision (not necessarily closest).

Its default behaviour is to call *get_mesh* and if a mesh is returned, it calls the mesh *ray_intersect_test*.

bsp_object::remove_from_bsp

Prototype
```
void remove_from_bsp()
```
Parameters
None
Return value
None
Remarks
This function removes the object from the bsp tree, by removing it from the linked list of elements from the bsp_node the object is in. After removing the object from the bsp tree, you can move it around and reinsert it in a new position.

bsp_object::save_params

Prototype
```
void save_params(char *file,char *sec)
```
Parameters

Parameter	Type	Description
file	char *	.fly file
sec	char *	section

Return value
None
Remarks
This function saves the object parameters into a .fly file.

bsp_object::step

Prototype
```
virtual int step(int dt)
```
Parameters

Parameter	Type	Description
dt	int	time interval in ms from last frame

Return value
If it returns TRUE, the object is repositioned in bsp tree; it returns FALSE if the object does not move.
Remarks
This virtual function is used for updating the object. The object must do whatever it has to do for the elapsed time interval (move, rotate, attack, ... whatever).

Its default behaviour is to move like a particle if not implemented by a subclass.

class class_desc

Definition

```
class class_desc
{
   public:
   virtual void *create()=0;
   virtual char *get_name()=0;
   virtual int get_type()=0;
};
```

Data members
None

Remarks
This class holds the description for the classes defined in Fly3D plug-ins. Each Fly3D plug-in will enumerate a fixed number of instances to this class and each will represent a game object. Its virtual functions are used to create and get information about the plug-in object class.

Methods

class_desc::create

Prototype
```
virtual void *create()
```

Parameters
None

Return value
Returns the pointer to the newly allocated class.

Remarks
This function creates a new instance of the described Fly3D plug-in object class. It allocates the new instance using the new operator and should be freed with the delete operator when not in use anymore.

class_desc::get_name

Prototype
```
virtual char *get_name()
```

Parameters
None

Return value
Returns a pointer to the name of the class being described.

Remarks
This function is used to get the name of the described class.

class_desc::get_type

Prototype
```
virtual int get_type()
```

Parameters
None

Return value
Returns the described class type id.

Remarks
This function is used to get the class id of the described Fly3D plug-in object class. Each Fly3D plug-in object must have an unique integer identifier.

class console

Definition

```
class console
{
public:
    int mode,time,nlines,linecount,winlines;
    char *buf[CONSOLE_MAX_LINES];

    char cmd_line[256];
        int cmd_pos;

        float dx,dy;

        console();
        ~console();

        void show();
        void hide();
        void draw();
        void step(int dt);
        float draw_text(float x,float y,char *text);

        void key_press(int key);
        void add_string(char *fmt, ...);
        int command_tokens(char *str,char **token);
        void command_exec(char *str);
};
```

Data members

Member	Type	Description
mode	int	console flags: (1 closing, 0 closed, 1 opening)
time	int	current animation time
nlines	int	number of lines in *buf*
linecount	int	current line number
winlines	int	number of lines currently visible
buf	char []	the console string history
cmdline	char []	the current command line
cmd_pos	int	the current command line cursor position
dx	float	cursor size in x
dy	float	cursor size in y

Remarks

This class implements the graphical game console. It enables you to type commands and execute them. Commands can create and delete game objects, change game object parameters, change current map and even save the current level state.

Methods

console::add_string

Prototype
```
void add_string(char *fmt, ...)
```
Parameters

Parameter	Type	Description
fmt	char *	string format and parameters

Return value
> None

Remarks
> This function adds a new string to the console history. It uses the printf syntax, so you can add formatted strings.

console::command_exec

Prototype
```
void command_exec(char *str)
```
Parameters

Parameter	Type	Description
str	char *	string to execute

Return value
> None

Remarks
> This function executes a console command.

console::command_tokens

Prototype
```
int command_tokens(char *str,char **token)
```
Parameters

Parameter	Type	Description
str	char *	string to be processed
token	char **	string tokens

Return value
> Returns the number of tokens found in the string.

Remarks
> This function converts a string into tokens (fragments the string at its spaces).

console::draw

Prototype
```
void draw()
```
Parameters
None
Return value
None
Remarks
Draws the console with its current number of lines and all text currently visible.

console::draw_text

Prototype
```
float draw_text(float x,float y,char *text)
```
Parameters

Parameter	Type	Description
x	float	position of text in x
y	float	position of text in y
text	char *	the text string

Return value
Returns the x position at the end of the printed text.
Remarks
This function draws a string of text in the console.

console::hide

Prototype
```
void hide()
```
Parameters
None
Return value
None
Remarks
This function closes the console. The number of lines in the colsole will decrease to 0 and the console will be closed.

console::key_press

Prototype
```
void key_press(int key)
```

Parameters

Parameter	Type	Description
key	int	pressed key code

Return value
None

Remarks
This function handles keyboard input to the console. It must be called with all pressed keys when console is on.

console::show

Prototype
```
void show()
```

Parameters
None

Return value
None

Remarks
This function tells the console to open. The number of lines in the console will start growing until it takes up one-third of the screen.

console::step

Prototype
```
void step(int dt)
```

Parameters

Parameter	Type	Description
dt	int	elapsed time is ms

Return value
None

Remarks
This function manages the animating of the console (opening and closing). It must be called every frame with the elapsed time for the console to open/close properly.

class directX

Definition

```
class directX
{
   public:
   int mpmode;
   int nplayers;
   player_data players[FLYMP_MAXPLAYERS];
   unsigned char diks[256];
   DIMOUSESTATE dims;

   directX(HWND hWnd,HINSTANCE hInst)
   { memset(this,0,sizeof(directX)); Init(hWnd,hInst); };

   void get_input();
   int  load_wav_file(LONG  cchBuffer,HPSTR  pchBuffer,LPDIRECTSOUND-
BUFFER *buf,LPDIRECTSOUND3DBUFFER *buf3d);
   void set_listener(float *pos,float *vel,float *Y,float *Z);
   LPDIRECTSOUNDBUFFER clone_sound(LPDIRECTSOUNDBUFFER buf);
   void set_master_volume(int volume);
   int init_multiplayer(char *netaddress=0);
   void free_multiplayer();
   mp_games *enum_games(LPGUID app_guid);
   int join_game(LPGUID game_guid,char *player_name);
   int create_game(LPGUID app_guid,char *game_name);
   char *get_player_address(DWORD dpid);
   void send_message(mp_msg *msg,int len,DWORD dpid=0);
   int get_num_messages();
   mp_msg *get_message(DWORD *size);
   int add_player(char *name,DWORD dpid,void *data);
   void *remove_player(int i);

   ~directX()
   { Release(); };
};
```

Data members

Member	Type	Description
mpmode	int	current multi-player mode. One of the following enumerated types: FLYMP_NOMP – no multiplayer FLYMP_CLIENT – running as client FLYMP_SERVER – running as server
nplayers	int	number of players in a multi-player game
players	player_data[]	player data array
diks	unsigned char[]	direct input keys array
dims	DIMOUSESTATE	direct input mouse state

Remarks

This class implements an interface with DirectX for input, sound and multi-player. A global variable named *directx* is the main interface with this class and must be initialised/freed with the *init_directx* and *close_directx* global functions.

Methods

directX::add_player

Prototype
```
int add_player(char *name,DWORD dpid,void *data)
```
Parameters

Parameter	Type	Description
name	char *	player name
dpid	DWORD	directplay player id
data	void *	pointer to specific player data

Return value

Returns the player index into the players array for the added player, and –1 if player could not be added.

Remarks

This function adds a new player to the current game.

directX::clone_sound

Prototype
```
LPDIRECTSOUNDBUFFER clone_sound(LPDIRECTSOUNDBUFFER buf)
```
Parameters

Parameter	Type	Description
buf	LPDIRECTSOUNDBUFFER	destination buffer for cloned sound

Return value

Returns the DirectX sound buffer pointer for the cloned sound.

Remarks

This function clones a sound buffer. Used for playing simultaneous instances of the same sound.

directX::create_game

Prototype
```
int create_game(LPGUID app_guid,char *game_name)
```
Parameters

Parameter	Type	Description
app_guid	LPGUID	IP address of server when starting a client. NULL for starting a server.
game_name	char *	game name

Return value

Returns TRUE is game creation is OK, FALSE if creation failed.

Remarks

This function creates a new multi-player game. It must be called from a server application and other clients will be able to join.

directX::enum_games

Prototype

```
mp_games *enum_games(LPGUID app_guid)
```

Parameters

Parameter	Type	Description
app_guid	LPGUID	application GUID. use FLYGUID for Fly3D games.

Return value

Returns pointer to the game's description class.

Remarks

Returns information on all games running on the selected server.

It is used for enumerating available games to join on a specific server.

directX::free_multiplayer

Prototype

void free_multiplayer()

Parameters

None

Return value

None

Remarks

Frees the TCP/IP connection used in multi-player games. It must be called when closing a server or a client that was playing a multi-player game.

directX::get_input

Prototype

```
void get_input()
```

Parameters

None

Return value

None

Remarks

This function gets the current key and mouse state. It fills the *diks* array with all current keyboard key states and the *dims* array with the current mouse state. It is required once a frame.

directX::get_message

Prototype
```
mp_msg *get_message(DWORD *size)
```
Parameters

Parameter	Type	Description
size	DWORD *	pointer to a DWORD to receive message size

Return value
Returns the message pointer.

Remarks
This function retrieves the first message in the application message queue. The size parameter will be filled with the actual size of the message.

directX::get_num_messages

Prototype
```
int get_num_messages()
```
Parameters
None

Return value
Returns the number of messages available in the message queue.

Remarks
You must call *get_message* as many times as the value returned by this function to clear the message queue.

directX::get_player_address

Prototype
```
char *get_player_address(DWORD dpid)
```
Parameters

Parameter	Type	Description
dpid	DWORD	directplay player id

Return value
Returns the IP address string for specified player.

Remarks
This function is used to query the IP address of one of the players in the current game.

directX::init_multiplayer

Prototype
```
int init_multiplayer(char *netaddress=0)
```

Parameters

Parameter	Type	Description
netaddress	char *	IP address of server when starting a client. NULL for starting a server.

Return value

Returns TRUE if initialisation is OK (TCP/IP installed), FALSE if unable to initialise multi-player.

Remarks

This function starts multi-player mode by initialising TCP/IP. It must be called before creating servers or connecting to a game.

It should be called with *netaddress*=NULL for creating a server.

When creating a client, set *netaddress* to the server address from where the games will be enumerated.

directX::join_game

Prototype

```
int join_game(LPGUID game_guid,char *player_name)
```

Parameters

Parameter	Type	Description
game_guid	LPGUID	game GUID to join
player_name	char *	player name

Return value

Returns the DirectPlay player id if game join is OK, 0 if unable to join.

Remarks

This function joins a multi-player game. It must be called with one of the games enumerated by the *enum_games* function.

directX::load_wav_file

Prototype

```
int load_wav_file(LONG cchBuffer,HPSTR pchBuffer,LPDIRECTSOUNDBUFFER
*buf,LPDIRECTSOUND3DBUFFER *buf3d)
```

Parameters

Parameter	Type	Description
cchBuffer	LONG	.wav file size in bytes
pchBuffer	HPSTR	.wav file bytes
buf	DIRECTSOUNDBUFFER **	destination direct sound buffer
buf3d	DIRECTSOUND3DBUFFER **	destination direct sound buffer 3D

Return value

Returns TRUE if loading is OK, FALSE on any error.

Remarks

Loads a .wav file stored in memory. It creates the direct sound buffer (**buf* and **buf3d*) to receive the sound. Note that the *buf* and *buf3d* parameters are pointers to pointers.

directX::remove_player

Prototype

```
void *remove_player(int i)
```

Parameters

Parameter	Type	Description
i	int	player index

Return value

Returns the data associated with the player when the player was created.

Remarks

This function removes a player from the game. The parameter *i* must be the index of the player in the *players* array.

directX::send_message

Prototype

void send_message(mp_msg *msg,int len,DWORD dpid=0)

Parameters

Parameter	Type	Description
msg len dpid	mp_msg * int DWORD	message to send length in bytes of message player to send message to: 0 – all players <>0 – player id of destination player

Return value

None

Remarks

This function sends a multi-player message. The message can have any size, but you must keep it as small as possible for a better performance. The message header must be as a *mp_msg* struct.

directX::set_listener

Prototype

```
void set_listener(float *pos,float *vel,float *Y,float *Z)
```

Parameters

Parameter	Type	Description
pos	float *	the listener position (pointer to 3 floats)
vel	float *	the listener velocity (pointer to 3 floats)
Y	float *	the listener up vector (pointer to 3 floats)
Z	float *	the listener front vector (pointer to 3 floats)

Return value

None

Remarks

Sets current sound listener attributes. All playing sounds will be relative to the listener position, velocity and rotation. If *vel* is (0,0,0), no Doppler effect is used.

directX::set_master_volume

Prototype

```
void set_master_volume(int volume)
```

Parameters

Parameter	Type	Description
volume	int	volume to set (negative value). Use 0 for maximum volume.

Remarks

Sets the master sound volume. Volume is a negative value with 0 being the maximum volume.

class face : public plane

Definition

```
class face : public plane
{
  public:
  vector *vert[3];
  vector edgenormal[3];
  vector vertnormal[3];
  vector color;
  int texpic;
  int lm;
  float uv[3][2];
  float lmuv[3][2];
  float emmradius;
  int lastdraw;
  int indx;

    int  ray_intersect(vector&  ro,vector&  rd,vector&  ip,float&
dist,float rad=0.0f);
  void inverse_map(vector& p,float& u,float& v);
  void forward_map(float& u,float& v,vector& p);
};
```

Data members

Member	Type	Description
vert	vector*[3]	pointer to the three face vertices
edgenormal	vector[3]	the three edge normals
vertnormal	vector[3]	the three vertex normals
color	vector	the face colour (r,g,b,a)
texpic	int	the face texture picture
lm	int	the face light map
uv	float[3][2]	the three vertex texture coordinates
lmuv	float[3][2]	the three vertex light map texture coordinates
emmradius	float	the face emmisive radius (if self-illuminated)
lastdraw	int	the last frame in which the face was drawn
indx	int	the face index into the faces array

Remarks

This class implements a 3D face with three vertices. Texture and light map can be applied to the face and functions for collision detection are also implemented.

If *emmradius* is >0, the face will cast light when static level light computation is calculated.

Methods

face::forward_map

Prototype
```
void forward_map(float& u,float& v,vector& p)
```
Parameters

Parameter	Type	Description
u	float&	point coordinate in u axis
v	float&	point coordinate in v axis
p	vector&	point in object space

Return value
None

Remarks
This function maps a point from light map texture space into object space.

The (u,v) pair define a point in the object's light map texture space that can be mapped into an object space 3D point.

This is used to find where a light map pixel is in scene coordinates.

face::inverse_map

Prototype
```
void inverse_map(vector& p,float& u,float& v)
```
Parameters

Parameter	Type	Description
p	vector&	point in object space
u	float&	point coordinate in u axis
v	float&	point coordinate in v axis

Return value
None

Remarks
This function maps a point from object space into light map texture space.

The *p* parameter defines a point in the object's space that is mapped into an object light map texture space 2D point.

This is used to find which light map pixel corresponds to a point in the face surface.

face::ray_intersect

Prototype
```
int ray_intersect(vector& ro,vector& rd,vector& ip,float& dist,float
rad=0.0f)
```

Parameters

Parameter	Type	Description
ro	vector&	ray origin
rd	vector&	ray direction
ip	vector&	intersection point
dist	float&	intersection distance
rad	float	intersection radius

Return value

Returns TRUE if an intersection is found, FALSE if no intersection is found.

Remarks

This function computes the intersection with the face.

If an intersection is found, *ip* will be set to the intersection point, *dist* will be set to the distance from the ray origin (*ro*) to the intersection point (*ip*).

If *rd* is normalized, the *dist* value will be in scene units, if not, it will be the distance divided by the ray direction (*rd*) length.

The *rad* parameter sets the collision radius. If >0, the collision will be tested for a sphere with radius *rad*.

class fly_pak

Definition

```
class fly_pak
{
  public:
char *buf;
    unsigned long pos, len;

    fly_pak();

    void seek(long offset);
    bool open(char *filename);
    void close();
    int read(void *dest, int size);
    void get_profile_string(char *section, char *key, char *dest);
    void get_string(char *dest);
    int get_int();
    float get_float();
    FILE *get_fp(char *filename);

    ~fly_pak();
};
```

Data members

Member	Type	Description
buf	char *	file buffer
pos	unsigned long	position inside buffer
len	unsigned long	length of buffer

Remarks

This class implements the loading of files. It should be used as it can read standalone files or files included in .fpk packages. The .fpk file is a group of files that are packed into a single file. When opening a file, first it tries to open the standalone file, and if it fails to find the file, it looks up the file path for a .fpk file that could contain the desired file.

Methods

fly_pak::close

Prototype
```
void close()
```
Parameters
None
Return value
None

Remarks

Closes an already opened file.

fly_pak::get_float

Prototype

```
float get_float()
```

Parameters

None

Return value

Returns a float loaded from the opened file.

Remarks

This function reads a float from the opened file. It is just like doing a fscanf(fp,"%f",&var).

fly_pak::get_fp

Prototype

```
FILE *get_fp(char *filename)
```

Parameters

Parameter	Type	Description
filename	char *	filename for the file to open

Return value

Returns the FILE* for the selected file.

Remarks

This function is used to get an standard FILE* for a file in a .fpk package.

fly_pak::get_int

Prototype

```
int get_int()
```

Parameters

None

Return value

Returns an integer loaded from the opened file.

Remarks

This function reads an integer from the opened file. It is just like doing a fscanf(fp,"%i",&var).

fly_pak::get_profile_string

Prototype
```
void get_profile_string(char *section, char *key, char *dest)
```
Parameters

Parameter	Type	Description
section	char *	section name
key	char *	key name
dest	char *	destination string

Return value
None

Remarks
This function works just like the GetPrivateProfileString Windows API function. It is used to manage .ini-type files and as .fly files are just text .ini files, it is used to load the .fly files.

fly_pak::get_string

Prototype
```
void get_string(char *dest)
```
Parameters

Parameter	Type	Description
dest	char *	destination string

Return value
None

Remarks
This function is used to load a string from the specified file. It works just like the fgets standard I/O function.

fly_pak::open

Prototype
```
bool open(char *filename)
```
Parameters

Parameter	Type	Description
filename	char *	filename for file to open

Return value
Returns TRUE if open is OK, FALSE on any error.

Remarks
This function opens a file (standalone or from a .fpk package). It first tries to open the file as a standalone file. If it fails to open it, it looks up the file path for .fpk files that may contain the desired file. All open files needs to be closed using the *close* method.

fly_pak::read

Prototype
```
int read(void *dest, int size)
```

Parameters

Parameter	Type	Description
dest	void *	destination memory pointer
size	int	number of bytes to read

Return value
Returns the actual number of bytes copied to the destination buffer.

Remarks
This function reads a specified number of bytes from the opened file into the *dest* memory buffer. If the number of bytes requested is more than the bytes available in the file, only the available bytes are copied and the number of bytes actually copied is returned.

fly_pak::seek

Prototype
```
void seek(long offset)
```

Parameters

Parameter	Type	Description
offset	long	offset to move from current position

Return value
None

Remarks
This function seeks the current file pointer just like the fseek standard I/O function. The *offset* can be positive or negative.

class fly_pak_util

Definition

```
class fly_pak_util
{
public:
    bool implode(char *folder);
    bool explode(char *filename);
};
```

Data members

None

Remarks

This class uses the fly_pak class to pack/unpack complete directories.

Methods

fly_pak_util::explode

Prototype

```
bool explode(char *filename)
```

Parameters

Parameter	Type	Description
filename	char *	filename for the .fpk file to unpack

Return value

Returns TRUE if unpacking was OK, FALSE on any error.

Remarks

This function unpacks a .fpk file, creating all files and directories included in it.

fly_pak_util::implode

Prototype

```
bool implode(char *folder)
```

Parameters

Parameter	Type	Description
folder	char *	folder to pack

Return value

Returns TRUE if packing was OK, FALSE on any error.

Remarks

This function packs all files from the selected folder (including subdirectories) into a single .fpk file.

class flydll

Definition

```
class flydll
{
  public:
  HINSTANCE hdll;
  char dll_filename[256];
  int nclasses;
  int (* num_classes)();
  class_desc *(* get_class_desc)(int i);
  int (* fly_message)(int msg,int param,void *data);
};
```

Data members

Member	Type	Description
hdll	HINSTANCE	instance handle of the plug-in dll
dll_filename	char *	file name of the plug-in dll
nclasses	int	number of classes implemented in the plug-in
numclasses	int (*)()	pointer to numclasses() function of the plug-in dll
get_class_desc	class_desc *(*)(int i)	pointer to get_class_desc() function of the plug-in dll
fly_message	int (*)(int msg, int param, void *data)	pointer to fly_message() function of the plug-in dll

Remarks

This class holds information for each Fly3D plug-in dll, including the number of classes implemented in the dll, and the pointers to the dll exported functions.

class flydllgroup

Definition

```
class flydllgroup
{
    public:
    int ndll;
    flydll **dll;
    int ncd;
    class_desc **cd;

    flydllgroup();

    void reset();
    int add_dll(char *filename);
    int delete_dll(char *filename);
    void move_dll(char *filename,int newrelpos);
    int send_message(int msg,int param,void *data);
    void load_all_classes(fly_pak *file);
    void load_classes(int d,fly_pak *file);
    void load_default_param(bsp_object *o,char *sec,fly_pak *file);
    void delete_class(bsp_object *o);
    void delete_references(bsp_object *o);
    bsp_object *add_class(char *name);

    virtual ~flydllgroup();
};
```

Data members

Member	Type	Description
ndll	int	number of Fly3D plug-in dlls in *dll* array
dll	flydll *	array of plug-in dll description classes
ncd	int	total number of classes implemented by the plug-ins in *cd* array
cd	class_desc *	array of class description classes

Remarks

This class implements a group of Fly3D plug-in dlls. Each Fly3D plug-in dll can enumerate any number of *bsp_object* derived classes.

The plug-in dlls are stored in the *dll* member variable and the classes implemented by them are stored in the *cd* member variable.

Methods

flydllgroup::add_class

Prototype

```
bsp_object *add_class(char *name)
```

Parameters

Parameter	Type	Description
name	char *	object class name to create an instance

Return value

Returns an instance of the class with the specified name.

Remarks

This function is used only by the flyEditor and creates a new object from a plug-in dll by just specifying the class name.

flydll_group::add_dll

Prototype

```
int add_dll(char *filename)
```

Parameters

Parameter	Type	Description
filename	char *	filename for the Fly3D plug-in dll

Return value

Returns TRUE if the dll was loaded OK, FALSE if not found or other error.

Remarks

This function adds a new Fly3D plug-in dll into the dll array. Its classes should then be loaded using the *load_classes* method.

flydllgroup::delete_class

Prototype

```
void delete_class(bsp_object *o)
```

Parameters

Parameter	Type	Description
o	bsp_object *	object to be deleted

Return value

None

Remarks

This function is used only by the flyEditor and deletes a object from the scene. It also clears any other object reference to the one being deleted.

flydllgroup::delete_dll

Prototype

```
int delete_dll(char *filename)
```

Parameters

Parameter	Type	Description
filename	char *	filename for the Fly3D plug-in dll

Return value

Returns TRUE if the dll was removed OK, FALSE if not found or other error.

Remarks

This function removes a Fly3D plug-in dll from memory. It removes all classes implemented by the dll from memory and frees resources associated with the dll.

flydllgroup::delete_references

Prototype

```
void delete_references(bsp_object *o)
```

Parameters

Parameter	Type	Description
o	bsp_object *	object whose references should be deleted

Return value

None

Remarks

This function removes any references to the specified object. It is used before deleting the object. All other objects that had pointers to this one will have their pointers set to NULL.

flydllgroup::load_all_classes

Prototype

```
void load_all_classes(fly_pak *file)
```

Parameters

Parameter	Type	Description
file	fly_pak *	.fly file

Return value

None

Remarks

This function loops on all Fly3D plug-in dlls included in the supplied .fly file and loads all classes from each of them using the *load_classes* method.

flydllgroup::load_classes

Prototype

```
void load_classes(int d,fly_pak *file)
```

Parameters

Parameter	Type	Description
d	int	dll index into dll array
file	fly_pak *	.fly file

Return value

None

Remarks

This function loads all classes from the specified Fly3D plug-in dll.

flydllgroup::load_default_param

Prototype

```
void load_default_param(bsp_object *o,char *sec,fly_pak *file)
```

Parameters

Parameter	Type	Description
o	bsp_object *	object to set parameters
sec	char *	section from .fly file to get parameters from
file	fly_pak *	.fly file

Return value

None

Remarks

This function loads all default parameters (*pos, vel, force, rot, life, colflag, mass, radius, bump, friction, active, latedraw*) for the specified object. All *bsp_object* derived classes (implemented in Fly3D plug-ins) have these 12 default parameters.

flydllgroup::move_dll

Prototype

```
void move_dll(char *filename,int newrelpos)
```

Parameters

Parameter	Type	Description
filename	char *	filename for the Fly3D plug-in dll
newrelpos	int	relative move

Return value

Returns TRUE if the dll was moved OK, FALSE if not found or other error.

Remarks

This function changes a Fly3D plug-in dll position (order) in the plug-in list. The order of plug-ins is important as the first ones will render first. The panorama.dll plug-in is usually the first (because it draws the background).

flydllgroup::reset

Prototype
```
void reset()
```

Parameters
None

Return value
None

Remarks
This function resets the class by freeing all allocated data.

flydllgroup::send_message

Prototype
```
int send_message(int msg,int param,void *data)
```

Parameters

Parameter	Type	Description
msg	int	message id
param	int	general parameter
data	void *	general data pointer

Return value
Returns a value from the plug-in dlls (0 if passed on all plug-in dlls, <>0 if some plug-in stopped message by returning <>0)

Remarks
This function is used to send messages to the plug-in dlls. It will send the message to all plug-in dlls included in the flydllgroup class. The data pointer can be used to send pointers to any type/size of data as all messages are local.

The send_message function will loop through all plug-in dlls loaded, and for each one, if the plug-in dll returns 0, the message passes to the next plug-in dll in the list; if it returns <>0, the send_message function stops and returns the value. So if return value is zero, it passed on all plug-in dlls.

class flyEngine

Definition

```
class flyEngine
{
  public:

  int cur_step,cur_step_base;
  int cur_frame,cur_frame_base;
  int cur_time,cur_dt;

  flydllgroup dll;
  console con;

  bsp_object *player;
  bsp_object *cam;
  vector frustum[5];

  bsp_object *excludecollision,*stepobj;
  bsp_object *elemdraw[MAX_ELEMDRAW];
  bsp_object *elemlatedraw[MAX_ELEMDRAW];

  int nelemdraw;
  bsp_object*elemdraw[MAX_ELEMDRAW];
  int nelemlatedraw[MAX_LATEDRAW_LAYERS];
  bsp_object*elemlatedraw[MAX_LATEDRAW_LAYERS][MAX_ELEMDRAW];
  int*facedraw;
  int nfacedraw;
  int*facedrawtransp;
  int nfacedrawtransp;

  char flysdkpath[256];
  char flyfile[256];
  char flydatapath[256];
  char flyfilename[256];
  char bspfile[256];
  char status_msg[256];
  char console_command[256];
  unsigned status_msg_time;

  float bboxdiag,viewmaxdist,viewmindist,
      camangle,aspect,geomdetail,curveerr,lmpxsize,detailtile,car-
toonwidth,shadowdepth;

  vector    bbox1,bbox2,bboxC,filter,background,cartooncolor,shadow-
color;

  int nodedrawcount,nodeonly,pvsoff,fog,mpdelay,
      antialias,amblight,mapmode,multitexture,
      shadows,noinput,wireframe,mute,clearbk,moving,
      appid,mouse,crosshairpic,crosshairsize,intropic,introtime,
```

```
          detailpic,hwlights,stencilcartoonpic,cartoonpicbsp;
      bsp_object *active_obj0,*last_active_obj;
      bsp_object *stock_obj0;
      mesh *model_obj0;
      sound *sound_obj0;
      bezier_curve *bezier_curve0;
      bezier_patch *bezier_patch0;
      bsp_object *shadow_obj;
      bsp_object *hitobj;
      mesh *hitmesh;
      int hitface;
      vector hitip;
      int status,fontspic,fonts_width[64],consolepic;
      vector *vert,*vertcolor,vertnormal;
      face *faces;
      int nvert,nfaces;
      int *edges,nedges,*faceedges;
      bsp_node *bsp;

      light_map *lm[MAX_LIGHTMAP];
      light_map_pic *lmpic[MAX_LIGHTMAP];
      int nlm,lmbase,nlmpic;

      light_map *fm[MAX_LIGHTMAP];
      light_map_pic *fmpic[MAX_LIGHTMAP];
      int fmbase;

      picture *piclib[MAX_PICTURES];
      int npiclib;

      char *pvs;
      bsp_node *leaf[MAX_LEAF];
      int nleaf,pvssizepvsrowsize;

      flyEngine();

      void draw_bsp(int mode=0);
      void draw_bsp_edges();
      int collision_bsp(bsp_node *n,vector& p1,vector& p2,int
elemtype=0,float rad=0.0f);
      int collision_test(bsp_node *n,vector& p1,vector& p2,int
elemtype=0,float rad=0.0f);
      void step(int dt);
      int step();
      void apply_bsp(bsp_node *n,vector& p,float rad,void *data,void
(*func)(void *data,bsp_object *e));
    void apply_bsp(bsp_node*n,vector*p,int np,void*data,void (*func)
(void*data,bsp_object*e));
      void send_bsp_message(bsp_node *n,vector& p,float rad,int msg, int
param,void *data);
```

```
int open_fly_file(char *file);
void close_fly_file();
int save_fly_file(char *file);
int add_lightmap(int sx,int sy);
void init_texture_cache();
void close_texture_cache();
void start_text_mode();
void end_text_mode();
void draw_text(int x,int y,char *text);
void draw_text_center(int x,int y,char *text);
virtual void set_status_msg(char *fmt, ...);
int get_picture(char *file);
bsp_object *get_stock_object(char *name);
bsp_object *get_active_object(char *name);
mesh *get_model_object(char *name);
sound *get_sound_object(char *name);
bezier_curve *get_bezier_curve(char *name);
bezier_patch *get_bezier_patch(char *name);
bsp_object *get_next_stock_object(bsp_object *o,int type=0);
bsp_object *get_next_active_object(bsp_object *o,int type=0);
int set_obj_param(char *objname,char *param,char *value);
int get_obj_param(char *objname,char *param,char *value);
int set_global_param(char *name, char *value);
int get_global_param_desc(int i,param_desc *pd);
void activate(bsp_object *d,int flag=1);
void set_camera(bsp_object *d);
bsp_node *get_random_point(vector& v,float mindist);
bsp_node *find_node(bsp_node *n,vector& v,float mindist);
int join_multiplayer(HWND hWnd,HINSTANCE hInst);
void close_multiplayer();
void check_multiplayer();

virtual ~flyEngine()
{ close_fly_file(); };
};
```

Data members

Member	Type	Description
cur_step	int	current step (each call to each object step function from each frame has an unique id)
cur_step_base	int	current step base (first step id for current frame)
cur_frame	int	current frame
cur_frame_base	int	current frame base (multiple renders are possible in different viewports)
cur_time	int	current time in ms

cur_dt	int	current elapsed time from last frame in ms
dll	flydllgroup	all Fly3D plug-in dlls in current scene
con	console	console interface
player	bsp_object *	current player bsp_object pointer
cam	bsp_object *	current camera bsp_object pointer
frustum	vector[]	the view frustum (an array of five 3D points)
excludecollision	bsp_object *	object pointer to be excluded from collision
stepobj	bsp_object *	pointer to object if inside some object step function
elemdraw	bsp_object *[]	array of elements to draw on current render
elemlatedraw	bsp_object *[]	array of elements to draw later on current render
nelemdraw	int	number of elements in *elemdraw* array
nelemlatedraw	int	number of elements in *elemlatedraw* array
facedraw	int[]	array of bsp faces to draw on current render
nfacedraw	int	number of faces in *facedraw* array
facedrawtransp	int[]	array of transparent bsp faces to draw on current render
nfacedrawtransp	int	number of faces in *facedrawtransp* array
flysdkpath	char []	path for the flysdk dir
flyfile	char []	path for the current .fly file
flydatapath	char []	path for current .fly file data dir
flyfilename	char []	filename for the current .fly file
bspfile	char []	bsp filename for the current .fly file
status_msg	char []	the current status string
status_msg_time	unsigned	the time of the status string message
console_command	char []	console command string, if <>"" command will be executed on next frame
viewmaxdist	float	near plane distance
viewmindist	float	far plane distance
camangle	float	camera angle in degrees
aspect	float	render view aspect ratio
geomdetail	float	geometry detail (objects subdivide maintaining a vertex distance < *geomdetail*)
curveerr	float	curve subdivision maximum error (curves subdivide maintaining this maximum error)
lmpxsize	float	desired size in scene units for the light map pixels (for the flyLight precomputation)
bboxdiag	float	scene bounding box diagonal
bbox1	vector	scene bounding box minimum point
bbox2	vector	scene bounding box maximum point
bboxC	vector	scene bounding box centre
filter	vector	current screen filter colour (draw over the hole screen)
background	vector	background clear colour
nodedrawcount	int	number of nodes drawn in last frame

status	int	if TRUE, status is draw
nodeonly	int	if TRUE, only the node containing the camera will be drawn
pvsoff	int	if TRUE, disables PVS culling
fog	int	if TRUE, enables distance vertex fog
mpdelay	int	delay between multi-player positional updates in ms (50 for 20 updates/sec)
antialias	int	if TRUE enables hardware anti-alias
amblight	int	ambient light (0–255) for the flyLight pre-computation
mapmode	int	map mode as bit array of 4 bits (0–15): bit 1 – texture map bit 2 – detail map bit 3 – light map bit 4 – fog map ex. mapmode = 1 means only texture map mapmode = 5 means texture map and light map mapmode = 15 means all maps
multitexture	int	if TRUE, enables multitexture support (up to 4 units)
shadows	int	if TRUE, enables dynamic shadows
shadowdepth	float	max distance for shadows
shadowcolor	vector	color for shadow polyons
noinput	int	if TRUE, all input is disabled (keyboard and mouse)
wireframe	int	if TRUE, renders to wireframe
mute	int	if TRUE, no sound is played
clearbk	int	if TRUE, clears the screen background prior to render
moving	int	if TRUE, some object is moving
cartoonpicbsp	int	1D picture for bsp cartoon texture
cartoonpic	int	1D picture for cartoon texture
cartooncolor	vector	color for cartoon edges
cartoonwidth	float	cartoon edges width
crosshairpic	int	picture for the cross-hair
crosshairsize	int	size for the cross-hair in pixels
appid	int	frontend application id
mouse	int	if TRUE, shows mouse cursor
hwlights	int	if TRUE, enable dynamic hardware lights for the dynamic objects
stencil	int	if TRUE, enables stencil buffer
detailpic	int	picture used for detail texture
detailtile	float	tile to multiply texture coordinates for the detail textures
active_obj0	bsp_object *	active objects linked list

last_active_obj	bsp_object *	last object in active object linked list
stock_obj0	bsp_object *	stock objects linked list
model_obj0	mesh *	linked list of models
sound_obj0	sound *	linked list of sounds
bezier_curve0	bezier_curve *	linked list of Bézier curves
bezier_patch0	bezier_patch *	linked list of Bézier paches
shadow_obj	bsp_object *	current object to cast shadows
hitobj	bsp_object *	current ray intersected object
hitmesh	mesh *	current ray intersected mesh
hitface	int	current ray intersected face
hitip	vector	current ray intersected point
fontspic	int	picture with the character fonts
fonts_width	int []	array with each font character width (for fonts not fixed size)
consolepic	int	picture used on the console background
intropic	int	picture used for opening level introduction
introtime	int	time in ms for the introduction animation
nvert	int	number of vertices in bsp tree *vert* array
vert	vector *	array of vertices for the bsp tree faces
vertcolor	vector *	array of vertex colours for the bsp tree vertices
vertnormal	vector*	array of vertex normals
nfaces	int	number of faces in bsp tree
faces	face *	array of bsp tree faces
edges	int*	array of bsp face edges (4*nedges*sizeof(int))
nedges	int	number of edges in bsp edges array
bsp	bsp_node *	the bsp tree root node
lm	light_map *	individual light maps (each light mapped face points to one of these)
lmpic	light_map_pic *	light map picture groups array (each light map points to one of these)
nlm	int	number of light_map classes in *lm* array
lmbase	int	offset into texture array for the light map pictures
nlmpic	int	number of light_map_pic classes in *lmpic* array
fm	light_map *	individual fog maps
fmpic	light_map_pic *	fog map picture groups array (each fog_map points to one of these)
fmbase	int	offset into texture array for the fog maps
piclib	picture *	array of pictures used as texture maps
npiclib	int	number of pictures in piclib array
leaf	bsp_node *	bsp tree leaf array
nleaf	int	number of leaves in bsp tree
pvssize	int	size of the pvs array in bytes
pvsrowsize	int	size of each pvs row in bytes
pvs	char *	pvs bit array

Remarks

This is the main interface with the engine. The global variable *flyengine* is initialised by the frontend and is from where all calls to the engine must be directed.

Methods

flyEngine::activate

Prototype

```
void activate(bsp_object *d,int flag=1)
```

Parameters

Parameter	Type	Description
d	bsp_object *	stock object to activate
flag	int	flag:
		1 – adds to bsp
		0 – not add to bsp

Return value

None

Remarks

This function activates an object from the stock. It clones the stock object and adds it to the list of active objects. If flag is TRUE, the object is also added to the bsp tree.

flyEngine::add_light_map

Prototype

```
int add_lightmap(int sx,int sy)
```

Parameters

Parameter	Type	Description
sx	int	x light map size (power of 2)
sy	int	y light map size (power of 2

Return value

Return the light map index into the light map array for the newly created light map.

Remarks

This function is used add a new light map to the light map array. Dynamic objects that can use light maps use this function to allocate its light map image.

flyEngine::apply_bsp

Prototype

```
void apply_bsp(bsp_node *n,vector& p,float rad,void *data,void
(*func)(void *data,bsp_object *e))
```

```
void    apply_bsp(bsp_node*n,vector*p,int    np,void*data,    void
(*func)(void*data,bsp_object*e));
```

Parameters

Parameter	Type	Description
n	bsp_node *	bsp root node
p	vector&	point
p	vector*	array of points defining a volume
np	int	number of points in p array
rad	float	radius
data	void *	general pointer data
func	void (*)(void *data,bsp_object *e)	call-back function

Return value

None

Remarks

This function is used to select objects inside a region. The call-back function will be called for every plug-in object (bsp_object derived) inside the region defined by the parameters. It is used by homing missiles, enemies and any object that needs to look around it. Even the fog maps use this function to select easily the faces to which it should apply the fog.

The region can be defined using a sphere of influence (p and rad) or a set of points (5 and define a frustum, 8 a box, etc . . .).

flyEngine::check_multiplayer

Prototype

```
void check_multiplayer()
```

Parameters

None

Return value

None

Remarks

This function is used to process multiplayer messages. When connected to a multi-player game, the function should be called every frame. It will get all the messages in the message queue and process them. System messages are processed and game messages are passed on to the plug-ins. This function is already called by the flyEngine step function if the multiplayer mode is on.

flyEngine::close_fly_file

Prototype

```
void close_fly_file()
```

Parameters

None

Return value
None

Remarks
This function closes the current loaded level, freeing all level data (models, textures, bsp, sounds, etc. . . . .).

flyEngine::close_multiplayer

Prototype
```
void close_multiplayer()
```

Parameters
None

Return value
None

Remarks
Closes multi-player mode, removing the player from the server to which it is connected. Join a game with the *join_multiplayer* function.

flyEngine::close_texture_cache

Prototype
```
void close_texture_cache()
```

Parameters
None

Return value
None

Remarks
This function frees the texture manager by freeing all texture maps, light maps and fog maps from the texture hardware. It deletes the *tc* global variable and sets it to NULL.

flyEngine::collision_bsp

Prototype
```
int collision_bsp(bsp_node *n,vector& p1,vector& p2,int
elemtype=0,float rad=0.0f)
```

Parameters

Parameter	Type	Description
n	bsp_node *	bsp root node
p1	vector&	first point
p2	vector&	second point
elemtype	int	object type modifier
rad	float	collision radius

Return value

Returns TRUE if a collision is found, FALSE if no collision is found.

Remarks

This function is used for collision detection between *p1* and *p2*. It finds the closest collision from *p1* to *p2* and returns the collision information in the following flyEngine members:

```
bsp_object *hitobj;     // object pointer
mesh *hitmesh;          // mesh pointer
int hitface;            // face index into mesh
vector hitip;           // intersected point in face
```

A faster version of this function is the *collision_test* function which returns the first collision from *p1* to *p2*.

flyEngine::collision_test

Prototype

```
int collision_test(bsp_node *n,vector& p1,vector& p2,int
elemtype=0,float rad=0.0f)
```

Parameters

Parameter	Type	Description
n	bsp_node *	bsp root node
p1	vector&	first point
p2	vector&	second point
elemtype	int	object type modifier
rad	float	collision radius

Return value

Returns TRUE if a collision is found, FALSE if no collision is found.

Remarks

This function is used for collision detection between *p1* and *p2*. It returns the first collision from *p1* to *p2* and is faster than the *collision_bsp* function.

flyEngine::draw_bsp

Prototype

```
void draw_bsp(int mode)
```

Parameters

Parameter	Type	Description
mode	int	drawing mode: 0 – standard 1 – cartoon

Return value

None

Remarks

This function recurses the bsp tree and select all bsp faces and dynamic object that are inside the current view frustum. Then, all faces from the bsp are drawn followed by all dynamic objects. Transparent faces and draw after the nontransparent ones and dynamic objects set to latedraw will be the last ones to render.

If cartoon mode is set, the bsp faces are drawn with the current cartoonpicbsp and then all edges from the bsp faces selected for drawing will be tested for outline by the current camera. If edge is found to be at a backface/frontface pair, the edge is draw as a black line.

flyEngine::draw_bsp_edges

Prototype
```
void draw_bsp_edges()
```

Parameters

None

Return value

None

Remarks

This function draws the edges (outlines) for the selected bsp faces. It is used by cartoon like bsp renders. The current *cartoonpicwidth* and *cartooncolor* flyEngine class variables are used and define the width of the lines and their colour.

flyEngine::draw_text

Prototype
```
void draw_text(int x,int y,char *text)
```

Parameters

Parameter	Type	Description
x	int	x screen coordinate for text
y	int	y screen coordinate for text
text	char *	text string

Return value

None

This function draws a string of text at the specified screen coordinates. The text is drawn as a set of texture mapped faces using the selected font texture in the flyEngine *fontspic* member variable. Before using this function, text mode must be started using the *start_text_mode* function.

flyEngine::draw_text_center

Prototype
```
void draw_text_center(int x,int y,char *text)
```
Parameters

Parameter	Type	Description
x	int	x screen coordinate for text
y	int	y screen coordinate for text
text	char *	text string

Return value
    None

Remarks
    This function draws a string of text centred at the specified screen coordinates. The text is drawn as a set of texture mapped faces using the selected font texture in the flyEngine *fontspic* member variable. Before using this function, text mode must be started using the *start_text_mode* function.

flyEngine::end_text_mode

Prototype
```
void end_text_mode()
```
Parameters
    None

Return value
    None

Remarks
    This function ends text mode and restores the camera to a perspective camera at the object selected from the flyEngine member variable *cam*. Start text mode using the *start_text_mode* function.

flyEngine::find_node

Prototype
```
bsp_node *find_node(bsp_node *n,vector& v,float mindist)
```
Parameters

Parameter	Type	Description
n	bsp_node *	bsp root node
v	vector&	point in world coordinates
mindist	float	minimum distance

Return value
    Returns the bsp leaf the point *v* is in.

Remarks

This function finds the leaf node for a given point. If the point distance to any plane is less than *mindist*, the leaf is rejected.

flyEngine::get_active_object

Prototype

```
bsp_object *get_active_object(char *name)
```

Parameters

Parameter	Type	Description
name	char *	object name

Return value

Returns a pointer to the given object or NULL if object not found.

Remarks

This function is used to get objects from the active objects linked list. It returns the object pointer for a given string-based name.

flyEngine::get_bezier_curve

Prototype

```
bezier_curve *get_bezier_curve(char *name)
```

Parameters

Parameter	Type	Description
name	char *	curve name

Return value

Returns a pointer to the given Bézier curve or NULL if curve not found.

Remarks

This function is used to get curves from the stock. It returns the curve pointer for a given string-based curve name. If curve is not in the curve linked list, it attempts to load the curve from disk.

flyEngine::get_bezier_patch

Prototype

```
bezier_patch *get_bezier_patch(char *name)
```

Parameters

Parameter	Type	Description
name	char *	patch name

Return value

Returns a pointer to the given patch or NULL if patch not found.

Remarks

This function is used to get patches from the stock. It returns the patch pointer for a given string-based patch name. If patch is not in the patch linked list, it attempts to load the patch from disk.

flyEngine::get_global_param_desc

Prototype

```
int get_global_param_desc(int i,param_desc *pd)
```

Parameters

Parameter	Type	Description
i	int	global parameter index
pd	param_desc *	pointer to param_desc to be filled

Return value

Returns the number of global parameters if called with *pd*=NULL

Remarks

This function is used to get the parameter description for any of the global flyEngine parameters.

flyEngine::get_model_object

Prototype

```
mesh *get_model_object(char *name)
```

Parameters

Parameter	Type	Description
name	char *	model name

Return value

Returns a pointer to the given model or NULL if model not found.

Remarks

This function is used to get models from the stock. It returns the model pointer for a given string-based name. Models can be .3ds or .fao files. If model is not in the model linked list, it attempts to load the model from disk.

flyEngine::get_next_active_object

Prototype

```
bsp_object *get_next_active_object(bsp_object *o,int type=0)
```

Parameters

Parameter	Type	Description
o	bsp_object *	object pointer
type	int	object type modifier

Return value

Returns the object next to the specified one or NULL if at end of list.

Remarks

This function is used to walk through the active object linked list. When called with o = NULL it will return the first object in the active objects linked list. When called with o <> NULL it will return the object following the object o in the active objects linked list. If the *type* parameter is <>0, only objects with that type id are returned.

Usually used like this:

```
bsp_object *obj=0;
while( obj=flyengine->get_next_active_object(obj) )
{
    // do somethig with object obj
}
```

flyEngine::get_next_stock_object

Prototype

```
bsp_object *get_next_stock_object(bsp_object *o,int type=0)
```

Parameters

Parameter	Type	Description
o	bsp_object *	object pointer
type	int	object type modifier

Return value

Returns the object next to the specified one or NULL if at end of list.

Remarks

This function is used to walk through the stock object linked list. When called with o = NULL it will return the first object in the stock objects linked list. When called with o <> NULL it will return the object following the object o in the stock objects linked list. If the *type* parameter is <>0, only objects with that type id are returned.

Usually used like this:

```
bsp_object *obj=0;
while( obj=flyengine->get_next_stock_object(obj) )
{
    // do something with object obj
}
```

flyEngine::get_obj_param

Prototype

```
int get_obj_param(char *objname,char *param,char *value)
```

Parameters

Parameter	Type	Description
objname	char *	object name
param	char *	parameter name
value	char *	string to receive the parameter value

Return value

Returns 0 if parameter was found and value is set, 1 if object not found and 2 if parameter not found.

Remarks

This function is used to get a string representation of an object's parameter.

flyEngine::get_picture

Prototype

```
int get_picture(char *file)
```

Parameters

Parameter	Type	Description
file	char *	picture name

Return value

Returns the picture index into picture array or −1 if picture could not be found.

Remarks

This function is used to get pictures from the stock. It returns the picture index for a given string-based picture name. If picture is not in the pictures array, it attempts to load the picture from disk.

flyEngine::get_random_point

Prototype

```
bsp_node *get_random_point(vector& v,float mindist)
```

Parameters

Parameter	Type	Description
v	vector&	point
mindist	float	minimum distance

Return value

Returns the bsp leaf the random point *v* is in.

Remarks

This function is used to compute a random position inside the level that is at least *mindist* away from any wall. The random position will be stored in the *v* parameter.

flyEngine::get_sound_object

Prototype
```
sound *get_sound_object(char *name)
```
Parameters

Parameter	Type	Description
name	char *	sound name

Return value
Returns a pointer to the given sound or NULL if sound not found.

Remarks
This function is used to get sounds from the stock. It returns the sound pointer for a given string-based sound name. If sound is not in the sounds linked list, it attempts to load the sound from disk.

flyEngine::get_stock_object

Prototype
```
bsp_object *get_stock_object(char *name)
```
Parameters

Parameter	Type	Description
name	char *	object name

Return value
Returns a pointer to the given object or NULL if object not found.

Remarks
This function is used to get objects from the stock objects linked list. It returns the object pointer for a given string-based name.

flyEngine::init_texture_cache

Prototype
```
void init_texture_cache()
```
Parameters
None
Return value
None
Remarks
This function initialises the texture manager. It loads all texture maps, light maps and fog maps into the texture manager and texture hardware. After calling this function, you can access the texture manager by the textcache derived class stored in the global variable *tc* allocated by this function.

flyEngine::join_multiplayer

Prototype

```
int join_multiplayer(HWND hWnd,HINSTANCE hInst)
```

Parameters

Parameter	Type	Description
hWnd	HWND	front-end window handle
hInst	HINSTANCE	front-end instance handle

Return value

Returns TRUE if a game is joined, FALSE on any error or join cancel.

Remarks

This function is used to join a multi-player game. A dialogue is shown with the player name and it lets the user select the server and the game to join. If a game is selected for joining, it loads the level the game is running on and returns TRUE. If the level is not in the user computer or the level name is not received, it returns FALSE and the game is not joined. When leaving the game, the multi-player mode must be closed with the *close_multiplayer* function.

flyEngine::open_fly_file

Prototype

```
int open_fly_file(char *file)
```

Parameters

Parameter	Type	Description
file	char *	filename for the .fly file to load

Return value

Returns TRUE if loading is OK, FALSE on any error.

Remarks

This function loads a level from a .fly file. It loads all resources associated with the .fly file (plug-ins, objects, object parameters, textures, models, bsp, sounds, etc...).

flyEngine::save_fly_file

Prototype

```
int save_fly_file(char *file)
```

Parameters

Parameter	Type	Description
file	char *	filename for the .fly file to save

Return value

Returns TRUE if saving is OK, FALSE on any error.

Remarks

This function saves the .fly file that represents the current loaded level. The .fly file is a .ini-like text file and includes information on all plug-ins used in the level together with all objects defined in each plug-in and its parameters.

flyEngine::send_bsp_message

Prototype

```
void send_bsp_message(bsp_node *n,vector& p,float rad,int msg,int
param,void *data)
```

Parameters

Parameter	Type	Description
n	bsp_node *	root bsp node
p	vector&	point
rad	float	radius
msg	int	message type
param	int	parameter
data	void *	general pointer parameter

Return value

None

Remarks

This function sends a message to all active plug-in objects inside the sphere of influence defined by the *p* and *rad* parameters. All plug-in objects (derived from bsp_object) receive the message through their *message* virtual function.

flyEngine::set_camera

Prototype

```
void set_camera(bsp_object *d)
```

Parameters

Parameter	Type	Description
d	bsp_object *	camera is set to view from the object

Return value

None

Remarks

This function is used to place the camera at a specified object. It computes the view frustum and sets the hardware projection matrix. All render calls after this function will use a camera placed at the object looking down its negative *z* axis.

flyEngine::set_global_param

Prototype

```
int set_global_param(char *name, char *value)
```

Parameters

Parameter	Type	Description
name	char *	global parameter name
value	char *	string with parameter value

Return value

Returns FALSE if parameter is not in the global parameter list, TRUE if parameter was found and value is set.

Remarks

This function is used to set a flyEngine global parameter from a string.

flyEngine::set_obj_param

Prototype

```
int set_obj_param(char *objname,char *param,char *value)
```

Parameters

Parameter	Type	Description
objname	char *	object name
param	char *	parameter name
value	char *	string to receive the parameter value

Return value

Returns 0 if parameter was found and value is set, 1 if object not found and 2 if parameter not found.

Remarks

This function is used to set an object's parameter from a string representation of its value.

flyEngine::set_status_msg

Prototype

```
virtual void set_status_msg(char *fmt, ...)
```

Parameters

Parameter	Type	Description
fmt	char *	printf-like parameter list

Return value

None

Remarks

This function is used to print out text to the status message area. The text is added to the console and also shown for a small amount of time in the screen status area. General game information is drawn here, for example connected players, kills, deaths, etc. . . . Use it just like a printf function with a variable number of parameters.

flyEngine::start_text_mode

Prototype
```
void start_text_mode()
```
Parameters
None
Return value
None
Remarks

This function starts text mode. It sets an orthographic camera and future rendering calls can use 2D vertices with screen coordinates. Use draw_text and draw_text center for drawing text with the current selected font in the *fontspic* flyEngine member variable. All status and 2D game interface must be drawn after starting text mode. Text mode is ended by calling the end_text_mode function.

flyEngine::step

Prototype
```
void step(int dt)
```
Parameters

Parameter	Type	Description
dt	int	elapsed time in ms

Return value
None
Remarks

This function is used to update the game after an elapsed time. The main loop from the front-end must call this function every frame (usually the render *DrawView* function calls it). The following order of operations is performed inside this function.

(1) Get current state for mouse and keyboard.
(2) For all light maps changed in the last frame, restore them to the original values.
(3) For all fog maps changed in the last frame, clear them.
(4) For each active object in the active objects linked list:
   if object *life*<0
      delete the object
   else
      increment *cur_step* variable
      call object step function
      if object step function returns true (moved), reposition it in the bsp
(5) Increment *cur_frame* variable.
(6) For all light maps changed in this frame, update them to the texture manager.

(7) For all fog maps changed in this frame, update them to the texture manager.

(8) Send the FLYM_UPDATESCENE to all loaded plug-ins (some plug-ins will draw the scene here)

(9) If multi-player is on, call *check_multiplayer* for processing multi-player messages.

(10) If multi-player is on and running on a client, check last player update message time and send a FLYM_MPUPDATE message to the plug-ins if the time from the last update is greater than the *mpdelay* variable.

(11) Calls the console step function.

class light_map

Definition

```
class light_map
{
public:
    vector v0, v1, v2;
    vector d0, d1, d2, normal;
    float det;
    float uv[3][2];
    int lastupdate;
    int pic;
    int offsetx,offsety;
    int sizex,sizey;
    int facenum;
    unsigned char *bmp;
    int bytespixel,bytesx,bytesxy;

    light_map(int f,int p,int x,int y,int sx,int sy,int bp=3)
    {
        facenum=f;
        pic=p;
        offsetx=x;
        offsety=y;
        sizex=sx;
        sizey=sy;
        bytespixel=bp;
        lastupdate=0;
        bytesx=sx*bp;
        if (bytesx&3)
            bytesx+=4-(bytesx&3);
        bytesxy=bytesx*sy;
        bmp=new unsigned char[bytesxy];
    };
    void map_point(float u, float v, vector &point);
    void set_base(face *f,light_map_pic *lmp,vector&
pos=vector(0,0,0));
    void illum(vector& pos,vector& color,float rad,int shadows);
    void load(light_map_pic *lmp);
    void save(light_map_pic *lmp);

    virtual ~light_map()
    {
        if (bmp)
                delete bmp;
    };
};
```

Data members

Member	Type	Description
d0	vector	light_map origin (0,0) in world space
d1	vector	light_map u vector (1,0) in world space
d2	vector	light_map v vector (0,1) in world space
lastupdate	int	last frame this light_map has changed
pic	int	light_map_pic index
offsetx	int	x offset into light_map_pic
offsety	int	y offset into light_map_pic
sizex	int	x size of light_map (power of 2 or not)
sizey	int	y size of light_map (power of 2 or not)
facenum	int	face index for one face using this light_map
bmp	unsigned char *	light_map bitmap
bytespixel	int	the light map bytes per pixel: 3 – RGB 4 – RGBA
bytesx	int	number of bytes per line (sizex*bytespixel aligned to 4 bytes)
bytesxy	int	total bytes of the light_map bmp (bytesx*sizey)

Remarks

This class implements a light map. Several faces (co-planar) can share the same light_map and many light_maps can share the same light_map_pic. Each light_map has an offset and size inside its light_map_pic.

Methods

light_map constructor

Prototype

```
light_map(int f,int p,int x,int y,int sx,int sy,int bp=3)
```

Parameters

Parameter	Type	Description
f	int	face using this light map (can be −1 for non co-planar faces)
p	int	light_map_pic for the light_map
x	int	x offset into light_map_pic
y	int	y offset into light_map_pic
sx	int	x size of light_map (power of 2 or not)
sy	int	y size of light_map (power of 2 or not)
bp	int	light_map bytes per pixel: 3 – RGB (light map) 4 – RGBA (fog map)

Remarks

Creates the light map and allocates the *bmp* array.

light_map::illum

Prototype

```
void illum(vector& pos,vector& color,float rad,int shadows)
```

Parameters

Parameter	Type	Description
pos	vector&	light position
color	vector&	light colour
rad	float	light radius
shadows	int	shadows flag: 0 – no shadows 1 – single object shadows 2 – global shadows

Return value

None

Remarks

This function dynamically illuminates the light_map pixels based on the above parameters.

light_map::load

Prototype

```
void load(light_map_pic *lmp)
```

Parameters

Parameter	Type	Description
lmp	light_map_pic *	light_map_pic with original light_map values

Return value

None

Remarks

This function restores the light_map pixels from the light_map_pic. Used when restoring a dynamically modified light_map.

light_map::map_point

Prototype

```
void map_point(float u, float v, vector &point)
```

Parameters

Parameter	Type	Description
u	float	point coordinate in the u axis
v	float	point coordinate in the v axis
point	vector &	point mapped in world space

Return value

None

Remarks

This function maps a point from the light_map (u,v) into world coordinate space.

class light_map_pic

Definition

```
class light_map_pic
{
  public:
  unsigned char *bmp;
  int sizex,sizey;
  int bytesx,bytesxy;
  int bytespixel;

  light_map_pic(int sx,int sy,int bp=3)
  {
    bytespixel=bp;
    sizex=sx;
    sizey=sy;
    bytesx=sx*bytespixel;
    if (bytesx&3) bytesx+=4-(bytesx&3);
    bytesxy=bytesx*sizey;
    bmp=new unsigned char [bytesxy];
  };
  virtual ~light_map_pic()
  {
    if(bmp) delete bmp;
  };
};
```

Data members

Member	Type	Description
bmp	char *	light_map_pic pixels
sizex	int	size in x (power of 2)
sizey	int	size in y (power of 2)
bytesx	int	number of bytes per line (sizex*bytespixel)
bytesxy	int	total bytes of the light_map_pic bmp (bytesx*sizey)
bytespixel	int	the light map bytes per pixel: 3 – RGB 4 – RGBA

Remarks

This class implements the light_map picture used when drawing. This picture can have several light_map pictures in it and many light_map classes will use a single light_map_pic.

Methods

light_map_pic constructor

Prototype

```
light_map_pic(int sx,int sy,int bp=3)
```

Parameters

Parameter	Type	Description
sx	int	size in x (power of 2)
sy	int	size in y (power of 2)
bp	int	the light map bytes per pixel: 3 – RGB 4 – RGBA

Remarks

Creates the light_map_pic and allocates the bitmap pixels.

class light_vertex

Definition

```
class light_vertex
{
    int nlights;
    vector pos[MAX_HWLIGHTS];
    vector color[MAX_HWLIGHTS];
    float radius[MAX_HWLIGHTS];
public:
    light_vertex() { nlights=0; };
    void add_light(vector& p,vector& c,float r);
    void init_draw(bsp_object *obj);
    void end_draw();
};
```

Data members

Member	Type	Description
nlights	int	number of active lights
pos	vector[]	position of active lights
color	vector[]	colour of active lights
radius	float[]	radius of active lights

Remarks

This class holds information on dynamic hardware lights. When a dynamic object receives a FLYOBJM_ILLUM message it adds the light parameters to this class with the *add_light* method. When rendering it calls the *init_draw* method before drawing the mesh to get the hardware lights in place. After finishing the render it calls *end_draw* to reset the hardware lights.

Methods

light_vertex::add_light

Prototype

```
void add_light(vector& p,vector& c,float r)
```

Parameters

Parameter	Type	Description
p	vector&	light position
c	vector&	light colour
r	float	light radius

Return value

None

Remarks

This function adds a new light to the light_vertex array of lights. If the maximum number of hardware lights is exceeded, the light is not added.

light_vertex::end_draw

Prototype
```
void end_draw()
```
Parameters

None

Return value

None

Remarks

Finishes hardware light illumination by disabling all lights initialised with the *init_lights* function.

light_vertex::init_draw

Prototype
```
void init_draw(bsp_object *obj)
```
Parameters

Parameter	Type	Description
obj	bsp_object *	object that is to use the hardware lights

Return value

None

Remarks

This function initialises and sets up the hardware lights stored in its light array. Each light is checked for shadows from the *obj* centre position to the light position. After calling this function all geometry drawn will be lit with stored lights. To end lighting, *end_draw* must be called.

class local_system

Definition

```
class local_system
{
   public:
   vector X,Y,Z;
   mat4x4 mat,mat_t;

   void update_mat();
   void rotate(vector& rot);
   void rotate(float ang,vector& v);
   void rotate(vector &v, vector &u, float maxang=360);
   void align_z(vector& z);
};
```

Data members

Member	Type	Description
X	vector	the X base axis
Y	vector	the Y base axis
Z	vector	the Z base axis
mat	mat4×4	matrix for rotating from local to global
mat_t	mat4×4	matrix for rotating from global to local

Remarks

This class implements a local system. A local system is defined by three perpendicular vectors (the base axis).

Methods

local_system::align_z

Prototype

```
void align_z(vector& z)
```

Parameters

Parameter	Type	Description
z	vector&	the vector to align the Z axis with

Return value
None

Remarks
This function aligns the *z* axis from the local_system with the supplied vector.

local_system::rotate

Prototype
```
void rotate(vector& rot)
void rotate(float ang,vector& v);
void rotate(vector &from, vector &to, float maxang=360);
```

Parameters

Parameter	Type	Description
rot	vector&	rotation vector in degrees
ang	float	angle in degrees to rotate around vector *v*
v	vector&	vector to define rotation of angle degrees
from	vector&	vector to rotate from
to	vector&	vector to rotate to
maxang	float	maximum angle of rotation around cross product of from and to

Return value
None

Remarks
This function rotates the local_system axis and redefines the local_system matrices.

The first one, rotates *rox.x* around the *x* axis, *rot.y* around the *y* axis and *rot.z* around the *z* axis.

The second one rotates *ang* degrees around a vector *v*.

The third one rotates from vector *from* to vector to, a maximum of *maxang* degrees. It rotates in the plane that contains the vectors *from* and *to*.

local_system::update_mat

Prototype
```
void update_mat()
```

Parameters
None

Return value
None

Remarks
This function updates the *mat* and *mat_t* matrices to represent the rotation defined by the *X*, *Y* and *Z* local system axis. If the axes are changed, this function needs to be called in order to have the *mat* and *mat_t* variables updated.

class mat4x4

Definition

```
class mat4x4
{
   public:
   float m[4][4];

   inline void null(void)
   { memset(&m,0,sizeof(m)); }

   inline void load_identity(void)
   {
      memset(m,0,sizeof(m));
      m[0][0]=m[1][1]=m[2][2]=m[3][3]=1.0;
   }
   void set_rotation( float ang, vector& dir );
   mat4x4 operator*(mat4x4& m1)
};
```

Data members

Member	Type	Description
m	float[][]	matrix elements

Remarks

This class implements a 4×4 matrix. The matrix can represent any linear transformation and is used for rotation, translation, scaling, etc. . . .

Example

```
mat4x4 m1,m2,m3;
m2.load_identity();
m3.load_identity();
m2.set_rotation(45,vector(0,0,1));
m3.set_rotation(30,vector(0,1,0));
m1=m2*m3;
```

Methods

mat4x4::load_identity

Prototype
```
inline void load_identity(void)
```

Parameters
   None

Return value
   None

Remarks

Sets the matrix to the identity matrix. The diagonal elements are set to 1.0 and all others set to 0.0.

mat4x4::null

Prototype
```
inline void null(void)
```
Parameters

None

Return value

None

Remarks

Sets all matrix elements to zero.

mat4x4 operators

Prototype
```
mat4x4 operator*(mat4x4& m1)
```
Parameters

Parameter	Type	Description
m1	mat4×4&	matrix to multiply current matrix

Remarks

This operator multiplies two matrices.

mat4x4::set_rotation

Prototype
```
void set_rotation( float ang, vector& dir )
```
Parameters

Parameter	Type	Description
ang	float	rotation angle in degrees
dir	vector&	rotation vector

Return value

None

Remarks

This function multiplies the current matrix by a rotation matrix of *ang* degrees around vector *dir*.

class mesh : public base_object

Definition

```
class mesh : public base_object
{
  public:
      int nv, nf;
      vector *vert;
      vector *vertnorm;
      face **faces;
      boundbox bbox;
      vector pivotpos;
      face *localfaces;
      vector color;
      float scrollu,scrollv;
      int lastdraw;

      mesh()
      {
        vert=0; vertnorm=0; faces=0; nv=0; nf=0; localfaces=0;
        color.vec(1.0f,1.0f,1.0f,1.0f);
        scrollu=scrollv=0.0f;
      lastdraw=0;
      };
      virtual ~mesh()
      { reset(); };

      void reset();
      virtual void draw();
      int load_3ds(char *name);
      void compute_normals(int flag=15);
      int  ray_intersect(vector&  ro,vector&  rd,vector&  ip,float&
dist,float rad=0.0f);
      int ray_intersect_test(vector& ro,vector& rd,float rad=0.0f);
      void illum_faces(vector& ip,float d_max,vector& c,int shadows);
      void implode(float mindist=0.1f);
    mesh *clone();
  };
```

Data members

Member	Type	Description
nv	int	number of vertices in the mesh
nf	int	number of faces in the mesh
vert	vector *	the vertices array
vertnorm	vector *	the vertex normals array
localfaces	face *	the faces array

faces	face **	the faces pointers array
bbox	boundbox	the mesh bounding box (aabb)
pivotpos	vector	the mesh pivot position
color	vector	the mesh colour multiplier
scrollu	float	texture coordinates scroll factor in u direction
scrollv	float	texture coordinates scroll factor in v direction
lastdraw	int	last frame the mesh was drawn

Remarks

This class implements a 3D mesh object. The mesh can have the faces defined in it (*localfaces*) or it can point to faces outside the mesh (from the bsp) by having the localfaces pointer set to NULL.

Methods

mesh::clone

Prototype
```
mesh *clone()
```

Parameters
None

Return value
Returns the pointer to the cloned mesh.

Remarks
This function clones a mesh (duplicates it) and all its attributes (vertices, faces, etc...).

mesh::compute_normals

Prototype
```
void compute_normals(int flag=15)
```

Parameters

Parameter	Type	Description
flag	int	bit flag defining what should be computed: bit 1: implode vertices (weld) bit 2: face and edge normals bit 3: vert normals bit 4: bounding box

Return value
None

Remarks

This function computes several mesh variables, for example face normals, vertex normals, edge normals, face connectivity and bounding box.

Use the *flag* parameter to do a partial and faster computation.

mesh::draw

Prototype
```
virtual void draw()
```

Parameters

None

Return value

None

Remarks

This function draws the mesh faces. The current colour and texture coordinates scroll factor are used to modify the mesh faces colours and texture coordinates.

mesh::illum_faces

Prototype
```
void illum_faces(vector& p,float d_max,vector& c,int shadows)
```

Parameters

Parameter	Type	Description
p	vector&	light point
d_max	float	light radius
c	vector&	light colour
shadows	int	shadow flags:
		0 – no shadows
		1 – shadow from specific object
		(flyengine::shadow_obj)
		2 – global shadows

Return value

None

Remarks

This function illuminates the mesh faces light maps. It is used only on meshes with light maps like the static bsp leaf mesh.

mesh::implode

Prototype

```
void implode(float mindist=0.1f)
```

Parameters

Parameter	Type	Description
mindist	float	distance threshold for welding vertices

Return value

None

Remarks

This function combines all vertices from the mesh that are closer than *mindist* into a single vertex.

mesh::load_3ds

Prototype

```
int load_3ds(char *name)
```

Parameters

Parameter	Type	Description
name	char *	filename for the .3ds file to load

Return value

Returns TRUE if loading is OK, FALSE if could not load the file.

Remarks

This function loads a .3ds file into the mesh. Vertices, faces, textures and texture coordinates are loaded and it also computes all face normals, edge normals and vertex normals.

mesh::ray_intersect

Prototype

```
int ray_intersect(vector& ro,vector& rd,vector& ip,float& dist,float
rad=0.0f)
```

Parameters

Parameter	Type	Description
ro	vector&	ray origin
rd	vector&	ray direction
ip	vector&	intersection point
dist	float&	intersection distance
rad	float&	collision radius

Return value

Returns TRUE if an intersection is found, FALSE for no intersection.

Remarks

This function computes the ray intersection with the mesh.

If an intersection is found, *ip* will be set to the intersection point, *dist* will be set to the distance from the ray origin (*ro*) to the intersection point (*ip*).

If *rd* is normalised, the *dist* value will be in scene units, if not, it will be the distance divided by the ray direction (*rd*) length.

The *rad* parameter sets the collision radius. If >0, the collision will be tested for a sphere with radius *rad*.

All faces from the mesh are tested for intersection and the closest intersection is returned. The *ray_intersect_test* function is a faster version that returns the first intersection (good for when you just need to know if there is an intersection and do not care where).

mesh::ray_intersect_test

Prototype

```
int ray_intersect_test(vector& ro,vector& rd,float rad=0.0f)
```

Parameters

Parameter	Type	Description
ro	vector&	ray origin
rd	vector&	ray direction
rad	float	collision radius

Return value

Returns TRUE if an intersection is found, FALSE for no intersection.

Remarks

This function tests for a collision with the mesh. It is faster than the *ray_inter-sect* function as it does not find the closest intersection, but returns at the first intersection encountered.

mesh::reset

Prototype

```
void reset()
```

Parameters

None

Return value

None

Remarks

This function resets the mesh, freeing all faces, vertices and vertex normals.

class mp_games

Definition

```
class mp_games
{
  public:
  int num;
  char name[FLYMP_MAXGAMES][128];
  int num_players[FLYMP_MAXGAMES];
  GUID guid[FLYMP_MAXGAMES];

  mp_games()
  { num=0; };
};
```

Data members

Member	Type	Description
num	int	number of games
name	char[][]	game names array
num_players	int[]	number of players array
guid	GUID[]	games GUID array

Remarks

This class is used to enumerate games on a specific server.

Use the *enum_games* function to get a pointer to this class. The class will be filled with information on all games available to join. Pass the *guid* field of the selected game to the *join_game* function to enter the game.

class mp_msg

Definition

```
class mp_msg
{
   public:
   DWORD type;
   DWORD from;
   char data[500];
};
```

Data members

Member	Type	Description
type	DWORD	message type
from	DWORD	directplay player id of the message sender
data	char[]	the message data (up to 500 bytes)

Remarks

This class implements a multi-player message. All messages must begin with *type* and *from* fields. The data field can be of any size up to 500 bytes.

class param_desc

Definition

```
class param_desc
{
public:
        char name[64];
        int type;
        void *data;

        char *get_string();
        void set_string(char *str);
};
```

Data members

Member	Type	Description
name	char []	the parameter name
type	int	the parameter type
data	void *	pointer to the parameter data

Remarks

This class holds information on Fly3D plug-in object parameters. Each class defined in a Fly3D plug-in (derived from bsp_object) can have any number of parameters. Each parameter must have an associated param_desc class describing its data.

The types of parameters available are:

>255 – parameter is a pointer to a class in the stock objects list that has this type id

<255 – parameter is a pointer to a class in the active objects list that has this type id

Type	Description	Data type	Data size (sizeof)
'a'	angle	float	4
'i'	integer	int	4
'f '	floating point	float	4
'v'	float vector (x,y,z)	vector	12
'c'	float color (r,g,b)	vector	12
'b'	Bézier curve	bezier_curve *	4
'h'	Bézier patch	bezier_patch *	4
'3'	3ds mesh model	mesh *	4
'm'	fao animate mesh	anim_mesh *	4
'w'	wav sound object	sound *	4
'p'	picture file	int	4
'o'	stock object	bsp_object *	4
'd'	active object	bsp_object *	4

Methods

param_desc::get_string

Prototype
```
char *get_string()
```

Parameters
None

Return value
Returns the parameter formatted as a string.

Remarks
This function is used to format a parameter as a string. It will get numbers, vectors, object names or file names depending on the parameter type.

param_desc::set_string

Prototype
```
void set_string(char *str)
```

Parameters

Parameter	Type	Description
str	char *	formatted string to set parameter from

Return value
None

Remarks
This function sets the parameter from a formatted string. The string can be a number, vector, colour, object name or file name depending on the parameter type.

class particle

Definition

```
class particle
{
  public
  vector pos, vel, force;
  float mass, bump, friction, radius;
  int life;
  int col_flag;

  int compute_collision(vector& p,vector& v);
  int step(int dt);
};
```

Data members

Member	Type	Description
pos	vector	position
vel	vector	velocity
force	vector	force
mass	float	mass
bump	float	bump factor (0 to 1): 0 – no bump 1 – maximum bump
friction	float	friction factor (0 to 1): 0 – maximum friction 1 – no friction
radius	float	radius
life	int	life in ms
col_flag	int	bit flag for collision: bit 1: collision on/off bit 2: collide and die

Remarks

This class implements a particle.

Methods

particle::compute_collision

Prototype

```
int compute_collision(vector& p,vector& v)
```

Parameters

Parameter	Type	Description
p	vector&	target position
v	vector&	target velocity

Return value

Returns TRUE if a collision was found, FALSE for no collision.

Remarks

This function is used to compute a collision for a moving particle. The *p* and *v* parameters are the new computed position and velocity parameters. If a collision is found between *p* and the current position, then both *p* and *v* will be modified accordingly.

particle::step

Prototype

```
int step(int dt)
```

Parameters

Parameter	Type	Description
dt	int	elapsed time in ms

Return value

Returns TRUE if particle moved, FALSE if particle did not move.

Remarks

This function updates the particle for a specified elapsed time. The particle will be moved according to its current velocity and the velocity will be updated using the current force and mass. If the collision flag is turned on, collision will be tested and the position and velocity will be changed based on collision point, normal, bump, and friction factors.

class picture

Definition

```
class picture
{
    public:
    char name[256];
    int sx,sy,bytespixel,size;
    unsigned char **buf;

    picture();

    int LoadTGA(char *file);
    int SaveTGA(char *file);
    int LoadPIC(char *file);
    int LoadJPG(char *file);
    int CreatePicture32(int xd,int yd);
    int CreatePicture24(int xd,int yd);
    void FreePicture(void);
    void ErasePicture(char c);

    virtual ~picture();
};
```

Data members

Member	Type	Description
name	char []	picture filename
sx	int	x size in pixels
sy	int	y size in pixels
bytespixel	int	number of bytes per pixel (24 or 32)
size	int	size in bytes for the image (sx*sy*bytespixel)
buf	unsigned char **	image pixels

Remarks

This class implements a picture with 24 or 32 bits/pixel. The picture pixels are allocated in a single array of bytes (*buf[0]*) and the other variables are just short-cuts to the picture lines (*buf[1]* to *buf[sy – 1]*).

Example

```
picture p;
p.LoadJPG("mypic.jpg");
p.SaveTGA("mypic.tga");
```

Methods

picture::CreatePicture32

Prototype

```
int CreatePicture32(int xd,int yd)
```

Parameters

Parameter	Type	Description
xd	int	x size in pixels
yd	int	y size in pixels

Return value

Returns TRUE if creation is OK, FALSE on any error.

Remarks

This function allocates the memory required for a picture with the specified dimensions. The buffer allocated is xc*yd*4 bytes.

picture::CreatePicture24

Prototype

```
int CreatePicture24(int xd,int yd)
```

Parameters

Parameter	Type	Description
xd	int	x size in pixels
yd	int	y size in pixels

Return value

Returns TRUE if creation is OK, FALSE on any error.

Remarks

This function allocates the memory required for a picture with the specified dimensions. The buffer allocated is xc*yd*3 bytes.

picture::FreePicture

Prototype

```
void FreePicture(void)
```

Parameters

None

Return value

None

Remarks

This function frees all data allocated by the picture.

picture::LoadJPG

Prototype

```
int LoadJPG(char *file)
```

Parameters

Parameter	Type	Description
file	char *	filename for the .jpg image to load

Return value

Returns TRUE if loading is OK, FALSE on any error.

Remarks

This function loads a .jpg image. The image can be a standalone file or it can be included in a .fpk package file.

picture::LoadPic

Prototype

```
int LoadPIC(char *file)
```

Parameters

Parameter	Type	Description
file	char *	filename for the image to load

Return value

Returns TRUE if loading is OK, FALSE on any error.

Remarks

This function is used to load an image. The extension is looked up and depending on the type of image (TGA or JPG) the appropriate loading function is called.

picture::LoadTGA

Prototype

```
int LoadTGA(char *file)
```

Parameters

Parameter	Type	Description
file	char *	filename for the .tga image to load

Return value

Returns TRUE if loading is OK, FALSE on any error.

Remarks

This function loads a .tga image. The image can be a standalone file or it can be included in a .fpk package file. Only 24 or 32 bits/pixel images are supported and they can be uncompressed or RLE compressed.

picture::SaveTGA

Prototype

```
int SaveTGA(char *file)
```

Parameters

Parameter	Type	Description
file	char *	filename for .tga file to save

Return value

Returns TRUE if saving is OK, FALSE on any error.

Remarks

This function saves a picture into an uncompressed .tga file. 24 or 32 bits/pixels images are supported.

class plane

Definition

```
class plane
{
    public:
    vector normal;
    float d0;

    inline float distance(vector &v)
    { return vec_dot(normal,v)+d0; }
};
```

Data members

Member	Type	Description
normal	vector	normalised plane normal
d0	float	smallest distance from plane to origin.

Remarks

This class implements a plane in 3D space.
Classes like the *bsp_node* and *face* derive from a plane.

Methods

plane::distance

Prototype

```
inline float distance(vector &v)
{ return vec_dot(normal,v)+d0; };
```

Parameters

Parameter	Type	Description
v	vector&	point from where distance is to be calculated

Return value

Returns the smallest distance from the specified point to the plane.

Remarks

This method calculates the perpendicular distance from the specified point to the plane.

If distance is zero, the point is in the plane surface.

A positive distance means the point is at the front of the plane (same side as the plane normal).

A negative distance means the point is at the back of the plane.

class player_data

Definition

```
class player_data
{
   public:
   DWORD type,dpid;
   char name[32];
   void *data;

   player_data()
   { memset(this,0,sizeof(player_data));};
};
```

Data members

Member	Type	Description
type	DWORD	player type (client or server)
dpid	DWORD	direct play player id
name	char[]	player name
data	void *	player generic data

Remarks

This class holds information on players in a multi-player game. Usually the *data* part of the class points to the player *bsp_object*.

class render

Definition

```
class render
{
   public:
   int type;

   virtual ~render()
   { ; };

   virtual int CreateView(HWND wnd)=0;
   virtual void DeleteView()=0;
   virtual void ResizeView(int sx,int sy)=0;
   virtual void InitView()=0;
   virtual void DrawView()=0;
   virtual void SetFullScreen()=0;
};
```

Data members

Member	Type	Description
type	int	render type: 0 – None 1 – OpenGL

Remarks

This is the base class for the render. The OpenGL implementation of the render is made by subclassing this class and implementing its virtual function in the selected graphics API.

A global variable named *render* is the main interface with this class and must be initialised/freed with the *init_render* and *close_render* global functions.

Methods

render::CreateView

Prototype

```
virtual int CreateView(HWND wnd)=0
```

Parameters

Parameter	Type	Description
wnd	HWND	view window handle

Return value

Returns TRUE if view is created, FALSE for any error.

Remarks

This virtual function should create the render view and attach it to the supplied window.

render::DeleteView

Prototype
```
virtual void DeleteView()=0
```
Parameters
None
Return value
None
Remarks
This virtual function should delete the render view and free any associated resources.

render::DrawView

Prototype
```
virtual void DrawView()=0
```
Parameters
None
Return value
None
Remarks
This virtual function is called to render the scene. Subclasses should do the following order of operations:
(1) Compute the elapsed time from last frame.
(2) Call *InitView* to initialise global render setting for the frame.
(3) Clear the Z-buffer, colour buffer if *flyengine->clearbk* is TRUE and stencil buffer if *flyengine->stencil* is TRUE.
(4) Call *flyengine->step* passing elapsed time (update all scene and plug-in objects).
(5) Swap buffers to display rendered image.

render::InitView

Prototype
```
virtual void InitView()=0
```
Parameters
None
Return value
None
Remarks
This virtual function is used to initialise the global default state for the render. It is called before starting each frame and is where all render general settings must occur.

render::ResizeView

Prototype
```
virtual void ResizeView(int sx,int sy)=0
```
Parameters

Parameter	Type	Description
sx	int	new size in x
sy	int	new size in y

Return value
   None

Remarks
This virtual function is used when the render view changes its size. It should resize the render view to the new dimensions defined by the *sx* and *sy* parameters.

render::SetFullScreen

Prototype
```
virtual void SetFullScreen()=0
```
Parameters
   None

Return value
   None

Remarks
This virtual function handles window/fullscreen changes. When called it must check the global variable fullscreen and:
   If it is 0, switch to window mode
   If it is 1, switch to fullscreen mode using the selected video mode defined in the *selvideomode* global variable

class renderGL : public render

Definition

```
class renderGL : public render
{
  public:
  HGLRC m_hRC;
  HDC hdc;
  HWND hWnd;

  renderGL()
  { type=FLY_RENDER_OPENGL; hdc=0; hWnd=0; m_hRC=0; active=1; };
  virtual ~renderGL()
  { DeleteView(); };

  int CreateView(HWND wnd);
  void DeleteView();
  void ResizeView(int sx,int sy);
  void InitView();
  void DrawView();
  void SetFullScreen();
};
```

Data members

Member	Type	Description
m_hRC	HGLRC	OpenGL handle
hdc	HDC	device context handle
hWnd	HWND	window handle

Remarks

This is the OpenGL implementation of the base render class. All OpenGL initialising and render view changes are implemented in its virtual functions.

A global variable named *render* is the main interface with this class and must be initialised/freed with the *init_render* and *close_render* global functions.

Methods

renderGL::CreateView

Prototype

```
int CreateView(HWND wnd)
```

Parameters

Parameter	Type	Description
wnd	HWND	view window handle

Return value

Returns TRUE if view is created, FALSE for any error.

Remarks

This is the OpenGL implementation for the *render* base class virtual function. This function creates the render view and attaches it to the supplied window.

renderGL::DeleteView

Prototype
```
void DeleteView()
```
Parameters

None

Return value

None

Remarks

This is the OpenGL implementation for the *render* base class virtual function. This function deletes the render view and frees any associated resources.

renderGL::DrawView

Prototype
```
void DrawView()
```
Parameters

None

Return value

None

Remarks

This is the OpenGL implementation for the *render* base class virtual function. It is called to render the scene and does the following order of operations:

(1) Computes the elapsed time from last frame.
(2) Calls *InitView* to initialise global render setting for the frame.
(3) Clears the zbuffer, colour buffer if *flyengine->clearbk* is TRUE and stencil buffer if *flyengine->stencil* is TRUE
(4) Calls *flyengine->step* passing elapsed time (update all scene and plug-in objects).
(5) Swaps buffers to display rendered image.

renderGL::InitView

Prototype
```
void InitView()
```
Parameters

None

Return value
None

Remarks
This is the OpenGL implementation for the *render* base class virtual function.
This virtual function is used to initialise the global default state for the render. It is called before starting each frame and is where all render general settings must occur.

renderGL::ResizeView

Prototype
```
void ResizeView(int sx,int sy)
```
Parameters

Parameter	Type	Description
sx	int	new size in x
sy	int	new size in y

Return value
None

Remarks
This is the OpenGL implementation for the *render* base class virtual function.
This function is used when the render view changes its size. It resizes the render view to the new dimensions defined by the *sx* and *sy* parameters.

renderGL::SetFullScreen

Prototype
```
void SetFullScreen()
```
Parameters
None

Return value
None

Remarks
This is the OpenGL implementation for the *render* base class virtual function.
It handles window/fullscreen changes. It checks the global variable fullscreen and:
If it is 0, it switches to window mode.
If it is 1, it switches to fullscreen mode using the selected video mode defined in the *selvideomode* global variable.

class sound : public base_object

Definition

```
class sound : public base_object
{
  public:
  int total_time;
  LPDIRECTSOUNDBUFFER buf;
  LPDIRECTSOUND3DBUFFER buf3d;

  sound()
  { buf=0; buf3d=0; total_time=0; };

  virtual ~sound()
  { reset(); };

  void reset()
  {
    if (buf3d) buf3d->Release(); buf3d=0;
    if (buf) buf->Release(); buf=0;
    total_time=0;
  }
  int load_wav(char *filename);
  sound *clone();
};
```

Data members

Member	Type	Description
total_time	int	the sound length in ms
buf	LPDIRECTSOUNDBUFFER	the DirectX sound buffer
buf3d	LPDIRECTSOUND3DBUFFER	the DirectX sound buffer 3D

Remarks

This class implements raw sound data. The sound can be loaded from a .wav file.

For playing multiple instances of the same sound, you must clone it and play the clones.

Methods

sound::clone

Prototype
```
sound *clone()
```
Parameters
None

Return value

Returns the cloned sound class pointer.

Remarks

This function clones the sound buffer for simultaneous sound playback.

sound::load_wav

Prototype

```
int load_wav(char *filename)
```

Parameters

Parameter	Type	Description
filename	char *	the filename for the .wav sound file to load

Return value

Returns TRUE if loading is OK, FALSE if the file could not be loaded.

Remarks

This function loads a .wav file (standalone or from a .fpk package).

sound::reset

Prototype

```
void reset()
```

Parameters

None

Return value

None

Remarks

Resets the class, freeing the DirectX sound buffers.

class static_mesh : public bsp_object

Definition

```
class static_mesh : public bsp_object
{
  public:
  mesh *objmesh;

  static_mesh()
  { type=TYPE_STATIC_MESH; objmesh=new mesh; };

  mesh   *ray_intersect(vector&  ro,vector&  rd,vector&  ip,float&
dist,int &facenum,float rad=0.0f);
  int ray_intersect_test(vector& ro,vector& rd,float rad);
  int message(vector& p,float rad,int msg,int param,void *data);

  virtual ~static_mesh()
  { if (objmesh) delete objmesh; };
};
```

Data members

Member	Type	Description
mesh	objmesh *	mesh with some bsp faces

Remarks

This class implements the bsp faces in a bsp leaf node. All leaf nodes have a *static_object* as their first *bsp_node* element in the *elem* linked list. It is just like a Fly3D plug-in object and is the only plug-in object already included in the engine dll.

Methods

static_mesh::message

Prototype
int message(vector& p,float rad,int msg,int param,void *data)

Parameters

Parameter	Type	Description
p	vector&	position
rad	float	radius
msg	int	type
param	int	parameter
data	void *	general pointer parameter

Return value
Returns 0 to continue the message chain.

Remarks

This function processes the messages sent to the bsp leaf faces. It handles static and dynamic lighting messages.

static_mesh::ray_intersect

Prototype

```
mesh *ray_intersect(vector& ro,vector& rd,vector& ip,float& dist,int
&facenum,float rad=0.0f);
```

Parameters

Parameter	Type	Description
ro	vector&	ray origin
rd	vector&	ray direction
ip	vector&	intersection point
dist	float&	intersection distance
facenum	int&	intersected face index into returned mesh
rad	float	collision radius

Return value

Returns the mesh object if a collision is detected, NULL on no collision.

Remarks

This function implements the ray intersection virtual *bsp_obect* function for the bsp faces included in a leaf node.

It passes the *ray_intersect* call to the same function from its *objmesh* member variable.

static_mesh::ray_intersect_test

Prototype

```
int ray_intersect_test(vector& ro,vector& rd,float rad)
```

Parameters

Parameter	Type	Description
ro	vector&	ray origin
rd	vector&	ray direction
rad	float	collision radius

Return value

Returns TRUE if an intersection is found, FALSE for no intersection.

Remarks

This function implements the ray intersection test virtual *bsp_obect* function for the bsp faces included in a leaf node.

It passes the *ray_intersect_test* call to the same function from its *objmesh* member variable.

class stripfan_mesh

Definition

```
class stripfan_mesh
{
    public:
    int nstripfan;
    int *stripfandata;
    int nvert;
    vertex *vertdata;

    stripfan_mesh()
    { nstripfan=0; stripfandata=0; vertdata=0; nvert=0; }

    void draw();
    mesh *build_mesh();
    vertex *add_stripfan(int nvert,int texpic,int lmpic);

    void reset()
    {
        if (stripfandata) delete stripfandata;
        if (vertdata) delete vertdata;
        nstripfan=0; stripfandata=0; vertdata=0; nvert=0;
    }

    virtual ~stripfan_mesh()
    { reset(); }
};
```

Data members

Member	Type	Description
nstripfan	int	number of strips and fans
stripfandata	int *	data for the strips and fans. 3 integers for each strip/fan.
nvert	int	number of vertices in vertdata array
vertdata	vertex *	vertices array

Remarks

This class implements a mesh made of strips and fans. Each strip/fan is made of an array of *vertex* classes.

The *stripfandata* is an array of integers with *nstripfan*3* elements. Each group of three elements defines a strip/fan as follows:

(1) The first element is the number of vertices for the strip/fan. If positive, it means a strip with *n* vertices. If negative, a fan with −*n* vertices.

(2) The second element is the texture applied to strip/fan. If −1, no texture.

(3) The third element is the light map applied to strip/fan. If −1, no light map.

Methods

stripfan_mesh::add_stripfan

Prototype
```
vertex *add_stripfan(int nvert,int texpic,int lmpic)
```

Parameters

Parameter	Type	Description
nvert	int	number of vertices to add
texpic	int	texture picture for this strip/fan
lmpic	int	light map for this strip/fan

Return value
Return the pointer to the actual vertices added for the strip/fan.

Remarks
This function adds a new strip or fan to the mesh. If *nvert* is positive, it means a strip, if negative, a fan.

Each strip/fan can have its own texture and light map. If strip has no texture or no light map, use -1 for the texture or light map parameter.

You must fill the strip vertices (position, colour, texture coordinate and light map coordinate) using the returned pointer. It points to an array of vertices of size abs(*nvert*).

stripfan_mesh::build_mesh

Prototype
```
mesh *build_mesh()
```

Parameters
None

Return value
Returns a mesh object representing the strip/fan object.

Remarks
This function converts the strip/fan mesh into a standard mesh.

stripfan_mesh::draw

Prototype
```
void draw()
```

Parameters
None

Return value
None

Remarks

Draws the strip/fan mesh.

stripfan_mesh::reset

Prototype
```
void reset()
```

Parameters

None

Return value

None

Remarks

This function clears the strip/fan mesh, freeing all allocated data.

class textcache

Definition

```
class textcache
{
   public:
   int curpic[MAX_TEXTURE_UNITS];
   int npic,curtextunit;

   virtual void use(int pic=-1,int textunit=0)=0;
   virtual void use_triangles(int pic=-1,int textunit=0)=0;
   virtual void init(int np,picture **pic)=0;

   virtual int add_picture(int sx,int sy,int bytespixel,unsigned
char *lm)=0;
   virtual void update_picture(int picnum,int sx,int sy,int
bytespixel,unsigned char *buf)=0;
   virtual void update_sub_picture(int picnum,int x,int y,int sx,int
sy,int bytespixel,unsigned char *buf)=0;

   textcache()
   {
     memset(curpic,-1,sizeof(int)*MAX_TEXTURE_UNITS);
     npic=0;
     curtextunit=0;
   };

   virtual ~textcache() { };
};
```

Data members

Member	Type	Description
curpic	int []	the current selected texture in each texture unit
npic	int	the total number of textures
curtextunit	int	the current selected texture unit

Remarks

This class is the base class for the texture cache (texture manager). Subclasses from this class should implement their functionality by implementing the virtual functions using the the selected graphics API.

Use the flyEngine *init_texture_cache* and *free_texture_cache* to initialise and free the global variable *tc* that is the main interface to this class.

Methods

textcache::add_picture

Prototype

```
virtual int add_picture(int sx,int sy,int bytespixel,unsigned char
*lm)=0
```

Parameters

Parameter	Type	Description
sx	int	size in x (power of 2)
sy	int	size in y (power of 2)
bytespixel	int	bytes per pixel (3 or 4)
lm	unsigned char *	picture pixels (sx*sy*bytespixel)

Return value

Returns the newly created picture index.

Remarks

This virtual function is used to add a new picture to the texture manager.

textcache::init

Prototype

```
virtual void init(int np,picture **pic,void *data)=0
```

Parameters

Parameter	Type	Description
np	int	number of pictures in pic array
pic	picture **	picture array

Return value

None

Remarks

This virtual function initialises the texture manager with a picture array. All pictures in the array will be loaded to the 3D hardware. For adding new pictures, use the *add_picture* function, for updating any picture pixels, use the *update_picture* and *update_sub_picture* member functions.

textcache::update_picture

Prototype

```
virtual void update_picture(int picnum,int sx,int sy,int
bytespixel,unsigned char *buf)=0
```

Parameters

Parameter	Type	Description
picnum	int	picture index
sx	int	size in x (power of 2)

sy	int	size in y (power of 2)
bytespixel	int	bytes per pixel (3 or 4)
buf	unsigned char *	picture pixels (sx*sy*bytespixel)

Return value
    None

Remarks
    This virtual function is used to update the picture in the picture manager with a new pixel array.

textcache::update_sub_picture

Prototype
virtual void update_sub_picture(int picnum,int x,int y,int sx,int sy,int bytespixel,unsigned char *buf)=0

Parameters

Parameter	Type	Description
picnum	int	picture index
x	int	x offset
y	int	y offset
sx	int	size in x (no need to be power of 2)
sy	int	size in y (no need to be power of 2)
bytespixel	int	bytes per pixel (3 or 4)
buf	unsigned char *	picture pixels ((sx*bytespixel aligned to 4 bytes)*sy)

Return value
    None

Remarks
    This virtual function is used to update just a part of a picture in the texture manager. Only the sub-picture pixels are passed. If *x* and *y* are 0 and *sx* and *sy* the size of the image, it will work just like the *update_picture* function.

textcache::use

Prototype
    `virtual void use(int pic=-1,int textunit=0)=0`

Parameters

Parameter	Type	Description
pic	int	picture index to select
textunit	int	texture unit to select

Return value
None

Remarks
This virtual function selects a picture to be used in the specified texture unit. The texture unit remains selected and active after the call. Calling this function with *pic* = −1 will disable texturing in the specified texture unit. The number of texture units available is at the *ntextureunits* global variable.

textcache::use_triangles

Prototype
```
virtual void use_triangles(int pic=-1,int textunit=0)=0
```

Parameters

Parameter	Type	Description
pic	int	picture index to selected
textunit	int	texture unit to select

Return value
None

Remarks
This virtual function selects a picture to be used in the specified texture unit. The texture unit remains selected and active after the call. Calling this function with *pic* = −1 will disable texturing in the specified texture unit. The number of texture units available is in the *ntextureunits* global variable. This is a variation of the use function that can be called between glBegin/glEnd pairs.

class textcacheGL : public textcache

Definition

```
class textcacheGL : public textcache
{
public:
   textcacheGL();
   ~textcacheGL();

   unsigned *tex;

   void init(int np,picture **pic);

   int add_picture(int sx,int sy,int bytespixel,unsigned char *buf);
   void  update_picture(int  picnum,int  sx,int  sy,int  bytespixel,
unsigned char *buf);
   void update_sub_picture(int picnum,int x,int y,int sx,int sy, int
bytespixel,unsigned char *buf);

   inline void use(int pic=-1,int textunit=0);
   inline void use_triangles(int pic=-1,int textunit=0);
};
```

Data members

Member	Type	Description
tex	unsigned *	the OpenGL texture handles

Remarks

This class is the OpenGL implementation subclassed from the *textcache* base class.

Use the flyEngine *init_texture_cache* and *free_texture_cache* to initialise and free the global variable *tc* that is the main interface to this class.

Methods

textcacheGL::add_picture

Prototype

```
int add_picture(int sx,int sy,int bytespixel,unsigned char *buf)
```

Parameters

Parameter	Type	Description
sx	int	size in x (power of 2)
sy	int	size in y (power of 2)
bytespixel	int	bytes per pixel (3 or 4)
buf	unsigned char *	picture pixels (sx*sy*bytespixel)

Return value

Returns the newly created picture index.

Remarks

This is the OpenGL implementation for the *textcache* base class virtual function. This function is used to add a new picture to the texture manager.

textcacheGL::init

Prototype

```
void init(int np,picture **pic,void *data)
```

Parameters

Parameter	Type	Description
np	int	number of pictures in pic array
pic	picture **	picture array

Return value

None

Remarks

This is the OpenGL implementation for the textcache base class virtual function.

This function initialises the texture manager with a picture array. All pictures in the array will be loaded into the 3D hardware. For adding new pictures, use the *add_picture* function, for updating any picture pixels, use the *update_picture* and *update_sub_picture* member functions.

textcacheGL::update_picture

Prototype

```
void update_picture(int picnum,int sx,int sy,int bytespixel,unsigned
char *buf)
```

Parameters

Parameter	Type	Description
picnum	int	picture index
sx	int	size in x (power of 2)
sy	int	size in y (power of 2)
bytespixel	int	bytes per pixel (3 or 4)
buf	unsigned char *	picture pixels (sx*sy*bytespixel)

Return value

None

Remarks

This is the OpenGL implementation for the *textcache* base class virtual function.

This function is used to update the picture in the picture manager with a new pixel array.

textcacheGL::update_sub_picture

Prototype

```
void update_sub_picture(int picnum,int x,int y,int sx,int sy,int
bytespixel,unsigned char *buf)
```

Parameters

Parameter	Type	Description
picnum	int	picture index
x	int	x offset
y	int	y offset
sx	int	size in x (no need to be power of 2)
sy	int	size in y (no need to be power of 2)
bytespixel	int	bytes per pixel (3 or 4)
buf	unsigned char *	picture pixels ((sx*bytespixel aligned to 4 bytes)*sy)

Return value

None

Remarks

This is the OpenGL implementation for the *textcache* base class virtual function.

This function is used to update just a part of a picture in the texture manager. Only the sub-picture pixels are passed. If *x* and *y* are 0 and *sx* and *sy* the size of the image, it will work just like the *update_picture* function.

textcacheGL::use

Prototype

```
inline void use(int pic=-1,int textunit=0)
```

Parameters

Parameter	Type	Description
pic	int	picture index to select
textunit	int	texture unit to select

Return value

None

Remarks

This is the OpenGL implementation for the *textcache* base class virtual function.

This function selects a picture to be used in the specified texture unit. The texture unit remains selected and active after the call. Calling this function with $pic = -1$ will disable texturing in the specified texture unit. The number of texture units available is at the *ntextureunits* global variable.

textcacheGL::use_triangles

Prototype

```
inline void use_triangles(int pic=-1,int textunit=0)
```

Parameters

Parameter	Type	Description
pic	int	picture index to select
textunit	int	texture unit to select

Return value

None

Remarks

This is the OpenGL implementation for the *textcache* base class virtual function.

This function selects a picture to be used in the specified texture unit. The texture unit remains selected and active after the call. Calling this function with $pic = -1$ will disable texturing in the specified texture unit. The number of texture units available is at the *ntextureunits* global variable. This is a variation of the *use* function that can be called between glBegin/glEnd pairs.

class vector

Definition

```cpp
class vector
{
  public:
  float x,y,z,w;

  inline vector()
  { ; };

  inline vector(float x0,float y0,float z0)
  { x=x0; y=y0; z=z0; };

  inline vector(float x0,float y0,float z0,float w0)
  { x=x0; y=y0; z=z0; w=w0; };

  inline vector(vector &v)
  { *this=v; };

  inline void null(void)
  { x=y=z=0; };

  inline float length(void)
  { return (float)sqrt(x*x+y*y+z*z); };

  inline void vec(float x0,float y0,float z0)
  { x=x0; y=y0; z=z0; };

  inline void negate(void)
  { x=-x; y=-y; z=-z; };

  inline void cross(vector& v1,vector& v2)
  {
    x=v1.y*v2.z-v1.z*v2.y;
    y=v1.z*v2.x-v1.x*v2.z;
    z=v1.x*v2.y-v1.y*v2.x;
  }

  inline void normalize(void)
  {
    float len=(float)sqrt(x*x+y*y+z*z);
    if (len==0.0f) return; x/=len; y/=len; z/=len;
  }

  inline float& operator[](int i)
  { return (&x)[i]; };
};
```

Data members

Member	Type	Description
x	float	vector coordinate in the *x* axis
y	float	vector coordinate in the *y* axis
z	float	vector coordinate in the *z* axis

Remarks

This class implements a 3D vector with four coordinates *x*, *y*, *z* and *w*. It is used for specifying points in 3D space, directions, velocity, force and also colour (*x* is red, *y* is green, *z* is blue and *w* is alpha). The *w* coordinate is usually set to 1.0 when using the vector to represent 3D points and from 0.0 to 1.0 when using it as the colour alpha value.

Methods

vector constructors

Prototype

```
inline vector()
{ ; };

inline vector(float x0,float y0,float z0)
{ x=x0; y=y0; z=z0; };

inline vector(float x0,float y0,float z0,float w0)
{ x=x0; y=y0; z=z0; w=w0; };

inline vector(vector &v)
{ *this=v; };
```

Parameters

Parameter	Type	Description
x0	float	coordinate in *x* axis
y0	float	coordinate in *y* axis
z0	float	coordinate in *z* axis
w0	float	coordinate in *w* axis
v	vector&	vector to clone

Remarks

Creates a new initialized or uninitialized vector.

vector::cross

Prototype

```
inline void cross(vector& v1,vector& v2)
```

Parameters

Parameter	Type	Description
v1	vector&	first vector for cross product
v2	vector&	second vector for cross product

Return value

None

Remarks

Sets the vector to the cross-product of two specified vectors.

x = v1.y*v2.z − v1.z*v2.y;

y = v1.z*v2.x − v1.x*v2.z;

z = v1.x*v2.y − v1.y*v2.x;

vector::length

Prototype

```
inline float length()
```

Parameters

None

Return value

Returns the length of the vector.

Remarks

This function return the length of the vector.

srqt(x*x + y*y + z*z)

vector::negate

Prototype

```
inline void negate()
```

Parameters

None

Return value

None

Remarks

Inverts all vector coordinates.

x = −x, y = −x, z = −z

vector::normalize

Prototype

```
inline void normalize()
```

Parameters

None

Return value
None

Remarks
Normalises the vector dividing each coordinate by the vector length.

vector::null

Prototype
```
inline void null()
```
Parameters
None

Return value
None

Remarks
Zero all vector coordinates.

vector::operator[]

Prototype
```
inline float& operator[](int i)
```
Parameters

Parameter	Type	Description
i	int	index into the vector (0 for x, 1 for y, 2 for z, 3 for w)

Remarks
Returns the indexed vector coordinate. Index must be between 0 and 3.

vector::vec

Prototype
```
inline void vec(float x0,float y0,float z0)
inline void vec(float x0,float y0,float z0,float w0)
```
Parameters

Parameter	Type	Description
x0	float	coordinate in x axis
y0	float	coordinate in y axis
z0	float	coordinate in z axis
w0	float	coordinate in w axis

Return value
None

Remarks
Sets vector coordinates.

Fly3D SDK tutorials

Tutorial 1   How to build a level model

Tutorial 2   More complex level modelling

Tutorial 3   Creating the level .BSP file

Tutorial 4   Creating the level script .FLY file

Tutorial 5   Creating the level light map .LMP file

Tutorial 6   Creating the level .PVS file

Tutorial 7   Adding Fly3D plug-ins

Tutorial 8   How to model a dynamic object

Tutorial 9   Creating a new Fly3D plug-in

Tutorial 10   Adding a new object to a Fly3D plug-in

Tutorial 11   Creating a player object

Tutorial 12   Creating a front-end

The tutorials are a very basic introduction to the use of FLY3D SDK; fuller documentation is available at www.fly3d.com.br

A.1 Tutorial 1 How to build a level model

A.1.1 Introduction

This tutorial describes how to build a level using 3D Studio Max and export it, using the supplied BSP export plug-in. If you have not got access to 3D Studio Max you can go direct to Tutorial 3 and use the supplied BSP files.

At the end of the operations exemplified in this tutorial, we have constructed the geometry of a level (stored as a .max file).

3D Studio Max operations

(1) Draw a plan view of the level using the line tool. The plan of the model must consist of a closed polygon.

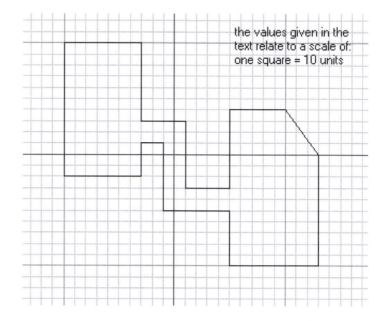

the values given in the text relate to a scale of: one square = 10 units

(2) Use the extrude modifier to convert the plan into a 3D model.

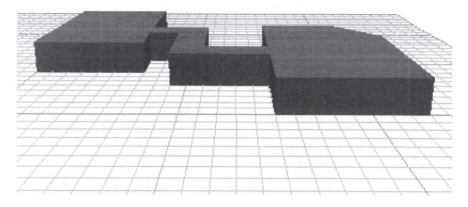

(3) Invert the face normals using the edit mesh modifier. This is done by selecting the face node in the edit mesh modifier, selecting all faces from the model with a selection window and then clicking the invert normal button from the edit mesh modifier. This is an important step, and converts the model from a normal 3D graphics object, with outwards-facing normals, to an interior.

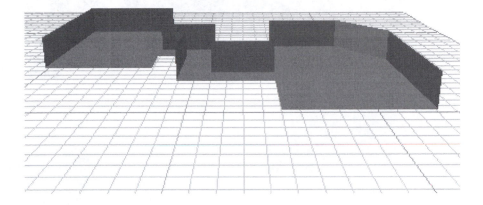

(4) Create the texture coordinates using the UVW Map modifier and select box mapping. Set the length, width and height to appropriate values for your level.

(5) Define the required materials using the standard material with bitmap diffuse mapping and apply it to the model. You can also apply different materials to different parts of the model.

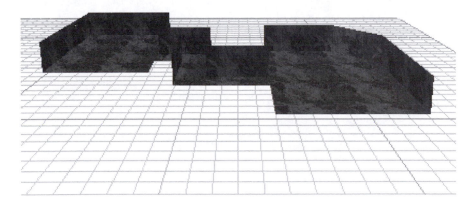

(6) Create some light objects (you can use simple small box objects, for example). Place the lights in appropriate positions and apply a standard material with self-illumination value larger than 0.

(7) Associate real dimensions with your model by setting the desired values in the Preferences menu on the general tab system unit scale. For example, for a wall of 50 units length, you might set 0.2 unit = 1 metre, making the virtual wall 10 metres long.

Tutorial 2 More complex level modelling

Introduction

This tutorial details a simple methodology for building a closed environment level.

At the end of the operations exemplified in this tutorial, we have constructed the geometry of a level (stored as a .max file).

The basic building block is a box. The level is constructed by joining boxes together, dragging vertices to convert the boxes into truncated rectangular pyramids, then deleting shared faces to create the final environment. An advantage of this construction method is that correct topology is maintained for the environment. This means that if a construction, such as that shown in the last figure from this tutorial is required, then the face normals will have the correct direction (the direction of the surface normals must be consistent with the rule that the entire environment must exhibit a single inside space and a single outside space). This rule is more difficult to guarantee as more complex shapes are used by an editor.

3D Studio Max operations

(1) Draw seven boxes as shown, using the box creation tool

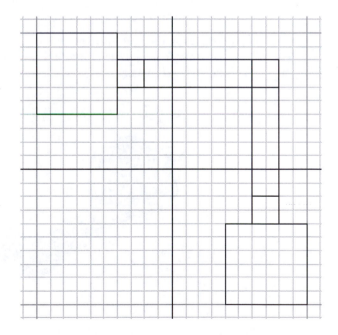

(2) Use the edit mesh modifier to move the vertices of boxes 2 and 6 as shown so that they align with the vertices from boxes 1 and 7.

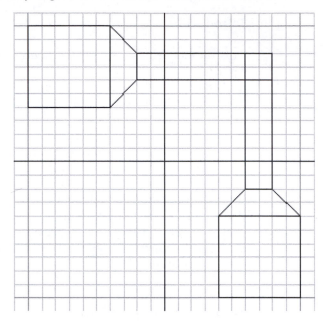

(3) Attach all boxes to each other using the attach multiple tool to create a single environment. All boxes now merge to form a single object.

(4) Use the edit modifier again to remove the six pairs of shared faces (note there are two triangles per face).

(5) Still using the edit mesh modifier, select all vertices and weld them with the weld vertices tool, deleting duplicated vertices (vertices that share the same position in space).

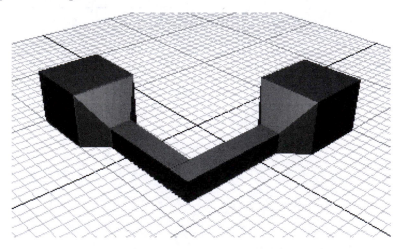

(6) Still using the edit mesh modifier, select all faces and invert their normals so that they point inwards.

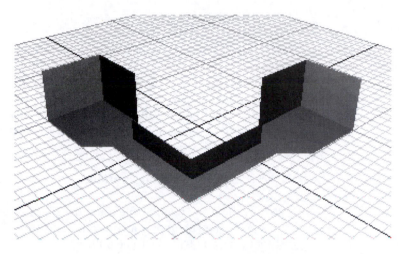

(7) Apply material and texture mapping coordinates using the material editor and UVW mapping tool.

(8) Create some light objects (you can use simple small box objects, for example). Place the lights in appropriate positions and apply a standard material with self illumination value larger than 0.

(9) Associate real dimensions with your model by setting the desired values in the Preferences menu on the general tab system unit scale. For example, for a wall of 50 units length, you might set 0.2 unit = 1 metre, making the virtual wall 10 metres long.

Tutorial 3 Creating the level .BSP file

Introduction

This tutorial explains how to export any 3D Studio Max scene into a Fly3D bsp file.

At the end of this tutorial you will have constructed a BSP tree to partition the space of the model, constructed a text file with information on the BSP statistics and a text file containing the list of images used as texture maps in the model faces. Each of these will be stored in files with extensions *.bsp*, *.log*, *.txt* and *.map*.

Fly3D export plug-in operations

Export the scene to a BSP file using the supplied export plug-in *expflybsp.dle*. Do this using the File/Export menu command and selecting the Fly3D BSP file type. This causes the BSP tree to be built.

Make sure to save the BSP inside the flysdk\data directory. Create a sub-directory in flysdk\data named *tutorial*. This where all level data from the tutorials should be be stored.

{To install the export plug-in, just copy the plug-in file to the 3ddsmax\plug-ins directory before opening 3D Studio Max}

At this stage, we set the options for the export file:

● Light Radius (metres): this parameter is multiplied by the self-illumination parameter value from the materials, giving the final light radius for the object. For example, specifying a light radius of 20 metres, a material with 50 per cent self-illumination gives a real light radius of 10 metres.

● Save # objects: this option saves all objects with names starting with the '#' character as .3ds files in the objects subdir from where the BSP file is being saved. Name all objects that will not be part of the BSP with this starting character as they will be used as dynamic objects (doors, player, guns projectiles, power-ups, etc. . . . .).

● Save BSP log: this option saves a *.txt* file with the same name as the BSP file, including information on the BSP construction, nodes and faces. This facility records the statistics of the BSP tree, which can then be examined for effectiveness.

● BSP planes:
  – face aligned: used for closed environments only, the level must present a single in/out volume. With this option, all BSP planes will be aligned with level faces, making a BSP plane for each plane defined by the level faces.

–   axis aligned: used for landscapes and free spaces. The bsp planes are aligned only with x, y and z axes. A maximum tree depth can be specified and will stop subdivision if that depth is reached. Landscapes are 2D bsp files that are good for race and strategy games. Freespaces are 3D bsp files used in space simulator and space strategy games.

A.4   Tutorial 4 Creating the level script .FLY file

A.4.1   Introduction

Writing a script consists of specifying the global level parameters, the plug-ins to be included in the level and enumerating the instances of the plug-in classes used in the level, with their parameter values. At the end of this tutorial you will have constructed a script with all the global parameters for the level which will be used in the lighting and visibility tutorials.

A.4.2   flyEditor operations

(1) Open the flyEditor.exe and click the new button.

(2) Save the new file to the same directory as the file from the previous tutorial (flysdk\data\turorial).

(3) Specify the BSP file to be used in the level, selecting the global tree item and double-clicking on the bspfile list view item. This will show an open file dialogue and you must select the BSP from tutorials 1 or 2.

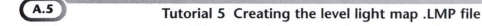

A.5 Tutorial 5 Creating the level light map .LMP file

A.5.1 Introduction

The operations in this tutorial effect the construction of the light maps that are used to illuminate the scene. At the end of this tutorial you will have created the light maps (stored in a *.lmp* file). This caches the illumination of all self-illuminated faces and light objects in the scene light maps.

A.5.2 Fly utilities operations

(1) Execute the flyLight.exe utility. In the flyEditor, use the Tools/Light menu option.

(2) Select the *.fly* file you created in Tutorial 3.

(3) Select the lighting options from:

- Shadows: shadows are calculated for each light map pixel (increasing the computation time for complex scenes).

- Connectivity: when off, this enables co-planar faces which are not connected to share the same light map. This means that the total number of lightmaps is kept as low as possible, although it also implies that many light map pixels will be redundant (mapping to space between such faces).

- Light Radius and Light Value: overwrite original setting from the materials to facilitate editing at this stage.

- Pixel Size: the desired light map pixel size. Small values will make the dynamic light slower.

- Ambient Light: amount of light to add to all light pixels (0 to 255).

(4) Press compute to start the lighting computations.

A.6 Tutorial 6 Creating the level .PVS file

A.6.1 Introduction

The operations in this tutorial calculate the PVS using the non-deterministic method described in the text. For a scene of high complexity, this program will run for several hours. After completion you will have computed all node to node visibility and enhanced the BSP tree with a connectivity matrix. The PVS will be stored in a file with extension *.pvs*.

A.6.2 Fly utilities operations

(1) Execute the flyPVS.exe utility. In the flyEditor, use the Tools/View menu option.

(2) Select the BSP file you created in Tutorial 1 or 2.

(3) Select the sampling cube resolution. For this tutoriual a 64 × 64 resolution is sufficient.

(4) Save PVSlog: this saves a *.txt* file with the same name as the BSP file including information on the PVS construction. This facility records the statistics of the PVS connectivity matrix, which can be examined for effectiveness.

(5) Visibility Sample Factor: a useful parameter that sets the volume sampling accuracy of the PVS calculation. The volume of each node is calculated and a sampling density specified (cubic metres/sample).

A.7 Tutorial 7 Adding Fly3D plug-ins

A.7.1 Introduction

At this point a level has been created and pre-processed but there are no dynamic objects included in the level and thus no game to execute. This tutorial enables experimentation with the supplied plug-ins to give an introduction to the nature of game development using plug-in architecture as a development tool.

After completing this tutorial you will have an executable game.

A.7.2 flyEditor operations

(1) Open the script file from Tutorial 4 with the flyEditor.

(2) Right-click the plug-ins tree item and select insert from the pop-up menu.

(3) An open dialogue will show up, and you should select the *walk.dll*.

(4) Now we need to create a new person object from the *walk.dll*. This will be the player. Right-click the *person* tree item and select insert from the pop-up menu. A new person object will be created and you can set its name to a chosen name like 'myplayer'.

(5) Fill in the person object properties in Table A.1 for your new player. Complex behaviour can only be achieved using a large number of parameters, but you can start using default values for them and experiment with different settings for parameters of your choice.

Table A.1 Person object properties for Tutorial 4

Parameter	Value	Description
colflag	1	sets collision on/off
mass	1	sets player mass (in this case >0)
radius	1	sets player collision radius (player collides as a sphere)
bump	1	bouncing factor (0.0 to 1.0)
friction	1	sliding factor (0.0 to 1.0)
active	1	activate on startup
height	18.5	player height (1.85m)
jumpforce	0.006	jump force (use space key to jump)
jumpforcetime	100	jump time
gravity	0.002	gravity applied to player
walkvel	0.2	walk velocity (use s, x, q, e keys to move)
rotvel	0.1	keyboard rotation factor (use arrows to rotate view)

mousespeed	0.2	mouse rotation factor (use mouse to rotate view)
zoomtime	300	zoom time in ms (use right mouse click to zoom)
zoomangle1	60	standard view angle
zoomangle2	20	zoom view angle
shield	1	player shield

(6) Press the Save and Restart button on the tool bar or select the File/Restart menu option to restart the scene (this will activate all objects set to activate on startup)

(7) Select the global tree view item and change the global parameters shown in Table A.2.

Table A.2 Global parameters for Tutorial 7

Parameter	Value	Description
viewmindist	1	near plane distance
viewmaxdist	1500	far plane distance
player	myplayer	sets the player object
camera	myplayer	sets the camera object
Camangle	60	player camera angle
Mapmode	1–15	selects mapping layers (bit flag):
		bit 1 for texture map
		bit 2 for detail map
		bit 3 for light map
		bit 4 for fog map
		use 1 for texture only
		use 15 for all mapping layers

(8) Now you are ready to walk around. Turn the render on by selecting OpenGL on the tool bar or using the menu render option. Start simulating, clicking the Simulate tool bar button or using the F4 key. You should see the level from the player's point of view in the render window (notice that as no birth pads have been created yet, the player will start up at coordinates 0,0,0 which must be inside the level).

(9) Select the render window by clicking on it (or use the TAB key) and you should be able to move around.

A.8

Tutorial 8 How to model a dynamic object

The most important factor that distinguishes a dynamic object from a static object is the texture map. It is important that one texture map be derived for the complete object for run-time efficiency.

The steps in buiding up a dynamic object are:

(1) Build a polygon mesh model.

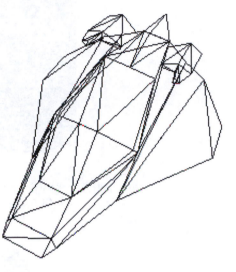

(2) Render orthographic views of the object (front, side, top, back, etc.). The number of views that will be required depends on the object complexity. All parts of the object must be visible and of sufficient projected area in 2D space.

(3) Use a painting package to paint the textures on the views.

(4) Create a single texture and copy/paste the required parts of the orthographic painted views into it. Notice that symmetric objects that have reflected textures should have both regions mapped onto the same area of the texture map. It is important for efficiency not to duplicate textures in the texture map.

(5) Use the supplied utility (ProgMesh.exe) to precisely position the texture coordinates for each of the model faces into the desired position in the texture map.

A.9 Tutorial 9 Creating a new Fly3D plug-in

A.9.1 Introduction

At the end of this tutorial you will have created a new Fly3D plug-in to be used in your games. The plug-in will implement a single game object named blink_light. The object will be a dynamic light source that constantly changes its radius based on a predefined time interval.

A.9.2 Visual C++ operations

(1) Open the Visual C++ Fly3D Plug-ins Workspace.

(2) Select the menu option File/New to create a new project.

(3) Select the projects tab and the Fly3D Plug-in Wizard.

(4) Set the project location to the flysdk\plugin path and name the project 'tutorial'. Make sure to select add to current workspace to keep all Fly3D plug-in projects in a single workspace.

(5) On the first wizard step, add a single class named '*blink_light*'

(6) On the second wizard step, add three parameters:

```
name: 'color'        type: color
name: 'illumradius'  type: float
name: 'blinktime'    type: int
```

(7) On the third wizard step, select the Fly3D SDK path and click Finish.

(8) You should now be able to compile the plug-in with no errors.

(9) Now we will add the blink light functionality. Open the *tutorial.cpp* file and add the following code to the *blink_light::step function*:

```
int blink_light::step(int dt)
{
  // compute current radius
  float r=illumradius*(flyengine->cur_time % blinktime)/1000.of;

  // illuminate around
  flyengine->send_bsp_message(
    flyengine->bsp, pos, r, FLYOBJM_ILLUM, 0, &color);

  // return 0 as we have not moved (changed position)
  return 0;
}
```

(10) If the *blink_light* is to be destroyed after, say, 30 seconds of illumination, set its life parameter to 30000 and add the following line anywhere in the *blink_light::step function*:

```
// subtract elapsed time from object's life
life-=dt;
```

When the *blink_light*'s life value turns negative, it will be destroyed by the engine.

(11) Use the ALT-F7 key to edit the project settings. On the link tab, change the output file name to '*../tutorial.dll*'. This will save the compiled *dll* to the flysdk\plugin directory with all other Fly3D plug-ins (make sure to change this option for the release and debug versions).

(12) Compile the tutorial (*flysdk\plugin\tutorial.dll* should be built) and we are ready to add the plug-in object to the level from previous tutorials.

(13) Run the plug-in (debug it) using the F5 key and select the *flyEditor.exe* to open (or just run a standalone copy of flyEditor if no debug is needed).

A.9.3 flyEditor operations

(1) Open the level .fly file created in previous tutorials and add the tutorial.dll to it just like in Tutorial 7.

(2) Add a new blink_light object and set its parameters as follows:

```
active = 1 (activate on startup)
color  = any colour you choose for the light, but not black!
radius = 100 (10 metres)
time   = 1000 (1 second)
```

This active parameters tells the engine to activate a copy of the object on scene start-up. If we set it to 0, the blink_light will be on the stock and can be used as a parameter in another game object or activated by another game object (and will not be visible until then).

(3) Run the level. You should see the blink_light illuminating the faces near its position (0,0,0). You can change its parameters and see the results in real-time in the render view.

A.10 Tutorial 10 Adding a new object to a Fly3D plugin

A.10.1 Introduction

After finishing this tutorial you will have added a new object to an existing Fly3D plug-in. The object we will add is a simple object that has a mesh representation and moves around bouncing on walls as a sphere.

A.10.2 Visual C++ operations

(1) Open the plug-in project created in last tutorial.

(2) Add a new type to the enumeration on the beginning of *tutorial.h*:

```
enum
{
   TYPE_BLINK_LIGHT=100000,
   TYPE_BOUNCE_MESH,
}
```

(3) Add the following lines to the end of the *tutorial.h* file:

```
class bounce_mesh : public bsp_object
{
public:
   bounce_mesh() { type=TYPE_BOUNCE_MESH; };

   // the object's mesh
   mesh *objmesh;

   // no step() is defined, using the particle base class step()

   // this will handle drawing and collision with the object
   mesh *get_mesh() { return objmesh; };

   int get_custom_param_desc(int i,param_desc *pd);
   bsp_object *clone();
};

class bounce_mesh_desc : public class_desc
{
public:
   void *create() { return new bounce_mesh; };
   char *get_name() { return "bounce_mesh"; };
   int get_type() { return TYPE_BOUNCE_MESH; };
};
```

(4) Add the following global variable to the beginning of the *tutorial.cpp* file:

```
bounce_mesh_desc cd_bounce_mesh;
```

(5) The exported *num_classes()* function in the *tutorial.cpp* file should look like this as we now have two classes:

```
__declspec( dllexport )
int num_classes()
{
  return 2;
}
```

(6) The exported get_class_desc() function in the *tutorial.cpp* file should look like this as we now have two classes:

```
__declspec( dllexport )
class_desc *get_class_desc(int i)
{
  switch(i)
  {
    case 0:
      return &cd_blink_light;
    case 1:
      return &cd_bounce_mesh;
    default: return 0;
  }
}
```

(7) Add the following lines to the end of the *tutorial.cpp* file:

```
bsp_object *bounce_mesh::clone()
{
  bounce_mesh *tmp=new bounce_mesh;
  *tmp=*this;
  tmp->source=this;
  return tmp;
}

int bounce_mesh::get_custom_param_desc(int i,param_desc *pd)
{
  if (pd!=0)
    switch(i)
    {
      case 0:
        pd->type='3';
        pd->data=&objmesh;
        strcpy(pd->name,"objmesh");
        break;
    }
  return 1;
}
```

flyEditor operations

(1) Open the level *.fly* file created in previous tutorials in flyEditor.

(2) Add a new bounce_mesh object and set its parameters as follows:

```
vel        = 0.1 0.1 0.1 (diagonal velocity)
mass       = 1.0 (object mass)
bump       = 1.0 (bumping factor)
friction   = 1.0 (friction factor)
radius     = 10 (the object collision radius)
colflag    = 1 (turns collision detection on)
active     = 1 (activate on startup)
life       = 30000 (bounce for 30 seconds and die)
objmesh    = select any 3ds file to be used as the object's mesh
```

(3) Run the level (setting the render and starting simulation).

(4) With the bounce_mesh object selected, click the activate button on the toolbar to add a new instance of the object to the simulation. You should see the bounce_mesh moving and colliding with the level walls.

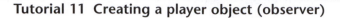

(A.11)
Tutorial 11 Creating a player object (observer)

(A.11.1)
Introduction

After finishing this tutorial you will have created a new game object that can be used as a player. The object will move around the level requiring keys and mouse to guide its movement.

Visual C++ operations

(1) Open the Visual C++ Fly3D Plug-ins Workspace.

(2) Select the menu option File/New to create a new project.

(3) Select the projects tab and the Fly3D Plug-in Wizard.

(4) Set the project location to the flysdk\plugin path and name the project 'observer'. Make sure to select 'add to current workspace' to keep all Fly3D plug-in projects in a single workspace.

(5) On the first wizard step, add a single class named 'observer'.

(6) On the second wizard step, add five parameters:

```
name: 'rotvel'  type: float
name: 'mousevel'  type: float
name: 'moveforce'  type: float
name: 'maxvel'  type: float
name: 'veldamp'  type: float
```

(7) On the third wizard step, select the Fly3D SDK path and click Finish.

(8) You should now be able to compile the plug-in with no errors.

(9) Open the *observer.cpp* file and put the following code over fly_message case FLYM_DRAWSCENE:

```
case FLYM_DRAWSCENE:
  // draws scene viewed from camera
  flyengine->set_camera(flyengine->cam);
  flyengine->draw_bsp();
  break;
```

(10) Make the *observer::init()* function as follows:

```
void observer::init()
{
  // initialise observer at random position in level
  if (flyengine->get_random_point(pos,10)==0)
    pos.null();
}
```

(11) Replace the observer step function with the following code:

```
int observer::step(int dt)
{
  if (node==0)      // if not in bsp (outside level on last frame)
    add_to_bsp(); // add it to the bsp as it might be inside now

  check_keys(dt); // process keys

  // damp velocity
  float len=vel.length();
  if (len<0.1f)
    vel.null();
  else
  {
    vel/=len;
    len-=dt*veldamp;
    if (len>maxvel)
        len=maxvel;
    if (len<0.0f)
        len=0.0f;
    vel*=len;
  }

  life=dt; // keep alive
  return particle::step(dt); // moves as particle
}
```

(12) Add the check_keys function as follows (also add its prototype to the *observer.h* file):

```
void observer::check_keys(int dt)
{
  // direct input keys
  unsigned char *diks=directx->diks;

  //  mouse smooth
  static int lastmouse[2][2]={ { 0,0 },{ 0,0 } },lm=0;
  float mousedx=(directx->dims.lX+lastmouse[0][0]+lastmouse
  [1][0])/3.0f;
  float mousedy=(directx->dims.lY+lastmouse[0][1]+lastmouse
  [1][1])/3.0f;
  lastmouse[lm][0]=directx->dims.lX;
  lastmouse[lm][1]=directx->dims.lY;
  lm=!lm;

  // process keys
  if (diks[0x38]) // ALT key
  {
```

```
      if (diks[0xcb]) // left arrow
          vel-=X*(moveforce*dt);
      if (diks[0xcd]) // right arrow
          vel+=X*(moveforce*dt);
      if (diks[0xc8]) // up arrow
          vel+=Y*(moveforce*dt);
      if (diks[0xd0]) // down arrow
          vel-=Y*(moveforce*dt);
      if (diks[0x1f]) // S key
          vel-=Z*(moveforce*dt);
      if (diks[0x2d]) // X key
          vel+=Z*(moveforce*dt);
    }
    else
    {
      if (diks[0xc8]) // up arrow
          rotate(-dt*rotvel,X);
      if (diks[0xd0]) // down arrow
          rotate(dt*rotvel,X);
      if (diks[0xcb]) // left arrow
          rotate(dt*rotvel,Y);
      if (diks[0xcd]) // right arrow
          rotate(-dt*rotvel,Y);
      if (diks[0x10]) // Q key
          vel-=X*(moveforce*dt);
      if (diks[0x12]) // E key
          vel+=X*(moveforce*dt);
      if (diks[0x1f]) // S key
          vel-=Z*(moveforce*dt);
      if (diks[0x2d]) // X key
          vel+=Z*(moveforce*dt);
    }

    if (diks[0x1e]) // A key
        rotate(dt*rotvel,Z);
    if (diks[0x20]) // D key
        rotate(-dt*rotvel,Z);

    if (mousedx) // mouse X
        rotate(-mousedx*mousevel,Y);
    if (mousedy) // mouse Y
        rotate(mousedy*mousevel,X);
  }
```

(13) Use the ALT-F7 key to edit the project settings. On the link tab, change the output file name to '../observer.dll'. This will save the compiled dll to the flysdk\plugin directory with all other Fly3D plug-ins (make sure to change this option for the release and debug versions).

(14) Compile the tutorial (*flysdk\plugin\observer.dll* should be built).

(15) You can now add this plugin to a level and set the global engine parameter camera and player to point to an active instance of the observer class. It will allow you to fly around the level with ease.

flyEditor operations

(1) Open the *flyEditor.exe* and click the new button.

(2) Save the new file (*observer.fly*) to the same directory as the file from the previous tutorials (*flysdk\data\tutorial*).

(3) Specify the BSP file to be used in the level selecting the global tree item and double clicking on the bspfile list view item. This will show an open file dialogue and you must select the BSP from tutorials 1 or 2.

(4) Now we need to create a new observer object from the *observer.dll*. This will be the player. Insert the *observer.dll* to the level by right clicking the tree item Plugins and selecting insert. Right click the new observer tree item and select insert from the popup menu. A new observer object will be created and you can set its name to a chosen name like 'myplayer'.

(5) Fill in the following observer object properties for your new player:

Parameter	Value	Description
colflag	1	sets collision on/off
mass	1	sets player mass (in this case >0)
radius	20	sets player collision radius to 2 m (player collides as a sphere)
bump	1	bouncing factor (0.0 to 1.0)
friction	1	sliding factor (0.0 to 1.0)
active	1	activate on startup
rotvel	0.1	velocity for keyboard rotation (arrows keys)
mosevel	0.1	velocity for mouse rotation
moveforce	0.01	force applied for movement (S, X and slide keys)
maxvel	0.5	maximum velocity for the observer
veldump	0.001	damping factor for observer velocity

(6) Activate an instance of the player by selecting the player and clicking the activate button on the toolbar (this must be done or you will not be able to set the camera and player global parameters to point to the observer as they can only point to active instances of objects).

(7) Set the following global parameters by selecting the Global tree view item:

Parameter	Value	Description
viewmindist	10	sets near plane distance
viewmaxdist	1500	sets far plane distance
camangle	60	set camera view angle
camera	myplayer	set camera object
player	myplayer	set player object
mapmode	15	view all mapping layers

(8) Now you are ready to fly around. Turn the render on by selecting OpenGL on the toolbar. Start simulating clicking the Simulate toolbar button or using the F4 key. You should see the level from the observer's point of view in the render window.

(9) Select the render window by clicking on it (or use the TAB key) and you should be able to move around using the S,X,ARROW keys

A.12

Tutorial 12 Creating a front-end

A.12.1

Introduction

After finishing this tutorial you will have created a new front-end executable. This front-end will be able to run any Fly3D level and is the simplest possible front-end. It creates a window, sets full screen mode, initialises the engine, loads a level and starts the game.

Visual C++ operations

(1) Open the Visual C++ Fly3D Workspace.

(2) Select the menu option File/New to create a new project.

(3) Select the projects tab and the Win32 Application type.

(4) Set the project location to the flysdk\frontend path and name the project 'flyfe'. Make sure to select 'add to current workspace' to keep all Fly3D front-ends projects in a single workspace.

(5) Select an empty project and add the following *flyfe.cpp* file to the project:

```cpp
#include <windows.h>
#include <Fly3D.h>

char szTitle[100]="MyGame Title";
char szWindowClass[100]="MyGame";

LRESULT CALLBACK WinFunc (HWND, UINT, WPARAM, LPARAM);
void LoadLevel (HWND, HINSTANCE);

int WINAPI WinMain (HINSTANCE hInst, HINSTANCE hPrev, LPSTR lp,
int nCmd)
{
  WNDCLASS wcl;
  MSG msg;

  // register window class
  wcl.style = CS_HREDRAW | CS_VREDRAW;
  wcl.lpfnWndProc = (WNDPROC)WinFunc;
  wcl.cbClsExtra = 0;
  wcl.cbWndExtra = 0;
  wcl.hInstance = hFlyInstance;
  wcl.hIcon = LoadIcon(NULL, IDI_WINLOGO);
  wcl.hCursor = 0;
```

```
          wcl.hbrBackground = (HBRUSH)(COLOR_WINDOW+1);
          wcl.lpszMenuName = NULL;
          wcl.lpszClassName = szWindowClass;
          if (!RegisterClass (&wcl))
          {
            MessageBox (0, "Can't register Window", "ERROR", MB_OK);
            return 0;
          }

          // create main window
          hFlyInstance = hInst;
          hFlyWndMain = CreateWindowEx(
                    0,
                    szWindowClass,
                    szTitle,
                    WS_POPUP,
                    0, 0,
                    GetSystemMetrics( SM_CXSCREEN ),
                    GetSystemMetrics( SM_CYSCREEN ),
                    NULL,
                    NULL,
                    hFlyInstance,
                    NULL);

          // load the level
          ShowWindow (hFlyWndMain, SW_MAXIMIZE);
          LoadLevel (hFlyWndMain, hFlyInstance);

          // main loop
          while (1)
          {
            while (PeekMessage(&msg, NULL, 0, 0, PM_NOREMOVE) == TRUE)
            {
              if (GetMessage(&msg, NULL, 0, 0))
              {
                if (flyengine &&
                    ((msg.message==WM_CHAR && flyengine->con.mode &&
          msg.wParam!=VK_ESCAPE) ||
                    (msg.message==WM_KEYDOWN && msg.wParam==VK_ESCAPE)) )
                      flyengine->con.key_press(msg.wParam);
                TranslateMessage(&msg);
                DispatchMessage(&msg);
              }
              else
              {
```

```
            // frees engine, render, directx and quits app
            flyengine->close_texture_cache();
            free_render();
            delete flyengine;
            free_directx();
            return TRUE;
        }
    }


    if (rend && flyengine)
      if (flyengine->step()) // simulate
        rend->DrawView(); // draw view


  }
}


// loads the menu level
void LoadLevel (HWND hWnd, HINSTANCE hInst)
{
  flyengine = new flyEngine;
  init_directx(hWnd, hFlyInstance);
  flyengine->appid=FLYAPPID_FLY;
  init_render(FLY_RENDER_OPENGL, hWnd);
  fullscreen=1;
  rend->SetFullScreen();
  flyengine->open_fly_file("menu/menu.fly");
  rend->CreateView(hFlyWndMain);
  flyengine->init_texture_cache();
  InvalidateRect (hFlyWndMain, 0, 0);
}
```

```
// main window message processing
LRESULT CALLBACK WinFunc (HWND hWnd, UINT mens, WPARAM wParam,
LPARAM
lParam)
{
  switch (mens)
  {
    // window resize
    case WM_SIZE:
      if (rend)
        rend->ResizeView(LOWORD(lParam),HIWORD(lParam));
      break;

    // window activation
    case WM_ACTIVATE:
      if (flyengine)
        if (LOWORD(wParam)==WA_INACTIVE || flyengine->con.mode)
          flyengine->noinput=1;
        else flyengine->noinput=0;
      break;

    // quit app
    case WM_DESTROY:
      PostQuitMessage (0);
      break;
  }

  return DefWindowProc (hWnd, mens, wParam, lParam);
}
```

(6) At the project settings change the following configurations in the Release and Debug versions:

- Add the path '..\..\lib' to the 'Additional include directory' and 'Additional library path'.
- Change the 'Output file name' to '..\..\flyfe.exe' so that the exe is placed with the other front-ends at the flysdk root path.
- Set the 'Object/library modules' option to 'fly3d.lib user32.lib'.

(7) Compile and run the new front-end. It will set full screen and run the menu.fly level.

References

Abram A. G., Westover L. and Whitted T. (1985). Efficient alias-free rendering using bit-masks and lookup tables. *Computer Graphics*, **19** (3), 53–9

Abrash M. (1997). Michael Abrash's Graphics Programming Black Book. Albany, NY: Coriolis

Akeley K., Haeberli P. and Burns D. (1990). *tomesh.c:* C program on SGI Developer's Toolbox CD

Appel A. (1968). Some techniques for machine rendering of solids. *AFIPS Conference Proc*, **32**, 37–45

Arvo J. and Kirk D. (1987). Fast ray tracing by ray classification. *Computer Graphics,* **21** (4), 55–64. (*Proc. SIGGRAPH '87*)

Assarsson U. and Möller T. (1999). Optimized view frustum culling algorithms, Technical Report 99–3, Department of Computer Engineering, Chalmers University of Technology, March

Atherton P., Weiler K. and Greenberg D. (1978). Polygon shadow generation. *Computer Graphics*, **12** (3), 275–81

Bar-Yehuda R. and Gotsman C. (1996). Time/space trade-offs for polygon mesh rendering. *ACM Trans. Graphics*, **15** (2), 141–52

Baraff D. (1990). Curved surfaces and coherence for non-penetrating rigid body simulation. *Proc. SIGGRAPH '90*, pp. 19–29

Bartels R. H., Beatty J. C. and Barsky B. A. (1988). *Splines for Use in Computer Graphics and Geometric Modeling.* Los Altos CA: Morgan Kaufmann

Bass D. H. (1981). Using the video lookup table for reflectivity calculations, *Computer Graphics and Image Processing*, **17**, 249–61

Bergeron P. (1986). Une version générale de l'algorithme des ombres projetées de Crow basée sur le concept de volumes d'ombre. MSc Thesis. University of Montreal

Bergland E. J. and Cheriton D. R. (1985). *Amaze: A multiplayer game. IEEE Software*, May, 30–9

Berman J., Bartell J. and Salesin D. (1994). Multiresolution painting and compositing. *Proc. SIGGRAPH '94*, pp. 85–90

Bier E. A. and Sloan K. R. (1986). Two-part texture mapping. *IEEE Computer Graphics and Applications*, **6** (9), 40–53

Bishop L., Eberly D., Whitted T., Finch M. and Shantz M. (1998). Designing a PC Game Engine, *IEEE Computer Graphics and Applications*, January 1998

Blau B., Hughes C.E., Moshell J.M. and Lisle C. (1992). *Networked virtual environments. Computer Graphics*, 1992 Symposium on Interactive 3D Graphics, March

Blinn J. F. (1977). Models of light reflection for computer synthesized pictures. *Computer Graphics*, **11** (2), 192–8

Blinn J. F. (1978). Simulation of wrinkled surfaces. *Computer Graphics*, **12** (3), 286–92

Blinn J. F. (1988). Me and my (fake) shadow. *IEEE Computer Graphics and Applications*, **8** (1), 82–6

Blinn J. F. and Newell M. E. (1976). Texture and reflection in computer generated images. *Comm. ACM*, **19** (10), 362–7

Blow (1998). A look at latency in games. *Game Developer Magazine*, July

Blumberg B. (1996). *Old Tricks, New Dogs: Ethology and Interactive Creatures*. PhD Thesis, MIT Media Lab., MIT, Boston, USA

Bouknight W. J. and Kelly K. (1970). An algorithm for producing half-tone computer graphics presentations with shadows and moveable light sources. *Proc. AFIPS, Spring Joint Computer Conf.*, **36**, 1–10

Brotman L. S. and Badler N. I. (1984). Generating soft shadows with a depth buffer algorithm. *IEEE Computer Graphics and Applications*, **4** (10), 5–12

Burka L. P. (1995). The MUDline 1995. http://www.apocalypse.org/pub/mudline.htm

Cabral B., Max N. and Springmeyer R. (1987). Bidirectional reflection functions from surface bump maps. *Computer Graphics*, **21** (4), 273–81. (*Proc. SIGGRAPH '87*)

Carpenter L. C. (1984). The A-buffer, an anti-aliased hidden surface method. *Computer Graphics*, **18** (3), 103–8

Catmull E. (1974). Subdivision algorithm for the display of curved surfaces. PhD Thesis, University of Utah

Catmull E. (1975). Computer display of curved surfaces. In *Proc. IEEE Conf. on Computer Graphics, Pattern Recognition and Data Structures*, May 1975 (Reprinted in Freeman H. (ed.) (1980). *Tutorial and Selected Readings in Interactive Computer Graphics*. New York (IEEE), pp. 309–15)

Catmull E. (1978). A hidden surface algorithm with anti-aliasing. *Computer Graphics*, **12** (3), 6–10

Catmull E. and Clark J. (1978). Recursively generated B-spline surfaces on arbitrary topological meshes. *Computer Aided Design*, **10** (6), 83–102

Chen S. E. and Williams L. (1993). View interpolation for image synthesis. *Proc. SIGGRAPH '93*, pp. 279–88

Chow M. M. (1997). Optimised geometry compression for real-time rendering. *Proc. IEEE Visualisation 97*

Clark J. H. (1979). A fast scan line algorithm for rendering parametric surfaces. *Computer Graphics*, **13** (2), 289–99

Cohen J. D., Lin M. C., Manocha D. and Pongami M. K. (1995). I-COLLIDE: An interactive and exact collision detection system for large scale environments. *Proc. 1995 Symp. on Interactive 3D Graphics* (Monterey CA) pp. 291–302

Cohen-Or D., Rich E., Lerner U. and Shenkar V. (1996). A real-time photo-realistic visual flythrough. *IEEE Trans on Visualisation and Computer Graphics*, **2**, (3), Sept.

Cook R. L., Carpenter L. and Catmull E. (1987). The REYES images rendering architecture. *Computer Graphics*, **21** (4), 95–102

Coorg S. and Teller S. (1997). Real-time occlusion culling for models with large occluders. *Proc. 1997 ACM Symposium, on Interactive 3D Graphics*, pp. 83–90 and 189

Cox M. G. (1972). The numerical evalutation of B-splines. *J. Inst. Maths. Applics.*, **10**, 134–49

Crow F. C. (1977). Shadow algorithms for computer graphics. *Computer Graphics*, **13** (2), 242–8

Crow F. C. (1981). A comparison of anti-aliasing techniques. *IEEE Computer Graphics and Applications*, **1** (1), 40–8

Crow F. C. (1987). The origins of the teapot. *IEEE Computer Graphics and Applications*, **7** (1), 8–19

De Boor C. (1972). On calculating with B-splines. *J. Approx. Th.*, **6**, 50–62

DeRose T., Kass M. and Truong T. (1998). Subdivision surfaces in character animation. *Proc SIGGRAPH '98*

Deering M. (1995). Geometry compression. *Proc. SIGGRAPH '95*, pp. 13–20

Diefenbach P. J. (1996). Pipeline rendering: Interaction and realism through hardware based multi-pass rendering. PhD Thesis (Computer and Information Science), Univ. Pennsylvania

Duchaineau M. A., Wolinsky M., Sigeti D. E., Miller M. C., Aldrich C. and Mineev-Weinstein M. B. (1997). ROAMing terrain: Real-time optimally adapting meshes. *Proc. IEEE Visualization 97*, October, pp. 81–8

Duff T. (1985). Compositing 3-D rendered images. *Computer Graphics*, **19** (3), 41–4

Duff T. (1986). Splines in animation and modelling. *SIGGRAPH Course Notes*, **15**

Dyn N., Levin D. and Gregory J. A. (1990). A butterfly subdivision scheme for surface interpolation with tension control. *ACM Trans. on Graphics*, **9** (2), 160–9

Evans F., Skiena and Varshney A. (1996). Optimising triangle strips for fast rendering. *Proc. IEEE Visualisation '96*, Oct, pp. 319–26

Farin G. (1990). *Curves and Surfaces for Computer Aided Design*. 2nd edn. Boston: Academic Press

Faux I. D. and Pratt M. J. (1979). *Computational Geometry for Design and Manufacture*. Chichester: Ellis Horwood

Fiume E., Fournier A. and Rudolph L. (1983). A parallel scan conversion algorithm with anti-aliasing for a general-purpose ultracomputer. *Computer Graphics*, **17** (3), 141–50

Foley J. D., Van Dam A., Feiner S. K. and Hughes J. F. (1989). *Computer Graphics: Principles and Practice*. Reading MA: Addison-Wesley

Forsey D. R. and Bartels R. H. (1988). Hierarchical B-spline refinement. *Computer Graphics*, **22** (4), 205–12

Fournier A., Fussell D. and Carpenter L. (1982). Computer rendering of stochastic models. *Comm. ACM*, **25** (6), 371–84

Fuchs H. (1980). On visible surface generation by *a priori* tree structures. *Computer Graphics*, **14**, 124–33

Funge J., Tu X. and Terzopoulos D. (1999). Cognitive modeling: Knowledge reasoning and planning for intelligent characters. *Proc. SIGGRAPH '99*, pp. 29–38

Funkhouser T. (1996). Database management for interactive display of large architectural models. *Graphics Interface*, 1–8

Garcia-Alonso A., Serrano N. and Flaquer J. (1995). Solving the collision detection problem. *IEEE Computer Graphics and Applications*, **14** (3), 36–43

Gortler S., Grzeszczuk R., Szeliski R. and Cohen M. F. (1996). The lumigraph. *Proc. SIGGRAPH '96*, pp. 43–52

Gottschalk S., Lin M. C. and Manocha D. (1996). OBB trees: A hierarchical structure for rapid interference detection. *Proc. SIGGRAPH '96*, pp. 171–80

Gouraud H. (1971). Illumination for computer generated pictures. *Comm. ACM*, **18** (60), 311–17

Gray J. (1968). *Animal Locomotion*. London: Weidenfeld and Nicolson

Greene N. (1986). Environment Mapping and Other Applications of World Projections. *IEEE Computer Graphics and Applications*, **6** (11), 21–9

Greene N. (1994). Detecting intersection of a rectangular solid and a convex polyhedron. *Graphics Gems IV*, ed. Heckbert, pp. 74–82

Haeberli P. and Segal M. (1993). Texture Mapping as a Fundamental Drawing Primitive. From: http://www.sgi.com/grafica/texmap/index.html

Haines E. (1991). Essential ray–convex polyhedron intersection. In *Graphics Gems II*, Arvo. J. (ed.) pp. 247–50. Boston: Harcourt Brace Jovanovich

Heckbert P. S. (1986). Survey of texture mapping. *IEEE Computer Graphics and Applications*, **6** (11), 56–67

Held M., Klosowski J. T. and Mitchell J. S. B. (1995). Evaluation of collision detection methods for virtual reality fly-throughs. *Proc. 7th Canadian Conf. Comp. Geometry*

Hoppe H. (1996). Progressive meshes. *Proc. SIGGRAPH '96*, pp. 99–108

Hoppe H., DeRose T., Duchamp T., Halstead M., Jin H., McDonald J., Schweitzer J. and Stuetzle W. (1994). Piecewise smooth surface reconstruction. *Proc. SIGGRAPH '94*, pp. 295–302

Hubbard P. M. (1993). Interactive collision detection. *Proc. IEEE Symp. on Res. Frontiers in Virtual Reality*, pp. 24–31

Hubbard P. M. (1996). *ACM Transactions on Graphics*, **15** (3), July, 179–210

Koestler A. (1967). *The Ghost in the Machine*. London: Hutchinson Pub. Group Ltd

Klosowski J., Held M., Mitchell J. S. B., Sowizral H. and Zikan K. (1998). Efficient collision detection using bounding volume hierarchies of k-dops. *IEEE Trans. On Visualization and Computer Graphics*, **4** (1), 21–36

Laird J. E. and Jones R. M. (1998). Building advanced autonomous systems for large scale real time simulations. *Proc. Game Developers Conf.* (Long Beach, CA), May

Landers J. (2000). Shades of Disney: Opaquing a 3D world. *Game Developer Magazine*, March

Lane J. M. and Riesenfeld R. F. (1980). A theoretical development for the computer generation and display of piecewise polynomial surfaces. *IEEE Trans. on Pattern Analysis and Machine Intelligence*, **2** (1), 35–46

Lane J. M., Carpenter L. C., Whitted T. and Blinn J. T. (1980). Scan line methods for displaying parametrically defined surfaces. *Comm. ACM*, **23** (1), 23–34

Lea R. L., Raverdy P. G., Honda Y. and Matsuda K. (1999). Scaling a shared virtual environment. Sony Computer Science Lab., Tokyo, Japan. http://www.csl.sony.co.jp/person/rodger

Lengyel J. and Snyder J. (1997). Rendering with coherent layers. *Proc. SIGGRAPH '97*, pp. 233–42

Levoy M. and Hanrahan P. (1996). Light field rendering. *Proc. SIGGRAPH '96*, pp. 31–42

Lewis J. P. (1989). Algorithms for solid noise synthesis. *Computer Graphics*, **23** (3), 263–70

Lin M. C. (1993). Efficient collision detection for animation and robotics. PhD Thesis, University of California, Berkeley

Lin M. C. and Gottschalk S. (1998). Collision detection between geometric models: a survey. IMA Conf. on Maths and Statistics

Lindstrom P., Koller D., Ribarsky W., Hodges L. F., Faust N. and Turner G. A. (1996). Real-time, continuous level of detail rendering of height fields. *Proc. SIGGRAPH*, pp. 109–18

Lippman A. (1980). Movie maps: an application of the optical videodisc to computer graphics. *Proc. SIGGRAPH '80*, pp. 32–43

Maciel P. W. and Shirley P. (1995). Visual navigation of a large environment using textured clusters. *Symposium on Interactive 3D Graphics*, April, pp. 95–102

Maes P., Darrell T., Blumberg B. and Pentland A. (1995). The ALIVE System: Full-body interaction with autonomous agents. *Proc. Computer Animation '95* (Geneva, April), IEEE Press

Mandelbrot B. (1977). *Fractals: Form, Chance and Dimension*. San Francisco CA: Freeman

Mandelbrot B. (1982). *The Fractal Geometry of Nature*. San Francisco CA: Freeman

Mantyla M. (1988). *Introduction to Solid Modelling*. Rockville MD: Computer Science Press

Mark W. R., McMillan L. and Bishop G. (1997). Post-rendering 3D warping. *Proc. 1997 Symposium on Interactive 3D Graphics*, pp. 7–16, Providence RI, April

McMillan L. (1995). *A List-priority Rendering Algorithm for Redisplaying Projected Surfaces*. UNC Technical Report 95-005, University of North Carolina

McReynolds T. and Blythe D. (1997). Programming with OpenGL: Advanced Rendering. From: http://www.sgi.com/software/opengl/advanced97/notes/

McReynolds T. and Blythe D. (1998). Advanced graphics programming techniques using OpenGL. *SIGGRAPH '98 Course Notes*. Also: http://www.sgi.com/software/opengl/advanced98/notes/notes.html

Megido M. (1983). Linear-time algorithms for linear programming in R^3 and related problems. *SIAM Journal of Computing*, **12**, 759–76

Miller G., Halstead M. and Clifton M. (1998). On-the-fly texture computation for real-time surface shading. *IEEE Computer Graphics and Applications*, March/April, pp. 44–58

Mirtich B. (1997). Efficient algorithms for two-phase collision detection. TR-97-23, Mitsubishi Electric Research Lab, available from: http://www.merl.com

Moore M. and Wilhelms J. (1988). Collision detection and response for computer animation. *Computer Graphics*, **22** (4), 289–98

Naylor B., Amanatides J. and Thibault W. (1990). Merging BSP trees yields polyhedral set operations. *Proc. SIGGRAPH '90*, pp. 115–24

Newell M. E., Newell R. G. and Sancha T. L. (1972). A new approach to the shaded picture problem. *Proc. ACM National Conf.*, pp. 443–50

Newman W. and Sproull R. (1973). *Principles of Interactive Computer Graphics*. New York: McGraw-Hill

Oppenheim A. V. and Shafer R. W. (1975). *Digital Signal Processing*. Englewood Cliffs NJ: Prentice Hall

Oppenheimer P. E. (1986). Real-time design and animation of plants and trees. *Proc. SIGGRAPH '86*, pp. 55–64

Peachey D. R. (1985). Solid texturing of complex surfaces. *Computer Graphics*, **19** (3), 279–86

Pedri P. (1999). Game Development in C++. http://www.ccnet.com/~paulp/GDCPP/GDCPP.html

Peercy M., Airey J. and Cabral B. (1997). Efficient bump mapping hardware. *Proc. SIGGRAPH '97*

Perlin K. (1985). An image synthesizer. *Computer Graphics*, **19** (3), 287–96

Perlin K. (1989). Hypertexture. *Computer Graphics*, **23** (3), 253–62. (*Proc. SIGGRAPH '98*)

Perlin K. and Velho L. (1995). Live paint: Painting with procedural multi-scale textures. *Proc. SIGGRAPH '95*, pp. 153–60

Phong B. (1975). Illumination for computer-generated pictures. *Comm. ACM*, **18** (6), 311–17

Piegl L. (1993). *Fundamental Developments of Computer-Aided Geometric Modelling*. New York: Academic Press

Porter T. and Duff T. (1984). Composing digital images. *Computer Graphics*, **18** (3), 253–9

Press W. H., Flannery B. P., Teukolsky S. A. and Vetterling W. T. (1988). *Numerical Recipes in C: The Art of Scientific Computing*. Cambridge, UK: Cambridge University Press

Rafferty M. M., Aliaga D. G., Popescu V. and Lastra A. A. (1998). Images for accelerating architectural walkthroughs. *IEEE Computer Graphics and Applications*, Nov/Dec, 38–45

Reeves W. T. (1983). Particle systems – a technique for modelling a class of fuzzy objects. *Computer Graphics*, **17** (3), 359–76

Reeves W. T. and Blau R. (1985). Approximate and probabilistic algorithms for shading and rendering structured particle systems. *Computer Graphics*, **19** (3), 313–22

Reeves W., Salesin D. and Cook R. (1987). Rendering antialiased shadows with depth maps. *Computer Graphics*, **21** (4), 283–91. (*Proc. SIGGRAPH '87*)

Regan M. and Pose R. (1994). Priority rendering with a virtual reality address re-calculation engine. *Proc. SIGGRAPH '94*, pp. 155–62

Reynolds C. W. (1987). Flocks, herds, and schools: a distributed behavioural model. *Computer Graphics*, **21** (4), 25–34

Rossignac J. (1999). Edgebreaker: Connectivity compression for triangle meshes. *IEEE Trans. On Visualisation and Computer Graphics*, **5** (1), Jan–Mar, 47–61.

Russell S. and Norvig P. (1995). *Artificial Intelligence: A Modern Approach*. Englewood Cliffs NJ: Prentice Hall

Schaufler G. and Sturzlinger W. (1996). A 3D image cache for virtual reality. *Proc. Eurographics '96*, August, pp. 227–36

Schroeder W. J., Zarge J. A. and Lorenson W. E. (1992). Decimation of triangular meshes. *Proc. SIGGRAPH '92*, 65–70

Schumaker R. A., Brand B., Guilliland M. and Sharp W. (1969). *Applying Computer Generated Images to Visual Simulation*. Technical Report AFHRL-Tr-69, US Airforce Human Resources Lab.

Scott N., Oolsen D. and Gannett E. (1998). An overview of VISUALIZE fx graphics accelerator hardware. *Hewlett-Packard Journal*, May, 28–34, http://www.hp.com/hpj/98may

Sederburg T. W. and Parry S. R. (1986). Free-form deformation of solid geometric models. *Computer Graphics*, **20** (4), 151–60

Seitz S. M. and Dyer C. R. (1996). View morphing. *Proc. SIGGRAPH '96*, pp. 21–30

Shade J., Gortler S., He L. and Szeliski R. (1998). Layered depth images. *Proc. SIGGRAPH '98*

Shade J., Lischinski D., Salesin D., DeRose T. and Snyder J. (1996). Hierarchical image caching for accelerated walkthroughs of complex environments. *Proc. SIGGRAPH '96*, pp. 75–82

Shoemake K. (1987). Quarternion Calculus and Fast Animation. *SIGGRAPH Course Notes*, **10**, 101–21

Singhal S. K. and Cheriton D. R. (1994). Exploiting position history for efficient remote rendering in networked VR. *Prescence: Teleoperators and Ves*, **4** (2), 169–99

Smith A. R. (1978). Color gamut transformation pairs. *Computer Graphics*, **12**, 12–19

Snyder J. M. (1992). *Generative Modelling for Computer Graphics*. New York: Academic Press

Snyder J. M. (1998). Visibility sorting and compositing without splitting for image layer decomposition. *Proc. SIGGRAPH '98*, pp. 219–30

Steed P. (1998). The art of low-polygon modelling. *Games Developer Magazine*, June, 62–9

Sutherland I. E. and Hodgman G. W. (1974). Reentrant polygon clipping. *Comm. ACM*, **17** (1), 32–42

Sutherland I. E., Sproull R. F. and Schumacker R. (1974). A characterization of ten hidden-surface algorithms. *Computer Surveys*, **6** (1), 1–55

Teller S. and Sequin C. H. (1991). Visibility pre-processing for interactive walkthroughs. *Proc. SIGGRAPH '91*, pp. 61–9

Thompson D'arcy (1961). *On Growth and Form*. Cambridge, UK: Cambridge University Press

Tu S. and Terzopoulos D. (1994). Perceptual modelling for the behavioural animation of fishes. *Proc. Second Pacific Conf. on Computer Graphics* (PG '94), Beijing, China

Van Hook D. J., Rak S. J. and Calvin J. O. (1994). Approaches to relevance filtering. 11th DIS Workshop, Sept.

van Lent M. and Laird J. (1999). Developing an artificial intelligence engine. *Computer Games Developer Conf.*, May

Ward G. J. (1994). The RADIANCE lighting simulation and rendering system. *Proc. SIGGRAPH '94*, pp. 459–71

Warnock J. (1969). *A Hidden-Surface Algorithm for Computer Generated Half-Tone Pictures*. Technical Report 4–15; NTIS AD-753 671, University of Utah Computer Science Department

Watt A. (1999). 3D Computer Graphics. Harlow: Addison-Wesley

Watt A. and Policarpo F. (1998). *The Computer Image*. Harlow: Addison-Wesley

Watt A. and Watt M. (1992). *Advanced Animation and Rendering Techniques*. Wokingham, England: Addison-Wesley

Weghorst H., Hooper G. and Greenberg D. P. (1984). Improved computational methods for ray tracing. *ACM Trans. on Graphics*, **3** (1), 52–69

Weiler K. and Atherton P. (1977). Hidden surface removal using polygon area sorting. *Computer Graphics*, **11** (2), 214–22

Williams L. (1978). Casting curved shadows on curved surfaces. *Computer Graphics*, **12** (3), 270–4

Williams L. (1983). Pyramidal parametrics. *Computer Graphics*, **17** (3), 1–11

Williams L. and Chen S. E. (1993). View interpolation for image synthesis. *Proc. SIGGRAPH '93*, pp. 279–88

Witkin A. and Kass M. (1988). Spacetime constraints. *Proc. SIGGRAPH '88*, pp. 159–68

Woo M., Neider J. and Davis T. (OpenGL Arhitecture Review Board) (1997). *OpenGL Programming Guide*. Reading MA: Addison-Wesley

Woodcock S. (1999). Game AI: The state of the industry. *Game Developer Magazine*, August

Zhang H. D., Manocha D., Hudson T. and Hoff III K. E. (1997). Visibility culling using hierarchical occlusion maps. *SIGGRAPH '97*, pp. 77–88

Zhukov S., Iones A. and Kronin G. (1998). Using light maps to create realistic lighting in real-time applications. *Proc. WSCG '98*. (Central European Conf. on Computer Graphics and Visualisation 1998)

Zorin D., Schroder P. and Sweldens W. (1996). Interpolating subdivision for meshes with arbitrary topology. *Proc. SIGGRAPH '96*, pp. 189–92

Index

AABBs 302, *303*, *439*, 443–8
AABBs, Fly3D 636–7
action games 370, 486
adaptive subdivision 140
addition, vectors 10, *10*
affine transformations 2, *44*, 45
agent architectures 493–8
agents 484–6, 496–7
    goal-based 491–3
    and hierarchies 490–3
    interactions 485
    reflex or reactive 491–2
AI *see* behaviour and AI
algorithmic operations 172
algorithms
    Bar-Yehuda-Gotsman 60–1
    culling *135*, *159*
    curve subdivision 46
    graph theory 60–1, *61*
    HSR 182, 185, 187, 189
    LOD 63
    non-u B-splines 101
    patch rendering 131
    patch subdivision 37
    patch to polygon 80
    polygon mesh render 189
    ray-convex 19
    screen space 189
    shading 2, 34, 37, 246
    shadow 329, 333–9
    skinning 42, *42*
    stripification 58
    tri-strip 58–9
    vertex insertion 157
aliasing 63, 216, 246–9, 251–2
ALIVE system 491–2
alpha blending 348
ambient light 195–7, 314, 321, 324
animal-human motion 393–5, 397
animated mesh, Fly3D 622–624
animation 32, 242–3, 337, 369–76
    shape changing 35
    visual disturbance 40
animators 368–9, 393–7, 399, 400
anti-aliasing 172, 245–69, 282, 318
arc length parametrization 46

arch, object 148, *149*, 150
architectures, AI approaches 487–90
artefacts 342, 344
    alias 247–9, 251–2
    image 245–6
    visual lighting 316
articulated structures 392–401, 445
artificial intelligence *see* AI
attributed tree 47
axes
    coordinate 46
    of rotation 5
    separating 450–1, *450*
    of symmetry 3, 174

B-spline curves 87–91, 102, 115–16
    locality 93
    non-rational 107
    non-uniform 96–101
    NURBS 106
    rational 106–7
    uniform 92–6
    variation 101
B-spline patches 115–16, 121, 124
B-spline surfaces 153–4, 156–7
back to front 346, 351–2
back-face culling 288–9
back-face elimination 179–80, 190
back-facing polygons 336, 360
basic maths, 3D space 1
basic maths engine, SIMD 22–30
behaviour-AI 368–9, 393, 484–515
Bezier curve, Fly3D 626–9
Bezier curve segments 88–90, 127
Bezier curves 82–92, 104–6, 108
Bezier method 109, 114, 118, 121
Bezier patch boundary 122, 127–30
Bezier patch, Fly3D 630–5
Bezier patch meshes 117, 123, 131
Bezier patch subdivision 158–9
Bezier patch surfaces 139–40
Bezier patches 81–2, 112–14
Bezier, Pierre 82–3, 113, 125
Bezier technology, games 139–53
bi-cubic parametrics *see* patches
bi-cubic patches *see* patches

billboards 541–3, 545–7
birds and fishes 493–5, 497–8
blending 348, 351–2, 364, 366
blurring *see* image blurring
bodies 437, 439
Boolean set operators 47–50
boundaries *see* patches
boundary model, vertex based 39
bounding boxes *see* AABBs;OBBs
bounding boxes, Fly3D 636–7
bounding spheres 190–1, 478–9
bounding volume geometry 302–4
bounding volumes 16–17, 20, 75–6
brightness, texture 315
broad phase, collisions 438–53
BSP faces-leaf node, Fly3D 732–3
BSP object, Fly3D 639–45
BSP technology, landscapes 292–4
BSP tree node, Fly3D 638
BSP trees 190, 272–3, 308
   collisions 438, 459–60
   exact visibility 312–13
   visibility 277–94
BSPs and PVS 295–6
buffers 349–50, 352, 354
bump maps 217, 227–31, 365–6
butterfly scheme 156–7, 168–9
butterfly subdivision 158–70

C++ programming, games 595–602
caching 315
CAD
   B-spline curves 101
   Bezier curves 79–84
   curve-to-surface 113
   IBR 567
   polygon mesh 33, 47
   rational curves 106, 107
   render surface 131, 138–9
   shadows 337
   subdivision 157
cameras 69, 174–9, 570
   interactive 477–8
   motion control 386–7
car simulation 473–7
Catmull 154–5, 157, 227, 254
client server, mp games 586–94
clippings 17, 205, 290
   algorithmic ops 189–93
   anti-aliasing 254
   environments 295–6
   maths 16
   rendering 273, 283
   shadows 336–7
   view 181–2, 185, 187
cognitive modelling 498–503
coherences 273, 445
   collisions 438, 440–2
   landscapes 69
   polygon render 190
   scenes 304–5, 311–12
collision detection 302, 437–66

control 369
   maths 14, 16
   model 32, 69
   render 270–4
colour
   aliasing 252, 253
   landscapes 69, 72
   lighting 315
   render 174, 198, 199, 214
colour maps 53, 216, 217, 227
comparative review, model 31–52
complex curves 88, 111
complex movement 373
complex objects 3, 9
   geometry 50
   landscapes 80
   polygons 32–4, 36
   rendering 280, 320
complex scenes 173, 180, 189
   alg ops 206, 209
   lighting 316
   visibility 270–313
complexity, visual 31
compositing 206, 347, 349
compression 53–6, 170, 516, 518–19
computer aided design *see* CAD
computer animation 82, 86, 125, 393
   control 368–9
   interact 467–8
   maths 16
   render 333
computer games 174, 180, 214, 224
   AI 485, 487, 491
   collisions 437–8
   control 403–5, 424
   interact 467–70
   lighting 320, 321
   maths 1, 139–53
   MP render 348, 360
   technology 516, 526
   visibility 270, 296
computer graphics 1, 245, 258, 401
   AI-behaviour 518
   alias 248–52
   camera 386
   dynamic 402, 403
   maths 9–10
   model 115, 125
   motion 369, 370
   polygons 31
   quality 33
   shadows 340
conceptual hierarchy mesh 37, *38*
conic sections 106, 107
connected quads, polygon mesh 59
connectivity 56–8, 66, 335
constant shading 72
continuous image domain 254
control grid, Bezier 124, 125
control, local 90, 91, 101, 121
control mesh 155, *156*
control points 101, 106, 114

control points *(continued)*
   B-splines 91–8, 100
   Bezier curves 84–91
   Bezier techno 148
   curve-surface 112
   patches 118, 120–8
   render 135
control polyhedra 107–8, 112–14
   patches 117, 130
   subdivision 153
controller module 467–70
convert patch to polygon 131–9
convert polygon-shaded object 172
convert solid-triangles 148, *149*
convex hulls 87, 90, 94, 136–137
convex objects 42, 439
coordinate axes 5, 46
coordinate spaces 2, 172, *173*, 174
coordinate systems 2–4, 7–9, 46, 190
   LH-RH *3*, 12
   local 173–7
   render 272, 316
   view 174–9
   world 176–7
coordinates 54, 66
costs 2, 32
Cox de Boor algorithm 101
creases, limit surfaces 157–8
cropping *341*, 342
cross-product vectors 11–12
cross-sections 83, 118–20
   model patch 117, 148
   sweeps 42–6, 82
cube convergence to cylinder 157
cubic curves 79
cubic mapping 233–5, 237
cubic spline *87*
culling
   BSP trees 282–3, 288–9
   collisions 439
   environment 295–6
   exact visibility 307–12
   maths *135*, 157, 159
   MP render 354
   polygon render 179–80, 190
   shadows 335–6
   visibility 271–3
curve continuity 100, 103, 108, 130
   B-spline 92–6
   Bezier 88, 89
   patch 121–2, 125
   subdivision 153
   to surface 111–13
curve, degree of 90, 91
curve interpolation 110, 125–7
curve network *128*, *129*
curve segments
   B-spline 91–5, 100
   patches 127, 129
   rational 107
curve splitting 134–5
curve subdivision algorithm 46

curved spine objects 43, 45, 324
curved surfaces 34, 36–7, 79
curves 91–103, 124
curves, B-spline *see* B-spline
curves, Bezier *see* Bezier curves
curves, parameter range 94–5, 97
curves, profile *see* profile
cylinders 106, 123, 137, 140, 157
   IBR 569–71
   mapping 221–2

data structures 1, 37–9, 270, 273
death match games 485, 586
decision cycles, AI-behaviour 491
deformations 108, 121–2, 125
depth comparison 342, 349
depth data 182, 185, 187, 551–9
depth field 363
Desk Top Publishing (DTP) 86
destroyable light sources 322
detail modulation 365
diffuse reflection 195–7, 199, 204
   light 315, 318
digitizers 32, 37, 41, 81, 127
direct-indirect illumination 195–6
directional light source 200, *201*
DirectPlay 587–8
DirectX interface, Fly3D 652–8
displacement 1, 4, 70–2, 217, 227
display surface 2, *173*
distortion 124–5, *186*
disturbance, visual 62, 246
downsampling bi-quad meshes 139–48
drawing objects 364
du Chaineau 72, 73, *74*
ducted solids 114, 137, 148, *149*
dynamic control 369, 402–36
dynamic lights 314, 318, 320–4
   polygon 173
   shadows 329, 341
dynamic lights, Fly3D 652–8
dynamic objects 173–4, 273–313
dynamic simulation 418–30, 467–70
dynamics theory, classical 404–5

economy 170, 316
edges, polygon 65–7
editing 80–1, 120–5
editors-modellers, software 51
efficiency 32, 35, 42, 270, 273, 439
elapsed time 370–2, 391, 479
encoding 54–7
engine architecture 595–616
engines 172, 315
environment maps 216–17, 221, 315
   compare 243–4
   cubic 233–5, 237
   lat-long 233, 237
   object 234–5
   reflection 231–8
   sphere 235–7
environments 2, 273, 331, 485

lighting 315, 318, 320
visibility 295–6
Euler 56, 59, 376–7, 431–3, 473
explosions 348, 388–92
extraordinary points 154–6, 158
extrapolation *see* mip-mapping
extrusion-lofting 43, 45, 52, 75
eye coordinate system 174–9, 187

Fann 124, *129*, 130
filtering 361
aliasing 247–8, 252–60
lighting 323–4
shadows 340–1
finite state machines (FSM) 486–90
first person shooter games 459–60
flame simulation 242–3
flat shaded polygons 204, 212, 214
flatness 138–9, 148
flight simulators 68–9, 178–9
collision 438
render 272, 280
Fly3D directories 666
Fly3D engine main interface 673–94
Fly3D face 659–61
Fly3D fans and strips mesh 734–6
Fly3D file loading 662–5
Fly3D globals
constants 618–20
functions 621
macros 620
variables 620–1
Fly3D objects
anim-mesh 622–4
base-object 625
bezier-curve 626–9
bezier-patch 630–5
boundbox 636–7
bsp-node 638
bsp-object 639–45
class-desc 646–7
console 648–51
directX 652–8
face 659–61
fly-pak 662–5
fly-pak-util 666
flydll 667
flydllgroup 668–72
flyEngine 673–94
light-map 695–8
light-map-pic 699–700
light-vertex 701–2
local-system 703–4
mat4x4 705–6
mesh 707–11
mp-games 712
mp-msg 713
param-desc 714–15
particle 716–17
picture 718–21
plane 722
player-data 723

render 724–6
renderGL 727–9
sound 730–1
static-mesh 732–3
stripfan-mesh 734–7
textcache 737–40
textcacheGL 741–4
vector 745–8
Fly3D plug-in dll 667–2
Fly3D plug-in object 714–15
Fly3D plug-ins 617, 638, 640, 646, 667, 714, 732
Fly3D SDK reference 617–748
Fly3D SDK tutorials 749–78
Fly3D SDKref
classes 617, 622–748
engine ref manual 617
Fly3D.dll library 617
Fly3D.h file 617
Fly3D.lib files 617
front-ends 617, 679
globals index 617
objects index 617
plug-ins *see* Fly3D
utilities 617, 666
Fly3D software
behaviour plug 604
C++ inheritance 604
design 604
fly engine 604–6
front-ends 610–16
game development 604
plug-ins 606–10
rendering 610–16
Fly3D software architecture 604–16
Fly3Dtut
dynamic objects 763–4
front-end create 775–8
level model build 749–52
level model complx 753–5
level script .Fly file 758
level.BSP file 756–7
level.LMP file 759
level.PVS file 760
player object new 770–4
plug-ins, add 761–2
plug-ins, new 765–6
plug-ins objects 767–9
fog 180, 290, 322, 364
fog maps 54, 322–4, 348
footprints, screen pixel *69*, 77
forces in dynamics 405–8
forward mapping 218–19, 317
four-D (projective) space 104
Fourier 70, 245, 248, 251–2, 256
Fourier techno 516, 518–19, 525–6
Fourier transform images 264–9
fractals 68, 70, *71*
frames 122, 190, 282–3, 516
free-form 82, 83, 120, 125
Frenet frame 46, *46*
frequency domain-spectrum 247–9

front-facing polygons 336, 360
fuzzy state machines (FUSM) 489–90

games 1, 218, 318, 320, 478, 602
    C++ programming 595–602
    characters 484–5
    Fly3D console 648–51
    Fly3D objects 646–7
    players 174, 369–70, 467
    technology 131, 174
    world 491, 496, 503
games applications 34, 40, 52, 170
    collision 439
    rendering 346
games engines see engines
games industry 31–2, 172–3
    motion 368, 393, 401
generators neg and pos 36
geometric operations 172–4, 189
geometric primitives 35, 47, 51–2
geometry 2, 44, 45, 302–4
geometry, CSG see CSG
geomorphs 66
global shape changing 123–5
glowing objects 348
Gourard shading 193–5, 201–4
    bump maps 230
    light maps 315
    lighting 322, 324
    maths 54, 110
    render 172, 212–13
graph theory algorithm 60–1
graphics 1
    anti- aliasing 245–69
    mapping 215–44
    polygon render 172–214
graphics APIs 172, 177, 178
graphics pipeline 40, 62
graphics processors 53, 80, 170
grids 68, 115–16, 123–5, 292

Haines ray-convex algorithm 19
haloes, explosions 348
hardware, 3D 172
height fields 68–9, 72–3, 76, 227
hidden surface removal see HSR
hidden surfaces 205–6, 208–11
hierarchical occlusion map 310–11
hierarchy 271–4, 279, 301–2, 312
    control 438–9, 444–5
highlights197 199, 201–2, 204
holes 48, 553, 555–6, 560
Hoppe 64–7
HSR 179–80, 182, 185, 187, 189
    polygons 204–12
    render 271, 273, 280, 305–7
    shadows 336–8
Hubbard time critic 440–2, 464–6
Huffman coding 55
human-animal move 393–5, 397, 403

IBR 216, 540–71
identity matrix 6
illumination 195–6, 315, 318, 330
image, aliased 362
image artefacts 245–6
image based rendering see IBR
image blurring 258, 264, 361–2
image generation 245, 569
image layering 548
image metamorphis see morphing
image planes 187, 246–7, 250, 296
image processing 516, 518, 531
image processors 250, 251
image pyramids 64, 310–12, 516–18
image rendering 346–7, 349–50
image synthesis 250, 251, 252, 256
image technology 525–6
image transforms 264–9, 516, 519
image, virtual 256, 256, 257
image warping 218–24, 260
images 34, 37, 54, 62, 311
implicit rep., objects **35–6**
instancing an object 3
Intel Pentium instructions 22
interaction 1, 467, 485
    case studies 470–6
interactive 106, 224
    control 369, 467–83
    modelling 81
    patch design 120–8
interior points 21
intermediate surfaces 220–4
interpolation 37, 81, 116, 186
    bi-linear 21–2, 316
    butterfly scheme 168
    control points 95–100
    curves 110, 125–7
    linear 370–3
    mapping 219–20
    motion 376–8
    shading 201–4
    subdivision 156–8
    surfaces 127–30
intersection testing see rays
intersections, ray see rays
inverse transformations 5, 9
isoparametric curves 133
isosurfaces 36

jagged edges 70, 249–50

k-dops 439, 443, 451
key frames 125, 402
keyboard-key press 470, 473
kinematic-motion ctrl 368–401, 467
knots 92, 94, 96–103, 106, 115–16, 122, 126, 128

landscapes 68–70, 292–4
laser rangers 32, 41–2, 125
learning architectures 505–15
learning back prop alg 515

learning neural nets 506–9
learning perceptrons 508–15
lens flare 314
level of detail *see* LOD
LH world coordinate system 2, *3*
light 314–16, 318, 321–2, 324
    fields 243, 321, 564–6
    Fly3D 695–700
light direction vectors 14, *15*
light intensity 194–6, 200–2
    shadows 329–30
light maps 54, 148, 173, 215, 243
    games 314–28
    render 348, 365, 367
    shadows 340
light objects 360, *360*, 361
light rays *187*
light reflect *see* reflected light
light sources 14, 174
    graphics 194–201
lighting 173, 314–22, 324, 326–8
    case studies 323–8
    environment 331
    in games 218
    resolution 80, 324, *325*
lights dynamic *see* dynamic lights
lights static *see* static lights
limit surfaces 153–4, 156–8
Lin-Canny features alg 438, 455–7
line segment subdivision *71*
linear axis cross section 118–20
linear filtering 324
linear interpolation 370–3
linear transforms 37, 45, 47, 317
    concatenated 7
    Fly3D 705–6
    rotations 2–9
    scalings 6–9
    shears 2
    translate 2–9
linearity test 46
list, linked polygon coords 37
list, polygon points 1–2
local coordinate 3, 7, 9, 173–7, 190
local reflect models *see* shading
local spatial curvature 37
local surface curvature 68, 133, 137
local system Fly3D 703–4
locality, butterfly scheme 168–9
LOD 53, 68–9, 72–3, 80, 131, 140, 170–1,
    263–4, 348
LOD algorithms 63
LOD processing 62, 63, 65
lofting 324
look-at point utility 177–8
loss *see* image compression
lumels 316–18
lumographs *see* light fields

magnitudes *see* lengths
map, texture *see* texture mapping
maps and filtering 324

maps and mapping *see* under name
masks, Catmull subdivision *155*
masks, modified butterfly *169*
maths, basic *see* basic maths
matrices 3–4, *6*, 7–8, 22
meshes 123, 131
    3D object Fly3D 707–11
    Bezier patch 113–14, 117
    butterfly refine *156*, 157
    compression 64
    downsampling 139–48
    optimization 64
    polygon 2, 11, 32, 218–27
    strip-fan, Fly3D 734–6
    transformation 64–5, 67
    warping, 2spline 535–9
message data
    compression 580, 581
    consistency 584–6
    predictive 581–4
minimal surface 122, *123*
mip-maps 63, 78, 323–4, 516, 518
    anti-aliasing 259–64
mirror vectors 14, *15*
mirrors 297, 352
missile trails 314
model shapes, interactive 80–1
modellers-editors, software 51–2
modelling 2–3, 34, 47, 81, 125, 174
modelling transformations 9
morphing 516, 518, 531–9
    2D images 533–5
    vertex 371
motion capture 368–70, 373, 392–3, 401
motion control 368–401, 403, 467
    AI 485–6
motion curve *374*
motion, smooth 125
movement, 3D objects 1
MUD game 573
    definitions 573–4
    delay origins 576–8
    delay semantics 578–80
    implement 574–6, 586–94
multi-pass rendering 346–7
multi-pass sampling 361–4
multi-pass shadow volumes 355–60
multi-passing, bump mapping 230
multi-player enumerate, Fly3D 712
multi-player game technology 572–94
multi-player message, Fly3D 713
multi-texture 363–7

narrow phase 438–9, 444
    collision 453–8
nets of patches 34
network interface, mp game 587–94
Newton, Isaac 404, 406–7, 473
noise function, spatial 239
normal vec perturb *see* displace
normal vector perturb *see* bump map
normal vectors, polygon 11, *11*, 12

normalization of vectors 11
normals 11, 12, 37, 174
    surface 12, 14, 17
notation, matrix 3–4
notation, subdivision 154–5, 158
numerical integration 403, 431–6
numerical milling machine 80, 81, 83
NURBS non-u rat B-spline curves 106

OBBs 304, *439*, 443, 445, 447–9
object boundary 275
object orientation 376
object position, locating 374, *374*
object rep 43, 270, 273, 275
    bi-cubic 31–7, 114
    CSG 32–3, 35, 37, 49–50
    implicit **35–6**
    mesh 32–4, 36–47
    patches 32, 34–5, 37
    spacial subdivision 35
object space 35, 121, 131–4, 136–8
    lighting 316–17
    mapping 218, *218*
    visible 274, 311–12
object surface 2, 81, 275, 317
objects 1–3, 32, 37, 114, 273
    base Fly3D 625
    clusters 272
    construction 51–2
    control of 467
    example 118–19, 148–50
    generation 41, 139
    hierarchies 272
    interactive 467, 478–9
    light 314–15, 320–2, 324
    matting 234–5
    motion of 368, 468
    mp render 348, 352, 360–1
    occupancy 274–5
    shadows 329, 341
    size projection 34
    in space 274, *274*
    subdivision 271
    visibility 312–13
    visualisation 117
objects, animated 174, 313–15
    collision 444
    interact 479
    light 320–2
    motion 369
    render 355, 361
objects, complex 32–4, 36, *50*
objects, complexity reduction 148
obstacles, avoidance of 491
occlusion culling 282, 308–12
occlusion maps 516–17
octree decomposition, scene 205
octrees 272–3, 275–8, 311–12
off-line animation 373, 402–3
offsets *see* world coord systems
opaque colour or objects 214, 348
OpenGL 177, 179, 346, 348–50

operations algorithmic 172, 189–212
operations geometric 172–4, 189
operations viewspace 179–89
ordering far and near 282, 284–5
orthogonal vectors 46
orthographic projection 184, 236
orthographic, undersampling 237

painting pack-alg 69, 282–3, 313
panoramas, compositing 571
parallelpiped 84, *84*, 87
parameter space 115–16
parametric surfaces 12, 131–9
parametrization *16*, 218, 375–8
    uniform 126
particle animation 387–92, 441, 493
particle collision, Fly3D 718–21
particles theory, classic 406–8
partition planes 281, 285, 289, 291
partitions 270–2, 274, 277–80, 292, 297, 306,
    313
patch surface 12, 81, 107, 116, 123, 131, 136,
    153
patches 59, 122–4, 316–17, 324
    Bezier 81–2, 113–14, 117
    bi-cubic 31–2, 34–5, 43
    boundary 112–13, 127–30
    deformation 108, 121–2
    derivative vec 109–10, 113
    flatness 132–3, 136–7
    joining 111, *111*, 113
    meshes 117, 131, 170–71
    min pixel area 138
    models 324–6
    net of 34, 120–5
    polygon convert 80, 131–9
    rendering 63, 131
    representations 80–1
    segments 116, *116*
    shape of 34
    splitting *132*, 133
    subdivision 37, 70, 227
    surface fitting 125–30
patchification *see* patches
perspective map 106, 260
perspective transformations 88
Phong shading 54, 110, 137, 193, 195
    contd 196–207, 213
    light 315–16, 324
    map 215–16, 244
photo-modelling IBR 566–71
photographic panoramas IBR 570
photography 33–4, 224–5, 566–7, 569, 571
piecewise polynomial curve 88, 91–2
pixels 21, 40, 42, 53, 62–3, 282
    aliasing 252–4, 258–60
    landscapes 69, 76–8
    light 318, 321–2, 325–6
    and picture Fly3D 718–21
    polygon render 193–201
    surface render 131, 138
    technology 516

planar
    curves 124, *124*
    graph 58
    impostors 543–5, 548
    patches 123, 124
    polygons 2
    reflections 352–5
    sprites 543, 548, *549*, 551
    surfaces 37, *38*
planar geometric projections 182–4
planar separator *see* graph theory
plane, 3Dspace, Fly3D 722
planes 77, 226, 316, 457–8
player data, mp games, Fly3D 723
plug-ins, Fly3D 667–2, 714–15
point light sources 331, 340
points 1, 2, 37
points control *see* control points
points set 1, 3
polygon count 31–3, 52, 62, 189–90
polygon facet net *see* polygon mesh
polygon facet vert *see* points set
polygon mesh 2, 11, 37–40, 59, 70–1
    graphics 172, 189
    mapping 216–17, 219
    model 79–82, 113–15
    patch surfs 117, 124
    render 131, 285–8
    scalability 170–1
    subdivision 153
polygonal facets 1, 36, 39, 70–1
polygonal objects 40–7
polygonal resolution 32, 34, 40, 42
    light 324–5
    model 131, 170
polygons 281–2, 316, 335–8, 341
    attributes 39–40
    edges 38–40, 65–7, 316
    light map corr 317–18
    normal vector to 11–12
    normals 37, 174
    point list 1–3, 37
    projection 317
    rendering 21
    size 37
    vertices 32, 37–41, 272
popping LOD switches levels 348
portal imagery with LDIs 558–9
portals 295–301
pre-calculation, bump mapping 231
pre-prepared animation 369
pre-scripted animation 369–6, 467
precalculated lights 173
profile curves 118–20
projection 182–3, 187
projection, 2D screen 1
projective transformations 218
PVS approach 295–9
pyramid, viewing 188–9
pyramids, detail 63, 65
pyramids, image 64

quadtrees 275–9, 526–8
Quake II and III 140, 496–7, 504
quality image 37, 62
quality object visualisation 117
quantization process Chow 55–6
quaternions, rotation 378–86

radiosity 189, 193, 215, 315–16, 330, 568
rail curve product surface 43–4
rational B-spline curves 106–7
rational Bezier curves 104
rational curves 88, 104–6
raw sound data, Fly3D 730–1
ray casting 14, 76, 340, 459
ray intersects 274, 279, 342, 439
    ray-box 20–1
    ray-convex 17–19
    ray-sphere 16–17
ray tracing 35, 189, 193, 215–17
    cntrl 439, 447, 465–6
    contd 231–2, 236, 244
    rend 274, 279, 315, 354
    technology 557
rays 14, 16, 76–8, 187, *187*, 321
real worlds 490–1
reference frame 122
refined patches 122–3
reflected light 195–6, 243, 315, 316, 329–30
reflected shadows 329–30, 340
reflected view 231, 243
reflection
    diffuse 315, 318
    models 11, 244
    planar 352–5
    vectors 14, *15*
region of influence 314, 321
regular grid, points 123
render pipe *see* graphics pipeline
rendered imagery 34, 541–77
renderers 32–3, 37, 39, 80, 203–4, 254–5
rendering 37, 172, 190, 313, 317
    base Fly3D 724–6
    efficiency 35, 42, 273
    examples 212–14
    feasability RT 32
    hardware *see* renderers
    IBR 564–6
    meshes 172–214
    multi-pass 346–7
    OpenGL Fly3D 727–9
    operations 173
    param surfaces 131–9
    patches 63, 131
    polygons 21, 189–90
    resources 547–51
    software 172
    speed-ups 273
    time 32, 60
represent, object *see* object rep
representation 1, 4, 35, 47, 49
resolution 32, 34, 40, 42, 80
RGB 347–9

RH world coordinate system 2, 3, 12
rigid bodies 370, 374, 376, 393
    classic theory 408–18
    dynamic control 404
robot flying object 479–82
rotation 3, 5, 43
    interpolation 376–8
    line transforms 2, 3, 5–9
    quaternions 378–86

sampling 237, 246–52, 316, 361–2
    frequencies 256
    sphere surface *237*
scalability 170–1
scale problems 40
scaling matrices 3
scalings transforms 2–7, 9, 88, 188
scan conversion 133, 317
scan line algorithms 205, 208–11
scan line renderer 39, 254–5
SCAR system 490, 495–97, 505
scenes 2, 9, 272, 275, 317, 330
    decomposition 272, 275
    hierarchy 271, *271*
    manage 190, 271–2, 274–5
    render 172–4, 190, 205
    subdivision 270, 274, 316
    visible 273, 280, 285–8
screen footprint *69*, 172
screen projection 1, 40, 172
screen space 173, 175, 182–7
    contd 189, 218
    landscape 68–9, 75
    surfaces 131, 138–9
    visibility 302, 308
scripting, explicit 468, *468*
search path length *278*
self-reflection 244
sensing role AI 503–4
shaded object 172
shaded surfaces 88
shading 12–13, 54, 72, 110, 137
    algs 2, 34, 37, 194, 246
    lighting 315, 317, 320, 324
    mapping 227, 230, 243–4
    polygon 172, 189, 193–205
shadow algs 329, 333–9, 344, 355
shadow volume 329, 334–7, 346, 357–60
shadows 321, 329–34, 336, 340–5, 362–3, 367
    edges 315
    mapping 244, 329, 348
shape 32, 34, 35, 47, 81
shape changing 35–6, 55, 80–1, 90, 116,
    123–5
shape surface 107–8
shears, transforms 2, 362, *363*
shiny objects 216, 231
ship death 477–8
shrinkwrap inverse map 221, 223–4
silhouette edges 227, 334–6
SIMD 22–30
single phase 438, 444, 459–66

situation calculus 498–503
skinning algorithm 42, *42*
skins 83
Snyder, J M 43, *44*
solids-revolution 37, 43, 114, 174
sort and sweep broad phase 445–6
source code SIMD basic engine 22–30
space 1–5, 35, 54, 125, 172–3
    2D 316
    4D projective 104
    domain rep 246, 248–9
    object 35, 121, 131–2
    parameter 115–16
    partitioning 277, 280
    screen *see* screen space
space curves 82–7
spatial coordinates 37
spatial curvature 37
spatial freqs 246–8, 258, 264–6
spatial noise function 239
spatial occupancy 272, 274
spatial orientation 5
spatial part 274, 297, 306, 438–9, 444,
    449–52
spatial subdivision 35, 273–4, 312
spatial variables 86
specular reflect 195–7, 201, 204, 231, 567
sphere bound vol 439, 443, 462–3
sphere influence 314, 318, 321–3, 340–1, 360
sphere influence visibility 291
sphere mapping 232, 235–7
sphere tree, collision 464–5
spheres, interaction 35–6
splines, cubic *87*
split curves 134–5
split and merge operations 74–6
split patches *132*, 133
split planes 277, 292–3
spotlights 321
state transition 479–80, 488–9
static light 314, 340
static objects 173, 314–15, 321–2, 329, 478
static objects, Fly3D 732–3
straight spine objects 43, *43*
strategy games 482, 526
strip structure polygon mesh 324
stripification algs 58, 170, 324–6
stylised rendering 213–14
subdivision 63, 110, 121, 227
    algorithms 37, 70
    Bezier techno 148–53
    BSP trees 278–9
    landscapes 70–1
    param 131, 134–5, 137
    RT render 270–1, 274
    surfaces 153–71
supersampling 254, 256–9, 361–2
surface domain 108
surface normal vectors 12, 14, 18
surface normals17 72, 110–11, 157
surfaces 2, 43–4, 81–3, 87–8
    attributes 174

B-spline 153–4, 156–7
bi-cubic parametric 12
contd 122–3
curved 34, 36–7, 63, 68
fitting 81, 125–31
interpolation 127–30
shape 107–8
sphere sampling *237*
subdivision 153–71, 227
surfaces patch 81, 107, 115–16, 121, 124, 131, 136
Sutherland 41, 191, *192*, 205
sweeping cross sections 42–6
switchable light sources 322
symmetry, axis of 3

tank object texture 224, *225*
teapots 113, *114*, 136, 528, *528*
tears from subdivision *134*, 137
terrain modelling 34, 72, 76
texels 261–2, 316–18
texture
    cache, Fly3D 737–40
    cache OpenGL Fly3D 741–4
    coordinates, interpol 66
    detail 315
    domains 3D 238–43
    elements *see* texels
    filtering 340–1
    patterns 221, 239, 258–9
    practical map 224–7
    solid 238, 241
    space 2D *see* two-D space
texture coordinates interpol 66
texture maps 14, 33–4, 40, 53, 63
texture maps 2D
    bilinear 219–20
    forward 218–19
    inverse 218–24
    meshes 218–27
    surfaces 220–4
texture maps
    aliasing 246, 258–64, 69, 76, 78
    lighting 315–18, 324
    mapping 215–27, 238
    multi-pass rend 363
    polygon 172, 176, 214
    shadows 329, 340–1
    techno 518, 526, 566
three dimensional 3D *see* three-D
three-D
    card 53, 173, 189, 193, 208
    geometry 2, *44*, 45
    graphics 1, 4, 9–10, 115
    objects 1–3, 35
    points set 3
    scenes 2, 9
    space 1–5, 35, 54, 125
    space curves 82
    transformations 2
three-D digitizers 32, 37, 41, 81
three-D face, Fly3D 659–61

three-D mesh Fly3D 707–11, 732–6
three-D object space 218, 238, 316
three-D StudioMax Fly3D 749–56
three-D vector Fly3D 745–8
time 440–2, 464–6
topic areas dynamic control 404–5
topology 153–4
transformations *see* transforms
transforms 108, 174–6, 178–9
    affine 2, *44*, 45
    concatenated 7
    contd 184–6, 187, 218
    curve 88
    inverse 5, 9
    linear 2–4, *6*
    matrices 5, 7, 8
    modelling 9
    perspectivd 88
    projective 218
    viewing 9
translational surface 130
translations *see* linear transforms
transparency 208, 283, 346, 348, 352
tree traversal 122, 283–8, 445
trees 247–77, 447–8, 451, 459–60
    attributed 47
    collision detect 464–5
    CSG *49*
tri-linear interpol 262–3
tri-strips 53, 57–60, 62, 170
tri-strips-fans, Fly3D 734–6
triangle
    bintrees 72–6
    meshes 56–63, 68
    scenes made of 317
    strips *see* tri-strips
    subdivision *71*
triangular facets 131, *132*
trivarate Bezier 124–5
turbulence, simulating 240–3
turret gun interactive 478–9
two dimensional 2D *see* two-D
two-D
    environment view 2
    screen projection 1
    screen space 218, *218*
    space 218, 238, 316
    techniques 516–39
    texture *see* texture space
typefaces 86, *87*

undersampling *237*, 246
uniform grid 68
uniform subdivision 140
UNISURF Bezier CAD system 82
user 32
    interaction 467
    interfaces 32, 42, 176
    projection *568*, 569
user-object
    animation 473–6
user-objectinteraction 467, 471–3

user-scene interaction 482–3
Utah teapot 113, *114*, 136

vectors
  addition of 10, *10*
  cross-product 11, 12
  direction 10
  dot-product 12, 13, *13*
  four coords Fly3D 745–8
  length (magnitude) 10
  matrix 22
  normals 11, *11*, 12
  orthagonal 46
  surface normals 14, *15*
  translation 3
  view 176–8, 199–200
vectors derivative *see* patch deriv
velocity vectors 471–4
vertex *see* vertices
vertex insertion alg subdivision 157
vertex normals 37, 67, 110, 137–8, 174, 201–3
vertex valence 156, *156*, 158
vertices
  buffers using 60–2
  colour 66
  connectivity 56, 58, 60
  coordinate data 54
  deletion *64*
  merging 52
  morphing 75, *75*, 371
  pixel *21*
  polygonal facets 1
  set 3D objects 2–3
  split 64–5
  structure polygon mesh 2
VFC 190, 289–91, 301–5, 308–12, 439, 463
view
  field 175
  interpolation 559–64
  morphing 561–4
  plane 175–7, 180–4
  space 173, 175, 179–89
  surface 172, 182
  vectors 176–8, 199–200
view coord system 9, 174–9, 184, 552, 554
view dependant light map 365–6
view frustrum 17–18, 173–6, *181*
  advance VFC 302–5

BSP trees 283, 289, 186–7, 190
  environment 296
  shadows 336
  trees 270–4
  visibility 311
view frustrum culling *see* VFC
view volume 270, 273, 289–90, 296–7, 302, 304
viewing 9
  direction 174–81, 283–4
  distance 40, 64, 68, 131
  motion control 368, *486*
  pyramid 188–9
  system 174, 175, 177
viewpoint 69, 76–7, 131, 172–9, 280–4, 306–7
virtual image 256–7
virtual reality 437, 490–1, 498
virtual tours 568
visibility 201, 270–313
visible scene sections 273
visual C++ ops Fly3D 765–8, 770–8
visual complexity – polygon count 31
visual disturbance 62, 246
volumetric rep 35, 49, 321–3
Von Neumann machines 486–7
Voronoi regions 455–7, 465–6
voxels 35–7, 56, 63, 76–8, 274–5, 451, *452*

walk-through flyby 386, 560, 568–9
warping 532–9, 551–6, 560, 567, 570
wavelets 516, 518–31
wedgie BV 75, *76*
weights control points 105–7
wireframing 33, 39, 114, 203, 212
world cord systems 2–9, 82, 110, 122, 174–7
  RH-LH 2–3, 12
world space 76, 174–5, 186, 199, 274, 318

z-buffering
  alg ops 204–12
  mapping 215–18
  mp render 346, 349
  rend example 212–14
  technology 516–17
  view ops 182, 185–9
  visibility 306, 311–12
zooming, user 526

IMPORTANT: READ CAREFULLY

WARNING: BY OPENING THE PACKAGE YOU AGREE TO BE BOUND BY THE TERMS OF THE LICENCE AGREEMENT BELOW.

This is a legally binding agreement between You (the user or purchaser) and Pearson Education Limited. By retaining this licence, any software media or accompanying written materials or carrying out any of the permitted activities You agree to be bound by the terms of the licence agreement below.

If You do not agree to these terms then promptly return the entire publication (this licence and all software, written materials, packaging and any other components received with it) with Your sales receipt to Your supplier for a full refund.

SINGLE USER LICENCE AGREEMENT

☐ YOU ARE PERMITTED TO:

- Use (load into temporary memory or permanent storage) a single copy of the software on only one computer at a time. If this computer is linked to a network then the software may only be installed in a manner such that it is not accessible to other machines on the network.

- Make one copy of the software solely for backup purposes or copy it to a single hard disk, provided you keep the original solely for back up purposes.

- Transfer the software from one computer to another provided that you only use it on one computer at a time.

☐ YOU MAY NOT:

- Rent or lease the software or any part of the publication.

- Copy any part of the documentation, except where specifically indicated otherwise.

- Make copies of the software, other than for backup purposes.

- Reverse engineer, decompile or disassemble the software.

- Use the software on more than one computer at a time.

- Install the software on any networked computer in a way that could allow access to it from more than one machine on the network.

- Use the software in any way not specified above without the prior written consent of Pearson Education Limited.

ONE COPY ONLY

This licence is for a single user copy of the software

PEARSON EDUCATION LIMITED RESERVES THE RIGHT TO TERMINATE THIS LICENCE BY WRITTEN NOTICE AND TO TAKE ACTION TO RECOVER ANY DAMAGES SUFFERED BY PEARSON EDUCATION LIMITED IF YOU BREACH ANY PROVISION OF THIS AGREEMENT.

Pearson Education Limited owns the software; You only own the disk on which the software is supplied.

LIMITED WARRANTY

Pearson Education Limited warrants that the diskette or CD rom on which the software is supplied are free from defects in materials and workmanship under normal use for ninety (90) days from the date You receive them. This warranty is limited to You and is not transferable. Pearson Education Limited does not warrant that the functions of the software meet Your requirements or that the media is compatible with any computer system on which it is used or that the operation of the software will be unlimited or error free.

You assume responsibility for selecting the software to achieve Your intended results and for the installation of, the use of and the results obtained from the software. The entire liability of Pearson Education Limited and its suppliers and your only remedy shall be replacement of the components that do not meet this warranty free of charge.

This limited warranty is void if any damage has resulted from accident, abuse, misapplication, service or modification by someone other than Pearson Education Limited. In no event shall Pearson Education Limited or its suppliers be liable for any damages whatsoever arising out of installation of the software, even if advised of the possibility of such damages. Pearson Education Limited will not be liable for any loss or damage of any nature suffered by any party as a result of reliance upon or reproduction of or any errors in the content of the publication.

Pearson Education Limited does not limit its liability for death or personal injury caused by its negligence.

This licence agreement shall be governed by and interpreted and construed in accordance with English law.